PRAISE FOR *DECEMBER 1941*

"Compulsively readable history of great sweep and startling detail."
— JON MEACHAM, FORMER EDITOR OF *NEWSWEEK* AND
PULITZER PRIZE-WINNING BEST-SELLING AUTHOR

"Riveting narrative history of America in the crucible of the Second World War. A real page turner. Highly recommended."
— DOUGLAS BRINKLEY, PROFESSOR OF HISTORY AT RICE UNIVERSITY AND
NEW YORK TIMES BEST-SELLING AUTHOR OF *THE WILDERNESS WARRIOR*

"Takes a new tack . . . about Pearl Harbor. Instead of just writing how it all went down, [Shirley's] book attempts to give readers a feel for how the country felt 70 years ago. He accomplishes that by providing anecdotal information from nearly 2,000 newspapers and magazines."
— *US NEWS & WORLD REPORT*

"Craig Shirley, known for creating a you-are-there atmosphere in his earlier books about Ronald Reagan's 1976 and 1980 presidential campaigns, has done it again."
— *WASHINGTON TIMES*

"A fascinating way to experience the look and the feel, the reactions and the emotion, the strategy, and the painful surprises of those 31 days."
— *NATIONAL REVIEW*

"Masterful . . . Shirley not only transports us back to that tumultuous time, but reminds this generation that denial about an enemy's intentions can have grave consequences."
— CAL THOMAS, SYNDICATED COLUMNIST

"It is terrific . . . tremendous report on that decisive month which changed America and the world."
— NEWT GINGRICH

"Every chapter is a day. I love in-the-moment history like this."
— CHUCK TODD, MSNBC

"Terrific piece of work!"
— ANDREA MITCHELL, MSNBC

DECEMBER
1941

31 DAYS THAT CHANGED AMERICA
AND SAVED THE WORLD

CRAIG SHIRLEY

NELSON
BOOKS

An Imprint of Thomas Nelson

Published in Nashville, Tennessee, by Nelson Books, an imprint of Thomas Nelson. Nelson Books and Thomas Nelson are registered trademarks of HarperCollins Christian Publishing, Inc.

Thomas Nelson, Inc., titles may be purchased in bulk for educational, business, fund-raising, or sales promotional use. For information, please e-mail SpecialMarkets@ThomasNelson.com.

Library of Congress Control Number: 2011940099

ISBN: 978-1-59555-457-4

ISBN: 978-1-59555-582-3 (TP)

Printed in the United States of America

13 14 15 16 17 RRD 6 5 4 3 2 1

Dedicated to family and friends who chose to serve . . .

Family

Henry Cone: Continental Army, First Company, First Regiment, Connecticut, 1775. Served: Siege of Boston, Battle of Bunker Hill. Third Regiment, Connecticut, 1776–1783. Served: Valley Forge and the Battles of Brandywine, Monmouth, and Long Island.

William Watkins: Continental Army, Fifth Company, Third Regiment, Connecticut, 1775. Served: Siege of Boston, Battle of Bunker Hill.

Andrew Cone: Served in the War of 1812.

ARM2C Ellsworth Abbott Shirley, USN, 43–45 (WWII KIA); Cpl. Edward Cone, USAAC, 43–45 (WWII); Seaman Gilbert Abbott, USN, (WWII); Cpl. Herbert L. Cone, USA, 46–48; PFC Ronald Lee Shirley, USMC, 46–48; Airman William Mackintosh, USAF, 49–53; RI Edward Bruce Shirley, USA, 49–51; Cpl. Fred R. Mackintosh, USAR, 52–58; Daniel Jacob, USAF, 52–54/USAFR, 54–59; F2 Louis Mackintosh, USN, 61–63; Capt. Gerald E. Eckert, MD, USAR; Seaman Kyle Richard Shirley, 73–74; Spc. 4 Michael L. Cone, USA, 72–75, (Vietnam); SSgt. Ronald J. Hauer, USAF, 77–81; SSgt Tracy A. Eckert, USAR, 80–04; Pvt. Timothy Naumann, USA, 97–08; Lance Cpl. Edward Nathan Shirley, USMCR, 99–05 (Iraq); Sgt. Sean Naumann, USMCR, 01–09; PV2 Ryan J. Cone, USA/SANG, 10–present (Afghanistan); HM Andrew Abbott Shirley, USN, 07–08; Cpl. Robert G. Eckert, USA, 06–10; SPC Holly F. Eckert, USA, 06–present (Afghanistan); AFC Zachary Shirley, USAF, 09–present (Afghanistan).

Friends

Capt. Ronald Reagan, USAR, 37–42/USA 42–45; Col. Jay Phelps Dawley, USA, 39–66 (WWII, Korea); Col. Richard Snyder, USAF, 40–65 (WWII, German POW); PFC Ralph Jefferson Turner, USA, 40–45 (WWII, Japanese POW); 2LT Robert J. Dole, USA, 42–48 (WWII); LTJG George H.W. Bush, USN, 42–45 (WWII); Sgt. Franklyn Nofziger, USA, 42–45 (WWII); HM Paul Laxalt, USA, 42–45 (WWII); MG John Singlaub, USAF, 43–77 (WWII, Korea, Vietnam); 1LT Frank Leonard, USAAC, 43–45 (WWII, German

POW); 2LT John David Dingell Jr., USA, 44–46 (WWII); ETM2C Richard Schweiker, USN, 44–46 (WWII); Lt. Col. Robert Gingrich, USA, 45–72 (Korea, Vietnam); Seaman Stu Spencer, USN, 45–46 (WWII); Sgt. Victor Gold, USA, 50–52; Gen. Paul Xavier Kelley, USMC, 50–87 (Vietnam); Capt. John McCain, USN, 54–81 (Vietnam War, Vietnam POW); 1LT Peter Hannaford, USAR/USA, 54–56; PFC Richard Glen Banister, USAR, 57–62 (Cuban Missile Crisis); Capt. James A Baker III, USMC, 52–54/USMCR; LCDR Frederic Johnson, USN, 55–76; PFC Stanley Gaines, USA/USAR, 57–64; Spc. 4 Fred Barnes, USA, 60–62; QM3 Robert Livingston, USN, 61–67 (Cuban Missile Crisis); Capt. Michael McShane, USAF, 66–72 (Vietnam); Cdr. Michael Phelps, USN, 66–69/MANG, 82–86; Col. Thomas A. Vaughan, USA, 68–71/ USAR, 71–98 (Vietnam); 1LT George W. Bush, USAFNG, 68–74; Lt. Col. Al Aitken, USMC, 70–90 (Vietnam, Mayaguez incident); Capt. Tom Finnigan, USAR, 71–81; Spc. 4 Kevin Kabanuk, USA, 72–74; Capt. Rick Perry, USAF, 72–77; Col. Robert Rowland, USMC, 73–98; Petty Officer 1st Class E6 Shirley Lawand Shammas, USN/USNR, 75–91; LC Kyle T. Fugate, USA, 86–09 (Afghanistan); LCDR Frank Lavin, USNR, 87–03; Maj. Stephanie Roell Fugate, USA, 95–04; Lt. Adam Paul Laxalt, USN, 05–10; HM2 Robert Staton, USN, 07–present; HM3 Fletcher Carson, USN, 07–present; 1LT Joseph M. Bozell, USMC, 07–present (Afghanistan).

CONTENTS

FOREWORD

It's strange what people remember and don't remember about December 7, 1941. I remember I'd just come out of the Belleview movie theatre in West Roxbury on Center Street, a part of Boston where I'd grown up. The name of the movie escapes me, but I remember going with my best friend, Fred Fettig.

When I read Craig Shirley's *December 1941*, I was amazed at the detail, the research, and the compelling nature of the story. I could not put it down, not only because I lived in that era, but also because it brought back so many memories and reminded me what America was all about in that time: the universal spirit of sacrifice and patriotism and heroism. It is a book I highly recommend. Shirley is a marvelous historian and storyteller, and *December 1941* is an invaluable contribution to American history. He also happens to be a good friend of mine. Military service and patriotism runs deep in his family as it does mine.

Growing up in Boston, attending the Patrick F. Lyndon School (where I learned to speak Latin), and being a lifeguard at the L Street Baths (which in those days had separate sections for women, men, and children) was a great time for me. We weren't rich by any means but my father, a teacher of military drills at Hyde Park High School, was a good provider. U.S. Army Major Albert J. Kelley also taught military history at two Boston high schools and was a reservist. He was a highly decorated and wounded veteran of the First World War. He'd been a company commander in Europe, where he was severely gassed by the Germans. Hard as it may be to believe for the men who served under my command in the Marine Corps, my nickname in those days was "Good Sam," given to me by my father.

My father was and still is my hero. I've known many men over the years whom I admired greatly: Ted Williams, Ronald Reagan, Paul Laxalt, George Bush, Tip O'Neill, and others, but like most American boys, my father was my idol.

December 7 was not cold and blustery as it normally was in Boston at that time of year. As I recall, the weather was quite mild. As an Irish Catholic, I'd been to mass that morning at Holy Name, where I served as an altar boy for Father Bryson. After the movie, I was in a hurry to get home to listen to one of my favorite shows, *The Shadow*, on the radio—we had no television. But someone on the street yelled out, "There's been a bombing against the United States!" No word of who had done it. I had to walk up a big hill, and it wasn't until I finally reached home that I heard word on the radio—the Japanese had just attacked Pearl Harbor.

My family—my mother, my brother, my two sisters, and my father—listened to WBZ radio as the news developed of the unprovoked attack on our army and navy there in Hawaii. We later learned how extensive the carnage was and how many other places in the Pacific the Japanese had attacked.

Later that afternoon, the phone rang. My father was to report for active duty immediately. For a kid at my young age, what did it all mean? I knew it meant something bad, because not long after my return home, my father had to leave. They called men like my father "retreads," which was pejorative, but he had heard worse over the years as an Irishman. He was one of five boys, all of whom went to college, which was simply unheard of in the early 1900s.

Even in the absence of my father, we had to get on with our lives in the new world war in which we found ourselves. It was total immersion—tearing down steel fences to get more materiel for planes, trains, trucks, and things like that. It was mandatory in those days for all boys in public school to get some form of military training as a part of the CMTC—the Citizens Military Training Camps. It came in handy, because at age thirteen, I was the light superintendent, responsible for walking the neighborhood every night and telling people to pull down shades. It was also my duty every couple of days to crawl up the tower on the American Legion building with binoculars to report every plane that was flying by and where it was going.

For all of us, it was the survival of America. That's the way we felt. That's how we acted. We were rationing food and gasoline. We were tearing down anything we did not need if we could use it to make things the soldiers did need. It was an all-hands situation, something the likes of which this country had never seen. People were willing to dedicate and devote themselves.

We had been devastated. The future was unclear. Our military was almost laughable. A power like Japan attacked us out of the blue, and we didn't know where it was going to end. They had done a lot of damage. *December 1941* reminds us of all this and more.

When you look at the number of people who went to war, look at the number of planes that were built and shot down, look at the number of ships that were launched and sunk, and look at the human life that was lost, it was all unspeakably big—the biggest occurrence our generation had ever experienced. We all suffered. We all sacrificed. You could not walk down the street and not see blue, silver, or gold stars in the windows of most houses. For a time, we had a blue star in our window, and then it came down to be replaced with a gold star.

Over the years I've often gone to military cemeteries both here and abroad, alone, walking along the graves and asking, "How are you, brother?"

"Where did you come from?"

"Did you have brothers and sisters?"

Those sacred markers from World War II don't represent all our honored dead, though, because nearly eighty thousand are still listed as Missing in Action, their remains never recovered. Eighty thousand American families never got a chance to say good-bye.

At the University of Massachusetts, my father's alma mater, is a plaque for those who graduated and later died in World War II. On that plaque is the name of Major Albert J. Kelley. My father. My hero. My inspiration.

General Paul Xavier Kelley, USMC
Arlington, Virginia
July 2013

PREFACE

I n 1941 a B-25 Mitchell bomber contained 107,156 rivets, each one inserted by hand. Often a woman's hand.

That year, there were as many people on the left, such as Lowell Thomas and Al Smith, who were part of the isolationist America First Committee as there were people on the right, such as Charles Lindbergh and Herbert Hoover.

The U.S.O. was created in 1941, as was the comic book character, "Captain America." The first time an organ was played at a baseball game was in Chicago in 1941, and the first television commercial aired was in 1941 to tout Bulova Watches. The "Red Ryder" BB gun was also first introduced in 1941.

In 1941, the United States of America went to war with the Axis powers, including Japan, Germany, and Italy, changing America radically and forever.

Just three days before the December 7 attack, President Franklin Roosevelt received a long memorandum marked "Confidential" from the Office of Naval Intelligence, reviewing at length all the subversive activities going on in America, including those emanating from the Japanese Embassy in Washington. "The focal point of the Japanese Espionage effort is the determination of the total strength of the United States. In anticipation of possible open conflict with this country, Japan is vigorously utilizing every available agency to secure military, naval and commercial information, paying particular attention to the West Coast, the Panama Canal and the Territory of Hawaii."[1] The twenty-six-page document went into great detail about the coordination between German and Japanese agents on U.S. soil. This previously undisclosed secret memo also reviewed the attempts by the Japanese to infiltrate labor unions, Latin American groups, and the National Association for the Advancement of Colored People.[2]

A second reference specifically to the Hawaiian Territory was made in the memo. "However, only the more important groups are of interest, since they are in a position to engage in espionage, sabotage and other acts inimical to the best interests of the U.S . . . . Each of these groups is at least strongly influenced if not directly controlled by similar ones in Japan."[3] The confidential document prepared for Roosevelt went into great detail regarding the Japanese civilian presence in Hawaii.

The response by the U.S. military, government, and citizenry to the events of December 7 was quick and decisive, even if it was also often bumbling and haphazard. "Everyone, I suppose, will be jotting down in a little black book somewhere the memories of Sunday, December 7—where they were, what they were doing, what they thought when they first heard of the war. Let me tell you—you don't have to make a note of those things. You'll remember them." So wrote famed sports columnist Bill Henry in his "By the Way" column in the *Los Angeles Times* on December 9.[4] This was true enough, but the entire thirty-one days of December 1941 were memorable, messy, historic, poignant, confusing, inspiring, depressing, and enduring.

After December 7, 1941, the policies toward the Japanese, Germans, and Italians living in America were harsh and comprehensive. But, because the government believed the Germans and the Japanese had incredible spy and sabotage networks operating in the United States and the Hawaiian Territory, the reaction by the government at the time, they felt, was justified.

At the end of December 1941, Americans still weren't calling it "World War II" or the "Second World War," though there were hints of the standard appellations to come. Even three weeks after America's entry into the global crisis, Americans were still calling it the "national emergency" or "the war." I didn't learn many of these and thousands of other things just from researching books during the development stages of *December 1941*; I learned many of these facts from the newspapers, magazines, and other publications of the era as well as confidential files from the FDR Library.

Washington Post publisher Phil Graham once said, newspapers were "the first rough draft of history." The phrase had been attributed to others before Graham, but he gets the credit for it.[5] So much of the sourcing for this book comes from hundreds of newspapers and thousands upon thousands of newspaper and magazine articles around the country and wire-service bulletins and radio dispatches and short-wave intercepts sifted through to build the following account. But private diaries, personal papers, and confidential and classified materials were also heavily relied upon for this story.

There never has been a book solely devoted to the month of December 1941, surely among the most important, decisive, and nation-altering thirty-one days in the history of the American Republic. There have been days, such as July 4, 1776; October 19, 1781; September 17, 1787; and April 15, 1861, that rank with December 7, but one is hard-pressed to think of another month as startling, compelling, interesting, critical, and inspiring as December 1941.

There have been many outstanding books written on World War II and the events leading up to Pearl Harbor, but never has there been a book about the days in America prior to December 7, 1941, and what happened to the country in the hours, days, and weeks after the attack. Suffice it to say, the country was decisively changed forever.

Never before or since has America been so unified. There were virtually no Americans against their country getting into World War II after the unprovoked attack by the Japanese at Pearl Harbor. One of the few was Congresswoman Jeannette Rankin, Republican of Montana. She voted against declaring war on Japan and would only vote "present" when FDR asked Congress for a declaration of war against Germany and Italy—after they had declared war on America. Someday someone will write a book about Ms. Rankin, exploring her reasons for not voting for war. They were principled, nuanced, and commendable. She was mistaken but she wasn't wrong.[6]

The goal here is to make the reader feel as if he or she is experiencing the day-to-day events as they unfolded. Some historians don't like to go into the arduous tasks of going through thousands of newspapers, preferring instead to rely on those bits and pieces of news reporting they may glean from other books. I did, and consequently the reader will find stories and information from the month of December 1941 they have never heard before. It makes for what I hope will be a fascinating book.

The careful reader will note that some styling and punctuation within quoted material varies, but that's because every effort was made to accurately reflect and duplicate the quoted material as it appeared in print at that time. Newspaper and magazine styles often varied (and still do).

Many sources were used in the writing of this book, from declassified material at the FDR Library to the personal files of Secretary of War Henry Stimson, the private diaries of White House staff, books, memoirs, and the like. The newspaper reporting of 1941 was both accurate and well-written but on rare occasions mistaken or incomplete. In these few cases, I tried to make clear that something was reported without actually confirming or denying it had happened, because I wanted to keep the reader in the moment. The search for history is the imperfect search for perfection.

Of my previous writings, many said they gave the reader a "you-are-there feeling," while another said I wrote like a sports writer, which I took as one of the best compliments I've ever received. The goal here was to impart new information while making the reading enjoyable. I wanted to do a story of America, to allow the reader to see the country through the eyes of the 130 million citizens who lived in the forty-eight states in that remarkable month of December 1941.

The goal was to write a book so that the reader could read and feel what their parents and grandparents and great-grandparents were reading and hearing and feeling and talking about at the time. About a time of war and peace and service and sacrifice and losing and winning and unity.

President Roosevelt, Prime Minister Winston Churchill, General George C. Marshall, Admiral Chester Nimitz, General Douglas MacArthur, and many others in both the Allied and the Axis powers are here. Prominent Americans including political leaders, actors, and athletes are here. Yet they are all merely supporting cast members in this drama.

The central and most important factor in *December 1941* is the United States of America.

Craig Shirley
Lancaster, Virginia

CHAPTER 1

THE FIRST OF DECEMBER

"U.S. and Jap Negotiations Continue"

Fitchburg Sentinel

"Britain Puts All Far East Areas on War Basis"

Tucson Daily Citizen

"Nazis See Fall of Moscow Near"

Idaho Times

"'Wise Statesmanship' Might Save Situation, Japs Tell Reporters"

Bismarck Tribune

America's 1,974 daily newspapers[1] were crammed with war news: Russian, German, British, Japanese, Italian, Free China, Vichy France, Netherland East Indies, and Serbian. Reports were thick with hostilities in the North Atlantic and the South Pacific, in Northwest Africa and Southeast Asia, in Western Europe and on the Eastern Front.

The Third Reich and the British Empire were engaged in massive tank battles along Africa's Mediterranean coastline. Marshal Henri Philippe Pétain, the puppet head of the Vichy French government, was reportedly in meetings with Adolf Hitler as a final step toward including France as part of the Axis powers' "New Order."[2] Several months earlier, in a bold military campaign that would have pleased the founder of the "First Reich," the Prussian king Frederick the Great, hundreds of thousands of German troops invaded Russia. Stalin cowered, and the maneuver looked like another brilliant offensive operation by Chancellor Hitler.

Maps of Asia, Africa, and Europe were frequently in the newspapers and magazines, showing American readers the German thrusts and surges across Europe, along with counterattacks by Britain and the Russians. Other drawings showed new incursions by the Japanese into China and Indochina, their designs on Thailand and the Burma Road. Giant arrows slashed across continents.

In Shanghai and Hong Kong, the British were eyeing fresh movements by Japanese troops. British troops in Hong Kong were ordered to return to their barracks, and a state of emergency was declared in Singapore. The Philippines also watched the Japanese with concern.

War was raging on the high seas. German "Wolf packs" preyed upon helpless civilian vessels with shoot-on-sight orders from Adolf Hitler himself, and thousands of tons of hardened steel had already been sent to the bottom of the Atlantic. Berlin was also making plans to take Surinam, a strategically important outpost on the Atlantic side of South America. "Bundles" were dispatched to Britain, and Greek war relief funds were raised courtesy of American charity for those besieged countries.

To slow the inevitable German advance on Moscow, the Red Army burned the homes of Soviet peasants by the thousands in hopes of denying Nazi forces any resources they might find in them. As a result, untold thousands of Soviet citizens were left homeless in the blinding white cold.

It was all just one more day in a new world war that had already been a fully involved inferno for over two years. And yet there was much more to come.

But there was no American war news. No Americans were fighting anywhere in the world, at least not under their forty-eight-star flag. Americans didn't want any part of this rest-of-the-world mess. They'd been through that thankless hell once before, in a global struggle that was supposed to make the world safe for democracy. Memories were still fresh of American doughboys fighting and dying in the trenches of European battlefields, only to result in the rise of distinctly undemocratic societies a generation later.

An entire world was truly at war, but the United States was sitting this one out.

On December 1, 1941, Americans simply referred to the unfolding hostilities as "the emergency" and went about their business, walled off from the clamor by two giant oceans. Christmas was coming, and the economy was showing signs of life for the first time in years. For over a decade, the country had staggered through the dark valley of the Great Depression, and it could finally see some sunlight. Americans planned to enjoy an uneasy peace and a modicum of prosperity.

The only place American troops could be found "fighting" was South Carolina, in war games supervised by one-star General George S. Patton Jr. Because of severe budget restrictions, the troops used fake ammunition. The brass wanted to conclude these maneuvers quickly so they and 300,000 participating troops could make it home in time for Christmas. But the faux battle was described as a "sham," with fistfights breaking out as parachutists landed, while "on to the field," as *Time* reported in the language of the era, "charged grease-monkeys and Negro engineers" armed with "rifles and clubs."[3] The army guaranteed they'd use real ammo for maneuvers scheduled in 1942.[4]

The navy's materiel situation was just a bit more promising. Rolling off production lines in Maine and San Francisco were new destroyers, the *Aaron Ward, Buchanan,* and *Fahrenholt.* Battleships in the works were the *Indiana, Alabama, Iowa, New Jersey, Wisconsin,* and *Missouri.* They were bigger, armed with more powerful guns than the fifteen battleships already in the fleet. "Meanwhile, Navy men find a particular comfort in their completed plans: as far as they know, the Japanese are planning nothing like them." The plan was for a two-ocean navy, an overall addition of 17 new battlewagons, along with "eleven more carriers, 54 cruisers, 192 destroyers, 73 submarines."[5] Also under development was a relatively small and light torpedo vessel known as the "PT-69." The Patrol Torpedo-69 was being developed by Huckins Yacht Corporation, one of three companies that recently received contracts to develop the next generation of PT boats. Though the PT-69's specifications were "a military secret," pictures and startlingly accurate estimates were printed in detail in *Time* magazine complete with speed, armaments, length, and construction, which was a plywood hull.[6]

The weather across the country was cloudy that day, from Abilene to Washington, D.C., and so was America's clarity about the threat from the East.

"Americans do not even seem worried by the prospect of war with Japan," *Life* magazine reported.[7] The reigning assumption was that if there was any action by the Japanese in the Pacific theater, it would be directed against Great Britain and the empire's outposts there. As a result, the British were beefing up their naval presence in the region, having recently dispatched large warships, including the *Prince of Wales*.[8] The British in Hong Kong ordered their garrison there to move into an "advanced state of readiness,"[9] and their troops in Singapore and Rangoon had also been so warned. As a precaution, the U.S. Army and Navy in the area were "ordered on the alert."[10] News photos of "Swarthy Punjabi sepoys"[11]—Singapore soldiers manning 40-millimeter guns—appeared in some American papers. Some 75 percent of the tin imported by the United States came from Singapore, so Washington had at least a passing interest.[12]

The American navy had been quietly moving munitions out of Honolulu and the tiny island of Palmyra to the British-held Fiji Islands and the Free French island of Caledonia to assist against possible Japanese strikes there.[13] The Americans had strengthened their military operations on Samoa, but the Japanese government made clear they too had parochial interests in the Pacific and vowed to keep the shipping lanes between their home islands and South America open. For average Americans, though, when they gave the Pacific a passing thought, it was only about palm trees and sandy beaches. The very word *pacific* meant tranquility, a peaceful nature.

Consequently, few in America paid any attention to an item buried deep in a United Press story from the evening of December 1, dateline Manila: "Sixteen Japanese heavy cruisers and aircraft carriers were reported by Manila to have swung southward. . . . Japanese reinforcements were reported landing in Indochina where there already were an estimated 100,000 troops."[14]

Another story, this one from International News Service, reported on the "precarious positions of the Philippines . . . under command of Lieutenant Gen. Douglas MacArthur" who was being "subjected to a horseshoe encirclement by Japan."[15] However, according to respected military analyst Dewitt MacKenzie, recent setbacks by the Nazis in Russia and Africa had led the Japanese to pull up because, he said, "Tokyo is anxious to evade conflict with America."[16] Indeed, representatives of the Japanese and American governments were in ongoing peace talks to gain clarity and iron out their differences.

Numerous newspaper reports and columns speculated on the intent of the Japanese government, and nearly all came to the conclusion that they had neither the will nor the industrial plant to move forward with any serious naval action in the Pacific. Furthermore, the Japanese navy was seemingly so weak the Nazis had deployed some of their ships to the Pacific to buttress their Axis ally. The Allies had lost track of a good portion of the German navy—they couldn't find many of their ships.[17]

When it came to the American ships, the conventional knowledge was that "[t]he Pacific fleet . . . has a decided superiority over the Japanese. . . . The Japanese would be hard put to replace their losses because of the lack of raw materials which they obtained from the United States and other western democracies." Few in America worried about the Japanese navy, though there were signs they should. Chillingly buried at the end of a piece by respected British correspondent Constantine Brown was this: "The Japanese have hinted . . . that they do have some juicy surprises if we decide to accept their challenge in the Pacific."[18]

Part of the source of the irritation between Tokyo and Washington stemmed from the Japanese invasion of China. The Japanese had invaded China in 1937 and proceeded to conduct genocidal activities on the Mainland. The Chinese had a strong lobby in Washington and America, as well as many sympathetic supporters.

In retaliation, the Americans slapped a boycott on products headed for Japan, including precious scrap metal. For the boycott to be lifted, the State Department set out four conditions to the Japanese. First, they had to withdraw as a member of the Axis powers. Second, they had to withdraw their forces from French Indochina and the Mainland. Third, they had to renounce aggression, and fourth, they had to "observe the principle of equal trade opportunity in the Pacific." Cordell Hull, the secretary of state, also offered the Japanese government $100 million if they would agree to switch from a wartime economy to a peacetime economy, but also sell war materiel to Russia in order to help Stalin fight Hitler.[19]

While talks continued with Japan, most eyes in America were fixed on Europe and the North Atlantic, not Asia or the Pacific.

The night before, the Germans had downed eight British bombers on a mission over Hamburg.[20] Over the previous weekend, the American merchant ship *MacBeth* was reported missing in the North Atlantic, presumed torpedoed.[21] U.S. ambassador to the USSR, Laurence Steinhardt, paid a worried visit to the White House to discuss the war in Europe with FDR;[22] and Nazi propaganda minister Paul Joseph Goebbels gave a talk at Berlin University in which he predicted that it was too late for the United States to do anything to prevent England's eventual defeat.[23] The plane of an American general, George H. Brett, head of the Army Air Corps, was shot at by Axis naval vessels as it crossed the Mediterranean.[24] Privately, Franklin Roosevelt had been telling aides since 1939 he believed the Nazis were bent on "world dominance."[25]

Not that America was ready for it.

Since dissolving its forces after 1919, there was little American military to speak of. The Army Air Corps had only 51,000 trained personnel as of June of 1940. On the other hand, the Royal Air Force had thousands of trained, battle-hardened men, and the German Luftwaffe had many more of their own. Both countries were far smaller than America in terms of population, and the U.S. planes were inferior to boot. American Curtiss P-40s were out-gunned and out-accelerated by the English Spitfires and the German Messerschmitts, and the P-40s couldn't achieve their altitude either.[26] Still, the American military was quite proud that their tiny air force operated out of what they called "dispersion fields," meaning their geographically scattered planes would not be subjected to mass destruction as a result of aerial bombardment.[27] They were also proud of their new glider schools.[28]

Lt. Gen. Leslie J. McNair observed that against Germany, the U.S. Army could "fight effectively but losses would be unduly heavy." And he lamented about the poorly equipped troops.[29] An army draft continued in America, but 1,400 American "boys" refused to report, declaring themselves "conscientious objectors." They were sentenced to Civilian Conservation Corps work camps around the country, where they picked up trash, planted trees, and served their time, for at least a year and in some cases, longer. Most were religious pacifists, including Mennonites.[30]

The army was also forcing 1,800 uniformed soldiers of the 29th Division out of service. All in excess of twenty-eight years old, they were deemed "over-age." Maj. Gen. Milton A. Reckord protested that it would take "weeks to build the division back to its peak."[31]

The navy was undermanned as well. Enlistments were so poor that Secretary of the Navy Frank Knox mused publicly that he might have to impose a draft for the blue-water service, something that had never been done before. The admirals thought the deficiency could be made up with better newspaper advertising campaigns and by "relaxation of health standards."[32] That might have explained why the navy called back seventy-seven-year-old Jesse "Pop" Warner as a chief boatswain's mate in San Diego. Warner had already served fifty-seven years in the navy, had a recent physical, and with the exception of upper and lower dental plates, was pronounced "fit for sea duty." He had originally enlisted in 1884.[33]

Americans were understandably gloomy or indifferent about world affairs, but things were bothersome at home too. The country was still feeling the effects of the Great Depression, and after the economy had made a gentle comeback several years earlier, it had slid back and had only recently perked up again. Unemployment hovered around 10 percent, though war production had begun to stabilize the economy.[34]

Despite their vow to stay out of "it," a war effort had been underway for a while now—allegedly only to aid the Allied powers. The "Arsenal of Democracy"[35] was reserved exclusively for friends of America, but there was some promising if slightly ironic upside to the early efforts. Just as Germany had pulled out of its own depression with a military buildup, so too did the United States. In California, for instance, industrial factories supporting the war effort numbered over 2,000 as of December, and wages were as high as $193 per week, although many employees were still scraping by on less than $40.[36]

It was a shaky and uncertain recovery. The stock market on December 1 was mixed, and Wall Street was mildly surprised that investors had not reacted more favorably to news of the Russian counteroffensive and of the Japanese desire to continue talks with Washington to try to effect a political solution to their disagreements. The market was at its lowest point since 1938, but there was no market averaging yet.[37] Stocks were broken down between railroads and industrials. In 1926, railroad stocks had been trading at over $102 per share, but by 1941, they were at $23 per share.[38]

Senator Sheridan Downey of California proclaimed that the 2 percent payroll tax was enough to fund the Social Security retirement system, which in 1941 provided a pensioner at age sixty with $36 per month for the rest of his life. With the tax scheduled to go to 4 percent in 1943, the trust fund would have more than enough to pay for the retirement of all Americans. But, Downey told a congressional committee, rather than depositing the taxes collected into Treasury bonds, it would be "more humane" to provide pensions for those elderly who were "slowly decaying and starving" on welfare rolls.[39]

A majority thought the Depression could last another ten years, and only 37 percent thought "that their sons' opportunities will be better than their own."[40] A majority also thought the New Deal would expand and exert evermore control over the American economy; that same majority also deemed it a good thing. But after thirteen years, the "new normal" of 1941 was to expect that nearly one out of five Americans would be perpetually unemployed, despite the best intentions of the New Deal.

The Roosevelt administration had pretty much run out of ideas (and the alphabet), content to simply keep throwing money at the problem and hypermanaging the economy through a weed patch of bureaus and administrative departments. No New Deal legislation had been proposed in Congress for over two years. As far back as "the winter of 1938–39, Roosevelt knew, but was not yet willing to say, that the New Deal, as a social and political revolution, was dead."[41] Washington was a bureaucratic mess and no one seemed to know what agency or department was responsible—or irresponsible—

for what. The Office of Production Management was fighting with the War Department over metals, as the allotment slated for farm equipment was being sucked up and sent to Great Britain.

The Rooseveltians ran roughshod over business. "For the first time during this emergency, the U.S. government forced the removal of a corporation executive from his own company," reported *Life* magazine. It seems that one F. Leroy Hill, president of Air Associates, a maker of airplane parts, "had been at odds with the National Defense Mediation Board." The army "fired" Hill from his own company, without ever appearing before a judge or jury. "When it finds a man that it likes, the Army plans to give the plant back to its owners."[42] The "mighty music" of America—as written by North Carolina's Thomas Wolfe—had been silent for over ten years.[43]

With all the news coverage of the war and the buildup at home, military and civilian culture mixed easily. The print ads in the nation's weekly and daily newspapers had broad military themes. The topic of national unity was deep throughout many, even in Parker Pen print ads, which depicted men in uniform right alongside civilians.[44]

The Ethyl Gasoline Corporation's ad told the story of an anonymous delivery man. "He's been delivering the goods for you and the folks next door for years. The lumber, stone, metal, glass of which homes are built. . . . Today, he's got an even bigger job to do—delivering the goods for Uncle Sam."[45] B.F. Goodrich pushed their rubber products via a heavy military thesis.[46] So did the automotive business. Plymouth was running ads for their 1942 model but also made it clear that the Chrysler Corporation manufactured "Army tanks, Anti-Aircraft Cannons, Army Trucks . . . shells and projectiles."[47] Chevy did the same thing. In fact, whether it was an Oldsmobile, a Ford, a De Soto, a Packard, a Nash, or a Buick, all their advertising had a martial theme, detailing how each manufacturer was contributing to the war effort.

Even bicycle manufacturers got in on the act. Columbia was promoting the idea of parachuting "leathernecks of the Marine Corps" along with bicycles that folded up and could "hit the silk," which upon landing "are assembled and ready to speed away on a lightning-fast maneuver."[48] Other manufacturers like Schwinn were just pushing bicycles for the Christmas season.[49]

But the combination of the war effort and the growth of federal power raised ominous flags as well. The Office of Price Administration warned that cars made after 1942 might be severely curtailed. A generic "Victory" model car was envisioned that would eliminate "double-bar bumpers" and would feature the "substitution of wool and rubber floor mats in favor of linoleum . . . elimination of all unnecessary gadgets such as clocks, cigar lighters, radios, dual tail lights . . . reduction in number of colors and the number of coats of paint." The OPM had already ordered a 50 percent reduction in the number of cars made for 1942 over 1941 because demand had gone up. It was contemplating prioritization of the civilian population to see who the government would allow to own a new car and who did not *need* to own a new car.[50]

Despite the rough economic times—or more likely because of them—American citizens went regularly to the movie theaters to escape. In every city, hamlet, and town, moviegoers saw their favorite actors and actresses in edifices such as the Strand, Paramount, RKO Keith, the Uptown, the Biograph, the Palace, and of course, the Bijou. Many theaters were truly palaces, elaborately designed, with heavy wood, brass railings, spit-and-shine ushers, dramatically large curtains, and colorful lighting. Uniformed boys and young men complete with caps and epaulettes opened doors, helped customers find seats, and pleasantly greeted all patrons as they entered. These theaters were designed for maximum comfort in order to make those attending feel special. Some were even equipped with the new-fangled air conditioning. By and large, kids went to the same movies as adults, and all forked over the 10 cents to see a movie; a double feature cost from 17 to 21 cents more. Saturday matinees for children usually ran a nickel.[51]

Americans dressed up in suits and ties and dresses to go to the movies. Everyone wore hats, and they always put on their "Sunday Best" to go to church, out to dinner, to take a train or an airplane. The whole idea was to make people think better of you as an individual. Good grooming permeated the culture, as did helpful advice and tips on landing a bride or groom.

Personal hygiene was also important, as consumers could purchase a "pro-phylactic tooth brush" and "tooth powder" for 47 cents.[52] Hair tonics such as Vitalis promised to keep men's hair in place, reduce dandruff, and "prevent excessive falling hair."[53]

Men did not go out unshaven, and only old men or psychiatrists had beards—though pencil moustaches, such as those sported by Clark Gable, Errol Flynn, William Powell, and Ronald Colman, were popular with movie actors and those who emulated their style. Women's role models were slim, chic actresses such as Barbara Stanwyck, Myrna Loy, and Greer Garson. Hem lengths were just below the knee, and women wore makeup, heels, girdles, and stockings before even thinking about going out in public.

The most popular movies in 1941 were *Sergeant York*, *The Maltese Falcon*, *Meet John Doe*, *Dumbo*, and the acclaimed masterpiece *Citizen Kane*. Along with *The Maltese Falcon*, *Citizen Kane* gave Americans one of their first tastes of film noir in which morality was ambiguous, human nature base, and all characters worthy of suspicion. These movies foreshadowed a post–World War II disillusionment, when in the late 1940s and early 1950s the traumatic mem-ories of battle and the haunting meaninglessness of the Holocaust provided plenty of fuel for dark and apprehensive films. But for now, such thoughts were only small gray clouds on an otherwise red-white-and-blue American horizon. Indeed, many movies in 1941 depicted unadulterated patriotism: for instance, *A Yank in the RAF*, *War Front*, *They Died with Their Boots On*, *Dive Bomber*, and *Buck Privates*, starring comedy duo Bud Abbott and Lou Costello.

As with most other years of the era, Hollywood churned out movie after movie, and the average American went to the theater twice a week. While at the theater, moviegoers could also watch serials such as the *Adventures of Captain Marvel*, *Dick Tracy*, *The Green Hornet*, and *Jungle Girl*.

Radio was also important to Americans, particularly the AM dial. Americans woke to farm reports and the weather, listened throughout the day to music and local programming often involving local children in contests, and settled into the evening with nationally broadcast adventure and comedy shows, such as *The Battling Bickersons*, the exploits of Jack Benny, and *Fibber McGee and Molly*. Up-and-comer Bob Hope made mil-lions of Americans laugh, while liberal columnist Drew Pearson and then-Populist columnist Walter Winchell made them think or simply get angry with their commentaries. Hollywood reporters like Hedda Hopper and Louella Parsons satisfied a taste for gossip, while others tuned their ears to the strains of Tommy Dorsey, Jimmy Dorsey, Harry James, Glenn Miller, Duke Ellington, Dinah Shore, Peggy Lee, Frank Sinatra, Harriet Nelson, Bing Crosby, and the great "Satchmo," Louis Armstrong. FM radio was not unheard of in 1941, just very expensive; an FM radio in 1941 could cost as much as $390, more than most people's wages in one month.[54]

CBS had inaugurated a new radio show just a year earlier, *Report to the Nation*. It was created in response to "the problem of allocating radio time to the numerous Government agencies that wanted it." Though the hour-long show covered Washington and the events there, it used "actors and actresses . . . about two-thirds are daytime Government employees" for its usual all-news and commentary format.[55]

Everybody smoked cigarettes in 1941, and everybody smoked cigarettes everywhere. In the movie theaters, in restaurants, on airplanes, in trains, at sporting events, at the office, even in classrooms, Americans smoked 'em if they had 'em. Favorite brands were Camels, Lucky Strike, and Chesterfield. Smoking had increased in America despite some then-obscure reports linking the activity with a shortened lifespan. The average American adult in 1940 consumed 2,558 cigarettes, double that of ten years earlier.[56] Ads pitched Camels as great Christmas gifts because their packaging was "so gay and colorful." They also contained "28 percent less nicotine."[57] Old Gold made it clear in their ads that smoking helped women lose weight.[58]

Technically, one had to be of an ambiguous legal age to purchase and smoke cigarettes, but it wasn't unusual to see young teenagers smoking cigarettes, and cigarette ads screamed out from every publication and billboard in America. Someone often really was calling for "Philip Morris," as the bellhop in the ad in every publication was. Smoking Philip Morris was important, as "eminent doctors" said it was easier on the throat than other "leading brands" because "all smokers sometimes inhale."[59]

Many ads also made clear the importance of a "good purge," which seemed very important in 1941. In one magazine ad for Kellogg's All-Bran cereal, the figure of a grey uniformed Civil War vet encouraged readers to "join the 'regulars' with Kellogg's."[60]

Sports fans had a lot to talk about. Football was in full swing, and fans were looking forward to the coming college bowl season, with Duke pitted against Oregon State in the Rose Bowl and Fordham versus Missouri in the Sugar Bowl. "As always, the selections stirred a few dissents."[61] The Yankee Clipper, Joe DiMaggio, had a newborn son, Joe D. III, with his wife, actress Dorothy Arnold.[62] And the "hot stove league" was hot with rumors that the great Jimmie Foxx was about to leave the Boston Red Sox and rejoin his old boss, Connie Mack, owner and manager of the Philadelphia Athletics.[63]

Other news of the day included a sixty-two-year-old North Carolinian mountaineer, Joe Downs, who wed fifteen-year-old Estelle Pruitt.[64] The photo of the scowling elderly man and his bucktoothed bride was published in hundreds of newspapers. In New York City, parents protested in front of Mayor Fiorello LaGuardia's home against the rising crime wave in the city's parks.[65] Six members of the Ku Klux Klan were convicted in Atlanta for conducting a widespread campaign of "flogging" people there—seizing people from their homes and whipping them. Despite pressure, Georgia governor Eugene Talmadge refused to pardon them.[66] He told them he'd once "helped flog a Negro himself" and then had the audacity to compare himself to the apostle Paul. "The Apostle Paul was a flogger in his life, then confessed, reformed and became one of the greatest powers of the Christian Church." Life magazine noted that Talmadge "frankly and deliberately stirs up racial hatreds."[67]

And 1940 GOP nominee Wendell Willkie decided to defend in the Supreme Court a self-admitted communist who had had his citizenship invalidated as a result of his political affiliations.[68]

The women's pages of the nation's newspapers were filled with articles on fashion, wedding announcements, landing a husband, and the proper conduct in the workplace. Life magazine detailed how Latin American women preferred wearing black and now it was taking over American women's fashions. "Black hats, black shorts, black slacks, black bathing suits, black skirts . . ." had all been inspired when a fashion designer saw "barefoot peasants of inland Mexico" attired in black.[69]

All newspapers had event-filled "Social Calendars."[70] A cartoon in the Greeley (CO) Daily Tribune women's page depicted a beat-up young woman, one eye blackened, head bandaged, and sporting a broken arm as she cheerily told three friends, "My boyfriend always starts a little spat just before Christmas."[71] But dozens of tamer cartoon strips were enjoyed by American parents and children: "Li'l Abner," about a hayseed in Dog Patch; "Alley Oop," a cave man in present times; "Blondie," a ditsy wife and her equally ditsy husband, Dagwood; "Prince Valiant," a knight of the Round Table; and "Bringing Up Father," about Jiggs and Maggie, two socialites seemingly caught in the time warp of 1922. Meanwhile, "Little Orphan Annie" was battling German spies in her comic strip and seemed to have a better plan for dealing with them than the U.S. government did.

Of course, Annie didn't have to worry about politics, and war is nothing if not political.

In May 1941, German U-boats sank an unarmed American freighter, the *Robin Moor*, and yet there was no great push to get America into another European war.[72] Few wanted war, and few believed it was coming to America.

Later in the year, Adolf Hitler upped the ante by ordering U-boats to fire on American naval ships. In turn, FDR ordered American vessels to defend themselves. On October 31, the Germans sank the *Reuben James*, an American destroyer, leaving a few dozen survivors. Earlier in October, German U-boats also torpedoed the USS *Kearny*, though she did not go down.[73] The *Kearny* had responded to the mayday call of a Canadian convoy, which U-boats were sinking at will.[74] The *Kearny* dropped depth charges, though it was not known if the American vessel sank any Wolf pack subs. The sea battle lasted three hours, with ten killed on the tough little American destroyer after being struck by a torpedo.[75] American freighter ships operating in the Atlantic began to outfit with fixed guns, and seven Americans serving in the British merchant marines were killed by enemy fire.[76]

Despite this Nazi aggression, there was no real groundswell for war with Germany; few really thought war was imminent. That's not to say that there were not strong opinions about it. The political factions were clear-cut on this. America had those, like Henry Luce, head of a powerful media empire that included *Time* and *Life*, who wanted to jump into the European mess with both feet. Others, like former ambassador Joe Kennedy, thought England was finished as a country and unworthy of support.

Kennedy's public utterances were increasingly construed as isolationist, even pro-Nazi. Though he sported a patina of Brahmin respectability, the Harvard-educated Kennedy made his fortune as a stock swindler, bootlegger, and movie mogul. In what would prove to be a lasting Kennedy hallmark, Joe cultivated powerful alliances with the press, particularly the newspaper baron William Randolph Hearst, who throughout the 1930s would dutifully print sycophantic stories about Kennedy's successes. The Kennedy paterfamilias would later abhor the liberalism of his sons, but in 1941 Joe was an archconservative and apologist for Hitler. FDR neither trusted nor liked the brash and ruthless Irishman and privately excoriated him. Kennedy became such an embarrassment to FDR that he was recalled as America's representative to the Court of St. James.

And yet, many Americans shared Kennedy's anti-interventionist view. Of this new war Americans would typically shrug their shoulders and say, "Well, I hope Roosevelt doesn't get us into it," or "Let's hope it doesn't come over here." All through the 1930s Congress passed—and Roosevelt signed as a nod to rural and Southern constituencies—various Neutrality Acts that banned certain forms of trade with Europe, particularly sales of military equipment. Other laws passed in the 1930s prevented U.S. troops from leaving North America.

The largest and most vocal opponents of joining the war were the members of the America First Committee, which had widespread and significant support, including famed transatlantic pilot Charles A. Lindbergh. The America First movement had sprung up after the German invasion of Poland in September 1939, heralding the beginning of the new world war in Europe. They possessed such influence over the foreign policy debate that FDR pledged to the nation's "mothers and fathers" during his 1940 reelection bid, "your boys are not going to be sent into any foreign wars."[77] Even as Hitler stormed across the European continent and England was fighting to the last, Americans were unmoved to get into it.

But by early 1941, FDR had craftily shifted the debate. The advent of Lend-Lease, a program to supply arms and equipment to American allies while staying otherwise uninvolved in the war itself, allowed America to avoid intervention as well as isolation. The old Neutrality Acts were abrogated, and Lend-Lease passed in March 1941.

It was originally pitched as a plan for Great Britain to operate on a "cash-and-carry" basis. But as Winston Churchill's government ran low on funds, the plan was radically altered so the English could "borrow" old American ships and other war materiel and pay the U.S. government later. Many editorialists squawked. So too did the America Firsters.

FDR, the old master, had sold his argument to Congress and the American people with the rather tenuous allegory that if your neighbor's house was on fire, you wouldn't refuse him your garden hose, because his house fire threatened your house. You wouldn't sell him the hose; you'd loan it and get it back when he was done. Of course, no one expected ships and other war materiel to come back in the same shape in which it had been lent. As Senator Bob Taft wryly observed, there were two things people did not return: used military equipment and used chewing gum. But that unappetizing comparison didn't stop FDR from carrying the day.

The morning of December 1, 1941, Americans still believed they would be able to avoid any of the conflict, but by that afternoon, things had noticeably changed. The morning papers carried headlines saying the Japanese wanted to continue talks. By the afternoon, many were reporting a worsening situation, especially after a 10:00 a.m. meeting between U.S. Secretary of State Cordell Hull and the Japanese envoys that took just over an hour. They had also met the day before, on Sunday, in an extraordinary and top-secret meeting.[78]

Hull had also met in secret with British ambassador Lord Halifax, where Halifax briefed Hull on British and Japanese developments in the Far East.[79] A reporter asked Kichisaburo Nomura if the Americans and the Japanese could reach some sort of accord, and the ambassador replied ominously, "I believe there must be wise statesmanship to save the situation."[80] And "Japan voiced a preference today for further negotiations with the United States for peace in the Pacific in place of war." This was despite "great differences in the viewpoints of the two governments."[81]

In a previous meeting, Special Envoy Saburo Kurusu gave some odd comfort to Hull, telling him, "You are on Hitler's list before us." The accepted wisdom was that the Japanese were "subservient" to Hitler and would not make a move without his approval, and that if things turned bad for Hitler on the Russian front, the Empire of the Rising Sun would shrink from any military actions against the British or the Free French in the Far East.[82]

The combustible premier of Japan, Hideki Tojo, was less sanguine. He'd just issued a statement announcing that "Japan will have to do everything to wipe out with a vengeance British and American exploitation in the Far East." He also used the word *purged* in reference to the Americans' and Brits' presence in the Far East.[83] Noncombatants in Shanghai and Thailand were warned by their governments to evacuate soon, including Americans.[84] The British were readying their forces to defend the Burma Road.[85]

Nomura was also asked about Tojo's over-the-top remarks and replied that the premier had been "'badly misquoted' in news dispatches." He was also asked about resuming negotiations with Secretary Hull and he replied, "They have never been broken off."[86] Most indications were that both parties wanted to continue negotiations to forestall any further problems in the Pacific. Indeed, it was reported that Japan wanted to continue negotiations for another two weeks, to reach a solution to the impasse.[87] The Japanese cabinet "had decided to continue negotiations despite great differences in the viewpoints of the two governments" after meeting in a "special cabinet session." This communiqué came from Domei, a Japanese government-run news agency.[88] Hull also met with the Chinese ambassador, Dr. Hu Shih, Australian minister Richard Casey, and Netherlands minister Dr. Alexander Loudon.[89]

Just a few days earlier, President Roosevelt had journeyed south to Warm Springs, Georgia, where he had availed himself of the hot mineral waters for years, in a vain attempt to cure his polio. He bought a house nearby that was nicknamed the "Little White House" by the press corps.[90] He was photographed carving a turkey for the patients at the Warm Springs Foundation, where together they were celebrating a "delayed Thanksgiving."[91] At a cocktail party in his honor, FDR downed several Old Fashioneds, his favorite drink, saw his former longtime secretary Marguerite "Missy" LeHand, now herself a victim of "acute neuritis" and a patient at Warm Springs, and ate heartily of the postponed Thanksgiving feast. FDR always had a big appetite and had several helpings of turkey, "gingered fresh fruit in cider . . . oyster-corn stuffing [and] pumpkin pie."[92]

The president had looked forward to spending an extended time in Georgia, until he took a confidential call over the weekend from Secretary of State Hull. Hull advised FDR that things in the Pacific had suddenly taken a turn, possibly for the worse.[93] He was in ongoing tense discussions with Special Envoy Saburo Kurusu and Ambassador Kichisaburo Nomura. Kurusu's wife was the former Alice Little of Chicago, Illinois. The men were photographed in America's newspapers, smiling, polite,[94] although it was also reported they had emerged from one meeting with Hull looking "grave."[95] All told, FDR was in Warm Springs for about twenty-six hours, got in only a short swim, and departed for Washington looking "grave."[96] Roosevelt's hurried departure on his special train, the *Ferdinand Magellan*, was "without the usual gay hand-waving to the crowds of back-country farmers, out to see the caravan whoosh past." He arrived at the White House at 11:30 the morning of the first.

By the afternoon of Monday, December 1, Americans knew about the call between Hull and FDR the previous evening and the president's speedy return to Washington as a result. Roosevelt was spotted looking "grim," an affliction that was apparently spreading. The *New York Times* reported that if negotiations broke down, "the American fleet in the Pacific . . . had instructions for . . . what to do if hostilities start."[97] It was later reported that FDR had met in secret with the chief of Naval Operations, Admiral Harold R. Stark.

Just the night before in Georgia, he'd given a startling speech in which he radically altered course, saying, "It is always possible that our boys may actually be fighting for the defense of these American institutions of ours" within the year.[98] It was the first reference to the possibility of American boys dying on another continent.

White House reporters knew of the president's return by the sudden appearance of his beloved Scottie, Fala. The dog trotted into a room full of reporters, barking and wagging his tail. "Ah, the President's home," said Mrs.

Roosevelt when she saw the dog.[99] The White House refused to say exactly why FDR had cut short his trip to Warm Springs.

Upon his return, FDR met in private with Hull in the Oval Office, after the secretary's meeting with the Japanese representatives. Several days earlier, Hull had given the Japanese envoys a response in writing, stating the Americans would not cease their embargo until and unless the Japanese withdrew their forces from China.[100] The Japanese made it clear they had no intentions of slowing their drive down the Asian continent, rejecting the U.S. position as "fantastic."[101]

Waiting on FDR's desk the morning of the first was a confidential memo from his "real world" eyes and ears, John Franklin Carter. The memo detailed the Japanese population along the Mexican border around Corpus Christi and Galveston. In summary, there were very few Japanese in the south of Texas in late 1941. "Everything very quiet along the border. There seems to be more anti-Japanese prejudice in Texas than in California, also more suspicion."[102] Most who saw FDR thought he looked good and healthy, even if he did not have the suntan he was usually known for, because of extra-long hours of work in the Oval Office.

The National Industrial Conference Board estimated that the "economic blockade" of Japan by the United States, Great Britain, and the Netherland Indies had "cut off 75 per cent of her normal imports."[103] Japan had a population in 1941 of 73 million occupying a land mass smaller than California.[104] The embargo was hurting the empire of Japan and her people, but it was also hurting American exporters.

An AP report clacked, "Whether the Japanese decision is a step toward a final settlement which conceivably might take Tokyo out of the Axis camp or a mere temporizing in the hope of a more propitious day for hard talk with the United States remains to be seen."[105]

FDR, after meeting with cabinet members about the Far East developments, saw his doctor that evening at 7:15 and then dined alone in his study at 7:30 before retiring at 11:00 p.m.[106]

Some afternoon papers reported the situation as "grave" and that no more talks between the Americans and the Japanese were contemplated,[107] while other reports said they wanted to continue them for "at least two weeks."[108] The headline of the *Panama City News-Herald* said, "Nazi Reversals Cause Japs to Ask More Time."[109]

Newspaper reports were often contradictory. But Americans also read of private meetings in the Philippines between Gen. Douglas MacArthur and Adm. Thomas C. Hart to discuss "emergency steps."[110]

CHAPTER 2

THE SECOND OF DECEMBER

"Japan Renews Talks, but Capital Is Skeptical"

New York Times

"U.S. Asks Japan to Explain Troop Moves"

Washington Evening Star

"All America Must Pull Together, Lecturer Warns"

Birmingham News

As the Christmas season grew closer, over 800,000 furloughs had been granted to America's soldiers and sailors, all of whom now would have to find a way home. A flight on Delta Airlines from Birmingham to Dallas was $32.[1] On American Airlines, a round trip flight between New York and Washington was $21.90.[2] These were considerable sums at the time, so for most people traveling by commercial air was out of the question.

What about the train? Because of Washington's bungling and unpredicted requisitions by the military, there was a shortage of railroad passenger cars. And the ride in some locales would be inhospitable. In New York, for instance, the Board of Transportation was to begin enforcing regulations prohibiting "smoking or spitting in stations, platforms and cars."[3] With no planes and few trains, soldiers had to either fight for a seat on a Greyhound bus or depend upon the generosity of private citizens with automobiles.

Because of regulations, military personnel were prohibited from hitch-hiking. A campaign in the Golden State was organized by the California Automobile Association to help soldiers and sailors avoid trouble. Motorists who volunteered could place on their windshield a sticker issued by the group that would tell young men in uniform that the driver was participating in the "Give Them a Lift" effort.[4]

Travel was on the mind of many. On the West Coast, residents of four counties in California and one in Oregon attempted to create the forty-ninth state of "Jefferson."[5] They were apparently upset about poor thoroughfare conditions and declared they wanted to secede "only on Thursdays to impress on their present States the seriousness of their petitions for improved roads and aid in development of resources."[6] Armed civilians stopped cars passing through their counties to hand them pamphlets.

Fortunately, the cars forced to sit and idle had plenty of gasoline, as did all Americans. This was true even though use was up sharply—11 percent—over the previous years, despite the admonitions by the government for Americans to use less. Total gas consumption for 1941 was projected to rise by 2.5 billion gallons from the previous year. But there were also, according to estimates, 2.5 million more cars on the road.[7]

The Traffic Subcommittee of the U.S. House released a report on the state of automobile traffic in Washington. The document said in no uncertain terms that "making recommendations for relief of the traffic problem in Washington properly emphasizes the need for long-range remedies rather than temporary palliatives if there is to be any reasonably permanent and effective cure of the city's parking and traffic ills."[8] The immediate construction of a subway was discussed as a cure.

Police in Kansas City were concerned with more mundane questions. They assembled a group of fifteen drivers and plied them with shots of whiskey each half hour "to determine at what stage of drunkenness a driver is at his worst." Of the fifteen, "one dropped out after a phone call to his wife, one fell asleep, three appeared still sober after seven drinks." Another complained he was a Scotch, not a bourbon, drinker. "Most of the men lost their driving judgment. But one improved for a time. His explanation: he was so nervous from being around cops that the liquor steadied him." Having reached no definite conclusions, the police packed the more or less drunk men into squad cars and drove them home.[9]

Worried about inflation settling in the auto industry, the Office of Price Administration fired a shot across the hood of auto manufacturers by announcing it would set a ceiling price on the cost of new cars. Said the head of the automobile section of the OPA, Cyrus McCormick, "The Government had the power to regiment the automobile industry to the nth degree."[10] Despite expressing personal concerns about such actions, his division went ahead with a complicated formula to regulate costs and production in Detroit that was even stricter than had been previously imposed.

Americans were keen on avoiding war and were for the most part unaware that it was coming their way. In the Philippines—relatively close to Indochina, where hundreds of thousands of Japanese troops were amassing—the Army Air Corps fighter planes under Gen. Douglas MacArthur's command were still lined up wingtip to wingtip at Clark Field. It was the same at Hickam Field in Honolulu, where hundreds of army and navy planes were also lined up in such a tight fashion.

Gen. Walter Short, in command of the army garrison in the Hawaiian Islands, was more worried about saboteurs than about aerial bombardment. *Sabotage* is derived from *sabot*, the French word for shoe. In an earlier era, when French factory workers were unhappy with their working conditions, they threw their shoes into the machinery. Short was more concerned about the thousands of Japanese workers on the islands throwing something at the military planes there on the ground than something hurling at them from the air.[11]

Also lined up—neat as you please—along "Battleship Row" in Pearl Harbor were American battleships, considered by most of the brass as the backbone of the navy. Battleships since the time of Stephen Decatur and John Paul Jones had borne the brunt of battles on the high seas. Most of the admirals in December 1941 were elderly men who viewed aircraft carriers as a passing fancy and not an important part of their operations. Serious navy men put their faith in battlewagons and not flattops.

Even so, Congress approved an additional $7 billion for new tanks, armaments, and other munitions, but the outlays would go to help Russia, China, and Britain.[12] Helping to foot the bill was the ever-present American taxpayer, purchasing Defense Stamps[13] from the government that could later be cashed in with interest.

The War Department and Washington were at the time teeming with corruption. Senator Harry Truman of Missouri, himself a product of the corrupt Tom Pendergast political machine in that state, was heading an investigation into the waste and fraud in the defense industry. Truman chaired an investigation of corporate suppliers to the U.S. military, spotlighting war profiteering and shoddy materials. His relentless inquiry ruffled feathers, but he didn't care, exposing one dirty and corrupt project after another. One construction venture for the army was supposed to cost $20 million, but five months later, cost overruns had shot the price tag up to $51 million. Dozens of contractors, including Ferguson-Oman and Taylor-Hale, overbilled and underdelivered, costing the taxpayer untold millions. The government was paying rent on equipment that wasn't worth the cost of the rental charge; other equipment was rented to the government and then hidden. It went on and on and on. One witness testified before the Truman Commission, "It seems to me all Ferguson-Oman officials and employees are organized to cost the Government every dollar they can."[14] As a result, Congress tightened military contracting practices.

Two other congressional committees were investigating a magazine that purported to have close ties to the Democratic Party and thus was strong-arming defense contractors into purchasing ads in the *Democratic National Press*. One knowledgeable source said their methods "would make Al Capone blush with envy."[15] It later turned out the publication had nothing to do with the party.

Yet another congressional investigation uncovered an apparently penniless man who somehow received a $200,000 defense contract for unspecified purposes and was using the money to entertain politicians and defense contractors in Washington at "championship prize fights."

"Investigators . . . have dug up considerable information about 'middle men,' 'brokers,' and 'go-betweens' who have neither manufacturing facilities . . . nor any legitimate connection with Government agencies. Yet they are said to haunt Washington hotels and ante-rooms in large numbers, seeking commissions on the basis of their alleged influence."[16]

Public monies were also appropriated for tens of thousands of houses on growing military bases, courtesy of the Public Buildings Administration. Thoughtfully, the PBA also hired a consultant for interior decorating, Miss Gladys Miller, but it wasn't made clear if she would personally redecorate every one of the forty thousand houses in the works. "She recommended . . . the purchase of furniture to scale with the rooms . . . gay, vivid colors to lend a cheery note; elimination of unnecessary objects." In addition to being paid by the U.S. taxpayer for her sage advice on paints, furniture, and spacing, she was also conveniently on the staff at New York University.[17]

The NFL title game was set for December 21, between the New York Giants and either the Green Bay Packers or the Chicago Bears, who still had one game left to play and were tied for the Western division championship. Depending on the winner, the game would be held either in Green Bay or the Windy City because of their superior records.[18] The American Professional Football League was considering expanding in order to compete with the National Football League. Washington could have used a new franchise after a dismal loss, which marked their worst record since 1935. They were scheduled to get a second pro team, which many thought the city needed given the sad-sack Redskins, often derided as the "Deadskins."[19]

In Manhattan, Tommy Manville, age forty-seven, a scion of the twenties era of "Wonderful Nonsense," professional inheritor, and reminder of why so many hated the rich, took a wife—his fifth—Bonita Francine Edwards, twenty-two, heiress to a Chicago lumber fortune. The couple met only four days before their betrothal. Manville said, "[L]ong engagements may be out of style," and Edwards confessed, "I'm not in love with Tommy—I'm just infatuated. I hope to fall in love with him after a while."[20] F. Scott Fitzgerald was right about the rich, and Manhattan was still ruled by the Vanderbilts,

Warburgs, and Astors, for whom the rules seldom applied because the rich were different—or at least always assumed as much about themselves.

On the other side of the rules spectrum, the first inductee under the new Selective Service act, buck private John Edward Lawton, said after a year as a dogface, "Army life is alright . . . but I don't think I'm exactly cut out for it."[21] Senator Henry Cabot Lodge told Republicans in Massachusetts that the United States needed a standing army of no less than 750,000 men, but if the country went to war, it might need on the order of 5 million men in uniform.[22]

At Jordan Marsh, a high-end department store in Boston, women's shoes were going for $7.50.[23] Customers looking for something a bit more affordable could turn to R.H. White's "bargain basement," where they could be purchased for $1.95.[24] Stockings at Jordan Marsh went for $1.15 a pair—the "philmy" kind—but "conditions may soon mean that silk top-to-toe stockings will be a luxury-memory."[25] "Health girdles" were squeezing American women for $7.00 apiece at Conrad's store in Boston.[26] In Washington, another expensive department store, Woodward & Lothrop, was touting men's dinner jackets for $75 for the "holiday season."[27]

The Office of Price Administration called on consumers to limit the wrapping on Christmas packaging. The call was issued by Lessing J. Rosenwald, director of the OPM's Industrial Conservation Bureau.[28]

But in her press conference, Eleanor Roosevelt suggested that Americans not be "too practical" in their gift buying. Gifts, she said, "should include those traditionally dispensed by Santa Claus." Mrs. Roosevelt revealed that the White House Christmas tree in the East Room would be "all white . . . and the White House will be decked out in holly, mistletoe and poinsettias. There'll be presents for the White House staff. . . . Just as on eight other Christmas Eves, the President and Mrs. Roosevelt will hang up their stockings at the big mantle in the chief executive's bedroom. There will be a sock, too, for Fala, just as there was last year when the President's Scottie got his first rubber bone." She told the reporters all of her shopping was nearly done.[29]

A delegation of Washington State Indians went to Washington to complain about government regulations that prevented them from purchasing liquor. A headline in the *Washington Post* read, "Indians Here to Demand Fire Water."[30]

William Henry Murray, a philosopher of sorts known as "Wild Bill," advised city folk to burn their paper money, "move to the country, can fruit and vegetables, and bury them in the ground to 'have something to eat when the trouble comes.'"[31]

Meanwhile, actress Tallulah Bankhead was hospitalized with the flu in Philadelphia, but it was reported that she was "much better after a day in an oxygen tent." Actor John Barrymore was also hospitalized, reportedly for an intestinal flu.[32] Though not reported, it was known they both drank deeply from the wrong bottle and often, although Bankhead's tastes sometimes ran more to cocaine and other drugs. She once quipped about cocaine not being habit-forming—"I ought to know, I've been using it for years."[33] Her father, William Brockman Bankhead, had been Speaker of the U.S. House from 1936 to 1940 until his untimely death, and she was frequently in Washington, partying from Anacostia to Bethesda, shocking women and delighting men.

In California, the first of the paper drives was announced, as there was a shortage of wood pulp in the country, according to the government. The Boy Scouts and the Salvation Army joined forces to collect old newspapers.

Federal taxes were scheduled to rise in 1942, but so too were many state and local taxes. For some in the higher brackets, they would only get one seventh of any raise, while the federal government would take the other six-sevenths.[34]

FDR officially signed legislation repealing portions of the Neutrality Act while also calling for the passage of legislation that curtailed strikes by unions in war-related industries.[35] But almost anything could fall under that designation, from agriculture to steel to newspapers. Yet another strike was threatened, this one by railroad workers. A deadline by the railroad union was set for December 7.

Meanwhile, a Japanese "expert" on America offered his assessment to his government on why America would be no competition for them in a war. "The national debt, a 'spoiled child' mentality, low national morale at the first defeat [Robert] Taft, [Gerald] Nye and [Charles] Lindbergh will lead a revolt, Roosevelt is a 'buffoon,' hesitancy, Americans excite easily and cool easily, disunity—with 20,000,000 Negroes, 10,000,000 unemployed, 5,000,000 trade unionists, inflation."[36] Taft, Nye, and Lindbergh were all leaders in the isolationist movement.

Many headlines referred to "Japs" or "Nips" (for "Nipponese"), and virtually every political cartoon of the era depicted the Japanese in the worst possible racial stereotype: short, squinty eyes, large glasses, buck teeth, in a menacing military uniform.

America and Great Britain considered and finally—after much haggling over fishing rights, fish oil, and wheat—aided Iceland under Lend-Lease, and troops from both countries were sent there, "all with a healthy taste for blondes." Iceland was the oldest democracy in the world, with a Parliament dating over one thousand years, the Althing. Despite rampant inflation, the Icelandic government "rejected price control-plans as smacking of State Socialism."[37]

While not the case in Iceland, America's and England's economies were heavily regulated and rationed. A black market thrived in the midst of the rationing, and in Britain a person could get everything from eggs, perfume, and lipstick to fruits, silk stockings, and clothes. Politicians' wives seemed to have no difficulty purchasing consumer items, including fur coats. Silk stockings were highly prized. Oranges—supposedly only for children— were consumed by all. With paper in short supply, the government ordered a "no-wrapping" rule, but this simply made it easier for thieves to identify what they wanted to steal. Shoplifting was rampant. False identity cards were sold by the thousands, allowing British subjects to register at multiple stores in order to purchase double or triple their allowed quotas of milk and other food stuffs.[38] The British experiment at managing the economy was an incomplete success.

Still, the Brits were facing the war, depravations, and bombings with a very proper stiff upper lip. The Royal Air Force had considered the stress young pilots must being going through before, during, and after the Battle of Britain, and set up psychiatric hospitals and counseling centers for the flyers, but no one partook. The facilities stood idle and were eventually converted to other uses. Understandably, one British pilot who crashed six times "went berserk."[39]

A British psychiatrist said that the lower classes handled stress better than the upper classes, as did children even more so than before the war, and those who did exhibit psychiatric problems were from broken homes and were not suffering as a result of the bombings. They even took to playing "air-raid games." Women too showed fewer signs of neuroses than before the war, it was felt, because the war gave them a new set of priorities and "pivotal values." "In London department stores, during heavy bombardment, the absence rate was lower than before."[40]

The American economy—especially outside of the industrial effort to support Great Britain and Russia—continued to suffer, and government agencies were created to help the small businessman. A premium was placed on advertising, as with the Hotel Pennsylvania in New York City, which offered "sterilized glasses in your bathroom" and the loan of "pajamas . . . a typewriter," or a "nonallergic pillow!" The ads were specifically targeted to businessmen traveling for the war effort, and a single room went for $3.85 per night and $5.50 per night for two. "The lobby, public rooms and restaurants are gay with new decorations." Glenn Miller was performing in the hotel's club room.[41]

The economy of the South was showing improvement as demand for cotton for military uniforms had jacked up the cost sky high. The price had reached a twelve-year peak, and farm income across the South was up substantially since the advent of Lend-Lease in early 1941.

On Capitol Hill, the House passed legislation regulating the importation of sugar from outside the country, while favoring and expanding quotas for domestic cane and beet sugar growers. The State Department opposed the action, seeing it as antagonistic toward potential war allies, but the Department of Agriculture supported it, seeing it as favoring domestic allies.[42]

For some, there was no Great Depression. The Andrews Sisters—LaVerne, Patty, and Maxine—sold their eight millionth record, for which Decca Records paid them the princessly sum of 2 cents per. They were harmoniously making on average $5,000 per week, before taxes.[43]

For American amateur and professional painters, it was another scene. Because so many of their canvases and brushes were imported from Ireland,

Belgium, and the USSR (there, brushes were made from Russian squirrels), they faced a shortage, and because so many of their paints contained precious metals such as zinc and cadmium—rare earth metals possibly needed for the war effort—they faced a possible confiscation of the metals by the government. "Manhattan's American Artists' Professional League recently petitioned Washington for cooperation in keeping artists supplied with their annual ration of paint (about a gallon apiece.)"[44]

America's parents and educators worried about the low reading proficiency of pupils. There were "16,000,000 illiterates in the United States—they cannot read beyond the fourth-grade reading level." Of all places, Harvard found that incoming freshmen had low reading acumen, and the school was forced to "start a course in reading fundamentals." Professor Reed Smith, sixty, of the University of South Carolina thought he knew the problem. "The old principle . . . that you can't sharpen an ax on a velvet grindstone has given place to the view that if the pupils don't like it, they shouldn't be required to do it . . . [T]he underlying assumption seems to be . . . that students will write clearly and correctly by some sort of blessed intuition if only the teacher does not depress them with such inconvenient and unprofitable matters as spelling, paragraphing, punctuation, sentence structure, grammar and the choice and order of words."[45]

On American campuses, there was growing agitation for war with Germany. At the University of Chicago, Professor Bernadette Schmitt said that "western civilization would not be safe until the German people were crushed on their own soil." She made her comments at the twenty-first annual meeting of the National Council for the Social Studies, gathering in Indianapolis.[46]

FDR had passed through Atlanta on his way to Warm Springs, but did not get off the train, though he did have his window open so he could be seen. On the way back to Washington, the curtains to his private car were closed. Had he stayed there, he might have tuned in to WGST to hear *Aunt Hattie* or *Man I Married*. The station was turned on at 6:00 a.m. and turned off at midnight. On 750AM, WSB, he might have heard the *Dixie Farm Hour*, or later, the soap opera *Guiding Light*, or later still, Fred Waring, a popular band leader. Like WGST, the station WSB also came on at 6:00 a.m. and "signed off" at midnight.[47]

One region where the economy—at least for the "nobility" there—was doing well was Hollywood. It was raking in millions each week, mostly for the "Big Five" studios: 20th Century Fox, RKO, Paramount Pictures, Warner Brothers, and Metro-Goldwyn-Mayer. Fifty-four actors made over $100,000 per year, but 50 percent of all the actors there had never made more than $10,500 per year. Indeed, the average annual income for over seven thousand extras "was $350.00."

Two-thirds of the producers in Hollywood made over $150,000, including the shy and retiring Orson Welles, for whom it was said, "There but for the grace of God, goes God." The "colony" was described as "nouveau riche, thriving . . . lacks lineage and decorum" whose power players "came from vaudeville, flea circuses, petty trade, other shabby zones of enterprise."[48] Hollywood did have to make some concessions to the world situation, including canceling the banquet at which the 1942 Academy Awards would be presented. Also, Los Angeles proclaimed "Medical Aid to Russia" day to raise money for Mother Russia and "Uncle Joe" Stalin.[49]

Citizen Kane's release was bitterly fought by the subject of the movie, William Randolph Hearst, and many movie houses in America did not show it for months—or at all. Hearst controlled a vast media empire and with it, enormous power. Deeply offended by Orson Welles's critical portrait of him, Hearst even made brazen threats to expose Hollywood scandals; studio heads offered to buy the film from RKO, at a price that guaranteed a small profit, if in return Kane were shelved or destroyed. Thankfully, RKO turned him down, and the movie that is consistently voted by critics as the Best American Film Ever Made lived on for posterity, to be endlessly explicated by intellectuals and studied in film classes ever after.

Citizen Kane debuted—"long-awaited" and "Nothing Censored!" said the Birmingham News—at the Empire Theater in Birmingham, Alabama, yet a local column panned not the movie but Welles himself, comparing him to Hitler. "Certainly he has applied almost Hitlerian policies in his approach to fame."[50] Admission was 30 cents. Another racy movie airing was *Honky Tonk*, starring Lana Turner and Clark Gable.

The power of movies in 1941 could not be underestimated. They enthralled all in America, were affordable, and theaters across the country were often the hub of social activity for families, boys and girls, children, social clubs, and fan clubs. One of the biggest stars of the era, Gable, took off his shirt in the movie *It Happened One Night* to reveal his bare and masculine chest. Unlike most men in America, he did not wear a T-shirt, and as a result, T-shirt sales dropped 40 to 50 percent in one year. The power of movies was such that Pope Pius XII devoted "a special papal encyclical to it." When classic novels such as *David Copperfield* and *Wuthering Heights* were made into movies, copies of the books flew off the shelves at public libraries and bookstores.[51]

Hitler remained a fascinating (if also feared, loathed, and later hated figure) for many Americans, and one of the most popular books of the time was *Total Espionage*, published by Putnam. The book detailed the rise of the Third Reich and the men behind it and especially how they had perfected the art of spying and intelligence gathering.[52] But Americans were also reading novels such as *Grim Grow the Lilacs*, *Forty Whacks*, and *Prescription for Murder*.[53]

News reports said the British had mounted a counteroffensive using American-made army tanks against the Germans in North Africa and that Russia was pushing back the German advance on Moscow, aided by the harsh Russian winter, just as it had aided Russia once before against Napoleon. But many of the news reports of Russian successes came from the Soviets' own state-controlled news agencies, including the Soviet Information Bureau, so it was difficult to know fact from fiction.

Double-talk from the Russians was the rule, rather than the exception. As they were claiming their hold on the port city of Rostov, it was reported that German troops had secured the town. The Russians had evacuated because of "unnecessary losses," but the Germans had taken "more favorable positions to meet the Russian assaults."[54] Of course, when it came to disinformation, the Germans were no pikers, and they matched the Soviets lie for lie in describing the Russian Front. A spokesman claimed German troops could see Moscow "with the aid of good field glasses."[55] All in all, reports from the winter battle were a mishmash of lies, distortions, half-truths, and prevarications. It was clear, though, that both sides had suffered horrific losses of men, many simply due to the bitterly cold weather, especially the Germans, who were underprepared for the Russian winter.

The battle could be heard in London, live, via radio. "The guns never cease. . . . The battle is fierce. The Germans are continually throwing in new troops," said an announcer on the scene.[56]

Meanwhile, Roosevelt spoke before the State Chairmen of Birthday Ball Committees, who were planning festive celebrations in each state for FDR's birthday in January, when he would turn sixty on the thirtieth.[57]

The birthday was celebrated in part to raise money for the March of Dimes, whose purpose was to cure infantile paralysis, and while nobody mentioned the president's affliction, many knew about it.

At home the debate continued over the America First Committee and its stances. Most of the debate focused on their high-profile members, especially Charles Lindbergh, but the membership also included former president Herbert Hoover, retired General Robert E. Wood, and 1936 GOP nominee Alf Landon, as well as Norman Thomas, a nationally known leader of socialism in America. Other prominent members included Walt Disney, Alice Roosevelt Longworth, and famed writers and liberals Sinclair Lewis and E. E. Cummings.

The GOP's 1940 nominee, Wendell Willkie, was a vicious opponent of the "Firsters." Formed only one year earlier, the organization had gained national prominence because of its mission and the people involved. Wood was a highly decorated veteran of the Great War and by 1941 was the chairman of the Sears & Roebuck Co.

The East and West Coast papers were generally more internationalist, while the periodicals from the center of the country generally opposed any U.S. involvement in the European war. As a result, America First was more popular in middle and rural America, less so in the metropolises of New York, Washington, Los Angeles, and San Francisco.

The America Firsters announced their intention to have as much influence over the 1942 off-year elections as possible by supporting candidates who "have kept faith with the people's mandate to avoid participation in the war." They would support any Republican or Democrat who opposed entry into the European war.[58]

If Henry Luce's *Life* and *Time* magazines could be reasonably described as pro-FDR and pro-intervention, the weekly magazine *Look* was a downright "pap" sheet for FDR, the Democrats, and the New Deal while ripping Republicans and anybody who stood in the way of the sophisticates of Washington and New York.

As with the Luce publications, nary a woman was found in the masthead of *Look* magazine, though women were often the most enthusiastic readers. The magazine was loaded with ads for Ipana Tooth Paste, Kleenex, Sal Hepatica (yet another laxative), movies such as *The Men in Her Life* starring Loretta Young, Listerine Tooth Paste, General Electric clocks, Chevrolet trucks (with the "Load-Master" engine), Colgate Dental Crème ("Scientific tests prove conclusively that in 7 out of 10 cases, Colgate Dental Crème instantly stops oral bad breath"),[59] Zenith radios, Pond's Vanishing Cream, Sanka Coffee, Ovaltine, General Electric vacuum cleaners, the U.S. Army Recruiting Service, and of course, cigarettes. Chesterfield cigarettes featured the beautiful actress Maureen O'Hara pitching them in the obliging carton size, which displayed photos of handsome young men in navy and army uniforms. The copy helpfully suggested, "[D]on't forget to mail them to the boys in the Service."[60] She was also found in the newspapers hawking Lux soap.[61]

One feature story in *Look* magazine was written by a "friendly critic of the New Deal" who nudged Roosevelt for not doing more to ramp up Americans' fears to help push them into the war as soon as possible.[62] Another was a profile of the many "dollar-a-year men" who had gone to Washington to man the New Deal. A survey was made, and some "288 Men, 1 Woman" were listed in the "dollar-a-year class."[63] Having made millions in other lines of work, they now stepped forward to "donate" their administrative and leadership skills to help Roosevelt implement the New Deal. This article was about Floyd

Odlum, who'd made millions on Wall Street, cashing out before the crash in 1929. He made his fortune by "pyramiding." The article said he cashed out because he'd been "expecting a crash."[64]

The ubiquitous celebrity story, this time covering the "Café Society" of New York socialites, appeared in *Look* with plenty of pictures of both the hoity-toity and the hoi polloi. Radio personalities such as Bob Hope and Jack Benny, showgirls such as Patricia Lee, gossip columnists, publicists, debutantes, columnist Walter Winchell, Betty Grable, and actor George Raft all made appearances in the fawning story.[65] It was harmless, but far more dangerous was an article that could only be labeled as propaganda, disinformation, and half-truths.

Under the appalling headline "Meet the Men and Women of Russia Whom Hitler Will Never Enslave," the article mentioned not one of the purges of the 1930s in which "Uncle Joe" Stalin put millions to death. It contained some of the most dreadful lies ever to appear in an American publication. "Russians Don't Like Slavery," said one subheading. The article claimed instead, "Only two decades ago they fought one of the bloodiest civil wars in history to free themselves from slavery to the Czar. They have not grown so used to the joys and dignities of freedom as to surrender them with apathy." And, "There are only 2,000,000 Communists in Russia." And, "These are people who have been living in a new world—suddenly given . . . a voice in their government."[66] It was atrocious.

Another article berated conservatives in England, containing one self-serving and arrogant quote after another attacking the conservatives, but never with attribution. The "article" was clearly made up out of whole cloth by Samuel Spewack, a dramatist.[67] He and his wife, Bella, were successful as Hollywood screenwriters, but their politics were hopelessly leftist.

More disinformation was forthcoming from *Look* when they did a long feature on how women now preferred cotton stockings to silk stockings. Because of the war effort, silk was in short supply. Silk was needed for parachutes and was regulated by the Supply Priorities and Allocations Board.[68] Cotton stockings were being churned out by experimental mills with the Department of Agriculture. To buttress the point of the article, actresses Rita Hayworth, Ann Sheridan, Dorothy Lamour, and Linda Darnell sported their "gams" in the hideous cotton covering for the benefit of photographers.

Of course, these women's legs were so beautiful, they could have been wearing cow hides and their legs still would have looked gorgeous. Unfortunately, also showing his legs for the article was Vice President Henry Wallace, who should have worn cow hide for the photograph.

In Washington, the chairman of the House Committee on Un-American Activities, Martin Dies of Texas, a Democrat, charged that "Communists and Criminals" had infiltrated the leadership of the American labor movement, specifically the Congress of Industrial Organizations, the principal umbrella group for organized labor.[69] The labor movement and the Roosevelt administration hated Dies. At the last minute, railroad workers gained huge concessions from the railroad companies, courtesy of a "compromise" hammered out by the government. The strike that had been set for December 7 was averted.

However, the army did discover a plot involving at least eighteen members of the Socialist Workers Party who were conspiring "to create insubordination in the armed forces of the Government." They were convicted in a trial in Minneapolis and faced up to ten years in prison. These were the first ever "convictions under the Smith amendment to the Sedition Act of 1861,"[70] which made it against the law to advocate overthrowing the government.

In the Mediterranean, the British government announced it had sunk three Italian naval ships headed for Libya where the Axis powers were fighting a furious tank battle with the British. The British ships suffered no damage or casualties in the battle.[71] Still, the Germans won a major victory in North Africa by cutting through British forces and "joining their two panzer divisions," and in the process the Brits were compelled to retreat from Rezegh and Bir El Hamed. The British forces, as a result of the maneuver, were encircled, with their backs to the sea. "A British spokesman . . . said the joining of the 15th and 21st Panzer Divisions had not in any way impaired British confidence." He said, "It could be termed a local German success."[72] The Germans accomplished this even as two Italian tank divisions fled the fight. Hitler's favorite general, Erwin Rommel, had engineered the counter-offensive. An embedded American journalist with the *Boston Globe* traveled for ten days with the British forces in Libya, noting that he had to get by on only two cups of tea per day, like everybody else, but "no other liquid."[73] The journalist Matthew Halton captured well the dangers and deprivations of war in the desert. It was not pretty or desirable. Roosevelt had already received several worried memos from the British ambassador Lord Halifax—Edward Wood—apprising him of the bleak situation in North Africa.[74]

With British forces spread across the world, Winston Churchill proposed an expanded draft of civilian men. Now, men from the ages of "18½ to 50" would be drafted for military service, but the British government hinted that men as old as sixty might soon be drafted. Previously, the draft had been of men from nineteen to forty-one years of age. The prime minister called it a "crisis of man power and woman power." The plan was also to draft unmarried women between the ages of twenty and thirty. The prime minister, what's more, warned of a possible invasion by the Nazis.[75]

On December 2, much of the public concern of the afternoon before over war with Japan had waned a bit. Maybe cooler heads were thinking. But some in Washington were mulling over the explosive statement by the Japanese: "The United States does not understand the real situation in East Asia. It is trying to forcibly apply to East Asiatic countries fantastic principles and rules not adapted to the actual situation in the world and thereby tending to obstruct the construction of the New Order. This is extremely regrettable."[76]

Franklin Roosevelt "politely asked" the Japanese government for an explanation of its intentions in Southeast Asia, specifically on new troop movements into Indochina and whether this was a prelude to an invasion of Thailand.[77] There were also reports that the Japanese army was practicing drills using parachutes in Kwangtung.[78] Furthermore, Japan was seizing private ships to use for their navy, and there were worries that if they seized Thailand, Japan could cut off the trade routes to the Indian Ocean.[79]

FDR's request was given to the Japanese consulate in Washington via Undersecretary of State Sumner Welles, who was filling in for Cordell Hull, whom the *New York Times* said was "indisposed."[80] As Welles entered the room for their thirty-five-minute meeting, Ambassador Nomura blurted out, "Nobody wants war." Welles later told reporters he could not disclose anything that had been discussed, but Nomura did. He said he told Welles, "War would not settle the issues anyway. Issues that cannot be settled by diplomacy cannot be settled by war."[81] Yet a huge chasm divided the two countries, and not just over their policies of talking to reporters. Some speculated that FDR was about to take control of the negotiations, personally.[82] The meeting with Welles was inconclusive, as they had not yet answered the president's question. But the *Washington Post* reported that FDR "assumed direct command of diplomatic and military moves relating to Japan and the lights of peace flickered low in the Orient."[83] "Mr. Roosevelt recalled that this Government had been somewhat surprised in June when Japan had sent troops into Indo-China, while discussions were going on here in an effort to reach an understanding for a permanent peace in the Pacific area."[84] As of December, the Japanese already had amassed a huge army, navy, and air force in the region, but was still adding to it. Roosevelt met with Henry Stimson, his secretary of war, and Frank Knox, the secretary of the navy. In a separate meeting, he met with Adm. Harold Stark, the chief of Naval Operations, and Hull in the second floor oval study of the private residence in the White House at noon, to discuss yet again the situation in Thailand. These meetings had not previously been disclosed to the press, with whom he met at 4:00 p.m.[85]

Roosevelt's alter ego, Harry Hopkins, who had been hospitalized for weeks at the "Naval Hospital," left his bed and met with the president over lunch on December 1, according to reports.[86] A Japanese official said they wanted to "make the United States reconsider Pacific problems."[87] The media—especially the Japanese press—began referring to the "A, B, C, D" coalition (America, Britain, China, and Dutch East Indies) and how they were conspiring against the Japanese. The administration also began referring to the State Department's document given to the Japanese as "principles for peace in the Pacific."[88]

Analysts argued that if Japan went ahead and invaded Thailand, they would gain an advantage in a final assault on the Burma Road, a vital thoroughfare used to supply the Free Chinese. If the Japanese seized the Burma

Road, it would put them in better stead to attack the British and Dutch, it would allow Japan to further interdict tin, rubber, and other resources going to America, and it would be more evidence that the Axis powers really did want to rule the world. Some speculation intimated that Germany was over-extended in North Africa and on the Eastern Front, so would be of little aid to Japan in their drive south and deeper into China.[89] But news reports continued that the Japanese cabinet wanted to proceed with peace efforts.

At his press conference, Roosevelt expressed hope for a speedy response from Tokyo, but said that it would be "silly" to set a deadline for a reply.[90] News reports said the Japanese could not get back to Roosevelt for "three days or more" because they were seeking "'clarification' of various points in Secretary of State Cordell Hull's statement on the American position."[91] Newspapers in Tokyo suggested that with the new British ships arriving in the South Pacific by order of the Admiralty and because of the heightened state of alert by the British, American, and Dutch forces, it was they who were agitating for a war and accused the British of planning to invade Thailand.[92] Japanese news agencies also flooded the airwaves with accusations against Australia and America.[93]

In fact, it was revealed that the navy had evacuated all 750 marines in Shanghai and they'd been redeployed in the Philippines, out of harm's way. They had crossed the China Sea—along with remaining American civilians—in two ships, the *President Madison* and the *President Harrison*.[94]

Americans worried that if Japan invaded Thailand, "it would enable Japan to menace American sources of tin, rubber and other raw materials essential for defense production, and, by giving Japan a firm hold in the South Pacific, jeopardize the future security of the Philippines."[95]

On the other hand, various government experts were reassured. "If the Japanese want to start something . . . we can bomb Japanese cities and war objectives from the Philippines easier than they can come this way in the air, since we have longer range, faster planes—the flying fortresses." The U.S. government was reportedly sending more armaments to the Philippines to rebuff the Japanese if they attempted an invasion. "The highest Army and Navy authorities here expect a Pacific war to be a series of quick and heavy air blasts, like tornados over Japan, the Philippines, Indo-China and Malaya," reported radio journalist Royal Arch Gunnison for the Newspaper Alliance.[96]

The Japanese newspaper, *Yomiuri*, compared their circumstances with America's in 1776.[97]

Expenditures by the federal government in 1941—ending with the fiscal year in November—revealed that the government was only collecting in taxes one out of every three dollars it was spending. The government had brought in taxes from June to October just under $3 billion, but had spent almost $9 billion. Government officials were not worried about the massive borrowing, however, because new taxes would go into effect in 1942 and discussions were underway for even greater taxing of the American people. In that five-month period, 70 percent of federal spending had gone to defense.[98]

Like all bureaucracies, the navy was often engaged in fights large and small. As they watched earth-shattering developments around the world, a fierce turf battle broke out over who would "operate the cafeteria in the Navy Department Building."[99]

The Navy Cafeteria Association operated the dining hall, but Secretary Knox wanted the Public Buildings Administration to take things over. The association bitterly fought the secretary. "Officers of the Cafeteria Association insist that the cafeteria, which has been under their operation since 1937, provides better food, larger portions and better service." The facility provided for twelve thousand meals per day, and to break the impasse, the matter was turned over to the sage council of the Judge Advocate General.[100]

Several days later, FDR received a memo from an aide about a "Mr. Davies" who was complaining that the navy had commandeered his yacht, but it was not seeing any action. "The Auxiliary Vessels Board ... which indicates that if acquired, she will later be restored and returned to her owner in the condition in which received by the Navy—if still afloat at that time."[101] He also received a more serious memo on the horrible conditions the Polish prisoners were subjected to by the Soviets. "As penalties food rations are reduced to 300 grams of bread and 200 grams of thin soup every twenty-four hours and [the Poles were] imprisoned in cold, wet dungeons."[102]

Secretary of the Navy Knox seemed not to worry about the abilities of the U.S. Navy. He'd just written an article for *American Magazine* saying the navy "is ready for any emergency in the Atlantic or Pacific."[103] But it was noted in another publication that "units of the Japanese fleet have been reported maneuvering north of British Borneo."[104] No one paid attention.

The shooting war on the water continued unabated, and Germany had the upper hand over the Allies. It was disclosed that the British aircraft carrier, *Ark Royal*, had been sunk by U-boats in the Mediterranean, with a number of planes appallingly still strapped on her decks.[105] German ships had also sunk a number of Australian ships, both military and civilian.[106] Berlin exulted that in a matter of weeks, they had sent to the bottom forty-eight merchant ships and eleven naval craft while damaging thirty-nine others. All told, the Germans had sunk 231,870 tons in November alone.[107]

America was starting to churn out "Liberty" ships, which would become the backbone of the merchant marines. In Baltimore, six of these workhorse boats were shortly launched, including one christened the *Roger B. Taney*.[108] Taney, a son of Maryland, had been chief justice of the U. S. Supreme Court less than a century earlier and was famous for delivering the majority opinion in the *Dred Scott* decision, which in essence codified slavery in America, saying that slaves were not people but property and thus could not sue in federal courts.

No American war or discussion of war would be complete without its politicization, and syndicated columnist Walter Lippmann did the trick. "A failure on the part of the Republican party to give the national policy wholehearted support, which, of course, includes outspoken criticism of incompetence, unwisdom and inefficiency, will have to be construed as meaning only one thing: that the party is gambling on the defeat of the United States and that it is staking its political future on a national disaster. If the Republican party in Congress merely sulks and opposes, waiting for trouble, and appearing to hope for trouble . . . the Republican party will have placed itself in the intolerable position of have a vested interest in the humiliation and defeat of the United States."[109]

Yet another columnist, Westbrook Pegler, took dead aim at Congress, calling members there a "miserable, fumbling, timid aggregation of political trimmers and panhandlers" who bowed down before organized labor. Members were incensed, including Clare Hoffman of Michigan, who said, "Oh, we can lick Mr. Hitler all right but he's 2,000 miles away. But Pegler's right here at home." Hoffman called for a congressional investigation of Pegler.[110]

Pegler also became a shrill critic of a young up-and-coming singer, Frank Sinatra. In a preview of later cultural phenoms such as Elvis Presley, the skinny kid from Hoboken, dubbed "The Voice," was making teenage bobby-soxers swoon at the Paramount Theater in New York City. Social conservatives such as Pegler saw Sinatra as a threat to decent society; it didn't help that Sinatra was Italian, a flagrant philanderer, and an outspoken liberal. Pegler referred to the singer in his columns as a "New Deal Crooner"[111] and a "Commie Playboy."[112]

In 1941, newspaper columnists wielded enormous power. Pegler and many other ink-stained wretches of the day delighted in taking potshots at the earnest do-gooder Sinatra, suggesting that he was a reprobate at best and a communist at worst. Sinatra's vicious and unfair treatment at the hands of the press in the early 1940s helped explain his lifelong animosity toward the Fourth Estate, especially in his later years when the political outlook of Ol' Blue Eyes grew decidedly more conservative.

While Pegler decried the self-absorption of Sinatra's screeching teenage fans, the self-absorption of Capitol Hill was long and legendary. Members were squawking about parking fees on the Hill, and Congressman Everett Dirksen, a Republican from Illinois, proposed price controls. He complained that while downtown garages charged 60 cents for eight hours, lots and garages on Capitol Hill charged at much as 25 cents for the first hour, 10 cents for the second hour, 5 cents per hour after that, a whole 5 cents more for eight hours.[113]

Washington was still hopeful for a workable solution to the crisis with Japan. Meetings took place and an exchange of documents continued between the Japanese embassy and the State Department, and the diplomats continued talking. Some publications took a decidedly "wait and see this will all blow over" posture on developments in the Pacific. Others, like the *Baltimore Sun*, were more breathless. "A single additional act of aggression by Japan may be sufficient to provoke instant large-scale retaliation by British forces—with the United States taking an active supporting role," greeted readers in the Charm City the morning of December 2.[114]

Roosevelt had had a light schedule that day, seeing no more than half a dozen people over the course of the day. He dined that evening with his personal secretary, Grace Tully, from 7:30 p.m. until twenty minutes after midnight. He then turned in at 12:35 a.m.[115]

In a fashion, tensions seemed to have diminished in twenty-four hours, and while coverage of the situation in the Far East continued by the nation's newspapers, it faded somewhat against the backdrop of the ongoing war in Europe. A columnist wrote, "If there is to be war, it will start under strange auspices. The American people have no hate in their hearts for the Japanese. For generations a mutual admiration has been developing between the two countries and, despite the differences in language and customs, some warm friendships have sprung up."[116]

CHAPTER 3

THE THIRD OF DECEMBER

"British Rush Troops to Libya"

Sun

"Nazis Rush Reinforcements"

Tucson Daily Citizen

"Tokyo Must Explain Actions"

Washington Post

"Airport Coffee Shop Refuses to Serve Colored Quartet"

Washington Evening Star

W inston Churchill, along with influential Jewish leaders in Great Britain, America, and Palestine, called for the creation of a separate "army of Jews" to fight in the war. Thousands of young men from Palestine, America, and other countries stepped forward to volunteer for the unique fighting force. "What people, what group have more at stake?" said Emanuel Neumann, an American Jewish leader. "Hitler has openly proclaimed the annihilation of European Jewry as one of his war aims." Henry Stimson, secretary of war, voiced his support. Ultimately, "entrenched bureaucrats" inside the British government threw enough monkey wrenches into the works, and the concept withered. One London bureaucrat smarmily said that the British government was fighting both the Nazis and "Zionism."[1]

Newspaper stories and editorials on the situation in the Pacific waned somewhat, as their attention was diverted to the Russian Front, the Atlantic, the Mediterranean, and North Africa, where the real fighting was going on. The situation there was simply more pressing.

More and more American correspondents were becoming embedded with Allied forces, especially with the British in North Africa, and poignant stories of heroism, humor, and sacrifice were appearing in American publications. One popular columnist, John Barry, sent back regular dispatches via his "War Diary" column.[2] Photos and their captions of the African war zone had to be approved by the British before being released for publication in the West.[3]

So it was with a good deal of news coverage that President Roosevelt publicly announced on December 3 that Lend-Lease aid would be extended to Turkey. In actuality, the U.S. government had been covertly aiding the strategically important country for some time, as it was a target for takeover by Germany. Roosevelt said, "The defense of Turkey [is] vital to the defense of the United States."[4] Billions under Lend-Lease had already gone to Great Britain, Russia, Free French operations, and other allies in the war against the Axis powers. Allegations arose that Washington was playing favorites with its lending and leasing policies, putting Great Britain ahead of the Soviets, but Roosevelt's spokesman, Stephen Early, dismissed them. Congress had just allocated $78 million more for Russia.[5] It was later revealed that under Lend-Lease, FDR was also aiding India.[6]

When it came to a president's ability to wage war, the *Baltimore Sun* editorialized in no uncertain terms, "We know from the experiences of other countries that Fascism results when the legislative branch of the Government surrenders to one man its powers to make decisions for the people. In the face of this same trend toward Fascism in America the immediate duty of the American people is to return to Congress only those representatives who faithfully execute the people's trust."[7]

Meanwhile, Edward R. Murrow of CBS, already a journalistic legend, was the guest of honor at a dinner at the Waldorf Astoria and in front of over one thousand celebrants said that "unless the United States enters this war Britain may perish." The establishment was out in full force to honor a charter member of the establishment; telegrams were read from FDR, the British ambassador Lord Halifax, Secretary of State Cordell Hull, and Brendan Bracken, the British minister of information. Murrow went on to say the war would be decided along the "banks of the Potomac" and not in North Africa or on the Russian Front.[8] By now, Halifax was sending daily confidential memos to Roosevelt, advising him on British advances and defeats.[9]

The Philippine government first issued a confusing statement from President Quezon as to where it stood in the Pacific mess; it was blamed on a medical condition for which he received a complete checkup. He then issued a loyalty oath to FDR—and to the United States.[10]

To checkmate German designs on Greenland, from where their subs and ships could more easily continue their now-unrestricted warfare against U.S. and British ships, the American military was contemplating its own bases along the east coast of Greenland, plus another on the island of Jan Mayen, in an area that had been discovered by Henry Hudson in 1607. Germany had already conquered Denmark and Norway, and its sights on Greenland were simply an extension of its plans to dominate the North Atlantic and, eventually, the world.[11]

The USSR, a large beneficiary of Lend-Lease, claimed anew to have successfully pushed back the German advance on Moscow and that their troops "were finding the frozen bodies of Germans wrapped in flimsy blankets; huddled in roadside ditches."[12] Russian troops also reported recapturing some towns first taken by the invading German army. Still, the information came from the state-owned media of the Soviet Union, and other news reports were less glowing about the Red Army's successes. A news report from the Associated Press said that German troops had broken through the Soviet lines and were advancing once again on Moscow.[13]

The British meanwhile were "reorganizing" in Libya,[14] mounting an effort at a counteroffensive against Gen. Erwin Rommel and his 16th Panzer Division and the rest of the German "Afrika Korps," as reported by Edward Kennedy, an "Associated Press War Correspondent."[15]

Consternation was running high in America over Europe and to what extent Congress and America would allow FDR to set national policy. Secretary of State Cordell Hull emphasized the disagreements with other countries, including "the basic doctrines of law, justice, morals and equality of treatment among nations—especially in trade—and settlement of controversies by peaceful negotiation rather than by force."[16] Hull, in private, was not confident about a favorable outcome in the Far East.[17] The issue of Japan, which had ebbed and flowed over the past several days, was beginning to flow again.

More bluntly, the senator from Montana, Burton K. Wheeler, Democrat and first among America Firsters, acidly said, "The President's foreign policy mean[s] the plowing under of every fourth American boy. The only time the administration has intimated that we should go to war with Japan is when the British Empire is threatened."[18] Everybody in the Roosevelt White House hated Wheeler. Wheeler had already announced he would investigate "interventionists" in Hollywood.[19] Just a year earlier, in 1940, John L. Lewis, head of the mine workers union and another isolationist Roosevelt-basher, had tried to convince Wheeler to run for president.[20]

In truth, Hollywood in 1941 was reluctant to take on the subject of fascism overseas and whether America should intervene in Europe's troubles. Germany was a huge and profitable market for American films, and the movie moguls were reluctant to alienate the cultural gatekeepers in Berlin. At the end of the day, Hollywood was first and foremost a business. When Charlie Chaplin's *The Great Dictator* was released in October 1940, many critics panned his satire of Hitler as left-wing propaganda, earning Chaplin the lasting enmity (and surveillance) of FBI director J. Edgar Hoover. It was only after America entered the war that suddenly Chaplin's film was seen as a courageous masterpiece.

For fifteen years, Sergeant Major Robert Smith, stationed in San Diego, had been a technical advisor to Hollywood on movies about the military. Smith observed that all inductees were essentially klutzes, both the real kind and the reel kind. He singled out actors Randolph Scott and John Payne as leading men who were "all thumbs."[21]

Nevertheless, the winds in 1941 were slowly starting to shift the weathervane of American opinion, as reflected by the drubbing that the America First Committee was taking from the commentariat. One columnist went so far as to suggest that the America Firsters were in league with Berlin. "It has begun blackmailing our Representatives and Senators with the threat that they will not be re-elected unless at this moment they play the Axis game. They are threatening the country . . . which would . . . lose us the war and lose us the peace. In the whole diplomatic game, the America First Committee has been the only ace in the hole for the Axis."[22]

On Capitol Hill, a much-debated bill on curbing strikes in war industries passed the House, 252–136. If it passed the Senate and FDR signed it, the measure would mandate a "60-day 'cooling off' period" before a union could undertake any strike in an industry that supported the war effort, and it could be argued that all industries somehow supported the war effort.[23] In San Diego, the U.S. Navy was concerned about a strike among shipyard workers. Some referred to union strikes as "sabotage."[24] Unsurprisingly, according to Gallup, large majorities of Americans opposed strikes in defense industries.[25] A ban on aid from the government to unions that affiliated or employed "members of the Communist party, the Young Communist League, and the German-American Bund" was also being discussed in the halls of Congress.[26] The *Los Angeles Times* editorially supported the measure, saying there was no "right to strike." "What about the right of self-defense and self-preservation which, though the first law of nature, these unioneers call it their right to deny and to imperil?" the paper stormed.[27]

The American labor movement had additional problems. Congressman Martin Dies said the Congress of Industrial Organizations (which later merged with the American Federation of Labor to become the AFL-CIO) was "marked by a coalition of Communism and criminality." High officials had been charged or convicted of "petty larceny, grand larceny, burglary, grand theft, carrying concealed weapons, assault and battery, robbery, white slavery, holdups, conspiracy, attempted arson, receiving stolen property, felonious assault, extortion and forgery."[28]

It wasn't just the unions that were seen as hotbeds of communist agitation. New York City was also concerned with the "Red menace" in their very own high schools, according to a report prepared by the New York state Senate. "Communist students in the New York City colleges and high schools are taught to lie, cheat and create disturbances in the classroom and on the campus. . . . Young Communist League branches are found in four colleges, nine high schools, teachers groups and the Navy Yard in Brooklyn." Teachers, students, and staff were suspended or fired as a result of the report and hundreds openly claimed membership.[29]

On December 3, the *Birmingham News* had a different take on New York: "The gay side of war—laughing soldiers, sailors and mariners promenading the streets, many with girlfriends clinging admiringly to their arms—is showing itself increasingly as the volume of American preparedness grows."[30] But the numbers weren't growing fast enough.

Roosevelt criticized the Selective Service for being too selective. Over 20 percent of men—nearly 200,000—were rejected because of "defective teeth." After the president intervened, the decision was to enlist the men into the army and then turn them over to the dental division for repairs.[31] A headline in the *Hartford Courant* said, "5 Negros Among 197 Given Tests" in a story about the draft in Connecticut. It also noted that "such things as fever, sore throats and certain correctible defects are reasons for temporary rejections."[32] In New Hampshire, the *Portsmouth Herald* announced that thirty inductees were being called and published the names of all thirty in the newspaper.[33]

In Georgia, 707 men received "greetings" from Uncle Sam. One of these was a man convicted for failing to keep his local "draft board advised of his address."[34] He was sent up for three years for draft evasion, but he pleaded that he'd tried to enlist a number of times. In court, the prisoner, Horace Woodrow Hampton, who had also been convicted twice of automobile theft, was advised that under a federal statue, inmates could be released if they went into the military.[35]

Mexicans who crossed the border and did not declare their intention to become U.S. citizens were exempt from military service. They could continue to live in Mexico and work in America, commuting each day.[36] But because defense contractors required most workers to have a birth certificate and the military required all personnel to have such documents, it created a land office business with the state agencies that handled legal documents.[37] Prior to 1941, birth certificates had not been much of an issue and people took prospective employees at their word as to where and when they were born.

There was a news report that covert Nazi agents were operating in Mexico City to recruit young Mexican boys—members of the "Mexican Sinarchists"—to Fascism and then send them overseas to join the Nazi cause. "A new pamphlet entitled, 'Mexico in 1960' contains a historical review indicating Sinarchist hostility to the United States," complaining about lands taken in 1847.[38]

Bad behavior did occasionally take place in America, as some men discovered it was easier to panhandle wearing a uniform. Some donned uniforms of the Royal Air Force and stood outside clubs and restaurants in New York, claiming they lost their wallets; kind-hearted civilians often bailed them out.[39] It also wasn't unusual for inductees to be found with syphilis.

Some men, especially farm boys wanting to get off the farm, enlisted rather than wait to be drafted, as enlistees got better treatment and a chance to learn a trade. One twenty-year-old who had just finished a three-year hitch signed up for another and said he liked the army and planned on being in it when he was fifty. "I don't know how to act around people," he told the *Los Angeles Times*.[40]

The U.S. government announced that the hulls for twenty-four "escort vessels" ordered by the navy would be built in Denver, Colorado—1,300 miles from the nearest ocean port. The initial budget was $55 million.[41] Part of the largess of the war effort also went to America's prisons. In Atlanta, a penitentiary received a bonus check from the government for the "outstanding work" by inmates there. The check was presented in person by the attorney general, Francis Biddle.[42]

Congress continued its investigations into corruption in defense contracting and discovered a "sub-subcontractor" who was taking kickbacks of nearly one-third of the contract he'd brought Remington Arms Co. of Connecticut and its subcontracted maker of "shell dies." The treasurer for the company said the sub-subcontractor, Leon K. Shanak, had performed "no service" and that the subcontractor, Trans-Continental, had provided nothing for the federal government.[43]

Washington "disqualified" 560 individuals for work because they failed to pass loyalty oaths to the U.S. government. This was out of a pool of 40,000 seeking jobs in defense industries. Arthur Flemming, a commissioner with the Civil Service, speculated, "Does [this] give evidence to you of some fifth column activities in the Government?" He answered his own query, "Certainly, if one studies our records, he would get some indication of that." Another 2,400 failed to pass "character investigations."[44] In London, a pacifist member of the House of Lords, the Duke of Bedford, was seated only after taking that country's loyalty oath to the king. The duke said he was only doing so to help some friends, who had been picked up by the government for violating "regulation 18B," which allowed the home secretary "to hold without trial anyone he regards as dangerous to the war effort."[45]

At the other end of the spectrum, Lady Astor—née Nancy Witcher Langhorne of Virginia—criticized Churchill for not including more women in the war effort. In a speech in the House of Commons, she said the prime minister should go "further in proposals to conscript women . . . If you don't conscript married women there will be great discontent."[46] Lady Astor had been born in the United States and like Churchill, she was nobody's fool. Like Churchill, she was a Tory, but unlike Churchill, she was beautiful. She was also the first woman to sit in Parliament, having succeeded her husband, Waldorf Astor.

Later, a poll of British subjects demonstrated wide support—55 percent to 35—for the conscription of women into the military; however, the vast majority—65 percent over 26—disapproved of women in combat. There were already a few women who were serving in harm's way, some "wo-manning" antiaircraft emplacements. "It is reported that women have been found to excel [over] men in the handling of complicated mechanical instruments and range finders."[47]

Americans were more chivalrous on the subject. In a *Los Angeles Times* poll, nearly 60 percent opposed drafting women into the military.[48] Of course, the nation's attitude about the sexes was hardly modern, as evidenced by syndicated columnist Dorothy Dix, who advised divorced women to buck up and accept the fact it was probably their fault that their husbands had left them.

"The discarded wife always poses as martyr and calls upon her friends and acquaintances to shed tears of pity over her. They look upon marriage as a gift in which the husband must give all while they give nothing."[49]

As a result of the Allied embargo of Japan, 75 percent of her imports had been cut, but that was only the beginning of its economic strain. Because of the shift in the Japanese economy to a war footing, billions of yen were being devoted to armaments, and annual rice production fell from 400 million bushels to 297 million because of the cutoff of fertilizers for farmers.[50]

The Japanese had still not answered President Roosevelt's question from the day before: what were their intentions in Thailand? The Thai government felt certain it knew the answer and issued an open invitation for help, assuming a likely and imminent attack. But diplomacy is a complicated art. "It is no secret here that the discussions have been severely hampered by the Japanese proclivity for combining peaceful words with warlike actions," reported the Associated Press from Washington.[51]

FDR "made clear that the objective which was sought meant that no additional territory should be taken by anyone," reported the *Los Angeles Times*.[52] But Roosevelt said his query "did not constitute an ultimatum."[53] He also complained that the Japanese people were not being made aware of Washington's position when it came to the Pacific and that the press there was only telling citizens of British military actions in the region. "The Chief Executive termed Japan a friendly power with which the United States was at peace."[54]

But the situation was dicier than a word like *peace* would indicate. The White House let it out that the administration might "abandon talks if good faith is not shown."[55] Yet there were still hopes for an "armed truce,"[56] though some of the striped pants set said the "crisis may come to [a] head within [a] few days."[57] Another group of diplomats said that FDR "placed Japan in a position where she must withdraw forces recently sent to and in transit to Indo-China and continue negotiations . . . or face . . . a possible war" with America.[58] Meanwhile, Japanese officials said Premier Tojo had been "misquoted" when he said that Americans and British had to be "purged"[59] from the Far East, and that a "subordinate official . . . did a clumsy job" of translating Tojo.[60] Later, the Japanese government denied outright that Tojo had ever said the word *purge*.[61]

An assistant secretary for the navy, Ralph A. Bard, said the situation in the Pacific was "a tinder box . . . waiting for a spark that will explode all over the eastern quarter of the globe."[62] But he also stated, like everybody else in the navy, that they do not "underestimate Japan's power" and "in the regrettable event of trouble in the Pacific, that trouble will not be a minor one."[63]

Despite FDR's assurance of a non-ultimatum, the *Washington Post* ran a story with a dire lede, dateline Washington, that appeared to blame Tokyo. "The issue of peace or war in the Pacific . . . may turn on Japan's reply."[64] The headline said, "Tokyo Must Explain Actions."[65] And the story detailed how FDR was waiting, how his question amounted to an ultimatum, even as he said in his press conference it did not. It also reported that Washington had set a deadline of December 15 as "zero hour." That was when the rice fields in Thailand were no longer flooded and the ground would be firm enough for mechanized vehicles.[66]

The paper ran a story, the same day, with an ominous headline, dateline Tokyo, that appeared to blame Washington. "The uncompromising attitude of Washington undoubtedly has dimmed any chance for success of the United States-Japanese negotiations, but Japan is determined that all avenues of a peaceful settlement be exhausted . . . informed sources said." The headline said, "Japan to Exhaust All Peace Avenues."[67]

As many times as FDR waved off speculation that any invasion of Thailand would lead to war, the *Post* speculated just as many times that an invasion would lead to "undeclared hostilities . . . general war in the Pacific." FDR also told reporters that "some progress" was being made in the peace negotiations and that it was his understanding the Japanese "would take no additional steps while the negotiations were underway."[68]

However his query was interpreted, by Tokyo or American newspapers, Roosevelt had good reason to be concerned. While the talks continued, one report came in saying, "A sizable Japanese naval force also is reported in Indo-China waters. . . ."[69] New reports coming from Saigon said the Japanese continued to amass extraordinary numbers of troops and supplies in Indo-China, along the Thai border. "The docks" in Saigon "are piled with drums of gasoline, trucks, guns and other equipment. Troops and supplies are arriving daily by ship and train at Saigon." Military experts thought the islands of the Dutch Indies would be the first target of Tokyo.[70]

FDR that day received a confidential memo from the Office of Naval Intelligence informing him about developments in the Far East, including troop movements into China and south, possibly as a prelude to invading Thailand.[71]

The British government was telling reporters that if Japan attacked their Far East outposts, America would jump into the fray, but this was wishful thinking, as Churchill had been agitating for months for direct involvement by America.[72] As much as the Japanese were provoking America, England was cajoling America. But it was also reported that the Dutch were pressuring London to go into Thailand to keep it from going to the Japanese, should they invade, much as FDR did with Surinam, taking it before the Germans could. The report out of Manila said a source close to the administration suggested that even if talks broke down between Washington and Tokyo, this would not presage a war between the two countries. "Washington sees no spark for an immediate Japanese-American war."[73] Even so, Americans were still evacuating Asia, many headed for the Philippines.

The *Chicago Tribune* was continuing to taunt FDR, contrasting his words of 1940—"I give you one more assurance your boys are not going to be sent into any foreign wars"—with his words of just a few days earlier—"It is always possible that our boys in the military and naval academies may be fighting for the defense of these American institutions of ours."[74] The paper stated its platform on the editorial page in one simple phrase: "Save Our Republic."[75]

Some former government officials seemed to be agitating for war with Japan. The former ambassador to Thailand, Hugh Grant, told the *New York Times*, "If the Japanese really want war, now is the time to let them have it. I believe we could smash them within a period of a few months with our superior air and naval forces."[76]

Another civilian, Senator Tom Connally, Democrat of Texas, gave a speech in Florida in which he thundered that the U.S. Navy "in the Pacific . . .

can shoot and shoot straight. That is my answer to the Japanese Premier." Connally threw some other choice barbs at Tokyo. FDR also sent a message to the United States Saving and Loan League, to whom Connally gave his incendiary remarks, but it was simply to praise them for their work in constructing "defense housing."[77]

After upbraiding FDR over his war-making powers, the *Baltimore Sun* then turned on a dime and taunted the Japanese. "By deciding to go on with the negotiations the Japanese statesmen are serving their own nation well. In ships, in planes, in all the stuff with which to make war, the United States grows stronger week by week. Both relatively and absolutely Japan grows weaker. The longer we can keep the Japanese talking, the greater the chance that they will finally understand that war with this country would be an undiluted disaster for them."[78]

The Japanese representatives in Washington, Ambassador Kichisaburo Nomura and "special envoy" Saburo Kurusu, told the Roosevelt administration they had transmitted the president's request for an answer on the Thailand question. Washington was suspicious of Kurusu, though. He'd only joined the Japanese embassy in Washington two weeks earlier and had been the representative of the empire of Japan in Berlin to sign the Tripartite Pact in September of 1940.

Maps in the nation's papers depicted the Far East with Japanese troop and ship emplacements, complete with the mileage by air from Tokyo to Singapore, Manila, and a newly mentioned potential target, Guam, an American territory. It was 1,600 miles from Tokyo to the tiny island in the Pacific.[79]

At Saks Fifth Avenue, Christmas ads were hawking lingerie for women, saying, "There is no shortage of pure silk."[80] Men in uniform were more pedestrian in their gift choices for Christmas. A poll conducted of soldiers said their preferences were "[m]oney, cigarettes, stamps, subscriptions to hometown newspapers, cookies and candy." Also shirts—but families were warned not to send striped or polka-dot shirts, as they were banned by the military, even when off duty.[81]

Macy's department store helpfully listed dozens of military posts and dates by which gifts had to be shipped to be there in time for Christmas. The store had its own "post exchange" to help family and friends get gifts headed for all forty-eight states.[82]

Another popular item for Christmas was a radio, and many houses had more than one. Emerson, Philco, and General Electric all touted AM radios that were as cheap as $16.95.[83] On WMAL in Washington, residents could listen to *Orphans of Divorce, Honeymoon Hill,* and *Quiz Kids.* On WRC, they could tune into *Guiding Light, Stella Dallas,* and at night listen to Eddie Cantor.[84] Shirley Temple was heard on stations across the country.[85]

In order to stay warm in December, many homes in the Washington area still used the relatively safe coal as opposed to natural gas. There was hardly a day that went by that the newspapers did not report on a home death via a natural-gas explosion or poisoning. A ton of good Blue Ridge bituminous coal—delivered—was $10, but if you wanted the small, "egg"-sized chunks for the stove, it was $10.50. The Blue Ridge Co. also delivered a full cord of firewood, stacked, for $7.50.[86]

The men in uniform were facing a traveling maelstrom to get home for the holidays, provided they were granted leave. It was expected that December of 1941 would be the heaviest travel month in years. Not enough planes were flying to accommodate everybody, railroads were scrounging to come up with extra cars, and an estimated 100,000 troops were expected to pass through Washington's Union Station over the Yuletide. The furloughs came in waves, staggered out over the month of December, beginning on the twelfth and extending to the twenty-ninth. Most of the G.I.s were looking forward to a two-week vacation.[87] Print ads suggested, "If he can't get home for Christmas—send a carton of Camels."[88]

One soldier (whose name was not revealed) who had taken his furlough a bit too casually years earlier tried to come back; having received a ten-day pass in May of 1919, he did not return to post for twenty-two years. While away, he got married, saw the country, and started his own business, but decided to return to Fort McPhearson to clear his record and serve his country as a mechanic. In truth, he tried to come back in 1919. After his pass was up, he returned to his duty station, but the army said they could not find his records proving he was a soldier in the U.S. Army. He was kicked out of the camp. Still, his conscience bothered him and, two decades later, he attempted to clear the matter up. He'd originally enlisted in 1915 and served under Gen. John J. Pershing in Mexico.[89]

The bureaucrats of Washington were in a quandary. A federal tax of $5 per car in America was costing the government more to enforce than it generated in revenue. Few wanted to repeal it, but no one could figure out how to distribute millions of windshield stickers, collect the tax, and still have money left over. Some suggested that additional revenues be raised so the Treasury Department could collect the tax. "If the Treasury is not given the money it needs to finance the collection . . . it cannot collect."[90]

Senator Walter George, Democrat of Georgia, fussed publicly that federal taxes on the American people had reached their limit, and the new borrowing to finance the New Deal and the war effort could mean pushing off repaying the debt, which would then "have to be amortized over the life of the present, the next and maybe the third generation." He projected that at the current rate the national debt could reach somewhere between $110 and $150 billion. Any future taxes could "tremendously [weaken] our whole economy."[91] But administration officials were already floating the notion of an additional tax of nearly $5 billion.[92]

Other congressional representatives were concerned that the huge outlays from Washington were only going to large corporations and that small businesses were missing in the equation, including getting the raw materials they needed to operate. The Office of Production Management said it was working on it. They had, they said, "10 different methods" and these "would be ready in four to five weeks." The navy said it was interested in helping small businesses, "but not at the expense of the defense effort."[93]

Nazi Germany's expensive war machine was also costly to their national economy, with two-thirds supported by tax revenue and one-third financed with borrowing, according to the Tax Institute at the University of Pennsylvania.

Economists noted, however, the indebtedness, borrowing, taxation, and spending were all controlled by the government in Berlin, and no amount of fiscal
or financial Keynesian excessiveness could stop a country from going to war if
the country truly wanted to go to war. "On the whole, the methods of German
war finance have neither been very radical nor have they been very different
from other countries. They contain very little of specific Nazi elements. Like
all other countries, Germany is financing the war on sound methods, mainly
by taxing much more heavily now than in the First World War."[94] Moreover,
Hitler had the firm backing of Germany's industrialists, notably the aristocratic Thyssen and Krupp families, who perhaps privately viewed the former
corporal from the Bavarian Army as a clown but also as a useful expedient for
ridding the country of unions, communists, and other undesirables. Germany's
industrial might was open at full throttle, for all-out war.

Because of the trouble obtaining precious metals from the Far East, the
United States began procuring these materials from Chile, and an agreement
between Washington and Santiago was established.[95] One congressman had
a novel solution to the metal shortage; he suggested melting down all the statues in the country, all ninety thousand of them.[96] Not even scarcity could
improve government efficiencies. A huge pile of scrap aluminum collected
by citizens at the urging of the government was sitting unattended in San
Francisco, "oxidizing under early winter rains on the lot where the metal was
dumped." An official with American Smelting and Refining Co. explained,
"We're awaiting orders from the government."[97]

The navy announced their $300 million effort at island building on Puerto
Rico had come for naught. The plan for years had been to turn the island into
an American outpost, complete with a thriving economy, English-speaking
citizens, clean living, and a modern military capability. The locals thought
otherwise. Indeed, "the headaches"[98] had been going on since 1898, when the
U.S. government took over the island. "Filth, some of the slimiest slums of the
New World, poverty, disease and a potent brand of Latin politics are still here,"
reported the *Washington Evening Star*. The appointed governor general, Dr.
Rexford Guy Tugwell, one of FDR's "original New Deal 'brain truster,'" was

at his wit's end and contemplated imposing a very un-good-neighborly martial law. Concerns about the "native population" birth and death rate were also heard.[99] It would not be the first time America had failed at nation building.

Farther south, the navy was finding Brazil to be a more hospitable partner, at least when it came to joint operations. With the blessing of the country, American ships patrolled the three thousand-mile-long coastline of the country, running at night under blackout conditions, watching for German ships and U-boats. The Brazilian government was also mobilizing their army, fearful of a German invasion.[100]

Ireland was officially neutral, but its hatred for Great Britain caused some of its citizens to cheer the Germans. Still, the Nazis attacked four Irish commercial ships, including passenger ships.[101] The German Luftwaffe also blasted and sank a British refrigeration ship, the *Meriones*, 7,557 tons, as it was stranded on the high seas. They also destroyed another British ship, the *Jessmore*, 4,099 tons.[102]

In the face of what was happening to Ireland and Britain, Navy secretary Knox coyly told reporters that the sinking of American vessels in the Atlantic had recently slackened, but without giving any reason why. When pressed by the scribes, he evasively said, "Make your own guess about that. There's a good story in it if you dig it up." But "the Secretary refused to say whether the Atlantic patrol of the United States Navy was being made more vigilant or whether repeal of the Neutrality Act had anything to do with the drop in the number of sinkings." He refused to say anything else about the ticklish situation in the Pacific or much else, except that he'd placed orders "for 5,334 vessels, costing $7,351,497,905 since January 1, 1940" or that "[n]early $1,000,000,000 has been spent for expanding shipbuilding facilities in that time," or that "27 combatant ships have been commissioned, 41 launched and the keels laid for 128."[103]

Loose lips indeed.

If enemy spies in the United States had missed anything, the last information hole was filled by Assistant Secretary for the Navy Lewis Compton, who said America was launching "a boat a day and the schedule will be stepped up to two a day by July. . . . He also revealed that Navy launchings are well ahead of schedule."[104] The *New York Times* joined in the fun, reporting on new battleships being launched and their locations, such as the

Indiana and the cruiser *Cleveland*.[105] Indeed, the *Los Angeles Times* had a large regular section in the paper, "Shipping News," in which construction, status, and launch information was all carefully and completely reported, along with "activities at Los Angeles Harbor." It also helpfully reported on "vessel arrivals and departures," including ships' complements, destinations, and estimated arrival times in other ports of call.[106] The Air Mail Schedule was also reported in detail.[107]

Mel Ott was named "playing manager" of the New York Giants, replacing Bill Terry, who was kicked upstairs to oversee the team's farm operations.[108] It was big news in the sports world. Less covered, Lou Boudreau was named player-manager of the Cleveland Indians.[109] Boudreau was part Jewish,[110] and for many Americans, this was meaningful, especially at this time in the world. At only twenty-four, Boudreau's announcement was duly noted, though he was an outstanding infielder and was already a part of history, helping to stop Joe DiMaggio's fifty-six-game hitting streak.

That year was an exceptional one for baseball, as not only did "Yankee Clipper" DiMaggio set a record for the next century, so, too, did Boston's Ted Williams, the last man to hit over .400 for a season. Baseball in 1941 was not only the "national pastime,"[111] it was the national obsession, and coverage of trades, drafts, and standings were often on the front pages of American newspapers, following the exploits of Bob "Rocket" or "Rapid Robert" Feller, a young sensational pitcher, who played for the Indians. In Washington, a journeyman front-office worker from the minor leagues, Calvin Griffith, was named as the traveling secretary for the Senators.[112] In Atlanta, fans had no major-league team to root for, but minor league baseball was as popular as it was in other secondary cities around the nation. Atlanta's fans rooted for the Crackers.

Football was still gaining a toehold, but the college game was more popular than professional football, which some regarded with suspicion. Considerable attention was focused on the "Negro college football championship," with the title game to be played before a sellout crowd at Memorial Stadium in Atlanta. The game would pit undefeated Morris Brown, located in Atlanta, against North Carolina College for Negroes, of Durham, now known as North Carolina Central University, also undefeated, though they had tied one game. The North Carolina squad was the champion of the "Colored Intercollegiate Athletic Conference."[113]

A one-hundred-year-old man, Joseph Punch, was making plans to wed a "child bride," Minnie E. Smith, age sixty-six. Punch was born in 1841 in Mississippi. Punch said his father had been a slave but gave no indication as to his own status in a Southern state twenty years before the Civil War.[114]

Progress in civil rights was slow at best in the North and had gone into reverse in the South. At Washington's National Airport, "The Southern Airs [sic], a well-known National Broadcasting Co. colored quartet . . . were refused table service at the coffee shop . . . because of a Virginia segregation law." The singers had driven to National from Williamsburg to catch a flight to Cincinnati, but it was canceled due to weather. The airport manager, John Groves, hid behind his little bureaucracy, claiming he did not know who had jurisdiction over the airport: the private owners of the coffee shop and restaurant, the Commonwealth of Virginia, or the District of Columbia. Waitresses had refused to serve the foursome. Representatives of the NAACP came to the airport to confer with the musicians and finally, accommodations were offered in the cafeteria, "which has permanent facilities for serving colored guests" but not in the main dining room of the airport or the coffee shop.[115] Refusing, the Southernaires departed, their dignity intact.

Yet contrary to what many people in the North thought, not everybody in the South was a racist. In Georgia, a prison camp warden, C. A. Jacobson, a white man, was sentenced to three years in the state penitentiary for the involuntary manslaughter of a black inmate, Louis Gordon, whom Jacobson had placed in a "sweat box." The jury deliberated for only forty minutes before convicting Jacobson.[116] And yet, lynching was prevalent in the South—a tragic fact about American society that Adolf Hitler delighted in pointing out to the world.

In Florida, in a war game exercise, a group of "Negro troops" successfully "captured" MacDill Field. "Shortly before 10 o'clock the invaders 'landed' from the bay, pushed through a gas barrage and smoke screen in utter darkness and had infiltrated the field before they were discovered."[117]

Military leaders in Japan were naturally calling for the United States to stop aiding Gen. Chiang Kai-shek's forces in China, to give up any presence or designs in the Far East, and to "retire, strategically and politically, to the Western Hemisphere." And in Washington, attention was fixed on the upcoming conference between President Roosevelt with Japanese ambassador Kichisaburo Nomura and special envoy Saburo Kurusu.[118] References to an old "Nine-Power Treaty," were thrown around diplomatic circles, but the Japanese said recent events had rendered it null and void.

Halfway around the world at another conference, five Nazi operatives in the Far East met in Shanghai, "anxious to patch up an understanding so that Japan's resources in men and weapons may be turned elsewhere against Germany's enemies."[119]

CHAPTER 4

THE FOURTH OF DECEMBER

"Defense Units Study Means to Protect Girls Hired by U.S."

Washington Evening Star

"Jap Evacuation Ship Sails after Mail Is Ordered Taken Off"

Tucson Daily Citizen

"America-Firsters Japan's Ace in Hole"

Atlanta Constitution

"Jap Press Hurls Bolts at Allied Powers in Crisis"

Birmingham News

An explosive twenty-six-page memo marked "CONFIDENTIAL" arrived at the White House from the Office of Naval Intelligence, analyzing "JAPANESE INTELLIGENCE AND PROPAGANDA IN THE UNITED STATES." Under the heading marked, "Methods of Operation and Points of Attack," it read, "The focal point of the Japanese Espionage effort is the determination of the total strength of the United States. In anticipation of possible open conflict with this country, Japan is vigorously utilizing every available agency to secure military, naval and commercial information, paying particular attention to the West Coast, the Panama Canal and the Territory of Hawaii." [1]

It also went into great depth about the subversive Japanese elements in the Hawaiian Islands. All the Japanese consulates on the West Coast were busily gathering information on the U.S. Navy, especially in the Pacific. One passage was underlined—perhaps by Roosevelt himself: "Recently it was brought to the attention of the Office of Naval Intelligence that out of a total of 198 postal employees in Honolulu, 51 have dual citizenship and that the foreman in the registry section, Ernest Hirokawa, is an alien Japanese. As a result of this discovery that registered mail for the fleet stationed in Hawaiian waters is not routed directly to the Pearl Harbor Navy Yard as a security measure." Chillingly, ". . . the [Japanese] Naval Inspector's Office . . . was primarily interested in obtaining detailed technical information which could be used to advantage by the Japanese Navy." [2]

Washington, D.C., was experiencing growing pains. The nation's capital was filling up so quickly with new bureaucrats and new bureaucracies that Congressman Jennings Randolph of West Virginia, no stranger to political opportunism, proposed moving all agencies out of Washington that were not directly related to national defense. Naturally, he had in mind moving large chunks of the government to his home state and produced the mayor of Elkins, West Virginia, John C. Freeland, to attest to how his town was ready to handle thousands of new residents. "The delegation traveled 200 miles, mostly over fogbound mountains, this morning to attend [Randolph's] hearing," as one report informed. [3] The word *decentralization* was introduced into the political lexicon. Suddenly, members of Congress had all sorts of ideas about moving around the bureaucracy and coincidentally, all these suggestions were in their home states.

A monument to that bureaucracy was the massive building being assembled just across the Potomac to house the War Department. Five-sided, many storied, many ringed, and with roads going everywhere, it was already named the War Department Building. The site was a giant mess, but it was envisioned to become the largest building in the world when completed. The traffic in the area had already been chaotic at best, and the gigantic construction endeavor only added to drivers' and commuters' headaches. To ameliorate the complaints of local residents, the military announced it would hold a briefing for the public on the building, its construction, and the new road system being built "at a meeting . . . at 12:30 p.m. at the Harrington Hotel." There, representatives of the Public Roads Administration, the Office of the Quartermaster General, architects, planning engineers, and top military brass explained the building, its workings, and answered all questions.[4] No one was satisfied.

The army also announced with great fanfare the purchase of almost thirty-nine thousand acres in rural Virginia to add to the existing Ft. A.P. Hill facility. The cost was $1,206,000.[5] Additional housing for nurses at Ft. Belvoir post, also in the Commonwealth, was announced, as well as expansion plans in other parts of the state.

Back across the river, the District of Columbia began to mandate fingerprints for business licenses, including "operators of massage, bowling, billiard . . . establishments, solicitors, private detectives, fortune tellers, clairvoyants and mediums . . . boxing promoters and applicants for liquor licenses."[6] The Young Democrats were planning to descend on Washington December 12 and 13, but they probably would not be fingerprinted.

Along with all the bureaucrats, Washington was filling up with women, as ever-more numbers of young ladies flooded into the nation's capital in search of employment with the national government on account of the war effort. The Consumer and Welfare Committee and the District Defense Committee of the city of Washington announced plans to form groups to meet them at the train and bus stations "in an attempt to keep girls . . . away from questionable rooming houses." Their stated goal was to call "attention to the bad character of some of the establishments encountered."[7] In simpler language, they wanted to keep these impressionable young girls—some literally just off the farm—from falling into prostitution. And the best way to promote clean living, it was thought, was by associating with decent people in decent parts of town with decent housing.

These were not "Rosie the Riveter" blue-collar laborers but instead "Tessie the Typist"—sprightly young girls in search of white-collar employment in steno pools, as clerk typists, filing clerks, secretaries, and certainly as "Girl Fridays," though undoubtedly there were more than a few men in Washington who wanted them for "Girl Friday Nights."

The problem was there was little good housing to speak of in Washington, which despite its status as the nation's capital was a dirty and humid backwater. Indeed, there has been little decent housing since its founding as the federal city—especially since the residents of the better neighborhoods fought the city's Zoning Commission when it planned to allow for rooming houses in their neighborhoods with zoning variances.

After a protracted fight and over objections from civic groups, the Zoning Commission shoved through the desired changes in the law and announced a new plan to allow up to four tenants to rent rooms in residential homes. It would only be "abandoned at the end of the national emergency proclaimed by President Roosevelt or by December 31, 1945, whichever date is reached first."[8] The lead editorial in the *Washington Evening Star* the next day was not about the war in Europe or the situation in the Pacific, but the decision of the Zoning Commission and the newspaper's concern about the new regulations.[9]

The state of affairs was worse in New York and other defense "boom towns" for young women. Though money was flowing out of Washington to defense contractors and as many as 1.5 million people had relocated to take jobs in national defense, "for the average woman and girl employee it's a story of inflated living costs and inadequate rates of pay." A study was issued by the U.S.O. and the Y.W.C.A. that said, "No one takes responsibility for their welfare, and girls, many of them never having held jobs before and drawn by the thousands into these boom towns, have found their wages, averaging from $18 to $20 a week, almost entirely consumed by board and high rentals, with little or no money left over for clothing and recreation . . . Involved is a pay rate of 40 cents an hour, 45 cents on night shifts with . . . facilities often so poor that the 'morale' service had put up tents with cots and equipment for doing laundry. . . . Girls are sharing not only rooms, but beds, with native commuters resenting intruders as 'trailer trash' and refusing to house single girls because they are waitresses or munitions workers."[10]

One could not help notice the change in Washington and across the country with the growing number of working women, and not just in the war effort. So many women now had jobs that department stores began having "Night Sales" to accommodate women who could not get out of the office for daytime sales. To keep the girls from being taken advantage of by renters, the city instituted rent control and appointed a "Rent Czar."[11] A number of profile stories were devoted to some of the young women who had streamed into Washington. They worked long days, socialized in the evenings, and did charity work, such as volunteering for "Bundles for Bluejackets," where they learned to knit windbreakers and sweaters for American sailors operating in the cold north Atlantic.[12]

Sumner Welles, the undersecretary of state, and his wife offered to the American Women's Voluntary Service the use of their stables on Massachusetts Avenue, but they were rejected, as they could only accommodate around two hundred girls, said Miss Anita Phipps, chairman of the A.W.V.S. On the morning of December 3, on the front page of the *Washington Post*, "an attractive girl . . . Miss Lila Quick, a 19-year-old Veterans Administration worker" was reported missing. Miss Quick had only arrived in the nation's capital several months earlier from Birmingham, Alabama.[13] The city also announced its "first woman air raid warden, Miss Mary Mason." She worked for the National Broadcasting Company as well as serving as a member of the Home Economics Association.[14]

The *Birmingham News* ran an entertaining regular feature on the front page entitled, "No Man's Land in Washington; Lulu Tells Betty What's Going On." In the guise of a letter, it opened, "Dear Betty, I have been too busy with defense work to write you lately. Let us make a New Year resolution ahead of time to write more often in the future. Speaking of the future, in some ways it looks brighter, in others more depressing. From all I hear, the 'peace emissary' from Tokyo, Suburo Kuruso, came to Washington just to stall for time. There are few persons here who believe his intentions were ever honorable. If all negotiations fail between Tokyo and Washington, then look out for trouble P.D.Q."[15]

Traffic fatalities had skyrocketed in Washington over just one year, possibly because more drivers were speeding, certainly because there were more drivers, and possibly because of the growing sense of crisis in the city. It was not unusual for a child, alighting from a school bus, to be mowed down by a car.

Perhaps some drivers had become impatient, as some most surely had when a convoy of two thousand cars "containing infantry and mechanized troops" rolled through Washington on a weekday "en route from the Carolina maneuvers to Camp Edwards, Mass. Washington traffic police routed the division over Key Bridge, Canal Road, Foxhall Road, Nebraska and Wisconsin Avenues to the District line." And later that afternoon, an additional 350 army vehicles were expected to make the approximate same route through Washington.[16]

In California, it was just the opposite. Drivers were pulled over for driving too slowly because of troop convoys or because their cars were "jalopies" that could not maintain a rate of speed.[17]

It didn't help matters when Washington and all of the East Coast were enveloped in the worst fog in years. The gleaming new National Airport, built near the banks of the Potomac River in 1941, was closed, as were airports from New York to Atlanta, but also west to Pittsburgh and Kansas City. The fog and "low lying smoke from defense-busy factories caused semi-blackouts." Ferryboats collided in Norfolk, five ocean-going passenger ships had to layup in the Chesapeake, and traffic ground to a halt for the day.[18] In Boston, the R.C.A. Company picked the foggy night to test out its new air-raid siren, and the moist air contributed to a weird sound that pierced Beantown. Across the region, people called the local police and fire departments asking what was going on.[19]

A senator from New York, James Mead, complained that men in uniform were being ill-treated in the District. On the floor of the Senate, Mead said that some Washington establishments "discriminated" against the military. A bill had been introduced earlier in the year that would "make it unlawful for any restaurant, hotel or other place of public assembly to bar men in uniform from its facilities or service."[20] A move was also afoot in Congress "to continue the fight for legislation giving residents of the District the privilege of voting...."[21] As it was the cold and flu season, the District Health Department and the

Pneumonia Control Committee asked sick people to stay home. As of 1940 in Washington, 80 out of every 100,000 individuals died of pneumonia.[22]

Congress was making plans to quit Washington sine die on December 20, giving members from long distances just enough time to get home to their districts, especially those traveling by rail, car, or bus. But before the Senate could depart, they would have to take up the bill regulating strikes in war industries, as labor unions were beginning to mount a lobbying campaign to defeat the controversial bill. Many were aghast it had so easily passed the House, with its overwhelming control by the Democrats, long aligned with the labor movement. But the unions found themselves on the wrong side of the patriotism argument. Industrial America saw the temporary advantage and they exploited it, pledging to put "patriotism above personal gain," and even William Knudsen, a high official with the Office of Production Management, said, "Let's, by the Almighty God, see to it that the boys, if they have to go, go with guns in their hands and not with a broom handle."[23] The War Department issued press releases claiming strikes had cost "7,000,000 man-hours."[24]

Henry Ford's plants in Detroit had already been partially converted to manufacturing to support the war effort. Ford himself was supportive. "[O]ut of the present conflict in Europe I see emerging a world federation, a union of all peoples in which there will be no customs, monetary or economic barriers," he said.[25] The Ford Motor Company was already churning out tanks and planes, but the old man was, as always, a visionary, quoting Tennyson's "Locksley Hall" speech of one hundred years prior.

At Union Station, where members of Congress and Washingtonians could catch trains leaving town, it was disclosed that government officials under the Wage-Hour Division were trailing Red Caps porters around to see if they were disclosing all their tips for tax purposes. "The checkers would dog the steps of the porters and compel them to disclose the amount of the tips they received. Arthur Brown, negro porter at the Camden Street Station . . . in Baltimore testified that the check system was a 'nuisance' which annoyed customers and Red Caps alike. He stated that Red Caps would do as well without any check system or guaranteed minimum wage." At the time, Red Caps could keep everything over 10 cents per customer to help with their luggage.[26]

The Washington social scene was in full swing in the early days of December, and the newspapers were filled with stories about this cocktail party, that black-tie dinner, and hoity-toity embassy parties. "Delightful Parties Held" and "Air Attaché and Mrs. Kenny Honored at Informal Party Given by Canadian Minister" were some of the headlines.[27] One party honoring "Senhor Paulo Bettencourt" and "Senhora de Bettencourt" was hosted by Nelson Rockefeller and "Mrs. Rockefeller."[28]

But one Georgetown socialite was having trouble with the help, according to the *Post*. "A popular Georgetown hostess tells this story on herself. Seems that along with a number of other Capitalites, she has had her share of servant trouble lately. A couple of days ago, however, she interviewed a colored maid whose qualifications appeared to be ideal. Arriving with the domestic for the interview was her brother." At the conclusion of the tour, the hostess welcomed the maid, telling her "you will feel like home here. 'She ought to,' put in the brother with a wide smile. 'She was bawned in this very room.'"[29]

In December of 1941, newspapers in America often published the impending military transfer of army personnel. In long columns, the names of men being assigned to the Medical Corps, the Infantry, the Coast Artillery, the Air Corps, the Ordinance Department, the Quartermaster Corps, the Dental Corps, the Field Artillery, the Veterinary Corps, and the Sanitary Corps were all right there in black and white along with the location of their new assignments. Anybody could read it, including jealous girlfriends, old enemies, collection agencies, and Japanese and Nazi spies.[30] The notion that anyone could enlist in the military, pack up their troubles, and get a fresh start was absurd.

The newspapers also thoughtfully listed shortwave radio broadcasts, including war news and broadcasts from London, Berlin, and "Tokio."[31] Also right there in black and white were details about how the navy's newest dive-bomber, the "HELL-DIVER," was being made in Columbus, Ohio, at a newly dedicated twenty-six acre facility. The plane, to be manufactured by the Curtiss-Wright Corporation, was a continuation of American pioneering in the new art of naval dive-bombing. The plant was opened by Rear Admiral John B. Towers, who helpfully told reporters, "Germany copied its dive-bombing technique from the United States Navy. Ernst Udet witnessed a demonstration of Navy dive bombing in this country eight years ago and took the idea back to Germany."[32]

The war continued its steady spread across the globe. In Lebanon, "war widows and orphans" of men who died fighting were receiving Red Cross aid.[33] President Fulgencio Batista of Cuba wanted his national legislature to grant him emergency powers to act in the event of hostilities. "He also declared that Cuba must be ready to carry out her commitment to the United States, with which the island's policy is linked."[34] The Argentine government was looking to clear up a previous misunderstanding with Washington, so as to gain access to its funds and pay for its own army.[35] Great Britain was moving ahead with declarations of war against "Finland, Rumania and Hungary." Churchill's policy was that "any man or state who marches with Hitler is our foe."[36] Finland had attacked Russia, an English ally.

The famed war correspondent, Royal Arch Gunnison, was in the Far East documenting, "Here in the Philippines the United States Army and Navy and the Filipino troops are on a 'war alert' 24 hours a day" and that the daily activities by America to strengthen its position in the region might dissuade Tokyo from military action." He was not hopeful, though, that the emperor would put a halt to his country's militarists. "It is not logic that will govern the Japanese. If they were logical, there would be no war."[37] Others in Washington's diplomatic circles were convinced that the Germans' complications in North Africa and the Russian Front would give the Japanese pause; that maybe there was a chance Hitler might not win the war, especially after two Italian divisions had surrendered to the Russians. Moscow issued a statement proclaiming that Josef Stalin was personally directing the Russian defense as "supreme commander in chief of the Red Army." The statement also claimed the Red Army had "severely defeated the Adolph Hitler Elite Guard."[38]

But Senator Claude Pepper of Florida, a staunch supporter of FDR in general and of Lend-Lease in particular, publicly predicted that the Vichy French government and the Japanese would engage in a "pincer" move into Thailand and toward the Burma Road.[39] Meanwhile, the Vichy French would support pinning down the British in Libya, thus reducing the armaments they could send to the Far East to strengthen their garrisons. But there were also rumors in Washington that the Japanese navy—thought to be a moderating force in Tokyo—was squabbling with the militarist elements inside the government. "[T]he conservative element struggles with the military group to prevent aggravation of the Pacific crisis to the point of war against the United States."[40]

This slim reed was grasped by many, that internal discord and food riots among the populace would prevent Japan from going to war. "If there is a ray of hope that a solution other than general war in the orient will be found, it rests on the uncertain attitude of the Japanese naval high command. . . . Reports to the State Department declare that riots, provoked by unemployment and shortages of rice and fish, the main staples of the Japanese diet, are rapidly spreading over the country."[41]

"Finally, Japan is confronted in the present situation with overwhelming naval and air supremacy of her potential enemies. An American fleet, bigger than her own, is poised at Pearl Harbor in the mid-Pacific."[42]

Suffice it to say, opinions as to Japanese intentions were sharply divided.

On December 3, the *Tatuta Mara*, a Japanese passenger ship, was stopped from departing San Francisco for Japan until sixty tons of U.S. mail destined for that country had been removed, though there was no mention of this being for security reasons. Because of the American embargo against Japan, longshoremen went aboard and off-loaded "a huge shipment of electric refrigerators, binoculars and electrical equipment." The ship also contained a large number of bankrupt businessmen who were going home to Japan after FDR had ordered a freeze of credit for Japanese in America. "One of the passengers was Jiuji G Kassai, member of the Japanese Diet, who warned the United States against going to war with the Japanese in a speech last week to the Commercial club."[43]

In Mexico City, it was reported that Japanese diplomats and their families, including the Japanese minister, were making hurried preparations to leave the country and head back to Japan. "In diplomatic circles, it was reported their decision was prompted by the arrival of a courier bringing from Washington confidential reports of the progress of United States-Japanese negotiations. A number of Japanese residents were reported to be trying to dispose quickly of their property preliminary to leaving."[44]

Japan also revealed that they had a response to the American position, though they did not indicate if they were responding to Secretary Hull's "principles for peace in the Pacific" of late November or the president's question on Japanese intentions when it came to Thailand of two days earlier. Whatever they were responding to, they let it leak out that Washington would not be happy with Tokyo's response.[45]

Thailand—renamed from Siam in 1939—was a prized possession for either side. The new name meant "Land of the Free," but the Japanese were thinking otherwise. It remained the only independent nation on the Asiatic Peninsula. "The nation's extensive mineral wealth includes tin, gold and silver, coal, tungsten, lead, antimony, copper, manganese, some iron and precious stones. Rubber production has been of increasing importance in southern and eastern Thailand."[46]

The mystery was cleared up when Tokyo rejected the Hull proposal, calling it "unacceptable" and saying that it could not serve as the foundation for "negotiations henceforth." It also did not address Roosevelt's question about Thailand. The Japanese news agencies, including Domei, let loose with a verbal blast against Washington. The newspaper *Asahi* claimed the Hull initiative was "'evident' that the United States was becoming 'more and more undisguised in her hostile activities against Japan.'"[47] After Hull said the two countries were at a near-breakdown in negotiations, the United Press called it "the strongest verbal whiplashing yet administered [at the] Tokyo government by an American official."[48]

The Japanese then floated the argument that they were amassing soldiers in Indochina as a security precaution to quell internal disturbances. "There have been no evidences of internal disorders . . . to warrant such extraordinary military and naval maneuvers," replied the *Washington Star*. The Vichy government had already signed over the former French colony to Tokyo. "Indo-China was taken over so easily that Tokio [sic] undoubtedly was encouraged to look upon further aggressive steps."[49] Still, the Japanese sent diplomats to

Indochina to give the whole situation a veneer of officialdom, rather than a blatant military incursion. Tokyo even produced a "neutrality" treaty between the Japanese and then-Silan signed in 1606.[50]

The Japanese government also broadcast over a radio in Hanoi that it would send no more troops into Indochina and further, the troops there would not be used to attack either Thailand or the Burma Road. They also disputed the number of soldiers FDR claimed were there.[51]

Before receiving the Japanese delegation in Washington, Hull met once again with FDR. Roosevelt then met with congressional leaders about the crisis in the Far East. Attending the meeting were Vice President Henry Wallace, House Speaker Sam Rayburn, and others. "Mr. Roosevelt told how the Japanese army twice had deliberately sabotaged peace negotiations with the United States just when these seemed to be going favorably." Hull echoed FDR's pessimism.[52] He had concluded that the Japanese had fully embraced "Nazi doctrine in tactics in the Far East." Also discussed was FDR's Lend-Lease announcement for Turkey.[53] The Germans were none too happy about Lend-Lease being extended to Turkey, storming, "[T]he last words have not been spoken in Defense Zone expansion" matters.[54] The Germans had designs on Turkey as a port on the Mediterranean.

Also in attendance was Senator Elbert Thomas, Democrat of Utah and chairman of the Senate Armed Services Committee. He had a kinder and gentler view of the Japanese, later predicting that shortly, the two powers would begin to cooperate against Germany and Italy. "Japan's Axis alliance is so unnatural and she is lonesome." Thomas made his remarks at a dinner in New York honoring a Soviet diplomat.[55]

A similar high-level meeting to the one convened by FDR at the White House took place in Tokyo, lasting two and a half hours and conducted by the "Privy Council, highest advisory organ of the empire to which Premier Gen. Hideki Tojo and Foreign Minister Shigenori Togo report in detail." The Privy Council in turn gave its advice to Emperor Hirohito. Pessimism filled the air in all the meetings and counsels in both Washington and Tokyo.[56] Meanwhile, Japan was working on creating a sham agreement with French Indochina, as it was ostensibly under Vichy control, which was under Berlin's control, but Indochina was already overrun with Japanese troops.

"Hull, in his press conference, specifically declared that Japanese policy is based on the doctrine of force and that this force is being wielded Nazi-fashion to attain political, economical, moral and social domination of the territory belonging to other sovereign nations."[57] The normally placid man was near to throwing up his hands, so frustrated was he with Tokyo. He was working to create a solution, but whatever he offered, the Japanese rejected and then blamed Washington for the continued stalemate.

A Japanese newspaper piled on. "If anything ruptures in the Pacific, the Anglo-American powers should take the responsibility."[58] Hull was a proud, successful, and patient man, but the Japanese intransigence had about beaten him.

British and Dutch commercial shipping in the Western Pacific effectively came to a standstill, in part because Nazi ships operating there were raiding them. British battleships had arrived in Singapore "but censorship cloaked that fact."[59] The Australians announced the loss of the cruiser, *Sydney*, after it was shelled by the German boat *Steiermark* in the Indian Ocean. The German vessel was actually a merchant ship that, when it was requisitioned and converted by the Germans, was renamed the *Kormoran*, but overwhelming majority of newspapers still reported it as the *Steiermark* had been "disguised as a merchantman" and opened fire on the Aussie boat. It was of little consequence that the German boat was sunk by the *Sydney* before she too went down.[60]

The Atlantic was no better than the Pacific.

By now, hope had faded for the recovery of most of the seventy-plus seamen who went down on the *Reuben James* in the North Atlantic, the greatest loss of naval personnel since the *Maine* went down in Cuba in 1898. A survivor, George Beasley, twenty-two, of Tulsa recounted, "We were swimming about 30 yards away . . . when she went down. Just as she slipped under, the depth charges went off. The ocean was thrown up in great wave, our raft was overturned and I was pulled under. About half of the men on the raft were drowned." Beasley was anxious to get back to sea.[61]

A month earlier, the U.S. government told the German government it would accept $3 million, cash on the barrelhead, for the previous sinking of the *Robin Moore*, which would settle all claims. The Germans then sank the American cargo carrier *Lehigh*, off the coast of Africa.[62]

Over the previous month, Germans had lost more ships than the British, but the British had lost more planes than the Germans. London reported it had lost three bombers over France, while "German planes bombed a port on the British southwest coast."[63]

December 4 was a bad day in California for military flyers, as several became lost in fog and perished. Out of the sky in Dublin appeared a German soldier, floating down in a parachute. The police arrested and booked him.[64] Winston Churchill's nephew, Pilot Officer Esmond Romilly, was declared missing in action after overseas air operations in the North Sea, flying for the Canadian Air Force. At twenty-two, he'd already been a bartender in Florida, lived in Alexandria, Virginia, with his wife, Jessica, a prominent London socialite, had been active in Socialist politics in England, and had fought on the Republican side in the Spanish Civil War.[65] Romilly was later declared dead.

America launched two more destroyers, the *Aaron Ward* and the *Buchanan*, in New Jersey, which was covered by many newspapers, including ship complements and armaments.[66] A wire photograph of an unusual view of the stocks and flukes of a giant anchor in the Pearl Harbor navy yard went out on all the wires, published in many papers. Again, photographers and reporters had unhindered access to American military installations and information.

The navy vessel *Salinas* was fired upon in the North Atlantic just a month earlier by German subs and the ship managed to limp into port, but not before returning fire on the subs, damaging one.[67] It was the first time the U.S. Navy had successfully fired upon and damaged a German vessel. American naval ships were under orders directly from FDR to defend themselves and had been for some time. The naval battle was heavily covered in all the newspapers. But if anyone really needed more detail on American vessels, all they had to do was pick up a copy of the publication *Jane's Fighting Ships*, easily available. "The publication . . . credits the *Salinas* with two 5-inch guns and three 3-inch anti-aircraft guns. Whether the latter could be depressed sufficiently for fire on a submarine would depend on whether they are of a late model."[68]

Photos of an unidentified British freighter being torpedoed in the Atlantic by a U-boat ran in newspapers on December 4. In Chungking, Chinese sources spotted forty Japanese warships in Vietnam's Camranh Bay. This fleet included at least one aircraft carrier and "45 planes aboard. The Japanese were hastily building an air base in Western Indochina near the Gulf of Siam

(Thailand) having impressed 5,000 native workers for the job." *Impressed* was a polite word left over from an earlier era that in fact meant "slavery."[69]

At the same time Seigo Nakano, a "pro-Axis political leader, was demanding the sinking of United States ships unless aid to China ceases."[70] The Maritime Commission urged the speedup of the production of Liberty ships, which were needed for transporting goods and war materiel. At the time, ships were "splashing" at the rate of one every seven months, but the goal was to streamline the process so that one could be launched every four months.[71]

In Nazi-occupied Belgrade, Serb guerillas were making the occupying German army's life miserable. "The Serbs were . . . harassing German patrols, cutting German communications and looting German supply trains." An initial report said the Serbs had inflicted six hundred casualties on the Germans. The Serbs, numbering around eighty thousand, led by Gen. Draja Mihailovic, "were locked in battle in the Yugoslav Valley of the Western Morava." The Germans were determined to wipe out every Serb as punishment for reprisals. The ragtag Serbs were fighting and winning against five Nazi divisions, heavily armed, with superior firepower.[72] The Nazis eventually lost four of five divisions before withdrawing.

Also, in a week's period of time, four German passenger planes between Belgrade and Ankara, Turkey, had crashed, and while some blamed the cold weather for causing engine failure, others blamed Serb saboteurs for the planes' demise.[73] Moscow also claimed credit for killing four thousand German troops, and the British claimed that Nazi planes accidentally killed or wounded sixty German prisoners who were being transported in freight cars to a camp in the Nile Valley.[74]

When it came to security, the American government wasn't completely feckless. "The United States yesterday added 189 names to its blacklist of individuals and firms in South and Central America alleged to be acting for the benefit of Germany or Italy."[75] The government had already assembled a list of two thousand persons of interest thought to be aligned with Italy and Germany. But apparently no Japanese interests were listed, even though America was not at war with any of the three principal countries of the Axis powers.[76] Many papers referred to it as a "Black List."[77]

In Paris, the German Gestapo set a deadline for those guilty of "terroristic acts against German soldiers." In recent days, a German doctor had been shot and a bomb had been detonated, killing two artillerymen. "The Germans have dealt sternly with previous attacks on soldiers. Fifty hostages were executed by German firing squads at Nantes for the assassination of the commander of that city and fifty others were executed at Bordeaux for the assassination of a German military lawyer."[78] In the occupied countries of Europe, it was not unusual for the Nazis to shoot one hundred civilians as reprisals for every action taken against a German national.

In the time since Nazi occupation of Paris, the city's population had sharply declined, from over 2.6 million in 1936 to just over 1 million as of the spring 1941. It was estimated that 1.5 million French had been deported to "German oflags and stalags."[79]

It turned out the House Military Affairs Subcommittee had only begun to scratch the surface when it came to Leon K. Shanack, the so-called "defense broker" whose exploits the papers had covered avidly the day before. It was subsequently revealed that Shanack was no piker when it came to bilking the American taxpayer and, in fact, had so far pocketed $97,959; he stood to collect another $91,990 in "brokerage fees" from Remington Arms for services rendered as a go-between with the Greenwich Machine and Tool Company of New York. It was later discovered that Shanack received even more fees from additional companies for other defense contractors.[80]

The economy wasn't in completely bad shape, even with a minimum wage of 30 cents an hour.[81] The newspapers abounded with bank ads for car loans and home loans, and pitched opening savings accounts with each, insured up to

$5,000 by the government.[82] At the People's Bank in Atlanta, they were paying 4 percent on a passbook savings account.[83]

Flush with defense dollars, New York was a downright party town. The Rainbow Room, a swank restaurant and nightclub with a revolving dance floor and live big band, located on the sixty-fifth floor of the Rockefeller Center, was the scene of lavish parties given by Manhattan's elite. "This is NBC, coming to you from the Rainbow Room" was a frequent phrase heard on national radio, causing a frisson of wistful yearning among ordinary Americans in the listening audience not privileged enough to be dancing there in formal attire to the strains of jazz kings like Tommy Dorsey or Harry James.

An astonishing story was reported at length in the *Chicago Tribune*, owned by Col. Robert McCormick, an isolationist whose Republican leanings were well-known, as was his opposition to FDR. Because of this, the paper's news gathering—which was often superb—was sometimes discounted by the more New Deal supplicant newspapers.

In an exclusive, lengthy, and detailed story, the paper reported that a secret "War Plans Division" was laying out how the United States government was preparing to create a massive armed force—over 5 million men— and would make a "supreme offensive effort" to enter the war on July 1, 1943. The document was called "Blueprint for War." A highly confidential letter was produced for the article from Roosevelt to Henry Stimson, secretary of war, urging he coordinate with Frank Knox, secretary of the navy, to formulate a grand plan for America's entry into the war. The main objective was the absolute defeat of Nazi Germany. "I wish you would explore the munitions and mechanical equipment of all types, which, in your opinion, would be required to exceed by an appropriate amount that which is available to our potential enemies," FDR ostensibly wrote the secretary of war.[84]

Just as astonishing, FDR's press secretary, Stephen T. Early, did not dismiss the explosive story out of hand, but simply said, "I am in no position to confirm or deny the truth of this story" and that there would be "an investigation." The War Department could only say, "No comment."[85] In Washington, at all times, "no comment" was a surefire confirmation that the allegation was true, as was any call for an investigation. Early went even further, defending the notion that FDR should be preparing for war. "An unlimited national emergency has been declared. If these divisions lacked plans to meet this emergency or any phase of it, they would be guilty of inefficiency."[86]

What rankled so many people was their perception of FDR's autocratic and secretive approach to governance and presumed preparations for war with Germany. Indeed, it came to light that he'd been arming Turkey for six months prior to announcing the extension of Lend-Lease to the beleaguered country, a promise he'd made to Churchill months earlier, even though there were forces in Ankara attempting an alliance with the Axis powers. Senator Robert Taft, Republican of Ohio, did not object, though. "I would much rather give aid to them than to Russia."[87]

Analysis in the Stimson document was cold and accurate. "By themselves, however, naval and air forces seldom, if ever, win important wars. It should be recognized as an almost invariable rule that only land armies can likely win wars."[88] It did recognize the political realities of December 4, 1941, when the document said, "It is out of the question to expect the United States . . . to undertake a substantial and successful" effort to enter the World War.[89] Astonishingly, war with Japan was only referred to as an aside, barely considered by the war planners.

Harold Ickes, secretary of the interior, outlined his own view of American foreign policy in a speech before the Jewish Community Council. "I know of no one, except the Nazis and the self-acclaimed but misnamed American Firsters, who is suggesting a negotiated peace, or who is likely to ask for a negotiated peace. I know the only way to prevent a war epidemic is through the establishing of democracy at the sources of war."[90]

On the East Coast, it was open season on the America First Committee, and syndicated columnist Dorothy Thompson said the group was "Japan's Ace in [the] Hole." The grassroots movement, she said, "creates in Tokyo the false impression that Japan can risk war with us."[91]

For good girls and boys expecting gifts from Santa (and with some assist from Mom and Dad), a "Slingin' Sammy Baugh" football made by Spalding was selling at the Plaza Sports Shop for $1.95, a Spalding "Babe Ruth" fielder's glove was $3.50, and boys' and girls' skates were selling for $6.95, available in either black or white.[92]

In Washington, in an era when downtowns were still vibrant and big department stores dominated shopping, men could shop at Frederick's for "nationally known Men's wear." For women, "Lysol for feminine hygiene" was being advertised under the heading, "Her Husband Was a Stranger." The dreadful ad copy continued, "His coolness was hard to bear. She blamed it on everything but the real cause—her 'ONE NEGLECT'—carelessness about feminine hygiene. You can prevent this threat to your romance. Do as modern women do. Use Lysol for your intimate personal care. Endorsed by many doctors." The ad was accompanied by the photo of an understandably stricken woman.[93]

For evening entertainment in Washington, patrons could enjoy the sounds of the Don Carper Four in the Café Caprice at the Roger Smith Hotel. "Dance to the enchanting rhythm . . . nightly at 10. . . . Tremendous Cocktails."[94] The hotel was located at Pennsylvania and 18th Streets, just two blocks away from the White House. Also open for business was the Pall Mall Room at the Hotel Raleigh, "with music by Bert Bernath and his Sidney Orchestra."[95] The Lounge Rivera, with dancing from "9 to 2" and music performed by Pete Macia's famous orchestra, was also a popular hangout.[96] For those whose dancing skills were suspect, they could always learn or brush up at any one of dozens of Arthur Murray Dance Schools around the nation.

There was also a great deal of cheer in South Carolina, where army troops finally finished two months of maneuvers. Some headed back to their bases, others to their homes for Christmas. "While music boxes blared in the smoke-filled cafes and taverns, long lines of soldiers impatiently stood on the sidewalks awaiting their turn to eat." The restaurants were so filled that many men ate standing up as "perspiring waitresses staggered under trays of food. . . . Last night was a barber's nightmare." Many of the soldiers had gone for over a month without a haircut but now "enjoyed the luxury of shaves and shampoos in warm water. Many waited three to four hours before getting a chair."[97]

A new and wholly ugly car was rolled off the assembly lines, the Crosley. "For Maximum Defense Economy, it costs 2/3 less to buy . . . up to 50 miles on a gallon . . . up to 40,000 miles on tires." The car sold for $447 but could be driven off the lot for just $149 down. It was being sold in Washington by the Manhattan Auto and Radio Co.[98] The car looked like it was made out of papier mâché.

A new cereal was unveiled, and to help boost sales they were selling two for one. The advertising claims suggested it did everything except cure the heartbreak of psoriasis. And it "sticks to your ribs!" too. What was this wonder food? "Shaped like cute little doughnuts . . . they stay crisp in milk." Its name was Cheerioats. Breakfast cereals were often marketed as edible medicine cabinets—to wit, Kellogg's All-Bran: "The better way to treat constipation due to lack of proper 'bulk' in the diet is to correct the cause of the trouble with a delicious cereal . . . eat it every day and drink plenty of water."[99] The brainchild of Will Keith Kellogg, prepackaged cereals such as All-Bran and Toasted Corn Flakes were considered nutritional innovations.

Virtually every newspaper of the era pitched a miracle cure for baldness. "More than a quarter-million persons have retained or regained good heads of hair by the reliable, proven Thomas method."[100] If Christmas cheer got to be too excessive, Americans could always turn to Phillips Milk of Magnesia, so they could "wake up clear headed after too much smoking, drinking, late eating." Apparently "alkalizing" one's "overindulgence" was the ticket.[101]

The scrap paper drive initiated in Washington just a day before and implemented mostly by children was a huge success. The tykes brought in tons of paper to recycling centers with the proceeds to go to local schools and PTAs.

In New York, the heavyweight champion of the world, Joe Louis, was looking forward to a title defense fight with Buddy Baer, brother of Max Baer, whom Louis had defeated several years earlier.[102] Both Louis and Baer had something to prove—Louis, the African American, and Baer, the Jewish American.

The *Atlanta Constitution* announced as part of the Christmas celebration it would serialize the Charles Dickens manuscript, *The Life of Our Lord*. Dickens had written it for his children and read it to them each Christmas, but asked that the book not be published until the last of his children had died. In 1933, the last of his children, Sir Henry Fielding Dickens, had passed away after a long and successful life.[103]

In Bogata, Colombia, the offices of the "anti-Nazi committee" were burglarized, and money was stolen that had been "collected during Anti-Hitler Week."[104]

In North Africa, British tank commanders still talked confidently of defeating Rommel, the "Desert Fox," but they would first have to involve Rommel in their plan, as he'd been pushing them all over North Africa and they were retreating right along the coast all the way to Egypt. Time may have been against Rommel, however, as the British navy's goal was total control of the Mediterranean so they could interdict German supply ships with impunity. The Germans were rushing supplies via plane and ship. Daily reports of the tank battles in North Africa often contradicted themselves, but both sides agreed that Rommel had crushed the New Zealand tank division aiding Great Britain.

Military service could be downright hazardous for the enlistee or draftee, but it could also be dangerous for the members of the Selective Service Board. In Athens, Georgia, former Major League pitcher William Austin "Cy" Moore struck the chairman of the local draft board when he questioned whether Moore's parents had given false documents as to their dependency on their son.[105] It could also be dangerous for the loved ones of potential inductees. In Los Angeles, a twenty-three-year-old carhop shot and seriously injured herself, greatly distraught that her boyfriend might be drafted.[106]

As with other newspapers around the country, the Boston Daily Globe reported on new assignments by troops and war equipment. "The newly organized Tank Destroyer Tactical and Firing Center has been stationed temporarily at Ft. George C. Meade, Md. according to a War Department announcement."[107] One G.I. from up north was so pleased with southern hospitality in Farmville, Virginia, he exclaimed, "If anybody mistakes us for southerners now, it will be OK."[108] Army chaplains were in short supply and a call went out for more men of the cloth to put on khaki and camouflage.

New York mayor Fiorello LaGuardia dedicated a new building in his city designed to house military personnel. He said that America was not "bluffing," that it may have been fooled in the "last World War" but would not be again. "We do not know what will happen tomorrow, next week or next month, but the United States Navy stands ready."[109]

The Globe also reported on new military construction with great fanfare.

"The United States submarine *Halibut*, 40th undersea boat to be built at the Portsmouth Navy Yard, was launched today. . . . Today's launching was the sixth of the year and establishes a new record for submarine construction. In 1940, there were four launchings. As soon as the ways were clear today, workmen began laying another keel in Uncle Sam's defense program." The story also detailed all the military brass in attendance at the yard in New Hampshire.[110] Yet another story detailed again how America expected to meet its goal of fifty thousand airplanes produced in 1942.[111] The military budget, it was announced, was almost $68 billion.[112]

When it came to telling America's enemies everything about the military, the *Los Angeles Times* was no slacker. A story went into great depth about "air-raid defense exercises" planned for the area in mid-December. It would involve hundreds of planes, as well as ground personnel and spotters. The planned drill was "similar to those in New York and other eastern cities during the last few months." . . ."[113]

"Taking part in the aerial portion of the tactical problem will be scores of planes from the 20th Pursuit Group, Hamilton Field, using P-40s and the 17th Bomber Group, McChord Field, Washington, in B-25s. The planes, it was learned, will fly as theoretical enemies as well as interceptors. Across a huge, kidney-shaped filter board, 120 women, plotters and tellers, will filter the information and pass it on to the information room."[114]

On tour was the typing champion of America, "a plump, brown-eyed girl" who could rattle off 150 words per minute, setting a per-hour record that had never been broken. "Miss Margaret Hamma" of Brooklyn was on a publicity tour to promote the new IBM electric typewriter.[115]

Actor Joseph Cotton reported that his car was stolen. Forty-eight hours later, it was discovered at the bottom of his pool. He'd failed to set the brake and it rolled backward, unnoticed.[116] The *Los Angeles Times* was celebrating its sixtieth anniversary.[117] The paper had seen much, and by 1940, the population of the city was just over 1.5 million citizens; a year earlier, water had begun to arrive at the city via the new Colorado River Aqueduct. That same year a heat wave kept the city hot under the collar, as the daytime temperature averaged "around 107 degrees for days and days."[118] The paper also reported on the "Latin American Queen" picked for the Rose Tournament Parade: Juanita Estela Lopez, "olive-skinned and dimpled . . ."[119]

In San Jose, a frustrated husband filed for divorce because his wife would not stop listening to the radio. His wife "Eva wouldn't clean the house, care for the children, cook my meals or talk to me," complained Max Barrott. Judge John D. Foley "awarded Barrott the divorce and his wife the radio."[120]

Knowledgeable observers tried to make some sense of Japan's actions. London had made it clear that any incursion into Thailand meant war with the British and that meant war with America as well. It would mean fighting a multifront war with countries that had more industrial capacity than Japan did.

"Japan is facing international economic siege and she is very vulnerable. If there was ever a country that needed to live on terms of peaceful trade with the rest of the world, it is Japan. Japan Proper has a population of 73,000,000 packed into an area less than that of California and far less rich in its material resources. Scarcely able to sustain herself in foodstuffs, she is heavily dependent upon imports of other raw materials. For such industrial and military necessities as petroleum, iron, steel, aluminum, lead, zinc, copper, tin, machine tools, wool and cotton she relied chiefly upon the United States, the British Empire and the Netherland Dutch Indies, nations which are now enforcing against her a rigid economic blockade." Imports from the United States had shriveled to nothing, from $18 million in September of 1940 to $500 in September of 1941. The country was also cut off from U.S. credit and the country lived and died by trade.[121]

"Japan, in the grip of her militarists, has chosen to seek the will-o'-the-wisp of economic self-sufficiency by the path of military aggression. Now, after four years of exhausting war, she finds her economic and industrial life strangling. She has made the tragic error of following a course of military aggression irreconcilably opposed to that kind of world. She can expect relief only when her national policies again permit peace-loving nations to do business with her, without risk to themselves, and in good conscience."[122]

Because of her own policies and myriad mistakes, Japan was now desperate. Washington was openly talking about a naval blockade of Japan, in cooperation with the British. "In that case ... the Roosevelt Administration would be disposed to ask Congress for an outright declaration of war, rather than to wage an undeclared fight."[123]

The peripatetic First Lady, tireless champion of social causes, was out and about as usual, appearing on national radio shows of her own, including a "Town Hall Meeting of the Air" broadcast over NBC. Her cohost was the famous photographer Margaret Bourke-White. The topic they addressed was "What Must We Do to Improve Health and Welfare of the American People?"[124]

While giving a speech in New York at a "symposium on 'Recent Immigrants and National Defense,'" Eleanor Roosevelt assured the audience that if war came, "aliens with good records ... need have no anxiety about being placed in United States concentration camps should this country declare war against their homelands."[125]

Italian, German, and Japanese Americans were relieved.

CHAPTER 5

THE FIFTH OF DECEMBER

"U.S. Proposals Downed by Japs"

Nevada State Journal

"Japanese Sea Talks Continue"

Standard Examiner

"Tokyo Envoy to Mexico Ordered Home
as U.S.-Japan Crisis Grows"

Sun

Scientists discovered in December 1941 that the sun was 100,000 miles farther away from the earth than previously thought. Rather than the formerly believed 92,897,416 miles, Dr. H. Spencer Jones, astronomer royal at the Greenwich Observatory in Great Britain just outside of London, calculated *Sol* was actually 93,003,000 miles from *Terra Firma*. Dr. Jones also made some discoveries about asteroids, which other scientists referred to as "the lice of the heavens."[1] Astronomers also enlarged their knowledge of sunspots.

During this time, astrophysical research was gathering momentum in an intriguing area: black holes. In a new line of exploration that was dismissed by the scientific old guard as erroneous and fanciful, more imaginative scientists were theorizing that when a star collapsed after a supernova, it created a sufficiently dense mass from which even light couldn't escape, deforming the fabric of space and time.

Despite the war, German and British astronomers continued to exchange information.[2] The world may have been on the brink of annihilation, but it was also on the brink of exciting new discoveries with enormous, lasting implications.

Science was advancing in others areas as well. In Los Angeles, an amateur "ham" radio operator, Karl E. Pierson, said he had developed important technology to quiet the static heard over broadcast receivers. Pierson had gained fame previously when he had been one of the last to hear transmissions from the lost aviatrix, Amelia Earhart, "on her fateful around-the-world flight in 1937." He also claimed to have received transmissions from Earhart after her plane went down.[3]

Because of the aluminum shortage in America, a new, strong, and flexible material was being perfected: plastic. Some scientists predicted a bright future for the revolutionary new synthetic product and for young men going into the business of polymer and acetate development. "Someday . . . bathtubs, caskets, automobiles and airplane sections may be made of plastic."[4] Plastic automobile bodies were also envisioned, but at the time, the material was mostly dedicated to the war effort.

Scientific advancement also extended to diet. Nutritionists in England, for instance, discovered that Rose hips were "20 times richer in vitamin c— the anti-infective vitamin—than orange juice, now scarce because of the war." The Ministry of Health initiated a "harvest of the hedgerows . . . to garner 500 tons of the rose fruit to be converted into a tasty health-giving syrup."[5] And scientists in Australia were working to perfect powdered beef and in one instance, a six-year-old can of powdered meat came out in perfect condition.

Dr. Karl Menninger, head of the American Psychoanalytical Association, produced a report explaining that man sought war because it was "a way to gratify subconscious desires to destroy and kill." Elaborating, Dr. Menninger said, "War appeals to people for the same reasons that the Fascist philosophy appeals to people. It stimulates the wish to exert power over other people, to be aggressive, dominant, commanding, possessive."[6]

Science was also unfortunately improving man's ability to wage war in the air, on the high seas, and over land. The American military announced the development of a fantastic new gun that could shoot down "anything that can fly and that is expected to prove a major factor in the war against Hitlerism." The announcement was made by Brigadier Gen. G. M. Barnes before a meeting of the American Society of Mechanical Engineers in the Hotel Astor in New York City. "Quantity production . . . will begin next month. The new weapon has a caliber of 4.7 inches or 120 millimeters. The characteristics of the gun are a carefully guarded military secret, but General Barnes discussed its history," reported the *New York Times*. Barnes elaborated, "Reports from abroad indicate that 90 per cent of the bombing over England and Germany has been carried out at altitudes not exceeding 12,000 feet" and the new gun would be effective "at higher altitudes, using a heavier and more effective projectile." So as to leave no doubt, Barnes went into even further detail for the benefit of casual and not-so-casual readers such as German and Japanese spies. Then General Barnes turned it over to Colonel L. B. Lent, chief engineer of the National Inventors Council, who "told the meeting that some 'revolutionary' new weapons submitted to the council were under test and development and 'someday soon may be heard from in tones not pleasant to the Axis powers.'"[7]

Unfortunately, a 70-ton "flying boat" built for the government by the Glenn L. Martin Co. caught fire and then ran aground in Baltimore harbor while conducting sea and air trials. A propeller flew off and hit the fuselage, causing the mishap, and the plane was badly damaged as other parts of it caught fire. The plane had been named Mars.[8]

For the first time in months, Washington was drenched by a really good gully washer, and a strange rainbow shone over the city for a brief time. The temperature on December 5 was unusually warm for the season—it was in the sixties.[9]

Because of better sanitation, including treated water and the improved methods of handling sewage and trash, American life spans had rocketed up in just a few short years. At the turn of the century, the average life expectancy for an American was around forty-four years of age, but by 1941, it had gone up to sixty-six years for women and sixty-three years for men.[10] And yet, Americans' diets were still questionable, as 50 percent of draftees were rejected, mostly due to poor nutrition, which was attributed to sub-standard household income. A Gallup poll found that four in ten American families were bringing in less that $25 per week and, as such, could not afford enough food. The residents of 12 million households went to bed hungry every night.[11]

There was still too little work to go around.

Many eyes were now on Thailand, and war seemed to move closer. "To most Americans, Thailand is still Siam. The name conjures pictures of white elephants, temple dancers and pagodas, rather than clashing empires. England declared months ago that Japanese invasion of Thailand would produce immediate collision with the armed forces of the British Crown." Japan propagandists continued their drumbeat that Thailand was threatened by outside forces. It was much the same argument Hitler made before invading Poland, Denmark, Norway, and Czechoslovakia, declaring he would be subjugating them for their own good.[12] The Japanese also claimed the number of troops they were sending into Indochina had been grossly exaggerated, and besides, they claimed, Thailand was a Buddhist country and thus anti-Chinese, and they, the Japanese, were there to protect Thailand.[13]

Syndicated columnist Walter Lippmann declared, "For the first time, the country is now on the verge of actual, all out war." Lippmann was the de facto voice of the "reasonable" establishment; his word carried clout. He saw another war coming for America not because of Lend-Lease or because of FDR's order to naval ships to fight back in the Atlantic, but because a fight with Japan would provoke America to jump in. In this, his was a voice both accurate and rare. He excoriated the isolationists and America First Committee for misunderstanding the situation in the Far East while focusing all their arguments on Europe.[14] Many saw Lippmann as little more than a shill for the Roosevelt administration when it came to intervention.

A large school of thought in American foreign policy also believed that Japan's society was overtaxed, having failed in four years to completely subjugate China. Large amounts of men and resources were being devoted to fighting a war without resolution and because of this, Tokyo could not seriously consider expanding the war any farther south.[15]

Yet other writers and observers saw the arrival of new British battleships in Singapore as another deterrent to Japanese actions against Thailand. "Political observers here say the arrival of the British fleet brought powerful new pressure on the Japanese in connection with the Washington negotiations and believe it may be decisive in forcing Japan to drop her plans for new aggressions and to begin a general retreat."[16]

A seesaw battle of public relations and war continued on the Russian Front, with the Germans claiming their big guns were raining shells on Moscow while the Soviets claimed the guns had been "silenced."[17] Temperatures on the Russian Front had reached 13 degrees below zero.[18] The British claimed to have repulsed two surges by the Germans in North Africa, though they conceded that Axis forces had "reoccupied the important Gambut supply base which the British captured in the early days of the Libyan campaign."[19]

Public relations battles were also raging in Washington, with isolationist Democrats and Republicans fighting with internationalist Democrats and Republicans. On the floor of the Senate, a sharp exchange took place between Senator Charles McNary of Oregon, a Republican, and Claude Pepper of Florida, a Democrat. Pepper charged his honorable colleague with being a "laggard in supporting the President's defense program."[20]

A grand jury had convened to investigate Nazi propaganda in the United States, and a star witness was Republican congressman Hamilton Fish of New York, an isolationist, whose chief aide had been indicted for perjury.[21] Fish represented a grand legacy, as his family boasted over one hundred years of political involvement.

Henry Stimson, the respected secretary of war, declared a war of his own against the *Chicago Tribune* for publishing the leaked documents on covert military planning by the U.S. government the prior day. Stimson did not deny their veracity and calmly said all contingencies were being explored, but he questioned the "wanting in loyalty and patriotism" of the newspaper for printing the story. Roosevelt had been asked about the report, but threw it into Stimson's lap to handle. Stimson did so, reading a long statement, lecturing the paper on proprieties in wartime and said his department was conducting an investigation. Capitol Hill erupted into a donnybrook over the *Tribune* story, while some charged that FDR was planning to give a "blank check" to Winston Churchill.[22]

Japanese propagandists and newspapers had a field day with the account. "Secret United States plans against Japan and Germany are exposed," blared a headline in the *Chugai Shogyo Journal*; yet other Japanese newspapers said the story demonstrated that America was not ready for war and that Secretary Hull was pursuing "dollar diplomacy." Japanese radio was little better, bashing America, spreading disinformation, playing the race and regionalism cards.[23]

A controversy over uniformed men and Washington's nightclubs had not died down, as both a general and a senator claimed their sons, both army privates, had been turned away and were told to go and change into civilian clothes before being admitted. Not to say there weren't plenty of other organized activities for soldiers and sailors.[24] The local newspapers listed dozens of locations of Service Clubs and U.S.O. clubs in Washington. At the Soldiers, Sailors, and Marines Club on L Street in the nation's capital, enlisted men found a "library, writing desks, table tennis, pool, radios, pianos, canteen, showers." The club was open twenty-four hours a day, seven days a week.[25] At many clubs, young single women put up Christmas trees, and if a homesick soldier or sailor had trouble finding a room in Washington, they could go to the hospitality committee in the District Building for help.[26]

Both Catholic and Jewish groups operated clubs for young servicemen as well. Over at the Bureau of Printing and Engraving, the Women's Battalion was sponsoring a dance. There were also dances at the Y.M.C.A., sightseeing tours of the area, teas, and lectures. There were also plenty of "Activities for Colored Service Men" in Washington, including an open house at the Phyllis Wheatley Y.W.C.A., religious services at various institutions, lodging at the Y.M.C.A. in Anacostia, and dances.[27] The *Washington Evening Star* referred to the minority clubs as for "colored," while the *Washington Post* referred to them as for "Negro."[28] Many political leaders, including no less a luminary than Eleanor Roosevelt, lobbied for greater civil rights for blacks. But those gains were to come much later. For now, Washington was still a part of the

South, a region where segregationist Jim Crow laws would continue to hold sway for the time being.

Despite his complaints about leaked documents, Stimson nonetheless "disclosed" in great detail army plans for training ten thousand new bombardier-navigators. He also announced plans for "52 'tank destroyer' battalions, and the conversion of two additional regular Army triangular divisions into fully motorized units. The infantry divisions to be motorized are the 8th, at Ft. Leonard Wood, Mo., and the 9th at Ft. Bragg, N.C. The action will double the number of such divisions on wheels, the 4th and the 7th already having been motorized."[29]

Military planners and civilians living and working in the areas of Arlington and Alexandria, Virginia, were still battling over the mishmash of new roads being proposed for the new $31 million War Department. When completed, "some 20,000 Government employees" were expected to work there, but "[i]t is estimated that more than 85,000 vehicles now pass the area of the new building daily."[30] The plan was for the entire building to be outfitted with air conditioning, which most federal buildings still lacked.

In New York, two shipping companies were indicted by a federal grand jury, "charging each with conspiracy to violate the Neutrality act by shipping abroad . . . material that might have been used by Axis powers."[31]

The presidents of the various South American countries were not lagging in their concern about a possible conflict between the United States and Japan. An "extraordinary meeting" was planned in Buenos Aires by the leaders of Brazil, Chile, Peru, and Argentina to discuss the matter.[32]

The District Court of Washington upheld "[t]he validity of covenants under which white owners agree not to sell land in Washington to colored persons . . . was voided when the Home Owners' Loan Corp. became owner of the property in question." A white family had "conveyed" property to a black family, but the white neighbors objected and brought a complaint to the city government. In simpler language, racism was still a protected institution in Washington, D.C.[33]

Ugly free speech was upheld in New Jersey, as the State Supreme Court voided a "race hatred law" aimed at the German-American Bund actively operating there, including holding rallies. Nine men "accused of making or promoting anti-Jewish speeches" were found to be innocent, as the state law "conflicted with constitutional guarantees of free speech." "The State's race-hatred law made it a misdemeanor to make utterances in the presence of two or more persons of 'hatred, abuse, violence or hostility' against any race, color or creed." The anti-Semites had been convicted, fined, and some sentenced to jail time before the upper court's ruling. "To denounce one's fellows or advocate hostility to them . . . is as revolting to any fair-minded man . . . yet . . . his utterances must be such as to create a clear and present danger that will bring about the substantial evils to society that the state has a right to prevent," wrote Chief Justice Thomas J. Brogan.[34] An appeal was under consideration.

The spirit of Christmas wisped thin in some places. A draft dodger of the World War, Grover Cleveland Bergdoll was denied parole by the War Department to be with his family for the holidays. He'd lived in Germany for many years, later coming home in 1939 with a wife, Berta, and six children in tow. Bergdoll "was convicted of desertion, escape and draft evasion during the World War" and was sentenced to seven and a half years at Ft. Leavenworth.[35]

The Vichy government was charitable when it announced that Americans located there could broadcast a twenty-word Christmas message to "10 friends in America provided the messages contain no politics or military information."[36] Meanwhile, the French Resistance, underground opposition to Nazi control in their homeland, continued to undermine the Axis powers in Paris. Another Nazi officer was shot "in the Rue de Seine Latin quarter of Paris" by a bicyclist who quickly fled the scene.[37] It meant fresh reprisals against Parisians, but the Resistance pushed on.

The Serbs continued to give the Germans fits even as "seven Nazi divisions . . . at least 100,000 men had been dispatched in an attempt to wipe out armed opposition to the Axis occupation." The dateline for the story was Jerusalem.[38] There were only sixteen shopping days left until the birthday of the celebrated son of Joseph and Mary, who had been born about six miles from there 1,941 years earlier.

An underground movement in Nazi-occupied Romania was also taking shape, with an unusual leader—none other than King Michael, a mere sapling of nineteen years, but a brave one at that. Together with his sweetheart, Irina Malaxa, they were actively arming, aiding, abetting, and plotting with the anti-Nazi guerillas growing in the country.[39]

The British government took to the airwaves and called for a "V for Victory" army of civilians in the occupied countries—estimated at 200 million—to switch over from "passive to active resistance. The time has come . . . over the B.B.C. for the army to form in small platoons . . . factory workers lose their tools and that office workers muddle and miscalculate."[40]

In other words, sabotage.

The Japanese government finally responded to President Roosevelt's question via the State Department about their intentions for Thailand. Brushing aside reporters and photographers, it was formally presented to Secretary of State Cordell Hull by Ambassador Nomura and Special Envoy Kurusu in a twenty-five-minute meeting "and after their departure, it was rushed immediately to Mr. Roosevelt's desk. The President also met Secretary Hull at a luncheon for a personal discussion of the document."[41] Hull was exhausted, but FDR was anything but. He was looking spiffy in a new green tweed suit, except for the black mourning armband he was wearing for the death of his mother three months earlier. When Hull walked in, FDR airily said, "What's cooking?"[42] Over the course of the day, FDR also met with various members of Congress, his staff, the cabinet, and also with a young congressman from Texas, Lyndon Johnson, who huddled with the president to discuss his running once again for the Senate in Texas. Johnson was described by the *Post* as the "fair haired boy of the Administration." FDR later met again with Hull for an hour and a half.[43]

In a long and sugary communiqué, Japan claimed their actions in Indochina had been because of Chinese troop movement—nothing more. The rambling text said "[t]hat no measure has been taken on the part of the Japanese government that may transgress the stipulations of the protocol of joint defense between Japan and [Vichy] France. Reference is made to your inquiry about the intention of the Japanese government with regard to reported movements of Japanese troops in French Indo-China.... As Chinese troops have recently shown frequent signs of movements along the northern frontier of French Indo-China bordering on China. Japanese troops with the object of mainly taking precautionary measures, have been reinforced to a certain extent in the northern part of French Indo-China.... As a natural sequence of this step, certain movements have been made among the troops stationed in the southern part of said territory. It seems that an exaggerated report has been made of these movements."[44] The Japanese had now formally offered yet another reason for their actions, and the missive was so reasonable, many thought something was up.

Following the message, a spokesman for Tokyo, Tomokazu Hori, also raised again the chances for peace in the region, saying that America and Japan would "continue with sincerity to try to find a common formula for a peaceful situation in the Pacific." He added that the administration had "misunderstood our fundamental policy" and that Washington and Hull "seem[ed] to allege that we are following a policy of force and conquest in establishing military despotism." Chillingly, he concluded, "If there is no sincerity then there is no need to continue the conversations."[45]

The U.S. government had no initial response, but rumors swept Australia that America and Japan were near to breaking off diplomatic relations, even as the U.S. government was attempting to allay fears that relations were in danger of imminently breaking down. Nomura tried his best too, saying, "[A]s far as we are concerned, we are always willing to talk—after all, we are a friendly nation." A news report further said, "Japan desired no precipitate action."[46] But in fact, a military skirmish had broken out in Manchukuo, China, near Vladivostok, between Russian and Japanese military forces. The Japanese dismissed them as "Soviet armed agitators."[47] The Japanese media then reported on a second incident involving Russian troops supposedly violating the border, and to many, it seemed a pretext, just as Hitler had done several years earlier in justifying his invasion of the Sudetenland area of Czechoslovakia.

A Japanese passenger ship was dispatched from Yokohama to Panama and Los Angeles to bring home its citizens as soon as possible. "Repatriation of Japanese nationals from strategic areas in and along the Pacific gained ominous pace today amid signs of deteriorating relations with the United States and associated powers."..."[48]

After the polite official response from Tokyo came the "unofficial" response from the Japanese news agency Domei. This time, the response was more dire, in snapping tones. "Japan cannot accept" Hull's proposal for peace in the Pacific.[49] "Such a document cannot serve as a basic datum in Japanese-American negotiations henceforth. Japanese-American conversations have taken place twice since the United States handed over to Japan the document in question . . . but there is no tangible evidence of progress of the negotiations."[50] The news agency then astonishingly quoted government officials saying that Hull's "unilateral disclosure . . . of details of the negotiations has made the situation still graver." Japan was accusing Hull of leaking their statements, which they had already released publicly.[51]

Piling on, they then accused the United States of "scheming to impose on Japan the provisions of old, obsolete principles which are incompatible with even the actual Far Eastern conditions of bygone days."[52] In short order, the Japanese had accused Washington of colonialism, plotting to invade Thailand, being too militant, not being militarily prepared, being too soft, being too hard, disinformation, of plotting to encircle Japan, and leaking to the media.

The initial move by the Japanese into French Indochina by citing a mutual defense arrangement was a charade. The Japanese had gone in because Hitler told the French to let them send in troops, but it was all cloaked in diplomatese.

Hull vowed not to respond but then did so, saying, "[A] general settlement in the Pacific still depended on Japan's acceptance of non-aggression policies outlined to the Japanese envoys last week." He also "described the months of . . . talks since April as a period of confusion arising from actions and statements at variance with the principles under discussions."[53] In short, Hull accused the Japanese of dissembling and prevaricating.

The British First Lord of the Admiralty, A. V. Alexander, offered up his two cents on the ticklish situation in the Pacific, warning the Japanese that "even at this late hour, aggression . . . will not pay. I had hoped that wiser counsels in Japan would prevail over those who appear to be leading her people into a new war of aggression. The threat has not abated and aggression may be imminent."[54]

In a marked change from only days prior, observers in diplomatic circles were now giving odds on war in the Pacific, with war occurring as a huge favorite, 100–1. Only a fool would bet on peace now, or at the very least ignore the warning signs. Even so, there was no national will to go to war. Yet some naïve residents of Capitol Hill believed it when administration officials told them, in confidence, that "war with Japan is not expected. The White House had privately told congressional kibitzers not to get too excited about the poker game with Tokyo. War was apparently not expected by the top-most authority."[55]

Of the 17 million men registered for the draft in America, approximately 10 percent had been classified as 1-A, and there were only 1.6 million men in uniform, barely enough to handle all the new operations the War Department had planned, with all its announced new equipment and pro-grams. To make matters worse, some 200,000 were scheduled to be dis-charged sometime in December because they were over twenty-eight years of age or had dependents.[56]

Oliver Wendell Holmes never said FDR had a "second-class mind, but a first-class temperament." He said that instead about FDR's cousin, Teddy Roosevelt.[57] Whether Franklin Roosevelt had a second-class intellect was arguable, but he was indisputably a man of immense charm and persuasion. As Winston Churchill said of his friend, "Meeting Franklin Roosevelt was like opening your first bottle of champagne."[58] FDR also had a very fine and enthusiastic mind when it came to details, especially about the navy, which he dearly loved and once helped run as assistant secretary of the navy under Woodrow Wilson.

At a press conference, FDR discussed in great specificity a recent fight on the high seas between the U.S. ship *Salinas* and German U-boats. This was a commander in chief with a firm grasp of operational detail: "Mr. Roosevelt said that during the World War the navy greatly overestimated the number of submarines it had sunk. He said he kept a set of figures on the reported sinkings and these totaled 725 German submariners at the end of the war.

Mr. Roosevelt added that it is silly to say a submarine has been sunk unless the person making the statement actually saw it sink."[59] Still, from the standpoint of Washington, the most important fighting going on was in the North Atlantic, after FDR had instituted Lend-Lease, after Hitler ordered his U-boats to sink "every ship with or without convoy that approaches Britain," after FDR issued his "shoot-on-sight" order to the American fleet.[60] However, he was not very forthcoming—by design—with the disappointed press corps.

The newspapers began keeping charts of ships lost and how much tonnage, like box scores of a baseball game.

A one-page memo marked "Confidential" was sent to Roosevelt disputing a rumor that Adolf Hitler had been shot. A garbled communication had previously said, "Big Chief shot down," but it was later disproven. (The memo was almost completely redacted.)[61] Also, the ever-present, seemingly daily memo from "there is more here than you realize" John Franklin Carter went into a recent unpleasant meeting with "Mr. Astor" (that would be Vincent) over recruitment of civilians in the New York City area. The memo was so circumspect, so guarded, wary, and inscrutable, one could be excused if he or she thought Carter was referring to underworld figures. "We . . . agreed as to future lines of cooperation and I arranged immediately to establish contact between him and the man who really heads my work in his area."[62]

On the same day, Roosevelt also signed a bill awarding $830 to a man who three years earlier had suffered personal injuries when "his right foot was crushed between a subway car and a loading platform" in the U.S. Capitol. FDR agreed that the government should pay the damages on the advice of the architect of the Capitol.[63]

That night, Eleanor Roosevelt entertained a Christmas party at the White House with 112 guests, but the president did not attend, preferring to have his supper on a tray in the private residence of the White House while working the phones.

To help reinforce the American army garrison in Manila, FDR ordered the 970 Marine Corps officers and enlisted men who had been stationed in Peking to leave immediately. That meant a big financial hit for these Americans; in

China, a dollar purchased about $18 in goods and services. Marines had been stationed in China for almost one hundred years, but FDR wanted them out before they became engaged in fighting the Japanese in China rather in the Philippines, where it was presumed they would be safer.[64]

Even with Chiang Kai-shek holding power and doing his best to hold off the invading Japanese, over the years, the American marines had quarreled and fought with Chinese nationals. However, some three hundred American pilots continued to fly with the Chinese nationals, having been encouraged by Washington to "resign" from the Army Air Corps, citing "arthritis" and "lumbago" but being told their rank would be waiting for them anytime their maladies cleared up.[65]

The Japanese had denied they had 80,000 to 100,000 troops in Indochina and they were right.[66] The number was more like 125,000, with another 150,000 in transit. "This force is composed of Japan's best divisions, veterans of the Chinese war, picked guards regiments from the islands, and some of the Kwantung army 'toughs.'"[67] People seemed to forget that Tojo and Hitler were soldiers in arms, bent on world conquest, and that if Hitler was capable of duplicity—then so too was Tojo. The Tripartite Pact bound them together in that mutual quest for world power. Some also foolishly thought that to fight one was not to fight both; but in fact, a fight with one was a fight with all the Axis powers.

Meanwhile, in Tokyo, the American ambassador, the skillful and experienced Joseph C. Grew, was just as frustrated as Cordell Hull. The Japanese were also violating the rule governing the treatment afforded diplomatic representatives. Grew found "himself in a complete diplomatic back-out. For several days he has not been able to transmit to the State Department other information than the official statements carried in the Tokyo press."[68]

The famed Karl Decker, "ace correspondent for William Randolph Hearst during the Spanish-American War," died at the age of seventy-three.[69] He was the reporter depicted in the movie *Citizen Kane* who sent a telegram to Charles Foster Kane informing him there was no war in Cuba, to which Kane replied, "You provide the prose poems, I'll provide the war." Indeed, the Hearst newspapers used the explosion of the USS *Maine* like a toy drum, beating America into the war. Over the years, questions revolving around the true cause of the *Maine* exploding have led to many investigations of the incident that while not providing indisputable evidence, have led to a consensus that the ship's destruction was caused by internal factors and not because of a nefarious bombing plot by the Spanish, but Hearst whipped up public opinion anyway. Decker had gallivanted throughout the world as an intrepid journalist, and his kind would soon become a dying breed.

Since 1932 and the subsequent rise of the New Deal, the Republican Party struggled for relevancy. For nine years, they had simply not been a part of the national debate, save for a few leaders like Senator Robert Taft and 1940 presidential nominee Wendell Willkie, who between them agreed on very little. The Young Republicans met in Kansas, one of only a handful of states Willkie had taken in the 1940 election. People in Republican circles looked back on the campaign and claimed it was close, but that was a relative concept. It was closer than 1936, when Roosevelt wiped the floor with Alf Landon, winning over 98 percent of the electoral vote; but the truth was he also skunked Willkie in 1940, taking 449 electoral votes to the Republican nominee's 82 and winning the popular vote by 10 percent.

At the GOP gathering in Topeka, Alf Landon and Joe Martin, minority leader in the House, exhorted the Republicans, but most simply claimed they were relevant when all evidence was to the contrary. Martin claimed the GOP was "a strong, virile, vigorous party destined to come back into power." He warned, "Wait till the people get their tax bills next March and in March, '43." This was the era before withholding; Americans could keep all their earnings until March, when they would receive a tax bill from the federal government for what was owed on April 15. Landon complained about government corruption, especially in national defense and that the "administration controls the radio" and eviscerated "one-man government."[70]

The majority Democrats were unconcerned about the minority Republicans. Indeed, there may have been more people in the Roosevelt family than there were in the entire GOP, as Eleanor Roosevelt purchased "bedroom slippers for 22 children" in her family, including both children and grandchildren.[71] She was also busy with Christmas entertaining in the White House, including those visitors from many of the foreign embassies in Washington, such as "young ladies from the Central and South American republics."[72]

Booze flowed freely across the country and in the White House for the season, and every publication was studded with ads for hard liquors, wines, and beer. One of FDR's first acts had been the repeal of the controversial Eighteenth Amendment, which attempted to prohibit alcohol in America. Many regarded it as one of FDR's greatest accomplishments, but the bitter enders of the Women's Christian Temperance Union hadn't given up. They issued a report saying that since 1933, Americans had consumed over $23 billion worth of booze, or 13,924,871,297 gallons of adult beverages.[73] Many Americans simply lifted their glasses at parties and toasted the president for his sagacity. At those parties, chocolate was plentiful and popular, going for 19 cents per pound. And for the next morning after too much drinking and eating, a tin of Anacin tablets sold for 14 cents.[74]

Along with the Republicans, the National Association of Manufacturers was struggling for relevance. Business, especially big business, had been a dirty word since 1929. Nonetheless, the N.A.M. at their annual meeting came up with some radical ideas for government that included: "Make investments attractive by allowing both business and individuals who risk their money to keep enough earnings to make the venture worthwhile." They also suggested, "Have tax policies which encourage, not penalize, reserves, and savings." They embraced radical ideas about government spending and regulations.[75]

By now, nearly everything was politicized or colored by the war. "Hitler's propaganda department went to some trouble recently to prove that Mozart was really a German and in that case it was all right for the citizens of the Reich to hear and enjoy the compositions of the great master." In fact, Mozart "was born in Austria in 1756."[76] In New York, a concert celebrating the composer's 150th anniversary of his death was held and conducted by Bruno Walter, a Jew who had fled Germany (where he was born Bruno Schlesinger).

Walter had been in Austria during the *Anschluss*, and though he was born in Berlin, he renounced his citizenship and sought asylum and citizenship in America, even after the Germans asked him to become an "honorary French citizen." Having conducted orchestras in Boston, Berlin, Vienna, Munich, London, and with the Detroit Symphony, Walter considered himself a citizen of the world, and an opinionated one at that. He hated jazz music, saying it was "like looking at Rembrandt through a distorted mirror." At the inspiration of the Salzburg Music Festival, he recommended listening to the works of Wagner, even though his music had become the unofficial music of the Third Reich. Walter said, "We are making war against the Nazis, not against the composers." He also called the war a fight "between the forces of good and evil."[77]

The same politicization applied to American movies and Hollywood. Nathan Golden, the motion picture consultant at the Commerce Department, reported that American films remained popular in Europe, even as some were not being shown because "the Nazis exercise a rigid censorship over the films shown in the conquered areas." Still, of those American movies that did air in Great Britain and other unoccupied countries, "export markets react unfavorably to pictures that play up scenes of sordid wretchedness, reckless lawbreaking, alleged social injustice, or any phase of squalid, shiftless life."[78]

Some things escaped the tar of war. Newspapers featured daily columns out of Hollywood, authored by Hedda Hopper, her hated rival, Louella Parsons, and Harold Heffernan. In these columns, Americans delighted to read about a lunch between Bob Hope and Rita Hayworth, or "Are Hollywood's 'name' ladies in the midst of a crackup epidemic?" According to Heffernan, Loretta Young, Irene Dunne, and Joan Fontaine were all showing the stress of movie making and all had been hospitalized or taken to bed for "protracted rest spells."[79]

Plenty of guidance columns filled the newspapers with advice for the lovelorn and information about personal hygiene, exercising, cooking, and

FDR's dog, Fala. And Mrs. Roosevelt's "My Day" was popular, as it was light on politics and heavy on her life as a wife, mother, and grandmother. When she did slip into politics, she made clear her opposition to women in combat, but was most definitely in favor of saving excess wrapping paper and string.[80]

"Animal interest" stories delighted readers, and one, about a dog named Sport, should have been shown to Fala so he could know how lucky he was. Sport was first run over by a train and lost an eye. Then he was run over by a car, but survived. Barely. Then Sport was run over by another car and lived long enough to be accidentally backed over by his owner's wife. Just as the dog's owner, Grover Lee, was digging a hole to bury the dog, Sport sprang to life and was seen later out hunting quail with his master in Georgia.[81] In New Jersey, a cat named Whitey fell forty-five feet into a dried-up well, survived the fall, and went three days without food or water before finally being rescued.[82]

On Friday, December 5, radio programming was light on news, heavy on the soaps, comedians, serials, and specials, such as Kate Smith's *All-American Football Team* and *The Lone Ranger*, although at 9:15 on WOL in Washington was a special, *What Price Defense?* featuring an interview with Emory S. Land, head of the U.S. Maritime Commission.[83] A new show was also debuting across the nation, *Shirley Temple Time*.[84]

Georgians were stunned to learn that ten state colleges in the university system were academically decertified because of "political interference" by the governor, Eugene Talmadge. A virulent racist, he charged the schools with "teaching of whites and Negros in the same schools." He attempted to take pro-integration members of the Board of Regents off and replace them with political cronies who would do his bidding. In retaliation, the Southern Association of Colleges and Secondary Schools stripped ten of eleven Georgia schools of their academic status and thousands of undergraduates were left high and dry. It was a huge issue in the state and indeed the entire South for days.[85]

Farmers were getting better prices for their crops than in previous years and at Christmas time were delighted to find that they, for once, had some "folding money" in their pockets. Employment—mostly because of the war effort—was up over the prior year, as was real income, and the Commerce

Department forecast heavier outlays for the Christmas of '41 than the previous year. However, the cost of living for the average American had also gone up 11 percent over the last twelve months.[86] The government urged consumers to control their spending, issuing guidelines and admonishing Americans to be careful with their money, while at the same time Washington was engaging in a massive bond drive, urging Americans to spend lavishly and buy as many defense savings bonds as possible, so the government could spend more on the war effort. Keynesian economics taught on the first day of class that government spending did not produce inflation, but consumer spending did.

Initial reports from the Treasury Department said the bond sales were strong, and the government was generating over $1 billion.[87] Preorders showed the danger of a possible oversubscription, but it also fit in with the new normal of America, circa 1941. The Great Depression was still a part of America's economic life, and few had escaped its terrors without being scarred for life. For every banker or Wall Street broker who jumped (no doubt cheered on by thousands), there were tens of thousands who lost their homes, their jobs, and their dignity, who scraped and struggled just to get a decent meal into their children once a day.

As money and hope flowed from the New Deal and the alphabet soup of agencies and bureaus created by FDR and his "Brain Trust," the country stabilized, but the economy did not expand and the days of "wonderful nonsense" of the 1920s were over. People who did have jobs saved their money, living on a "cash basis," and that included purchasing government bonds, many thinking that it would help stabilize their government. But because of government programs and the new frugality, there was not much in the way of consumer borrowing, which also hampered economic growth. No one wanted to be caught with too much debt and too little cash ever again. And it was a simple and direct act of patriotism for liberals to support FDR, and for conservatives to support their constitutional government.

The privately held Alabama Power Company took out newspaper ads to announce that the power restrictions had been lifted and its customers were invited to "unrestricted use of electricity service."[88] The company clearly was attempting to encourage customers to use more electricity as a means of generating additional profits. The order came down from Washington's Office of Production Management, which seemed to have its hands in everything. Georgia Power also ran identical ads announcing "Blackout lifted."[89] Again, the national government was sending conflicting signals.

Even so, a spiffy double-breasted suit for a boy was retailing for $9.88, while "Longies" were going for $2.98 apiece.[90] All the department stores in the country touted long, "leisure hour" robes for women, in the style made famous by Rita Hayworth and other Hollywood actresses. The hemline of skirts and dresses had already moved up to just below the knee. Also, long hair was very much in style for women, especially younger women. Hair was up for evening and formal occasions but curled and coiffed and about the shoulders during the day. Of course, no stylish woman went out in public without a hat. Neither did men. American women's hair styles were only regulated by popular fashion, unlike in Japan, where the government only allowed four approved hair styles for women.

At Rogers Jewelers in Boston, a five-tube countertop radio—a Superheterodyne—could be purchased for $9.95, or just 50 cents down and 50 cents per week.[91] General Electric lightbulbs, the 40-, 50-, and 60-watt versions, were going for 13 cents apiece, while the 75- and 100-watt bulbs were going for 15 cents per.[92] In Philadelphia, bags of mail stolen nearly ninety years earlier—long before the Civil War—were found in an attic of a home. All the envelopes had been opened in an obvious search for money, but the real value now laid in the stamps.[93] Philatelists like FDR drooled at the thought of poring over the thousands of canceled envelopes.

Tens of thousands of American G.I.s were traversing the country, the lucky ones on their way home in time for Christmas. It was not unusual to see convoys of hundreds of trucks and thousands of uniformed men heading for their home base before heading home. For most, home was priority, war a distant thought.

But news dispatches on December 5 said the American flyers fighting with the Chinese were just "itching" to get after Japanese pilots. Also the story noted that the Japanese had not yet taken the Burma Road using airplanes for aerial bombardment campaigns because they hadn't thought of that "vital overlooked method of attack."[94]

And the *Los Angeles Times*, in an editorial on the whole matter of Japan and the United States, wrote on Friday morning that while war could be imminent, it appeared "that nothing decisive will be forthcoming till next week, if then."[95]

At week's end, the editorial pages of America's newspapers were filled with speculations and analysis of the preceding several days. Nearly all concluded that the country was moving closer to war with Japan. All the pieces speculated on Thailand, Indochina, the Philippines, Singapore, and other locales in the Far East. With the exception of some internal documents generated by the navy, including ones from Adm. Husband Edward Kimmel, newly installed head of the Pacific Fleet based on Pearl Harbor, no one else was speculating on whether the Japanese might strike elsewhere.

Japan's consulate in Mexico City was being hurriedly evacuated, and the staff had at first requested visas from the U.S. government to leave for Japan via Los Angeles, but they were then advised by their government that they would depart from Mexico, via the port at Manzanillo. The Japanese minister to Mexico, Yoshiaki Miura, worriedly stated, "Only God knows how this crisis will be resolved."[96]

CHAPTER 6

THE SIXTH OF DECEMBER

"Joint U.S.-Japan Commission
Is Proposed to End Deadlock"

Atlanta Constitution

"Japanese Plea of Self-Defense Coldly Received"

Washington Post

"Britain Takes Up Battle Posts in Far East as Crisis Grows;
Tokyo Reply Keeps Door Open"

Christian Science Monitor

"Far East Makes Ready for War"

Fairbanks Daily News-Miner

Bob Feller, standout pitcher for the Cleveland Indians, made his major league debut in 1936 at the age of seventeen. But after a meeting with Lt. Commander Gene Tunney, now the director of the navy's physical conditioning program, he announced that he was planning to enlist early in the U.S. military reserves. Back home at his father's farm in Van Meter, Iowa, "Rapid Robert" reasoned that because he expected to be classified 1-A in February of 1942 anyway, he might as well beat the crowd. Feller was intrigued by the idea of being a reservist while still pitching for the Indians on his days off from the military. He paid a visit to the Army Air Corps at Wright Field in Ohio, as he was interested in flying planes, having already taken lessons and soloed.[1] Both the army and the navy had pursued Feller "concerning his plans for entertaining" their troops.[2]

British actor and captain David Niven was just as patriotic. He had it written in his contract that wherever he was making a movie, he had to be allowed to leave if he was called up to join his regiment.[3]

The USS *Arizona* was the pride of the American navy. At 31,400 tons, she was larger than many other battleships in the American fleet. She was older too, having had her keel originally laid in 1916 at the Brooklyn Navy Yard. Her early days were spent close to home, patrolling the waters off the Atlantic coast, her shakedown cruise a quick jaunt to the Caribbean. The *Arizona*'s home port was Norfolk, Virginia, until 1921, when she was transferred to Southern California, sometimes making the journey to Hawaii and back. In 1929, she went back to Virginia to be reoutfitted and modernized, which took two years. In August of 1931, she returned to the West Coast and from there was ordered to reposition to Pearl Harbor in 1940, on direct command of the president.

The navy had seventeen battleships, all told; some launched as long ago as 1912, as the *New York* and the *Texas* were. The *Arkansas* had been launched in 1911. In fact, the fleet was very old, with only the *North Carolina* and the *Washington* splashed in the previous year. Virtually all the battle-ships had been built during or just after the Great War. The Japanese had five fewer battlewagons, but they tended to be newer and of heavier tonnage. The United States' seven aircraft carriers were newer than the battleships, but the *Lexington* and the *Saratoga* were both launched in 1925. The *Enterprise* and *Yorktown* were built in 1936 and the *Wasp* in 1939. Japan also had seven carriers, but again, they tended to be bigger and lighter and thus faster than their American counterparts.[4] The United States had more heavy cruisers than Tokyo, eighteen to twelve, but overlooked was the fact that Japan only had one ocean to worry about. The United States had two—or more—with which to concern itself.

On December 6, there were dozens of large and small ships along with four subs moored at Pearl Harbor: eight battleships, two heavy cruisers, six light cruisers, and twenty-nine destroyers, as well as a handful of ELCO PT boats, ocean-going tugs, minesweepers, minelayers, seaplane tenders, repair ships, and two general store ships along with one hospital ship, the *Solace*. A destroyer, the *Helm*, was underway at sea; another, the *Ward*, was patrolling the entrance to the harbor at Pearl.[5]

Three carriers had also been stationed at Pearl Harbor: the *Enterprise*, under the command of Captain George D. Murray; the *Lexington*, under the command of Captain Frederick C. Sherman; and the *Saratoga*, with Captain Archibald H. Douglas at the helm.[6]

Less than two weeks earlier, on November 28, Adm. Husband E. Kimmel sent Adm. Bill Halsey and the *Enterprise* on an errand to deliver Marine Corps fighter planes to Wake Island.[7] On December 5, Kimmel ordered the *Lexington* to transport twenty-five scout bombers to Midway Island.[8] The *Saratoga* had also left Pearl Harbor for repairs at San Diego.[9]

The "carriers vs. battleships" debate continued unabated and unresolved within the American navy. The Japanese had pretty much decided that the airplane was the weapon of the future, while the navy was pushing ahead with plans to build eighteen carriers—by 1945.

The foreign correspondent for the *Sun* newspaper of Baltimore, Marc T. Greene, submitted a story "by mail," from Manila, which reviewed the American military situation in the Pacific, especially with regard to the airplane. "The rapid expansion of American air strength . . . in the southern and central Pacific area is giving immense satisfaction. . . . The recent acquisition of such islands as Palmyra and Johnston, in easy touch with our Hawaiian bases constitute the most recent evidence of that."[10] Readers were reassured of American air dominance in the Pacific.

The secretary of war, Henry Stimson, one of the cooler and more respected heads in Washington, nonetheless found himself in a fog, though not yet of war. He was on a military plane headed to Washington from New York, but the low-hanging clouds that had enveloped the city the day before were still too thick, so the flight was diverted to Richmond; upon landing he found he had no way to get back to the nation's capital. Stimson, seventy-four years of age, did what any resourceful person would do; the cabinet official on whose shoulders would fall the burden of the surely coming war stuck out his thumb and hitched a ride back to Washington.[11]

Another form of debate was the soapbox kind, taking place on the street corners of America, including Fifth Avenue in New York. There, proselytizers and preachers, orators and lecturers, along with just plain cranks, attempted to convince small crowds of the curious to either be pro-intervention or anti-intervention, and, depending on which side of the soapbox, either denouncing FDR or praising him, denouncing Stalin or praising him, denouncing Charles Lindbergh and the America First Committee or praising them. Law enforcement tolerated them as long as no violence broke out and nobody tried to sell anything without a license.[12]

On December 6—as with every Saturday—many newspapers ran quotes in advance from the sermons that priests, pastors, ministers, and reverends would give the following day. Nearly all dealt harshly with Adolf Hitler, war, and realistically about the human condition and the eternal struggle of free men against tyranny. Though they followed the teaching of a martyr, they did not preach martyrdom for their flocks but instead exhorted them to fight. Said the Reverend Louis St. Clair Allen of the Brooklyn Methodist Church: "The cross has not departed out of human affairs. If an enemy persists in destroying us, our only recourse is slavish submission, death or defense of liberty. I do not choose death or submission. I believe we must give ourselves for our liberties."[13]

Little had changed as far as America was concerned by Saturday, December 6. Diplomats and political observers were still kicking the embers and reading the tea leaves of the conflicting messages sent by the Japanese over the previous few days. Yet another Nipponese source accused America of trying to "pass the buck" in the Far East, whatever that meant.[14] President Roosevelt had convened his weekly meeting with the cabinet on Friday, and afterward the White House said it would have no further comment on a new 150-word official Japanese communiqué.[15]

So reporters went to Cordell Hull, who said he had nothing to say and referred them back to the White House. Official Washington, for once anyway, had nothing to say on a grave matter, including in the editorial pages of most newspapers, which had no new take on the grim matter in the Pacific. The *New York Times* did take a hard line, urging FDR to stand by the government of the pro-American Chiang Kai-shek forces in China. But even spokesmen for the Third Reich had no comment regarding matters in the Far East. The *Christian Science Monitor* said the situation was "momentarily in suspense."[16] The *Monitor*, based in Boston, occasionally ran editorials in German, as there was a heavy Germanic population in the area.[17]

Another editorial took the U.S. government to task, though, for not being frank and transparent in announcing the military buildup during the emergency. In fact, back in October, FDR had prohibited any more announcements on the production of new airplanes, but publications kept announcing them anyway. The *Monitor* concluded, "[T]hose in the opposition camp argue that a full exposé of America's skyrocketing production might have persuaded the Japanese to forgo further aggression in the Far East."[18]

The Japanese were sticking to their guns, though, saying the troops sent to Indochina were to protect Thai security and that they had the permission of the Vichy French government to move troops into Indochina because of Chinese troop movement in the region. They also introduced a new argument, their own version of a "Monroe Doctrine": the affairs of the Far East were of no concern to Washington.[19]

Tokyo conveniently overlooked—or expected America to overlook— the fact that Vichy France was a wholly owned subsidiary of Adolf Hitler, including all French possessions and military hardware, or that America's Monroe Doctrine said nothing about the United States abusing or invading her neighbors.

The British had been supplying Chinese forces along the Burma Road, and more and more analysts thought invading Thailand to then cut the strategically important venue was the real goal of the Japanese.[20]

Some of the Saturday newspapers reviewed the impasse, hashing it over. "An uneasy peace hung over the Pacific today as the United States waited for Japan to makes its choice between conciliation or further attempts at conquest in the Far East."[21] Negotiations that had started seven months earlier had made no progress whatsoever, but both sides acknowledged they were learning more about the negotiations from the newspapers than from the actual meetings and documents.

Suddenly out of Tokyo came a new proposal, courtesy of a member of the influential Privy Council. Count Kentaro Kaneko suggested a "Japanese-American Commission to iron out the Pacific deadlock." Kaneko, eighty-eight years old, was respected and a student of American culture. He suggested officials from various walks of life be appointed to the commission. The *New York Times* saw hope in the proposal, writing, "[A]n impression prevailed in diplomatic circles that something approaching a status quo may have been reached temporarily that might permit the exploratory conversations to continue with less disturbance."[22]

However, Japanese nationals were being hurriedly withdrawn from Panama, British North Borneo, Malaya, India, Ceylon, and other countries, just as they had already begun withdrawing diplomats from Mexico.[23] Also, the Japan Institute in New York announced abruptly it would close and the director and his immediate staff would depart for home, while another "132 Japanese nationals . . . applied for passage back to Japan." However, approximately two thousand Japanese nationals in the greater New York area had no plans to repatriate as far as anybody knew.[24]

A government spokesman in Tokyo, Tomokazu Hori, held a press conference and said it was all just one "big misunderstanding on the part of the United States government regarding our policy in the Far East." Washington "seems to allege that we are following a policy of force and conquest in establishing a military despotism."[25]

Australia had some reason to believe that about the Japanese and hastily reconvened their War Cabinet as a result because the "Pacific crisis had reached a new and graver stage." All Christmas leaves were canceled for Aussie troops, "a million gas masks for the civilian population" were ordered, and their naval ships were being convoyed to the Pacific, though an official said all the precautions did not "'mean that war is inevitable' with Japan." But there was internal debate in Australia over the government's power to conscript men of fighting age, and whether Australians should fight for England, just as there had been during the Great War. The Aussie Labor Party opposed the draft, declaring "a volunteer army is always more effective."[26] War measures were also taking place in Thailand, "the most directly menaced," as well as the Netherland East Indies.[27]

The Churchill government implemented its own emergency measures in the Far East, including "recalling all fighting men to their posts" in Singapore and prepared for a "state of readiness." The British referred to Singapore as their "Gibraltar of the Orient." It was announced the sale of gasoline would be suspended in Shanghai, which had become a virtual ghost town, as commercial shipping had slowed to nothingness over the past several months. Those not of British ancestry were forbidden from leaving British Malaya, and rumors swirled that Manila would soon be evacuated of noncombatants. The Associated Press also reported, "Without explanation, Japan recalled two attachés of the Japanese government in Washington. (The German radio identified them as military attaches, Col. Tadamuri and Lt. Col. Ariuo Uehida.)"[28]

In character, the Australian government issued a blunt statement: "We are fully alive to the Japanese threat and are not afraid of it."[29] The pro-West Chinese government of Chiang Kai-shek also issued a statement, predictably leveling Tokyo, calling its response to FDR "an insult to the intelligence of the American people."[30]

Many in the West felt that the combined military forces of the "ABCD" powers, as Tokyo called them—American, British, China, Dutch—were more than a match for the Japanese should they press on with their invasion and consolidation of the Far East. In the Philippines alone there were "a dozen divisions, one American and 11 Filipino, several hundred planes, two heavy cruisers, several destroyers and 18 submarines."[31]

Douglas MacArthur was confident his forces would repel any Japanese attack on the Philippines and that he was "well-prepared . . . to meet land onslaughts from the Japanese in the event that military folly leads Japan to war with the United States. . . . The air arm of America is a long one. From the Philippines it can sweep to and over Japan with ease, and back to its insular bases."[32] But Japanese air officials brushed off MacArthur's swagger, authoritatively pointing out that the B-17 planes under his command were of the older "B and C type with a range of 2200 miles which is insufficient to Japan, from Manila, and return."[33]

Some, however, were worried instead about the power of the Japanese fleet and counseled a more aggressive posture by the American navy. The notion was floated of moving the American fleet stationed at Pearl Harbor to the Philippines to help MacArthur stave off an invasion, but "this could not be brought to the Philippines without great danger, because the cruising range of the fleet is only 2500 miles, and it would be necessary to make one jump of more than that distance without refueling. . . . This would be a risky operation for it would require the use of the whole American battle fleet and would leave the West Coast open to Japanese raiders. It probably will not be tried."[34]

A new $8 billion defense bill had passed the House 309–5 and was headed for the Senate, where its passage was all but assured.[35] America Firsters or no America Firsters, no one on either side of the aisle was going to allow themselves to be accused of being unpatriotic, or miss out on federal contract goodies for their states.

The funding bill could not have come along at a better time, as a new report out by the U.S. Senate scored the army for pitiable recreational facilities at bases across the country. With the exception of Ft. Meade, all had extremely poor sporting facilities. Camp Davis in North Carolina had eighteen basketballs but no basketball courts. Pine Camp in New York had plenty of baseballs and bats, but no baseball fields. Camp Blanding in Florida, with a complement of fifty thousand men, had "no basketball courts, no football fields, no handball courts, no gymnasium—but 25 chapels." A congressman called the situation "ridiculous."[36]

The navy did a far better job of taking care of their personnel, especially their officers, than did the army. The navy's air base in Miami looked like a "superswank country club." It had tennis courts, bars, squash courts, a movie theater, and swimming pools (one for officers and cadets and the other for enlistees) for the pilots to enjoy when not in training.[37] The competition between the army and the navy, and the Marine Corps and the navy, was not without basis, as the other two branches thought the navy elevated themselves to be the royalty of the American military. But navy pilots could also be dangerous and foolish. Two pilots were released from a navy brig after an investigation in which they had clearly been hot dogging in Alabama, when they flew too low over a turnip field and decapitated a woman with the wing of their plane, according to news reports.[38]

The navy was also building dozens of temporary structures on the Mall between the Lincoln Memorial and the U.S. Capitol. The Public Buildings Administration said these structures could be torn down faster than they were built and the plan was to do just that after the "emergency."[39]

For the first time in FDR's nine years in office, unemployment was slowly tracking downward, after years of joblessness in the high teens and low 20s. The economy had perked up considerably as a result of the war effort, with the government plowing billons into defense contractors. Yet, as corporations began to finally show a profit after long years of languishing, Washington began talking up a new tax on corporate dividends, cutting into investors' profits.[40] Congressman Carl Vinson of Georgia was touting legislation that would cap corporate profits, with the excess turned over to Washington, even as Wall Street had been dwindling down since September.[41] But the guns-vs.-butter-vs.-success issue seemed settled to the Brain Trusters of the New Deal. Government would dispense and control all.

Regardless, a profound shift was occurring in the administration's priorities that met sharp resistance from the eternally crusading First Lady and her allies among the more liberal New Dealers, such as Vice President Henry Wallace. Funding for social programs was increasingly subordinated to ramped-up preparation for what seemed like inevitable war. The more conservative advisers and cabinet members in FDR's orbit, always ambivalent about the New Deal anyway, were starting to win the day, as the president shifted his attention from domestic concerns to the existential threat posed by geopolitical crises abroad. By 1941, the pendulum was swinging away from butter, and inexorably to guns. Ironically, the transition to rearmament also provided a Keynesian spending boost that helped ameliorate unemployment. A lasting structural change to the American economy was unfolding.

That said, doubts at the time persisted about the viability of capitalism. Even owners and operators of private business, such as C. M. Chester, chairman of General Foods and a high official in the National Association of Manufacturers, told their annual gathering that the "free market must prove itself." The redoubtable *Wall Street Journal* was crammed with stories specifying how government was regulating businesses, pressuring them, harassing them, but also contracting with them. On Friday the fifth alone, dozens of government contracts were announced, many of them with clothing companies such as the D. & D. Shirt Co. of Pennsylvania for 50,000 flannel shirts for $24,500; 10,000 khaki shirts from the Philadelphia QM Depot for $5,345; $2,250 to the Marine Tobacco Co. for "Tobacco, cigarettes and cigars"; and $34,510 to the Gillette Safety Razor Co. of Boston for 2,285,250 safety razors.[42]

The American ambassador to Great Britain, John C. Winant, had no doubts (and no understanding) about Moscow's commitment to the free market. He ludicrously told a prominent Jewish leader, Rabbi Morris S. Lazaron, "that Russia has turned her back on Communism in respect to the work of the individual, religious liberty and the employment of the talents of man."[43]

Audaciously, the Third Reich announced that because of the "black list" of pro-German business in the Americas produced by Washington, they would ask for reparations from the U.S. government to pay for business "losses . . . after the Reich wins the war."[44] An authoritative new book, *The Structure of Nazi Economy*, authored by Maxine T. Sweezy and published by the Harvard University Press, was released to favorable reviews. "As a critical study it should be of considerable interest to students of economic affairs, who will find Miss Sweezy's discussion of Nazi policy in terms of Keynesian theory particularly rewarding," wrote a reviewer in the *Christian Science Monitor*.[45] The book took no political position but was simply an exhaustive look at the German economy under Hitler.

Up on Capitol Hill, a House committee was continuing their investigation into Nazi propaganda in America and was uncovering an astonishing amount of material, as well as evidence that both Italy and Nazi Germany were sending a tremendous amount of money to America to fund anti-interventionist movements including the "Citizens No Foreign War Coalition."[46] Led by Martin Dies, a Democrat from Texas, the House Committee on Un-American Activities had discovered so many German agents operating in America and so much activity, he was actually worried about the formation of a Fascist political party in America.[47]

One of the organizations being investigated by the Dies Committee was the America First Committee itself, worried that it was a front group for the German Bund. It was estimated that "twenty-five percent of America First membership were Nazi sympathizers." The rest were simply "honest American isolationists."[48] What's more, "It is understood that the committee also has amassed a considerable amount of information about Japanese activities in the United States. This, however, has been withheld in view of the delicate situation." Dies was further investigating "365,000 persons ostensibly Communist sympathizers."[49] Dies was heavily investigating labor unions, which his fellow Democrats—including more than a few at the White House—found grating.

A suspected pro-Soviet group, Fight for Freedom, was under investigation by HCUA for its ties to Moscow. Another group, the Washington Youth Council, was also decidedly pro-interventionist. They heard from Senator Claude Pepper of Florida, who brought down the house when he shouted, "Adolf Hitler is a devil from hell! You had just as well try to make peace with the devil!" Pepper warned against Hitler gaining a "foothold in South America." Other speakers included representatives of England and China.[50]

What Dies and his committee did not know was the Japanese consulate in Honolulu was just a few blocks from the harbor, had a magnificent view of the fleet, and was a beehive of espionage, with detailed reports going daily to Tokyo, via radio, telegram, telephone, and the U.S. mail.[51] Nor did he know that the United States was hip-deep in Japanese agents and sympathizers.

Because of their poor recruiting numbers, the navy announced that enlistment into the reserves would be cut from a minimum four-year obligation to a two-, three-, or four-year obligation. Joining the navy and seeing the world was not the cup of tea most young American men dreamed of. That could have something to do with German submarines, though not all Wolf pack U-boats were skippered by courageous men either. The British Admiralty released the story of a U-boat that was forced to the surface as a result of repeated depth charges dropped. The commander jumped into the water before his sub was sunk by the British; some of the crew were lost. This particular German commander had no interest in going down with his ship.

Nazi policy toward German Jews was even more cowardly than the sub's captain. Yet another harsh edict was issued in Berlin. Jews could no longer sell their own property without "official permission" from the state. The reason given by the Nazis was that Jews were selling their possessions in a manner "that is threatening to upset existing market regulations for their respective articles."[52] "This statement . . . refers to the sale of furniture, clothing, china, rugs and similar articles by Jews who have been expecting their turn to be expelled from the Reich capital."[53]

Curiously, American Jews were not nearly unified in their approach or attitude toward Hitler, internationalism, or Roosevelt. In 1941, a considerable number of Jewish Americans were financial supporters of the America First Committee or simply pacifists that blanched at the idea of getting involved in the European conflict. A leading Jewish intellectual and member of the Roosevelt administration, Jerome Frank, published a book in 1938 entitled Save America First. In his book, Frank spoke for many, calling for "100 percent American—Western Hemispheric—isolation as the only safe way to save America. . . . It by no means [argued] for pacifism, but it warned against the propaganda of American Anglo-philes, Communists and sentimental internationalists."[54]

Frank later admitted that he and others did not see Hitler for the evil monster he was in the early days and that, in fact, many Jews had at first supported Benito Mussolini. "We thought Hitler was a paranoiac buffoon with mad bad dreams of world conquest which could never come true and he was no menace to the United States. We deplored as needlessly provocative the speeches of Secretary [Harold] Ickes criticizing Hitler."

Frank was not alone, as he recounted other Jewish members of the administration embracing isolationism. One of the biggest proponents of the America First committee was Lessing Rosenwald, one of the richest Jews in America. Frank wrote all this in a long and provocative article in the *Saturday Evening Post.* "Strangely enough, there is a group of wealthy Fascist Jews in America—a group not large in number and who have escaped public attention for the most part. Hitler is alright, they believe, except for his anti-Jewish 'mistake.' Even this, they half forgive because, they say, too many Jews had participated in the German democratic government established after [the] World War . . . or the German Communist movement."[55]

Frank also identified another troublesome group in America, the Christian Mobilizers, a virulently anti-Semitic group that passed out "Buy Christian" signs for window display. From the right, lecturers warned darkly about the "fifth columnists" inside the U.S. government, pro-communist forces bent on a marriage between Washington and Moscow.[56]

In his piece, Frank also covered an even far more dangerous group, the German Bund. "It will help . . . to consider the Americans who are classified as German Americans. There is, unfortunately, a small percentage of such citizens who are merely Germans in America. They are hyphenates. They part their American citizenship in the middle. Their wholehearted loyalties are not given to the United States. Some of them . . . would like to see this country dominated by the Nazis."[57]

Of the many controversial members of the Roosevelt cabinet, Interior Secretary Harold Ickes was at the top of the list. His official responsibilities were the natural resources of the country, but he expanded his portfolio to include foreign policy, trade, Jewish affairs, immigration, gas rationing, whatever caught his attention. Widely regarded as effective and brilliant and a marvelous public speaker, he was just as effective at rubbing others the wrong way. Clare Boothe Luce once caustically said of Ickes that he had "the mind of a commissar and the soul of a meat axe."[58]

Ominously, the very first American concentration camp was opened for business on Long Island. Named Camp Upton, it had extremely high fences topped with barbed wire, machine gun nests, and was built to house up to seven hundred "aliens."[59] Meanwhile, the British began rounding up aliens of every stripe, from Finns to Romanians to Hungarians, all countries with governments allied with Nazi Germany, all countries on which England had declared war. In the initial sweep, Scotland Yard arrested two hundred suspects.[60]

The East Coast was still recovering from an oil shortage that dated back to the summer of 1941, when some tankers were diverted to England to help fuel the British military effort. Fingers had been pointed at Interior Secretary Ickes, who some thought unnecessarily alarmed Americans along the Eastern Seaboard by exaggerating the situation and arbitrarily closing gas stations when he should have been calming fears.[61] There had been a brief congressional investigation, but before it really got under way, the "crisis" had passed.[62]

Making matters worse was the government's order for the oil companies to reduce the lead content in ethyl gasoline for the war effort. All sacrifices, it seemed, were made for the "emergency" or the "war effort." Lead had been added to gasoline for years, as it reduced engine knocking while improving engine efficiency. With the reduced lead content, drivers would have to use more gas, which was going for as much as 20 cents per gallon.[63]

The war effort permeated nearly all advertising content, as with General Motors Trucks, billed as "Partners in Power for the nation's defense."[64] And if the male reader wasn't sure about how to enlist in the war effort, the U.S. Army was running ads everywhere for recruiting purposes, claiming over 100,000 vacancies for "picked young men" and listing various recruiting offices in Boston, Baltimore, Atlanta, and other locations. Young men who signed up right away could expect as a private to make up to $105 per month, "plus uniforms, board, lodging and medical care."[65]

American G.I.s could always count on enjoying a good bowl of Campbell's Chicken Noodle Soup or any of the other twenty-one soups available in a can, including asparagus, Consommé Madrilène, or the good old standby, tomato.[66] Campbell's had been an American institution since a few years after the Civil War, when the company was launched.

A new cigarette was being marketed: Spud menthol Imperials, which helped relieve a sore throat, a dry throat, a hoarse voice, or a "thick taste in the morning."[67] At Landsburgh's jewelry department in Washington, "lovely monogrammed 10-piece cigarette sets" were going for $1.79. Their suggested gift for men was a cigarette box and nine ashtrays.[68] As a suggestion for Christmas gifts, Kelly Kar Co, in Los Angeles, offered five hundred used automobiles, the prices ranging from $25 to $1,500.[69] But most everybody in the West was making sacrifices.

Canada was shipping huge amounts of foodstuffs to Great Britain to help feed the troops and civilian population. They were shipping so much cheese to England, Canadians were experiencing their own shortage.[70] America was sending massive amounts of food to Great Britain and the USSR as well as other participants in Lend-Lease. As a result, the U.S. government was calling on American farmers to increase their output by 15 percent in 1942. "Reports from England state that cheese, dried milk, evaporated milk, dried eggs, fruit and tomato juices, poultry, meat, bacon, lard and pork products are most urgently needed." Corrugated paper boxes, "cellophane," tin foil, and other packaging materials were in short supply in America because so much had been shipped overseas.[71]

There were only nineteen shopping days left until Christmas, and Americans were making many of their purchases at the growing number of chain department stores. Sears & Roebuck had been around for years, but others that also dotted the cities and towns of America included F. W. Woolworth, Montgomery Ward, the S.S. Kresge Co., and the Ben Franklin Five and Dime.

In a story earning a minor headline in the *Washington Evening Star*, the works of a "colored artist," William Smith, went on display in the Library of Congress as announced by the librarian there, Archibald MacLeish. Smith had been near homeless, living in the basement of a theater, subsisting on potatoes, when he got some help up from the Karamu House, a "negro cultural and art center."[72]

As on most Saturday evenings, Americans were either going to the movies or listening to the radio. Nationally syndicated shows included *Quiz Kids*, Bill Stern's sports show, Guy Lombardo's Orchestra, and a top favorite, *Your Hit Parade*, which featured all the top songs of the week. Also heard on many stations around the country on Saturday the sixth was the show *Hawaii Calls*, which featured native Hawaiian music broadcast live from the Moana Hotel on Waikiki Beach, hosted by local personality Webley Edwards.[73]

Late in the evening of December 5, over Italian radio and later picked up by NBC, it was broadcast that large numbers of Japanese ships were sighted north of Luzon and "south of Formosa."

Meanwhile, in Honduras it was revealed by the government that Nazi provocateurs had been attempting to destabilize their government as well as other Central American countries "to fight against the United States."[74]

Hitler, though, was greatly occupied with the Russian Front, and went on radio in Berlin to announce he was throwing 1.5 million fresh troops, as well as one thousand big guns and eight thousand tanks, into the fight against Stalin. "It now appears that the Red capital now faces its hour of greatest peril."[75] The tenacity of Germany led Senator Burton Wheeler of Montana to predict that FDR would send at least a "token army" to England, "if the war lasts."[76]

The Russian winter had now registered 31 degrees below zero, even as the Third Reich was marching once again toward Moscow, though the Soviets were heavily bombing German truck columns. Hitler was caught in the very pincer he wanted to avoid, with British bombers walloping Berlin every night from the West and a protracted struggle against the Russians in the East. Still, the predicament did not stop Germany from sinking five British ships—including a submarine—in the first few days of December just off the coast of England.[77]

Hitler frankly was hoping his Japanese allies would push their invasion of China harder and cross through to Russia, creating a two-front war for Stalin. Nazi Germany had already taken 600,000 Russian troops prisoners of war, and had moved them to camps inside of Germany, where they were treated poorly, at least as compared to the treatment afforded British POWs. Germany claimed they had, all told, imprisoned 3 million Russian troops.[78]

The Germans and Russians traded charges of atrocities committed against their soldiers by the other side.[79] The *New York Times* reported of "cannibalism" among the Soviet prisoners, according to the International Red Cross.[80] The Third Reich put many of their prisoners to work in their war industry. "In the great armament plants in Saxony opened for a glimpse to the foreign press, thousands of non-Germans [labor] . . . over roaring abrasive machines . . . then trudge off to their barracks quarters, within the confines of the factory. Besides the silent Poles wearing a purple and yellow letter 'P' on their chests, sit those other former British allies, Croats of former Yugoslavia."[81]

Churchill's government had to imprison one of their own, Adm. Sir Barry Domvile and his wife, Lady Domvile, accused Nazi sympathizers. Lady Margaret Domvile was a German national and her husband had, in 1937, journeyed to the Third Reich as a hunting guest of Heinrich Himmler, head of the odious Secret Police. Though retired, the admiral had once headed the office of British Naval Intelligence. The couple were both active in "the Link," an Anglo-German group. Domvile had twice been a guest of Hitler's, including a visit to Salzburg, just one month before the war began. Admiral Domvile was incarcerated in Brixton Prison, along with his son, while Lady Domvile was held in Holloway Prison.[82]

As a new professional football league was contemplated, the NFL's regular season was scheduled to end December 7. The Washington Redskins, 1941 also-rans and patsies to the Bears in the 1940 championship game, losing 73–0, the most lopsided game in league history, were scheduled to play a meaningless game at Griffith Stadium at 1:00 p.m. against the Philadelphia Eagles.[83]

Starting at quarterback for the Eagles was Jack Banta, a college star whom the Redskins had drafted and then treated badly, and now Banta was aiming for revenge.[84] Redskins fans were in no way fanatical about their team. The town was simply too transient; the owner, George Preston Marshall, too odious; the team too spotty; but it was a pleasant way to pass a Sunday afternoon for the high and mighty of Washington, including government officials, military brass, and the like.

Also a bit undependable was the forty-seven-year-old ditzy socialite Tommy Manville of New York City, who just days after marrying twenty-two-year-old (asbestos) heiress Bonita Edwards found himself divorcing his fifth wife. For his troubles, Manville agreed to pay his wife a $200,000 settlement, not including alimony for their two-week marriage.[85] Just as their May-December marriage had been covered in all the papers, so was their May-December divorce.

Rita Hayworth, dubbed "The Love Goddess" by drooling newspaper columnists, was the top-of-the-heap, flavor-of-the-month, toast-of-the-town actress and celebrity in December of 1941. Her photos and articles appeared everywhere, and readers of family newspapers learned all there was to learn, including her weight, which was 118 lbs.; her height, which was 5'6"; and her measurements, which were 35-25-35.[86]

Charles J. Pietsch of the Gideons met with the chaplain of the navy, Robert D. Workman, in Washington to present him with a Bible to give to the president. Pietsch was the Gideons' representative from Hawaii.[87]

The weather across the East Coast, which had been unseasonably warm, all of a sudden turned much chillier, especially in Washington, where administration officials also braced for the worst in the Far East. "Certain extremely well-informed American officials are ... convinced that Japan will start a fight in the near future."[88] Golfers had been on the links well into winter in the East because of the mild temperatures, but now they retreated to their favorite 19th hole.

A correspondent for the New York Herald Tribune, Wilfred Fleisher, who had spent several years in Japan, bluntly told a group in Washington that the United States and Japan were "at the end of negotiations."[89] Indeed, most headlines across the country said war between Great Britain and Japan was imminent in the Pacific.

But the "World Golden Rule Foundation" called for a week of "Self-Denial and Generosity" and designated the next seven days for seven occupied countries, beginning on the seventh, which had been proclaimed to be "Chinese Day."[90]

A more authoritative source, a Chinese diplomat, Dr. Wel Tao-Ming, said Japan was running a "bluff."[91] Dr. Tao-Ming said Japan's expansionist policies had reached the end of their supply lines, and while the island nation had harbored dreams of controlling access to natural resources it did not possess, they had pursued their course out of weakness and not strength. "My personal opinion . . . is that the Tojo Cabinet is a bluff. . . . In our struggle of more than four years, we have drained them, both militarily and economically, to such an extent that they have neither war materials nor man power left to launch into an adventure on a grand scale in other zones."[92]

Japan had hundreds of daily newspapers, most of which strongly reflected the policies of the government of Gen. Hideki Tojo. Of the deteriorating situation in the Far East, one Japanese paper said, "Japan might be forced to abandon her peaceful endeavors." With all the arrogance he could muster, a member of the Tojo Cabinet declaimed, "We watch tensely to see whether Mr. Roosevelt or Mr. Churchill will commit an epochal crime and further extend the world upheaval."[93]

CHAPTER 7

THE SEVENTH OF DECEMBER

"Extra! War!"

San Francisco Chronicle

"Japs Attack Manila, Far East Crisis Explodes"

Marysville Daily Forum—Extra!

"War! Oahu Bombed by Japanese Planes"

Honolulu Star-Bulletin 1st Extra

"U.S. at War! Japan Bombs Hawaii, Manila"

Washington Post Extra

"Navy Is Superior to Any Says Knox"

New York Times

Sunday in America was a day for relaxing, whether you followed the fourth commandment or not. It was a day for church, for family meals, for reading the newspapers, listening to the radio, going for long walks, for afternoon naps, for working in the yard and visiting with neighbors.

Sunday, December 7 was different.

Ten days earlier, on November 27, Chief of Naval Operations Adm. Harold R. Stark and Chief of Staff of the U.S. Army Gen. George C. Marshall authored a two-page memo stamped for their commander in chief "Secret." It read: "Subject: Far Eastern Situation."[1]

"If the current negotiations end without agreement," they wrote, "Japan may attack: the Burma Road; Thailand; Malaya; the Netherlands East Indies; the Philippines; the Russian Maritime Provinces." The memo then went on to discount why the Japanese would attack most of the cited strategic locations. "There is little probability of an immediate Japanese attack on the Maritime Provinces.... The magnitude of the effort required will militate against direct attack against Malaya and the Netherlands East Indies until the threat exercised by United States forces in Luzon is removed. Attack on the Burma Road would, however, be difficult and might fail. Occupation of Thailand gains a limited strategic advantage as a preliminary to operations against Malaya or the Netherlands East Indies, might relieve internal political pressure, and to a lesser extent, external economic pressure. The most essential thing now, from the United States viewpoint, was to gain time. Considerable Navy and Army reinforcements have been rushed to the Philippines but the desirable strength has not yet been reached. Of great and immediate concern is the safety of the Army convoy now near Guam, and the Marine Corps' convoy just leaving Shanghai. Ground forces to a total of 21,000 are due to sail from the United States by December 8, 1941, and it is important that this troop reinforcement reach the Philippines before hostilities commence."[2]

"Precipitance of military action on our part should be avoided so long as consistent with national policy. The longer the delay, the more positive becomes the assurance of retention of these Islands as a naval and air base. Japanese action to the south of Formosa will be hindered and perhaps seriously blocked as long as we hold the Philippine Islands."[3]

"After consultation with each other, United States, British, and Dutch military authorities in the Far East agreed that joint military counteraction against Japan should be undertaken only in case Japan attacks or directly threatens the territory or mandated territory of the United States."[4]

"It is recommended that: prior to the completion of the Philippine reinforcement, military, counter-action be considered only if Japan attacks or directly threatens United States, British, or Dutch territory . . . in case of a

Japanese advance into Thailand, Japan be warned by the United States . . . that advance beyond the lines indicated may lead to war; prior to such warning no joint military opposition be undertaken."[5]

Significantly, no mention was made by Stark or Marshall of any other American military installation in the Pacific region, including Hawaii.

Adm. Husband E. Kimmel, newly installed commander of the Pacific Fleet in Hawaii, had obsessed for months about a Japanese naval attack on the American fleet at Pearl Harbor, located on the south side of the island of Oahu, up a narrow and well-protected channel.[6]

A navy report had been given to him detailing how the Japanese could pull off such an attack on the base. The report said the Japanese would attack on a weekend and would not declare war first. Outside of those in the "war gaming" sections of the military, no one in or outside of government had given the notion of an audacious daytime bombing on a weekend even a passing thought. There had been only one blackout drill on Oahu—in May the year before—to simulate response in an attack.[7]

An extraordinary Sunday meeting was requested by the Japanese embassy in Washington with Secretary of State Cordell Hull. The meeting was set for 1:00 p.m. (EST). It would be 7:30 a.m. in Honolulu. In 1941, Hawaii was in its own "half time zone." Tokyo had already reassigned some of their Washington envoys back to Japan.

Just one day before, Hull had told reporters that he anticipated no further meetings with his Japanese counterparts.[8] Privately, Hull had already told Henry Stimson, "I have washed my hands of it and now it is in the hands of you and [Frank] Knox—the Army and the Navy."[9]

Most American newspapers Sunday morning were by and large quiet when it came to the Pacific crisis. The *Honolulu Advertiser* was covering local news involving housing issues, a display by the Shriners, and the typical international war news coming from Russia, Germany, and England.[10] There was also a special feature on where children could see Santa Claus—from 11:00 a.m. to 5:00 p.m. that day—in front of a fake fireplace in the lobby of the newspaper office.[11] Another front-page story reported on the newly formed "Razor Blades for Britain Committee in Hawaii," which was taking up a collection because blades could no longer be purchased in England, as all steel was being devoted to their war effort. "All razor blade donations . . . must be new," the story cautioned.[12]

Inside, stories and features favorably reviewed the movie *A Yank in the R.A.F.*; announced clipper tours between Hawaii, the West Coast, Midway, Wake Island, and the Philippines; and detailed the ongoing prostitution problems in Hawaii. On page seven was a feature, "Week's War Review." The column opened by saying, "A critical week of war news was highlighted by heightening tension in the Pacific, but no new developments towards war."[13]

In the *Washington Star*, only one story was devoted to the Far East, while the rest of the war and foreign news was about the Russian Front, North Africa, and the North Atlantic. The other news of the day covered sports, the weather, traffic reports, human-interest stories, metro articles, editorials, and columns. The most human of human-interest stories ran across the wires on Sunday morning about the death of a ninety-seven-year-old man, "Ray Fritman, who had spent a lifetime seeking his true identity. . . . He became lost during a parade in New York in 1852 and never saw his parents again." He got his name from an orphanage in New York, fought in the Civil War, and later taught school in Indiana.[14]

When there was news in some papers about the crisis with Japan, it was tucked among all sorts of other stories. However, buried on page three of the *New York Times* was an ominous piece, dateline "Tokyo, Sunday, Dec. 7." The headline read, "Japanese Herald 'Supreme Crisis.'" The account was on the United Press wire. "Japan indicated early today that she was on the verge of abandoning efforts to achieve a settlement of Pacific issues by diplomatic negotiation [in] Washington." The story further detailed Tokyo's anger over Russia's apparent decision to throw in her lot with the "ABCD" powers of America, Britain, China, and the Dutch and oppose Japan in the Far East. But also a Japanese government official said, "[T]he time for alteration of the Thai Government's neutrality is believed at hand."[15]

The Thai government announced a state of emergency, and despite the claims of Tokyo, the Thais said they were not worried about the British. However, the British were worried about the Japanese. Civilians through-out the Far East had been told to evacuate and all British troops had been recalled, some picked up in bars and clubs in Singapore and taken back to their respective bases and ships. Twenty Japanese nationals had been taken off a ship headed for Bangkok and detained by the British.[16]

England's military commanders planned an "all hands on deck" meeting for December 8 to game out the dire situation.[17] One fact was becoming increasingly clear: Britain was now incapable of defending its Far Eastern prizes—especially oil, the greatest prize of all. To defend its empire against the resource-hungry Japanese, the British desperately needed the assistance of its rich cousins across the Atlantic, something President Roosevelt well understood.

On Saturday evening, December 6, FDR sent a message directly to Emperor Hirohito, "an unprecedented action—as disturbing reports reached the State Department that two large and heavily escorted convoys were seen yesterday morning steaming into the Gulf of Siam, which washes the shores of Thailand."[18] The contents of the president's message to the emperor were not revealed at the time. Later it became known—it was utterly respectful and solicitous of the emperor. Words such as "friendship" and "virtue" and "wisdom" littered the missive, but also words like "fear" and "concern."[19]

"Only in situations of extraordinary importance to our two countries need I address to Your Majesty messages on matters of state. I feel I should now so address you because of the deep and far-reaching emergency which appears to be in formation. Developments are occurring in the Pacific area which threaten to deprive each of our nations and all humanity of the beneficial influence of the long peace between our two countries. These developments contain tragic possibilities." Roosevelt politely raised the subject of China *and* Indo-China and expressed concern over Japan's military incursions in those two countries. "During the past few weeks it has become clear . . . that Japanese military, naval and air forces have been sent to Southern Indo-China in such large numbers as to create a reasonable doubt on the part of other nations that this continuing concentration in Indo-China is not defensive in its character." Roosevelt reviewed other matters in the area including the Philippines, the East Indies, and Malaya and the apparent Japanese designs on these countries as well. "I am sure that Your Majesty will understand that the fear of all these people is a legitimate fear in as much as it involves their peace and their national existence. I am sure that Your Majesty will understand why the people of the United States in such large numbers look askance at the establishment of military . . . bases manned and equipped so greatly as to constitute armed forces capable of measures of offense." He assured Hirohito that the United States and the other countries of the region had no warlike designs on Japan.[20]

Roosevelt closed with a plea. "I address myself to Your Majesty at this moment in the fervent hope that Your Majesty may, as I am doing, give thought in this definite emergency to ways of dispelling the dark clouds. I am confident that both of us, for the sake of the peoples not only of our own great countries but for the sake of humanity in neighboring territories, have a sacred duty to restore traditional amity and prevent further death and destruction in the world."[21] The telegram was sent at 6:00 p.m. Washington time on the sixth, but there was no evidence Hirohito ever saw it.

Even with the details of the message then unknown to the public, it was clear to most that the Roosevelt administration felt some sort of breakthrough was still possible in the Far East that might relieve the pressure cooker it had become. "The dispatch of the President's message was announced after a day in which appeared some slight hopes that the crisis with Japan would subside and that conversations could be resumed . . . on some satisfactory lines."[22]

Only once before, on December 13, 1937, had Roosevelt communicated with Hirohito. That was when the Japanese had bombed an American ship, the gunboat *Panay*, while she sailed in Chinese waters. That message was delivered verbally to the Japanese ambassador in Washington and "it produced results, and the United States received satisfaction for the *Panay* attack."[23] The new Roosevelt initiative was interpreted to reflect his dissatisfaction with Tokyo's military maneuvers in the Far East and as a last ditch effort to restart the talks.

Following FDR's plea, observers agreed, "The next step, it was felt, is wholly up to Japan . . ."[24]

"The message also was viewed as possibly a step of last resort to avert an open break with Japan since it was considered unlikely that Mr. Roosevelt would communicate directly with the Emperor unless virtually all hope had been abandoned of a satisfactory adjustment of Japanese-American difficulties through the usual diplomatic channels."[25]

While coverage might have otherwise been slight, every radio and newspaper in America covered in detail Roosevelt's olive branch to Japan the morning of December 8, though not all reported on the "two large and heavily escorted Japanese convoys . . . steaming toward the Gulf of Siam (Thailand) this morning."[26] Another large convoy featuring six aircraft carriers heading southeast from Japan and briefly reported on six days earlier had not been seen or heard from since. Kimmel had received a notice on December 2 that this Japanese task force, moving at flank speed, around 24 knots, had been lost to American trackers.[27]

The American military policy in the Far East had never been completely clear, and Roosevelt never articulated specifically that if Japan went ahead and invaded Thailand, the United States would get into a shooting war with Tokyo. But everybody assumed Thailand was the line in the sand, especially since the British had made clear their intention to attack Japan if Thailand were invaded.[28]

The Japanese press meanwhile continued to pound the United States, accusing Washington of stalling and "insincerity," though without elaborating.[29] Domei, the government-owned news agency, announced that the Japanese government, from Premier General Hideki Tojo to the foreign minister to the navy minister Vice Adm. Shigetaro Shimada "'would speak the whole truth about the current international situation as well as the Japanese-American talks' in speeches Monday."[30]

The Japanese, having invaded China, incredibly called for "self-determination" for the Chinese and had used this as yet another reason to tell Washington to butt out of the affairs of the Far East.[31] They also blasted the "sensationalism" of American "press and radio," but that was nothing new. American politicians had complained of this for years.[32] The War Department had done a little saber-rattling of its own and called attention to new bases it was building in the Aleutian Islands, a potential threat to Japan.[33]

Yet another Japanese spokesman, Dr. Morinosuki Kashima, unsurprisingly blasted the United States and its "offensive attitude diplomatically, politically and strategically." News reports confirmed that "certain attaches of the Japanese Embassy in Washington had been shifted, but reasons for the move were not specified." Other unexplained actions by the Japanese were reported, including the recall of the heads of steamship offices in Bombay and Singapore.[34]

Australia was actively preparing for war and ordered "nonessential" civilians to leave the Philippines immediately and that an evacuation might be necessary.[35] The British were still furiously evacuating Singapore, sending trucks around the city to pick up soldiers and sailors.[36]

On the other side of the world, Great Britain declared war against Finland, which had become an "ally" of the Third Reich. "Each of the German satellite states had refused ultimatums that they halt hostilities against Russia, Britain's ally." Immediately, the British government arrested 150 Finns "who will be removed later to concentration camps," while "[n]ewly designated 'enemy diplomats' prepared to leave London."[37]

In concert with the British declaration of war, FDR put Finnish ships in American ports in New York, Philadelphia, Boston, and Baltimore under "protective custody."[38] Finland's president Risto Ryti received "a telegram of independence day congratulations from Adolf Hitler."[39] In the Mediterranean, another German ally, the Vichy government of France, activated its fleet there to assist the Nazis and Italians against "British piracy."[40]

The British scored some heavy air wins over Libya, due to the new American plane, the Tomahawk fighter, obtained under Lend-Lease.[41] Also under Lend-Lease—and because of the wheat surplus in America—a large shipment was headed for Russia that Moscow had purchased using American credit.[42]

But the relentless German counteroffensive on Moscow was scoring results, in spite of the claims from the Soviet-controlled state media. "Moscow appeared tonight to be in her direst peril . . . the Russian capital had become the target for 1,500,000 advancing troops, 8,000 tanks and 1,000 guns."[43] The Nazi panzer groups were a mere forty miles from the Soviet capital; the huddled residents of the besieged city could hear the Germans' heavy guns in the near distance. For the Russians, all appeared lost—until temperatures plummeted and the historical military asset that some refer to as "General Winter" emerged from his slumber. The "iron willpower" of the

Nazi Supermen, ill-protected in lightweight uniforms, was about to face the supreme test.

The day before, navy secretary Frank Knox released a report he'd prepared for FDR that stated America's fleet was "superior to any" in the world and that it had recently been "placed on a war footing with full personnel manning the ships of three fleets," including the Pacific fleet in Hawaii. "I am proud to report that the American people may feel fully confident in their Navy." It is, he said, "without superior. On any comparable basis, the United States Navy is second to none." Knox concluded, "In the Pacific, the strategic importance . . . with development of the islands guarding the approach to the Navy's defense in the Hawaiian area with the resultant safety of the Pacific Coast, are obvious."[44]

It was good PR, but there were problems, particularly with enlistments. Because of the ongoing recruiting difficulties of the navy, it was announced that physical standards would be reduced and young men heretofore disqualified for "varicocele, hydrocele, hernia, nasal deformity, seasonal hay fever not accompanied by asthma, and undernourishment," would now be admitted. The navy had already lowered the standards for bad teeth.[45] A December 2 memo from Knox spelled out the problem. In one month, the net gain for navy personnel from October to November of 1941 had gone up by only 6,921 men, from 280,184 to 287,105. His report to FDR was signed, "Very Respectfully."[46]

Badly needed by the navy were men with radio experience, and a public plea was issued. "Men experienced either as amateurs or professionals in operation and maintenance of radio equipment are urgently needed by the navy and will be given ratings upon enlistment as radiomen, second class." The navy had an immediate opening for one thousand enlistees, as long as they were high school graduates or "actively engaged in radio repair or service work . . ."[47]

The army, too, was having difficulty meeting its announced goal of 2 million men in uniform and a "new class of 21-year-old youths will be called up for possible military service at least by July 1 of next year." The army was experiencing a "shortage of man-power . . . many local [draft] boards throughout the country are rapidly drawing to the end of their lists of potential Class 1-A registrants." Class II-A and Class II-B men might be reclassified as 1-A. In Washington, over four thousand healthy young men were classified as II-A or II-B.[48]

Captain Dickinson S. Pepper of Walter Reed Hospital berated young doctors who, while in medical school, received deferments and were then "shirking" their duty. "I cannot believe that the medical student of today appreciates the crisis that confronts our Nation," he said.[49]

The nation's women were not shirking. In full-page ads, Revlon Nail Enamel and the Beauty Salons of America featured actress Joan Crawford doing her bit for the war effort. "Morale is a woman's business. The way you look affects so many people around you.... To them, a woman's beauty stands for courage, serenity, a gallant heart ... all the things that men need so desperately these days. So the time spent in your favorite beauty salon every week isn't selfish or frivolous. It's part of your job of morale."[50]

At 3:42 a.m., the *Condor*, on patrol outside the entrance to Pearl Harbor, spotted an unidentified and unauthorized midget submarine. Later that morning, at 6:45 a.m., the *Ward* fired on and hit yet another mysterious midget submersible. The young captain with the perfectly nautical name of William Outerbridge ordered his number three deck gun to fire on the unknown submarine. Outerbridge reported, "We have attacked, fired upon, and dropped depth charges on sub operating in our defensive zone."[51] A report was made to naval authorities at Pearl Harbor, but no action was taken.

Scout planes from the *Enterprise*, some two hundred miles out and heading back to Pearl Harbor after making her delivery, spotted Japanese bombers and escort planes over the Pacific at 6:15 a.m., heading southeast. Radio confusion between a scout plane and the "Big E" prevented it from taking any action.[52] Adm. Bill Halsey and his aircraft carrier had been due back at Pearl Harbor the morning of December 7, but a storm had waylaid them, and they would now not arrive until the afternoon.

At St. Agnes Episcopal Church in Washington, sitting in a pew alone and deep in prayer was Viscount Halifax, the British ambassador to the United States. As "Father DuBois reached that part of the service where he prayed 'for guidance for all Christian rulers,' Viscount Halifax was visibly and deeply moved."[53]

In the predawn of December 7, the first wave of planes from six aircraft carriers had become airborne and headed for the island of Oahu. Their code several days before if diplomacy failed was "Climb Mt. Niitaka."

At Opana Point Radar Station, set on the highest point on the island of Oahu, two young army privates, Joseph L. Lockard and George Elliot, noticed what looked to be a huge grouping of planes headed for the island. A call was placed around 7:00 a.m. to Lt. Kermit Tyler, who was the morning duty officer, informing him of "many planes." Tyler, thinking the two were seeing a squadron of American B-17s due in that morning, told them to forget about it. They turned off the radar and went to breakfast. An earlier radar "blip" had also been ignored.[54]

A private pilot was up for a quiet and leisurely flight over Honolulu early that morning. Ray Buduick, a lawyer, expected to have the airspace all to himself and his seventeen-year-old son, Martin.[55] Shortly after takeoff, he realized that his expectations were wrong. All of a sudden, the skies over the island were filled with hundreds of airplanes. "A private plane owner reported he was given a salute of machine-gun bullets by the Japanese planes. His craft was damaged but he managed to land."[56]

A female flight instructor, Cornelia Fort, in her early 20s, was also aloft, giving a lesson, when she was overwhelmed with hundreds of planes bearing a red flaming ball.

A squadron of Japanese fighter planes, being faster than the bombers, arrived at Oahu at 7:30 and orbited the island for twenty-five minutes while they waited for the slower planes to catch up.[57]

On a beach in Santa Monica, a group of sun worshipers was out early playing volleyball when one of them heard something over the radio and tried to catch the attention of the others. But they were disinterested at the moment in anything other than the outcome of their morning match.[58]

The first wave of 183 planes, including dive bombers and torpedo planes on approach to Oahu, continued unmolested and basically undetected. They'd been transported in secret since November 26, at 0900, having departed their home waters of Tankan Bay. The six carriers, *Akagi, Kaga, Soryu, Hiryu, Shokaku,* and *Zuikaku,* could deploy hundreds of war planes. They were under the orders of the fleet commander, Isoroku Yamamoto, and the command of Chuichi Nagumo. The massive fleet halted in mid-ocean to refuel on December 3. The standing order was radio silence and, if not recalled by Tokyo, to attack.

As they flew over the island, on their approach from the north, over the sugarcane and pineapple fields, they saw no puffs of antiaircraft black smoke in the sky, no airplanes rising to meet their challenge. Realizing they had succeeded in their audacious sneak attack on the American fleet, the code indicating their achievement was transmitted: "Tiger! Tiger! Tiger!"[59]

"Tora! Tora! Tora!"

Along the Waikiki beach, some early morning fishermen were out. "Downtown nothing stirred save an occasional bus." Then came the Japanese planes. "They whined over Waikiki, over the candy-pink bulk of the Royal Hawaiian Hotel."[60]

A commercial liner just making port from San Francisco slipped into the harbor at Honolulu. Thinking themselves lucky to be witnessing naval war games, what with the planes diving overhead and all the puffs of black and white smoke, "[s]cores of delighted passengers crowding the deck remarked that it was mighty fine of the United States Navy, timing it so nicely with [their] arrival."[61]

Initial reports out of Hawaii were light. The first bulletin went out over the local airwaves, garbled, not from a military source or official government spokesman, but from a broadcast personality, Webley Edwards, who hosted the popular radio show *Hawaii Calls* on CBS, which was heard all over the mainland.[62]

"Attention. This is no exercise. The Japanese are attacking Pearl Harbor. All Army, Navy and Marine personnel are to report to duty."[63] Shortly thereafter, a government-ordered blackout was secured on Hawaii, but long-distance phone calls, telegrams, or messages from ham radio operators continued.[64] The phone lines eventually became jammed as the navy was frantically using them.

But this didn't stop anybody from hearing about the attack all across the mainland. It went out over the airwaves, repeatedly, with regular programming interrupted, on every radio station in America. News spread by word of mouth, from neighbor to neighbor, parents to kids. The words *Pearl Harbor* were questioningly and angrily on everybody's lips. In the living rooms of America, people huddled around Philco or General Electric radios, listening to war news that for the first time directly involved the American people. On the sidewalks, people huddled around car radios, listening to the flash bulletins.[65]

The headlines of the morning newspapers of December 7, 1941, contained no news about the surprise attack on Pearl Harbor, as they had gone to press hours before the attack. Plus, there was a five-and-a-half-hour difference between the East Coast and Hawaii. But by that afternoon, hurriedly rushed "Extra!" editions of newspapers were printed in large-point type by the droves, nationwide.

At the meaningless football game at Griffith Stadium in Washington between the Redskins and the Philadelphia Eagles, twenty-seven thousand attendees—including many military personnel and journalists—"were the last to know anything about the world-stirring events."[66] Throughout the game there was no announcement whatsoever through the loudspeakers, although radio broadcasters in the booths continually were breaking into their accounts of the game with war bulletins. Listening on the radio, fans heard, "Japs bombed Pearl Harbor—Japs make direct hit, killing hundreds." People in the bleachers heard none of this. The famed sports reporter Shirley Povich of the *Washington Post* recalled that a colleague had received a private message from his newspaper. "The Japanese have kicked off. War now!"[67]

In the interval after the first half, it became evident to the football fans that something extraordinary was in progress. Throughout the intermission and the second half there were constant calls over the public address system for various newspapermen, believed to be at the game, to get in touch with their offices immediately and for high-ranking army and navy officers to call their departments. "Important persons were being paged, too many important persons to make it a coincidence." In the first half, the chief of the Bureau of Ordnance with the navy was paged. So too was a high official with the Philippine government. Of the flock of cameramen there to cover the game, by the second half only one lone photographer stood vigil, the others sent to the Japanese embassy and others now to more interesting and important locations.[68]

As the rumor of war spread, the seats emptied. One enterprising wife sent her husband, who was attending the game, a telegram. "Deliver to Section P, Top Row, Seat 27, opposite 25-yard line, East side, Griffith Stadium: War with Japan Get to office." The Redskins ownership later said using the PA to announce the war news was against its management's policy.[69]

It was reported initially that the Japanese had struck at 7:35 Hawaiian time, 1:05 (EST).[70] According to *A Battle History of the Imperial Japanese Navy*, the time was 7:55 a.m., local time.[71] Because Hawaii had gone into a news broadcasting blackout, it is likely that there were many in the scattered Hawaiian Islands who did not know about the attack until nearly everybody in the world knew about it.

In all, some 353 Japanese fighters and bombers descended on Oahu, more than 3,500 miles from their homeland.[72] "An NBC broadcast said Japanese planes—estimated as many as 150 in the opening assault—struck at Ford Island in Pearl Harbor."[73] Initial reports said the planes appeared over the harbor out of the south coming over Diamond Head. Civilian locations were also bombed and strafed. One of the first to die in the attack may have been a ten-year-old Portuguese girl.[74]

A reporter for the International News Service, Richard Haller, filed this report:

Japanese warplanes brought sudden death and undisclosed destruction to the beautiful Hawaiian Islands in their sudden raid this morning. A flotilla of planes bearing the Rising Sun of Japan on their wingtips appeared out of the south while most of the city was sleeping. The planes dove immediately to the attack on Pearl Harbor and Hickam field, the giant air base lying nearby. . . . Three battleships were struck as they lay at anchor in the naval base. One . . . was reportedly set afire. Another . . . we hear has been sunk along with another warship. There was no confirmation of the sinkings by officers of the Fourteenth Naval District. . . . I wasn't able to confirm reports that Japanese paratroopers had landed. But the report spread through Honolulu like wild fire. There were rumors that a number of prisoners were taken. From the rooftop of the *Honolulu Advertiser* building I saw a thick pall of smoke rising from the Pearl Harbor and Hickam field areas. Three separate fires were raging there. A staggering series of explosions came shortly after 10 o'clock when the attack was already two hours old. Army authorities later reported that a direct torpedo bomb hit had been made on the Hickam field barracks. The army said it was feared that 350 men had been killed. A few minutes later the Japanese planes, flying at an immense altitude returned over Honolulu. . . . Waikiki, the world famous resort beach, was also subjected to sudden attack as the raiders tried to silence the big guns of Fort DeRussy, guarding the entrance to Honolulu Harbor. . . . The raiders fantailed over the residential districts and dropped what appeared to be incendiary bombs over Pacific Heights and Dowsett highlands. Some fires were ignited.[75]

Associated Press reporters in New York could clearly hear over the phone the bombing in the background, as an unidentified local NBC reporter standing on the roof of a building, microphone in hand, "radioed direct from the scene." He noted that although two local broadcast stations had reported on the raid, local citizens did not heed the warning to take cover until the sound of bombs was heard.[76] Some did not go home but instead to the hills over the harbor, to get a good look at the ensuing battle.[77]

The reporter from the local NBC affiliate then said, "We have witnessed this morning the attack of Pearl Harbor and a severe bombing of Pearl Harbor by army planes, undoubtedly Japanese. The city of Honolulu has also been attacked and considerable damage done. This battle has been going on for nearly three hours. One of the bombs dropped within fifty feet of the KGU tower. . . . It is no joke; it is a real war," he said, before his connection died.[78]

A few minutes later he began broadcasting again. "We have no statement as to how much damage has been done, but it has been a very severe attack. The army and navy, it appears, now have the air and sea under control." Then his line went dead, this time for good.[79] John Daly of CBS also broadcast early reports from the scene for a time.[80]

Right in the middle of the attack, a squadron of B-17s making a refueling stop on their way to the Philippines from San Francisco arrived as Japanese war planes buzzed around them. The squadron was commanded by Major Truman Landon, who remarked, "Hell of a way to fly into a war! Unarmed and out of fuel!"[81] Radio station KGU in Hawaii had kept broadcasting all night so the B-17s could use their radio locators.

The Japanese planes did likewise.

FDR and the War Department were hampered by misinformation coming out of the Pacific. Nearly all initial reports were sketchy, incomplete, and often woefully false. One news report said that the *Oklahoma* and the *West Virginia* battleships were engaged in sea action against the Japanese.[82] Another said Japanese planes had glided in over Pearl Harbor so as to escape detection.[83]

Wild speculation was one thing; the lack of full information and detail was another. One of the first "Extra" editions out was the *Maryville Daily*

Forum based in Missouri. Over the top one-third of the broadsheet read in huge, old Western-style wanted-poster type face, "Japs Attack Manila"[84] with the subheads "Reports Stagger London"[85] and "Far East Crisis Explodes!"[86] Another said, "Little information is immediately available regarding the strength of the Japanese air attacks."[87]

An Associated Press wire story with the dateline of Honolulu carried the headline "Two Japanese Bombers Appear over Honolulu; Unverified Report Says a Foreign Warship Appears Off Pearl Harbor." The excited reporter filed his story via the transpacific telephone cable as the battle was actually taking place. The story noted that no bombs had apparently been dropped on Honolulu and that civilians were being taken off the streets by military personnel. The initial report noted there were no casualties yet known.[88]

Within minutes, the AP story made its way around the world, with reactions from Berlin, New York, and Washington. America's great and loyal ally, Russia, was quiet on the attack. The Third Reich had no comment initially, and the story out of the nation's capital announced that President Roosevelt had called for an "extraordinary meeting of the cabinet for 8:30 p.m. tonight and to have congressional leaders of both parties join the conference at 9 p.m."[89]

Another local report was filed, this one by Frank Tremaine via the United Press: "Flash—Pearl Harbor under aerial attack. Tremaine." His initial dispatch was sent via cable to UP offices in San Francisco and Manila. Subsequently, he filed additional reports as his wife, Kay, sent them along.[90]

A newlywed couple, Wallace Holman and Rosalie Shimek, had been married the day before in Baltimore and spent their honeymoon in New York City at the Roosevelt Hotel, where that evening they listened to Guy Lombardo perform. The next day they were strolling along a street in New York, startled as furious shopkeepers began throwing out anything that bore the brand "Made in Japan." No one knew where Pearl Harbor was, including the couple, and one merchant told them it was "off New Jersey."[91] But all knew America had been attacked by Japan. A little boy, Gerald Eckert, in Rochester, New York, heard about an attack on Pearl, but wondered why the Japanese were attacking the old lady down the street whose name was Pearl.[92]

Rumors mixed easily with reports. One said the Japanese fleet, having blasted the navy out of the water at Pearl Harbor, was now steaming north to the Aleutian Islands to attack military outposts there. Yet another said that American ships were in hot pursuit of the Japanese fleet now heading for its home waters.

In Washington, the formerly sleepy town quickly began to take on a war atmosphere, as pedestrians huddled around cars to listen to the radio, citizens called newspaper offices, hungry for details, and others called to inquire about the location of air-raid shelters. "The shrill voices of newsboys calling war extras broke the ordinary Sabbath evening calm."[93] In bold type, the *Washington Post's* extra edition boomed, "U.S. AT WAR! JAPAN BOMBS HAWAII, MANILA."[94]

As soon as Roosevelt had been notified by Secretary of the Navy Frank Knox, he summoned his press secretary, Stephen T. Early, who then called together the White House press corps to make an official announcement at 2:22 p.m., Eastern time.[95] "The Japanese have attacked Pearl Harbor from the air and all naval and military activities on the Island of Oahu, principal American base in the Hawaiian Islands," said Early, reading from a statement given to him by the president. Early responded to the first question, "So far as we know, they came without warning."[96]

Some 150 tense reporters were in attendance then, and throughout the day. The White House became the country's hub for information on unfolding events. Roosevelt remained in his private library in the second-floor residence, taking reports and meeting with staff, including his "two secretaries, Marvin McIntyre and Maj. Gen. Edwin S. Watson."[97] The president "ordered war bulletins released at the White House as rapidly as they were received. A sentence or two was added to the story of the surprise attack every few minutes for several hours."[98]

Early called press conferences all throughout the afternoon, and reporters ran back and forth from their cubbyholes to the press secretary's office, writing fresh copy or issuing radio broadcasts with each new announcement.[99] As each new development was ready to be announced, a Secret Service man would stroll across the hall and remark, 'Press Conference!' setting off a stampede for Early's desk."[100] Telegraph boys rushed about.

At each press conference, Early would attempt to elaborate on the coordinated and unfolding attacks by the Japanese throughout the Pacific. In case no one missed the duplicity by the Japanese, he said,

> So far as is known, the attacks on Hawaii and Manila were made wholly without warning when both nations were at peace, and were delivered within an hour or so of the time that the Japanese ambassador and the special envoy, Kurusu, had gone to the State Department and handed to the Secretary of State Japan's reply to the Secretary's memorandum of November 26. As soon as the information of the attacks . . . was received by the War and Navy Departments it was flashed immediately to the President at the White House. Thereupon and immediately the President directed the Army and Navy to execute all previously prepared orders looking to the defense of the United States. The President is now with the Secretary of War and the Secretary of the Navy. Steps are being taken to advise the congressional leaders.[101]

At 3:18 p.m. Early's personal secretary told the reporters the attacks were apparently still under way. Halfway through the afternoon, Early appeared to retract the story that Manila had been bombed, but later retracted the retraction.[102]

Unfortunately, there was no plan for the defense of the United States. The navy in the Pacific was either obliterated or scattered, and the Army Air Corps in Oahu had simply been annihilated. A second wave of 171 planes then hit Hawaii. And then another round of news came, this time confirming the worst fears: "Admiral C. Bloch, commandant in Hawaii had reported 'heavy damage' to the islands, with 'heavy loss of life.'"[103]

As the second wave continued the attack on Pearl Harbor, the governor of Hawaii, John Poindexter, was on the phone with Roosevelt.[104] A bomb went off in front of the governor's mansion at Washington Place, killing a man. Another detonated close to the offices of the *Honolulu Advertiser*. A woman was killed when the Waikiki section of Honolulu was bombed.[105] Poindexter had been appointed territorial governor by FDR, but within a few months, he would be replaced by a military government in Hawaii.

Early or his secretary, Miss Ruthjane Rumelt, held press conferences at 2:22, 3:18, 3:22, 3:33, 3:57, 4:45, 6:00, 6:08, and 6:24. It was 3:33 when he announced that a Japanese sub seven hundred miles off of California had fired on a transport, crippling it. It was 3:57 when he announced the emergency meeting with the cabinet and congressional leaders. At 6:00 p.m., he announced that another over-flight of Japanese planes was preparing yet again to hit Pearl Harbor. He later had to retract it, saying that the White House and the War Department were attempting to separate fact from rumor, but because they had not been able to reach the commanders of the navy and army in Hawaii, "[t]he President is, therefore, disposed to believe, and is rather hopeful that the . . . report is erroneous." At 6:08, he reported that unidentified planes had been spotted over Guam. At 6:24, he announced Guam had been attacked.[106]

While the news buzzed, other issues needed to be addressed. One of the first people FDR met with after his phone call from Knox was Charles Fahey, solicitor general of the United States. The two met "to discuss what steps were to be taken against Japanese aliens in the United States."[107] The same question was being considered and answered in other quarters as well. According to one story datelined Norfolk, Virginia, the director of public safety there, Col. Charles B. Borland, "immediately ordered the arrest of all Japanese nationals in this strategic naval center" as soon as he'd heard of the attack.[108]

On the streets of America, strangers were talking to strangers, and some compared the atmosphere of hotel and movie lobbies, restaurants, and clubs to that of London during the German blitz two years earlier. "Something of the strange psychological phenomenon . . . Folks wanted to be together. A sense of comradeship . . . was apparent."[109] Americans across the country attending Sunday movie matinees were surprised to see the film stopped, the managers walk out on stage, and news reports read to them of the bombing of Pearl Harbor.

Pedestrians lined Pennsylvania Avenue and the streets on both sides of the White House, including West Executive Avenue between the State Department and the Executive Mansion, but Secret Service agents and police officers later closed the perimeter around the area. As night fell, the crowd moved across the street to Lafayette Park. "Some stood on the running boards of the cars. Some climbed the stone abutments of the iron fences. Some stood in the middle of the thoroughfare. Some held their children on their shoulders. But all kept quiet and all looked at the lighted windows, with no eyes for anything else." A visitor from Colorado, Dorothy Quine, was in the crowd. "I can't understand it when Kurusu is here talking about peace," she said.[110]

At the Soldiers, Sailors, and Marines Service Club in Washington, a sign was posted: "All Servicemen Are Due in Camp at Reveille Tomorrow. Signed, Secretary of War." The servicemen, like everybody else, were stunned at the attacks and yet cocky too. "The men at the club last night were generally grim and confident of a quick American victory."[111]

The military ordered all personnel into uniform, immediately. Many military men had been working in "civvies" instead of their uniforms at their defense jobs for years to avoid making the town look "militaristic." That would all change.

Then an oddly worded paragraph appeared in an AP story: "There was a disposition in some quarters here to wonder whether the attacks had not been ordered by the Japanese military authorities because they feared the President's direct negotiations with the Emperor might lead to an about-face in Japanese policy and the consequent loss of face by the present ruling factions in Japan."[112] The story seemed to be trying to pin the blame for the surprise attack on President Roosevelt because he reached out to Hirohito the night before.

Vice President Henry Wallace was in New York, but he caught the first available plane back to Washington and arrived at 6:00 p.m. that evening. Wallace went directly to the White House where he and the cabinet met alone with FDR, beginning at 6:40 p.m. Wallace then attended the second meeting that included members of Congress. FDR still had time to make his near-daily visit to the White House physician at 5:50 and was, according to records, there for over an hour.[113]

As members of Congress and the cabinet arrived that night at the White House, the crowds outside cheered. The first to arrive was a now former isolationist, Senator Hiram Johnson of California, smoking a cigar, saying nothing.[114] Longtime internationalists gloated, if under their breaths. "What a sight. The great isolationist ... All the ghosts of isolationism stalk with him, all the beliefs that the United States could stay out of war if it made no attack," penned Richard Strout, famed writer for the *Christian Science Monitor*.[115]

Roosevelt had been in meetings off and on for a reported ten hours from the time the White House had first learned of the attack. It was in these meetings that he received a report from Gen. Douglas MacArthur that Japanese planes were also over Luzon and that they had bombed several American airfields in the Philippines.[116] "Upon being advised of the attack on Pearl Harbor, Hawaii, Lieut. Gen. Douglas MacArthur ... placed his entire command on the alert."[117] But the planes at Clark Field remained parked wingtip to wingtip, and many were easily destroyed by the Japanese.

MacArthur told reporters there would be no censorship in the Philippines, as was instituted in Hawaii, and announced he would hold press conferences every half hour. He told reporters that his commanders were already making preparations for the internment of Japanese nationals and captured Japanese soldiers. "We are calm and confident," the general said.[118]

During the Japanese attack on Manila, Don Bell broadcast live from a bunker crammed with army personnel. Calmly, Bell said, "Perhaps ladies and gentlemen, you can hear the sound of those Japanese bombers again. Apparently the raid is not over yet."[119]

In meetings with FDR were Henry Stimson, Cordell Hull, other members of the cabinet and Congress, as well as Army Chief of Staff George C. Marshall. "The president reviewed for them all information received ... and gave them also other information not yet verified and which at the time had to be classified as rumor. The President told them of doubtless very heavy losses sustained by the Navy and also large losses sustained by the Army on the Island of Oahu."[120] At 9:15, the navy issued a press release, announcing it had no information on casualties in the Pacific.[121]

Roosevelt took a break from the afternoon meetings and began dictating his remarks to Grace Tully, his personal secretary, to deliver to Congress the next day.

In his landmark book *White House Ghosts*, Robert Schlesinger described the scene. "Shortly before 5 pm . . . Roosevelt summoned Grace Tully to his study. Reports had been coming in from a smoldering Pearl Harbor all afternoon and the president finally had a moment to reflect on the speech he would give the next day to Congress and the nation. Tully found him behind his desk. Two or three piles of notes were neatly stacked in front of him and he was lighting a cigarette. 'Sit down Grace. I'm going before Congress tomorrow. I'd like to dictate my message. It will be short.' He took a long drag from his cigarette."[122]

The president had dinner at around 7:30 that evening.[123] His son, James, dined with him. At 8:30, he met once again with high government officials "in the second-floor red-room study"[124] and gave it to them right between the eyes. "FDR told the Cabinet and congressional leaders the full scope of the disaster—battleships sunk, planes destroyed. . . . He said it would be very difficult to mount a retaliatory attack on Japan and that the way ahead was long. He said it was very unpleasant to be a war president, according to a diary account of the meeting written that evening by Agriculture Secretary Claude Wickard."[125] Wickard noted, "The Secretary of the Navy has lost his air of bravado. Secretary Stimson was very sober." FDR also indicated that while he did want to speak to Congress the next day, he was not sure he would ask for a declaration of war. At one point, Senator Tom Connally "exploded," storming, "Where were our forces—asleep?"[126] When they departed, FDR took a nap and then awoke to work again on his remarks. Then, "in the small hours, he went to bed, slept for five hours."[127] As the officials left the White House, Richard Strout said, "They won't talk. They went in grim, they came out glum."

It was announced that evening the president would speak to a joint session of Congress and the American people the next day, the eighth, at 12:30 (EST). Eleanor Roosevelt was surprised at how "serene" her husband was. "I think it was steadying to know finally that the die had been cast."[128]

One of the last persons to see Roosevelt that evening was his coordinator of information, William "Wild Bill" Donovan, who later went on to form the Office of Strategic Services. He'd become a trusted advisor to the president and was not part of the original "Brain Trust" around Roosevelt. Donovan was respected, in part, for having won the Congressional Medal of Honor in the Great War.[129] Roosevelt also saw Edward R. Murrow late that evening, just before he retired at 12:30 a.m.[130]

The lights of the Navy Department glared all night, burning the midnight oil, and one officer said the reports on the commercial airwaves were "surprisingly close" to the official reports. Like other military men, naval officers had not worked in uniform for a long time, preferring to blend into the culture of Washington by dressing like ordinary civilians. Now, one quipped of uniforms coming out of storage, "There'll be the worst smell of mothballs around here tomorrow."[131]

Cots were brought into the munitions building, where the army was also working all night, including Secretary of War Stimson. They, too, were deluged with phone calls asking about loved ones in Hawaii and around the Pacific. The army, like everyone else in the government, had no answers to give them. The munitions building was surrounded by machine guns.

The crowd in Lafayette Park remained late into the night of December 7 and began singing "God Bless America."[132] Wickard memorialized how calm FDR was and how impressed he was of the president. "As I drive home, I could not refrain from wondering at the fates that caused me to be present at one of the most important conferences in the history of this nation."[133]

Japanese prime minister Hideki Tojo went on state radio and told the Japanese people, "I hereby promise you that Japan will win final victory" and reminded them that in 2,600 years, they had never lost a war.[134] On the other hand, they had never actually declared war on an enemy before engaging in an attack on them either.

The Japanese propaganda agency, Domei, announced at 6:00 a.m., Tokyo time, that "naval operations are progressing off Hawaii, with at least one Japanese aircraft carrier in action against Pearl Harbor."[135]

Tojo met with the Japanese cabinet one hour later, and after that short meeting, U.S. ambassador Joseph Grew and British ambassador Sir Robert Leslie Craigie were "summoned" to an audience with the foreign minister, Shigenori, to give them Japan's formal reply to Cordell Hull's missive of November 26. The reply rejected Hull's four points for peace in the Pacific.[136]

Over at the Japanese embassy at 2514 Massachusetts Avenue NW in Washington, reporters and curious onlookers watched the bonfire on the back lawn, as diplomats and officials burned thousands of documents. "Members of the Embassy staff . . . burned their code books in an outside fire behind the Embassy. . . . Newspapermen watched while the Japanese secrets were fed into the crackling flames."[137]

A crowd of about a thousand watched from the sidewalk, occasionally booing or taunting Japanese officials as they entered the compound, but no violence took place, as some in the White House had feared. Several young men yelled, "That's democracy for you! They kill us and we protect them." Another screamed, "We ought to kill them instead of guarding them."[138]

Several deliverymen knocked on the door in vain. Finally, a note was posted on the door to the embassy, though it was in Japanese. It said, "If you have business here, please use the side entrance."[139] But no one was allowed to leave, including the Irish maid, who wept to police that she had six children and a husband at home to feed. "With a noticeable brogue," she implored the Secret Service agents to let her go, but to no avail.[140]

"Police were assigned to guard the Japanese, German and Italian Embassies," but the Japanese had already taken precautions and hired "30 private detectives for the same job."[141] The State Department was already making plans for the safe passage of Japanese embassy officials to Tokyo, but it was not clear yet if the Japanese government was making the same provisions for their American counterparts.

Nomura and Kurusu glumly watched the blaze from inside the legation. All reports said they were truly shocked over the attack on Pearl Harbor. "If several sources of information can be believed, they knew nothing of what their army and navy were preparing while they were conducting diplomatic negotiations."[142]

Embassy Row was a hubbub of activity with all the tourists, cars, reporters, police, Secret Service, and a few actual residents of the palatial buildings that lined the northwest end of Massachusetts Avenue. Lord Halifax was working in his library at the British embassy when he learned of the attack. He immediately called Churchill by radio-telephone, and this was how the British learned of the attack by the Japanese.[143] The British prime minister had already given a stirring speech to the Parliament. He and FDR spoke by transatlantic phone, and "they discussed a synchronized declaration of war on Japan."[144]

The FBI straightaway arrested a Japanese national, the first of many,

Kiyoshi K. Kawakami, at his home on 3729 Morrison Street NW. "Officials later declined to reveal what had become of him." The provost marshal general of the West Coast, Alaska, the Canal Zone, and Hawaii, Allen Gullion, ordered "a general roundup of all 'previously known suspicious aliens.'"[145] But this was only the start.

In Baltimore, a group of boys hung "an effigy of a Japanese bearing the sign, 'This Jap Tried to Invade the U.S.'"[146] Sometime during Sunday, a clipper plane coming in from San Francisco with twenty-eight passengers and eleven crew members landed safely "at an unnamed airport in the Hawaiian Islands." Still unknown was the status of a Japanese ocean liner in the middle of the Pacific with many Americans on board.[147]

No one expected war like this. On December 7, Gen. H. H. "Hap" Arnold, chief of the Air Corps, was quail hunting in California, accompanied by Donald Douglas, president of Douglas Aircraft. The pair's location was so remote that a local sheriff had planes drop notes on the two men, alerting them to the new war.[148]

If Arnold was caught unawares, so was the beautiful city of Honolulu. "Honolulu isn't built for war," wrote Elizabeth Henney in the *Washington Post*. "White, gleaming, tropical buildings in the heart of the city (perfect targets) give an impression that joy and beauty are important, even more so than business." Sure, the harbor was right there, but the locals also celebrated "Boat Day," and when employers were informed that someone was coming in via a liner or a clipper plane, Henney said, "One is given time off to meet them and welcome them with fresh flower leis. Friendship is that important. There are no ragged beggars on the streets of Honolulu, but there are flower venders, selling leis, gardenia ones with two dozen or more blossoms for a quarter. And now, when the great black drops hurtle from the sky, ripping the gay red and blue tiles from the buildings, stilling songs and laughter, blasting soft bodies to shreds, what is the answer to Honolulu's question: 'Why this to us?' We have welcomed the Japanese race with the others that came. Our creed has been that of friendship."[149]

The Japanese attacked the Philippines. They attacked Wake Island. They attacked Thailand. They attacked Hong Kong. They attacked Malaya and British troops in Singapore. They attacked U.S. Marines stationed in China. They attacked Guam. They attacked Midway Island. They attacked Shanghai. They attacked Pearl Harbor.

"The purpose of the Japanese in striking at Pearl Harbor is obvious. The vast area of the naval base, 1,735 acres, with 250 buildings and 15,000 linear feet of berthing space, is a natural target, as it is the most complete naval base owned by this country, the center of Pacific Fleet operations, and possesses many vulnerable features which are well and easily recognized."[150] It was all so obvious as the day closed. But no one saw it coming the day before.

A White House memo had been quickly prepared for FDR telling him what he already knew about the attack, but this memo had some inaccuracies. "At least two aircraft were known to have a swastika sign on them."[151] On balance, though, the memorandum was pretty accurate. Another fascinating memo was a transcription of a conversation at 6:40 p.m. between the president and Henry Morganthau. Morganthau routinely had all his phone conversations transcribed, and though FDR had prohibited him from doing so with their phone calls, he did record one on this day, memorialized for history. The secretary of the treasury informed Roosevelt that he'd frozen all Japanese funds, had secured the border, and had doubled the guard at the White House while closing off adjoining streets. "We are not going to let any Japanese leave the country or to carry out any communications," Morganthau said, and FDR only said, "I see" to that.[152] FDR got a bit heated about making the White House look like an armed camp.

As Admiral Kimmel watched from a window in his office, which overlooked the harbor, the horrific butchery of the men and ships of the navy, a round of ammunition came crashing through the window and exhausted itself after tearing a hole in his white dress uniform.

Kimmel muttered, "It would have been merciful had it killed me."[153]

CHAPTER 8

THE EIGHTH OF DECEMBER

"U.S. Declares War on Japan"

Birmingham News

"Japan Wars on U.S. and Britain;
Makes Sudden Attack on Hawaii;
Heavy Fighting at Sea Reported"

New York Times

"Japanese Aliens' Roundup Starts"

Los Angeles Times

On the morning of December 7, isolationist America was at peace, desperately trying to stay out of the conflict. By the morning of December 8, internationalist America was at war and became forever an altered country.

From coast to coast and beyond, army and navy forces went on a "wartime footing."[1] That was just the beginning. "Censorship was established on all messages leaving the United States by cable and radio."[2] Christmas leaves were canceled for the military. Borders closed. Roadblocks erected. Armed guards posted everywhere. Blackouts ordered. Japanese nationals rounded up. All radio communication from and to Hawaii was suspended indefinitely.

The Coast Guard stepped up guarding, well, the coast. And governors were "asked" to call up the Home Guard.

America was about to formally enter its Second World War, and yet as of the 8th, no one was actually referring to the new conflagration as such. "Tonight the war becomes a World War in grim earnest," opined the *Los Angeles Times*.[3] The *Sun* of Baltimore got closer, writing, "Japan's declaration . . . puts the United States into this second and most terrible war of the nations."[4]

In the moments after the Japanese attack on Pearl Harbor, some Americans, mindful of the Orson Welles's nationally broadcast ruse of 1938, when he turned H. G. Wells's book *War of the Worlds* into a seemingly real-life invasion by Martians, thought this was another hoax. "That was the reaction of civilians and military men alike as the news of Japan's attack . . . became public. It was a study in human refusal to believe harsh truth."[5]

On the front page of the *Los Angeles Times* on the morning of December 8 was a box notice from Brigadier Gen. William O. Ryan, commander of the Fourth Interceptor Command. "Air Guards Attention! To chief observers: All observation posts: A.W.S. (Aircraft Warning System). You are directed to activate your observation posts immediately and to see that the post is fully manned at all times."[6] The West Coast of the United States was over 2,500 miles from Hawaii and thousands more from Japan, but with so little hard information coming out of the Pacific, the military wasn't leaving anything to chance. On the morning of December 7, the American military was asleep, rhetorically and behaviorally. Twenty-four hours later, everybody was at or headed for their battle stations.

Initial news reports of the massive and unprovoked attacks by the Japanese throughout the Pacific were all over the place, and many news stories, short on accuracy or facts, were full of speculation, half-truths, and outright guesses. Others only scratched the surface. An observer said publicly it was nuts to have lined up airplanes wingtip to wingtip. But then criticism of the U.S. Army stopped.[7]

One thing *was* for sure, though: the Japanese had been planning and practicing precision bombing for months, the evidence being the carnage they'd inflicted all over the Pacific and especially Pearl Harbor. They knew their targets cold. In those few Japanese planes shot down in Hawaii was detailed information on the location of the various ships, armaments, crew complements, and other important specifics.[8] "The Japanese radio reported that Nipponese warships had surrounded Guam and said all big buildings on the island were ablaze."[9] It also claimed the Pan Am Airways base on the island had been destroyed, its gasoline stores aflame.[10]

"Japanese bombers, following up earlier successes in the two-day Battle of the Pacific, raided Manila in the darkness of night, dispatches from the Philippine Capital disclosed this afternoon. The heavy attack opened shortly after midnight Tuesday, Manila time (11:00 a.m., Washington time). Dispatches telling of the raid followed acknowledgment earlier in the day at the White House that the Japanese raid on Pearl Harbor yesterday had resulted in the sinking of 'one old battleship' and serious damage to other war craft. There were casualties of 3,000 on the Island of Oahu, the White House said, and nearly half are dead."[11]

This story in the December 8 afternoon edition of the *Evening Star* in Washington did not even touch on the real story of the bloodbath wreaked by the empire of Japan; at Pearl Harbor, Hickam Field, Ford Island, various other locations on the island of Oahu, and a half-dozen additional strategic locations in the Pacific. Hickam had cost $22 million to build.[12] Although, the report did near accuracy in saying, "Blood was spilled heavily in a war which Tokyo did not declare until three hours after Japanese raiders struck soon after dawn yesterday."[13] General Tojo went on the radio and blamed the Americans for provoking the Japanese into attacking the Americans. Audaciously, he said, "Japan has done her utmost to prevent this war."[14]

Fully twenty-four hours after the attack, White House press aide Stephen Early understatedly told reporters, "The damage caused to our forces in Oahu in yesterday's attack appears more serious than at first believed."[15] Early was the first White House official called by FDR,[16] after the president had been told by Secretary of the Navy Frank Knox of the attack at 1:40 p.m.[17] Eleanor Roosevelt had been hosting a private luncheon, and FDR was in his Oval Study having lunch with friend and confidant Harry Hopkins,[18] who was living for a time in the private residence of the White House along with his motherless daughter.[19] Hopkins doubted the initial report. FDR did not.[20] The appalling message via radio to Knox from Rear Adm. Patrick Bellinger was: "Air Raid Pearl Harbor. This is no drill."[21]

Along about the same time, Ed Chlapowski, in the navy only a year, stationed at Pearl Harbor, also sent a message: "This is no drill. Pearl Harbor is being attacked by the Japanese. This is no drill."[22]

Congress had passed a law in 1798 that was later amended and called the Espionage Act of 1918. "All information relative to strength, location, designation, composition and movement of United States troops or Army transports outside the continental limits of the United States are designated by the War Department as secret and will be so considered under the law."[23] The U.S. government announced that violations of the Espionage Act carried the death penalty.[24]

The War Department issued an order to all three military branches to institute strict censorship in the Canal Zone and Hawaii, as well as the Southern Pacific coastal region covering Southern California.[25] Additionally, all outgoing mail and other communication by men in uniform would be heavily checked so as not to reveal any sensitive information to people outside the military. The American media were asked "to cooperate in observing the restrictions against publication of secret information."[26]

Roads were cleared in California by the state police to allow antiaircraft guns to get to their destinations. On the West Coast, "special patrols [were] set up in Japanese sections." The military police were ordered to "arrest all persons 'previously designated' as suspicious characters."[27] The president's personal bodyguard, Tom Qualters, tracked down and found the Japanese correspondents for Domei and took away their White House Correspondents' Association press passes.[28]

Another order was issued from the government ordering all companies engaged in manufacturing munitions to go on a twenty-four-hour production schedule.[29] Round-the-clock armed military guards were posted all over government and war manufacturing facilities. In Washington, police leaves and vacations were canceled.[30]

America was at war with Japan, although a formal declaration had not yet been offered to Congress by the president of the United States, who was scheduled to address the members at precisely 12:30 eastern standard time at their invitation.[31] The president had not formally told Congress he would ask for such, but few doubted he would and some speculated that a declaration should also be made against Italy and the Third Reich.

Roosevelt awoke at first light, "examined latest war dispatches, conferred with military and naval leaders, completed his draft of the message to Congress . . . conferred with Mayor La Guardia on civilian defense on the Pacific Coast."[32] FDR, as a political payoff, had appointed Fiorello La Guardia as head of Washington's Office of Civilian Defense.[33]

Winston Churchill beat FDR to the punch; the British government declared war on Japan several hours before America did, as they too had been underhandedly attacked. Churchill and Roosevelt had spoken by transatlantic phone Sunday night. The next morning the prime minister went before Parliament, war was declared, and by 7:00 a.m. Washington time, "a note was handed to the Japanese Charge d' Affaires . . . [in London] 'stating that in view of Japan's wanton acts of unprovoked aggression the British government informed . . . that a state of war existed between the two countries.'"[34] The prime minister had pledged to declare war on Japan "within the hour" if the empire attacked the United States, and he was off by only a few.[35]

Costa Rica and the Netherlands Indies also declared war on Japan before the United States. In Costa Rica, the government began arresting Japanese workers laboring in cotton and rice fields and "seized on suspicion of espionage" a Japanese fishing boat.[36] China also declared war on Japan but threw in Italy and Germany for good measure.[37] Australia also declared war on Japan before the United States did.[38] Nicaragua's president general Anastasio Somoza announced his country would also declare hostilities on Japan.[39] Canada threw in with America's lot.[40] Local Number 1,442 of the United Brotherhood of Carpenters, located in Chattanooga, Tennessee, issued a statement that they too were declaring war on Japan.[41] The secretary of the union, Roy E. Hayes, said, "With the power vested in my office . . . a state of war does exist between this union, 1,442, and the present Japanese government."[42]

Because of the news blackout clamped on Hawaii, the extent of the devastation was still not generally known, nor did anyone know where the Japanese might strike next; this only added to the surreal sense and abject fear. Nothing was getting out of the Pacific by the afternoon of December 7. Some in America were openly speculating that the Japanese might capture one or more of the Hawaiian Islands, including the main island, which according to sources had no defenses whatsoever.

Twenty-four hours earlier, no one thought it possible that a massive Japanese convoy featuring six of their first line aircraft carriers could cross an ocean—stopping to be refueled along the way—traveling thousands of miles, undetected, to Hawaii. Now everybody was contemplating the prospect that Japan could and would strike the West Coast of the United States. The distance from Tokyo to Honolulu was 3,860 miles, but from Hawaii to San Francisco, it was only 2,397 miles.

Unsubstantiated stories and rumors were rampant, including that the Japanese had attempted to also invade British Borneo,[43] that the battleship *West Virginia* had been sunk, that the *Oklahoma* was ablaze and subsequently sunk, that a civilian ship, the *President Harrison*, had been seized by the Japanese while in Chinese waters, that a U.S. transport, the *General Hugh Scott*, had been sunk, and that another transport carrying lumber was sunk just a little over a thousand miles off San Francisco.[44] A different report said the Japanese were parachuting into Hawaii and that saboteurs were running amuck there.[45]

Roosevelt received yet another memo from the ubiquitous John Franklin Carter clearly generated several days before the attack; it went into great detail about the racial composition on Hawaii, the number of Japanese, and where their loyalties lay. "There will be, undoubtedly, planted Japanese and agents who are there for the purpose of sabotage. The danger of espionage is considerable. This is especially the case as many Navy wives are over-garrulous with regard to their husbands' departures and where they are going." A reference was made speculating about "the Japanese fleet appear[ing] off the Hawaiian Islands."[46]

The *Washington Post* reported that the attacking planes had been "land-and-sea-based" and that the planes had taken off from the Marshall and Caroline Islands, which had been turned over to the Japanese by the Germans at the conclusion of the last war.[47] The Associated Press also reported that four-engine bombers had been used in the attack, but this was no idle mistake.[48] If the Japanese already had long-range bombing capabilities, they could—at least theoretically—reach the West Coast of the United States. The *Post*, going for the same three cents as every other paper in the country cost, had a banner at the top of the fold that said, "Keep It Flying! The *Post*'s suggestion: Let the Stars and Stripes fly from every building in Washington today, the symbol of America united!"[49]

Additional stories reported that the U.S. military had downed "many Jap planes" in the battle over Hawaii.[50] Others said the Japanese had parachuted into Manila and they'd used mustard gas in their invasion of Malaya.[51] Hundreds of rumors went out over the airwaves, including one that said Germany had participated in the attack on Hawaii.[52] Another said on NBC radio out of Manila that "Germany soon will follow Japan in a declaration of war on the United States."[53]

The Japanese also claimed they had sunk an American carrier off the mouth of Pearl Harbor with one of their submarines and that they had captured dozens of commercial vessels. Some disinformation was coming directly from the White House, as Press Secretary Stephen Early reported that American forces had destroyed "a number of Japanese planes and submarines."[54] Another rumor was the U.S. government would hold the Japanese diplomats Kichisaburo Nomura and Saburo Kurusu in effect hostage until the government was assured that Ambassador Joseph Grew and his staff were safely out of Japan.[55]

An AP story erroneously reported, "At sea the United States Fleet apparently had engaged the enemy. Destroyers steamed full speed from Pearl Harbor, and spectators reported seeing shell splashes in the ocean. Unconfirmed reports said the attacking planes came from two enemy aircraft carriers and probably these and other enemy ships were being fought by the American ships."[56] Yet another story said that as of December 8, "American operations against the Japanese attacking force in the neighborhood of the Hawaiian Islands are still continuing."[57] Also, errant wire stories claimed that British and American forces had sunk many Japanese ships,[58] and the *New York Times* erroneously reported that "four engine dive bombers" had been used at Pearl Harbor.[59] The paper furthermore mistakenly said that "four submarines were destroyed" by the U.S. Navy.[60]

The *Sun* reported "an oil tank there was seen blazing and smoking. An unconfirmed report said one ship in the harbor was on its side and four others burning. . . . In Washington, some hours later, the War Department gave the White House a preliminary estimate that 104 were dead and more than 300 wounded."[61]

Unconfirmed reports from Panama and London said a Japanese aircraft carrier operating off Hawaii had been "sunk by United States Navy ships." The word "unconfirmed" filled hundreds of out-of-breath news stories. However, one story on the AP wire, dateline Honolulu, was accurate. "Japanese bombers, striking lightning-like aerial blows from off the Pacific, brought death and destruction . . . to this mid-Pacific island fortress and vacation paradise. Scores of men in United States uniform, as well as civilians, died under the savage blows which shattered the Sabbath morning peace and spread the European war to the vast expanse of the Pacific Ocean."[62]

Thousands of concerned citizens gathered in front of the White House on December 7 and 8, quietly peering through the wrought iron fence. Pennsylvania Avenue was jammed with cars until the police closed it. The sidewalk in front of the White House was also closed, so the curious gathered along West Executive Avenue. Thousands more were on Capitol Hill as the members, the Supreme Court justices, the guests, and the president of the United States made their way there. There was a real fear of a Japanese terrorist attack in Washington. "Her undercover agents, a suicide squad, might . . . arrange a surprise here."[63]

Berlin and Rome were surprisingly cautious in their public statements, not immediately rallying to the cause of their Axis ally, Japan. But a radio report in Rome monitored by CBS said that the two Axis powers were indeed at war with the Allies because of the actions of the Japanese.[64] But who knew? Disinformation was more plentiful than information, and the Japanese were filling the airwaves with claims both true and false. "Japanese headquarters said the United States aircraft carrier sunk was the victim of a submarine off Honolulu and that many merchant ships had been captured in the Pacific."[65]

There still had been no mention of the exact extent of the damage in Hawaii, and as far as anyone in the United States was concerned, the *Arizona* had come through unharmed.

In Tokyo, some forty-five American diplomats, led by the estimable Joseph Grew, were stranded in the middle of a war in the middle of a hostile power.[66] Grew had been ambassador to Japan since 1932, with a long career serving both Republican and Democratic presidents, including Wilson and Coolidge.

The Japanese had maintained fifteen consulates in America and the territories, including San Francisco, New York, Mobile, Seattle, Philadelphia, New Orleans, Galveston, Portland, and Pearl Harbor. All these localities had significant naval bases or manufacturing facilities, not so coincidentally. At some, including the one in New Orleans, crowds gathered to boo and hiss the Japanese until local police dispersed them.[67]

On the West Side of New York City, a Japanese national was severely beaten by some street toughs, who screamed, "Why don't you go where you belong?" The Japanese man checked himself into a hotel with a fractured skull.[68] Stones were hurled through the plate-glass window of the Taijo Trading Company at 121 Fifth Avenue.[69]

The Japanese had attacked with lightning speed and precision, although their attempts so far to take Singapore were faring poorly; the British "cut to pieces" the invading Japanese troops while they waded through the surf.[70] Eventually, they took the strategically important area and, having planned ahead, dropped leaflets "announcing the seizure of the settlement but urged people to go about their business and remain calm."[71]

Another report said that American planes in Manila took to wing in search of Japanese targets.[72] Manila was no stranger to war. It was here in the harbor, in 1898, that Commodore George Dewey engaged the Spanish in the kick-off battle to the Spanish-American War. Since that war's conclusion, America had had a military presence there. Germany had not taken part in the Pacific attack, as some stories had it, but the Third Reich was taunting America via the airwaves.

FDR had his eye on the ball, though, as his White House claimed that Germany "pushed" the Japanese into the attacks in the Pacific.[73] Indeed, Japan radio issued a broadcast claiming Germany would join the war within twenty-four hours.[74] In fact, Berlin had wanted the Japanese to prosecute the war in China further, march across Asia, and eventually catch Moscow between the Axis forces. But Roosevelt knew that to win the new world war, America would have to engage the Germans and Italians eventually. Still, in his speech to Congress, he refrained from mentioning the other Axis powers. He only discussed Japan, even as Germany and Italian officials offered cooing words of support for Tokyo and called FDR a "shylock."[75] The spokesman for the Third Reich backed away from an actual military commitment to Japan, though.[76]

Because of the European war and Hitler's unrestricted warfare in the North Atlantic, FDR had already declared "an unlimited state of national emergency" on May 27, 1941.[77] Three weeks later, on June 16, the U.S. government ordered the eventual closing of all German consulates on U.S. soil.[78]

Time stopped in America at 12:30 eastern standard time on December 8 as everyone tuned in to listen to the president of the United States address a joint session of Congress with an elegantly simple five-hundred-word avowal.[79]

Street commerce stopped; traffic stopped. Many schools had already closed, some fearing Japanese attacks; the public schools in Oakland, California, shut down in response to a report that a Japanese carrier lay off San Francisco. The district attorney said he had closed the schools based on the recommendation of the Office of Civilian Defense in Washington.[80] Newspapers were already printing helpful stories on the various time zones of the east coast, the west coast, Hawaii, and Tokyo, along with an explanation of the International Dateline. When it was noon in Washington, Japan was fourteen hours ahead, but Honolulu was nineteen and a half hours behind Tokyo. And Honolulu was five and half hours behind Washington. All papers had the standard "Man on the Street" reactions to the attack, but women were interviewed as well. That day the Honolulu Star-Bulletin printed three "Extra!" editions—all told 250,000 newspapers. With the radios often shut off, residents were desperate for news.[81]

First thing Monday morning, Wall Street plunged except for commodities such as beef, wool, and steel, which climbed dramatically.[82] Then the traders stopped to listen to their president.[83] Congress opened at 12:00 noon with a prayer, offered by the Senate chaplain, the Reverend ZeBarney T. Phillips, asking for national unison.[84]

A now former isolationist, GOP congressman Joseph Martin said of the new unity, "There is no politics here. There is only one party when it comes to the integrity and honor of this country."[85] FDR's remarks would be broadcast live on NBC, CBS, and Mutual Radio.[86]

"Promptly at noon the big glass doors at the White House swung open, six limousines drew up, and President Roosevelt came out."[87] He was walking, using the painful leg braces, but did not speak. "The car, bearing the White House insignia, started at once for the Capitol." In the other cars were "Mrs. Roosevelt, Mrs. Dorothy Brady, Mrs. Stephen Early, Grace Tully . . . General Edward M. Watson and Captain John Beardahl, the President's military and naval aides."[88]

FDR was attired in the familiar dark blue cape.

Silent crowds encircled the White House, watching the procession, with little doubt as to what their president was going to ask of their Congress. Telegrams of support and shock had already flooded the White House. "The messages came from Governors, Mayors, religious leaders, heads of civic movements, newspaper editors and radio broadcasters, many offering their personal services."[89]

A resolution offered at noon for a joint session of Congress was quickly approved.[90] The galleries were packed, and crowds outside were kept two blocks away from the Capitol. Police even checked those favored with a pass every few feet. The Diplomatic Corps began to file in, except the Chinese ambassador, Hu Shih, who was detained briefly by a guard, until a senator interceded.[91] Seated together were Gen. George C. Marshall, Adm. Harold Stark, and Maj. Gen. Thomas Holcomb, commandant of the Marine Corps.

The president departed the White House at 12:10,[92] still tinkering with his remarks on the way to the House chamber where he was about to speak to a solemn, angry but resolute audience. In his car, he "sat back in the deep cushions . . . adjusted his big dark Navy cape."[93]

The running boards on Roosevelt's car were draped with Secret Service agents, three on each side, and four were inside the car. "The men in the" limousine "held sawed-off riot guns. Those outside carried .38-caliber service revolvers."[94]

Soldiers guarded each doorway in the Capitol and credentials were demanded while FDR waited in the Speaker's office. The Senate marched into the House Chamber. Then the Supreme Court came. A committee, chosen by the Speaker, then escorted the president to the rostrum. They were John McCormack, the House majority leader; Joseph W. Martin, House minority leader; Robert Doughton, chairman of the House Ways and Means Committee; Alben Barkley, Senate majority leader; Charles McNary, Senate minority leader; and Senator Carter Glass of Virginia. The same man, Garrett Whiteside, a House clerk in 1917 and now a Senate clerk in 1941, who had delivered the 1917 document to President Wilson, this time typed the address for President Roosevelt.[95]

"When all are seated, the speaker announces the President of the United States. Cheers, applause, more cheers, and Franklin D. Roosevelt, with a tired and worn face, is ascending the ramp which is always provided for him. When the president took the stand, every man, woman and child, every Republican, isolationist (on Saturday), Roosevelt-haters and Democrats stood as united Americans and cheered for their president." Some in attendance discovered to their embarrassment they were crying, until they saw others around them crying as well.[96]

FDR was accompanied by his eldest son, James, to the rostrum. James, a captain in the Marine Corps, was in his blue dress uniform. "The President stood erect, his head held high. He spoke in clear, measured words to a chamber in which there was not even the sound of a deep drawn breath or the rustle of a woman's skirt."[97] He "gripped the reading clerk's stand, flipped open his black, loose-leaf schoolboy's notebook."[98]

The floor was crammed with senators and congressmen and other dignitaries as they had rushed back to Washington beginning the afternoon before, as soon as they heard about the attacks. Reporters caught up with Senator Harry Truman in St. Louis, just as he was about to board a flight for Washington the day before. "It's for the welfare of the country that we must declare war and put Japan in its place," he said. Wendell Willkie, the 1940 GOP nominee, who had attacked FDR, accusing him of wanting to send American boys into the European war, now said, "I have not the slightest doubt as to what a united America should and will do."[99]

The galleries, which could only hold five hundred people, were filled to capacity, but not with the general public, as the Capitol had been closed off to private citizens;[100] they were gathered outside on the lawn of the Capitol.

Instead, only VIPs and those receiving permission and a special pass could be there to see history unfold.

The rotunda had been closed and barriers and cable ran everywhere on Capitol Hill, cordoning off the tourists and merely curious. The crowd on Capitol Hill was larger than eleven months earlier when FDR had been inaugurated for a third time, and many had been waiting since early in the morning to see him arrive. As many as five hundred District cops and the Secret Service were crawling everywhere.[101] Seated in the gallery next to Eleanor Roosevelt, who was in a black dress that gathered at the neck and wearing her favorite silver fox furs, was Edith Wilson, the widow of Woodrow Wilson, in a maroon dress, matching hat, and white gloves.[102] Their fashions were duly noted by society writers.

Twenty-four years earlier, on April 2, 1917, Edith Wilson had sat in the House chamber, listening to then-President Wilson solicit Congress in a long speech for a declaration of war on Germany.

Seated behind Mrs. Wilson was Mrs. Hull. Also in attendance were Harry Hopkins, the cabinet, and the Diplomatic Corps, excluding the Japanese envoys. The audience rose as the cabinet and members of the Senate filed in. "The atmosphere of the Capitol was grave, but for the first time in years there were no doubts."[103]

The chaplain, Phillips, opened with a short prayer.

Since 1932, "There was in the United States a tradition of silence about the physical affliction of President Roosevelt, an implication that it would be tasteless ever to mention the misfortune that galvanized his energies, transformed his personality and therefore the subsequent history of the United States."[104] The newsreel cameras and the attending journalists never recorded that FDR had been wheeled to a side door leading to the House of Representatives, given a chance to lock in his leg braces, and then stood before the Congress of the United States, the citizens of America, and the struggling peoples of the world.

"With infinite slowness, limping from side to side, Roosevelt came up the ramp to the dais, one arm locked in his son's, the other hand feeling every inch of the long sloping rail." At the dais, he fiddled with his glasses and opened the binder of the short speech that would change the world.[105]

Then Speaker Sam Rayburn simply announced, "The President of the United States!"[106]

After a pause, Congress stood and cheered wildly and long, as FDR stood before them."They cheered him again and again. Every space was filled, every doorway jammed. People were standing packed into the corners of the House floor, in tiers, one row behind another, as at a parade. They were standing on chairs, on sofas, on the narrow ledge of the panels of the wall itself."[107] The ovation was unlike any the old building had ever heard before.

FDR asked for an American declaration of war against the empire of Japan. The room was deadly quiet as he began in a grim tone. His speech was broadcast live on every imaginable radio network, filmed and photographed by every imaginable news agency. His voice was sonorous, the cadence and pitch, perfect:

Yesterday, December 7, 1941—a date which will live in infamy—the United States of America was suddenly and deliberately attacked by naval and air forces of the Empire of Japan.

The United States was at peace with that nation and, at the solicitation of Japan, was still in conversation with its government and its Emperor looking toward the maintenance of peace in the Pacific. Indeed, one hour after Japanese air squadrons had commenced bombing in the American island of Oahu, the Japanese Ambassador to the United States and his colleague delivered to our Secretary of State a formal reply to a recent American message. And while this reply stated that it seemed useless to continue the existing diplomatic negotiations, it contained no threat or hint of war or of armed attack.

It will be recorded that the distance of Hawaii from Japan makes it obvious that the attack was deliberately planned many days or even weeks ago. During the intervening time the Japanese government has deliberately sought to deceive the United States by false statements and expressions of hope for continued peace.

The attack yesterday on the Hawaiian Islands has caused severe damage to American naval and military forces. I regret to tell you that very many American lives have been lost. In addition American ships have been reported torpedoed on the high seas between San Francisco and Honolulu.

Yesterday the Japanese Government also launched an attack against Malaya. Last night Japanese forces attacked Hong Kong. Last night Japanese forces attacked Guam. Last night Japanese forces attacked the Philippine Islands. Last night the Japanese attacked Wake Island. And this morning the Japanese attacked Midway Island.

Japan has, therefore, undertaken a surprise offensive extending throughout the Pacific area. The facts of yesterday and today speak for themselves. The people of the United States have already formed their opinions and well understand the implications to the very life and safety of our nation.

As Commander-in-Chief of the Army and Navy I have directed that all measures be taken for our defense. But always will our whole nation remember the character of the onslaught against us. No matter how long it may take us to overcome this premeditated invasion, the American people in their righteous might will win through to absolute victory.

I believe that I interpret the will of the Congress and of the people when I assert that we will not only defend ourselves to the uttermost but will make it very certain that this form of treachery shall never again endanger us.

Hostilities exist. There is no blinking at the fact that our people, our territory and our interests are in grave danger. With confidence in our armed forces—with the unbounding determination of our people—we will gain the inevitable triumph—so help us God.

I ask that the Congress declare that since the unprovoked and dastardly attack by Japan on Sunday, December seventh, 1941, a state of war has existed between the United States and the Japanese Empire.[108]

Roosevelt's six-and-one-half-minute address was interrupted several times with ovations and cheers and whistles and rebel yells from Congress and again, at the end, sustained applause was heard as he waved his hand to the members.

Roosevelt often wrote his own speeches, or at least provided substantial edits. The president's original manuscript of his address revealed the sheer power of words. He initially wrote December 7, 1941, would be a day that would live in "history," but he later crossed out that word, inserted a proof-reader's caret, and scribbled "infamy."[109] As Mark Twain once said, "The difference between the almost right word and the right word is really a large matter—'tis the difference between the lightning bug and the lightning."[110] In his speech to Congress on December 8, the president had captured lightning in a bottle. Churchill, who had long lobbied for America's entry into the war, was jubilant. And the American media was breathless.

The United Press reported, "Democracy was proving its right to a place in the sun with a split second shiftover from peace to all-out war."[111] Journalist Louis M. Lyons of the *Boston Daily Globe* was on hand, one of the few privileged reporters allowed to sit in the eighty-six seats in the press gallery that five hundred other journalists were denied. Of the crowd in the House Chamber, Lyons wrote, "All rose in a mighty crash of supporting applause as he asked in one simple sentence that Congress declare a state of war exists between the United States and Japan."[112]

The war resolution (in language identical to 1917, with the exception of substituting Japan for Germany)[113] passed the Senate thirty-two minutes after FDR's speech to the joint session began and less than fifteen minutes after he concluded his impassioned remarks.[114] The refrain "Vote! Vote! Vote!" echoed throughout the chamber.[115] It passed the House twenty-two minutes after that.[116] The Senate vote was 82–0 for war with Japan. The House vote was 388–1 for war with Japan.[117] In 1917, Congress had debated for four days to go to war with Germany. This time, they did so in a little over forty minutes.[118]

There were still some in Congress now, who had been in Congress then, who had voted against war with Germany. Not this time. Even the most rabid isolationist, anti-Roosevelt Republican voted to go to war with Japan. Save one. The one dissenting vote was Jeannette Rankin from Montana. She had voted no once before, in 1917 when Congress was asked to vote on the Declaration of War. At that time she stood weakly, and said, "I want to stand by my country but I cannot vote for war." Then she broke out in tears.[119] This time there were no tears. But boos and hisses rained down on the silver-haired woman. A Democratic member could be heard saying sarcastically, "Sit down sister!"[120] Speaker Rayburn gaveled for the chamber to come to order.

Rankin had remained seated, along with Congressman Clare Hoffman, Republican of Michigan, while everyone else stood as the president entered the

House. Hoffman would later go on to become a vocal opponent of government-initiated fluoridation and polio immunization. Rankin was the daughter of a rancher, a Republican, a pacifist, a suffragette, and utterly principled. She'd first been elected in 1916 and in 1917 had voted against entry into the European war. In 1918, she lost a primary bid for the U.S. Senate. She kicked around for twenty years, working on social causes, until once again elected to the House in 1940. After her vote against war with Japan, she was essentially hounded out of office and did not bother to seek reelection in 1942. Following the vote, she told reporters, "As a woman I can't go to war and I refuse to send anyone else."[121]

Both houses of Congress adjourned almost immediately after passing the war resolution. Very little discussion had taken place in either body prior to the vote. Of the thirteen senators and forty-two representatives who missed the vote due to distance or illness, all declared they would have sided with FDR to go to war. Several rushed back, only to walk onto the floor as the voting had finished.[122]

At 4:10 eastern standard time that afternoon, Roosevelt signed the declaration of war against Japan at his desk in the Oval Office. In cursive he wrote, "Approved—Dec 8th 4:10 p.m. E.S.T. Franklin Roosevelt."[123] Also signing the Declaration of War, as stipulated by the Constitution, were the vice president and Senate president Henry Wallace, at 3:23; and Sam Rayburn, Speaker of the House, at 3:15.[124] Roosevelt was photographed surrounded by congressional leaders while he signed the document.

As the New York Times reported, "The United States went to war today as a great nation should—with simplicity, dignity, and unprecedented unity. The deep divisions which marked this country's entrance into the wars of 1776, 1812, 1861, 1898 and 1917 were absent. Overnight, partisan, personal and sectional differences were shelved."[125]

After the leaders departed, Roosevelt took an hour-long nap on the sofa in the Oval Office. "When he arose he checked reports again (still piled with bad news)."[126]

And then, everything changed in America.

All troops out on passes were immediately recalled to their posts. All leaves and furloughs were canceled and men ordered to return to their duty stations immediately. Military posts were closed to civilians. Nationwide, recruiting offices were flooded with applications for all three branches. "Young boys of 'teen age' and grizzled veterans of the last war—swamped Army, Navy and Marine recruiting stations here today, ready to give their lives if need be to whip Japanese. White and colored, the uneducated and professional men, joined together."[127]

The recruiting office of the navy in Washington usually had three applicants on an average morning, but this morning, two hundred young men showed up. The phones of recruiting offices across the country began ringing Sunday afternoon. The navy was accepting candidates from the ages of seventeen to fifty, the marines sixteen to thirty.[128] The first elected official to volunteer was Senator Albert "Happy" Chandler, Democrat of Kentucky, who was a veteran of the last war.[129] Recruiting offices also offered training for women in "first aid, diet and canteen ambulance corps."[130]

Boston Red Sox slugger Ted Williams had been classified 3-A, but his draft board in Minneapolis announced that he would shortly be reclassified as 1-A.[131] Every newspaper carried photos of young men gathering outside of recruiting offices. Women descended in droves onto defense training centers in New York, asking, "What can we do?" "You can wash dishes," answered a member of the American Women's Voluntary Services. Shortly, the contributions of American women would become more substantive. "A police instructor for women air-raid wardens opened his usual Monday morning meeting with the words, 'our subject for today is incendiary bombs.' His class was most attentive."[132]

While voting to declare war on Japan, Congress had also voted for supplemental funds for the war effort and a bill to "freeze" all currently enlisted men into the services "for the duration of the national emergency."[133]

After the bill signing, FDR met with the Soviet ambassador, Maxim Litvinoff; La Guardia; and the chairman of the Red Cross, Norman H. Davis.[134]

The mayor of San Francisco declared a state of emergency and ordered a halt to all strikes in his jurisdiction while calling for thousands of Civil Defense volunteers. The metropolis had an especially heavy concentration of Japanese citizens, and city fathers feared sabotage.[135] Big tuna fishing boats owned by Japanese in Monterey were ordered to stay at their berths or anchorage. The West Coast felt doubly vulnerable to sabotage and the possibility of a Japanese invasion. Blackouts were ordered up and down the coastline. A "Jap Boat" was spotted off Laguna Beach "flashing messages to the shore from that point." The local police issued an APB to find and apprehend the vessel.[136]

Government officials began to discuss the possibility of rationing commodities such as rubber, tin, and gasoline. The government also took out ads in newspapers, calling for blacksmiths, boat builders, machinists, boilermakers, and other skilled labor for work in the Panama Canal Zone. The pay was good, too, as much as $1.66 per hour.[137] Air-raid warden schools were opened in Rhode Island. Stevedores called off their strike in New London, Connecticut.[138] Harvard hosted a debate on its role in the war, "its role in a country at war," and what the war meant to Harvard. Dean Paul Buck foresaw no "radical change" for his school. More practically, Emerson College "suspended classes" and hosted a pro-American rally. "An American history exam was canceled while war in the Pacific made current history."[139]

Roosevelt immediately ordered the arrest of all Japanese "dangerous to the peace and security of the United States," said Attorney General Francis Biddle. At the time, ninety-three thousand Japanese had registered with the government as a result of the Alien Registration Law.[140]

The FBI was ordered to implement the arrests. Almost immediately, 738 Japanese aliens were picked up and the bureau had another 50,000 on their watch lists.[141] The government also began rounding up Japanese "in the jurisdiction of the Fourth Army, which takes in the west coast and Alaska, and the Hawaiian and Canal Zone departments."[142]

Those arrested were placed in "immigration detention centers" and from there would be turned over to the U.S. Army. The U.S. attorney in charge of the program announced his office would remain open twenty-four hours per day until further notice. They already had in custody 1,200 Germans and Italians locked up in facilities in Montana and North Dakota.[143]

In Baltimore, a municipal judge, William Coleman, was supposed to preside over a pro forma citizenship swearing in ceremony. But instead, he denied the thirty-four individuals of German, Italian, and Finnish origin their application to become U.S. citizens.[144] At the time, Japanese could not become American citizens. Over the objections of President Calvin Coolidge, Congress had passed the Asiatic Exclusion Act in 1924.[145]

A number of Japanese nationals were arrested in New York under the Enemy Alien Act and taken to Ellis Island for holding. Japanese newspapers were ordered closed.[146]

The secretary of the treasury, Henry Morgenthau, announced "the seizure of all Japanese banks and business in the United States," to be carried out by his agents.[147] He warned "that anyone hiding or destroying, or helping anybody else to hide or destroy, any of the Japanese property ordered seized would be risking ten years in prison."[148]

Morgenthau also ordered all communication with the empire of Japan banned as well as commerce under "Section 3 of the Trading with the Enemy Act."[149] The order covered all indirect commerce or communication as well. He also closed the borders of Mexico and Canada to all Japanese nationals and placed a ban on any financial transaction in America by "Japanese aliens." Those intercepted at the borders were detained and additional security was added.[150]

Additionally, Morgenthau ordered the impoundment of over $131 million in Japanese holdings in U.S. banks, and all exit visas out of the country were canceled for Japanese nationals. Customs officials were ordered to stop and detain any Japanese national from leaving the country. Morgenthau's order was complete, absolute, and harsh. "All general licenses, specific licenses and authorizations of whatever character are hereby revoked in so far as they authorize, directly or indirectly, any transaction by, on behalf of, or for the benefit of, or any national thereof." The order was not only aimed at preventing commerce with Japan; it also prevented the conduct of commerce by Japanese citizens in America or any territory controlled by the United States. The United States had $217 million in banks and holdings in Japan, and all assumed they would freeze those as well.[151] Morgenthau hinted that his actions might also apply to Germans and Italians.[152] It was unclear how the new edicts from Washington would affect second-generation Japanese Americans, known as "Nisei."[153]

One Japanese-American, grasping at straws, speculated that it might have been possible for the Germans to get hold of Japanese planes to carry out the attack. Another young Japanese man, a truck driver, said, "This is it. I guess I'll join the Army." He meant the American Army."[154]

Public facilities around the country immediately took on a "nation at war" cast. There was an increased military presence, and spontaneously, Americans began showing up at Red Cross stations to donate blood for the war effort. As men returned grimly to their bases, the *Los Angeles Times* noted, "There were no gay farewells in sharp contrast to the usual scene of men returning to duty."[155]

Brandishing M-1 rifles, the standard military issue, affixed with bayonets, armed marine, army, and navy guards stood at post around Washington's government buildings, including the Capitol, something that had not been seen since 1917 and before that, since 1865. They were under orders to be "strict." Carrying full field packs and wearing steel helmets, they were on guard twenty-four hours a day.[156]

The phrase *war footing* was injected into the lingo, while the word *theater* took on a whole new meaning. Rather than the local movie theater, now it was used in the context of "Pacific Theater" and "European Theater."

An increased police existence was noticeable in Washington, as were increased Secret Service agents, though not as noticeable. But in other cities and towns, the reality of men and women in all sorts of uniforms and others wearing officious badges and armbands took root. The civilian guard around the Boston Navy Yard was doubled and other precautions were taken, including increasing the boats patrolling the Inner Harbor and "guarding of the different Japanese business concerns in the city proper. Guard[s] posted at the Emperor Hirohito Club, Braddock Park, South End, headquarters for the greater Boston Japanese." Riot squads were also reconstituted in Boston, and an air-raid system was announced.[157]

The America First event scheduled for Boston Garden was scheduled for the coming Friday evening. Lindbergh was slated to speak, along with other leading isolationists. Mrs. Sohler Welch, head of the Boston office, sheepishly said, "If they do go through, I imagine the plans will have to be radically altered."[158] Other America Firsters came forward and issued statements of support for FDR, including Herbert Hoover, Gen. Robert Wood, and Alf Landon.[159] Senator Gerald Nye, however, accused the United States of "doing its utmost to provoke a quarrel with Japan" and said that America was being led around by the nose by Churchill and the British. He said the attack on Pearl Harbor was "just what Britain had planned for us. Britain has been getting this ready since 1938." Even knowing of the attack, Nye went forward with an America First speech in Pittsburgh.[160] An antiwar rally in Baltimore, sponsored by the Keep America Out of War Congress, featuring noted socialist Norman Thomas, was also slated to go forward.[161]

The Coast Guard issued a sweeping order preventing any ship from departing Boston Harbor, and all sailing permits were confiscated. The order affected several ships carrying war materiel under Lend-Lease. The FBI also ordered the Boston and Maine railroad not to sell any tickets to Japanese citizens, and conductors were instructed to notify the local police of any Japanese on board any train.[162]

In New York, ships in the harbor were put under extra guard, and police closed the Nippon Club. "Twelve Japanese who were there when the police came were escorted to their homes." The State Department ordered the halt of all ships departing from New York for foreign ports. "New York City policemen extended their visits to all Japanese restaurants in the five boroughs. They permitted diners to finish their meals, then escorted owners and their staffs to their homes. Various Japanese commercial units seemed to have had some official signal of what was to come. Many did not renew leases."[163] Government officials seized control of six Japanese banks based in New York.[164]

Adm. Adolphus Andrews, commander of the North Atlantic Coastal Frontier, was in charge of protecting New York Harbor, though he was not too concerned about an attack. Asked why, he replied nonchalantly, because "there is no Japanese Navy in the Atlantic."[165]

Those Japanese apprehended by FBI agents were told they were "prisoners of the Federal authorities" and then removed via paddy wagons and patrol cars after they were allowed to pack a suitcase. Upon arrival, their background records were checked and then they were "taken to the Barge Office at the Battery and to Ellis Island by ferry." Many "underwent extended questioning. Federal stenographers and clerks were called in to [record] the pedigrees of the prisoners. All the prisoners were treated with every courtesy, although they were well-guarded." Many of the Japanese nationals seized by the government hadn't been to their native country in years. "Some of the Japanese were crestfallen, some were smiling, but none offered resistance."[166]

Revisions to the Draft Act were being hurriedly contemplated as the quota for January was not big enough. The pool of eligible young men needed to be expanded, especially as the first solid casualty reports were slowly coming in from Hawaii. First Lt. Hans Christiansen, a marine aviator, of Woodland, California, age twenty-one, was killed. Sergeant James Guthrie of Republican Grove, Virginia, an Air Corps engineer, was killed. No age given. Private George G. Leslie of Arnold, Pennsylvania, age twenty, with the Army Air Corps, was killed. Dead American boys came from other small towns including Ravenna, Ohio; Janesville, Wisconsin; and Bloomfield, New Jersey.[167] The lists were swelling as bodies were still being recovered in Honolulu and elsewhere. Nearly all killed were little more than small-town boys; no one in America yet knew the full story of the thousands of deaths of military and civilian alike. The first Hawaiian casualty may have been a civilian, Bob Tyce, who owned a civilian airport on Oahu. He was seen attempting to "hot prop" the propeller of a plane, but was strafed from the air by a Japanese fighter.[168] The naval department put out a statement asking reporters to stop making inquiries about the status of military personnel. The department would only respond to the inquiries of families.[169]

Nor did Americans fully understand yet that the Japanese had practically declared war on America two hours after the attack on Pearl Harbor. Curiously, Tokyo instituted complete wartime blackout measures, but Washington did not do so immediately. Bridges and important points of transportation in Maryland and Virginia were put under guard. Air raid wardens prowled the streets of Washington, yet without proper identification papers some were stopped for questioning by the police as "suspicious characters."[170]

The America First Committee began to quickly melt away, as all now previous isolationists issued statements supporting the war and the president, and denouncing Japan. The group's inspirational leader, Charles Lindbergh, in Chicago—ground zero for the isolationist movement—issued a terse, (and some thought) ungracious statement. "We have been stepping closer to war for many months. Now it has come and we must meet it as united Americans regardless of our attitude in the past toward the policy our Government has followed. Whether or not that policy has been wise, our country has been attacked by force of arms and by force of arms we must retaliate. Our own defenses and our own military position have already been neglected too long. We must now turn every effort to building the greatest and most efficient Army, Navy and air force in the world." The famous aviator then took his family to Martha's Vineyard and went into seclusion, accepting neither telegrams nor phone calls.[171]

The National Committee of the Communist Party, headquartered in New York, also issued a statement supporting the United States.[172]

A Christmas charity drive for children sponsored by NBC, the *Star* newspaper, and the Warner Brothers Theaters was "suspended . . . because of the war."[173] The federal government and military installations went into lockdown mode, and only those carrying special passes could be admitted. National Airport went on a "wartime basis" as "special attention was being paid to anti-sabotage patrol."[174] Attention was also being paid to gas lines, water lines, and electrical plants to guard against sabotage. All across the country, war emergency committees and regional defense councils and the like were hurriedly organized.[175]

At 11:00 p.m. on December 7, a partial blackout was ordered for Washington, but it looked more like a "dim out" to officials. "Residents—at least some of them—did as they were requested and snapped off lights in their homes or pulled the shades down." But much of Washington was still brightly lit, from the great chandelier in the White House to the U.S. Capitol.[176]

Mrs. Roosevelt, in her weekly Sunday evening radio broadcast, had called on American women to "rise above their fears" and support their sons in the services and help support the morale of their families. "Many of you all over this country have boys in the services who will now be called upon to go into action. You cannot escape a clutch of fear at your heart and yet I hope that the certainty of what we have to meet will make you rise above these fears."[177]

The First Lady told her listeners that she too had a son in harm's way. "I have a boy at sea on a destroyer. For all I know he is on his way to the Pacific." Mistakenly, she also said that the president had been meeting with the Japanese diplomats at the very time Japan was attacking. In closing, she said, "To the young people of this nation I must speak tonight. You are going to have a great opportunity—there will be high moments in which your strength and your ability will be tested. I have faith in you! Just as though I were standing upon a rock, and that rock is my faith in my fellow citizens."[178]

General Motors declared it was putting all its plants on "full war status."[179] The United Brotherhoods of Welders, Cutters and Helpers—which had scheduled a nationwide strike for the following week—called it off.[180] The War Department issued orders to defense contractors that workers in those plants "be required to work as many additional hours as is necessary to get the day's work done. Additional overtime work and second and third shifts must be arranged. Our production must be put on a 24-hour-a-day basis."[181] The War Department also ordered all defense plants to take steps to ensure that sabotage did not befall them.

Soon, there would be plenty of work for all Americans. Pearl Harbor was the final nail in the coffin of the Great Depression; shortly, the problem wouldn't be creating enough work—it would be finding enough workers.

In Abilene, Texas, "the only Japanese soldier in the 45th Division was a prisoner in the Camp Barkeley stockade today. He is doing six months at hard labor for desertion. Headquarters said he refused to tell a court martial where he had been during two months absence."[182]

In Panama and Alaska, and at a military installment in Sacramento, blackouts were ordered. Antisubmarine netting was spread across the San Diego harbor.[183] Over one hundred Japanese civilians were picked up in the Canal Zone, in part because the canal was an inviting target for sabotage. The Japanese minister demanded their release, but it fell on deaf ears.[184]

The naval base at Puget Sound announced it would shoot down any plane flying overhead. All private aviation was canceled in the United States by the Civil Aeronautics Authority and licenses were suspended. Only commercial and military planes were allowed aloft.[185] Fishing boats in San Francisco harbor were ordered to stay at anchor, and the lights on the Golden Gate Bridge were turned off. On the Bay Bridge, cars were allowed to pass except those containing Japanese. These were stopped and questioned. The new water aqueduct in Los Angeles was put under guard. Cargo ships in Los Angeles, San Francisco, and other West Coast harbors were "bottled up."[186]

The downtown area of the city was clogged with traffic, but citizens were warned to stay at home. "Then came a reaction as truly American as apple pie." The word on the street was, "They started it—we'll finish it!"[187] Four thousand antiaircraft troops were deployed around the city, and the navy ordered a blackout of the harbors at Long Beach, San Pedro, and Wilmington. The city also ordered the darkening of street lights[188] and . . . airfield landing lights were turned off. "[There were] Black-outs, wild rumors of approaching aircraft."[189]

Reeves Field was closed around 11:30 a.m. on the seventh "as word of the attack on Honolulu was received. Gates to the field were closed, all leaves were canceled, all visitors were banned and those within the gates were subject to questioning before they were permitted to depart."[190]

A national call was issued for volunteer amateur radio operators and airplane spotters. The first request the government made of the ham radio operators was to switch off their crystal sets to clear the airwaves so Washington officials could better monitor enemy transmissions from inside the United States.[191]

The real story of the events in Washington, Tokyo, and the Pacific were only beginning to emerge by December 8 and would not be entirely unraveled for some time. In short, the Japanese military attacked unarmed civilians and unprepared and unaware military outposts without first declaring war. The time in Washington was 1:05 p.m.

Secretary of State Cordell Hull had been in conferences Sunday morning with Secretary of the Navy Frank Knox and Secretary of War Henry Stimson for three hours, beginning at 9:45 a.m. At 1:00 p.m., Japanese ambassador Nomura requested an immediate appointment with Hull.[192] The fourteenth part of the long message from Tokyo had arrived and it concluded, "The Japanese government regrets to have to notify hereby the American government that in view of the attitude of the American government it cannot but consider that it is impossible to reach an agreement through further negotiations."[193] It could be interpreted many ways, and only one as a declaration of war. Countries had broken off negotiations in the past, had withdrawn envoys, all without going to war.

The meeting was set for 1:45, but Nomura and fellow diplomat Kurusu were fifteen minutes late. They then cooled their heels in Hull's outer office for another fifteen minutes. The meeting started at 2:15 and lasted only ten minutes. The pair presented an ultimatum from their government.[194] Just before meeting with Nomura and Kurusu, Hull learned of the attack on Pearl Harbor in a startling phone conversation with the president.[195] The meeting, suffice it to say, was short and unpleasant. *Time* magazine said the statement they'd delivered was "an incredible farrago of self-justification and abuse."[196]

The Japanese envoys departed, photographed curiously smiling, while surrounded by dozens of scowling reporters and photographers,[197] though it was not clear the diplomats knew that their country had attacked America. These photos became infamous, further inflaming the already inflamed American populace. Most people didn't follow the diplomatic interplay between the two countries, the boycotts, the invasions, or the subtle and not so subtle military moves. Then came a declaration by the emperor of Japan, Hirohito, which was picked up, translated, and then broadcast by NBC radio. Surprising no one, Hirohito told his listeners, "We by the grace of Heaven, Emperor of Japan and seated on the throne of a line unbroken for ages eternal, enjoin upon thee, our loyal and brave subjects. We hereby declare war upon the United States of America and the British Empire."[198] From there, Hirohito made his case against America and England while crafting essentially a "pep talk" for the Japanese people. Servicemen—many of them sailors—teemed Times Square and other city gathering places where they read newspapers, some anxious to go to war with Japan. "'We can whip them in no time,' was a common remark sailors made."[199] Of course, none of these young men had ever been to war, nor did they realize the Japanese population had been making sacrifices since the invasion of Manchuria in 1931, and the Japanese troops were battle-hardened from that incursion as well as the invasion of China in 1937.

The Japanese had, by best estimates, somewhere between three and five thousand fighter planes and sixty-six divisions or 1.8 million men in uniform, not including the twenty divisions occupying Eastern China as well as others in Indochina, Formosa, and other locales. Also, "the Japanese fleet [was the] world's third largest," consisting of "eleven capital ships with [others] nearly ready; eight or nine aircraft carriers plus three carriers converted from merchantmen; forty-four to forty-six cruisers . . . about 126 destroyers and sixty-nine or seventy submarines, some of them large craft of long range probably now operating in the Eastern Pacific."[200] The Japanese had a hell of a fighting force and no one was going to "whip them in no time."

Most Americans could not find Pearl Harbor on a map before December 7, 1941. One congressman lamented that Pearl Harbor should have been put in the middle of the United States rather than the middle of the Pacific. The *Washington Post* made reference to "Bickam Field,"[201] while the *New York Times* called it "Hickman."[202] It was Hickam Field.

But Americans did understand fair play and playing by the rules. Fair play was ingrained in Americans, as was American Exceptionalism and Manifest Destiny. Editorials across the nation freely used the adjectives "sordid," "deceitful," "consummate duplicity," "perfidy," "treachery," "unscrupulous," and others far worse in describing Japan's actions.

All made it abundantly clear to their infuriated readers that Japan had declared war after attacking America. While most of the immediate information coming out of the White House was inaccurate, their initial estimate of the dead in Hawaii, three thousand, was fairly correct.[203] None of the names of the American ships hit by the Japanese were released by official sources.

Roosevelt—at least outwardly—took the crisis in stride. "Deadly calm" was how Eleanor Roosevelt described him. "He was completely calm. His reaction to any event was always to be calm. If it was something that was bad, he just became almost like an iceberg, and then there was never the slightest emotion that was allowed to show."[204] Secretary Morgenthau suggested more protection for FDR, but he balked. "You've doubled the [White House] guard," said the president. "That's all you need."[205]

Editorially, every paper in the country called for American victory and denounced the Japanese in the harshest and sometimes most personal terms. The *Los Angeles Times* called the Japanese a "mad dog . . . a gangster's parody." The *Philadelphia Inquirer* called them "war-mad." The *St. Louis Globe Democrat* accused Tokyo of "international rapine."[206]

A palpable rage against the Japanese was everywhere. "Let the Japanese Ambassador go back to his masters and tell them that the United States answers Japan's challenge with steel-throated cannon and a sharp sword of retribution. We shall repay this dastardly treachery with multiplied bombs from the air and heaviest and accurate shells from the sea." The author of this "bombastic" statement was seventy-four-year-old Tom Connally of Texas, a member of that deliberative body known as the United States Senate.[207]

American boys had grown up playing cowboy, and the rule was you didn't shoot anyone in the back, even an Indian. Boys did not sucker punch other boys. You gave your opponent a chance to defend himself. American girls had grown up learning good manners and the rules of life. Dirty play and breaking the rules was frowned upon. Chivalry and good manners reigned in American culture in 1941. Men held doors for ladies. Ladies acted like ladies. Men and women abided by the rules of courtship and life. It was the American way. Now, Americans were storming mad. "We'll mop them up," said one. Another said, "I've got a brother somewhere on the Pacific. . . . I just hope he gets three or four of those yellow rats." Yet another said, "Now we've got to go get those yellow rice eaters." Mrs. A.V. B. Gilbert of Clifton Road in Atlanta said, "The Japanese are despicable people." Barney Oakes, a salesman, said, "The Japs will find those were expensive warships they sank."[208] American public opinion was uniformly anti-Japanese, to say the least, and some of it quite ugly.

The Japanese had not played by the rules. They had assaulted America without provocation, without declaring war. They had deceitfully attacked America on a Sunday, and in 1941, America was for all intents and purposes a Christian country.

The lead editorial of the *Los Angeles Times* pulled no punches. "Japan has asked for it. Now she is going to get it."[209]

CHAPTER 9

THE NINTH OF DECEMBER

"New York Has Two Air Raid Alarms;
Planes Reported Near"

Birmingham News

"Frisco Drives Off Japanese Raiders"

Boston Globe

"Pacific Battle Widens; Manila Area Bombed"

New York Times

"More Planes Off Frisco, New Raid Alarm Sounded"

Sun

T wo days after the attack on Pearl Harbor, America was in a panic. A war that had been oceans away now appeared to be on the country's doorstep. News stories raced across the United States of more imminent assaults, including on New York.

"The great metropolitan area of New York City was put on an air-raid alert twice within an hour shortly after noon Tuesday amid varying unconfirmed reports of an imminent attack by hostile planes," ran the Associated Press wire. "The vast stretch of Long Island from the city to Montauk Point also braced itself for the reported possible attack. A million schoolchildren in New York and thousands on Long Island were sent home. Army planes took to the air after the first alarm was sounded. . . . We have information that a squadron of planes is headed toward Long Island. Make all necessary preparations, if identified as enemy planes," heard police patrolmen on their car radios.[1]

No one seemed to know where the reports of the unidentified planes came from. Citizens were confused, not knowing what the sirens were for, and others claimed they didn't hear the sirens. But this did not stop city fathers from going into a full-fright lockdown. Many New Yorkers, however, took it in stride, ignoring the air-raid sirens, going about their business. In Times Square, people took a decidedly "so what?" attitude. It was much the same in Brooklyn, Queens, and Harlem.[2]

A policeman boarded a bus full of passengers and told them they had to get off and take shelter, but no one moved. Stymied, he said, "What was I to do? Use my gun on them?" A pretzel vendor got into an argument with another police officer who ordered him off the street, but the vendor, with hot wares to sell, won the argument, not budging.[3] "Spotters" were searching in the sky, armed with field glasses, looking in vain for enemy fighters. Cops tried to get people off the streets and into shelters, while civil defense volunteers tried to get customers in department stores and restaurants to lie down on the floor.[4] "In at least one fashionable East River apartment, women volunteer wardens . . . ran through the building, breaking up early bridge games and rousing late sleepers; soon the halls were filled with women in dressing gowns, with cold cream on their faces."[5]

Military planes at Mitchell Field took off, searching for enemy planes. Radio beams that planes "rode" into airports were shut off. The *New York Times* said planes were guarding the city for "air raids," antiaircraft guns had been deployed, and the police and fire departments were trying to figure out how to efficiently notify the eight hundred schools in the area.[6] The paper also published a special feature, "What to Do in an Air Raid."[7] New York City did not have air-raid sirens in any of the five boroughs, so a Rube Goldberg operation involving the sirens on police squad cars and fire engines, in concert, was employed.[8]

Unsubstantiated rumors continued to wash all over America. A story opened in the *Los Angeles Times*, "As battle comes close to the Pacific

Coast . . ."[9] Boston also went on the alert, thinking it too was under imminent attack. The "approach of enemy planes" was heard broadcast over the radio. "New Englanders suddenly were confronted with the possibility that the war was about to burst on them with terrible realism."[10] Sirens in Beantown wailed for over an hour.

Civilians were barred from the Boston Navy Yard. Area schools were closed and children sent home. The Coast Guard "canceled all liberty" on reports that enemy planes were headed for Boston.[11]

In New York, guardsmen stepped up their patrol of the harbor and were on the lookout for "incendiary" bombs.[12] The docks were covered with armaments and one well-placed bomb could send the whole thing up. Fourteen thousand workers at the Bethlehem Steel Company at the Quincy, Massachusetts, shipyard were sent home. Antiaircraft guns were deployed along the New England coastline.[13] Teachers in the Boston schools were reported crying. "Conditions of near-panic were reported in several places . . . [amid] wild rumors that the Japanese were in New York, among other rumors."[14] Cars, headed for Boston, were halted in Cambridge.[15]

The head of the Bay State's Committee on Public Safety, J. Wells Farley, said, "Remember—panic is the worst danger."[16]

On the other side of the country, in San Francisco, a woman, Marie Sayre, was shot and wounded by a member of the Home Guard when her husband failed to stop their car as ordered as he approached the Golden Gate Bridge.

In newspapers across the land, it was reported that there were "unidentified planes" over San Francisco; the planes were never identified, nor did they take any hostile actions. When the army claimed that thirty planes had flown over the "west coast sector," consequently an air-raid signal was sounded and the civilian population went into hiding.

Searchlights lit up the sky as the air raids sounded at 2:39 a.m., adding to the sense of panic.[17] The whole thing earned screaming headlines in American newspapers even though there was no real evidence that the planes were, in fact, the enemy. Gen. William Ryan claimed they had been turned back at the Golden Gate Bridge. Still, he did not know to whom the planes belonged. "They weren't Army planes, they weren't Navy planes, and you can be sure they weren't civilian planes."[18] No one could account for the mystery aircraft that mysteriously vanished southward.

Also on the West Coast was a persistent rumor of an enemy aircraft carrier nearby. General Ryan maintained that enemy ships had been "detected . . . about 100 miles at sea."[19] Then it was reported over the radio that the military was searching for "two or three Japanese aircraft carriers and some submarines reported operating off the coast." Some supposedly saw fifteen planes flying south toward San Jose. "The lights went off in Oakland and most of her sister cities . . . and there were strange reports of planes being heard overhead but no confirmation."[20]

Military planes were sent aloft in wild goose chases looking for phantom ships and planes, but none were found. Stories also circulated that Japanese attacks on the Aleutian Islands and Canada were imminent.[21] Alaska was on full alert status.[22] Rumors begat fresh rumors. In this case, it was that the Japanese carriers in California waters were there to try to "panic" Washington "into calling [the] fleet back home,"[23] presumably to join in the search for the phantom ships and phantom planes. The country was utterly convinced that the Japanese were on the brink of attacking and possibly invading the West Coast of America, or were plotting to engage in a harassing naval action, much as the Germans had been doing in the North Atlantic for nearly a year.

Cities including San Francisco were completely blacked out at night, and many imposed curfews. In Seattle, a mob took to the streets and smashed the windows of store owners who were not complying with the blackout orders. "The crowd, urged on by shouting women," totaling one thousand people, broke the windows of some thirty shops and stores that had left some lights on.[24] Many radio stations, including those in Seattle, were ordered to stop broadcasting after 7:00 p.m., except those used to transmit official business to the worried citizenry.[25] Blackouts were ordered in nearly every city on the West Coast, along with the U.S. capital on the East Coast. In Washington, "Autoists should use only their dim lights and drive slowly, spotlighting of bridges and public buildings must cease, all theater marquees must be turned out, all show windows must be darkened and outside advertising put out, street lights will be dimmed, although traffic lights will stay on; citizens must pull their window shades down."[26]

In Manila, a radio correspondent had to debunk a rumor that American planes had bombed the Japanese cities of Tokyo, Kobe, and the island of

Formosa, which was in Japanese hands. This was after CBS had reported that the bombing had taken place.[27] Another rumor was "Japanese planes were reported off Panama."[28] Military officials in Boston later claimed the air-raid alarm was just a "dress rehearsal" and there had been no approach of planes.[29] The civilian government had not been let in on the army plan, which had made the announcement. It was the same in New York. The "air raid" was a hoax concocted by the military.[30]

Another rumor making the rounds—fifth-hand—was that the Japanese had told Adolf Hitler six days earlier that they were planning to attack.[31] Another was that Germany was getting ready to declare war on the United States, and Berlin chortled that the United States was now facing a "two-front war." Another tale was that Christmas leave was still on, on schedule and as planned, for the military.[32]

The initial reports that Japanese troops had parachuted into Hawaii were now largely dismissed. More likely, it now seemed, observers saw the parachutes of Japanese pilots who had bailed out of their planes due to antiaircraft fire.

It was also whispered in Walter Winchell's column that Charles Lindbergh and Anne Morrow Lindbergh were contemplating a divorce, as she'd become fed up with his politics and his ego. The worm was turning for the once-unassailable aviator hero who had crossed the Atlantic. Winchell was enormously influential, and he both shaped and reflected public opinion. His trademark staccato voice on the radio riveted listeners throughout the nation. A supporter of FDR who morphed into a red-baiting reactionary after the war, Winchell was a feared and fearless reporter who could make or break careers. His reportage was a mix of politics, opinion, hokum, sensationalism, and celebrity dirt.

Forty-eight hours after the attack, Washington would neither openly confirm nor deny the details of the assault.

The Japanese claimed they'd sunk the *Oklahoma* and the *West Virginia*,[33] while other rumors said the *Pennsylvania*, another battleship, had been sunk. Then the Japanese upped the ante, saying they had destroyed eleven ships including "four battleships, an aircraft carrier and six cruisers . . . more than 100 American airplanes." The White House stuck to their story of only a couple of ships being badly damaged and some planes being "put out of commission," although the number of dead had been upped to 1,500.[34] "Just what the condition of the United States Pacific fleet is at the present time has not been revealed by Washington." FDR, however, did make a reference to "severe damage" in a press conference.[35]

About the only thing the White House would say about Pearl Harbor was that an old battleship had capsized and a destroyer was lost, along with some smaller ships. They did concede the damage "appears more serious than at first believed."[36]

Stephen Early announced that FDR would take to the airwaves on December 9 at 10:00 p.m. (EST) to lay out a "more complete documentation" of the events in Hawaii the previous Sunday. Roosevelt was scheduled to speak for a half hour, and it would be carried live on all networks nationwide.[37] His day on the ninth was occupied with reviewing reports and meeting with the military brass.

During the day on the ninth, the president held a press conference in which he "outlined in general terms a broad program for intensification of military production efforts." He also discussed the attacks in general, but did not address any specifics, begging off until more information was forthcoming. He also bristled when the reasons for the attacks were brought up. According to one report, "Mr. Roosevelt resentfully remarked that neither he nor any member of Congress knew the reasons at present for the Japanese success in surprising the American defenders of Pearl Harbor. He was even more resentful when told that rumors were spreading that an important percentage of the Navy personnel in Pearl Harbor had been given week-end leaves." Reporters also pressed him on releasing war information.[38]

Within hours of the attack, hundreds of volunteer-staffed "Defense Centers" opened around the country. More popularly known as "canteens," they operated as a resting area for troops on their way to their posts.[39] Magazines and newspapers were available to peruse. Mostly women worked at these, serving coffee and doughnuts, giving out writing papers to the young G.I.s so they could write home. It was this way all over the country. In Atlanta, "hundreds of women of all ages, gray-haired grandmothers and young high school girls, swarmed into the American Women's Voluntary service headquarters."[40]

Meanwhile, the White House continued the drumbeat against Germany, claiming Berlin had "pushed" Tokyo into the attack as a way of cutting off Lend-Lease. FDR and Winston Churchill issued a joint statement saying the "Anti-Axis world" would prevail in the global conflict.[41] Churchill had just received word that ten RAF planes had been shot down over France, and renewed Nazi bombs rained down again on his war-torn island. German planes had also sunk four commercial ships off the coast of Scotland.[42]

Washington was confronting the very real prospect of having to foot the bill for a worldwide war. Since early 1941, the country had been subsidizing the British, the Russians, the Free Chinese, the Free French, the Turks, and other anti-Axis powers under Lend-Lease. But now, the newest price tags were coming in and estimates as high as $150 billion to pay for the whole war were floated. The cost of the final year of the "first World War" was approximately $18 billion, as reported in the *Birmingham News*. This may have been the first public reference to the Great War as the "first,"[43] the implication being, of course, that America had just entered the second.

The country was already paying for a new war and with heavy interest too. The first official casualty list from the Pacific was released from the War Department. The list of thirty-seven names included officers and enlisted men. The very first name released was Second Lieutenant Robert H. Markley. His nearest living kin was his father, Arthur H. Markley, of Nardin, Oklahoma. The first enlisted man was "Private Robert G. Allen. Nearest relative, Mrs. Sarah T. Allen, mother, Sims, Ind."[44] Ages were not given. They were all men, and nearly all came from the small towns and villages of America. Another casualty was Private Dean Cebert of Galesburg, Illinois. Also lost was a navy chaplain, Robert Carl Cornelius, of Buffalo, New York.[45] Of the thirty-seven initially announced dead, "six were commissioned officers, four of the Air Force and two of the infantry. All 31 enlisted men were of the Air Force."[46] The very same reporter for the Associated Press, Horace A. Lowe, who had the same sad job of reporting the initial casualties of the Great War, now reported on the new American losses.[47]

Condolences from the government to the next of kin began arriving in mailboxes throughout the United States. The letters were personally signed, long, individually typed. "The adjutant general of the Army, in each case, notified the next of kin of the deep regret of the Secretary of War at the death of this soldier in the defense of his country."[48] Only later, with so many young boys killed or missing in action, would Uncle Sam resort to Western Union telegrams, with hundreds of thousands of saddened parents and family members reading, "We deeply regret to inform you that your son . . ."

Elected officials also debated the duration and cost of the war, with some saying it could take up to six years. Senator Robert Taft said it might also cost the lives of 2 million young American boys. The Selective Service, with the permission of Congress, altered the draft laws to allow the military to keep in uniform all men for the duration of the war and for six months thereafter. No more two-year hitches.[49]

Everywhere, efforts to get Americans to purchase war bonds were stepped up. Eventually, the bonds would become a part of the fabric of the society, appearing in movies and newsreels, endorsed by Hollywood celebrities, sports heroes, and other noteworthy Americans. Appeals screamed from posters on every bus and lamp post, in the lobbies of movie theaters, and from magazines and newspapers and on the radio. The U.S. Treasury pleaded with Americans to buy more defense bonds and stamps. "War needs money. It will cost money to defeat Japan. Buy defense bonds or stamps today. Buy them every day if you can."[50]

Everybody, it seemed, wanted to pitch in for the war effort. In Texas, the senior class at Baird High School decided to forgo a planned class picnic and use the $37.50 instead to purchase bonds.[51] In New York, the Society of Composers, Authors and Publishers made an appeal to its membership to come up with patriotic songs of the kind heard during the Great War.[52] The government also announced plans to recruit private pilots to form a civil air patrol.[53]

On the byways of America, it was impossible for a man in uniform to wait for more than a few minutes while hitchhiking, even though hitchhiking was prohibited by the military. Volunteers poured forth from American Legion halls and from Boy Scout troops. The navy asked women to come forward and knit socks, turtlenecks, and watch caps. Sewing needles at the ready, they turned out by the thousands.

In Birmingham alone, over 600 men showed up to volunteer for military service in just a few hours, but officials estimated that less than 150 would qualify, because many were too young or too old, had dependents, had infirmities, or did not qualify because of the results of the findings of "mental tests." Those under twenty-one would have to get parental approval before they could join. The navy's recruiting offices nationwide were open twenty-four hours a day, seven days a week. Meanwhile, "veterans of the first World War and Spanish-American War insisted that they weren't too old."[54]

Men were attempting to enlist in large numbers all over the country. Boston's recruiting offices were overrun with cheering young men, and a thousand showed up at the navy's Federal Building offices. It was the same with the marines, the army, and the Coast Guard. Many waited for hours in line, "laughing, joking, discussing each new war bulletin," while tickets for food were handed out and women, from the Boston Red Cross, supplied the young men with coffee and doughnuts.[55]

City boys, who had once turned their noses up at military service, were clamoring for the chance to serve. L.A. was officially put on a war footing, and ironically, the Lindbergh Beacon atop City Hall was turned off, though not because the aviator was associated with anti-Roosevelt policies, but because the light would be an easy target and signal for enemy planes.[56] In Syracuse, New York, Chapman W. Schanandoah, thirty-five, "an Onondaga Indian, whose tribe, as one of the Six Nations of the Iroquois Confederacy, opposed the Selective Service Act, was among the naval volunteers."[57]

Detroit Tigers star Hank Greenberg, an army reservist, was expecting to be called up, as was heavyweight champ Joe Louis. Indeed, a day later Greenberg announced, "I'm going back in. We are in trouble and there is only one thing to do—return to the service." In doing so, he would be giving up a reported annual salary of $50,000.[58] Greenberg was a class act. So too was Louis, who was honored by Count Basie and Paul Robeson with his own song, "King Joe."[59]

In London, thousands of young American men who had joined the RAF or the British army were champing at the bit to get out of the English military and join in the fight against the Japanese. "The American Embassy was besieged with inquiries from Americans eager to get back home and fight in an American uniform."[60]

Farmers were now urged by the Department of Agriculture to plant "fence-post to fencepost" in order to feed and clothe a hungry army and navy and much of a hungry world. A premium was also put on cotton. Because of lost tax revenue, the government asked merchants—focusing on Alabama—to notify officials of excessive sales of sugar to the makers of down-home adult beverages. Joe Rollins, head of the U.S. Alcohol Unit, "announced . . . a plan to obtain cooperation of merchants in reporting sugar sales to moonshiners."[61] Officials also worried about shortages of dairy products in America because so much butter, eggs, and milk were being shipped to England under Lend-Lease.[62]

The AFL and the CIO pledged to do their utmost to put a halt to all wildcat strikes during the emergency.[63] A walkout in lumber yards around San Diego was canceled. Even John L. Lewis, head of the United Mineworkers, a Roosevelt-basher and a Republican, offered his support to the war effort.[64] In Minneapolis, a dozen members of the Socialist Workers' Party were sentenced to sixteen months and one day in prison for advocating the overthrow of the U.S. government. They had promoted using violence in so doing.[65]

Some aggressive internationalists were arguing that the United States ought to go ahead and declare war on Germany and Italy. Syndicated columnist Dorothy Thompson penned, "We have got to dispose our common forces in a world war. Therefore, the only logical answer to Japan's declaration of war against us is to reply with a declaration of war against the Axis, for Japan's war is an Axis war."[66]

Indeed, buried in Henry Stimson's private papers donated to Yale University was a draft of a declaration of war against all three Axis powers and not just Japan.[67] Clearly, it had been hotly debated, but in the end, Roosevelt decided to declare war only on Japan, even as Winston Churchill had been nagging him about Europe and North Africa as well. FDR was being well served, however, by men like Cordell Hull and Stimson. He even got a fan telegram from an obscure New England newspaper publisher, William Loeb.[68] Another concluded his letter to Stimson saying, "V for Victory, and also for Veng[e]ance!"[69]

Henry Stimson had been secretary of war as a young man under

President William Howard Taft and again as an old man under President Franklin Delano Roosevelt. In between he'd been secretary of state under President Herbert Hoover. Handsome, distinguished, and mustachioed, Stimson had been a soldier and a statesman, serving both Republican and Democratic presidents. At one point, he'd even had a doctrine named after him. In 1936, he wrote a prophetically titled book, *The Far Eastern Crisis*.[70] He was born to wealth, attended Harvard and Yale, earned Phi Beta Kappa, and could have lived the leisurely life of Jay Gatsby but instead devoted his life to public service. His wife, Mabel, was the granddaughter of founding father Roger Sherman, but Stimson himself could not father children, as a case of the mumps as an adult left him sterile.[71] Stimson loved his country and would come to be known as one of the greatest public servants in its history, along with Ben Franklin, John Hay, Colonel Edward House, George Kennan, and John Foster Dulles.

Buried in the *New York Times* was a curious story, headlined "Anti-Japanese Society Aide Claims He Warned Stimson." It said, "Evidence that Japan was planning [the] thrust at the United States as long ago as late August was disclosed today by Kilsoo K. Haan, Washington representative of the Sino-Korean People's League, a volunteer anti-Japanese society. Mr. Haan released to *The New York Times* a copy of a letter he said he had sent to Secretary of War Henry L. Stimson on Oct. 28, in which Koki Hirota, former Foreign minister, was reported to have given members of the Black Dragon Society a rather accurate forecast of the hostilities and preparations therefore . . . Mr. Haan's letter said in part: 'Information: Hirota . . . now the 'big stick' of the Black Dragon Society, in their Aug. 26 meeting, told of the news that War Minister Tojo has ordered a total war preparation to meet the armed forces of the United States in this Pacific emergency. Tojo is said to have told him of the Navy's full support of his policy against America. The most suitable time to wage war with America is December, 1941, or February, 1942.'"[72]

There was never any evidence that Emperor Hirohito was aware of, or read, Franklin Roosevelt's eleventh-hour plea to renew the talks between the two aggrieved nations. In fact, the Japanese government refused to acknowledge

that they had even received it and, as with all diplomatic cables, it was supposed to be sent via the ambassador of record in a given country, in this case,
Joseph Grew.[73] On Saturday the sixth, Grew was listening to a broadcast radio
out of San Francisco. The signal was so strong it could be heard all the way
to the American embassy in Tokyo. Grew was startled to hear a news report
about an important message sent to Hirohito from the president, which had
been released to the American media, but he knew nothing about it himself.
He told his staff that the radio transmission from the State Department may
have been deliberately interfered with.[74]

Had Hirohito received FDR's message the evening of December 6 and
been moved by it, he certainly had it in his power to recall the fleet heading
for Pearl Harbor. The Japanese people did not even know, for several hours
after, of the attack by their country on American and British military forces.
Around the time of the attack, a Tokyo radio station was broadcasting a lecture by a university professor on "Good Morals."[75]

Two days later, the text of the message from FDR to the Japanese emperor
on December 6, which was nothing but solicitous, respectful, and worried,
was released by Washington. It spoke of the long friendship between the two
countries. Grace Tully said it had been drafted by Cordell Hull himself.[76]

Of course, it was pure State Departmentese, flowery, fulsome, excessive,
and effusive, when plainer and blunter talk might have caught the attention of
Tokyo. American presidents had fought for years with the stuff churned out
by the striped-pants set at the State Department, and FDR was no exception.
He knew when it was time to be solicitous and when it was time to hit an
opponent over the head with a two-by-four. Still, there was never any evidence that Hirohito ever saw the missive; he had the same problem as FDR—
too many meddlesome bureaucrats.

Washington was bracing for both Japan and Germany to widen the war
quickly. In the Pacific, commercial vessels were warned to be on the lookout
for Japanese ships, and mines littered the sea routes and harbors. In the North
Atlantic, officials were expecting the Germans to step up operations there.
"Official observers in the capital expect the Japanese action to be followed by

an all-out German attack in the Atlantic, with German submarines operating near the United States coasts."[77]

The Optimists Club was appropriately meeting as scheduled at the Mayflower Hotel at 12:30 on December 9. They had much to consider.[78] Almost forgotten for a moment in America was the war raging on the European and African continents, so focused were Americans on the new war in the Pacific, where thousands of Japanese troops were landing daily at Manila and Japanese planes were conducting an unremitting bombing raid. A CBS correspondent there said it was a "bad dream." Midway Island was also still under attack as of the eighth, while Japanese radio was claiming they had taken Wake Island and Guam.[79]

Two days after the coordinated attack, the Axis power was still laying waste to the men and materiel of the American military. In Guam, a wire story said the Japanese had sunk the navy minesweeper *Penguin*, all 840 tons of her. There were survivors, but in the battle to take Guam, civilian employees of Pan American Airways had been killed.[80] Guam's garrison was practically nonexistent, "virtually defenseless."[81] Guam had been discovered by Magellan in 1521, and under the Treaty of Paris ending the Spanish-American War in 1898, it became a U.S. possession.

An old American aircraft carrier, the *Langley*, was also rumored to have been attacked while in Philippine waters, but then it was later revealed that the ship had not been hit.[82] Japanese forces, though, had apparently landed on the Philippine island of Lubang. It was reported the invading force was assisted by Japanese fishermen.[83]

Thailand had already surrendered.[84] The Japanese were also prosecuting the war farther south, attacking Australian outposts, and had renewed their bombing of Singapore as well. Hong Kong was bombed twice on the eighth.[85] Japanese civilians in Singapore "gathered in leading . . . hotels and geisha houses and indulged in boisterous drinking parties," so excited at the looming Japanese bombing of the city.[86]

The newspapers were loaded with bad news from the Pacific. A foreign correspondent, Vincent Sheehan, who had just returned from the Far East, told an audience at Bryn Mawr College that America was staring at defeat. The United States, he said, will "have the greatest humiliation in its history" when the citizens learned of the "staggering number of . . . battleships lost" in the attack. "I'm telling you, responsible people in Washington expected last night that eastern cities would be bombed." A report was circulating that Germany was planning to attack the United States without a formal declaration of war.[87]

The postmortems on December 7 were starting to roll in, and they were uniformly bad for the U.S. military and especially Adm. Husband E. Kimmel, commander of the Pacific fleet at Pearl Harbor, and Gen. Walter Short, in charge of the army forces stationed in Hawaii. The country needed scapegoats and unfortunately for these two men with exemplary careers, it would fall to them to eventually take the blame, though they had been caught in the dark as much as anyone else in the military or the civilian government.

On December 7 and 8, the media attention focused on Kimmel was universally positive. The *Baltimore Sun* called him "two-fisted . . . a reputation of being one of the toughest in the service." Kimmel, fifty-nine, had been appointed commander in chief of the Pacific fleet on February 1, 1940. His commendable service record was there for all to see and no one in the hours after the attack said anything against him.[88] At least publicly. But this would change rapidly. Within hours and with no evidence, Congressman John Dingell of Detroit took to the floor of the House and called for his court martial.[89]

Dingell "proposed to demand that court-martial proceedings be instituted against . . . Lt. Gen. Walter C. Short . . . Maj. Gen. H.H. Arnold . . . Maj. Gen. George Brett . . . and Admiral Husband Kimmel, commander of the Pacific fleet."[90]

The halfcocked Dingell, after some vicious comments about the services, had to be reeled in and reprimanded by Congressman Alfred Lee Bulwinkle of North Carolina, who said, "It is the patriotic duty of every American, especially every congressman, to be guarded in his words in order not to give aid and comfort to the enemy." Bulwinkle was met with applause on the House floor, in violation of decorum.[91] Vague party lines were forming, with some Republicans defending Kimmel and some Democrats pummeling him.

But others in Congress were already asking navy personnel uncomfortable questions, including wanting them to "explain how Japanese penetrated

Hawaiian defenses."[92] The House Naval Affairs Committee requested that Adm. Harold Stark, chief of Naval Operations, and navy secretary Frank Knox appear before a hearing on the tenth to discuss what happened in the Pacific. Stories that a "large portion of the Pacific fleet has been wiped out" floated across the nation's capital.[93] Conspiracy theories began to circulate among isolationists that FDR had let the attack happen to bring America into the war. Although now debunked by the facts, those theories persist to the present day. FDR's anguish at the attack seemed sincere enough; aides and confidants have since reported in their memoirs that the president pounded the table as he pored over Pearl Harbor damage assessments, agonizing over every loss, demanding to know how this could have happened to his beloved navy.

People wanted to know why planes were helplessly lined up wingtip to wingtip, making it easy for Japanese bombers and fighters to destroy en masse. Others wanted to know what had happened with the newfangled radar that had recently been installed on Oahu that was supposed to pick up large scale numbers of planes, or why the spotting stations failed to note the large numbers of Japanese planes, or how a flotilla of Japanese ships had crossed thousands of miles undetected.

Yet another postmortem delved into the psychology of attacking America on a Sunday, speculating it was a way in which to adversely affect American morale. Plus, it was the optimum time in which to attack, as it was "the custom of the American military services to grant as much leave as possible on Sundays and rest at ease in barracks or aboard ship."[94]

Some recounted the time of an earlier naval battle between the United States and Japan in 1863. An American sloop, the *Wyoming*, was approaching the coast of Japan. Three Japanese ships with superior firepower engaged the *Wyoming*, but due to the better marksmanship of the Americans, they won the contest.

Another take on the "Who shot John?" aspect of the new war came from the *New York Times*, a take more sympathetic to the Japanese point of view than the Grey Lady's readers probably shared: "Throughout this year the crisis developed, with Japan always reaching out farther. The United States froze all Japanese credits in this country, cut off her supplies of oil, scrap iron and other war materials, and stopped buying Japanese silk. Britain and the

Netherlands Indies followed suit. These economic measures were followed by military moves in which the country strengthened its forces in Hawaii, Manila and other Pacific bases, and the British sent a fleet to Singapore, with both countries shipping heavy strength in bombing planes to the Far East. As these measures tightened, Japan protested against economic strangulation and military encirclement."[95]

The Japanese had also signed the Tripartite Pact with the Axis powers in September of 1940, had invaded Manchuria in 1931, invaded East China in 1937, quit the League of Nations in 1933, signed the anti-Comintern pact with the Third Reich, sunk an American naval ship on the Yangtze River in 1937, engaged in a military buildup, occupied French Indochina—and through her fascist government had become increasingly hostile to the West.

It was becoming increasingly clear why the Japanese had struck, or some so thought. In short, the Japanese saw the American and British military presences in the Pacific and the Far East as threats to the desires for an empire that exceeded the home islands of Japan. It was also becoming clear that Japan, in the twentieth century, had never troubled herself with actually declaring war before attacking an opponent. In 1904 her navy attacked the Russian Fleet at Port Arthur before war was declared. In 1931 she struck at Manchuria, in 1932 at Shanghai, and in 1937 at Peiping without warning.

The details of Secretary of State Cordell Hull's meeting with Ambassador Kichisaburo Nomura and Special Envoy Saburo Kurusu of two days earlier were just beginning to be made clear to the American people, along with the documents they had handed him after Japan attacked Pearl Harbor.

Hull, seventy, was a courtly gentleman, a career diplomat respected on both sides of the aisle for his acumen and calm demeanor. Not this time. The extraordinarily long "Memorandum" given Hull accused America of wanting war while Japan wanted "world peace." The duplicity and revisionism was astonishing. The document stated, "Ever since [the] China affair broke out owing to the failure on the part of China to comprehend Japan's true intentions . . ."[96] In point of fact, Japan had invaded the sovereign country of China four years earlier, and in the process, had butchered thousands of innocent civilians. As far as the Chinese were concerned, there was no misunderstanding. They understood perfectly well what the Japanese military was up to. The Japanese accused Washington of "impractical principles" while applauding themselves for signing the Tripartite Pact with Germany and Italy in the interest of peace. They also criticized the United States for objecting "to settle international issues through military pressure" and also attacked America for "pressure by economic power." Hull's frustration with Japan had been growing for months. Some afternoons he liked to relax over a game of croquet. But each time he hit his ball, he would yell "Japan" in frustration.[97]

Hull digested the long, mendacity-laden document and then exploded. "In all my 50 years of public service I have never seen a document that was more crowded with infamous falsehoods and distortions—infamous falsehoods and distortions on a scale so huge that I never imagined until today that any government on this planet was capable of uttering them."[98]

That was during the day of December 7. That evening, around 6:00 p.m., he blasted the Japanese again for the "treacherous and utterly unprovoked attack upon the United States."[99]

The details of the proposal Hull had made to the Japanese were also revealed; in exchange for withdrawal of their forces from China and Indochina and for signing a nonaggression pact with other Pacific powers, America would release frozen Japanese assets, sign a new trade agreement with the Japanese, and lift the trade embargo. The Japanese rejected the offer outright.[100]

And now eighty-eight years of an uneasy friendship that had existed between the two countries since Commodore Matthew Perry sailed into Tokyo harbor in 1853 was over. Before that historic meeting, Japan had been under self-imposed isolation for more than two hundred years, turning away all would-be suitors. Perry's hailed diplomacy was the beginning of an "Open Door Policy" and trade, and good relations had flourished between the two countries. When war broke out between Japan and Russia in 1904 (during which Japan also attacked without a declaration of war), America made favorable loans to Tokyo. And at the Portsmouth Peace Conference in 1905, President Theodore Roosevelt "was a strong factor in the favorable peace terms won by Japan."[101] Roosevelt later won the Nobel Peace Prize for his actions at Portsmouth.[102]

Along with Japanese nationals, German and Italian nationals came under greater government scrutiny. The Federal Bureau of Investigation announced the initial arrest of 350 "dangerous aliens," including 300 Germans and 50 Italians "listed for arrest."[103] Police in the Canal Zone began to detain Italians and Germans along with Japanese nationals.[104] In Alabama, seven individuals were deemed "dangerous aliens"; five Germans, one Italian, and one Japanese were arrested. The policy coming out of Washington was "that all aliens, especially Japanese, were under the strictest observation of government agents."[105]

Francis Biddle, the attorney general, declared "hearing boards"[106] would be arranged to consider the case of some Japanese picked up, but he also cautioned, "'Even in the present emergency, there are persons of Japanese extraction whose loyalty is unquestioned;' he added that it would therefore be 'a serious mistake' to take any action against these persons and asked State and local authorities not to take such action in their communities without consulting the Department of Justice."[107]

The FBI disclosed that by the ninth, "700 to 1,000 Japs [had been] locked up as 'dangerous to security.'" It was also revealed that 391 Japanese had been arrested in Hawaii, and 345 on the mainland had been arrested in the hours after the bombing of Pearl Harbor. They were placed in "temporary detention stations, principally on the West Coast."[108]

The Home Office in London also declared it was arresting Japanese nationals, starting with the staff members of Domei, the government-owned propaganda agency. Going further, the British issued an order for "all Japanese over the age of 16" to "report as soon as possible to the nearest police station" and produce "their registration certificates."[109]

In the United States, the Civil Aeronautics Authority ordered all commercial airlines to disallow Japanese nationals to purchase tickets or fly with them.[110]

In Los Angeles, as in every other major and minor city in America, efforts to deal with Japanese nationals accelerated. In that city alone, it was estimated there were some forty to fifty thousand Japanese. "A military quarantine was set up around Terminal Island, in Los Angeles Harbor, home of a large Japanese fishing fleet." Traffic was prohibited from entering or leaving the island, and fishing boats were ordered back to their docks, where government officials took control.[111] Maps, binoculars, and radios in the possession of Japanese were ordered confiscated. "Stop all Japanese" was the standing order.[112]

It was the same in San Francisco. The city instituted "a special squad of fifty extra policemen" to guard "the Japanese colony, which covers thirty-six square blocks and has about 7,000 residents. Agents of the FBI picked up a small group for questioning."[113] But one *New York Times* story suggested the FBI initially had a plan to incarcerate all Japanese living in America.[114]

Because of the heavy concentration of war industries in California, combined with the large Japanese population, officials worried about the possibility of sabotage, and extra security was ordered around all plants. Mrs. Roosevelt had already jumped into the whole issue of how Japanese, Italian, and German Americans would be treated, saying, "She saw absolutely no reason why Japanese with 'good' records—meaning 'no criminal nor anti-American record'—had anything to fear." Biddle did say, however, that the mass arrests of Japanese citizens in the Canal Zone and Hawaii were inevitable.[115]

Though large numbers of Japanese were rounded up nationwide, the government said it was interested in only a small number of potential threats to American security among the thousands. "The alien census last year listed about 92,000 Japanese, 90 percent of who live on the West Coast, and for months the F. B. I. has been preparing a list of those to be picked up immediately in the event of war." The Alien Census Act also provided for the fines, imprisonment, and deportation of any Japanese who failed to register. In 1941, Washington had far more powers to deal with Japanese than it did in 1917 to deal with Germans living in America.[116]

From corner to corner of the country, pledges of fidelity to the war effort came from labor groups, corporations, Filipinos in Los Angeles, "Americans of Korean descent," and the Japanese-American Citizens League.[117] The Japanese diplomats in many of the consulates in the United States were truly astonished at their country's actions, and many openly questioned their own government. The Japanese consul general in San Francisco, Yoshio Muto—the majority of newspapers referred to as Joshio Muto—called the attack "unimaginable."[118] Kenji Nakauchi, the general consul in Los Angeles, actually apologized for his country's actions. "What can I say except that I am quite sorry!" When asked about roundups and internment camps, he said he saw "no reason why thousands of Japanese should be imprisoned." Nakauchi pointed out that Germans and Italians in Vancouver were not imprisoned when Canada went to war with the Axis powers.[119]

Ashamed of his country's actions, one Japanese national attempted hari-kari by cutting himself with "a pocketknife and with a needle." Matsuabo Matushita told police, "My country has done wrong attacking the United States of America." It was reported, "[T]he wounds were slight."[120]

A news report in the *Evening Star* said, "It is extremely difficult for Americans to distinguish their enemy, the Japanese, from their friends, the Chinese," according to a Smithsonian anthropologist, Dr. Ales Hrdlicka. Only after a period of time, he said, can Anglos tell the difference by "facial expressions, mannerisms and ways of speech." He said they, along with Filipinos, "all came from the same Mongoloid stock and have the same general physical characteristics." Several Chinese in Washington had been embarrassed since the war started by being mistaken for being Japanese. A Chinese reporter arrived at the White House with a note pinned to his lapel that read, "Chinese reporters—not Japanese—please."[121]

In New York, Chinese-Americans received buttons to wear to distinguish them from Japanese nationals. The blue buttons were distributed by the United Chinese Relief and proclaimed, "Thumbs up for China." It was reported that "many Chinese, mistaken for Japanese, had been mishandled."[122] A full-page ad appeared, sponsored by United China Relief calling for the defeat of Japan. Officials of the organization included Pearl S. Buck, John D. Rockefeller III, David O. Selznick, Wendell L. Willkie, and Mrs. Franklin D. Roosevelt.[123]

The FBI seized the offices of Japan's consulate general on Fifth Avenue to "begin impounding papers and records." Morito Morishima, head of the office, was interrogated by the agents and his possessions examined. In those, agents with the "alien and sabotage squads" found "twenty film negatives of scenes in New York and Washington," including "the Washington monument, bridges in Washington and New York, and the New York skyline . . . and one that appeared to be of a dam or reservoir."[124]

Attorney General Biddle, concerned over the "wholesale arrests" of Japanese aliens, issued a statement saying that only the FBI could make such arrests[125] and any suspicion of nefarious activities should be reported to the local FBI office. U.S. attorneys were instructed to pass the message along to state and local authorities to let the FBI handle the Japanese roundup.

Apparently the FBI had been making lists of Japanese aliens for months.

Across the country there was an outpouring of volunteers. Dozens of armed men showed up at the Hall of Justice in Los Angeles, reacting to an erroneous radio story that said the Civilian Defense Council asked them to come forward.[126] Units of the State Guard were activated, and the Armory in Los Angeles was put under twenty-four-hour guard.[127] The Motion Picture Producers Association "made available scores of studio trucks for the detail."[128] New York police were overrun when they put out a call for airplane spotters, and "40,000 civilian observers" went on "24-hour duty" in "13 East Coast States."[129] The acting mayor of New York, Newbold Morris, told listeners they could expect a "'token visit' from Axis bombers at any time."[130]

The navy's intelligence office in Los Angeles was sealed up tighter than a drum, and the uninvited were turned away, albeit politely. But down the hall were the navy's public relations offices, whose doors were wide open. "Well, after all, there is a difference between the Navy's intelligence office and its publicity bureaus," a reporter wryly noted.[131] However, with the new flood of enlistees, what the navy needed more than anything else were good typists.

The navy banned cables to and from Hawaii and the Philippines, and Uncle Sam banned outright the sending of any news whatsoever to Japan, Germany, Italy, and Finland.[132] The service also asked the press to take care in stories given to them by the next of kin about servicemen who had been killed or wounded, or about the location of their current billet. And never were the names of ships to be published in connection with any sailor. "Voluntary censorship" was bandied about, but the government also warned of enforcing the 1918 Espionage Act.[133]

State and local agencies swung into service quickly, motivated as much by fear, anger, and disinformation as patriotism. Defense preparations were being organized in every city, town, village, and hamlet of America. Volunteer guards were placed around utilities. Judges and magistrates swore in citizens to pledge to defend America. Police stations were swarmed with volunteers. A volunteer auxiliary police force was forming in Los Angeles, with thirty thousand citizens wanting to sign up.[134]

The dome to the state house in Sacramento was blacked out, and all forest lookout stations went on a 24/7 basis.[135] The Boulder Dam was also put under twenty-four-hour guard, and Route 93, which crossed over the dam, was closed to traffic.[136] New York mayor Fiorello LaGuardia, head of Washington's Civil Defense program, issued a six-point program for "civilians in areas subject to possible aerial bombing." Rule number one was "Keep Cool. Above all, keep cool. Don't lose your head."[137] People stopped working to listen to war news, colleges let students out of class to listen to speeches by FDR, and pedestrians gathered around parked cars to listen to the radio. The war was everywhere and was quickly being injected deeply into the body politic of America.

And yet life went on. Hedda Hopper's Hollywood gossip columns appeared nationwide, Americans went to movies, went to work, went to church, went on with their lives, albeit with a shadow looming over all people and all activities.

"There's a war on!" was a refrain that was only beginning to be heard. Movie theaters began to paint over the upper lights of their marquees in order to lessen the chance of them being seen from the air. People were spending a lot more time looking up in the sky. Women's silk stockings—"a prized possession this year"—were still available at J.J. Haggarty department store in Los Angeles, but this wouldn't last.[138]

Nash was touting their newest car, claiming it would get "25 to 30 miles on a gallon!" and had air conditioning.[139] Marriage announcements and marriages and Christmas parties continued. Advice columns, such as "The Gentler Sex" by Malvina Lindsay, informed women readers of "the desperate wife who decides to have an affair because of her husband's infidelity."[140] It foreshadowed the sea change in sexual attitudes and activity on the home front, when men went off to war and left their wives and girlfriends behind. After the war, when confronted with pregnant wives, many returning G.I.s never properly did the math and assumed that the babies were theirs.

Meanwhile, frostbite sailing races were still being held on the Chesapeake, Christmas shopping went on, women still bought fashionable shoes, men bought pipes and trench coats and "snoots" at Macy's and jewelry for their wives at Garfinckel's department store, accidents happened involving drivers and pedestrians. The Women's Pages (later known in the post-war world as "Style" sections) carried new recipes and fashion tips. One advice columnist, Dorothy Dix, admonished her female readers, "Men are slaves to beauty, yet when they marry they pass looks up."[141] Babe Ruth signed a movie deal with Samuel Goldwyn to appear in a film about his former teammate, Lou Gehrig.[142]

Yet there would be a real and tangible and permanent change in America. "Textiles, wool and cotton goods will become scarce," cited the *Wall Street Journal*.[143] The paper noted that soon leather would also be in short supply.

The paper forecast what no one else in journalism had yet. A radical change in America was coming. "War with Japan means industrial revolution in the United States. The American productive machine will be reshaped with but one purpose—to produce the maximum of things needed to defeat the enemy. It will be a brutal process. It implies intense, almost fantastic stimulation for some industries; strict rationing for others; inevitable, complete liquidation for a few."[144]

Americans would also have to learn to do without or with less—or find another source or substitute—of products that had come in from the Far East. "Primarily, these are rubber and tin. Secondarily, there is coconut oil, tungsten, chromium, copra, tung oil, palm oil, manila hemp, jute, graphite. Sugar too.[145] Civilian use of Copper, Lead, Zinc and other vital metals to disappear."[146] The nonmilitary use of copper, as an example, was prohibited or severely curtailed for "building supplies and hardware, house furnishings and equipment: dress accessories: jewelry, gifts and novelties: burial equipment: automotive, trailer and tractor equipment, and a miscellaneous list which runs from fire-fighting apparatus, toys, beauty parlor equipment, barber shop supplies, bicycles, chimes, bells, keys, and a host of other items." Five hundred and fifty thousand tons of copper would be needed for shell casings and cartridges in 1942.[147]

Chrome would also shortly be curtailed. It was used for automobile bumpers, bun warmers, toasters, coffee thermoses, irons, and had dozens of other nonmilitary applications. Welders, who had threatened a strike, now called for burning their American Federation of Labor membership cards.[148]

American housewives tossed in the sponge when told there would be a severe curtailment of sponges. Not only would the war cause disruption in supply, but a blight in the Atlantic had wiped out whole beds. Back then, sponges were not made synthetically.

During the American embargo of Japan, the administration had decided not to include oil, as the country was wholly dependent upon oil imports from the United States and cutting it off might cause too much shock to the Japanese economy. All bets were off now, on that score, but no matter. Because of frugal policies, Japan had a stockpile, according to estimates, of up to a two-year supply of the precious liquid.[149]

The shipping schedules for commercial ships were radically changed to suit the new priorities. First, they would no longer be published in the newspapers. Second, the war effort took priority. Also, because of the war conditions in the South Pacific, it would take twice as long for merchant ships to traverse the distance due to the presence of Japanese submarines. Also, the military expected a 50 percent reduction in the transport of nonmilitary items.[150] The government announced "secret plans" to secure defense factories from saboteurs under the Plant Protective Service.[151] Aviation fuel took a front seat to refined gas for the civilian population. Because of the high performance nature of aircraft engines, they required additional lead in the gas to prevent what could be dangerous engine-knocking, which meant the American car driver could look forward to their engines knocking for the duration of the emergency.

The industrial might of America had been ramping up for the past year, due to Lend-Lease, but now it would be turned up several more notches. A beneficiary of American generosity was the Free French government led by Charles de Gaulle, which a day after everyone else, declared war on Japan.[152]

Yet there was a spiritual change in the country as well. "The tentacles of a great crisis are reaching down into the hearts and minds of all the people. And the full measure of the impacts upon the nation can be determined only with realization that a great international crisis has come to force readjustments in the lives and thoughts of all individuals."[153]

The attack changed American attitudes and outlooks forever. Since the end of the Great War, America had become an increasing isolationist country, and it was reflected in her policies of high tariffs and tight immigration policies, as well as the Neutrality Acts of the 1930s. Americans told themselves that they were protected by two great oceans and nothing could ever befall their homeland. Columnist Walter Lippmann called the image of us sitting comfortably isolated and protected by the oceans a "deadly delusion."[154]

The war in Europe often seemed very far away, with little impact on the daily lives of American citizens. But now, there was a new unity in the land not seen in its history. The factionalism that had been a hallmark of Americanism had dissipated. "Behind this determination stand not alone the members of our government. Behind it, dedicated with them to the extirpation of the counterpart in the Pacific of the criminal architects of ruin, pillage and slaughter in Europe, stand a people united as never before."[155]

It was war. "This is the World War in the complete and literal meaning of the words—a war which can end only in our victory or in our defeat."[156]

Deep in some newspapers of America, it was reported that German embassy officials in Washington were burning papers as "bits of charred paper floated down" to the street. A truck arrived to deliver brown wrapping paper. A "society reporter" visited the embassy, and the charge d'affaires, Hans Thomsen, said, "Have you come to say goodbye?" To which she replied, "Well, have I?" Thomsen demurred, only saying it was "a little premature."[157]

In Berlin, an official of the Third Reich told the Associated Press that his country was preparing to issue a "clarifying statement" on the war between the United States and the empire of Japan.[158] The spokesman said America had been the aggressor in the Pacific, and according to the terms of the Tri-Partite Pact, Germany and Italy were duty bound to come to the assistance of their ally. Secretary of State Cordell Hull jumped into the fray and said he too had heard rumors that Germany was about to declare war on America.[159] The White House announced that FDR was going to address not only the Pacific but Europe in his radio broadcast, including a "Nazi pattern." Elaborating, the Washington Evening Star reported, "There was a strong implication . . . that

Mr. Roosevelt's words tonight will be virtually a declaration of war against Nazi Germany."[160]

And then a reporter for NBC, David Anderson in Stockholm, broadcast a story in which he "predicted" Germany would declare war on the United States "within a few hours."[161] He elaborated, saying that American embassy officials in Berlin were already evacuating. And unconfirmed reports said a meeting was planned the next day in the Reichstag. A performance in the Kroll Opera House in Berlin was canceled because this was where the Reichstag met.[162]

CHAPTER 10

THE TENTH OF DECEMBER

"US Warships in Battle Off Manila, Berlin Says"

Sun

"Roosevelt Sees a Long, World-Wide War;
Japanese Invade Luzon, Fight in Manila;
2 Big British Warships Sunk, Tokyo Says"

New York Times

"Japs Sink Two British Dreadnaughts"

Birmingham News

Franklin Roosevelt appeared in good spirits and good health to the reporters who filed into the Oval Office. FDR was dressed in a grey suit, white shirt, black tie, and black armband for his mother, Sara, who'd died the previous September. "He was smoking a cigarete [*sic*] in an ivory holder . . . and he chatted smilingly with correspondents."[1] "He looks fine," one reporter whispered to another and it was noted "there were no haggard lines in his face. His color was good. There was about him a calm confidence." Another was heard to say, "He thrives on activity—and he has plenty of it now."[2]

He'd been confined to a wheelchair for years, only occasionally using the painful leg braces when in public. In all of his years in the presidency, he'd only been photographed in the wheelchair maybe three times. Secret Service men routinely confiscated photographs and negatives, and the White House press corps was in on the cover-up, berating new members not to photograph the crippled and confined president.[3]

The security around FDR had increased appreciably, as reporters were asked repeatedly to show their press credentials before being allowed into the briefing with the president.[4] Yet by that evening during a long radio broadcast, the wear and burden of the war and the long day showed in his face. As time went on, the stress of the war years with its never-ending long days and long nights, combined with his endless smoking of Camel cigarettes, contributed mightily to FDR's decline in health. Several years into the war, a young reporter assigned to the White House beat was appalled during his first day on the job when he realized the haggard, sallow-skinned, and decrepit man sitting before him was the president of the United States.[5]

But at the dawn of the war, and flexing his new powers, FDR issued a proclamation saying that "all alien enemies are enjoined to preserve the peace . . . and to refrain from crime against the public safety and from violating the laws . . . and to refrain from actual hostility or giving aid or comfort to the enemies of the United States." It was also noted that "violators [would] be interned."[6] Japanese subjects were prohibited from leaving Hawaii, and local military commanders in the battle zones were given wide latitude to imprison those they deemed a threat.[7] Nationals from all three countries who were in America were "liable" as far as the government was concerned, especially Japanese, because "an invasion had been perpetrated upon the territory of the United States by the Empire of Japan."[8]

The edict put a halt to the process for nearly 500,000 Japanese, German, and Italians wanting to live or stay in the United States. J. Edgar Hoover was keeping FDR apprised of the FBI's efforts, via Maj. Gen. Edwin M. Watson. "I thought it might be of interest to the President and you to have the inclosed [sic] charts before you, which show the number of Japanese, German and Italian aliens taken into custody by the FBI as of December 9. This gives the exact location of the number apprehended and places at which they were apprehended." The memo was accompanied by a detailed chart of the forty-eight states, denoting pickups.[9]

The administration was also getting ready to ask Congress for virtually unrestricted powers, including the ability to send arms and other support materiel to any country fighting the Axis powers and not just against Japan.[10] The White House was seeking nothing less than authoritarian powers in the conduct of war. It went even further.

With the help of the Federal Communications Commission and the War Department, the White House in essence nationalized the nation's radio industry. "President Roosevelt signed an executive order late today . . . to designate radio facilities for use, control or closure by the War or Navy Departments. . . . The effect of the order is to give the Government freedom to step in and supervise directly or make use of all radio facilities of the Nation."[11] The order also allowed "other agencies of the government" to step in and take control of private radio broadcasting facilities.[12]

FDR was drawing broad support from many corners. Gen. John J. "Black Jack" Pershing, America's only five-star general, still on the active duty roster at the age of eighty-one, sent the president a letter, offering his services. FDR responded kindly, calling him "magnificent. I am deeply grateful to you . . . under a wise law, you have never been placed on the retired list."[13]

A dispute among constitutional scholars broke out over exactly when America went to war with Japan, fueled by FDR's language proclaiming "a state of war has existed" even though Congress had not formally declared war on Japan at the time. Most agreed that a state of war did not come into actual existence until 4:10 p.m. on the eighth, when the president actually signed the proclamation of war. Whatever the variances, all agreed that the president's powers were now vastly expanded. "Statutes which operate in such periods authorize the President to take over transportation systems, industrial plants, radio stations, power facilities and ships, and place some controls on communications systems," reported the New York Times.[14]

The mobilization of the political and business class to fight a highly industrialized global war, combined with the concentration of power into the hands of the commander in chief, was profoundly changing what had once been Fortress America. It marked the beginning of what would later be known as the Imperial Presidency. The expansion of presidential powers in response to Pearl Harbor also presaged the postwar national security state, in which civil liberties were sometimes curtailed. This was all to come. But in December 1941, it was already clear to ordinary and powerful citizens alike that a major shift in American society was underway and that the republic as originally envisioned by the Founding Fathers was giving way to something different.

A quote from Alexander Hamilton from *Federalist 74* was bandied about to support the contention that wartime conditions allowed for the expansion of executive powers: "The direction of war implies the direction of common strength; and the power of directing and employing the common strength forms an unusual and essential part in the definition of the executive authority."[15]

Most believed President Roosevelt now had enhanced and broadened powers not only over the military but the citizenry, the economy, and labor as well. One euphemistic new example: "The Secretary of War may rent any building in the District of Columbia."[16] In other words, the federal government now had the right to commandeer private property. Indeed, in his press conference, FDR suggested that a seven-day workweek in the war industries might be necessary and proposed convening a conference of business and labor to discuss the matter. The word *parley* was used, but in fact there would be little to discuss.[17] He also floated the idea of a "Conference on the Defense of [the] Western Hemisphere."[18] Also proposed was the notion of "enforced savings" of the average worker that would automatically deduct "10 to 15 percent of all income and wages."[19]

The issue of who exactly was an American also came up in debate. The law said Japanese could not become naturalized citizens "under provisions of the act of Feb 18, 1875 amending the act of July 14, 1870 limiting naturalization to white persons or those of African descent." Open to question was whether a child born in America, of Japanese parentage—called "*Nisei*"—was considered a naturalized American.[20]

The government was now monitoring or restricting the movements of over 1 million individuals, virtually all of Japanese, German, and Italian heritage. As of December tenth, the attorney general's office said they had now picked up over one thousand foreign nationals. FDR's proclamation instituting prohibitions on those still roaming free, including the ability to possess a firearm, "ammunition, bombs, explosives or material used in the manufacture of explosives; shortwave radio receiving sets; transmitting sets; signal devices; codes or ciphers; cameras; papers; documents or books in which there may be invisible writing; photograph, sketch, picture, drawing, map or graphical representation of any military or naval installations." The directive went on with even more specifics and restrictions.[21] Arrests continued. "A Japanese was seized near Oakland Airport and another was arrested near the scene of an early morning fire in Oakland."[22]

Hawaii had the same concerns, only magnified. The territorial governor, Joseph Poindexter, appointed by FDR, worried about "the conduct of Hawaii's 37,000 Japanese aliens and 100,000 American-born Japanese."[23]

Also open to question was how to deal with approximately fifty Japanese diplomats still in the country. Cordell Hull made an appeal to a neutral European country to act as the go-between involving the two warring countries.

American diplomats were still in Tokyo as well, including Ambassador Joseph Grew. There was also the matter of approximately five thousand Americans on Japanese soil. But there were only a few neutral countries in the world now, including Switzerland, Spain, Portugal, and Sweden.[24]

Tokyo meanwhile announced there were 1,270 Americans, British, Canadians, and Australian citizens in Japan.

In reply, the Japanese announced they would abide by the Geneva Convention and allow U.S., British, and Canadian diplomats safe passage to a neutral port of call.[25] But the Japanese government also announced it had arrested one hundred American and British nationals.[26] Thousands of other noncombatant Americans were spread throughout the War Zone, and the British government reminded the Japanese government of the Conventions and the Geneva Protocol of 1925 strictures against the use of chemical weapons.

Allies initially rounded up 25,000 Japanese in Davao in the Philippines and another 100,000 at Bilibid prison in Manila. In Davao, Japanese "have submitted peaceably. Some appeared voluntarily at concentration centers."[27]

Also worrisome for Washington was that while few of her naval officers spoke Japanese, "a vast number of [Japan's] military officers . . . speak English. This is bound to give Nippon an edge in questioning war prisoners, translating intercepted messages and in obtaining information from material found on men fallen in action."[28]

The questions were why did it happen and how did it happen? Pearl Harbor had often been referred to by the navy as "the Gibraltar of the Pacific."[29] Just one day before the attack, Secretary of the Navy Frank Knox had issued a statement saying the navy was ready.[30] It was more than just being "back-stabbers-in-the-dark," as the Los Angeles Times described the new enemy.[31] Senator Burton Wheeler of Montana said the Japanese "must have gone crazy."[32] Winston Churchill had warned for more than a month that the Pacific was a powder keg waiting to explode.

Pearl Harbor was a vitally important outpost for the American military and thus a direct threat to Japan's designs on an empire stretching up and down the Asian east coast and spreading into the Philippines and the Pacific. This answered some of the "why," although it was far more complicated. After all, the Japanese had already invaded China, Manchuria, and French-Indochina, and many presumed America would also tolerate the invasion of Thailand. Deeper issues were involved.

Why did the Japanese attack America and Great Britain? One answer was the character of the military men running Japan. "These men are the most reactionary school. They have long been practically at grips with Emperor Hirohito, trying to divest him of actual state authority, reduce him to helpless isolation in the palace, and to restore an aristocratic regime tantamount to the old-time Shogunate under which for 250 years, ending around 1870, Japan was locked away from the outside world."[33]

The biggest fascist of all, Prime Minister Hideki Tojo, was the major-domo in all military and political affairs in his country. As a fascist, militarist, and overtly nationalistic, Tojo wasn't hard to figure out, as his defense for keeping troops in China was the positive impact it had on Japanese military morale. His nickname was "The Razor." When he became prime minister in

October 1941, he was assigned the task of evaluating the negotiations with the United States to see if peace was possible but within a matter of days signed off on the audacious plan to launch a sneak attack against America.

Why did the American military fail to see the threat posed? Why did American diplomats and politicians fail to remember that Japan, in her long history, had never actually declared war on an opponent before attacking that opponent? Why did American politicians and diplomats fail to recognize just who and what was running the show in Tokyo? "The real rulers of Japan have been a clique of army and navy officers whose thought processes, fanatical, mystical, belong in another age. They are a direct throwback to the Shoguns, Diamyos, and Samurai who ruled in ancient and medieval times. . . . They were Fascists before Mussolini, National Socialists before Hitler."[34]

But the Japanese people were also a proud and courageous race. They were unyielding and Tokyologists knew that, for the Japanese, "national suicide would be preferable to yielding."[35] The word *fanatical*, used to describe the Japanese, was cropping up in more and more articles. The Japanese had often been poorly and cruelly portrayed in the political cartoons of American newspapers, but now it took an uglier, racist turn. A hated caricature was emerging of the average Japanese citizen and certainly the Japanese military. The president of Tufts University, Leonard Carmichael, accused the Japanese race of being "infected with madness."[36] Political cartoons routinely depicted the Japanese in the most vicious possible manner: short, "bifocals and bamboo," squinty-eyed, often with a knife in the back of Uncle Sam, egged on by caricatures of Hitler and Mussolini.

Still, the bigger question on the minds of Americans and official Washington was how were the Japanese so successful in sneaking up on Hawaii? Sure, it was a big ocean, but it was also a big armada and should, some thought, have been spotted by navy or civilian ships or planes. Pan American flights over the Pacific were routine, and the military on Oahu did have planes and ships dedicated to be on the lookout for potential threats from the sea. Indeed, one that had landed in the middle of the battle over Oahu made its way safely back to San Francisco, while another, along with twenty airline personnel, successfully escaped from Guam.

One expert said the navy suffered from "Scapa Flow." Scapa Flow was where the Germans surprised and sank the British *Royal Oak* in early October of 1939, at a time when the Brits should have known better. The *Christian Science Monitor* acidly wrote, "Why the American Navy permitted itself to be surprised in the Pacific will take some major explaining from a command which almost at the same moment was declaring its marine forces 'second to none' in the world."[37]

The army, along with the navy, seemed confused as to its next step. The army oddly announced that it was not planning any type of offensive operations against the Japanese any time soon.[38] A White House source elaborated, saying nothing on the scale of the 2 million doughboys sent to Europe in 1917 was being contemplated. And while it was the Japanese who had attacked America, "the most formidable enemy still is Germany."[39] Stories circulated that Germany was planning on aiding the Japanese with military hardware. Adm. William D. Leahy supposedly had told a journalist four years earlier that Japan needed to be corralled. In 1937, isolationists labeled him a "warmonger."[40]

The blame game and the "I knew it all along" parlor room nonsense were only beginning to gain a head of steam. Some of the headlines: "While Japan caught the United States Navy napping at Hawaii," "U.S. Learns Lesson in Attack,"[41] "U.S. Navy Caught Off Guard,"[42] and "Preparedness of Defenses is Questioned in Washington: Capital Hears Queries About Functions of Hawaii Off-Shore Patrol."[43] Conclusions were being jumped to all over the place, and the navy was increasingly under attack by American politicians and editorialists and not just Japanese militarists. "Also heard in the rising uproar were proposals for a housecleaning of the Navy Department, beginning with the Secretary, Frank Knox."[44]

FDR was asked at his press conference the day before who was to blame, and he bristled at the offending reporter. A reporter also complained that it seemed to him the War Department had clamped down on all information, but Roosevelt smiled and "told the correspondent his toes hadn't been stepped on."[45] "Asked if it would be the policy to make public no bad news, the President answered in the negative, but added that the rule of accuracy and determination not to aid the enemy would be the standard of measure." He also shot down the notion that some papers were unhappy with the policy, noting that he'd also "heard other reports where the shoe was on the other foot."[46]

Along with the finger-pointing, conspiracy theorists started coming out of the woodwork. Senator Guy Gillette, Democrat of Iowa, claimed he'd been told by a source that the State Department had been told by another source that the Japanese would attack America in either December 1941 or January of 1942.[47] No doubt there had been formal and informal warning about the Japanese, and the Allied Signals Intelligence had decoded transmissions between Tokyo and their embassy in Washington, but nowhere in those transmissions was it explicit that Japan was going to war with the United States. The War Department had issued "war warnings" to the field commanders, including Admiral Kimmel and General Short, but none of those ever mentioned Hawaii.[48] Roosevelt himself had been given several top secret memos alerting him to the possibility the Japanese could attack the Philippines or Hawaii, but in the end, everybody just could not fathom it. All thought the Japanese's next target was Thailand. It was one of the greatest bait and switches in world history.

Experts on the Far East weighed in, saying the attack was to break up a suspected blockade of Japan, before the Allies and the United States could get it going in earnest. Others, including Kimmel, thought FDR was being deliberately provocative, when the president personally ordered the fleet moved from San Diego to Oahu early in 1941.[49] He also complained of being kept in the dark about the increasing diplomatic difficulties between Washington and Tokyo and implied that had he known, he would have taken steps to protect the fleet.

With perfect hindsight, the *Washington Post* opened its lead editorial of December 8 by saying, "The Japanese attack on Hawaii began precisely as many Navy and Army officers predicted it would." The editorial did not name these visionary individuals, and there was no reporting before December 7 in the *Post*, or any paper in America for that matter, about their warnings of a possible attack in the Pacific by Japan.[50] The paper, however, being located in the nation's capital, was marinated in the "as I said before" *tuchas*-covering culture of the town.

The *Post* also had an aggressively pro-Roosevelt, pro-interventionist editorial policy with a habit of patting itself on the back. "This paper has gone on that assumption since Hitler and the Italians leagued themselves with the Japanese" that war was inevitable and it would not be confined to the

European powers. In arguing for a swift entry into the war, it said, "This is our rendezvous with destiny."[51] Their crosstown rival, the *Washington Times-Herald*, was a vicious and bitter opponent of FDR, the New Deal, Lend-Lease, and internationalism. The paper was owned by newspaper mogul Col. Robert McCormick, whose opposition to FDR was reflected deeply in all his papers.

Adding to Americans' doubts about the world situation was the fact that while their government was telling them one thing, other sources were telling them something quite different. Network radio correspondents were reporting in great detail about destruction in Manila, while the War Department was saying the Philippine base in question was operational—or saying nothing at all. "Continuing as it did, the silence created a growing possibility that the public would simply begin to believe all rumors, simply because no facts were made available to controvert them."[52] The Japanese were dropping propaganda leaflets by day and flares at night, to illuminate bombing targets. There was constant chatter going around that German pilots were participating in the attack, flying Japanese warplanes.[53]

Americans did not know of the six separate military targets successfully hit in Oahu by the Japanese, or of the near-complete destruction or disabling of twenty-one vessels in the American fleet, or that over three hundred first-line Air Corps and navy planes had been destroyed, or that three thousand of the fellow countrymen had been brutally killed only because they wore a uniform and happened to be in the wrong place at the wrong time.

There was no news coming out of Hawaii about the extent to which the Japanese had succeeded, including the murder of 1,177 sailors and marines assigned to the *Arizona*, which having taken a bomb into her magazine, exploded in an earth-shattering fireball and sank to the bottom of the harbor. Nearly the entire crew was lost.

Hawaii was under martial law, and retail stores were ordered closed so the civilian government could order an inventory of available food supplies. The White House said repairs on the damaged ships and planes were in effect and replacement planes were being "rushed" to Hawaii, but the fact was Pearl Harbor, Ford Island, and Hickam Field were only beginning to pick up the pieces. Dead and missing soldiers and sailors were still unaccounted for, and investigations hadn't even gotten underway. A sad epilogue to December 7 was that a squadron of six planes from the *Enterprise* was on approach to Pearl Harbor after a vain search for the Japanese ships, and despite being told repeatedly they were "friendlies," they were shot down by panicked U.S. sailors. Only one of the six planes landed safely.[54]

Honolulu wasn't completely caught unaware of Japanese intentions. For some time, residents of Oahu had been warned what to do in case of attack, to "lay in emergency food supplies," and warned they might have to evacuate to the mountains should war come to their island. "It is safe to say that no other American community was as well prepared for war as was Hawaii."[55] Ironic.

The risk was great after December 7 of another Japanese attack on Hawaii, so Americans thought. "Unless the naval patrol around Hawaii, and indeed around the fringe of American islands farther west can be made more effective, periodic harassing attacks on Hawaii are practically certain."[56] Secretary Hull said publicly he expected more surprise attacks on the part of the Japanese. And fresh claims by the Japanese included the sinking of a "mother ship" and the downing of an American plane near Hawaii.[57]

The Japanese were crowing now; what was left of the American fleet was no match for their intact fleet in the Pacific. "This force would be regarded as utterly inadequate to accomplish any successful outcome in an encounter with the thus-far-intact Japanese Fleet."[58]

As of the tenth, the war news only became more depressing. The Japanese sunk two huge British battleships, the thirty-five-thousand-ton *Prince of Wales* and the thirty-two-thousand-ton *Repulse*, in the same Pacific battle. Hundreds of men were lost, and the *Repulse* went down immediately after the torpedo- and dive-bomber planes had attacked. The ships, without air cover, were simply sitting ducks to air attack. Winston Churchill was truly stunned at the news. "In all the war, I never received a more direct shock," Churchill wrote in *The Grand Alliance*.[59]

He was down to only nineteen battleships. The Japanese claimed they'd also sunk the *King George V* battleship.[60] It was learned that two British islands in the Pacific, Nauru and Ocean, were under attack by the Japanese.[61] Both were small, but both were strategically important, as part of the Gilbert Island chain halfway between Hawaii and the Philippines. The Japanese had also apparently seized a British airfield located in the northern Malaya Peninsula area.

Japanese troops stormed ashore at Luzon in the Philippines. They were also "in force in Malaya," as reported from Singapore.[62] "Bitter fighting continued throughout the night and today."[63] The Japanese claimed they bombed Clark Field and Nichols Field in the Philippines again and shelled Midway Island, as well as shooting down nine American planes over Wake Island. The Japanese navy had also captured over two hundred commercial ships of all countries, all in the waters off the China Coast and southward.

American fighter planes were off the ground in Manila and finally engaging the enemy; however, there was respect for the Japanese fighters. One American flyer described the opposing planes as "plenty good and heavily armored."[64]

The Japanese took possession of the *President Harrison*, with a complement of U.S. Marines on board.[65] They were tightening their grip on Thailand, sending in more troops, and tightening their grip on Bangkok.[66] Shanghai was also now firmly in Japanese hands.[67]

FDR received classified daily reports from London on the situation in the rest of the world. The reports were frank and disheartening. In all world sectors, the Axis powers were on offense and the Allies were on defense. "Heavy air attacks . . . A small enemy force landed . . . German progress . . . Battle casualties . . . German . . . long range bombing force on Eastern Front is still being vigorously pursued . . . seriously damaged by bombs."[68]

New casualty reports were coming in from Hawaii. Leading the latest list was Sergeant Walter R. French, twenty-nine, of Delphos, Ohio. He was in the Medical Corps. The War Department acknowledged a mistake, in that Wilbur Carr, nineteen, of Franklin, Ohio, was not dead as his parents had previously been told. Young Carr was alive and well.[69]

In New York, for the first time in thirty-five years, the huge lighted clock at the top of the Colgate-Palmolive-Peet building was darkened as a precaution.

Handbooks were issued to all the schools in New York City, outlining air-raid procedures for the children, teachers, and administrators.[70] The U.S. Capitol was darkened for the duration of the war and the floodlights, which had illuminated the great building for years, were turned off.[71]

In the face of depressing news came more depressing news. The thirty-second president had taken to the airwaves the night before from the Oval Room of the White House to give his fellow countrymen a more fulsome report on the attack on Pearl Harbor, the situation regarding the Japanese, and to generally buck up morale, but also to let the American media have it right between the eyes.

He might have started out looking crisp and alive that morning, but Roosevelt looked fatigued at the end of December 10, with dark circles under his eyes. He was still attired in a grey pinstripe suit, but it now looked baggy and loose. His remarks could be heard over most of the free world and parts of the non-free world, except Vichy France, which jammed the NBC transmission. The American radio audience was estimated to be 90 million citizens. In 1941, the population of the United States was 130 million.[72]

He opened, blasting Tokyo, saying, "The sudden criminal attacks perpetrated by the Japanese in the Pacific provide the climax of a decade of international immorality." Early in his remarks, he made a compelling case that the Japanese, Germans, and Italians were all the common enemy of the United States and that each of them was a threat. "It is all of a pattern," he said.[73]

Then, "We are now in this war. So far, the news has been all bad. We have suffered a serious setback in Hawaii. Our forces in the Philippines . . . are taking punishment but are defending themselves vigorously. The reports from Guam and Wake and Midway Islands are still confused, but we must be prepared for the announcement that all these three outposts have been seized. The casualty lists of these first few days will undoubtedly be large."[74]

He assured loved ones that the dead of family members would be made known to them as judiciously as possible and that "they will get news just as quickly as possible." Roosevelt turned his attention to all the disinformation being spread around. "Most urgently, I urge my countrymen to reject all rumors. These ugly little hints of complete disaster fly thick and fast in wartime. They have to be examined and appraised. As an example, I can tell you frankly that until further surveys are made, I have not sufficient information to state the exact damage which has been done to our naval vessels at Pearl Harbor. Admittedly the damage is serious."[75]

"I cite as another example a statement made on Sunday night that a Japanese carrier had been located and sunk off the Canal Zone. And when you hear statements that are attributed to what they call 'an authoritative source,' you can be reasonably sure from now on that under these war circumstance the 'authority source' is not any person in authority." Clearly, Roosevelt had become angry with all the innuendo and false information over the past several days and warned that a lot of the disinformation could be coming from the Japanese as a means of sapping American morale. "This is an old trick of propaganda which has been used innumerable times by the Nazis."[76] And then he took on the national media.

"To all newspapers and radio stations—all those who reach the eyes and ears of the American people—I say this: You have a most grave responsibility to the nation now and for the duration of this war. If you feel that your government is not disclosing enough of the truth, you have every right to say so." And then he dropped his anvil. "But—in the absence of all the facts, as revealed by official sources—you have no right in the ethics of patriotism to deal out unconfirmed reports in such a way as to make people believe they are the gospel truth. The lives of our soldiers and sailors—the whole future of this nation—depend upon the manner in which each and every one of us fulfills his obligation to our country."[77]

Then he swung into an impassioned defense of Lend-Lease, contending the program had bought the Allies time against the Axis powers. "Precious months were gained by sending vast quantities of our war materiel to the nations of the world still able to resist Axis aggression." FDR moved to the heart of his remarks, telling Americans what they had learned and what they must do. "I repeat that the United States can accept no result save victory, final and complete. We have learned that our ocean-girth hemisphere is not immune from severe attack." And finally, "We are now in the midst of a war, not for conquest, not for vengeance, but for a world in which this nation, all that this nation represents, will be safe for our children." He made no bones of his intentions, saying, "We expect to eliminate the danger of Japan, but it would serve us ill if we accomplished that and found that the rest of the world was dominated by Hitler and Mussolini."[78]

Concluding, Roosevelt said, "So we are going to win the war and we are going to win the peace that follows. And in the difficult hours of this day—and through dark days that may be yet to come—we will know that the vast majority of the members of the human race are on our side. Many of them are fighting with us. All of them are praying for us. For in representing our cause, we represent theirs as well—our hope and their hope for liberty under God."[79] The White House was flooded with letters and telegrams praising FDR, supporting his efforts. Many volunteered to do what they could do for the war effort.[80]

That evening FDR dined alone, went for a swim, and "went back to his desk, the war dispatches, phone and radio communiqués."[81]

Despite FDR's plea, the country was overrun with rumors. The day after the president lectured Americans about not engaging in unfounded gossip, it became clear the East Coast scare of planes about to bomb New York, Boston, and Washington of the day before was indeed a rumor that had raced out of control and was passed along by radio, government, and military sources. "The story grew from mouth to mouth. Newspapers and radio stations could not deny it. They could get no authentic information one way or another. The War Department's statement that it had not originated the report could not be interpreted as a denial."[82]

What began as an innocent phone call to Mitchell Field turned into confusion. A man had called the First Army Office in New York, innocently asking about "any truth in a report that bombers had been sighted. He said he had heard it in a radio broadcast from Washington." From there it went to the airfield commander to whom it was somehow announced that the War Department *had* an "enemy plane approaching the coast."[83]

This quickly metastasized into a "phony tip," which then set off a panic of wailing sirens and general confusion that affected millions along the East Coast, for no reason whatsoever. Panicky housewives called husbands at work, pleading for them to come home. Others called newspapers wanting to know where bomb shelters were located. Three hundred planes stationed at Mitchell Field on Long Island took to the air, looking for nonexistent enemy planes. On the fears of eminent attack, the stock market declined deeply. The War Department did not apologize for causing so much of the problem, but newspapers did print notices telling readers how to react in the future to air-raid warnings.[84]

The whole thing "at noon yesterday threw the Atlantic Coast from Portland, Maine to Norfolk into a confusion which, in some places, bordered on hysteria. Somehow somewhere—so the story went—an unidentified enemy airplane had been sighted over the sea. It was all an extraordinary comedy of errors superimposed on a people stunned by the events of the last two days into an exceptional state of suggestibility."[85]

The fallout over the supposed sighting of enemy planes over San Francisco continued. The army denied it was a dress rehearsal or a hoax, as those in New York, Boston, and Washington found out. In San Francisco, they stuck by their story.[86]

There, Gen. John J. Dewitt emphatically, loudly, and scarily berated the civilian population for not reacting sooner and with more alacrity to the warnings and air-raid sirens, going so far as to say that it would have been "a good thing" if some bombs had indeed dropped, as a way to awaken the populace. "He denounced as 'inane, idiotic and foolish' those who refused to believe there was real danger." He warned of "death and destruction." He told people to "get the hell out" if they didn't start to take things more seriously. He said he hoped for enemy bombings. "It might have awakened some of the fools in this community who refuse to realize this is a war." He said a bombing was "imminent." He told FDR the fact that there had been no sabotage by Japanese in San Francisco was evidence that it was coming soon. He favored the forced internment of all Japanese living in America.[87] Dewitt was widely praised. Dewitt was also a nutcase.

Congress was actively engaged in the war now. On the ninth, the Senate had passed a number of war-related bills and then adjourned at 2:08 that afternoon. But the House had their nose to the grindstone, passing bills and holding hearings until they adjourned at 4:47.[88] The Senate Naval Affairs committee met for over an hour behind closed doors where they learned more details about the coordinated attacks. Opinions, however, were out in the open. "Members left this session saying that they were 'stunned' by what they had heard. Though some committeemen had indicated that they went to the meeting prepared to criticize, they left pledging full cooperation in meeting new Navy demands.[89] Others were panicky, though. One senator advocated seizing every questionable piece of property in the Western Hemisphere such as French Guiana from which airplanes could be launched to bomb America.[90]

The House committee with oversight of the navy held a closed-door meeting but was scheduled to hold a hearing the next day as well. They were still trying to pin down Secretary Knox and Admiral Stark on a mutually agreeable time to testify.[91]

The issue of secrecy arose. Senator Charles Tobey of New Hampshire, who three days earlier had been an isolationist and a Republican and who was now an internationalist and a Republican, shocked his colleagues when he said, "But when a thing is a fait accompli, and when, as reported on the floor of the Senate in conversation today, a large part of the Pacific fleet is wiped out—and that is a fait accompli, the enemy certainly knows that—the American people and their representatives in Congress ought to know it." A colleague attempted to shush him, but Tobey kept flapping his gums.[92] Other members of Congress were just downright mad. Congressman Emanuel Celler lost his temper so badly, the House actually went into a brief recess until he cooled down. Celler was angrily calling for all isolationists to apologize to Roosevelt.[93]

With America's eyes on the Pacific, across the Atlantic, the Nazis were only beginning to employ their politics of hate. The pawn Vichy government, at the direction of Berlin, rounded up some eleven thousand communists and "Jews who entered France since January, 1936." The reason being, according to Vichy head Marshall Pétain, they were to blame for the attacks on German officers in Paris. "Attacks against officers and soldiers of the armies of occupation constitute a national danger for France." Pétain said investigations "have proven Jews, Communists and foreigners to be responsible." He went so far as to send Adolf Hitler a telegram, offering his "condolences" over the attacks on German officers by Parisians.[94]

But the real target was France's Jewish population. "The announcement also says that all Jews who have entered France . . . are to be either incorporated in working formations or confined in concentration camps. The measure is described as applying Jews in the occupied and unoccupied zones alike."[95]

This dispatch in the *New York Times* ended hopefully. "Despite the severity of these measures there is a strong feeling here tonight that the execution of hostages will not resume."[96]

The situation in Berlin continued to disintegrate rapidly. American journalists, some of whom the Third Reich had successfully feted over the past several years, convincing them of the superiority of the "Thousand Year Reich" and that National Socialism was the only way forward, now ordered these same scribes confined to their homes.

Throughout the 1930s and up to 1941, American journalists stationed in Paris and Berlin fed their newspapers back home a steady diet of stories, many of them puff pieces, about the fascist celebrities in their midst. The American public couldn't get enough "Hitlerania" from these reporters. Many of them were lazy and besotted hedonists, a little too enamored of café society. Others, such as William J. Shirer in Berlin, would go on to chronicle the rise and fall of Nazi Germany with brilliant distinction. But now, neither the hacks nor the professionals were allowed to go to their offices. Nazi officials claimed it was a retaliatory strike because, supposedly, Nazi reporters had been arrested in the United States.

Berlin also wasn't too fond of FDR's remarks of the previous evening.[97]

There had been no slackening or shortage of young men wanting to enlist, and in many areas even more young men turned out day after day. "All recruiting records of the nation's armed forces were shattered . . . as thousands of men attempted to enlist for combat duty in the Army, Navy, Marine Corps or Coast Guard."[98] It appeared that America would need every man possible for all the battles coming down the road.

Not just in the Pacific either, but maybe in North Africa and Europe; it was reported that the American embassy in Rome was burning papers "in preparation for severance of American diplomatic relations with the Axis."[99]

CHAPTER 11

THE ELEVENTH OF DECEMBER

"Germany and Italy Declare War on U.S. and Sign New Axis Alliance"
Evening Star

"United States Declares War against Germany and Italy"
Robesonian

"Naval Base, Air Depot at Manila Aflame after Merciless Attack"
Atlanta Constitution

The formalities began on the morning of December 11, 1941, when German and Italian diplomats paid a call on Secretary of State Cordell Hull to advise him of their governments' decision to declare war on the United States of America, something Hull and the world already knew. Now the whole world would be completely aflame.

After declaring war on America, Adolf Hitler and his fascist factotum, Benito Mussolini, gave ranting speeches in their respective capitals to appreciative and cheering audiences.[1] Hitler announced that "the war would determine the history of the world for the next 500 to 1,000 years. This," he said, "has become the greatest year of decision by the German people." The Japanese ambassador was seated at the Hitler speech; their fates were now joined.[2]

The führer elaborated his reason for war with America, saying, "If anyone said the cultural values have been brought back from America to Europe, it was only the invention of a decayed Jewish mixture."[3] Hitler viewed America as too decadent and lazy to fight a global war effectively—certainly too weak to go up against the so-far unbeatable Wehrmacht. In Hitler's febrile mind, American society was rotted from within by a mongrel Jewish-Negroid race that was addicted to pleasure and the sort of jazz music that was now banned in Germany. Unbeknownst to him, German youth surreptitiously gathered in jazz-listening clubs at great personal risk to savor that same music in still-urbane places such as Berlin.

America was a paper tiger poised to fall; that was apparent to Hitler, who declared that Italy and Germany were now bound to Japan in a "death pact."[4] The strutting and hyper-macho Mussolini, in addressing a crowd of 150,000, simply called it a "steel pact."[5] Like Hitler, Mussolini also went after FDR. "One man, one man only, a real tyrannical Democrat, through a series of infantile provocations, betraying with a supreme fraud the population of his own country, wanted the war and had prepared for it day by day with diabolical obstinacy."[6] Hitler also threw back in Washington's face the leaked War Department document of several days before, which had claimed that the U.S. government was mobilizing for a conflict against Germany to begin in 1943.[7] Secretary of War Henry Stimson had prepared a document at FDR's request, outlining what it would take in terms of money, manpower, and materiel if the United States entered the war, but it was certainly not a declaration of war.[8]

Concluding, Hitler modestly remarked, "I am now the head of the strongest military force in the world, of the strongest air force and the most gallant navy. Behind me is the National Socialist Party with which I grew great and which grew great with me and by me. I thank the President and I thank God for the opportunity given me and the German nation that our generation, too, may write a page in the book of honor of German history."[9]

None of this was news to either Franklin Roosevelt or Cordell Hull. The speeches themselves happened about thirty minutes before the nations' diplomats arrived—and news, even then, traveled fast. Roosevelt and Hull had known this was in the offing and even wanted to get into the war to help Britain. In *Our Country*, Michael Barone wrote, "The United States entered 1941 with a president who was determined to bring the country to the defense of Britain. . . ."[10]

So, it was not surprising that Hull took the whole matter with a bit of nonchalance. He didn't even bother meeting with German first secretary Herbert von Strempel (who was suspected of funneling money to pro-Nazi groups in America)[11] and Chargé d'Affaires Hans Thomsen. They arrived at 8:30 a.m., thirty minutes after Hitler's announcement. Hull was not there, and the two diplomats waited an hour before meeting with Ray Atherton, chief of the European Division. Atherton took the note and said his acceptance of it was only the formalization of the undeclared war that had existed between the two countries since 1939—in retrospect, an astonishing statement. Hull then arrived, but through an aide he informed the two Germans that he was "too busy with important matters to see them."[12] Hull was frostier than the Washington weather, which was only in the low twenties. The *New York Times* reported the only excitement generated at the State Department was from the "correspondents and photographers seeking information and pictures."[13]

The message Hull refused to accept came from Foreign Minister Joachim von Ribbentrop, via their ambassador to America. It was the same as which von Ribbentrop had given personally in Berlin to the American representative, Leland Morris,[14] and Chargé d'Affaires George L. Brandt around the same time. America had not had an ambassador to Germany since 1938, when Hugh Wilson had been recalled for discussions and never returned.[15]

Like the Japanese declaration, the German avowal accused the United States of all manner of things including "having violated in the most flagrant manner and in ever-increasing measure all rules of neutrality in favor of the adversaries of Germany." The missive elaborated, saying, "Although Germany on her part has strictly adhered to the rules of international law in her relations with the United States during every period of the present war, the Government of the United States from initial violations of neutrality had finally proceeded to open acts of war against Germany. The Government of the United States has thereby virtually created a state of war." The statement concluded by breaking off diplomatic relations between the two countries and "as from today, considers herself as being in a state of war with the United States of America."[16]

The situation between Washington and Berlin had been deteriorating for several years, at least since the Munich Conference in 1938, when Roosevelt had publicly urged Hitler not to seek any more territory. In April 1939, FDR had actually offered Hitler economic assistance in exchange for Germany to abide by "10-year[s] of peace and disarmament."[17] By the fall of 1941, the two countries were at war in nearly all respects, at least on the high seas, with Hitler's "unrestricted warfare" directive on all American vessels,[18] both military and commercial.

Some slow-learning observers complained that Germany was in complete violation of the Versailles Treaty ending the Great War, but it was beyond moot at this point. A war machine of terrifying abilities had been assembled and was led by a madman.

Later that morning, around 10:40 a.m., Italian ambassador Prince Colonna arrived at the State Department but only delivered a verbal message of the Italian pronouncement of war on America. This time, only the lowly political adviser to Hull, James Dunn, granted an audience to the Italian. Dunn told Colonna, with all the contempt he could muster, that the United States "fully anticipated that Italy would follow obediently along" the lead of Germany.[19] Apparently Colonna had to be roused for the meeting. Earlier, reporters had banged on the door of the Italian embassy in Washington, only to be greeted by a servant wearing an apron who replied, "The boss is still in bed."[20] Following the formalities, all representatives agreed to surrender their diplomatic credentials, and all parties agreed to the safe and speedy passage of nationals to their respective countries as proscribed by the rules of international law.

Hard as it was to comprehend, the goal of the Geneva Conventions had been to civilize war.

That afternoon, Roosevelt sent a communiqué to the Hill, along with a request for resolutions of war against Germany and Italy. It said:

> On the morning of December 11, the Government of Germany, pursuing its course of world conquest, declared war against the United States. The long-known and long-expected has thus taken place. The forces endeavoring to enslave the entire world now are moving toward this hemisphere. Never before has there been a greater challenge to life, liberty and civilization. Delay invites great danger. Rapid and united effort by all the peoples of the world who are determined to remain free will insure a world victory

of the forces of justice and of righteousness over the forces of savagery and of barbarism.

Then concluding, FDR wrote, "Italy also has declared war against the United States. I therefore request the Congress to recognize a state of war between the United States and Germany and between the United States and Italy."[21]

The *New York Times* noted that while "all over the city the Stars and Stripes flew proudly from public buildings,"[22] the vote in Congress came amid a "grim mood."[23] But it was also a determined mood. Unlike the vote on war with Japan, Congress this time passed the declarations without opposition, as Congresswoman Jeannette Rankin squeakily voted, "present."[24] The people of Montana had been apoplectic over Rankin's vote several days earlier against war with Japan.[25] This time, the Senate voted 88–0 for war with Germany and 90-0 for war with Italy. Two members had been in *abstentia* but apparently in town for the vote on Germany; but they made it back in time for the vote on Italy. Those two were Democrats William Smathers of New Jersey and Charles Andrews of Florida, who both "arrived in the Senate chamber just too late to vote for war against Germany, but were recorded in the Italian count."[26] Again, as with the vote on Japan, some members were missing but sent messages indicating they would have voted in the affirmative.

The silent galleries in the House were not filled to capacity as they were on the eighth, but present were British ambassador Lord Halifax and Archduke Otto of Austria.[27] Halifax had recently journeyed to Detroit, only to be pelted with eggs by isolationists there. He took it in stride at the time by saying, "My, those people certainly were good shots."[28]

While there was nearly 100 percent unanimity in the country to going to war with the hated Japanese, Americans were somewhat more ambivalent about going to war with Germany and Italy, even as the Third Reich had just sneakily torpedoed American military and commercial vessels, much the same as the Japanese had at Pearl Harbor. There were many German Americans and many others who saw Hitler as anti-communist (but pro-socialist) and who knew he had revived the German country. This made some Americans more dubious about the European war. And by and large, Americans had never had anything against Italy. What's more, the East Coast cities of America teemed with their own "Little Italy" sections. Still, despite the ambivalence, not one newspaper of record editorialized against the declarations of war. From Chicago to Minneapolis to Seattle to New Orleans, all praised FDR, all condemned the Axis, and all exhorted Americans to do their utmost to win.

With the two war resolutions in hand, the president first balanced his cigarette holder on the edge of his desk and then signed them, muttering, "Everything seems to come in threes." He then asked Senator Tom Connally for the time, and "with lips drawn back from clenched teeth," Roosevelt scribbled it on each piece of historic paper, along with his distinctive signature.[29] About a dozen members of Congress were there in the Oval Office, and the room was deadly silent. He signed the declaration of war against Germany at 3:05 p.m. and the declaration of war against Italy at 3:06 p.m. From the time his message had been read to Congress at 12:21 p.m. until he signed the resolutions passed by both houses of Congress, America had gone to war with two more countries in less than three hours.[30]

Congress also voted to take the handcuffs off the president. Quickly, they voted to allow U.S. troops to go beyond the constraints of the previous law that barred them from leaving the Western Hemisphere.[31] The House that morning had opened with a prayer by the chaplain, Rev. James S. Montgomery, "with an appeal for divine aid for the nation."[32]

Calls for a formal investigation into the attack on Pearl Harbor were growing louder. Senator Charles Tobey, Republican of New Hampshire, having earned headlines for himself the previous day with his unremitting attacks on the military and his near-leaking of sensitive military information to the press, called yet again for an inquiry and again let the world in on confidential information. "Senator Tobey asserted that the fleet's listening devices 'weren't working,' that the ships 'lay at anchor and no steam up' and that more ships were sunk than had been disclosed by Roosevelt." When asked by a colleague where he'd gotten his information, Tobey replied he'd gotten it from two other colleagues. Tobey told reporters, "I wouldn't want to tell all I've heard on the floor of the Senate." He blasted the navy for allowing a "disaster that's almost unspeakable."[33]

Democratic senator Scott Lucas of Illinois rose to angrily challenge Tobey, warning him that it was "a serious thing to indict anyone until you know what you are talking about." He said Tobey "does not know what he is talking about and he admits he does not. You, Mr. Senator from New Hampshire, are no naval strategist." Lucas was just warming up, furiously and repeatedly attacking Tobey. When Tobey asked Lucas to yield—a cherished and time-honored senatorial privilege—Lucas refused to give him the floor.[34] Tobey was one of the most unpopular men in Washington.

Yet Tobey was not the only senator raising hell. It was bipartisan. Senator Frederick Van Nuys, Democrat of Indiana, charged the military with "criminal negligence." He said it was the responsibility of Congress to get to the bottom of the matter. But Van Nuys himself also trafficked in rumors, as he told reporters "he had heard reports the British military intelligence service had warned the American forces that an attack by the Japanese might be imminent."[35] Meanwhile, Frank Knox and Admiral Stark had still not appeared before any congressional committees.

In his syndicated column, "Washington Merry-Go-Round," Drew Pearson tsk-tsked, "Alibis cannot very well explain away how both Army and Navy Intelligence had their guard down so carelessly when Japanese planes swooped down out of the early morning sky at Hawaii on Monday." He then eviscerated navy intelligence as being dominated by "royalty," where family connections, breeding, and good table manners were more important than skills and, well, intelligence. Navy intelligence, Pearson charged, was dominated by "wealthy young blue-bloods. Only members of the best families can qualify for Military Intelligence, and how much they know about the life around a Japanese waterfront is questionable."[36]

Following Tobey's tirade, another Republican, Minority Leader Charles McNary, who had been Wendell Willkie's running mate in 1940, offered into the record a resolution of unanimous support for FDR by the GOP members.[37] Later that day, the chairmen of the Republican and Democratic parties, Joseph Martin and Edward Flynn, respectively, exchanged telegrams in which they pledged to set aside partisan differences for the duration of the war. They also sent a telegram to the president, indicating their peace accord and then suggested that the headquarters for both parties in Washington be turned over to non-partisan activities to support the war effort. Roosevelt accepted their pledge and suggested the facilities be converted to civil defense.[38] Martin said, "Republicans will not permit politics to enter into national defense."[39] It would remain to be seen how durable this peace would be.

As politicians were making accusations and conjectures and suppositions about the attack on Pearl Harbor, other individuals were pointing out that the navy's patrol planes in the days leading up to December 7 went out each day, at exactly the same time and followed the same route, each day. The theory was the Japanese could have timed their approach and attack when the patrol planes were not in the area. One officer said, "You could set your watch by those flights."[40] Given the fact that the Japanese consulate was a stone's throw from the harbor on Oahu, and from which there was a considerable amount of spying going on, it was one of the saner theories.[41] Secretary of War Henry Stimson, much esteemed by all in Washington, stepped into the fray when he asked Congress not to investigate any dereliction of duty at Pearl Harbor and instead leave it to Roosevelt to get to the bottom of it and take action if deemed necessary. "We don't even know yet all the details of the fight in Hawaii," he sagely pointed out.[42]

Naval officers were still marveling at the accuracy of the Japanese attack at Pearl Harbor, but with little photographic evidence and shaky firsthand evidence, some guesstimated that the Japanese must have flown planes into the American and British ships. Another theory was the Japanese had developed some horrific new bombing technology, possibly based on a "magnetic principle" to account for their uncanny accuracy at Pearl Harbor.[43] Worse, the New York Herald-Tribune reported that "an informed source" said the Japanese were making plans to launch suicide bombers at the West Coast.[44]

Abruptly, all three congressional committees, which had begun preliminary investigations into "what happened in Hawaii," shut down. "The House Navy Affairs Committee abandoned an investigation," and its chairman, Carl Vinson, Democrat of Georgia, said there were no plans to reopen the nascent inquiry. Meanwhile, Senator Harry Truman, Democrat of Missouri, announced his Senate Defense Investigating Committee would cease any further inquiry into the surprise attack, as would the Senate Naval Affairs Committee.[45] The wagons of the bureaucracy were being circled, and editorials across the nation applauded the decision to forestall any investigation.

Stimson would only concede that there had been a "heavy loss of planes" in Hawaii and then said oddly that the loss "is being made good at the present time."[46] The United States and Great Britain had adopted radically different methods in alerting the civilian population as to military reversals. Whereas Washington was under a near-standing order to stay mum on specifics of losses, Winston Churchill believed instead in hitting the British subjects right between the eyes, withholding nothing, reasoning this would rally the civilian population to greater resistance, as opposed to obfuscating. "No one can underrate the gravity of losses inflicted on the United States nor underrate the length of time it will take to marshall the great forces necessary in the Far East for victory," said the prime minister.[47] With the sinking of the *Repulse* and the *Prince of Wales*, Churchill immediately went to Parliament to tell the members in person and in detail.[48] With the loss of the two ships came the deaths of nearly 600 men and officers,[49] including a personal favorite of the prime minister, Admiral Sir T. S. V. Phillips.[50]

Churchill was also forthcoming about reversals in North Africa. "The Libyan offensive did not take the course its authors expected, although it will reach the end at which they aimed," he said. Of course, England had several more years of experience in these matters than did the U.S., and it was harder to explain away German airplanes overhead bombing London than it was an attack 6,000 miles away in the middle of an ocean. Still, Churchill was stricken over the twin losses, according to correspondence with Roosevelt.[51] A survivor of the sinking of the *Repulse* was Cecil Brown of CBS, who'd been embedded on the ship.[52] Another embedded journalist, O. D. Gallagher of the International News Service, was on the *Prince of Wales* and found himself bobbing in a life preserver in shark-infested waters. Of the attack and his long hours waiting to be picked up, Gallagher wrote, "The physical hell created by the Japanese attack was matched by a psychological hell."[53] The British so embraced the hard truths that even the Christmas card put out by the Admiralty reflected on the loss of the two ships.[54]

In Washington, officials deliberated on the need for air-raid shelters and "pontoon bridges across the Potomac River and other emergency plans. . . ."[55]

Treasury officials discussed the possibility of higher taxes with members of Congress.[56] And a plan to fingerprint and issue government identity cards was thrashed out in Congress "as a measure of protection against saboteurs and as a means of speedy identification of hostile agents."[57]

Moreover, in the nation's capital, the Office of Production Management announced that it was ordering Detroit to cut construction of automobiles scheduled for January of 1942 by 50 percent.[58] The *Washington Post* reported that the United States was making plans to issue an outright ban on the sale of new tires and would confiscate all imports in order to conserve rubber for the war effort. The government also announced that it might freeze tin stocks to prevent speculation.[59] The decree came from the Director of Priorities, which was a part of the Office of Production Management.[60] Only the orders for automobiles from defense contractors would be processed. The government came down hard on tire manufacturers, warning them to surrender their inventories. They were told to "cough up" or else. Americans would have to learn how to patch and re-patch flat tires; used tires were exempt from the edict.

Washington bureaucrats also "ordered a 75 percent reduction in the manufacture of coin-operated gambling machines and juke boxes because the metal is needed for the war industries."[61]

A rumor going around D.C., promulgated by Eleanor Roosevelt, was that the president had met with a Japanese diplomat on December 7, but in fact there had been no such meeting. "Imagine the nerve of that man sitting with my husband in the White House when Japanese bombs were falling on our boys! And when I came in he got up and actually bowed and was full of smiles," she told audiences.[62] The First Lady had apparently been misinformed. Doris Kearns Goodwin, in her Pulitzer prize-winning *No Ordinary Time*, explained that "the only explanation is that Eleanor mistook the Chinese ambassador, who had stopped by to see the president shortly after noon, for the Japanese ambassador."[63]

It also leaked out that there had been a contentious debate a year earlier over the oil embargo of Japan, with Harold Ickes, Robert Morganthau, and Frank Knox on one side, arguing for the embargo; and Cordell Hull on the other side, against it. FDR eventually sided with the pro-embargo faction in his cabinet, but only after Japan had stockpiled enough of the precious liquid to conduct extended war operations.[64]

The day before the war declaration by Germany and Italy, FDR had convened his "inner war cabinet" for an hour-and-a-half meeting at the White House beginning at noon. "Those present at the meeting . . . included . . . Hull and Stimson . . . the acting Secretary of the Navy, James V. Forrestal, Admiral Harold B. Stark . . . General George C. Marshall . . . and Sumner Welles, Under-Secretary of State." During this meeting, the final touches were being added to FDR's "battle room" in the West Wing of the White House.[65]

In addition to a flurry of memos about the disposition of the *Sea Cloud*, a yacht that had been requisitioned by the navy and owned by a wealthy individual, Roosevelt also had to put up with Harold Stark, who was a racist and a bootlick. "Dear Mr. President, You are not only the most important man to the United States today, but to the world. If anything should happen to you, it would be a catastrophe. I do not say this to you because of my own personal relationship, but as a cold-blooded fact. I have said if I were Hitler and were timing it, and he probably has timed it, that I would have ready a spectacular raid on the United States—Washington, New York, or somewhere. Please . . . let somebody provide . . . a place where, in case of an air raid or any other disturbance, not only your safety, but the precious hours of sleep which you need and which are probably too few, would be provided for against any disturbance of any kind." [66]

The news coming from the Philippines and the entire Pacific was becoming gloomier as the battle for Wake Island raged on, and the Japanese were advancing toward General Douglas MacArthur. The Japanese took the airport on Luzon by parachuting in thousands of troops. "More than 100 bombs were dropped in the first hour of the attack."[67] The Japanese were invading Luzon and inexorably driving toward Manila. Furthermore, Tokyo claimed to have sunk a U.S. battleship and submarine in the area, though neither was identified. Berlin radio reported that the Japanese had sunk an American aircraft carrier, the *Lexington*, which, if true, would have been a devastating blow. But both Tokyo and Berlin were schooled in psychological warfare and, in the days after December 7, flooded the airwaves with disinformation.

It also appeared that the British "Gibraltar of the Far East," Singapore, was about to fall to Tokyo.[68] The great fear among G.I.s was falling captive to enemy hands. The Japanese believed no man should ever allow himself to be a captive of another man, and in their culture, it was better to die than to live with the shame of being a prisoner of war. Personal suicide had an honored place in the Japanese culture. Trouble was, they imposed this view onto their enemies, and it would shortly become known how monstrously cruel and cold-blooded the Japanese were toward American, British, and Australian POWs. Furthermore, Americans did not realize how racist many of the Japanese military leadership were. They hated Anglos, Chinese, Koreans— anyone not of the Japanese race and culture.

The bad news kept coming. The Japanese took the American consulate in Hanoi and arrested the U.S. representative there, O. Edmund Clubb, along with his staff.[69]

Americans could take some cheer in the sinking of a large 29,000-ton Japanese battleship, believed to be the *Haruna*.[70] But in a bombing raid on Manila and Cavite, the Japanese claimed they'd destroyed dozens of parked American planes. Cavite was aflame. Still, a spokesman for MacArthur told reporters, "'The situation is completely in hand' and that Japanese forces along the coast were being mopped up."[71] Roosevelt had once said of MacArthur, "Never underestimate a man who overestimates himself."[72]

Roosevelt also once told a crony that Huey Long and MacArthur were the most dangerous men in America.[73] There was no doubt, though, that MacArthur was a national hero, an image fostered in part by his aggressive press staff. For example, the week of December 8, there was the general, heroically photographed on the cover of *Life* magazine with the caption, "Commander of the Far East."[74] The magazine effusively called him a "stickler for sartorial splendor." The fawning profile was written by Clare Boothe Luce, wife of *Life* publisher Henry Luce.[75]

The U.S. Army continued to run print ads asking for recruits, but it was a waste of time. None of the branches could process the incoming deluge of applicants fast enough.

The first member of Congress to be called up was a young and lanky congressman from the Hill Country of Texas. An FDR and New Deal man through and through, Lyndon Baines Johnson, was ordered to report in San Francisco for active duty at the 12th Naval District, with the rank of lieutenant commander.[76] The day after FDR's address to Congress, Johnson went to see Admiral Chester Nimitz, also from the Hill Country of Texas, and asked Nimitz to sign the paperwork placing him on active duty.[77]

It wasn't as noble as it appeared. It was really about making himself look good to his constituents. Johnson successfully wheedled and schemed and pulled strings to keep himself out of the war zone and off any ship; ultimately, he only saw the most minimal of duty, sometimes seeming more like a tourist in the Pacific than a fighting man for the navy. He and his aide, John Connally, found time to tour nightclubs in California and hire a Hollywood photographer to take pictures of them in their navy dress uniforms.[78] After the war, the driven young congressman would prove his relentless ability to get what he wanted as senator and then president.

The sale of defense bonds quickened even as the newspapers were still hawking Christmas gifts. Suggestions for gifts that men could give their wives included diamond rings, going for as much as $29.00,[79] and "Barbizon gowns," elaborately designed slips and lingerie.[80] Also being hawked were fur coats from $59.95 up to $325.00 at J. Fred Johnson & Co. in Kingsport, New York.[81] Racial stereotypes also filled the newspapers. In the *Evening Star*, the D. L. Bromwell Co. was advertising the "Darkey Hitching Post," a racial caricature of a black lawn jockey in the form of a small yard statue.[82] Haley's Car Service ran an ad with a drawing of a Japanese man in the now-familiar distortion complete with oversized eye glasses, evil-looking eyebrows and a large and mean smile.[83] Other popular choices were Old Spice aftershave in an elaborate box set for men, and sleepwear for women.

Approaching the holiday season, U.S. Agriculture officials assured American households that there was no need to worry about food scarcity, despite gossip going around. "They pointed to America's bulging granaries and well stocked pastures, and confidently seconded President Roosevelt's declaration that 'there is enough food for us all' and more left over to send abroad. Only in the case of spices . . . and some luxury items imported [from] the Far East is there the possibility of a restricted supply."[84] In California "alien Japanese"-grown vegetables were taken off the market even though there was plenty of demand. "At present, no transactions are being made and none are legal with alien Japanese," said a produce official. Also, there was fear of poisoned vegetables coming from alien Japanese farms making their way into stores there.[85]

Housewives were stocking up for the Christmas holidays and would need plenty of sugar for pastries. Sugar was fetching 15 cents for a two-pound bag, two cans of Del Monte Bartlett peaches were 29 cents, and "Flako" pie crust was 11 cents a package.[86] A quart of 90-proof rum was going for $1.99, though food prices had skyrocketed in the past year.[87]

Corn was emerging as a vitally important staple of the diet for civilians and G.I.s, as well as important feed for livestock. From corn, scientists could extract oil, sugar, and starch along with "a multiplicity of chemicals used in everything from textile and drug manufacture to leather tanning and explosives."[88] Fortunately for the war effort, corn harvests for 1941 had gone through the roof, with billions of bushels generated.

At the McCord radio factory in Detroit, new helmets were being developed for the military. For over twenty years, American G.I.s had still been using the old "doughboy" helmets of the Great War, which when turned upside down, looked like a chamber pot. The new helmets were stronger, more comfortable, and most importantly, provided more protection to the American soldier.[89]

The head of the Office of Production Management, William Knudsen, held a press conference in which he not only called for a doubling of the production of four-engine bombers, from 500 to 1,000 per month, but also for a "168-hour, 7-day work week." Industries that needed to be stepped up, he said, were "guns, planes, tanks, ammunition and shipbuilding." Plants for the construction of aircraft would be located inland, away from easy enemy air attacks.[90] Also in Detroit, the Nash-Kelvinator Company was churning out airplane propellers. A week earlier, Nash-Kelvinator had been making cars and appliances.[91] America's peacetime industrial might was rapidly becoming a wartime "Arsenal of Democracy."

America easily outstripped the Axis powers in the production of steel and in the mining of sulphur, which was needed for gunpowder. Indeed, up until December 7, much of the world's exports of sulphur came from the United States.

The newest casualty lists rolled in from the Pacific, and now death announcements were beginning to appear in local newspapers. War Department letters were arriving at the homes of grief-stricken parents and newly minted widows. In small-town America in 1941, there were few secrets; when someone learned of the loss of a beloved boy, within minutes neighbors knew and would come over to offer condolences. Shortly thereafter, the family minister or priest or rabbi was at the home to help console the suffering parents and forlorn family.

The local newspaper would invariably find out and write up a small story of the boy who'd died, giving his rank and service of record, along with a photo from the family (if possible) and a quote from the boy's high school football coach or scoutmaster. Headlines such as "Two Alabamians Die in Fighting around Hawaii"[92] or, "Lynn, Hingham Youths Killed at Honolulu"[93] appeared in papers around the country.

After the initial gasping shock from the mailman—who painfully knew he was the unwilling messenger of death—came the realization that their son was never coming home again, never bounding into the kitchen again, asking what was for dinner. A boy who had left home, tousle-haired, full of adventure, freckle-faced, toothsome, the light of his parents' lives, the joy of his grandparents, the secret love of the girl next door, was now dead. His Christian name had often been an afterthought. He was not John but "Johnny." He was not Edward but "Eddie." He was not Thomas but "Tommy." Or he might have had a nickname—Butch, Dutch, Mick, Duke, or Barney.

Now the boy would never know the love of a good woman or watch his son take his first step or play catch with that son. He would never see the first time his son would put a razor to his face, watch a daughter go off to the prom, walk her down the aisle, or know the quiet pride of being a good man among the uncommon men of his country.

Grey hair would never be combed. His parents would never hold him again, hug him again, and dry his tears again, even as they could not stop their own. The pain and the feeling of emptiness and helplessness were unbearable for the thousands of inconsolable parents and grandparents and brothers and sisters. Everybody had a sick, wrenching, and wretched feeling in the pits of their stomachs. Some filled theirs with alcohol to deaden the pain. Some mothers' hair went white in a matter of days. Some simply withdrew. None would ever get over the loss of their boy.

It was so final, so useless, so stupid, so heartrending. But it was also as necessary as it was tragic.

Private William T. Anderson of Quantico, Virginia, was first on the new lists of dead soldiers, though the names were not released in alphabetical order. His nearest relative was his now grief-incapacitated father, Herbert C. Anderson.[94] This roll call of the dead came from the army and announced eighty-seven more men killed in Hawaii. The list was of three officers and eighty-four enlisted men. Under the heading, "More Victims," a second list of eleven men killed was released, but it was also announced that Private Robert R. Niedzwiecki of Grand Rapids and Private Raymond C. Joiner, of Henderson, North Carolina, who had both been reported as killed, were in fact alive, much to the relief of their families.[95] The parents of Wilbur Carr of Franklin, Ohio, were also relieved to find that the reports of their son's death had been premature.[96]

Another tragic Pearl Harbor death was that of Rear Admiral Isaac Campbell Kidd, fifty-seven, the first flag officer to die in the Pacific. Kidd had reported for duty on Oahu in February of 1940. He was a chief of staff and an aide to the commander of a battleship group in Pearl Harbor, though the War Department did not release the name of the ship on which he lost his life on December 7.[97] (It was later learned that Kidd was on the bridge of the *Arizona* where he assumed command, trying vainly to get it up to battle stations. When the ship exploded, he was killed and his remains never recovered.) For years, Kidd had warned to deaf ears to watch out for the Japanese and was regarded in the navy as an expert on the emerging enemy. His son, Isaac C. Kidd Jr., was scheduled to graduate the following week from the Naval Academy in Annapolis, just as his father had in 1906. Admiral "Captain Kidd" was later posthumously awarded the Medal of Honor.[98]

In unoccupied Vichy France, it was reported that, under the pretext of the charge of subversion, eleven Frenchmen were shot by Germans. Elaborating, the Associated Press story stated, "Reports from the occupied zone said police made mass arrests in southern France and ear-marked hundreds of Jews and 'Communists' for concentration camps."[99]

While diplomats in Berlin were going through the formalities, the Nazis were less formal and cordial to American journalists and citizens. In retaliation for the arrest of German nationals in America, the Third Reich arrested the precise number of Americans residing in their country, including four Associated Press correspondents.[100] Tit for tat, the government there announced that for every German arrested in America, they would arrest an equal number of U.S. citizens.

As of the eleventh, U.S. attorney general Francis Biddle announced that the Justice Department and the FBI had picked up "865 Germans, 147 Italians and 1,291 Japanese as enemy aliens."[101]

There was also the very real problem of what to do with the possessions of the Axis powers that had fallen into American hands. After delivering the message of war from Mussolini, members of the Italian embassy were furiously trying to sell their cars. Embassy officials were also stocking up on American vitamins by having a delivery boy from a nearby pharmacy make repeated trips to and from the facility, loaded down with "boxes of vitamin pills."[102] Several days later, an exchange of journalists took place between Germany and the United States, although a New York Times reporter, Guido Enderis, was exempted by the Nazis and allowed to stay on in Berlin.[103]

A new government office, similar to the Alien Property Custodian agency set up during "World War I," was created in the United States to handle the property of the soon-to-be leaving foreign diplomats, as revealed by the Washington Post. The Post's use of a numbered war was possibly the first iteration in print.[104]

The nation's capital was expanding its scope and realm of inquiry. "The Department of Justice turned its attention today to disloyal Americans," which the Boston Evening Globe referred to as "potential Benedict Arnolds."[105] The Los Angeles Times called them "quislings."[106]

The notion of Nazi spies let loose in America became a preoccupation of not just the FBI but also of popular culture. This was epitomized by the release of the farcical, "You Nazty Spy!", a Three Stooges short subject film, produced by Columbia Pictures in January 1941, in which the hapless ringleader Moe Howard actually performed an astonishingly realistic imitation of the führer. As far as these three Jewish former vaudevillians were concerned, satire was the best way to answer the absurdities of Nazism.

Now that war was official, the movie moguls in Hollywood—the vast majority of them Jewish—eagerly embraced what they saw as their patriotic duty and shed any inhibitions they may have had about taking on Germany. These immigrants (mostly from poor provinces in Russia) also saw the war effort as their golden opportunity to prove their *bona fides* as assimilated American citizens. Americans were about to be inundated with a sea of flag-waving, patriotic celluloid, much of it stridently propagandistic.

The phrase "Fifth Columnists" kept coming up in news dispatches. The expression had its roots in the Spanish Civil War and referred to subversive elements inside a country who were working with outside agitators or revolutionaries. The worry in America was that Fifth Columnists were working clandestinely to help the Axis powers through sabotage and subversion. But Biddle said that FBI director J. Edgar Hoover had assured him there were no Fifth Columnists operating in the United States.[107] Yet in Miami, officials discovered a train trestle wired to explode with dynamite, its wires and batteries set to detonate.

The Justice Department contradicted itself and said that no lawful American could be arrested, though for what it was not specific.[108] It also decided to suspend the naturalization citizenship of over 450,000 Japanese, Germans, and Italians born in America.[109]

Tensions mounted in the country, and sometimes it seemed as if everyone was a suspect. Brush fires on the coast of Washington State were suspected by local police to be signal fires for approaching planes. "The fires were in the form of arrows" pointing to a naval base and Seattle.[110]

No one was yet using the word "paranoia" in describing Americans after December 7. After all they'd gone through in just a scant several days, their skittishness was understandable. The Navy Department announced it had mined the New York Harbor and warned commercial vessels to take care while approaching and departing the port.[111] It also announced that due to the constrictions of war, fallen sailors and marines would be temporarily buried "where they died . . . They will be buried with full military honors."[112]

The nation's capital was just as skittish. In addition to armed navy guards posted at all federal buildings, machine-gun nests went up around town as well, including on the Memorial Bridge, which connected the town to Arlington National Cemetery and Virginia. Civil-defense units were organized in all cities, big and small, all locales nationwide.[113] In Atlanta, "Immediate organization of an Atlanta Emergency Defense Corps, dedicated solely to the protection of the lives and properties of Atlantans" was urgently reported by the *Atlanta Constitution*.[114] To answer the propaganda campaigns being ginned up by Tokyo and Berlin, it was urged "that men trained in public relations and publicity work [could] constitute a counterforce against subversive propaganda."[115]

Though under martial law, military and civilian officials were incrementally loosening things in Hawaii. Stores had begun to open, and though the naval facilities of Ford Island and Hickam Field were smoldering still, there was only light damage to civilian areas. A phone call was even allowed from a man on the islands to his brother in California, but it was closely monitored by navy censors. "He was given permission to talk to his brother on condition that nothing was said about the weather, military conditions on the island, cables, letters, or the war in general."[116]

Following the scares of two days earlier, newspapers began publishing guidelines for the dos and don'ts of civilian defense. Helpful tips included: "Don't believe or spread rumors . . . Don't mention air raids in the presence of small children . . . Don't rush into the street if an air raid should come."[117] A columnist for Baltimore's *Sun* told readers, "Fear is one of the most contagious of diseases, and the individual should remember that, if he breaks down, the man next to him is very likely to follow suit."[118]

Other news stories contained helpful suggestions on "How to Teach Yourself to See Better in Blackouts." "Blackout seeing is practically the reverse of daylight seeing. It is done not only with a different part of the eye—but with a different and special set of nerve endings."[119] It was urged that children's energies be focused on "knitting and dishwashing."[120] And, "Don't expect all news to be good. We are at war. Mistakes and accidents are inevitable, some battles may be lost." At this point and for some time, all American military battles would be lost.[121]

Only four days into a great new world war, America was losing. Terribly.

So it was well-received news when the songwriters of America began churning out quickie songs to boost the national morale. "Tin Pan Alley's batteries, featuring saxophone and fiddle rather than bugle and drum, are ready to open fire on Japan." The papers reported that thousands of songwriters were flooding the offices of song publishers with tunes like, "You're a Sap, Mr. Jap" and "The Jap Won't Have a Chinaman's Chance" and "Good Bye Mama, We'll See You in Yokohama." The president of Broadcast Music, Inc., which put out the call, was Sam Lerner, who had a slightly more famous brother, Jay.[122]

Anti-Japanese sentiment was manifesting itself in other ways as well. The annual Japanese Cherry Blossom Festival in Washington was changed instead to the "Oriental Cherry Blossom Festival." Vandals also cut down four Japanese cherry trees, originally planted in 1912 as a gift from Tokyo, along the Tidal Basin in the nation's capital. Inscribed on the trees was "To Hell with the Japanese."[123] Two of the destroyed trees had been planted when Mrs. William Howard Taft attended the ceremonies commemorating the gift. When FDR ordered the building of the Jefferson Memorial in 1939, some outraged Washington women chained themselves to the trees one cold morning because some would have to be bulldozed before the memorial could be built. An enterprising government staffer took steaming pots of coffee to the tree huggers, who drank the proffered liquid happily and excessively. The staffer then waited for nature to take its course, at which time the bulldozers moved in. [124]

Department stores across America were taking Japanese products off their shelves, "some of which were destroyed and the remainder placed in storage." Some merchants were rebuked by patrons for displaying "Japanese" goods, which were, however, Chinese, as proved by the "Made in China" label. Dance bands were not playing "Japanese Sandman." At the Freer Gallery of Art, Nipponese paintings, sculptures, and representations were removed. The gallery had been "world famous for its Oriental collection."[125]

G.C. Murphy, a national chain of five-and-dime stores, was one of the first to remove all their goods manufactured in Japan. At another, Woolworth's, a clerk laughed about burning up a Santa Claus made in Japan.[126]

Other welcome news, which helped distract Americans, was that Hollywood was continuing to churn out flicks. Walt Disney, a genius and true American original who had invented the color cartoon and feature-length cartoon, had just released *Dumbo* when his studio was commandeered by the military on December 8. (It was adjacent to the vital Lockheed air plant, and his site was needed as a primary defense station.) He halted most other work at his studio to finish his next feature-length cartoon, *Bambi*, before accepting a commission from the Naval Bureau of Aeronautics to make twenty animated training films. These were the first in a flood of Disney films in aid of the war effort (both live-action and cartoons).[127]

Greta Garbo and Melvin Douglas were starring in a racy new comedy, *Two-Faced Woman* (it proved to be a flop and Garbo's last movie),[128] and gossip columnists spotted Walter Pidgeon, Richard Ney, and Greer Garson taking a respite from the filming of their new British wartime movie, *Mrs. Miniver*.[129]

Baseball legend Babe Ruth was headed to Hollywood "to play in the Lou Gehrig picture [*Pride of the Yankees*]. It will be an enriching experience, no doubt," said the Bambino.[130] A new comedy was released, *Look Who's Laughing*, starring Edgar Bergen, the famed ventriloquist and actor, and popular comedic actress Lucille Ball. Millions of Americans went to the movies each week to see cartoons, serials, newsreels, and feature presentations—in 1941, the greatest source of popular visual entertainment.

But these distractions did not negate the horrific reality unfolding across the globe. After announcing their "death pact," the three Axis allies strengthened their agreement by also announcing a "no separate pledge." In essence, "the agreement bound them not only to make war indissolubly together, but also to make peace after it in a common front."[131] FDR also made a pact, but with Chiang Kai-shek and his forces in China battling the occupying army of Japan. He told the generalissimo they had a "common enemy."[132]

The speculation that German planes had been used at Manila and in other battle zones was regularly dispelled now as experts began asking rational questions, including how the planes would have gotten to the Far East anyway, what with the British naval blockade and the very remote possibility they had been flown all the way from Germany to Japan. It was established shortly thereafter that no German planes or pilots had participated in any battle in the Pacific, nor had four-engine bombers been used at Pearl Harbor by the Japanese. The Germans weren't needed, as the Japanese seemed to be doing a thorough job all by themselves.

Manila, Luzon, and other parts of the Philippines were under sustained and numbing attack by round-the-clock Japanese bombing, despite the whistling-past-the-graveyard talk of "Dugout Doug" MacArthur.

The psyche of the country was badly battered. Since the morning of the seventh, all the news had been dire, except Roosevelt's spectacular declaration of war against Japan. The daily reports of Nazi gains, of British losses, of false alarms, of casualty reports, of rumors, innuendo, gossip, indecision, inaction, roundups, cancellations, and detentions were wearing down a population that had been battered for over a decade since the onslaught of the Great Depression.

At the end of 1941—just when, for the first time since 1929, unemployment had dipped below 10 percent,[133] when war seemed a faraway proposition, and when America had two oceans to protect her—an unwanted war had overrun the country. Now, even the White House was undergoing evening blackouts, and plans were made to move the original copies of the Declaration of Independence and the U.S. Constitution from display in the Library of Congress to a secure location in Maryland. The documents creating the very foundation of the government were put in hiding, as officials feared their destruction by bombs or saboteurs.[134] Hiding one's government was not cheery news. Mrs. Roosevelt hated the wartime precautions used in the White House, especially the long and dour blackout drapes.[135]

Apartment buildings on the East and West Coast were organizing their basements as bomb shelters, complete with stocked food and toys for children. The Seventh Wonder of the Modern World, the Panama Canal, was closed each evening.[136] Preparations were going forward for the construction of bomb shelters in the greater Los Angeles area. One proposal was for shelters to be no more than 300 feet apart from each other.[137] Yet another air-raid

THE ELEVENTH OF DECEMBER | 249

warning struck terror into Southern California. At night, unidentified planes flew over the entire coast that was blacked out, and radio stations went off the air after announcing the raid. "Anti-aircraft and machine gunners scrambled to their weapons at Ft. MacArthur, which was promptly placed on an 'alert' basis."[138] The planes went unidentified and no bombs fell.[139]

During the state-wide blackout, car accidents were reported, and several drivers were killed as a result. Airplanes headed for Los Angeles were diverted to other cities, as the radio beam at the airport had been turned off. The fact that a noisy electrical storm happened along at precisely the wrong time did not help Southern Californians' jittery nerves.[140] New York had experienced three false air-raid warnings in just a couple of days, including one during rush hour on the morning of the tenth.[141] The city was still trying to clean up the mess and the confusion, even as hotels in the five boroughs were making their own plans for air raids.[142]

Across the country, Americans were asked to stay off the telephone line, so as to not tax the phone system. Far more stringent sacrifices and huge mistakes would follow shortly. Government officials in New England sheepishly announced that they had frankly botched the faux air-raid alert of several days earlier.[143] Citizen confidence in government was waning in some quarters.

The news of the war and the incompetence of America would get worse, much worse, before it got better.

CHAPTER 12

THE TWELFTH OF DECEMBER

"Army Death List from Hawaii
Reaches 155, Still Incomplete"

Evening Star

"Knox in Honolulu"

Atlanta Constitution

"Plan Bared for Mobilizing Men, Women"

Boston Daily Globe

These early days of the war were among the very worst. As of the twelfth, Wake Island was still holding on—but just barely—and in a press conference, FDR praised the beleaguered marine garrison fighting there. The British conceded that operations were not going well in the Malaya-Thailand sector and that the Japanese "had dented British defense lines in the jungles.... Heavy fighting continued."[1] Hong Kong was closer to being occupied by Japanese troops, who were also coming ashore on the Philippine main island of Luzon, where most of the commerce and population were located. The Japanese claimed they had destroyed over two hundred Americans planes, the vast majority still on the ground. Also, "the Japanese attacked Olongapo, 50 miles west of Manila, one of the most important naval installations in the Philippines [and] the province of Batangas and Clark Field, 40 miles north of Manila."[2]

Some unconfirmed reports said Japanese pilots were flying their planes into American targets, and Admiral Thomas Hart, commander in chief of the Asiatic Fleet, said the Japanese inflicted "very great damage. There was a considerable loss of life, more among the civilians in the city of Cavite than among the naval personnel."[3] Whereas General MacArthur was confident, Hart could only muster a languid, "We shall do our best" statement.[4] For his part, Winston Churchill more confidently told Parliament, "We are all in this. Not only the British Empire now, but the United States are fighting for life. It would indeed bring shame upon our generation if we did not teach them a lesson which will not be forgotten in the records of 1000 years."[5] Churchill for his part had been jubilant about the Japanese attack on America. "Churchill regarded the Japanese attack as Britain's salvation. He recalled in his memoirs the emotion he felt at hearing the news: 'We had won the *war* . . .'"[6]

The night of the seventh, he was having a depressing dinner with Averill Harriman and American ambassador John Winant. A butler brought in a small radio, and Churchill fiddled with the dials, finally getting it turned on. When he heard the report, Churchill immediately called FDR via the transatlantic line: "What's this about Japan?" Roosevelt confirmed that Japan and America were now at war: "We are all in the same boat now," FDR told the British prime minister.[7]

As of the twelfth, the Russians had still not decided if they would declare war on Japan. Joseph Stalin was locked in a fight to the death with Germany along a 1,800-mile front and was terrified that if he declared war on the Japanese, they would invade Siberia, opening a two-front war. The German offensive, Operation Barbarossa, involved 4.5 million German soldiers,[8] and Russia needed all the men they had in uniform to stave off the assault. Russia could barely muster the forces to withstand the German invasion, so it was open to question whether Russia could even send troops to meet the Japanese. As of December 1941, the outcome of the German offensive was still uncertain, and the smart money was on Hitler's army. However, it did appear as if Germany had slowed for the winter, unable to continue its assault because of the brutal Russian cold. But the army of the Third Reich remained in place, hunkered down, with Moscow still in sight.

Out of the midst of the war gloom came some somberly and disquietingly good news with the announcement of the first American hero of the "New War."[9] Captain Colin P. Kelly Jr. had been the pilot of the plane that had sunk the Japanese battleship *Haruna*, and his name had been released for radio and newspaper reports. Kelly's type of aircraft was unidentified in news reports, as was the cause of his death, but it was made known he had scored "three direct hits on the Japanese capital ship."[10] Kelly's tragic heroics were a bit of good news in the morass of the unremittingly bad reports and bulletins going around in America. But in this, the first naval battle between America's forces and the Japanese, other ships had slipped away, avoiding greater losses for the enemy. In addition to everything else, luck seemed to be on Tokyo's side.

Another little bit of heroic news was the report of the Pan Am Clipper that had escaped Guam, shot up by the imperial navy. It had managed to limp back to San Francisco with the passengers—all employees of the airline who had been stationed on the island—safe and unharmed. It was a story of great courage involving the pilot, who had to engage in some fancy flying to escape the war zone. Left behind at Guam were hundreds of civilians, though, as well as a handful of U.S. Marines.[11]

Interestingly, commercial flights by Pan Am continued in the Pacific, although along new routes and with new passengers: military men. "No commercial passengers or private materials are accepted for the time being on the Pacific," the air service company said, although flights for private citizens would continue along the east and west coasts of the United States.[12]

The sad realization of another world war was beginning to settle in. Americans were stoic and resolved, though, even as they were facing the unknown. President Roosevelt proclaimed, "The eleventh of December, 1941, will be recorded in history as the date marking the formal beginning of the Great War to preserve this world as a living space for free men. For Americans, there is a certain measure of comfort to be derived from the fact that we are formally at war . . . At long last we know where we stand and we know what has to be done."[13] Before the eleventh, America had only been at war with Japan, and it was still a matter of consternation for many Americans as to whether their country should get into the European war. The surprise declaration of war by Germany and Italy committed America to a wholly different kind of war, a completely "undiscovered country" of death and destruction.

Only days into the new world war, very few in America really knew yet what would have to be done, the sacrifices that would have to be made, the carnage and slaughter of millions of civilians by the Axis powers, the untold millions of deaths of young men in uniform on both sides, and how this war would change the world—and their nation—for all time.

America's fighting men had already died in wartime since the attack on the seventh, and many more would die in the days, months, and years ahead in war zones around the world; but thousands of fighting men also died in accidents right here in America. Not a day went by that did not include bulletins of military airplanes crashing in Norfolk, Miami, and Texas or accidental drownings or accidental shootings in and around the other hundreds of military installations. So many domestic military plane crashes occurred that guidelines were issued instructing civilians on how to help downed pilots escape from the crafts and their harnesses. The sacrifice of these servicemen who were stateside was no less than those of their brothers in harm's way across the rest of the world.

Everybody was coming to understand the rationale behind the Japanese attacks. It was not insanity. The scheme was a blending of their own philosophy of attack first and declare war later. The goal, by utilizing the Nazi blitzkrieg—lightning war—had been a quick decapitation of the American military in the Far East with the hope that Washington, left virtually defenseless to an invasion of the West Coast, would sue for peace. Then the empire of Japan would have the entire western Pacific to itself, with its weak governments and rich natural resources.

Some Americans were also coming to recognize that the arrogance and braggadocio of the American navy before December 7—that the U.S. Navy was superior to that of the Japanese—had been a myth. "The sea power of the United States and the sea power of Britain were inferior to Japanese sea power in the Pacific last week; they are still inferior, though even more so, today."[14]

The fact that many ships in the spring of 1941 had been repositioned to the Atlantic had further weakened the American naval presence in the Pacific. "The attack on Hawaii was a serious military defeat, bordering on a disaster. For a nation of less strength, it might have been an irretrievable disaster. This blunt fact cannot be concealed, even though full details have not been made public, for obvious military reasons."[15]

It had been five days since the attack on Pearl Harbor, and Americans still had few hard details of the attack, but they had heard rumors of additional attacks there. No photographs of the aftermath appeared in the nation's publications.

Other than the names of the battleships *West Virginia* and *Oklahoma*, which had appeared in early stories, no subsequent bulletin contained any details about the damage done at Pearl Harbor by the Japanese. "There probably is good reason for suppressing temporarily the Pearl Harbor statistics, since the Japanese can only guess at what damage they did—until they have time to hear from their spy system in the islands. But the whole story should be told reasonably soon," opined the *Los Angeles Times*.[16]

After being picked up in the shark-infested waters of the China Sea, war correspondent Cecil Brown filed a harrowing story of the head-shaking loss of the British ship *Repulse*.[17] "In [a] float, a young midshipman, with a hole in his side big enough to put a fist in sat silently, clenching his teeth. Some men had the skin scalded from their backs, but made no complaint."[18]

Japanese planes had first set the ship aflame, and then, like sharks smelling blood in the water, more planes swooped down. The ease with which the Japanese had sunk the giant battlewagon only added to the sense of vulnerability all Americans felt. Allies were also taken aback at the ferocity at which the enemy soldier waged war. Japanese society, with its emphasis on consensus, had subsumed the needs of the individual. Dying for the greater good of the group was honorable. This social value was the product of centuries of feudal warfare; after a long tradition of devastating civil war and the Way of the Shogun, the small and crowded island nation of Japan had learned to survive by placing great value on social peace and the sublimation of egoism. "They die with the same fervor in battle as the Mohammedan. . . . This national characteristic of the Japs may prove a great factor in the Pacific fight," said an expert on the Far East to a group of businessmen in Alabama.[19]

One newspaper, more blunt and concise in its assessment of Japan's edge in waging war, simply described the enemy as "short and sturdy."[20]

It was slowly dawning on navy officials and an American public that had been weaned on the unsinkable-battleship theory that—after December 7 and the subsequent and apparently all-too-easy sinking of the *Repulse* and the *Prince of Wales*—the day of the mighty warship had passed. The airplane, whose development as a war weapon in the Great War had only scratched the surface, would rule this new war.

The old Spads and Fokkers and Nieuports of years earlier lumbered along at not much over 100-miles-per-hour and were weapons of short-range capability. They mostly fought each other. Now, the Japanese, the Germans, and the British all had superior fighter planes and bomber planes. They were equipped to take on other planes and targets on the ground and the high seas. These planes and their pilots had advanced training techniques, bombing sights, long-range capabilities, high altitudes, and, most importantly, speed. Some of the fighter planes of 1941 cruised at well over 320 miles per hour and in dives and dogfights could approach 340 miles per hour or more. America was developing the B-17 and other durable high-level bombers but was woefully behind on fighter planes. The navy in some cases was still flying biplanes.

Originally established as a part of the U.S. Army in 1907, America's aviation force in the years leading up to 1941 went by a number of different titles and was placed under various parts of the army. One of its most familiar titles, the U.S. Army Air Corps, was used from July 2, 1926 to June 20, 1941. The air corps fought during World War II as the Army Air Force. The service name that we all know today, the U.S. Air Force, didn't become its own service until after the war in 1947, gaining special strategic prominence in the post–World War II nuclear age.

But in 1941, Hermann Göring's mighty Luftwaffe ruled the skies. The British already had lost two aircraft carriers to German aerial assault, the

Courageous and the *Glorious*, though British planes had helped sink the great German battleship *Bismarck*. Of course, the Italian navy, such as it was, had nearly been blown out of the water by British airplanes in the Mediterranean. One editorial bluntly and accurately said, "The war with Japan is an air war."[21]

In Europe, the Germans had perfected the use of military aircraft in their blitzkriegs across the European continent, and though they had mostly abandoned the Battle of Britain, the unremitting aerial assault might have succeeded had not Hitler abruptly changed the bombing targets from military to civilian out of a spiteful desire to demoralize the British populace. The bombing of the military targets was nearly wiping out Great Britain's ability to produce and get aloft her Spitfire and Hurricane fighter planes. By changing targets, Hitler gave the English a chance to rebuild their industrial plants, and the bombing of civilians in London did nothing more than anger the stubborn and resolute British.

Understatedly, David Lawrence wrote in the *Evening Star*, "The bomber may decide this war."[22] The British were engaged in daytime bombing of German naval installations at Wilhelmshaven and Emden, but planes were also being used to observe German ship movement.[23] The fear was, with American and British ships now occupied in the Pacific, the Germans would step up their naval operations in the Atlantic.

A new idea was mulled over in Washington to expand a Selective Service for all able-bodied men *and* women from the ages of eighteen all the way up to sixty-five, even more all-encompassing than the British draft.[24] "We undoubtedly are soon going to consider the registration of women," said Brigadier General Louis B. Hershey, director of the Selective Service Administration. He estimated there were about 20,000,000 who could serve in some way, either replacing men in factories, enlisting in civil defense or with the armed services in noncombatant capacities.[25] Then Congress introduced a bill to draft able-bodied men, but the actual training would be of men ages nineteen to forty-five; however, Hershey said that a "boy of 19 would not be sent into combat service." He elaborated on an expansive draft. "This registration is necessary to get an overall picture of the manpower of the country."[26] Earlier notions about the drafting of women were set aside for the time being.

But, five days after Pearl Harbor, recruiting offices across the nation were still being mobbed. It wasn't just the quantity of the young men eager to enlist; it was the quality as well. Prior to the seventh of December, most of the enlistees were poor, unhealthy, and relatively uneducated country boys, looking frankly for a way to get off the farm, to get a bed, decent medical attention, and three squares a day. Get up at 6 a.m.? Big deal. These boys had been doing it all their young lives and for no pay from Daddy either. Being in the army with clean uniforms, clean sheets, hot-water showers, and weekends off was like a vacation for a lot of these down-at-the-heels farm boys.

Now a new kind of young man was enlisting. The average recruit was twenty-one, had at least a high school diploma, and was considerably healthier than his country cousins. "The Army expects 50,000 volunteers in December, twice the November total. The more exacting Marine Corps has 4,000 in sight, also doubling last month."[27] At one recruiting station, a navy yeoman was admitting young men for enlistment when he was stunned to look up and see his own son signing.[28] The army also put out a call for 10,000 women to sign up as much-needed nurses, and the Red Cross issued an urgent alert for blood donors.[29]

Not everybody wanted to serve. "Dallas Thompson, 21, colored, was sentenced today to serve from one to three years in jail on a guilty plea of violating the Selective Service and Training Act of 1940. The presiding judge told him, 'The Army doesn't need a fellow like you.'" According to the story, Thompson pretended he could not read or write when apparently he could do both perfectly well.[30]

That some black American men were reluctant to serve in the U.S. military was understandable. The military was still segregated, and black soldiers got the bum equipment, the bum food, the bum assignments, and were generally treated like bums. Their treatment in the Great War had not been forgotten. "Blacks had volunteered to serve in a segregated army for a segregated government, confident that after the war their sacrifices would be rewarded. When black veterans returned in 1919, they got a nice parade through Harlem and nothing else—no jobs, no challenges to segregation, no progress."[31]

Still, over the course of the new war, over 2.5 million black Americans registered to join in the fight, and those enlisting in South Carolina received Bibles courtesy of the American Bible Society.[32] The account of this new war would later be replete with stories of young African American men overcoming the Germans, overcoming the Japanese, and overcoming their own country.

An eighteen-year-old boy quit his job at the engine house of the New Haven Railroad and left a note for his pals.

"To my buddies at the roundhouse. I was born in America. I enjoyed more privileges than any boy anywhere in the world. I had free speech; the right to choose my religion. I worked where I pleased and spent my money where I pleased. Yes, I did enjoy myself. I had liberty, fought and paid for with the blood of my forefathers. We all realize that this God-given liberty which we enjoy is in serious danger of being destroyed forever. But we know that it will never be destroyed while boys like you and I can prevent it. That is why I left my job here and enlisted in the United States Marines today. As our beloved President said last night, if I have to pay the supreme sacrifice to defend our liberty, I will consider it a privilege. So, until I see you again, have hope in us; we will not let you down."[33]

The letter was signed Tom Mahoney. Young Tom's father had served in the navy in the last war. The son would only have a short period of time to become a man. "One day at war in Manila had made tough, determined soldiers out of a good many American youngsters who only yesterday were just kids in soldiers' uniforms."[34]

Bond sales were high as Americans were rushing to banks and post offices and other locations to buy up the notes which lent to their government billions of dollars, to be paid back later with interest. At all levels and among all groups, everyone wanted to pitch in some way, somehow, for the war effort. Congress was also exploring new "war taxes," possibly totaling as much as $6.5 billion, to be paid in lump sums by businesses and individuals.[35] Every December, newspapers carried ads reminding citizens their taxes were due before the end of the year. The concept of "withholding" had yet to be introduced by the federal government and later also adopted by those state governments that imposed income taxes.

Volunteering for civil defense, which hundreds of thousands and possibly millions of Americans did, was not for the faint of heart nor those lacking commitment. Long hours were spent training civilians on spotting and discerning enemy versus friendly planes, operating gas masks, handling crowd control, and doing potentially dangerous work. Over the course of the hostilities, thousands of civilians died in war work.

In Arlington, Virginia, "more than 1,000 volunteer air raid wardens were sworn in last night after sampling odors from four different types of gases available for present-day warfare and witnessing the extinguishing of an actual incendiary bomb."[36] Groups organized themselves in order to volunteer. Catholic women's groups, Boy and Girl Scouts, Job's Daughters, Masons, Daughters of the Nile, Kiwanis Clubs, and Lions Clubs, these and more stepped forward. Everywhere CD (Civil Defense) workers scanned "the sky for enemy bombers."[37]

Construction began on a bomb shelter at the White House, between it and the Treasury Department in "the underground space" that once "housed the Treasury Department vaults." But Grace Tully could never understand why the bomb shelter—which FDR had resisted anyway—had "open sky above and it was never explained to me why the protective structure had this weakness."[38]

Boat owners on the Mississippi, on the coasts, and on the Potomac River also volunteered to guard bridges and report suspicious activities. The Coast Guard Auxiliary organized much of this work.[39] Snafus happened everywhere, but Americans were sincere in their desire to pitch in. New guidelines were published advising people how to deal with air raids, including how to protect their pets. If in a car, they were to pull over and turn off the lights. If as pedestrians no shelters were available, readers were advised to "Lie Down."[40]

Women's silk stockings were making their farewell appearance, as the important material was needed for parachutes. Replacing them, along with the cumbersome garter belts and hooks, were "Spunsters" made from nylon, a synthetic material. American men lamented the passing of the day when the wind would whip a woman's skirts up, revealing the sexy ensemble. Woodward and Lothrop Department Stores began hawking for all their female customers the new "bright little brief panties" that women skaters had used. Later, they became known as "panty hose."[41]

The national government claimed that the initial roundup of suspected aliens was nearly over, but "additional arrests may be announced during the next few days," the office of the attorney general said. But the *Los Angeles Times* then reported a "Jap and Camera Held in Bay City"; the man had been taking photos of the city from Twin Peaks. And then another story appeared on how "two Japanese yesterday were taken into custody . . . with maps of Los Angeles County and Japanese literature in their possession."[42]

Princess Stephanie Hohenlohe, a member of the Hungarian royal family visiting the United States, was picked up by the FBI. "Once reputed a friend of high Nazi officials and a colorful figure in European political intrigue . . . the short, red-haired [woman] was sent to the United States Immigration Station at Gloucester, NJ." A Republican member of Congress urged the FBI to arrest prominent labor leader Harry Bridges, along with other "dangerous aliens."[43]

A Chinese man, Samson Lee, recounted all the problems he had on a simple train trip from Hartford to New York and back and how ticket agents, conductors, and others demanded repeatedly he show proof that he was Chinese and not Japanese. Fortunately for Mr. Lee, he did have such proof. In frustration, he said, "Perhaps I should just wear a sign around my neck to say I am a Chinese." He had his own cultural observances of the differences between the Japanese and Chinese. "One great difference between the two people is in their manners. Japanese are very boorish compared to the polite Chinese gentlemen. Most other people do not like them so very much."[44]

Lee's troubles were nothing compared to the unidentified Chinese man whose body was found in Seattle, nearly decapitated. According to officials, he may have been mistaken for a Japanese "secret agent."[45] But in a case chalked up to "racial hatred," a Filipino man attacked a Japanese man with a knife as the two rode on a Pacific Electric Railroad car.[46]

In Washington, the State Department was also asking Americans to forgo serving on any "free movement" committees "or groups representing foreign countries whose activities are contrary to American policies."[47] Loosely translated, the government did not want Americans to get caught up in ethnic politics but instead pledge "100 percent unity" to America. The State Department went even further, saying "the government does not look with favor on any activities designed to divide the allegiance of any group of American residents between the United States and any foreign government in existence or in prospect."[48]

The government agencies also asked Americans to "rat out" their fellow citizens. "The Department of State is glad to be informed of the plans and proposed activities of . . . organizations representing such movements." The government was not going to tolerate any "split loyalty."[49] As if to buttress its point, the FBI in Los Angeles arrested Robert Noble, a "self-styled admirer of Hitler," and charged him with "making seditious and disloyal utterances in wartime. If convicted, Noble could go to jail for up to twenty years."[50] In Boston, a "radio transmitting set" and the owner, an "alien," were seized. In the Italian section of Beantown—the North End, once home to the likes of Paul Revere—a cache of "twenty shotguns and rifles and fifteen revolvers" was also taken by G-men, and the owner, an "Italian alien," was arrested. Those taken into custody could not meet with journalists, photographers, or "the general public."[51]

More and more, Washington, D. C., was becoming an armed camp, a city expecting to be under siege at any second. Atop the Commerce Department citizens could plainly see machine-gun nests, and within days, the nests were atop all federal buildings. More "dry run" blackouts were planned for the town, and it was proposed that the front and back bumpers on all cars be painted white, along with white lines on roads and sidewalks, so as to guide pedestrians and drivers to air-raid shelters.[52]

The commander of the Coast Guard, Admiral Richard R. Waesche, warned Congress of the likelihood of disruption. "Enemy agents may start an epidemic of fires and explosions in vital defense centers at any time." The concern was of sabotage, the kind that had taken place during the last war.[53]

It was clear that this war was a new kind of war, one that would require new approaches. The War Department organized a "Battle Room" in the White House, complete with "telephones and other modern instruments of communication. . . . Army and Navy officers plotted movements on maps. . . . [It was] a unique communications center across the hall from [the president's] office at the White House." During the Spanish-American War, President McKinley had a war room, but it contained only maps.[54] With its communications tools, FDR's became a real nerve center. All this would cost a lot of money, and Congress passed a new appropriations bill totaling $10 billion. But this was only the beginning. General Motors had already begun retooling its operations under Lend-Lease and a $720 million contract from Washington to churn out machine guns, diesel engines for tanks, and "Allison" engines for aircraft.[55]

Some worried about FDR's expanded new powers, especially those over radio properties by government officials, and then it was subsequently announced by the Federal Communication Commission "that the Army and Navy would take over some facilities and close others. It was officially denied that this was censorship." The head of the FCC, James Branch Fly, got a bit testy and said, "It does not mean any general taking over of radio is contemplated. . . ." The industry fell right into line, raising nary an objection. "On the heels of this action Neville Miller, president of the National Association of Broadcasters, urged all broadcasting stations to exercise unusually careful editorial judgment in selecting news.'"[56] The edict did not apply to newspapers, though, and their independence was reasserted in a decision by the Supreme Court that upheld their right to criticize and comment on government.

Unlike most other papers, the *Washington Post*—which had generally been supportive of FDR—came out four square against government censorship. "The people . . . are adult . . . they are entitled to know what is going on. This newspaper . . . hopes that the President will entrust the information job to men who are wise and technically proficient rather than to officers who are neither."[57]

On the West Coast, a lower court had ruled that the *Los Angeles Times* could not comment on the proceedings of a trial there, but the upper court overruled it. It was a significant decision for a free press.[58] Even so, editorialists routinely applauded the government's new abilities. Said the *Birmingham News*, "We shall have to live, perhaps not literally but surely in spirit, as if we were under martial law—subordinating absolutely everything, as far as possible voluntarily, to the gigantic effort we must make in order to survive. The soft talkative days are gone, and the hardest days we have ever known since Valley Forge have begun."[59]

Indeed, just a few days later, the War Department rolled out new proposals "for prompt suspension of radio broadcasting operations when enemy air raids are threatened anywhere in Continental United States." It was put into effect immediately. "The orders apply to standard broadcast, high frequency, television and relay broadcast stations." Stations were even given scripts to read before going off the air. "At this time, ladies and gentlemen, radio station _____ is temporarily leaving the air in conformity with the national defense program. Keep your radio on so that upon resumption of our service we may bring you the latest information."[60]

Everywhere the word *sacrifice* was on everybody's lips. In Alabama, the "Add a Plate Club" was started to encourage families to invite enlisted men to dinner. The club hoped the goodwill would spread across the country.[61] And it did, for the most part—except in Paterson and Jersey City, New Jersey, where five men who operated a fraudulent charity for kids that took in over $290,000 and gave out a little more than $2,000 for "Crippled Kiddies" were sentenced to long prison stretches and heavy fines. But in New York City, the offices of the Civilian Defense Volunteer Committee were "flooded" with volunteers, up to 100 per hour.[62]

Others worried about a new kerfuffle involving Eleanor Roosevelt, when she somewhat facetiously advised that young American women learn how to drink so they could better adopt male roles on the home front. Temperance groups were not enamored of the advice of Mrs. Roosevelt, whose stance in this regard was ironic because she often frowned on her husband's favorite vice, cocktails promptly at 5:00 p.m., a cherished habit that the president referred to as "fivesies."[63] FDR, in need of temporarily forgetting the enormous burdens on his shoulders, would ebulliently mix drinks in the Oval Office and delight in swapping gossip with his staff. The puritanical Sara Delano Roosevelt, mother of the president, was known to have once remarked, "Franklin, haven't you had enough of your cocktails?"[64]

If power added to FDR's worries, it didn't stop him from accumulating it. He had switched roles, as the press described it, from "Doctor New Deal" to "Doctor Win the War." The United States was not the only representative form of government to have voluntarily given up power to the chief executive. Both Australia and Great Britain had done much the same, and the contradiction was lost on everyone. The Allies, to combat the dictatorial, militaristic regimes of the Axis powers, had resorted to more authoritarian forms of government. A bill was offered in Congress to further expand the president's powers, including the ability to "redistribute the functions of the various government agencies" and also the ability to award no-bid contracts. But, "the most important [proposal] would allow censorship of communications by mail, cable or radio transmitted to any foreign country."[65]

Absent from Washington for several days had been Secretary of the Navy Frank Knox. He'd failed to respond to congressional inquiries (until they had been squashed) and did not appear in any news stories. He had been absent from the all-important meeting at the White House the day before, sending the "acting" navy secretary. It was then learned that Knox had covertly shown up in Hawaii to conduct his own investigation of what happened and to prepare a briefing and report for President Roosevelt. The navy chief arrived in Hawaii the evening of the eleventh.[66]

By December 12, nearly all of the Pan-American countries had fallen into line behind the United States. From Argentina to Guatemala, most declared war on Japan, Germany, and Italy. This was important because it negated the chance of a power, friendly to the Axis, establishing military bases and harbors from which they could wage a harassing and easier war against the United States.

The war bureaucracy in Washington was growing exponentially. Congress, under its own assault of phone calls and visits and letters from worried constituents, voted an appropriation that would allow each senator to have an aide at the princely sum of $4,500 per annum.[67]

The war bureaucracy was also expanding its rule over the private sector. Previously, Washington had directed Detroit to cut production of new cars by 25 percent in December and by 50 percent in January 1942 because of the steel and rubber shortages. Buick had already begun its ad campaign in the *Saturday Evening Post* and other publications touting its new "automatic drive" under the slogan, "Better Buy Buick."[68]

Now the Office of Production Management (OPM)—another New Deal holdover—ordered Motor City to halt the production of new cars altogether by some plants. It stated that "a changeover to defense production would be accomplished as rapidly as possible after Government orders are received." General Motors was hit hard, and Chevrolet, Oldsmobile, Fleetwood, and Fisher body plants were shut down immediately. Chrysler also had to shut down its De Soto, Dodge, and Plymouth plants.[69] Indeed, war planners actively considered halting the production of all new cars by February of 1942.[70]

Ironically, as the government was ordering Ford, General Motors, and Chrysler to gin up seven-day-a-week production schedules to turn out war materiel, all the companies were engaged in immediate and massive layoffs of skilled car makers and assembly-line workers. Shortly, International Harvester and Bell Aircraft, along with dozens of other manufacturers, would go on seven-day production schedules.[71] At the top of the list, as ordered by OPM, were antiaircraft weapons. All through the years of the New Deal, officials of the OPM had used phrases like "oversupply" when referring to labor in America. No longer. Now the military had first dibs on all healthy young American males.

In a press conference on the twelfth, just five days after the attack, FDR asked American newspapers not to publish the casualty lists from the Pacific anymore. He clarified his request by saying "that it might be permissible for individual papers to print individual stories that a person had been notified that a relative was a casualty." The *Evening Star* in Washington also reported, "The next of kin and dependents of naval casualties are being notified and are being asked not to divulge the name of ship or station to which the relative was attacked."[72] But Roosevelt's request was too late to stop the publication of the newest casualties in Hawaii announced by the army, losses that totaled 155 dead: 146 enlisted men and 9 officers. Wounded men were not announced, but the army made clear that many of these would not survive.[73]

At his meeting with reporters at the White House, the president went out of his way to single out Senator Charles Tobey for harsh criticism. Tobey had been on the warpath, engaged in a blame game of the military, especially of Admiral Kimmel. "President Roosevelt today joined in a bitter denunciation of uninformed criticism of the conduct of the Pacific fleet. 'He repeated somebody's gossip, he made it as a statement of fact which he had no right to do whatsoever,' the Chief Executive said."[74]

He also told the gathering that he thought, for the time being, the forty-hour work week would be sufficient. This was part of the deal the government had worked out with labor. In exchange for this from the government, labor would put a stop to all strikes during the emergency.[75]

Kimmel now issued his first public utterances since the attack on Pearl Harbor the previous Sunday, but rather than point fingers or attempt to explain what happened, he instead commended "the men of the Navy, Marine Corps and Army. We Americans can receive hard blows but we can deliver harder ones. In these days when we face the task that lies ahead with calm determination and unflinching resolve it is truly great to be an American. Instances of valor were so great in number that they are too many to enumerate. The same sort of selfless courage was displayed then that will win the war."[76]

The panic of the prior day over dynamite found on a train trestle in Miami was cleared up. As reported by the Associated Press, "A 38-year-old colored man confessed yesterday, the FBI announced, that he set a charge of dynamite on a Florida East Coast Railway trestle, then reported it to the police in the hope he would become a hero and receive a reward." Stokes McCreary was charged with the violation of the "anti-sabotage statute."[77]

Newspaper articles of the era routinely identified the race of African Americans as either "colored" or "negro" in reporting exploits both good and bad. Whites were never identified as white, and the papers almost never covered Hispanics. It wasn't just the newspapers that were segregated. So too was Washington, essentially a Jim Crow town. "Blacks looked out on a city that was rigidly and thoroughly segregated. Throughout the city, [the] hotels, restaurants, movie theaters, libraries and taxicabs refused to serve blacks."[78]

The war and the military had swiftly become a deeply and tightly woven stitch in the American cultural fabric. There was virtually no place anyone could turn now and not be reminded of the war—even children, even on Santa's lap. In Atlanta, a department-store Santa Claus was entertaining kids, listening to their Christmas wishes, playing his role to perfection, when his mood suddenly changed, becoming somber and stoic. Stepping out of character, he began to read to the children a letter from one of his three sons, all of whom were in uniform.

> Dearest Dad,
>
> There is a war on and I am now in it, but that must not be a cause for you to worry. Of course, there is danger and there will be more danger to come but if I am to die a soldier's death, so be it. . . . You must think of me as doing my duty to God and country. Be brave and show outward pride, that the mite of humanity you helped bring into the world is now a soldier doing his part of defending our great and wonderful country. . . . You must pray, not only for me and others in the Army, but for the innocent women and children who will have to endure untold suffering from this fight for freedom of religion, speech and democracy. I am not afraid to die for this. . . .
>
> Until then I remain and always,
> Your Loving Son.[79]

The letter was not unique. Hundreds of thousands of mailboxes were filled each day with letters to and from G.I.s, and within a matter of months, millions of mailboxes would be filled with long missives from sons and daughters in uniform in the far-flung regions of the globe. Uniformly, the letters were tender, funny, inquisitive, brave, confident, patriotic, self-deprecating, and well-written.

Public education in America in 1941 was the best in the world, and dedicated teachers led by rote, by repetition, and by discipline mixed with a healthy dose of tenderness and the knowledge that the hand that rocked the cradle truly ruled the world. A high-school diploma was a hard-earned document and those young Americans who received a diploma had language skills, writing skills, citizenship skills, geology, biology, physics, Latin, Greek, and an expansive list of books read. According to the U.S. census, only 24.5 percent of young Americans received a high-school diploma in 1941,[80] and less than 5 percent completed four years of college.[81] All in all, well-educated, even erudite and mannerly, young men and women came out of high school, ready to go out into the real world and contribute to society.

America in 1941 was a do-it-yourself enterprise, despite the welfare state created by the New Deal. People still looked to themselves to solve their own problems. Many schools still used the McGuffey Readers, which had worked so well for their parents and grandparents, to help young students expand their vocabularies. The "Palmer Method" of cursive writing was taught, over and over and over, and penmanship across the culture was generally excellent. Men and women took pride in their cursive script and their ability to write numerous letters each day. Because the rule was, if you got a letter, you had to send a letter. At three cents for a first-class stamp, letters were frankly practical as well. Long-distance phone calls were hugely expensive, car travel was for sensible reasons, such as going to work, and flying on planes was for businessmen and G.I.s but not for the average citizen's pleasure. Taking a train or a bus trip was a big deal, and people dressed accordingly.

Letters were the standard form of personal communication for private citizens and government officials alike. The worst to receive, of course, was the telegram from Uncle Sam: "We regret to inform you that your son . . ."

CHAPTER 13

THE THIRTEENTH OF DECEMBER

"Saboteurs Light Flares in Blackout at Manila; Sentries 'Shoot to Kill'"

Atlanta Constitution

"4000 Japs Drown"

Boston Evening Globe

"Weather Bureau Halts Forecasts"

Los Angeles Times

"House Gets Bill to Register All Men 18 to 64"

New York Times

Amid all the bad news in America emerged a small bit of comic relief. In San Francisco, the Japanese proprietors of dry cleaning establishments were apprehended, and all of their assets, financial and otherwise, were confiscated or frozen by government officials—including the clothing of their customers, who, predictably, got hot under the collar. "The United States attorney's office, besieged with irate demands for a ruling, said Washington would probably issue an order allowing persons to submit affidavits declaring that their pants—and coats and vests—were not Japanese assets."[1]

Clothing and closets were on the mind of other government pen pushers, especially the nosy officials of the Census Bureau. Originally mandated by the Constitution to count the population once every ten years as a means of apportioning congressional representation, bureaucrats had expanded the mission over the years into something considerably more intrusive: to gain demographic data on the American people. Incredibly, government poll takers in the 1940 census asked American men and women how many individual articles of clothing they owned and how many they purchased each year. "Census Bureau officials declare they have found the explanation for cluttered clothing closets in the American home; people just buy more than they need." Apparently the government thought that women who annually purchased "four dresses; 16 pairs of stockings; 4 pairs of shoes; 2 hats; one pair of gloves; 1 blouse; 1 apron or smock; 7 lingerie items; 1 sleeping garment" were buying too much.[2] The breakdown of men's clothing purchases was just as conservative as the women's, but they too got a lecture from meddlesome census officials.

Americans accepted constitutional provisions to create armies and navies in order to protect them, their freedoms, and their livelihoods, but it was open to question how much Americans needed or wanted the government's sartorial advice or input on the condition of private closets. To civil libertarians, it was more worrisome than laughable.

Some of the wartime black humor coming from government was just in bad taste. A prankster at the Tennessee Department of Conservation asked for a requisition for 6,000,000 licenses at $2 apiece for hunting "Japs." The response from another bureaucrat was in equally bad taste: "Open season on 'Japs'—no license required."[3] Political correctness was still decades away.

Other government agencies reacted petulantly as well. The Maritime Commission changed the name of a large packet ship from the *Japan Mail* to the more palatable *China Mail*.[4] The merchant marines also "weeded out" Japanese, German, and Italian nationals from service, even taking those already on ships, off.[5] Of more immediate importance, the attorney general's office made a new announcement that over 2,500 aliens had been arrested, not including those in the Canal Zone or the Philippines.[6] In the Canal Zone, dozens of Japanese civilians had been arrested, taken from their homes and placed in "quarantine stations, a tent city mushroomed to accommodate the aliens and alleged Axis sympathizers as roundups began."[7]

Also, forty-three Americans in Hawaii were "placed in custody," suspected of subversive activities against their country.[8]

American allies in Cuba, Nicaragua, and Mexico also began the roundup of Nazi diplomats and those alleged to be supporters of the Axis powers, including Japanese fishermen on the west coast of Mexico who were "suspected of 'espionage.'" President Batista of Cuba seized all Axis possessions and was holding all Axis personnel on the Isle of Palms, some forty miles south of Cuba.[9]

In the "funny, dumb, and dangerous" category was the story of a housewife in Detroit. Mrs. Donald de Rusha had been walking along the shore of Lake St. Clair when she happened upon a "gadget." While she did not know what it was, she thought the fifty-pound object would make a nice doorstop. The object was an undetonated piece of military ordinance.[10] Luckily, her error was pointed out in time and no one was hurt.

Even as war and enemies—real or imagined—dominated the thoughts of the citizenry, people still enjoyed distractions to take their minds off the crisis. A long running "soap opera" was the ongoing private/public tale of poor little rich girl Gloria Vanderbilt, thin, pretty, an inheritress, and hugely controversial as the granddaughter of a robber baron and the daughter of two supremely narcissistic and unbalanced parents.

Gloria herself was a bad news buffet. At only seventeen years of age, she was in the newspapers constantly, photographed in skimpy cocktail dresses at nightclubs in New York and Los Angeles. On the twelfth, it was announced that she was going to marry a man fifteen years her elder, Pasquale Di Cicco, who had already been married, divorced, and, as a Hollywood agent, romantically linked to a number of other women—none of whom stood to inherit another $4 million when they turned twenty-one, however.[11]

Poor Gloria's life had already been a mess-and-a-half. Her mother had been declared unfit when Gloria was a child, and the court remanded her to an aunt. Gloria's life up to that point had been a movable feast of wine, men, and scandal. Americans, by and large, followed her car wreck of a life with salacious and prurient *schadenfreude*. It was all outrageous stuff in 1941, a time when society regarded the lowbrow hijinks of high society with an almost Victorian sense of propriety.

In the *Atlanta Constitution*, as in many other newspapers around the country, there were listed the "Downtown Theatres," "Night Spots," "Neighborhood Theatres," and "Colored Theatres." The movies shown at the theaters for black Americans were generally low budget, little known, or had already been shown first in the "whites only" movie houses. These included *Wyoming Wildcat, Buck Benny Rides Again* (starring Jack Benny and his manservant, Eddie "Rochester" Anderson), *Beat Me Daddy*, which was the name of an Andrews Sisters song, and *White Eagle*, of cowboys-and-Indians genre. In the heart of Dixie—Atlanta—one of the most popular black movie houses was named the "Lincoln."[12]

Besides celebrity scandals and movies, another pastime available to Americans, and indeed the world, was the Geminids meteor shower, which appeared every December and promised to be especially brilliant this time around. Some theologians believed this meteor shower was what led three kings to a small manger one thousand nine hundred and forty-one years earlier.

Newsreels detailing the December 7 attacks were beginning to hit America's movie houses. "War took the play in all newsreels on programs opening yesterday at movie theatres."[13] No actual footage of Pearl Harbor was shown for obvious reasons, and most of the news shorts dealt with the history of the relationship between the United States and Japan. The "March of Time" newsreel was judged to be among the better of those shown, but Fox also produced some that were informative. However, in each case, only the shots of civilians in action in Honolulu were shown—almost nothing about the navy or the Air Corps.

Of course, none of the newsreels reported on the *Arizona*. It was nearly a week after the attack when the name of the ship finally appeared in the newspapers, though it was a wire story of a London report of a Japanese propaganda claim. American editors ran the item, but some ran it with headlines that doubted its veracity. "Reuters today quoted a Japanese naval communiqué broadcast from Tokyo as saying that the 32,000-ton United States battleship *Arizona* had been sunk in action in Hawaii. The *Arizona* was launched in 1915, and its normal complement is about 1,359 men."[14]

But the story, fourth-hand, was generally treated as an unfounded rumor except by the *Boston Globe*, the *LA Times* and the *New York Times*, all of which gave the Japanese claim a bit more veracity. As the *Birmingham News* noted, "It has been an Axis technique to make spectacular war claims, especially naval, in hopes of learning the true results of attacks from its adversaries' denials."[15]

The Japanese also claimed they had hit Honolulu again at the same time that Secretary of the Navy Frank Knox was conducting his investigation. But this was, like so much other radio traffic, chalked up to propaganda. Still another rumor was going around Washington that "as long ago as November 15 Government officials had received confidential and reliable information from Tokyo pointing out that Japan had definitely decided to wage war on the United States, even before it sent Saburo Kurusu with a badly camouflaged peace dove to Washington." But this conspiracy theory had it that Japan's Black Dragon Society was behind the attack on America.[16] The attack had been planned for months, but the Japanese fleet did not leave the home waters until November 26.

Finger-pointing was continuing in Washington, albeit in softer tones now. The last refuge of patriotism had cloaked any meaningful questions about culpability in either the civilian government or the War Department about the attack on Pearl Harbor. The War Department was still sticking to its story that only one destroyer had been sunk and one battleship "capsized" at Pearl Harbor, but even after almost a week had passed, less information, not more, was forthcoming. The old adage, "the first casualty of war is truth," was proving true enough.

After his quick trip to Oahu to meet with navy officials there and to inspect the damage, Knox returned to Washington. He ducked reporters, who clamored for a comment, saying only, "I will not have statements to release until after a conference with the President."[17] The weather in Washington was a bit harsher than what Knox had left behind in Hawaii, where it was always clear and sunny. On the thirteenth, Washington was paralyzed by cold rain, snow, sleet, and freezing temperatures that forced government workers to keep their cars at home and call cabs. The problem was, for every cab there were dozens of impatient federal workers.[18]

In Knox's absence, President Roosevelt was meeting daily—even hourly—with his military planners and leaders. At his request, Congress authorized a huge boost in the navy's budget to allow an increase in the surface fleet by 30 percent—a tip-off to the unspoken damage done at Pearl Harbor. He'd also sent to Congress a report on the history of U.S.–Japanese relations and the progress of Lend-Lease.[19]

Planned additions to the navy included at least seven new battleships, six new aircraft carriers, twenty-seven new cruisers, eighty new destroyers, and forty-seven new submarines.[20] All told, the new complement of ships would add some 900,000 tons to the fleet.[21]

For the first time, the gates to the once-accessible White House were closed. The wrought iron fence that had gone up some years earlier with its large gates had always remained open, until the twelfth when they were permanently shut. Now anyone wanting to get into the White House complex had better show a "pass with picture engraved on it" to be admitted. And no longer would "cabs, private cars, delivery wagons" be allowed to enter.[22]

FDR was thirty-five minutes late to his weekly Friday gabfest with reporters, something he normally was on time for. But he did have a country at war to run.[23] FDR enjoyed an easy repartee with reporters; he was a smooth pro at manipulating the Washington press corps with humor and flattery. His powers of obfuscation were truly impressive. He could charm the pants off "the boys" of the Fourth Estate, who eagerly scribbled down his insouciant witticisms, while at the same time telling them absolutely nothing of substance. FDR was widely revered at the time, but certainly not by everyone. Regardless of ideological viewpoint, one fact was clear: throughout the Depression and now on the cusp of global war, Roosevelt's energetic activism, his irrepressible confidence, and his effervescent charm reassured a frightened nation when it needed it most.

His totalitarian counterparts overseas starkly reflected the sort of leadership that America could have born when the economic system collapsed in the 1930s. Now that total war had broken out among the great powers, a tale was making the rounds that Hitler and Stalin were engaged in a deal that would halt the Nazi invasion and they would sign a peace accord. Some wondered how true it was and if it was a factor in Stalin's still not declaring war against the Japanese, as all other Allies had already done. The Nazis were still pounding the British in North Africa, claiming to have downed seven planes and that "British troops were bombed and shelled successfully."[24]

The air-raid drills had not gone well in Los Angeles. In fact, they were an unmitigated disaster. Glitch followed glitch. Mistake followed mistake. There were car accidents in which people were killed because of the doused street lights but no clear rules on operating cars at night without headlights. Rather than reassure the civilian population, all the practice blackouts did was add to a sense of "hysteria." The general in command, W. A. Ryan, frustrated, said any future blackouts would "be ordered only when danger from air attack was actual."[25] The county fire warden complained that the sirens on his fire apparatus had worn out because they had been overused.[26]

The newest panic in Los Angeles had begun when a flashing yellow light had been misinterpreted to mean "raiding party on the way." The yellow light was only supposed to mean "alert," while a blue light would signal "blackout." Everybody was thoroughly confused. Half the city responded poorly, and the other half didn't know what to do. Civilians were ordered off beaches, and then the order was rescinded. Proprietors of commercial establishments saw their lights smashed by law enforcement officials if they were not turned off within the prescribed three minutes given. In some cases, the broken lights increased the risk of fire. Huge fines and jail time of up to 180 days were proposed for those who violated the rules, whatever they were. In one instance, the only arrest made was that of a drunken man.[27] It was never really a blackout; the street lights remained on because they operated on 800 different timers strewn across the city. As no one had been forewarned of the practice blackout, no one was available to turn off the timers. Because of the strict rules against driving in some areas, work crews could not get to municipal lights to turn them off. The owners of billboards also were never told of the blackout drill.

It wasn't that the citizenry didn't want to cooperate. It was the politicians and the military that could not coordinate their actions, especially since they were still attempting to devise a uniform code for alerting the public. Rules would also have to be established for doctors making house calls during blackouts and air raids.[28]

In Long Beach, factory workers began the long process of painting thousands of windows black to help facilitate round-the-clock production.[29] A system of lights, bells, whistles, and horns was eventually established and then never used. But the coast guard issued new regulations "to prevent aliens from escaping on vessels leaving Los Angeles Harbor."[30]

The blackout in California went from the coast to 100 miles inland. Yet a fourth blackout was imposed on the City by the Bay and this one did not go any better than the previous ones. It too was marred by accidents, "violence," and, of course, new rumors of unidentified enemy planes.[31] It was finally decided that to avoid any confusion, all vehicular traffic had to pull off the road and stop for the duration of air raids and blackouts.[32] Fines and jail time were imposed on violators.

All told, eight ports of call were designated "defensive sea areas" by an executive order from President Roosevelt. This meant they were closed for the duration of the war. The three on the West Coast were San Francisco, San Diego, and Puget Sound. On the East Coast, Portland, Maine; Portsmouth, New Hampshire; Boston; and Narragansett Bay, Rhode Island, were all closed to commercial boat traffic that did not have the proper authority.[33] The San Francisco Bay was closed to all boat traffic except military vessels. "Any ship entering the bay will do so at its own risk. No non-government vessel may enter or navigate on these waters without specific permission from the Government," reported the *San Francisco Chronicle*.[34]

Baltimore city fathers saw the silliness over blackout drills taking place in other cities around the country and wisely announced their own dry run, but ten days in advance, giving all enough time to prepare.[35]

San Diegans went through their own panicky air-raid warning when "something" was sighted "out there" off the coast.[36] Whatever "something" was, something disappeared, unidentified. Yet another air-raid drill in New England had also gone poorly and several motorists were badly injured from driving their cars with the headlights off.[37] Blackouts were also risky because not everyone played nice when they did occur, especially thieves. The owners of jewelry and fur stores in New York City were advised to remove their merchandise during the blackouts, as theft had been a common occurrence in London during the raids there.[38] New York City also issued a brochure with verbiage that seemed terrifyingly prescient, even visionary. The title of the pamphlet was "If It Comes" and it read in part: "New York City is in little danger of attack from airplanes. But such an air attack is not impossible. New York, as the nerve center of the nation, presents a tempting target which might justify an enemy in taking great risks. We must prepare now against this possibility of aerial attack."[39]

In another security measure, the United States Weather Bureau said it would suspend public announcements of weather forecasts. "This action is being taken to prevent the flow of valuable data to enemy analysts." The service did say, however, it would release weather data on the weekend for "winter sports conditions."[40] Newspapers no longer would contain any specific data, and radio certainly would not broadcast any specifics on weather forecasts.

For many, though, the war had gotten out of control when it was announced that New Orleans had canceled its annual Mardi Gras. Soberly, city officials said the massive street party "would not be consistent with the present state of the nation."[41] The bacchanalia of the Big Easy was now a bust.

Meanwhile, churches in New York were preparing for bombing attacks. Different religious denominations had differing guidelines for clergy and parishioners. The chancery of the New York Catholic Church said that in the event of an air raid, congregants were excused from completing Mass but priests were not. The priests had to complete their services, even if bombs were raining down from the heavens.[42]

New York, like Los Angeles, had been pretty much of a disaster in its practice drills. The irony was that the head of the nation's civil defense program, Fiorello La Guardia, was also the mayor of New York. A later blackout drill in New York proved to be more organized. "Brightly lit marquees and lobbies of theatres along West Forty-fifth Street—in the heart of the city's Great White Way—[were] blacked out." Ten theaters were holding plays that night while the blackout occurred, even as the audiences were in their seats and the performers were on stage. The shrines of the American theater established their own guidelines for air raids and blackout drills, just as the churches of New York had.[43]

Some were speculating that the unidentified planes spotted earlier in the week over Los Angeles and San Francisco were scout planes for the Japanese, but it remained a mystery with speculation that the planes were American aircraft from one of the many military airfields on the West Coast. Some ludicrously suggested that, in remote regions of the United States, there existed "secret airfields" that the enemy was using.[44] And there was also a considerable amount of disinformation still out about the raid on Hawaii.

New reports said there were six separate attacks at Pearl Harbor, the first at 7:55 a.m. and the last two at 7:15 p.m. and 9:10 p.m.[45] The Japanese government also told their populace that they'd bombed New York City. Twice.[46]

Battery-powered radios were now being pitched as Christmas gifts touting their ability to get the latest news on air raids, even if the electricity went out. To accommodate holiday shoppers, street parking was banned all throughout the downtown areas of Washington, including "both sides of F Street, NW from Sixth to Fourteenth Street."[47]

It was also decided to go ahead with the annual Christmas tree lighting on the South Lawn of the White House, presided over by the First Lady and the president with a twist: "The tree-lightening [sic] ceremony will follow a patriotic theme.[48] The invocation will be offered by the Most Reverend Joseph M. Corrigan, rector of Catholic University, while the benediction will be given by the Reverend Oscar F. Blackwelder, president of the Washington Federation of Churches. The carols to be heard would include 'Joy to the World,'"Adeste Fideles,"It Came Upon the Midnight Clear,' and 'Silent Night, Holy Night.'" It would be just too crushing to American morale to have the symbol of Christianity doused by the enemies of Christianity. Events were planned throughout Washington, D.C., for men in uniform, so as to ensure that none of these young men would be alone if possible. Outdoor Christmas lighting for private residences and businesses in Washington was banned, however.[49]

Mrs. Roosevelt, meanwhile, was on a West Coast tour, discussing civil defense, meeting with Red Cross officials, and meeting with defense council officials in San Diego. While there, she visited her son John and his wife.[50]

The unanimity across the country in support of war against the Axis powers was no less than astonishing. From July 4, 1776, to December 6, 1941, the country had been more or less divided over all matter of things, and compromise was the glue that held together America.

Compromise as a watchword, though, had been replaced by compel. The American people were compelled mostly by their own free will (along with a generous amount of peer pressure) to support their president and their government as never before. The *New York Times* sent reporters all over the city to sample opinion, and what they discovered was no less than amazing. "There was no disunity; there was a fusing of people of all groups, all classes, all nationalities, all races, into a feeling of national solidarity. There was no panic; there was the quiet refrain, 'They started it; we'll finish it.' There was no hysteria; there was the cold-voiced slogan, 'Remember Pearl Harbor.' There was no more isolationism or pacifism; there was a united people, ready and willing to back up the President of the United States and the armed forces to the limit."[51]

The president of the Life Underwriters Association of New York, Miss Beatrice Jones, said "the Jap attack was something that had to happen to bring the American people up with a sharp turn . . . to impress on them the soft days are over."[52] A pacifist group, the Mothers of American Sons, voted to disband and turn their assets over for the purchase of war bonds.[53] And General Robert Wood, national chairman of the America First Committee, announced its formal dissolution once and for all by an act of its committee. Wood issued a statement urging all Americans to get behind the war effort, something not thought possible a week before in anybody's worst nightmare.[54] Adding to this was the unity among the twenty-one countries of the Western Hemisphere. They were 100 percent unified in opposition to the Axis.[55]

Deeper into the polyglot culture of urban America, some wondered about the attitudes of Italian Americans and German Americans. Generally speaking, the Italian Americans in New York's Little Italy and Harlem professed their loyalty to America, denounced Mussolini, and took his picture down or turned it to the wall. German Americans, by and large, were supportive of their adopted country as well, but some "dyed-in-the-wool Nazi types sullenly said nothing but looked daggers at American inquirers." Visitors to New York, where a great many German Americans lived, discovered that while most German Americans applauded the United States, they did not do so with the same vehemence as the Italian Americans.[56]

To underscore the observations of the reporters, a nest of German spies, including several women in New York, had been caught some weeks earlier and convicted by the government for passing along state secrets to Berlin. The case was thin, and it may have even involved entrapment by the FBI. The presiding judge may have tipped his hand on the flimsiness of the government's case when he advised the jury, "men are not sent to jail for their opinions in this country. A man is entitled to believe that the German race is a superior race . . . that the world was created in order that the German race might dominate it. So long as he does nothing to carry those views into effect to the detriment of the United States."[57]

The jury deliberated for eight hours before convicting all fourteen defendants on both counts of conspiracy.[58]

Private pilots had been grounded since the seventh, and the Civil Aeronautics Board began background checks on the 94,000 licensed pilots in America, investigating their "character and loyalty to the United States."[59] The Civil Aeronautics Administration (CAA) slowly began lifting restrictions on those whose backgrounds checked out, but it limited recreational flying to a "ten-mile radius of the base of operations" and mandated that any distance flying must first be approved and a strict flight plan filed and obeyed. The CAA also reserved the right to confiscate any plane "piloted by an alien or suspected alien."[60]

Government officials were moving in other directions as well to prevent sabotage. In Massachusetts, guards were placed around drinking water supplies and plans were made for the inspection of milk pasteurization facilities.[61] Civilians were warned that if water supplies were interrupted due to poisoning or bombing, they would have to get by on three pints a day. Under the state and local committees on public safety, new precautions were being instituted daily. "Crack Army Crews" were at the ready, manning antiaircraft batteries and searchlights twenty-four hours a day, seven days a week.[62] Atop many buildings in the greater Boston area could be seen the antiaircraft guns and the men assigned to them, and there were "secret storage places for ammunition within speedy delivery distance of anti-aircraft gun establishments."[63]

Cameras were banned at the East Boston Airport after someone was spotted taking pictures of government planes there.[64] The navy also announced that all navigational lighting and radio beacons along the Eastern Seaboard might be turned off for the duration of the national emergency. Boston, like Washington and other locales in America, was quickly becoming an armed camp. "Sights, sounds and smells of the Army have become a part of the daily life for city dweller and suburbanite alike."[65]

Civilian Defense insignias began to sprout up across the Boston area and around the country on armbands and helmets, on posters and public buildings, all showing what would become the iconic simple letters "CD" inside a equilateral triangle inside a circle. Other patches designated specialties such as "Auxiliary Police," "Auxiliary Fireman," "Bomb Squad," "Fire Watcher." The insignias began in Massachusetts but spread quickly across the country, along with the specified duties and ranks of the volunteer arm of government.

Sober Bostonians were relieved to see a Guinness beer advertisement touting beer's healthful benefits because of its "barley, hops . . . yeasts."[66] Others were curious as to what the pacifist Norman Thomas planned to say at Harvard, which was still examining what the war meant to Harvard.[67] Sophisticates descended from the *Mayflower* exhibited their own form of nativism when the Museum of Fine Arts closed to the public its "Jap art treasures . . . for the duration of the emergency," according to the *Boston Evening Globe*.[68]

Some miles away on Cape Cod, the Selectmen who governed Provincetown voted to shut off the light at Pilgrim Tower. The monument had been dedicated years earlier by Teddy Roosevelt. A couple of townsfolk complained that the light at the top of the monument was weak, while the North Truro lighthouse was enormously powerful. But it was turned off, even as the Truro light was kept on.[69]

As if to underscore the danger involved, the famed insurance company, Lloyd's of London, canceled its policy of insuring American property.[70] Also, a black market for the sale of automobile tires was emerging, and Justice Department officials were busy keeping track of this. A rationing system was hastily arranged.

Although Washington had ordered the "fixing" of many goods and services in the economy, a federal judge nonetheless ordered fines against the "Big Three": Reynolds Tobacco, Liggett and Myers Tobacco, and American Tobacco also for "price fixing," conspiracy, and monopoly of the cigarette market in America. In each instance, the fine against each company was $5,000.[71] The government also fixed the prices of most oils and lubricants, but not butter, salad dressing, or shortening.[72]

Officials in California had originally blocked the vegetables produced by local Japanese farmers from being shipped to market for fear of poisoning. But Uncle Sam jumped in and gave these very same farmers a pass to continue operating and shipping their products to market. There were just too many military bases in the Golden State that were dependent on the farmers for fruits and vegetables: "to put them all out of business would interfere with the normal economy of the region . . . the Treasury . . . issued an order exempting them from the restrictions which now apply to all other Japanese aliens." The Treasury Department also issued an order allowing the Japanese access to their frozen bank accounts—but only $100 per month.[73]

In New York, the FBI, based on a "telephone tip from a man who spoke in broken English with what seemed to be an Italian accent," was looking for some WPA workers who had been overheard by the tipster, plotting to blow up the Coney Island police station.[74]

There were newspapers in America in 1941, and there were tabloids in America in 1941. The *Washington Post*, the *New York Times*, the *Wall Street Journal*, the *Evening Star*, and the *Christian Science Monitor* were for the most part sober, serious, and down-to-earth papers, which more calmly reported the facts of the war and the government—their editorial policies notwithstanding. Then there were the tabloids, such as the *Boston Daily Globe*, the *San Francisco Chronicle*, the *Los Angeles Times* and the *Chicago Tribune*, which tended toward screaming headlines and stories that were thin on facts but long on hyperbole. To examine the San Francisco or Los Angeles tabloids on December 13 would be to convince the reader that America and the Allies were winning, that all was calm and well. In reality, while the Americans still held Wake Island and the Philippines, it was only a matter of time before the superior numbers of the Japanese military would overwhelm these two territories as well as others in the western Pacific.

More honest observers knew and reported the reality: just days in America was losing the war. "American armed forces battled Japanese attacks on three sides of Luzon Island." It was also reported the Japanese were on the offensive in the jungles of Malaya, their tanks rolling.[75]

The stock and commodities markets were slapdash. There were so many factors, including price controls on some commodities, production controls on others, plus the unsettling war news, along with new announcements coming out of Washington. It was not a good time to be in the market. A chart of the market from 1914 to 1941, showing the index of industrial production, demonstrated a steady gain over three decades, even with the big dip at the onslaught of the Great Depression. Industrial stock prices for the same period, however, showed a huge peak in 1929 and then a precipitous decline all through the 1930s. Even with production up from 1937 on, stocks still fell. Airplane stocks were flat too. Eastern Airlines, Western Airlines, Trans World Airlines, American Airlines, United, all showed minimal growth.

Smoking was allowed on all flights, in all sections, at all times. Some preferred "Kool" cigarettes: its advertising said an overwhelming majority of smokers—83.2 percent—agreed that the menthol brand eliminated "smoker's hack!"[76] Others preferred to give cartons of Philip Morris as gifts wrapped in "gay Holiday packings,"[77] while others still thought a carton of Old Gold's in the "gay, NEW . . . YULETIDE CARTON," which offered "New Smoking Happiness," looked just fine in Santa's holiday sack.[78] The best slogan of the season may have been for the Proctor toaster: "Merry Crispness."[79]

But the best ads artistically were still the Coca-Cola seasonal, featuring a hale and hearty Santa enjoying a bottle of the world-famous drink. Their longtime slogan was, "The pause that refreshes."[80]

There could be no pause in the war as the navy conceded that Guam was "probably taken" by the Japanese. "The Navy announced today it was unable to communicate with the Pacific island of Guam by either radio or cable and added that the capture of Guam by the Japanese was probable."[81] Some 400 navy men and around 155 marines were left to defend the garrison on the island. The loss of the small but strategically important island was devastating. "Similarly, Wake and Midway may fall despite heroic resistance. The Navy had already reported that in one 48-hour period, the Japanese attacked Wake four times by air and once by naval units, but that during the latter assault, a Japanese light cruiser and destroyer were sunk by aerial counterattack by the Wake Marine garrison." Wake was nothing but a little "V-shaped" island in the middle of the Pacific, 2,400 miles west of Hawaii. Strategically, it was anything but nothing.[82] Palmyra, only hundreds of miles south of Hawaii, was also an attractive target for the Japanese.

The frankness of the navy was uncharacteristic of how the military was handling other setbacks.

During the previous evening, Japanese night bombing had obliterated parts of Manila around Clark Field. At first report, 75 civilians were killed and another 300 wounded. The U.S. Army continued to issue bulletins claiming that the Japanese landings north of Manila on Luzon had been repelled and that American G.I.s were once again "mopping up" the area.[83] The Japanese claimed otherwise, saying publicly that their forces were making their way inland on the big island of Luzon toward Manila.

The British, more experienced in global war and hence a bit more frank than the Americans, admitted that operations were not going well in the Hong Kong sector, that the Japanese were on the offense, and that the Brits were withering under the pounding. The Japanese agreed. "Japanese Army headquarters declared the fall of British crown colony of Hong Kong was imminent following complete Japanese occupation of Kowloon whose 4-mile-long and supposedly impregnable defenses have been battered down."[84] The Japanese littered the area with propaganda dropped from airplanes designed to inflame racial tensions between the Chinese and the British.

It was announced, however, that Dutch submarines had sighted and sunk four Japanese troop transports on the east coast of Borneo. Torpedoes were fired, and 4,000 Japanese troops were sent to the bottom of the Pacific.[85] In an "exclusive" story for the *Boston Evening Globe*, the "Jap Naval Attache at Vichy" denied that pilots for his country were using the planes as "human torpedoes," calling it a "myth." The paper also claimed that neither Washington nor London was pressuring Moscow to get into the fight against the Japanese.[86] The same day, however, the *Washington Post* ran a story saying, "Tokyo admits using 'human torpedoes.'"[87] It was the war's first confirmation of kamikaze pilots.

Reporters caught up with the widow of Captain Colin P. Kelly Jr., the twenty-six-year-old West Point grad and pilot who was credited with the sinking of the *Haruna*. Mrs. Marion Kelly was calm, saying, "I know he's happy," of her now-deceased husband. Photographed on her lap was one-and-a-half-year-old Colin P. Kelly III, nicknamed "Corky." His mother bravely, if also forlornly, continued, "And Corky will be proud too." The mother and son had little choice as the most important man in their lives was dead. There was little left in the emptiness except pride and pain, a Gold Star in a window to replace the Blue Star that had previously been displayed, and, under the improved pension legislation for war widows, $42.50 a month for the rest of Mrs. Kelly's life or until that time as she remarried, from a grateful government.[88] But the curly headed, handsome young pilot with the wide-set eyes would never walk through the door of his home again, never again throw his arms around his wife, never again have a son bound up into a warm embrace.

Unfortunately, the Kellys would be one of the first of many who would bravely tell reporters how "proud" they were of the men in their family who had fallen in the new war.[89] The first Gold Star of World War II had already been awarded to the mother of Private Joseph G. Moser by Mrs. Mathilda Burling, president of the Gold Star Mothers of America.[90]

The tradition of the first war had been revived. Blue stars in the front windows of American homes denoted a family member in the service. Silver stars were for a family member who'd been wounded. And then there were the Gold Stars. So many more sad stories were yet to come of dead soldiers and sailors.

CHAPTER 14

THE FOURTEENTH OF DECEMBER

"Civil Service Law Bars Aliens from Federal Payroll"

Boston Sunday Globe

"San Francisco's Women Get Ready to Fight"

San Francisco Chronicle

"U.S. Flyers Battle Japs in Manila Raid"

The Sunday Star

"Japanese Report Fate of Hong Kong Sealed"

Los Angeles Times

S even days after the surprise Japanese attack on Pearl Harbor, 836 days after the surprise German attack on Poland, and three days after Nazi Germany and fascist Italy declared war on the United States, an observer needed a scorecard to tell who, around the globe, was at war with whom. The Associated Press went so far as to use a sports metaphor in calling it a "lineup."[1]

At war with Germany, Italy and Japan: *the United States, Great Britain, Canada, China, Free France, the Netherlands, Netherland Indies, New Zealand, Poland, union of South Africa, Costa Rica, Cuba, Nicaragua,*

Dominican Republic, Honduras, Haiti, El Salvador, Guatemala, and Panama.

At war with Germany, Italy, and their European allies only: *Soviet Russia, Belgium, Czechoslovakia, Ethiopia, Greece, Luxembourg, Norway, Yugoslavia.*

At war with the United States, Britain, and Russia: *Germany, Italy, Slovakia, Rumania.*

At war only with Russia and Britain: *Finland, Hungary.*

At war only with the United States and Britain: *Japan, Manchukuo, Bulgaria.*

Broken relations with Germany, Italy, and Japan: *Mexico.*

Broken relations with Japan only: *Colombia.*

Broken relations with the United States: *Hungary.*

Expressing "solidarity" with the United States: *Argentina, Brazil, Bolivia, Chile, Ecuador, Paraguay, Peru, Uruguay, Venezuela.*[2]

Not mentioned were Ireland and Vichy France—which was little more than a hand-puppet for Berlin—although there were some in the West still under the illusion that the Marshal Pétain government could or would stand up to the Axis powers.

Joseph Stalin still had not decided to declare war on Japan, still looked out for his country's own interests, and still demanded Lend-Lease help from America. He was angry that, despite his country's enormous sacrifices in staving off Hitler's Operation Barbarossa, he seemed to be getting little help in return from America and the Brits. A delusional paranoiac by nature, Stalin began to suspect that the Allies intended to let his country bleed at the hands of the Nazis. After all, in Stalin's mind, his partners of convenience—America and Britain—were capitalists and, as such, could not be trusted. Indeed, one of his greatest fears was that FDR and Churchill would eventually make common cause with Hitler, and all three would then pursue him. Stalin trusted no one, as reflected by his incessant, murderous purges of millions of innocent people. Meanwhile, the Irish, blinded by an age-old hatred of the English, could not see that the Third Reich was their enemy too. The island of Eire remained neutral.[3]

Argentina, though expressing solidarity with the United States, was thought among the knowledgeable in Washington circles to have strong Nazi leanings.[4] To be sure, South America was riddled with Nazi spies and sympathizers, making that region a prime surveillance target for both the FBI and later FDR's foreign spy agency.

What with countries at war and with all of the borders and bureaucrats and bribes needed to get from locale to location, noncombatants and civilians queued up in ports of call and airports, in terminals and in train stations. They waited interminable hour upon interminable day upon interminable week, without transit visas, trying to get out, get in, get going, get back, get home. "Lisbon has been crowded for many months with persons who have gone there in the hopes of getting transportation to America via the Pan American clippers or ships of the American Export Line."[5] Somewhere, Bogie and Bergman were stuck too and time went by.

Just hours after the German army said it was hunkering down for the long Russian winter and awaiting spring to renew its offensive operations, came fresh stories declaring the Russian army now had the Nazis on the run, at least outside of Moscow. But, as much of the reporting came secondhand from Stalin's propaganda machine, it was unknown what was true and to what extent it was an exaggeration. "The German high command said early this week that with the settling in of winter, Nazi troops had entrenched themselves and that Moscow and Leningrad could not be taken before spring."[6] The *New York Times* accurately digested the Russian propaganda and said, "It seems unlikely that the Germans have suffered real disaster the red Army avers." Hitler claimed the German army would regain the offensive after the winter snow melted.[7]

The Nazis were continuing their purges in other occupied areas, such as in Vichy, where resistance members were shot for possessing guns or holding a different political view or simply being of another race—basically, anyone who wasn't a Nazi. "In the unoccupied zone, roundups of Jews, Communists and 'terrorists' generally continue day by day."[8]

It was later revealed that over a hundred non-Aryans were lined up and shot by the Nazis. The occupying Nazi General, Otto von Steuelpnagel, signed an order levying fines of one billion French Francs "exclusively" against Jews in Vichy. The order never elaborated what the fine was for, although bulletins pasted all over Paris made clear, the Nazis were not done with the matter—they were on the hunt for more "anarchists." Also, by von Steuelpnagel's order, "A large number of criminal Judeo-Bolshevik elements will be deported to hard labor in the eastern territories. Other deportations of still greater numbers will follow."[9]

The Nazis also began registering Americans in Germany, but oddly, only those over the age of fifty and under the age of fifteen.[10]

Yet another American pilot emerged as an early hero of the war. This one was John G. Magee Jr., a pilot/poet in the best tradition of Antoine de Saint-Exupery. He was the son of a rector of St. John's Episcopal Church in Washington. Impatient to get into the fight, young Magee had joined the Royal Canadian Air Force months earlier, and while the details of his death were not revealed, he too had "slipped the surly bonds of Earth . . . and, touched the face of God."[11]

Curiously, as one city after another had stumbled and bumbled its way through air-raid drills and blackout drills, the nation's capital had yet to complete a first, true dress rehearsal. As of the thirteenth, one was not planned for several weeks, even though the head of the local civil defense warned that without complete cooperation, "failure . . . may mean the blasting out of life or property."[12]

The city had good reason to protect property, and not just the public property of the government, either. Many private insurance companies had stopped writing policies or canceled policies on "war risk" homes and businesses located in Washington. "The majority of the reputable companies closed their books with the first rain of bombs on Hawaii."[13] Consequently, the federal government took $100 million and created a "nation-wide war insurance system to pay the private owners of homes, farms or factories in the Continental United States for damage or destruction resulting from enemy aircraft."[14] The new government bureau, the War Insurance Corporation, also covered crops and fruit orchards.

The federal city for years had been a sleepy, fevered, malarial swamp, appallingly humid and hot in the summer. It was situated on the Potomac River, which had become a slow-moving cesspool. Sewage was dumped in from homes upstream: from Georgetown, whose sewage drained right into the river; from the Army base at Ft. McNair; and from the Anacostia River, which fed into the larger Potomac. Until a WPA project built the Tidal Basin to control the river, it often overflowed its banks, sometimes even as far as the White House, and everything reeked. Between the New Deal, Lend-Lease, and now a new war, the town had changed radically.

David Brinkley memorably wrote in *Washington Goes to War*, "A languid Southern town with a pace so slow that much of it simply closed down for the summer grew almost overnight into a crowded, harried, almost frantic metropolis struggling desperately to assume the mantle of global power, moving halting and haphazardly and only partially successfully to changing itself into the capital of the free world."[15] Because of the advent of air conditioning, it was at least tolerable in the summer months now. But on this Sunday, December 14, it was doused by heavy sleet that knocked down the phone lines.

British diplomats had so hated being posted to Washington that they were paid extra, the same as if they were assigned to a war zone.[16] Now, Washington was ground zero for a world war zone. The town was radically altered, forevermore.

The town took soldiers and sailors, not only of America, but of America's allies, to its bosom. British and Australian enlistees were truly amazed at how hospitable Washington was. "Decent, that's what these people are. Why, there are more conveniences for service men here than I've ever found anywhere," said one Australian soldier.[17]

There were canteens where men in uniform could listen to music, write letters, put their feet up. There were dances at churches and civic centers, there were of course bars on every corner, but there were also lectures and concerts, historic tours and church services. At the Botanic Gardens, there was a poinsettia display, and a variety show at the Washington Hebrew Congregation.[18]

The cities of America, and especially Washington, had transformed into one big "R and R" station for men in uniform. The town bristled with a military presence, and the navy's PBYs routinely took off and landed on the Anacostia and Potomac Rivers.

The war had radically changed life in the military and aboard ship as well, especially in a combat zone. Censorship was widely employed in letters to and from sailors. It was not at all unusual for gobs and swabs to open their "V-Mail," only to find it already read by navy censors. Sensitive information such as the names of cities and ships, as well as details about other sailors, were neatly cut out of the letter with scissors. The same treatment went double for outbound letters. In a letter home, a sailor wrote, "We hear on the radio that the U.S.S. ___ was sunk. We couldn't send out any message because it would give our position away to the Japs."[19] Wives and girlfriends were advised not to put multiple lipstick kisses on the outside of letters as it could be interpreted to be code.[20]

As a consequence of rumors, the postmaster general had to go so far as to issue a statement saying there would be no censorship of in-country mail.[21]

Civilians were also admonished to be careful what they said and to whom, especially "ship movements or other information which might be valuable to the enemy. You are violating the security of the United States and endangering the lives of your fellow Americans if you fail to observe . . . precautions." A Five Point Plan was released, all of it urging civilians in each of the points: "Don't discuss . . . . concentrations . . . movements . . . new weapons . . . naval personnel."[22]

In other words, shut up.

But, curiously, newspapers were still publishing the billeting and deployment of individual G.I.s, naming names and destinations.

More guidelines were issued for blackouts. "Matches and cigarettes used on open streets are easily spotted by rooftop watchers." Eleanor Roosevelt advised Americans that the government was worried about poison gas attacks, implying that the Japanese had used gas against the Chinese. She also suggested that in order to keep children calm, parents should teach them "war is a game."[23] Long stories appeared advising people on how to deal with a gas attack by the

Japanese. Evacuation plans were developed, and Congress debated the bill to fund gas masks for the civilian population. Initially, the government wanted to distribute 38 million gas masks along the East and West Coasts.[24]

Bombing chitchat continued endlessly. In the militarily unimportant area of San Joaquin Valley, a mass exodus of farmers and farm workers ensued after rumors spread that they were about to be bombed.[25] Still, there was reason to be concerned. Law enforcement officials found evidence of attempted sabotage at dams in both California and Maryland. Advice columnists and veterans of the London bombings urged Americans that work was the best therapy for getting over the bombing jitters. When asked by the Gallup polling organization, a plurality of Americans on both coasts believed they might be bombed.[26] Stories appeared in newspapers on the "dos and don'ts for handling fire bombs," giving readers tips on what to do should one fall in a backyard undetonated. "Suppose an incendiary bomb fell in your vicinity, what would you do?"[27] Some training sessions to teach civilians how to handle undetonated bombs were called by the dubious moniker, "skull practice."[28]

The president's eldest son, James, went on active duty for the marines. In short order, all four Roosevelt boys would be in uniform, John, Elliot, and Franklin Jr. The recruiting offices of the country were still being inundated with applicants, some of whom had been sent away more than once due to the outpouring. "Boys" and "white-haired men" continued to show up.[29]

One young man in New York was so deeply moved by the war and the sacrifices of his fellow Americans that he changed his status from conscientious objector to 1-A. "In the face of this dastardly inhuman attack . . . I feel my stand as a conscientious objector in untenable. I feel proud to admit that I have made a mistake in taking the impractical stand of pacifism and repudiate it without the slightest reservation or hesitation. I stand ready to serve!" The wire story did not release the name of the young man for obvious reasons.[30]

In newspapers throughout the country, stories of young men (and some women) in the war zone or in flight school or gunnery school or boot camp or nursing school began to appear, generated by proud parents and other family members.

And more were turning up dead. A headline in the *Atlanta Constitution* read, "Georgian Killed in Hawaii Attack." It told of Lt. Ralph Hollis of the navy.[31] On the front page of the *Birmingham News* was another headline, "Lauderdale Negro Killed in Naval Engagement," its story telling of twenty-three-year-old Anthony Hawkins Jr. who had "died in action" in Hawaii.[32]

In Lynn, Massachusetts, the parents of Army Private Leo E. A. Gagne were making plans for his mass. He'd been killed at Hickam Field in Hawaii. The outpouring of friends and strangers, like everyplace else in America, was awe inspiring. "Members of his grief-stricken family had hardly made announcement of their plans to have a mass celebrated in the hero's memory when veterans of World War I offered to join them by paying military honors." Also, the local Veterans of Foreign Wars and the American Legion, along with community groups, came out to pay tribute and console the grieving family. The burial would not be anytime soon, however. "The body will not be returned to this country until hostilities have ended, according to the War Department."[33]

High school students were assembling stretchers and first-aid chests for carrying bandages and medicines.[34] In Miami, a blind man offered his services and those of his seeing-eye dog to help people in blackouts.[35] Boy Scouts were distributing 5 million air-raid posters.[36] Yet another newspaper account told of a senior class deferring the $37.50 collected for a trip to the purchase of war bonds instead.[37] Meanwhile, school kids in New York could be heard singing, "Hi-ho, hi-ho, we're off for Tokyo, to bomb each Jap, right off the map, hi-ho, hi-ho."[38] Such stories appeared by the thousands.

Civic mindedness was deep in the culture now. While not necessarily the clean-living model, a nonetheless patriotic group of strippers at the Follies Theatre in Los Angeles, led by Miss Dorothy Darling, pledged they would purchase $500 worth of war bonds each week.[39]

Nationally, the American Automobile Association organized an effort to drive women and children to and from military bases while also transporting soldiers and sailors to their new duty stations.[40] Virtually everyone was supporting the war effort now.

The final nail was driven in the coffin for the America First Committee. They'd already folded their tent, but not before the storefront of the New York office was besieged with "junior clerks, office boys and stenographers [who] made it a point to pass by the . . . office during the lunch hour and by, shouted remarks and finger postures added to the discomfiture of the staff." A "for rent" sign was hung in the window.[41]

A week earlier, the organization had bragged about setting up shop in every congressional district in the country, as a means of pressuring federal candidates into adopting their nonintervention agenda. Now the organization was deader than a doornail, and the former head of the organization, General Robert E. Wood, offered his services as a former military commander to President Roosevelt.[42] Wood was a highly decorated and much-esteemed veteran of the Great War.

Congress was nearing passage of a new Selective Service Act, the word "selective" being, by and large, window dressing. The aim was to scoop up as many males as possible. The 1-A classification referred to all able-bodied young, male American citizens between the ages of eighteen and forty-four years of age. The classification of 2-A was reserved for men whose work was considered essential, including many professional baseball players after January of 1942. The classification of 2-B was for men working in war industries, and 3-A was for married men.[43]

Government officials made it clear, however, that any jobs in the private sector filled by women would be vacated for men once they returned from combat.[44] But a federal circuit court of appeals made clear that there was no college deferment for studies or athletics. A football player at Gonzaga University sought to defer being drafted until he finished his gridiron career, but the court threw him for a loss.[45] Also, the U.S. Golf Association and the PGA mulled over suspension of the pro links tour for the duration of the war, and military leaders called for cancelling the Rose Bowl.[46]

The PGA considered a suspension, in part because of tour crowds on the West Coast. "Japanese planes have been seen reconnoitering over San Francisco. Machine gunners and bombers have a fondness for targets of that nature," reported the *Sunday Star*.[47] The amateur and professional tennis tours made no indication of canceling their seasons. Bobby Riggs was the number one ranked player in the world.[48]

Movie director Frank Capra was anxiously awaiting his orders. His *Meet John Doe* had premiered in May. On the twelfth, five days after Pearl Harbor, he'd accepted a commission as major in the Army Signal Corps, and on the thirteenth he'd wrapped principal photography on *Arsenic and Old Lace* with Cary Grant and Priscilla Lane; only editing remained.[49] Capra had already served in "World War I" (as the *Los Angeles Times* called it) as a math instructor at Ft. Scott in San Francisco.[50]

Soon, General George C. Marshall would give the talented young filmmaker a vital assignment: to create a documentary series called *Why We Fight* that explained to Americans the stakes involved in this world war, outlining the differences between American democracy and the totalitarian systems overseas.[51] Meanwhile, in case anyone in Tinseltown didn't get the message, big prints ads were purchased, telling readers, "All theatres are open and operating as usual! Even during Blackouts the show goes on as usual, with outside lighting curtailed in cooperation with the Citizens Defense Committee."[52]

War work was proving deadly, and not just for those in uniform. At a munitions plant in Iowa, a massive explosion killed nine and badly injured twenty.[53] Over the course of the war, thousands of civilians would be killed in the war industry or because of new procedures. In Los Angeles, a man fell into a culvert and drowned during a blackout.[54] With many of the ships in the sea lanes running without lights, a collision involving a commercial vessel, the *Oregon*, and an unnamed navy ship off of Nantucket resulted in the death of seventeen sailors.[55] Risk came with the territory for all Americans nowadays.

If American sacrifices and rationing were austere, Canada's were downright Scrooge-like. The country rationed gasoline and prohibited the manufacturing of "bicycles, tricycles, children's metal wagons, ice skates, roller skates, beds and furniture and appliances of every sort made of metal, such as electric broilers, fans, grills, irons, electric tea kettles and a host of other metal objects of everyday use are not to be manufactured except by permit."[56]

While Americans would not experience gasoline rationing (not yet, anyway), the quality of their gasoline would go down. The anti-knocking ingredient—tetraethyl lead—that gave gasoline the octane so needed for automobiles was considerably more essential for the high performance engines of American airplanes. It would also mean that miles per gallon would drop significantly.[57]

Questions arose again, about food and food supplies. During the Great War, American housewives had experienced food shortages and "to a housewife, a world war is a world war." Government officials cooed that this time it would be different. Supplies were high, sugar could be expected to continue arriving from Hawaii, and new oils, to replace coconut and palm oil from the Far East, could be acquired from South American countries. Also, Americans were told foodstuffs would not be shipped overseas in the quantities of the last war. Still, this did not stop the rush of food buying, especially of flour, canned vegetables, and sugar (with good reason). Soap manufactures and sugar producers were rationing sales to wholesalers, in the hopes of stopping hoarders.[58] The Office of Production Management moved in and banned sugar-hoarding outright.[59] Then the government moved in and curbed the shipment of sugar altogether. Rationing began. "The federal restrictions are aimed chiefly at candy and soft drink manufacturers and bakeries."[60]

War was also costly. It would be financed with bonds and taxes and bank loans. The nation's banks as of the tenth had assets of $3.8 billion: "This indicated that the banks still have vast idle funds for financing the war."[61] And yet every day there were fresh stories in the papers about the young and old, the poor and rich, black and white, male and female, all purchasing defense bonds, some with their last few dollars.

Now, on a war footing, the country was divided into nine regions in order to facilitate military and civilian responses to possible attacks. The country was not divided on the economy, however. By a better than 2-1 margin, Americans supported wage and price controls as a means of combating inflation as well as "war profiteering."[62]

The cost of living had been rising, doubling in less than six months with no compelling argument other than government control offered.[63]

In New York, bulldozers moved in to knock down the last of the 1939 World's Fair exhibits, including a pavilion created by the Japanese government to symbolize the eternal friendship of the American and the Japanese people.[64] The World's Fair had showcased many technological marvels and was enormously popular. It was at this venue that Radio Corporation of America (RCA) introduced television to the American public, an astounding invention that had to wait until war's end to come to fruition.[65] In 1941, the Fair's disintegrating remnants stood as a poignant reminder of a more peaceful and productive direction that the world could have taken, but didn't.

Even a week after the attack on Pearl Harbor, public information about the health and well-being of men and women in uniform only trickled out. In one case, a happy family received a telegram announcing that not only was their son-in-law safe, but he and their daughter—stationed in Oahu—had had a healthy baby boy.

The parents of Myrtle M. Miller of Baltimore were also delighted, as Myrtle, an army lieutenant and nurse stationed in Hawaii, was also "well, safe." There was no doubt that young American men bore the brunt of the fight, but a goodly number of women too had been at the scene of the battle. Myrtle's father said that his daughter stated, "If war should come, I will follow the boys. They will need help, and I feel it is my duty to do whatever is in my power to do."[66] Miss Miller's words were not just those of a woman or a nurse or a member of the army, but those also of an American.

The names of some of the army pilots who managed to get their planes into the air on December 7 were released by General Walter Short, who was still in charge of the army post in Hawaii. Head of the list was Lt. George Welch, twenty-three, a native of Delaware, who managed to shoot down four Japanese planes, one number short of making him an "ace." The photos of half a dozen army pilots, including Welch, who had fought Japanese in the skies over Oahu, were widely reprinted. "Lt. Louis M. Sanders . . . engaged Japanese plane and shot it down. Second Lt. Kenneth M. Taylor attacked six Japanese planes; shot down two. . . . Lt. Gordon H. Sterling Jr., Second Lt. Phillip M. Rasmussen, Second Lt. Harry W. Brown . . . ." All were cited for "Spectacular Heroism."[67]

All were handsome young men with full heads of hair, square-jawed, all-American, each with a Tom Sawyer-glint of mischievousness in his eye.

Indeed, the Sunday papers were filled with pro-Allied stories, as if the government had done an information dump of positive news in order to buck up American morale. Stories told of how Americans flyers downed a handful of planes in dogfights over Pearl Harbor on the seventh, how American forces had supposedly hurled Japanese invaders back into the sea from their assault on the Philippines, and how British and Dutch forces were supposedly mounting counteroffensives against the Japanese and Germans. The articles were so glowingly positive about the Allies' counteroffensive and bravery one could have been excused for thinking Japan would sue for peace within a matter of days.

The women's pages of the papers all featured energetic women volunteering, stepping forward for civic work, helping in their communities. In Georgia, dozens of women patiently took classes to learn Morse Code, tapping out dots and dashes, or more accurately, "dit's" and "da's." The women attending were described as "busy housewives" and "women" who "ranged from sweatered and socked school-age youngsters to grey-haired matrons." Classes had been pulled together by the American Women's Volunteer Service.[68]

This World, the Sunday magazine section of the *San Francisco Chronicle*, simply reprinted on its cover the first Associated Press alert on the attack at Pearl Harbor. "Bulletin Honolulu, Dec. 7—(AP)—At Least Two Japanese Bombers, Their Wings Bearing the Insignia of the Rising Sun, Appeared over Honolulu at about 7:35 a.m. (Honolulu Time) Today and Dropped Bombs."[69]

The ever-so-popular comic strips of America—many newspapers carried up to four pages daily—were the last to reflect the war culture. Cartoonists often drew their strips weeks in advance, so it was difficult to take advantage of current events to build into their storylines. So, while war was on everybody's else's lips, in "Wash Tubbs," "Boots and Her Buddies," "Superman," and "Joe Palooka," all the heroes and heroines of the comics went about their lives, fighting bandits, shady Hollywood directors, and other scofflaws. Cartoonists had not used their strips to promote a political agenda; though within a short time, they would be fighting Nazis and Japanese spies, especially in "Captain America," whose very creation was as a result of the war.

Theodor Seuss Geisel—who later became known as the gentle and kindly favorite of kids, "Dr. Seuss"—was drawing some of the toughest and most vicious anti-Nazi and anti-Japanese cartoons in the country.[70]

Roosevelt was getting a clearer picture of the damage at Pearl Harbor, as Frank Knox explained in a confidential, nineteen-page memo to FDR. Scribbled at the top was a note by Roosevelt: "Given me by F.K. 10p.m. Dec 14 when he landed here from Hawaii. FDR." The memo also went into some graphic explanations over the poor response of the navy and the poor displacement of aircraft. "At neither Army or Navy fields were planes dispersed." Of the few Japanese planes shot down, "American radio and other American built equipment was recovered from the wreckage." And, "The *Arizona* is a total wreck, her forward magazine having exploded after she had been damaged by both torpedoes and bombs."[71]

One week after the seventh, all the Sunday papers contained retrospectives and analyses of the attack, the war, and the future conflict. Many of them were pure spitball, and others still didn't have the full details of the war and the attack at Pearl Harbor. Several newspapers ran profiles of Admiral Yamamoto, not altogether unfavorably. One story noted he "does without the eye-glasses that mark most Japanese."[72]

The *Los Angeles Times* reported that Japanese radio was claiming that Admiral Kimmel had been killed at Pearl Harbor while aboard the *Pennsylvania*, which, according to the Japanese, had also met its demise.[73] Kimmel was alive and kicking, but the fact that the Japanese knew the *Pennsylvania* was the admiral's flagship demonstrated how much they knew about the American navy.

Some pieces accurately reviewed the importance of the tiny specks of islands in the Pacific to the war for both sides. The vast majority of Americans had never traversed the Pacific, and it was hard to describe or comprehend its massiveness. It was half again the size of the Atlantic, and planes, ships, and submarines could not roam with impunity. They needed to be refueled, and the men needed time to get their feet on dry land at periodic breaks. If the United States was overlaid on the Pacific, it would stretch only from the Philippines to the Marshall Islands.

Islands that Americans had never heard of before, such as Guam and Johnston, and Palmyra, were all of a sudden known and vitally important. "At the war's start naval bases were being constructed on Midway, Wake, Johnston and Palmyra Islands. Channels were being cut through the coral reefs and coral heads were being taken out of lagoons to provide take-off areas for fully loaded planes."[74] Japan controlled many islands in the Western Pacific and was now attempting to run America off the central Pacific islands. There was concern they would also seize the Aleutian Islands in the cold North Pacific and, from there, establish bases closer to the West Coast of America.

The *Boston Sunday Globe* featured a column by Owen Scott who, without quoting an authoritative source on the record or on background, said that the country could not possibly begin to engage the enemy in any meaningful way before 1943. Also, "it will be in 1945 before the United States has its Navy operating in a two-ocean basis with full strength in both." He furthermore claimed the war would be won with technology and manpower.[75] American Exceptionalists would have begged to differ.

Yet other stories delved into how America would administer an occupied Europe, once the war was won. Considering how badly things were actually going, this was as astonishing as it was presumptuous. Still, not a soul in the country believed that the United States would not win in the end.

Newspaper and magazine ads for Christmas gifts included toy airplanes for boys and "pajama dolls" for girls.[76] There were ads selling military uniforms, ads pitching washing machines, pianos, tile for concrete floors, and sewing machines; ads for church services and social events and lectures and field trips filled the papers too. Men were urged to please their wives by taking dance lessons at the Arthur Murray Studios.[77] They were also urged to purchase "gift nylons."[78] Birth announcements and marriage license applications filled newspapers, as did the ads for "naughty Can-Can"[79] underwear for women.

Debutante balls went forward, and the Elks, the Knights of Columbus, the Eastern Star, and the Colored Masons all met, elected officers, and stepped up their charitable works. The V.F.W. and the American Legion nationwide made their impressive pool of military talents available to civil defense.

The book review sections of all Sunday papers were eagerly read. John Steinbeck's newest novel, *Sea of Cortez*, was favorably reviewed in many, as were *Wolf in the Fold* by Nellise Child and *The Young Churchill* by Stanley Nott. The new novel *Storm*, by George R. Stewart, was reviewed but not altogether favorably. The best-selling novel was *The Keys of the Kingdom* by A.J. Cronin, and the best-selling nonfiction book was William Shirer's *Berlin Diary*.[80]

At the President Hotel in Atlantic City, rooms for the Christmas season were going for $4.50 for a single and $7.00 for a couple, per night.[81] All the Sunday broadsheets had extensive travel sections featuring resorts and hotels and articles on voyages and destinations.

The top ten movies of 1941 were announced. *Citizen Kane* topped the critics' list, but every film on the list would soon become a classic, from *The Philadelphia Story* to *The Maltese Falcon*.[82] Hollywood and the U.S. government had already begun recruiting and organizing "bond drives."

Some of the first actors and actresses to sign up for the bond drives were Mickey Rooney, Clark Gable, Bette Davis, Spencer Tracy, Bing Crosby, Judy Garland, and Jimmy Cagney. Also a young, up-and-coming actor, Ronald Reagan, though in the army reserves, had been turned away three times for active duty because of his extremely poor eyesight. It was so bad upon testing that, without contacts or glasses, he could not distinguish a tank unless it was less than seven feet from him.

Slowly, the references to the Great War as "World War I" were beginning to seep into news reporting. No one in Washington ever sent out a memo, but over time, all were coming to see that the "War to End All Wars" had simply been a prelude to a new world war. A columnist for the *San Francisco Chronicle*, Carolyn Anspacher, opened her piece by penning, "Eternities ago, during a conflict now designated as World War I . . . "[83] But Blair Bolles opened his Sunday piece by calling this the "119th week of World War II," making the case it had begun with the invasion of Poland in September of 1939, which of course was true.[84]

The fourteenth of December also marked 142 years to the day since the greatest and most indomitable American ever, George Washington, had passed away. Neither Washington nor his country would or could ever be denied.

As the British had learned beginning in 1776—and the Axis powers would in the near future—the American spirit was an indomitable thing.

CHAPTER 15

THE FIFTEENTH OF DECEMBER

"Knox Reveals Six U.S. Warships Lost in Hawaii Attack"

Yuma Daily Sun

"Japanese Pounding Hong Kong"

Evening Star

"United States Lend-Lease Aid
Now Totals $1,202,000,000"

Lethbridge Herald

"2,727 Officers, Men Killed 'Not on Alert,' Secretary Declares"

Evening Star

I n Lisbon, the port was a madhouse of clamoring humanity, with thousands trying to flee Nazism. The last ship of the American Export Line was about to set sail for the United States before the harbor closed. Only Americans and British subjects with passports and transit visas were allowed aboard. No Germans were allowed, even if they opposed Hitler, and all those German citizens in Portugal wanted nothing to do with the Third Reich. The "pitch blackness of Nazified Europe" was what they now faced.[1]

Still, with their Aryan features, they had a chance to survive in Germany or on the European continent, provided they used their wits. For others, the prospects were terrifying. "Many refugees from Germany were affected. Some 600 Jewish refugees from various countries now in Portugal feared that new developments might cut them off from escape from Europe."[2] The tales of those left behind ripped at the heartstrings: the elderly couple who had hitchhiked for seventeen days, hiding in cellars, in haymows; fathers trying desperately to get their children and wives to safe passage. Left behind were "kings and dukes, ministers of state, and men of letters, businessmen and just ordinary people, some fleeing because their lives were in danger; others because they shared in the panic that was in the air. There was tragedy and despair, generosity and kindliness, mixed unhappily with selfishness. Lisbon has become just another trap from which, this time, there may be no escape."[3]

As the last ship sailed over the Western horizon, "It is hard to imagine the tragedy of the moment for many thousands of human beings from all over Europe. At any moment, the fate of thousands of helpless fugitives from the Nazi 'New Order' in Europe may be sealed."[4]

Also behind enemy lines (or soon to be) were American Christian missionaries throughout the Far East. The Catholic Church had by far the most, with nearly 1,300 priests, brothers, sisters, and scholastics scattered across the region. There were also a couple hundred Baptist missionaries.[5] Prayers were offered for their safe return.

Despite their early successes, General Tojo warned the Japanese people at a public rally of a long and brutal war with the Americans. In America, *Life* magazine opined, "Close observers of Japan have said for years that if that country ever found itself in a hopeless corner it was capable of committing national hari-kari by flinging itself at the throat of its mightiest enemy. Japan has found itself in just such a corner . . . Japan's daring was matched only by its barefaced duplicity."[6] But Tojo also bragged to the Japanese Diet that the American and British fleets in the Pacific had been "crushed."[7]

Midway Island was still in U.S. hands as of Monday, the fifteenth, but FDR had already cautioned the American people that all of the central Pacific islands—save the Hawaiian Islands—and all those of the Far East could fall to the Japanese. In his way, he too was warning his people of a long and brutal conflict and that the news would get worse before it got better. Guam had already fallen, and with it, the fates of 155 marines and 400 navy men were now in the hands of their captors, who did not have a good track record when it came to POWs.[8]

Across America, the refrain "Remember Pearl Harbor!" was heard more and more. It followed in the tradition of other American battle cries: "Give me liberty or give me death!" from Patrick Henry; "Don't give up the ship!" from Captain James Lawrence in the War of 1812; "Remember the Alamo!" from General Sam Houston, before the 1836 decisive battle of San Jacinto in the Texas War of Independence; and "Remember the *Maine!*" which found its origins in a gin mill in New York in 1898, shortly after the explosion of the ship in Havana harbor, which sparked American eagerness for the Spanish-American War. (Whether or not the Spanish or their allies had planted a bomb on the *Maine* was open to question, as it was not unusual for ships of the day to see faulty boilers explode, but for men like William Randolph Hearst, the propaganda value was too attractive to quibble over details such as welders' seams or the efficacy of iron bolts.)

Time magazine observed that never had the people of America been this united. "What would the people . . . say in the face of the mightiest event of their time? What they said—tens of thousands of them—was: 'Why, the yellow bastards!'"[9] December 7 had become indelible.

Everybody knew where they were on December 7 when they heard the news of Pearl Harbor. There were but a few dates in American history for which someone could say, "I remember where I was when I heard . . . ."

December 7, 1941, was now at the top of the list.

FDR had yet to meet with navy head Frank Knox, but the rumor out of Washington had it that the navy thought it might be possible to refloat and refit some of those ships hit by the Japanese. Because the harbor was relatively shallow and because the Japanese bombers had ignored the dry docks, the damaged and sunken ships would not have to be towed the 3,000 or so miles to San Diego.

Still, the fact that repairs were being discussed and that the president had met with Admiral Samuel Robinson—head of the Navy's Bureau of Ships, which was responsible for construction and maintenance—was confirmation to the casual observer that severe damage had occurred at Hawaii.[10]

All major publications had done profiles of the military brass, including Admiral Ernest "Rey" King, Admiral Harold "Betty" Stark and Admiral Husband "Kim" Kimmel. Kimmel had been featured on the cover of *Time* magazine the second week of December.[11] Stark had picked up his nickname while an underclassman at Annapolis.[12] *Time* wasn't afraid of controversy, even as it had a tendency to shill often for the Roosevelt administration. Its reporting could be terse, mincing few words. In their November 10 issue, they referred to the *New Republic* magazine as "pinko," suggesting the publication was soft on communism.[13]

Life and *Time* magazines took up Kimmel's cause, but they were only two of a very few to do so. Defending the increasingly beleaguered navy man, *Life* wrote, "Admiral Kimmel had not been given enough patrol planes to spot enemy carriers a night's steaming away."[14] Still, "there was speculation whether Knox's investigation would lead to changes in either army or navy command in the Hawaiian area."[15]

On Sunday evening, the fourteenth, Knox—upon his return from Hawaii—gave his report to Roosevelt in a short meeting of thirty minutes. FDR studied it into the evening.[16] Knox's return to Washington was not announced until after he left the White House that evening. Then on Monday, eight days after the attack, some of the brutal truth was revealed to the American people.

President Roosevelt sent a report to Congress on Monday detailing that Japanese submarines had been used, something not previously confirmed. Elaborating, he said, "The actual air and submarine attack on the Hawaiian Islands began at 1:20 p.m. Washington time on Dec. 7." Enraged, he said that it was well over three hours after the attack before U.S. ambassador Joseph Grew was notified by the Japanese that they had declared war on America. He also observed that "Japan . . . accepted the German thesis of racial superiority and extreme nationalism." Japan, he noted, had proclaimed itself in 1937 to be of a superior race when compared to any other country "of the Orient."[17]

The document Roosevelt sent to the Hill was essentially a recitation of the steady decline of the relations between the two countries, brought on by Japan's growing militarism. News reports described the president's tone in the document as "bitter." The climax of the FDR's communiqué exclaimed that "there is the record, for all history to read in amazement, in sorrow, in horror, in disgust!"[18]

The report had been sent in part to placate some in Congress who had been agitating for more details. However, those congressmen knew they had to tread lightly in their criticism. Senator Charles Tobey of New Hampshire, who just a few days earlier had created a scene on the floor of the Senate over the attack by calling for the heads of everybody in the military, was publicly rebuked by the American Legion of his own state, who called on him "to demonstrate undivided allegiance to our country . . . by supporting the proper civil and military authorities of this country."[19]

Knox huddled again that morning of the fifteenth with the president for "two hours and 25 minutes" before meeting in a room packed with reporters and photographers. "Knox looked pale and haggard as he talked to the press in his office."[20] The report was startling. The massacre was widespread. FDR called it "barbaric aggression."[21] Americans were prepared to hear of a couple hundred killed. They were not prepared for thousands. "The casualties crept from rumor into uglier-rumor: hundreds on hundreds of Americans had died bomb-quick, or were dying, bed-slow."[22]

The bottom line was that far more men had been killed or wounded than previously thought and far more ships had been destroyed or damaged than previously reported. Knox's report only dealt with the navy's losses and only mentioned the army planes and hangars destroyed, although he did say that "army losses were severe."[23]

Knox told reporters that six American warships had been destroyed in the attack. He "declared that the Navy was not on the alert . . . that the Pacific fleet lost the battleship *Arizona*, three destroyers and two lesser craft . . . . Knox disclosed for the first time that the Navy had suffered 3,385 casualties in the Hawaiian attacks—2,729 officers and men killed and 656 wounded—

fatalities in the sudden attack." He elaborated, saying, "Officers 91 dead and 20 wounded: enlisted men 2,638 dead and 636 wounded."[24]

Still, all the details would not be revealed to the American people, "and no complete report is promised."[25] The other capital ship he named besides the *Arizona* was the *Oklahoma*, along with four smaller ships; the *Cassin*, the *Shaw*, the *Downes*, and the *Oglala*. Not revealed was the number of civilians killed by the Japanese.[26]

Knox did say the *Arizona* was lost due to a direct hit by the enemy, and he dispelled the rumors that the Japanese had any kind of secret weapon or that they had used anything other than single-engine aircraft. Knox said the American forces destroyed three Japanese submarines and forty-one planes. He also claimed that the remaining American ships were at sea, searching out the enemy.[27]

Unpromisingly, he told reporters, "We are entitled to know if (a) there was any error of judgment which contributed to the surprise [and] (b) if there was any dereliction of duty prior to the attack."[28]

The secretary of the navy also made it clear that Japanese espionage had played a significant role in the attack, feeding the imperial navy constantly with updated information on targets and movements.

He finished the grim report by saying, "In the Navy's gravest hour of peril, the officers and men of the fleet exhibited magnificent courage and resourcefulness during the treacherous Japanese assault on Pearl Harbor. The real story of Pearl Harbor is not one of individual heroism, although there were many such cases. It lies in the splendid manner in which all hands did their job as long as they were able, not only under fire but while fighting the flames afterwards and immediately starting salvage work and reorganization."[29]

Knox paid tribute to an unnamed young seaman who, on his own, manned a machine gun and fired the first shots of America in the new war against Japan, "even before general quarters was sounded." He also paid tribute to the unnamed captain of a battleship who stayed at his post even as "his stomach was laid completely open by shrapnel burst."[30]

Before departing, Knox told the reporters there would be an investigation into the military leadership in Hawaii, directed immediately by the president.[31]

December 15 was "Bill of Rights Day," a national holiday commemorating the first Ten Amendments to the U.S. Constitution. Individual rights and freedoms took on a new meaning this time around, however, and President Roosevelt gave a one-hour address, broadcast live from 10 p.m. to 11 p.m. on all radio networks. FDR, concerned about the agitated state of Americans, used his remarks to warn against "inflamed or hysterical action."[32] CBS Radio also broadcast a special entitled, "We Hold These Truths," starring Lionel Barrymore, Walter Huston, and Edward G. Robinson. Always on the lookout to promote young starlets, a Hollywood studio depicted Gene Tierney in a low-cut white dress, holding an oversized version of the document. Constitution meet Cheesecake.[33]

The year 1941 was also significant as it was the 150th anniversary of the ratification of the Constitution by the Commonwealth of Virginia, in 1791, "which completed the necessary action on the Bill of Rights and gave it the full force and effect of the Constitution." Celebrations of the day were far and wide, involving public and private schools and towns and communities. Vice President Henry Wallace laid a wreath at the grave of George Mason, the Father of the Bill of Rights, at the Founding Father's home in Gunston, Virginia. The governor of Virginia, James Price, also spoke, and a ceremony took place at the tomb of the newspaper editor, John Peter Zenger, "the editor whose trial established the freedom of the press." The Librarian of Congress, Archibald MacLeish, was the mastermind behind the big day.[34]

The original Bill of Rights contained twelve amendments, but the two regulating the pay and the size of Congress were thrown out. As for the ten amendments that formed the final Bill of Rights, in light of current events, few if any people openly commented on which of those were effectively overlooked by the war effort.

A new document was also signed, but among Allies of a different sort. Together, America, Great Britain, the Netherlands, Russia, Free China, and others met in London and signed a mutual war pact declaring that none of the signers would embark on a separate peace agreement with any of the Axis powers.[35]

On both sides now, it was all-for-one-and-one-for-all war, as representatives of the Axis powers met in Berlin to map out *their* war strategies.[36] In Syracuse, New York, representatives of the Six Nations of the Iroquois Confederacy met as well to decide their next move. These six independent nations had declared war on Germany in 1917 and were gathering once again to determine if they as a group would declare war on the Axis.[37]

Eight days after the attack, the White House was in a full lockdown. Papers and passes were demanded. Cops and military police roamed ubiquitously, stopping everyone, guns bristling. "Soldiers with sub-machine guns," the *Los Angeles Times* bluntly noted.[38] On the White House grounds, guard towers had been built and one-inch steel cables ran every which way, controlling the flow of foot traffic.

Security measures continued unabated. In Santa Barbara, miles and miles of federal parklands were closed to the public, including the Santa Ynez River locale. "Public entry is not to be permitted until the close of the war."[39] Entry to the Chesapeake Bay was tightly restricted by navy vessels. "Boats ordered to stop shall comply immediately on pain of being fired on."[40]

The New York state government announced that, in order to save steel, motorists would only be required to have license tags on the backs of their vehicles, thus saving annually two thousand tons of the important metal. However, there would be no corresponding reduction in licensing fees.[41] It was enough to drive any man to drink, except for German nationals in New York. These "Nazi Citizens," as the *New York Times* called them, were prohibited by the state of New York from owning liquor licenses.[42]

In short order, the federal government ordered a halt to the manufacture of all new pots and pans and kitchen appliances made of iron or steel, and the industry should "discontinue the use of brightwork or trim containing copper, nickel or aluminum."[43] However, a "war train" of sorts—but really called the "Defense Special"—was already touring the country, showing businessmen what the military needed to have manufactured. On the train, organized by the Office of Production Management, were blueprints and prototypes of fashioned metal parts.[44]

The culture had changed so deeply that *Time* magazine devoted a long article to the advantages of arc welding in the building of planes and ships.[45]

Washington was seizing an increased number of neutral or civilian ships, including those of allies, under the nautical rules of "angary." Maritime Law provided for a nation, during wartime, to take any and all vessels in order to defend itself. Still, the oceans would shortly be crammed with American-made ships. In anticipation of all that new construction, the industry estimated it would have to recruit over a million workers within a year to meet the military and commercial needs of the country.[46] The demand for shipyard workers was such that agriculture officials anticipated a farm labor shortage.

The navy began awarding what would become their famous "E" flags to civilian industries—and not just shipbuilding—denoting their "Excellent" work. Workers and management alike took real pride in flying these flags at the front of their plants.[47] The growing patriotism in America was such that, at the Hatfield Wire and Cable Company in New Jersey, during the morning Pledge of Allegiance, two of the 350 employees refused to salute Old Glory. Three hundred and forty-eight employees went on strike as a result and said that, unless the two were fired, they would not go to work. The two (who cited religious stipulations) were dismissed.[48]

Sunday also found 80 percent of General Electric employees at their posts, working yet another full day. The employees of the big corporation had already voted to work a six-day week but here they were, on the seventh day, working hard in Schenectady, Bridgeport, Philadelphia, and dozens of other locations around the nation. The company employed 125,000 workers.[49]

The war industry continued to be dangerous for civilians and would be, throughout the years. At a plant in New Jersey, an explosion "blew an employee to bits" and injured forty others. The FBI and the navy opened an investigation to see if sabotage had been the cause of the blast.[50]

After a call for donors, the Red Cross was awash in the blood of American civilians. Local chapters were overrun with so many people walking in, they were asked to call ahead and make an appointment.[51]

America of 1941 was all slang, all the time. In the patois of the era, Americans had not "washed out" nor had they made a "hash" of things. Carl Sandberg once famously said, "Slang is language that takes off its coat, spits on its hands, and gets to work."[52] Coffee was "Joe"; and breakfast, lunch, and dinner were "three squares." Sailors were "swabs" and "gobs" and soldiers were "dogfaces" and marines were "jarheads." "When one soldier tells another 'our bean-gun grub was shrapnel, cream on a shingle, and ink with side arms,' he's merely saying the meal from the rolling field kitchen included baked beans, creamed beef on toast and coffee with cream and sugar."[53] An unknown or pushy girl was "sister."

Among civilians, "patch my pantywaist" meant being amazed, and "hoy-toytoy" was a good time. "Futzing around" was wasting time, and "dig me?" was do you understand? A "yum yum type" was a good-looking individual, and "shove in your clutch" meant get going.[54] A "G.I." of course was slang for "government issue." Later, as the massive war effort generated its inevitable moments of chaos and confusion, harsher slang would emerge that had currency for many years, such as SNAFU (Situation Normal, All F—ed Up).

Many G.I.s were going to get their Christmas furloughs after all. For those who were not released, the individual bases and the local USOs would do their best to ensure the young men a modicum of a Merry Christmas: after all, they were expecting packages from home, many of those packages containing cartons of cigarettes.

Cigarettes of every style, brand, and packaging were available to every civilian and G.I. in America. The refrain, "Smoke 'em if you've got 'em," became an unofficial military slogan, as superior officers would bark this refrain to enlistees when they went on break. Because cigarettes were included in rations and readily available in military PX commissaries, the federal government all but recommended, encouraged, and endorsed cigarette smoking by men and women in the military. One brand with their own pitch was "Juleps," which contained a "hint of miracle-mint."

Advertising encouraged "chain smoking" of Juleps for those who thought they smoked too much of another brand. They were also recommended for "the boys at camp." Spud cigarettes also billed themselves as good for a sore throat. So did Regent cigarettes.[55] And Philip Morris.

There was never a general outbreak of violence against Japanese Americans, Italian Americans, and German Americans, but the Japanese Americans living loyally in the United States had more to fear and thus more to lose than the others for obvious reasons. There were the occasional stories, such as the Japanese man in California who showed up dead in a canal in his car, either because of an accident or foul play.[56] Still, U.S. attorney general Francis Biddle, concerned that the civilian American population would take out their ire on the wrong people, issued an important statement on the matter: "The United States is now at war. Every American will share in the task of defending our country. It is essential that we keep our heads, keep our tempers— above all, that we keep clearly in mind what we are defending. The enemy has attacked more than the soil of America. He has attacked our institutions, our freedoms, the principles on which this nation was founded and has grown to greatness. It therefore behooves us to guard these principles most zealously at home."[57]

Biddle reminded Americans that "aliens form 3½ percent of our population," while restating that only those aliens with malice in their plans need fear the federal government.[58]

Japanese Americans in Los Angeles opened up their own pro-American storefronts and announced they would rat out any Japanese they thought "who by word or act consort[s] with the enemies." They also came up with their own loyalty pledge.[59] Little Tokyo in Los Angeles was a ghost town; shops had been forcibly closed as the Treasury Department had ordered Japanese citizens to stay off the streets. Christian Japanese groups formed support groups. Japanese had some reason to be bitter toward the United States. Since 1924, with the passage of the Japanese Exclusion Act, only 100 Japanese individuals per year were allowed U.S. citizenship.[60]

For the eighth day in a row, the Japanese pounded both Hong Kong and the Philippines. In Manila, General MacArthur had the added problem of subversive elements on the island facilitating the Japanese offensive, as well as problems with some of the local native tribes and anarchist groups. The Japanese were attempting to incite a riot against the American military. Japan's propaganda agencies claimed their military was making progress in both battles, as well as all of Malaya, where they were advancing toward Singapore.[61]

Even the stiffest upper lipped Brit was not hopeful about the outcome in either Hong Kong or Singapore, even though the Free Chinese were waging a furious battle against the Japanese. The *Christian Science Monitor* reported, "British troops admittedly were withdrawing from Kowloon. . . . Britain admitted that Japanese troops once again had gained ground in . . . North Malaya. . . . Britain admitted that its garrison at Victoria, southeastern Burma, was withdrawn following Japanese landings. . . ." According to London officials, the withdrawal from Kowloon was "according to plan."[62] It was a somber forty-sixth birthday for King George VI, who marked it with his wife, Queen Elizabeth, and his daughters, Princess Elizabeth and Princess Margaret.[63]

MacArthur issued yet another statement saying the situation was "well in hand both on the ground and in the air."[64] In fact, the conditions in Manila had deteriorated so critically that the national legislature was meeting in a basement and the Japanese had established three different beachheads on the main island of Luzon. The only encouraging news was that Filipino troops had won a fight against Japanese parachutists in the hills outside of Manila. The Allies had already declared Thailand as a lost cause, and Shanghai had fallen quickly.[65]

In the European sector, the German bombing of London had ground to a halt. Whereas London was bombed some 19,000 times in the month of September 1940, by September 1941 it had "only" been assailed from the air about 1500 times.[66]

The Allies did get some good news from North Africa, where the Brits had regained the offensive against Rommel, aided in part by Indian troops, which must have been particularly galling to the racist Hitler. "The Indians captured 21 Axis officers and 350 men. . . ."[67] Also, American planes had mounted a small counteroffensive in the China Sea, apparently hitting several Japanese ships.[68]

Deep in the hills of Yugoslavia, Serbian guerrillas were also giving the Germans fits, staving off division after division totaling several hundred thousand troops—eighteen total by December of 1941. They were completely stymied by Draja Mihailovic, the heroic Serb general who commanded a force of less than 80,000 men.[69]

Greek guerrillas were also wreaking havoc with Germany's plans for their country, and despite their best efforts, the German Army and Italian Army could not dislodge them. In the face of widespread food and arms shortages, the Greek people were starving and, by estimates, receiving only around 250 calories a day whereas, before the war, they were getting "between 3,000 and 4,000 daily."[70]

After meeting with Knox, FDR had lunch with his 1940 Republican opponent, Wendell Willkie.[71] No eyebrows were raised whatsoever. FDR's press secretary, Stephen Early, joined them. The Indiana businessman had run a personality campaign in 1940; no one could ever out-personality Roosevelt. The Republican Party of the era was a confusing mishmash of internationalists and minimalists, New Dealers, and the like. It had no coherent organizing philosophy and thus was more akin to a loyal half-opposition. The Democratic Party in 1941 was all over the feeble and flaccid GOP.

Willkie lost decisively even as FDR was seeking a third consecutive term, something no previous occupant of the White House had probably ever really considered and certainly not sought. (Ulysses S. Grant had sought a third term, though not consecutively.) Willkie was a Republican New Dealer and fervent internationalist who often spoke up in favor of Roosevelt; many wondered if he'd wandered into the wrong political headquarters as a young man. Willkie later penned a best-selling book, *One World*, which stood as one of the great exhortations ever written for a coming-together of humanity—or just a big collectivist secular humanistic world. Take your pick.

Willkie was recruited to supervise a labor-business conference called by the White House for the following week, but it leaked out that he might take on even bigger responsibilities.[72] The fact was, FDR and Willkie genuinely liked and respected each other.

As with all his days now, Monday was another busy one for Roosevelt as he announced that Lend-Lease to the Allies would continue now that America was officially in the war. He also nominated twenty-five army men to "temporary appointment" as generals. The Senate would have to approve these promotions, including that of Col. Theodore Roosevelt, son of Teddy Roosevelt and a distant cousin of FDR.[73] Eleanor Roosevelt wrapped up her extended West Coast tour, traveled by train to Portland, and met with civil defense officials the day before. All this was recorded in her widely syndicated column, "My Day."[74] She arrived back at the White House just after 2:00 p.m. on the fifteenth.[75]

The Honolulu that Knox had left behind had changed a great deal in a very short period of time. A once happy, open, casual, and relaxed town was now paranoid, closed, and insecure. A curfew kept everybody off the streets at sundown. Movie theaters and restaurants stopped their businesses in time for patrons to leave and get home. Bars were closed; people did their drinking at home. Trenches were everywhere, as were barbed wire and barricades. Guards patrolled the streets, and "the use of a pocket flashlight or a match is likely to bring a bullet." Dinner parties and cocktail parties were a thing of the past, unless the host and hostess were willing to put up their guests overnight; cars were not allowed on the roads after sunset. Even so, many owners had painted over their headlights. Daytime driving was allowed, but gas sales were limited to half a tank, and the radio kept telling listeners to cut their driving to the bare minimum.[76] However, limited service on Pan

American airlines began again between Honolulu and the West Coast, and for the first time in two weeks, the radio station KGU, a part of the NBC empire, returned to the airwaves.[77]

San Francisco was just as panicky as Honolulu. Constant air-raid warnings, blackouts, and rumors of enemy planes and ships had about frazzled the nerves of the average San Franciscan. So, when flares appeared in the night sky, they were rumored to have dropped from enemy aircraft. It was just one more headache citizens did not need. City fathers canceled the annual East-West Bowl game, one of the biggest college football games of the year. Los Angeles also canceled the Rose Bowl and the Rose Bowl Parade. The Rose Bowl was moved to the East Coast and would be played at Duke University on January 1.[78] Still, the NCAA saw its role become more important, as the distraction of athletic competition would be helpful to the nation's morale.

The U.S. Maritime Commission announced that from now on ships would no longer be launched with any sort of pomp or ceremony. No pretty girls breaking champagne over the bow, no glitzy send-off. Ships would just roll off into the water for immediate sea duty, when finished.[79]

There was a war on, you know.

The gloomy news continued unabated from the Pacific. Washingtonians learned of two more of their young men killed: a navy pharmacist, Robert E. Arnott, twenty-one, who had married Loretta Houser of Silver Springs, Maryland, just the previous May; and Lt. Albert Gates of the navy, who was a native of the District and had once been an instructor at Annapolis.[80]

For the tiny town of Canton, Mississippi, population 6,500, it was even worse. In all of "the first World War," the town had lost but one son. On December 7, it lost three sons at Pearl Harbor. The town's eight churches dedicated their services to Eugene Denson, 22; Keith Joyner Jr., 24; and James Everett, 29. All were U.S. Army soldiers.[81]

Slowly, a new point of view on the attack was advanced in political and diplomatic circles around the country. The first was the damage could have been far worse. All the first-line carriers were at sea and so escaped unharmed. The Japanese never bombed the fuel and ammo dumps, and many of the ships hit could be repaired, as it turned out. If the Japanese had caught the fleet flat-footed at sea, some speculated, the loss could have been 30,000 men and not 3,000 men.

Many in the military political and diplomatic classes also believed that America would have to join the fight sooner or later. What better way to get into a war than with the civilian populace completely united, ready to make any sacrifice, and with the moral high ground of indignation? The Japanese attacked without the decency of the government declaring war on America, first. America was a victim, was angry, knew it was a morally superior country to the Axis powers, and knew what must be done to win the thing.

If there was ever such a thing as a "Good War," then this war met that definition. Said the respected journalist David Lawrence, "It was a stiff price to pay—but unity came that way. Thus someday the historians of the present epoch will speak of last week's events. For it is difficult to realize what a profound change the Japanese attack on Hawaii has made in American policy and American attitude toward things outside the United States."[82]

The Allies were a force for moral good in the world, and the Axis powers were a force for evil. The eternal struggle between good and evil had taken on a new form. Rarely could a conflict of such carnage be labeled a "Good War," but this was one of them.

The Nazis weren't merely a conquering national power—they were a warning from history, a lesson as to the human potential for evil brutality. In 1941, not even the worst cynic could possibly imagine just how brutal the war would turn out to be.

CHAPTER 16

THE SIXTEENTH OF DECEMBER

"Wandering Jews"

Time

"New Powers Voted for President"

Yuma Daily Sun

"Yamamoto Planned Assault; Seeks to Take White House"

Christian Science Monitor

Buried on page sixty-seven of *Time* magazine was an article meanly entitled "Wandering Jews," covering the release of a 151-page report issued by Manhattan's Institute of Jewish Affairs. The document was horrendous in its content. "Not a Jew is left in Memel and Danzig. The number of Jews in Greater Germany has dropped from 760,000 to about 250,000 since the Nazis came to power. Warsaw's ghetto had more than ten times as many deaths (4,290) as births (396) last June. In all Poland, Jewish deaths since the start of World War II have been five times the normal rate—300,000 in two years."[1]

According to the magazine, "The volume covers 8,500,000 Jews in 16 countries [and] totes up the first full balance sheet on what remains of Jewish life on the Continent." Italy had passed racial segregation laws in 1938, forcing many Jews to change their religion to Christianity in the hopes of emigrating to Central or South America. "Rumania's five-day pogrom last January was featured by 'kosher butchery,' a monstrous parody of the Jewish ritual for killing animals by throat-slitting. All Jewish men from 18 to 50 years of age have been drafted for forced labor. Their daily food ration is one-eighth of that provided for a Rumanian soldier." In Czechoslovakia, the report noted there had been "no Jewish problem . . . prior to Munich. Afterwards, the Nazis' Aryanized an estimated $1,000,000,000 worth of Jewish property."[2] *Aryanized* in this case was a euphemism for *stole*.

The startling report went on to detail how, under Chancellor Hitler, the number of physicians and attorneys in Berlin and Vienna had declined from more than half to nearly non-existent. "Today there are no Jewish business enterprises in Germany, no Jewish lawyers, craftsmen, actors or musicians.... With the exception of the manual labor which they perform upon a virtual slave basis, the Jews have been completely eliminated from the economic life of greater Germany. Nearly a million European Jews had to flee their homes between 1933 and 1940. Most had gone into the Soviet Union and the United States had only allowed in 135,000 over that seven year timeframe."[3]

There in black and white was the documentation of the systemic elimination of Jews from Europe. There was no "Jewish question." Anybody with half a brain knew what was happening to the Jews of Europe.

Other countries, including those in Central and South America, had changed their policies, halting Jewish immigration, walling them into Hitler's clutches. Official Washington and London "have creaked and groaned in the long-winded process of turning out their passports to freedom."[4] The port of Lisbon, the last chance for those escaping Hitler, had closed, and Gestapo agents roamed the city. Some Jews committed suicide rather than fall into the hands of the vile Third Reich. "Scenes at the Portugal frontier were indescribable. Piled up . . . a dirge of human mass pressing to get through. Some went back home, trusting in the promises of Nazi agents."[5]

Neither *Time* magazine nor possibly any other publication of note in America took any editorial position on the atrocious, unspeakable, revolting, repellant, and heartbreaking document. It was duly noted and then dropped out of sight. The relative silence of the rest of world was not lost on Hitler, who interpreted it as tacit approval of his genocidal "Final Solution."

The city of Boston had finally installed air-raid sirens on the roof of the Tower Building where the police headquarters was located. But almost nobody around town could hear the four big speakers. Later, more were added at strategic points around the city. Stores across the nation were reporting a brisk business for "blackout cloth," which homeowners used to cover windows from inside. As a result of the big demand, supplies ran short.[6] Also, a "booming" business in the construction of cheap fallout shelters in people's basements was emerging. For a couple hundred dollars, companies would pour two thick cement walls in your very own basement.[7]

It could have been a moot point as many municipalities changed their policies on air raids and children in school. Several weeks earlier, they were encouraging parents to retrieve their children during an air raid, and now they were telling them schools would be locked down and children kept until the danger had passed. Officials were also recommending that adults seek the nearest basement and not try to make it home.[8]

Astonishingly, the federal government was making plans to "register" children as part "of a program being worked out by the United States Children's Bureau and the Office of Civilian Defense for the protection of youngsters in American cities in event of air raids and especially if it should become necessary to evacuate them." Katherine Lenroot, the director of the effort, said it was in response in part to a school that told children to "go hide in the woods" during an air-raid test. She was confident that parents could be "reassured," even if children were removed, because the government would take care of all their needs.[9]

And yet it didn't stop there. Boston Harbor was essentially closed. All-night boat traffic was banned, and daytime coming and going was severely restricted. Fishing boats were tightly regulated, and space along the piers from which they sold fresh fish was all but eliminated.[10] As on the West Coast, the Weather Bureau on the East Coast announced that atmospheric reports were now a "war secret."[11]

Boston's brouhahas went beyond the war; one major fight was over the attempts by some, including doctors, to legalize the "dissemination of birth-control information."[12] William Cardinal O'Connell, archbishop of Boston, was mounting a loud campaign against changing the law. Another controversy was how to deal with Boston's long-festering South Side. After "generations of neglect," government officials said the crime-infested area was "heading toward ruin because of congestion, deterioration and bad living conditions." A report was shot through with "overcrowding, disorder, litter." Part of the recommendation for cleaning up "Southie" included a "need for fewer saloons."[13]

Even louder than any of these controversies and certainly the ineffectual air-raid sirens was a big rally for Russia held in the Boston Arena. Ten thousand people turned out to pony up $35,000 in cash to aid the collectivist state. Guest speakers were Joseph Davies, former ambassador to Russia, and Ivy Litvinoff, wife of Russian ambassador Maxim Litvinoff. She told the throng, "I wish Mr. Stalin could see it."[14]

Davies, in a burst of exuberant class-warfare candor, said, "God bless you cold-hearted Boston people. . . . You may be the home of the Cabots and the Lodges but we know . . . beneath their capitalistic hearts were people who believed in democracy and liberty, freedom and courage."[15]

At the time, many on the American left were quite naïve about the real nature of the Soviet state. Many liberals and intellectuals, who should have known better, perceived it as a worker's paradise; it was only after the war that the true horrors of Stalin's repressive regime came to light. The muckraking journalist Lincoln Steffens famously asserted, after visiting communist Russia: "I have seen the future, and it works."[16] The ordinarily perceptive Steffens could not have been more mistaken. But in 1941, with Stalin's Red Army serving as the bulwark against the Nazi onslaught, the prize-winning reporter wasn't alone in his delusions. Even FDR viewed Stalin as an avuncular fellow with whom he could do business, referring to the murderous dictator as "Uncle Joe." The ugly realities of the Gulag would eventually emerge for the entire world to see.

Meanwhile, outside of Beantown, a class of sixty volunteer women graduated from fire school. Upon receiving their diplomas, they gave a demonstration in which they practiced jumping "into nets from second-story windows, carrying hose lines up fire ladders and smothering 'bomb' fires, the women demonstrated what they had learned in the six weeks' course in all forms of fire-fighting."[17]

Just up the road from "the Hub," Dartmouth College announced it was contracting its academic schedule, canceling the Christmas and spring break vacations so graduating seniors could enlist five weeks earlier. Nearly all college campuses were hotbeds of patriotism and volunteerism.[18] The president of the University of Alabama told his students, "We have an intelligent, patriotic government in Washington. . . . My appeal is to stick by the government, the President and Congress."[19] Yale University passed a resolution supporting the war.[20] The municipal colleges of New York City—Queens, City, Hunter, and Brooklyn—all reported a tremendous upswing in volunteerism and in war bond and war stamp purchases.[21] A coed at the University of Georgia wrote a sweet and patriotic poem that was reprinted in many newspapers. From the last stanza:

> So this Christmas I'm not asking for a brand-new car,
> NOT even champagne nor caviar,
> I'll be perfectly frank and play my hand
> All I want is a brand-new man.[22]

The weather across America had turned cold, and even in the Deep South temperatures were dipping into the twenties.

In preparation for the winter, the city of Washington instituted its annual snow removal plan, requiring citizens to move their cars off all major thoroughfares—about eighty-five miles, all told—from 2 a.m. to 8 a.m. The city's refuse department was hopeful that its snow removal this time around would be an improvement over previous years. "The city is better equipped this year than previously to meet a snow emergency."[23]

In the face of the indifference by American leaders, a large gathering was announced for later in the month, organized by American Jewish groups, to take place in Madison Square Garden. A leader of the event said, "The Garden rally also will respond to a moving call recently received by American and British Jewry from Jews in the Soviet Union . . . . [T]he troubled experiences of racial and religious minorities at the hands of Hitler has been brought home to all of us by the events of the past few days."[24]

Rallies and prayer vigils were increasing across the country. The day before, 3,000 people of varying faiths came together at the National Cathedral in Washington to pray for "victory and peace."[25] Speakers included priests, ministers, and rabbis. The Right Reverend James Freeman broke down crying, as he quoted a sonnet written by John Magee Jr., a pilot who had been killed the week before while flying for the R.C.A.F. Young Magee's father was also a minister with a congregation in the nation's capital, though he did not speak.[26] A Catholic church in Los Angeles had been holding a prayer vigil ever since the attack, serving communion each day.[27]

But not all men of the cloth were supportive. In New York City, a minister resigned his position because he would not "use his ministry to 'bless, sanction or support war.'" The Reverend John Haynes Holmes, who was "a director of the American Civil Liberties Union ... asserted that the American people were not guiltless in a war."[28] Meanwhile, in Germany, Dr. Hans Kerrl, the Nazi minister of religious affairs, died unexpectedly. He expired, out of favor with Hitler, as he'd been unable to stop Catholic and Presbyterian criticism of the Third Reich.[29]

One nagging question involved the soon-to-be-passed draft registration act before Congress. Would the government really draft, for military service, men in their forties and even older? Government officials stepped forward to say that it was unlikely that anyone under the age of twenty-one or over the age of thirty-five would be taken in for active duty service. Eighteen-year-olds would not be drafted, but they were free to register and shortly become active-duty members of the military.[30]

Officials said that the government would register all men between the ages of eighteen and sixty-four so they could have a handle on how many men were available for potential military service. In any case, special training had to be added to the navy's boot camp because more than 10 percent of inductees did not know how to swim. Instructors basically taught the landlubbers a rudimentary dog-paddle stroke, but the real goal was to teach them how to stay afloat for long durations without life preservers. Sinking was not an option.[31]

Recruiting offices continued to be heavily patronized by eager young men, and in some cases men more eager than young. In New York, a father and son appeared together to enlist. They were both accepted and were sent into the service together.[32] However, the policy of allowing family members to serve on the same ship or in the same unit would change shortly.

An unexpected—but certainly welcomed—enlistee was Clarke H. Kawakami, who'd been the Washington correspondent for Domei, the Japanese state-run media agency. He resigned his position in protest, calling the attack "the blackest and most shameful page in Japanese history."[33] The War Department played his story way up, seeing the propaganda value of young Kawakami joining the U.S. Army, despite his having attended Harvard.[34]

New York, Illinois, Pennsylvania, and Ohio were leading the way with new enlistees, but the sons of all states were doing their level best to get into the military. As tens of thousands of young men were streaming into the army, a two-year veteran was leaving, thanks to being ratted out by his own mother. At the age of fourteen, Lynn Vinson had somehow conned the military and enlisted. Two years later, his mother went to the commandant of Camp Robinson in Arkansas with the proof that her son was underage. Vinson was given an honorable discharge but vowed to get back in as soon as he could.[35]

In spite of the national emergency, over 500,000 men in uniform would be granted a furlough to go home for Christmas and sample their mothers' cooking and their fathers' advice.[36]

Many for the last time.

Publications across the country were crammed with notices and announcements for civilians, particularly for defense rallies and classes in such subjects as "incendiary and explosive bomb demolition" and "poison gas analysis."[37] In cities with tall buildings, there was a real fear that flying glass in a bombing raid could maim dozens, if not hundreds.

Food and transportation were always issues, and many stocked up on canned goods, just in case. Families made their own plans on what to do in case of an attack. Along with the men and women of America, children barely into their teens also stepped forward. In New York City, "250 boys and girls between the ages of 13 and 17 assembled . . . in Queens . . . to be instructed on the requirements of junior air wardens." Right off the bat, the seriousness was made clear when an instructor told them, "If any of you are here seeking telephone numbers or dates go right home and remain there. We don't want you. This is not a social affair but the grim business of war."[38]

Around the country, more and more factories and plants were operated on a more rapid schedule. At many, the workers voted to "donate" their Sundays to the government and work for nothing. In Massachusetts, textile plants sought approval from the state to allow women to work past 10 p.m., and in New Hampshire, the governor waived the rule forbidding women and children from working more than 48 hours per week, as long as they worked in a war-related industry.[39] Even the Eureka vacuum cleaner company had switched over to defense manufacturing.[40]

The Red Cross, the police, all the federal, state, and local agencies that dealt with volunteerism, the private organizations such as the Legion, women's groups, the Boy and Girl Scouts—all reported a tremendous upswing in Americans stepping forward. The Grand Exalted Ruler of the Benevolent and Protective Order of Elks, John McClelland, sent Roosevelt a telegram pledging that 500,000 Elks would take up activities to protect America.[41] It was assumed the Moose Lodges of America would also stampede into volunteer offices.

All the activities were duly reported in the nation's periodicals. Page after page after page of the papers covered both the war front and the home front. And yet again, a newspaper noted the death of a sailor at Pearl Harbor. The New York Times reported that "45-year-old" Edwin J. Hill, chief boatswain, "was killed during the Japanese attack." Hill left behind a wife and three children.[42]

Over the weekend, a bravely forlorn message was issued by the Department of the Navy: "Wake and Midway Continue to Resist." The two tiny islands—little more than lumps of coral atolls rising a few feet out of the ocean—had been shelled and bombarded for days by Japanese planes and ships. The battling marines of Wake were referred to as the "Devil Dogs" in the papers. A radio transmission was sent to Honolulu by the tough marines. When asked if there was anything the beleaguered men needed, the reply came, "Send us some more Japs."[43]

Rumors continued to swirl of a "shakeup" in the navy's high command in the Pacific, and no less an authority than the *Army and Navy Register*, an influential journal, speculated that the American ambassador to Vichy, Admiral William Leahy, was the top dog to take over from Admiral Kimmel.[44]

San Franciscans suffered through yet another blackout as the military claimed again that enemy planes had been spotted over the city. There was still confusion in California about headlights, cars, and driving during blackouts. Some drivers thought it was okay to drive if they covered their headlights with blue tint and others if they turned off the headlights, so the rule had to be clarified, yet again: no driving during blackouts.[45] Period.

With much of the Far East and Europe cut off from the rest of the world due to war, shortwave radio took on a new importance. As Americans listened to NBC or CBS or Mutual broadcasts, often the announcer would source their reports as "Berlin radio" or "Stockholm radio," as the networks had set up "listening posts" along the East and West Coast of America. "Today, these listening posts with their batteries of radio receivers listening to the short wave transmissions of the world are proving extremely valuable now that the fact of belligerency with all the Axis powers has cut off the American sources of news."[46]

The war effort would cost much more than what taxpayers were kicking in, but as of December, economists estimated that only 20 percent of the economy was devoted to that purpose,[47] unlike Great Britain, where more than 50 percent of the national economy was used for their national purpose.[48] Still, America's economy was much larger than that of England's and certainly larger than Germany's or Japan's. Like a large ship, a large economy could not be turned on a dime, yet even so, the rapid revamping of the country's industrial complex and the redirecting of resources were impressive.

Private and commercial aircraft were increasingly recruited for the war effort. American Airlines took out ads in publications in the Northeast, including the *New York Times*, to advise travelers that flights to "Syracuse, Rochester and Buffalo," as well as other cities, had been canceled or postponed. "The airplanes usually utilized for the operation of these flights have been assigned to the performance of an administrative mission for the transportation of national defense supplies."[49]

Much of the war effort would come from higher taxes; therefore, articles began popping up cautioning taxpayers to set aside enough money to comply and to make their once-a-year lump sum payment or quarterly payment. "Now is the time to figure your tax and begin putting away a little money each week to pay it," it was advised. The policy of the government was to collect taxes on March 15 of each year. The marginal tax rate began at $750 per year for single individuals and $1,500 for married couples. If the wife made less than $750, it was still mandated that the income be reported. The government figured to bring in around $1 billion on March 15, but taxpayers had a choice to file their taxes on the calendar year or, if they were a small businessperson, on their own fiscal year.[50] The government was not only coming down hard on taxpayers, it was also coming down hard on people who disagreed with it under the old Anti-Sedition Acts of 1917. G-men picked up a Kansas City lawyer, Herman D. Kissenger, charging him with being a "long time sympathizer" of the fascist governments of Germany and Japan. He'd written a letter to Congressman John Dingell, Democrat of Michigan, in which he advocated the impeachment and court-martialing of Congress and the president. The U.S. attorney for the area said a federal grand jury would be assembled to consider the government's case against nutty letter-writing.[51]

In Chicago, when Roosevelt appeared on the screen in a movie house newsreel, Edward A. Loss Jr. booed him and was fined $200 by a municipal court judge, "the maximum" for disorderly conduct.[52] In Topeka, a mother was sentenced to one year in prison "because of the alleged failure of her two young sons to salute the American flag in school. The boys, Clinton and John H., were made wards of the court by Juvenile Court Judge Roy N. McCue, who said [Lucille] Meyer 'was guilty of encouraging the children in the contributing to their delinquency.'"[53]

The government was moving to seize a billion dollars' worth of Axis property in America. The attorney general's office created "a special force of G-men . . . to impound the enemy owned property."[54] Much of the impounded property was eventually liquidated, but the government still had property seized in 1917 and had yet to release it because it lacked the authority, even after the Armistice.

There existed a real threat to America from spies and Fifth Columnists. Federal agents raided and seized the offices of the German American Bund, the German American Business League, and the newspapers they published in New York. A notice was posted on the door: "This property is under the control of the United States Government. All persons are hereby prohibited from entering the premises under penalty of law. H. Morgenthau Jr., Secretary of the Treasury."[55]

Roosevelt received a short, contradictory memo on the matter of spies operating inside the United States. It said, on the one hand, that Frank Knox was overblown in his public allegations but, on the other hand, that "considerable danger of sabotage to strategic points [was] left unguarded."[56]

In California, a German baron, Ernest Frolich de Meyer, was arrested wearing the uniform of a U.S. Army officer. When federal agents raided his apartment in Hollywood, they found navy and Marine Corps uniforms, "a short wave radio set and what appeared to be data on coast defenses."[57]

Government bureaucrats, in order to control supply and demand, debated full-blown wage and price controls and "consumer rationing cards," but these were ruled out for the time being.[58] Still, the Brookings Institute, which was advising the government on such matters, said the country could not have rationing without price controls, and it could not have price controls without rationing. Brookings advocated both.[59]

The federal government could also be inadvertently dangerous and often clumsy, even scary. In Los Angeles, a man awakened to find a live antiaircraft shell weighing fifteen pounds in his backyard, undetonated.[60]

The government was, in addition, nearly omnipotent. On final passage, Congress, by voice vote, approved new legislation granting FDR all the war powers given Woodrow Wilson in World War I. Plus, FDR could now issue noncompetitive contracts and reorganize the government as he saw fit and without the approval of the courts or Congress. He could regulate all the transactions of the government, and he could censor just about anybody and anything.[61]

The irony was lost on the citizenry that Roosevelt now wielded more power over the American people than King George III ever dreamed of, on his best days.

That evening, FDR and Eleanor dined with Henry Stimson, Grace Tully, and actor Melvyn Douglas at 7:30 p.m. Douglas excused himself at 9:15 p.m., and the Roosevelts turned in at 12:15 a.m. Throughout the month, though, Roosevelt dined or met, often alone, with women: "Miss Margaret Suckley" on the nineteenth, "Mrs. Mary Eben" on the eighteenth, "Mrs. Dorothy Brady" on the twenty-first, "Crown Princess Martha of Norway" on the tenth and again on the fourteenth. Unescorted women, both married and single, were frequent guests in the private residence of the White House in the month of December 1941.[62]

American and Chinese pilots began airlifting civilians out of Hong Kong, as the prospects for holding the city dimmed in the face of the continued onslaughts. The Japanese had mounted an all-out assault by land, sea, and air to take the prized British possession once and for all. "The Japanese opened a general . . . offensive against Hong Kong . . . to take the British crown colony . . . the fate of the colony would be decided in a matter of days."[63] The Japanese also claimed that they'd wiped out an entire British mechanized division; it "had been destroyed" on the Malayan peninsula.[64] The news was equally bad in other Far East sectors of which London had control; Churchill's government hinted that some could fall. British resistance in Hong Kong was crumbling.

Meanwhile, "Japanese forces operating on Luzon are advancing according to plan, 'crushing enemy resistance at every point,' army imperial headquarters said today. Bombers which attacked air bases on central Luzon Saturday destroyed forty United States bombers and fighters on the ground and set fire to three other aircraft, it asserted. Barracks, the announcement continued, were destroyed in a raid on United States military headquarters."[65] American resistance in the Philippines was crumbling.

Adding insult to injury, Tokyo announced it had seized 225 American and British merchant ships. They also claimed that twenty-one American and British naval vessels had either been destroyed or badly disabled since the opening of the war, less than two weeks past.[66]

Plans for a supreme Allied War Council were moving ahead. FDR had met with representatives of all the Allied powers at this point to work out the broad outline of such an organization. Roosevelt had already discussed it by transatlantic telephone with Churchill and had met with the Lord Privy Seal, Major Clement Attlee, to flesh out the concept. The problem was, Russia was still dillydallying about actually declaring war on Japan. The best Moscow could say was the Allies "could reasonably look forward" to Russia jumping into the Pacific war.[67]

The Russians for their part had successfully mounted a drive to push back the dug-in German Army from just outside Moscow and Leningrad. Initial news reports closely resembled the propaganda coming from Stalin's government, but as more independent sources confirmed, it became clear the Russians had gained an offensive. However, it was important to remember the Russians were still fighting on their own terrain and the Germans had driven hundreds of miles deep inside Mother Russia.

A British attempt to mount a counteroffensive in Thailand was repulsed by the Japanese, and the Japanese claimed to have sunk another British ship, though the name was not released.[68] Also, Vichy France announced it was intending to halt diplomatic relations with the United States, as a result of the seizure of several of its ships in American ports.[69]

On the more hopeful side, American forces were claiming to have sunk four Japanese troop transports operating near the Philippines, but again no details were released.[70] Admiral Yamamoto seemed unconcerned. He'd written a letter sometime earlier to a friend, which the Japanese state propaganda agency, Domei, released. In it he said, "Any time war breaks out between Japan and the United States I shall not be content merely to capture Guam and the Philippines and occupy Hawaii and San Francisco. I am looking forward to dictating peace to the United States in the White House in Washington."[71]

Lofty ambition, that.

Even before the war had begun in earnest, a group of educators had met in Riverside, California, to plan for world peace. Organized by the Institute of World Affairs, they sponsored a weeklong series of talks, roundtable discussions, and panels. Nothing was concluded except that an "international governing commission" would be necessary to run postwar Germany, if only because "Germany must be humiliated and made to realize it mustn't molest people," according to one participating academic. Another educator observed that "while Germany may have foisted upon the world its Jewish . . . problem, the world must realize that it has a German problem to solve."[72]

One thing at a time.

Roosevelt was right when he warned the country that the news would become bleaker before it became brighter.

CHAPTER 17

THE SEVENTEENTH
OF DECEMBER

"Women Demand to Be Drafted"

Christian Science Monitor

"Japanese Ships Shell Two Hawaiian Islands"

New York Times

"Widows to Be Given Adequate
Support from U.S. in New War"

Birmingham News

"Speed War Output President Demands"

Evening Star

"Justice Roberts Heads Pearl Harbor Inquiry Board"

Washington Post

A Penny a Plane Club formed in Marshall, Texas. City fathers asked the residents if they would donate one penny for every enemy plane downed by the Americans. The club had started in Argentina and was wildly successful. There, residents of the country amassed a membership of 50,000 and "made possible the purchase for the British of a fighter plane costing $75,000 each month." The chief organizer of the American effort, Harry Adams, had been told of the success of the Argentineans and thought it could spread throughout the United States.[1]

Money seemed to be flying out of the pockets of the American citizenry, seemingly all for the war effort. Some banks actually ran out of government bonds because demand was so high. Nonetheless, a goal of $1 billion a month in bond sales was announced by Washington. Three businessmen in Connecticut began a new *Arizona* fund to raise money to build a new battleship to replace the one sunk by the Japanese.[2]

The city of Washington was awash in letters, all containing contributions to "Uncle Sam" from patriotic Americans. Some envelopes contained a penny. Others contained up to $200. Written on many of the envelopes was "Remember Pearl Harbor!" Children sent letters, businessmen sent letters, housewives sent letters, families and local clubs sent letters. An elderly man sent $25.00 with a note regretting that he was too old to fight. A woman sent $5.00, saying if it purchased just one bolt for an airplane, it would make her happy. Hairdressers sent their tip money, as did waiters and waitresses. Treasury officials said there were too many letters, making it impossible to count how much money had been received.[3]

Within America, a deep wellspring of charity had always existed. It was just one of the many qualities that made it unique among countries throughout the history of the world. But this outpouring had been unmatched in the history of the republic. The pain and anger of the citizenry had been channeled into positive actions, and perhaps Christmastime helped season the era with the kindness, love, and brotherhood demonstrated by a Jewish carpenter one thousand nine hundred and forty-one years earlier.

A little girl sent a letter to Santa asking that he forgo toys for her this year, and instead, make "every country free."[4] A dying man left his estate to an aeronautical library for young boys so that books could be "loaned to anyone by mail, without charge."[5] Even Congress—at least the House—got in the spirit of giving and sacrifice as Speaker Sam Rayburn, Democrat of Texas, announced there would be no Christmas vacation for the members—not even the three-day recess usually granted.[6]

Money was also flying into the pockets of some of Washington's biggest lobbyists. Tommy "The Cork" Corcoran had just steered a $21 million dollar loan to a new business "syndicate formed to produce manganese," from the Reconstruction Finance Corporation, or RFC, for which he pocketed a handsome fee of $65,000, an amount that was more than the vast majority of Americans would make in their lifetime. He told the Truman Investigating Committee that he'd picked up over $100,000 in lobbying fees over the past year.[7]

It was never really suggested that Corcoran had any special pull in Washington simply because he was part of the FDR Brain Trust,[8] and for a time he actually resided at 1600 Pennsylvania Avenue, NW; moreover, he said the fact that he was once counsel to RFC had nothing to do with the loan he'd secured for his client.[9]

Later, Truman learned to despise Corcoran as much as FDR loved him.

Charles West, another close adviser to Roosevelt, was suing a company for $700,000. He claimed they had rooked him out of his fees after he had arranged for federal business for them.[10] Most other Americans were less selfish.

Heavyweight champ Joe Louis and challenger Buddy Baer agreed to a title fight under the condition that the proceeds would go to the Navy Relief Fund. They raised thousands. They then met in a second bout and donated those proceeds to the relief fund as well, approximately $90,000 from both contests.[11] In gratitude, the Internal Revenue Service for years after the war pursued Louis, claiming the donated money had been income to him.[12]

In Los Angeles, star pro football running back Jackie Robinson was thrilling fans of the Los Angeles Bulldogs. The Bulldogs were one of the many flimsy professional gridiron teams that had sprung up around the West and the South in the late '30s and early '40s, and Robinson, in an athletic class of his own, ran roughshod over opponents. Robinson would later switch games and break the color barrier in Major League Baseball after the war.

By 1942, Louis, Baer, and Robinson were all in uniform.

Clark Griffith, the owner of the Washington Senators, announced that he wasn't going to make an announcement about some important news regarding his baseball team because of the war. "In another week or so, we'll be veterans in the war and people will want to look at the sports pages as a change." Fans hoped whatever change was coming would be on the mound, as only the pitiable Philadelphia Athletics and the even more pathetic St. Louis Browns had worse pitching.[13]

The annual East-West Shrine college game held in San Francisco had been moved to New Orleans because of the apparent risk under which the West Coast was still operating.[14] As a result, other high school, college, and professional sports events were also canceled or moved. With the baseball season over, the son of San Francisco, Joe DiMaggio, the "Yankee Clipper," was voted Outstanding Male Athlete of 1941, besting Ted Williams, the "Splendid Splinter." The winner the previous year had been Tom Harmon, "Old Number 99," the famous end of the Michigan football team.[15]

But the big unanswered question was whether or not Major League Baseball should be canceled during the national emergency. The owners had already met in Chicago with no decision reached, preferring instead to see what Washington said. "End of major league baseball for the duration is being feared . . . as a result of what already has happened to the sports programs on the Pacific Coast," the Boston Globe observed.[16] In 1917, the game had been confronted with the same problem, but the government told owners to keep playing, as it was too important to the nation's morale. Even so, a month was sliced off the schedules during that war. If the 1942 baseball season went forward, the minor leagues figured to take a hit, what with so many of their players young, single, and 1-A healthy. There were vague reports about future meetings between baseball leaders and governmental leaders.

The news from the world of sports that Americans did not get through newspaper or magazines, they could get from radio. Radio was simply the most dominant cultural force in America, even more than the movies, magazines, or the broadsheets. The role of radio as a form of news and entertainment in the American home could not be overstated. Radios were in the living room, the bedroom, and the kitchen. Radios were in cars and restaurants. They were simply everywhere, and everybody listened, especially now.

Radio had been the main form of entertainment for Americans since the early days of the Great Depression and even before. Many was the lonely pensioner who got by each night listening to Bob Hope or the "Texaco Hour" or "Our Miss Brooks" or the orchestra dance music, broadcast from a hotel in any given city in America. Only one's imagination limited what a radio show could do; the creative men and women could make the kids sitting around the living room believe Superman was really flying or ghouls were really at their door, or Little Orphan Annie was really meeting with the president.

Yet the entertainment side of the radio shied away from the war until *Fibber McGee and Molly* took up the subject. Fibber wanted to buy a globe, and Molly warned him to buy it with Japan still on it, before the Allies bombed it into smithereens. Bob Hope then jumped into the fray, telling audiences, "We may have to black out our lights, but we will never black out our sense of humor." Another was a bad routine between Jack Benny and Dennis Day. That did it. By mid-December 1941, radio, like everybody else in America, had gone to war.[17]

Congress passed a law that would provide for six months' salary and give lifetime pensions to the families of the soldiers and sailors killed at Pearl Harbor. The salary was straightforward, but the pension was a more complicated system, based on widows' ages, and how many and how old the servicemen's orphans were.[18]

It ranged from a low of $30 per month to a high of $83 per month. It was a part of the Soldiers and Sailors Relief Act, but some additional laws also kept men in uniform from being harassed by collection agencies and lawsuits, and under certain circumstances prevented a war widow from being evicted if she was behind in her rent.[19]

Mr. and Mrs. Max Mueller of Omaha were notified that two of their sons, Henry, nineteen, and Erwin, seventeen, had both been killed at Pearl Harbor. The last the parents knew, both boys were assigned to the *Arizona*.[20]

More details were slowly being released from Hawaii, including the recovery of a "suicide submarine," one of three suspected subs thought to have participated in the attack at Pearl Harbor. A "midget submarine," it carried a two-man crew and ran on batteries. Its range was so limited that it could not make it back to a safe port. The three subs and crews who were believed

Top left: ARM2/C Ellsworth Abbott "Barney" Shirley, USN. Killed in Action January 1945.

Top right: President Roosevelt signs the Declaration of War with Japan on December 8, 1941.

Bottom: Sugar rationing creates long lines at home.

The attack on Pearl Harbor

December 7, 1941

IF YOU CAN'T GO ★ BUY WAR BONDS

THIS HOTEL PLEDGES A 100% PAYROLL

OUR BONDS ARE THEIR SECURITY!!

SERVICE ON THE HOME FRONT

★ CITIZENS DEFENSE CORPS
★ CITIZENS SERVICE CORPS
★ AMERICAN UNITY
★ SALVAGE PROGRAM
★ VICTORY GARDENS

WPA

There's a job for every Pennsylvanian in these CIVILIAN DEFENSE EFFORTS

PENNSYLVANIA STATE COUNCIL OF DEFENSE
CAPITOL BUILDING,   HARRISBURG, PENNA.

AIR RAID
PRECAUTIONS

KEEP COOL

DON'T SCREAM

DON'T RUN

PREVENT DISORDER

OBEY ALL INSTRUCTIONS

PENNA ART WPA

FEDERAL · USA WORK WPA · THEATRE

IF YE BREAK FAITH

BE CAREFUL

NEAR MACHINERY

help US

PRESERVE FOOD

your SURPLUS...

JOIN UP NOW AT
615 REAL ESTATE TRUST BLDG
PENNYPACKER 5718
RUTH G.H. STRAWBRIDGE
CHAIRMAN

COMMUNITY FOOD CONSERVATION INC.
COOPERATING WITH
PHILADELPHIA COUNCIL OF DEFENSE   PENNSYLVANIA STATE COLLEGE
CHURCH ORGANIZATIONS   WORK PROJECTS ADMINISTRATION
GARDEN CLUB   NAVY LEAGUE SERVICE

"CENSORED"

Pvt. John Doe
U.S. Army.   FREE

Mrs. John Doe
1000 Silence St.
New Orleans, La.
U.S.A.

EXAMINED BY 42

LET'S CENSOR
OUR CONVERSATIO
About the WA

WPA WAR SERVICES of LA

Do with less—
so they'll have
enough!

RATIONING GIVES YOU YOUR FAIR SHARE

504

NAVY DEPARTMENT
Office of Naval Intelligence
Washington, D. C.

~~CONFIDENTIAL~~

December 4, 1941

Subject: JAPANESE
DURING

Note : Prepare
Intelli

The Kurusu
year of intense
terns, condition
and extent of th

As Ambassa
tember 1940, bu
top-flight dipl
Chicago, and Ho
was Minister to
a director of

Methods of Oper

With tens
anese Governme
quate to meet
coincident wi
Nomura, diplo
organize and
relax the for

Designe
and commerci
intelligence
liminary mea
instructed t
as over the
U.S.S.R. in
For this wo
to send com

~~CONFIDENTIA~~

505

to spread as much political propaganda as possible throughout the United
States by means of personal contacts with members of the press and persons influential in American politics and business.

The focal point of the Japanese Espionage effort is the determination of the total strength of the United States. In anticipation of
possible open conflict with this country, Japan is vigorously utilizing
every available agency to secure military, naval and commercial information, paying particular attention to the West Coast, the Panama Canal
and the Territory of Hawaii. To this end, surveys are being made of
persons and organizations opposing U. S. intervention in the present
European War, and close attention is being paid to all anti-Jewish, Communist, Negro and Labor Movements.

Although not yet fully developed, this new Espionage organization
is characterized by a high degree of decentralization. The activity of
the Military and Naval section, which is divided into a number of different groups, is supplemented by the work of independent agents, and the
general pattern includes individuals, small groups and commercial organizations functioning separately and energetically. In the background
lies the Imperial Japanese Government exercising direct control over individuals and organizations through the Embassy and the Consulates.

The new program envisages the use of citizens of foreign extraction, aliens, communists, negroes, labor union members, anti-semites,
and individuals having access to Government departments, experimental
laboratories, factories, transportation facilities, and governmental organizations of various kinds. Nisei (second generation) Japanese and
alien Japanese residents have not been overlooked. Realizing, however,
that its nationals in this country would be subject to prosecution "in the
event of a slip," the Japanese Government has advised extreme caution in
their employment.

In the event of open hostilities, Mexico will probably be the Japanese Intelligence nerve center in the Western Hemisphere, and in anticipation of war, U. S. - Mexican Intelligence routes are being established.
This network, covering Argentina, Brazil, Chile, Peru and the Central
American countries, will come together in Mexico City, and Japanese cooperation with the German and Italian Intelligence organizations is expected. Such co-operation has been discussed in Tokyo with representatives of the Axis powers and the plan is said to have been approved by
them.

At the present time, the District of Columbia, New York City, New
Orleans, Los Angeles, San Francisco and Seattle are the espionage centers
in the United States with Mexicali, Baja California and Vancouver,
British Columbia important boundary outposts.

-2-

...we here highly resolve that these dead
shall not have died in vain...

REMEMBER DEC. 7th!

Discovered in the FDR Library by
researcher Andrew Shirley after being
declassified some years ago, this top secret
twenty-six page memo from the Office of
Naval Intelligence to the Roosevelt White
House on December 5th, 1941 laid out
the possible targets for Japanese Attack
which included the Panama Canal and
Pearl Harbor. Clearly, Roosevelt and the
American military had at least an inking
of the attack that come just two days later.

*Courtesy of the Franklin D. Roosevelt Presidential
Library and Museum, Hyde Park, New York.*

Americans aid the war effort by collecting shoes, stockings, and cooking grease.

PLEASE DRIVE CAREFULLY
MY BUMPERS ARE ON THE SCRAP HEAP

Top: Actress Rita Hayworth participates in the scrap metal recycling campaign by donating her car's bumper in response to the call for bumpers and other non-essential metal car parts for the war effort in Hollywood, CA, Oct. 4, 1942.

Bottom: Women enter vocational schools to learn war work.

to have engaged in the attack on Pearl Harbor knew they were on a one-way mission from which they, in all likelihood, would not return alive. A photo of the recovered sub that had washed ashore appeared in the papers.[21]

Submarines had been an important part of the story of the North Atlantic for some time. German "Wolf pack" U-boats had been sinking everything in sight; however, subs had not yet become important in the fight for the Pacific, except when the story was bad. That day, a confidential memo from the secretary of the navy to FDR advised the president that the American naval sub presence in Manila was now tenuous. "How much longer the submarines can base at Manila is problematical."[22]

Also, the American Asiatic fleet was down to "one patrol bomber squadron . . . 2 cruisers, 8 destroyers, 3 gunboats, several minesweepers . . . surface vessel lack fighter aircraft defense, and cannot operate in areas where dominated by enemy aircraft strength."[23]

This story line would eventually change. For the first time since the beginning of the war, American naval forces began to report sea action by American submarines in the western Pacific, adding that they had performed well enough but had little to no support from American planes or surface ships. The overall news from the region continued to be nearly all bad for America.

"Japan's assault on the Philippines slacked off . . . but defense forces regard the respite as only temporary. Most observers said the letup probably meant that the Japanese were moving additional forces and supplies into position off the island coasts, resting pilots, overhauling planes and marshaling gasoline, bombs and ammunition for new and powerful attacks." The situation was anything but "well in hand."[24]

The British were "having difficulty in Borneo, Malaya, and Hong Kong, and the American possessions of Johnston and Maui Islands in the Hawaiian area were shelled by Japanese naval craft." Also, "Wake Island and Midway were reportedly raided again . . . [S]evere fighting continued in northern Malaya, where Japanese troops continued to push southward toward Singapore, now using one man tanks. At Hong Kong, Japanese naval vessels were reported . . . to have joined the attack on the British Colony. The Japanese claimed they had sunk one gun boat and six torpedo boats and damaged a destroyer and three other vessels in Hong Kong waters."[25]

Lord Halifax, the British ambassador to the United States, said of Hong Kong, "We must be prepared for its fall" and proclaimed that it had no military value.[26]

Apparently, the attack on Maui had only been some Japanese torpedoes that hit the loading docks of a pineapple company; but still, Maui was part of the Hawaiian chain and only a hundred miles southeast of Honolulu. Also, a military airfield and "fleet anchorage" were located at Lahaina Roads there.[27] It was the first attack on the Hawaiian Islands since the seventh, and that alone made it terrifying. Johnston Island was described by navy officials as being hit much harder than Maui, and more importantly, that was the first time it had been bombed. Johnston Island was "discovered" by the British ship Cornwallis in 1807.[28] Some speculated that the Japanese were hitting many different locations in hopes of sending the navy off on a wild-goose chase.

The British were doing their utmost to hold onto Singapore, but this hold seemed more tenuous by the day. A knowledgeable source said, "British lack of naval superiority has changed the entire situation in Northern Malaya."[29] If Singapore was taken, it would be catastrophic to the cause of the Allies. If Singapore went, the rest of the Western Pacific could fall like dominos into Japanese possession.

There was a growing suspicion that the Roosevelt administration, being heavily influenced by Winston Churchill, was more interested in first investing resources in the Atlantic and Europe and that the Pacific would have to wait. Two days later in an unsigned White House memo dated December 19, titled "First Priority of Military Strategy," the answer came in the next line: "The Defense of the Atlantic Area between the United States and the United Kingdom." Both Africa and "the Pacific area" were noted as "secondary areas."[30] The condition of the Pacific was described as "bleak."[31]

Meanwhile, the governments of Turkey and Ireland restated their decision to stay neutral. Ireland also refused to allow the Allies to use its ports. Vichy France also claimed to be neutral, although with hundreds of thousands of

German troops in the country and Marshal Pétain at Hitler's beck and call, it was a joke. Conversely, Free French forces in Morocco, Algeria, and other locations were bravely working against the Germans, who were tightening their grip on the region. An underground movement in France was growing. Audaciously, they had detonated a bomb in Paris, killing six Gestapo agents and one German general. New reprisals came in the form of rounding up as many as 4,000 suspects including, of course, Jews. "This group included some of most influential and wealthiest Jews in Paris."[32]

Halfway around the world, another courageous group was fighting the odds. A small assembly of twelve Indians led by one British lieutenant furiously fought off a much larger force of Japanese in Kota Bhara, in Malaya, before finally succumbing.[33] The civilian evacuation of Malaya had already begun. "There definitely is danger—a real threat to Singapore by land," a British dispatch read.[34]

Meanwhile, it was rumored that Hitler had come close to suffering a nervous breakdown, frustrated with the lack of progress on the Eastern Front. His doctors told him to go to Berchtesgaden, his spectacularly scenic mountain retreat in Bavaria, for rest.[35] There, the would-be ruler of the world would gaze at the soaring peaks and become lost in reveries of his own megalomania. Meanwhile, in the field, his soldiers were behaving with characteristic thuggery. Three precious Russian shrines, the home of Tolstoy, the cottage of Anton Chekov, and a museum dedicated to Tchaikovsky, were evilly sacked by Nazi troops.[36] In a confidential memo to Roosevelt from the British Embassy, the document said the German generals had decided to "try to stabilize their Russian front." The document also pointed out that the Russian air force had gained air superiority over the Germans, in part because they knew more about handling equipment in the freezing cold than did the Germans.[37]

There was no rest for the Poles under the heel of Nazi governor Hans Frank, an eager and enthusiastic supporter of Hitler's genocidal policies. While grinding Poland into the ground under his iniquitous administration, "hundreds of children between the ages of 14 and 16 have been executed for their political activities, including membership in the Boy Scouts. A Polish official said in one town, 100 Scouts were executed in the central square and a nine-year-old boy was shot because he destroyed a Nazi propaganda poster."[38]

Secretary Knox had not been entirely forthcoming in his report on the damage at Pearl Harbor, but he had said all along he wasn't going to reveal everything, in the name of security. The *New York Times* said his report was "undoubtedly an understatement of the damage done."[39] The Japanese, of course, were claiming much more damage at Pearl Harbor and in the Philippines than Washington was, but this time, the Japanese estimates were closer to the truth than the American revelations.[40]

The casualty report was as accurate as could be expected in those days after the attack, but Knox said at the time the government would not release all that they knew, and now, once again, some members of Congress were agitating for a full inquiry. Knox also did not release the names of any of the deceased, but he did meet with key congressional representatives in secret. His report was long on heroics but short on specifics, such as the story of the four ensigns who, when their captain went down, supposedly guided their destroyer out of the harbor in an attempt to track down the enemy.[41]

Capitol Hill was sharply divided, with some members eviscerating Knox. One said that America needed a new secretary of the navy. Supporters of the White House had hinted for several days that Roosevelt would soon order an investigation. Other members of Congress said if they went forward, they would not ask Knox to testify about his own findings. But another, Senator David Walsh, Democrat of Massachusetts, said they might have to "investigate the investigation."[42] Walsh had been a bitter opponent of Lend-Lease and was a fervent isolationist—until December 7. The call for a congressional inquiry had been safely bottled up for over a week, but it was beginning to escalate again. Knox had also claimed that the navy was at sea looking for the Japanese; that was true in only the barest sense.[43]

The chairman of the Senate Foreign Relations Committee, Senator Tom Connally, Democrat of Texas, was not satisfied in the least with Knox's limited report. "The statement . . . that neither the Navy nor the Army was on the alert at Hawaii when it was attacked by the Japanese is amazing. It is astounding. It is almost unbelievable. The Navy of John Paul Jones and that of Dewey must wear crepe. The old Army must carry an arm band. The loss of life is staggering."[44]

At the same time, photos of B-17s on the ground, aflame, at Hickam Field on Oahu were appearing in the newspapers. Photos of other damage done at Pearl Harbor began appearing, but nearly all were of civilian centers and homes. Only a few photos of damaged planes were released; there were no photos of ships.

It was also reported that a Japanese pilot on December 7 landed his troubled plane on the island of Niihau, two hundred miles northwest of Oahu. Without phones or radios, these islanders knew nothing of the morning's attack. There the pilot encountered a native islander, Benny Kanahele. After being shot by the pilot three times, the large Hawaiian grabbed the pilot and rammed his head into a stone wall, killing him.[45] "The pilot shot me . . . in the ribs, hip and groin. And then I got mad. I threw him against a stone wall."[46]

Benny was reported to be a woman but was in fact a man.

So as to head off any congressional investigations into the attack at Pearl Harbor and to control the controversy, FDR went ahead and appointed his own Joint Inquiry Board, a blue ribbon commission made up of five men.[47]

They were to take the preliminary (and to many, unsatisfactory) findings by Knox numerous steps further and take the heat off the administration. A justice of the U.S. Supreme Court, Owen J. Roberts, would chair the panel, and he immediately promised there would be no "whitewash" of the events or those responsible. The other four members were all respected career military men.[48] They included retired Admiral William Standley, who was the former Chief of Naval Operations, retired Rear Admiral Joseph Reeves, retired Major General Frank McCoy and Brigadier General Joseph McNarney, who served with the Army Air Corps.[49] Admiral James Richardson was expected to be one of the appointed; however, he was in hot water with FDR after telling the president it was a mistake to move the fleet from San Diego to Hawaii.[50] Roberts had a distinguished career, including his prosecution of Teapot Dome while he served as a federal attorney. Yet even with their careers of accomplishment, having been appointed by FDR, they were his men, beholden to him. "The membership of the Board satisfied Administration leaders in Congress, for it was announced that any Congressional action would be delayed until the Board had had any opportunity to study and act."[51]

At his press conference, announcing the board of inquiry, the president spent considerable time speculating about espionage activities in Honolulu prior to December 7. Roosevelt had met with General George Marshall and Secretary of War Henry Stimson as well as other military brass, just that day, to come up with the board; these men were described as "gloomy" when spotted leaving the Oval Office.[52]

The move by FDR, however, did not satisfy those on the Hill who did not consider themselves "administration leaders," but there was little they could do. Congressman Martin Dies, Democrat of Texas and chairman of the House Committee on Un-American Activities, squawked that his own investigation into subversive Japanese elements operating in the United States had been shut down at the request of Roosevelt and Cordell Hull the previous September.[53] He said that "his committee had information which 'clearly indicated a planned attack on Manila and Pearl Harbor.'"[54]

Heading off a congressional probe was exactly what the administration and the military wanted. Two items of immediate concern to investigate would be (1) a fresh claim by Hull that he notified government officials in late November of his concerns that events in the Pacific would take a turn for the worse and (2) that, apparently, several radio stations in Hawaii had continued to broadcast in Japanese, even as the last planes were departing Oahu and headed back to the six Japanese carriers.[55]

At the business and labor conference that had convened, FDR told both sides that all strikes must cease for the duration of the war. Even with the new laws on the book, there had been wildcat strikes around the country. He also called for round-the-clock production. The country, he said, has "got to do perfectly unheard of things."[56]

The longshoremen sent FDR a telegram pledging not to strike during the emergency.[57] Yet what got everybody talking was the olive branch offered to the American Federation of Labor by the Congress of Industrial Organizations. Jaws dropped throughout the labor community. The two collective bargaining agents had been feuding for years, but because of the emergency, a slight thaw had developed in their previously frosty relations.

Washington also announced an extension of the new tire ban to be made permanent starting January 4. No new tires or tubes could be manufactured for civilian use, only to fill those orders coming in from the military.[58] Additional articles appeared in the papers advising consumers how to protect their tires, how to make them last, and how to make effective repairs. More government directives were forthcoming about the whole matter of tires and tire maintenance.

As the towns and cities of America struggled to perfect their blackouts and air-raid drills, advice was offered on protecting the family animals from falling bombs. The American Red Star Animal Relief organization sent out notices regarding horses, dogs, and cats. It informed owners that animals were important to morale and that there was no need to kill them, as many in England had done by the thousands with their own animals in the early days of the Blitz.[59]

Inland waterways were not overlooked when it came to security. Officials in the Empire State instituted tight navigation policies over the St. Lawrence River. New York City seemed to have finally outpaced the other cities when it came to organizing its air-raid policies. First, the city worked with the newspapers to get the stories right once and for all, including the rules. Second, the drills were announced well ahead of time. "A test of the most powerful siren in the city, the steam-driven device on top of the Consolidated Edison Company's plant at First Avenue . . . will be made at 4 o'clock this afternoon and will be followed at 4:15 p.m. by the testing of two of the seventy new 'sirodrones' acquired by the city this week for air-raid alarms." Specific details followed, and the boxed item ran on the front of newspapers.[60]

On the West Coast, the mystery plane puzzle had still not been solved, but as the days grew shorter, the issue of instituting a form of "daylight savings" was debated, especially in Los Angeles, where the Board of Supervisors decided to implement it for the county. It would allow citizens to get to work and back home during daylight hours. Hollywood studios had already implemented their own work schedule, which began the workday sooner but ended it sooner too.[61]

With FDR's new authority under the War Powers Act granted him by Congress, some Americans may not have agreed altogether with the new policies, but they understood the sentiment of their Allies down under. The headline in the *Christian Science Monitor* said it all: "Australians Give Up Liberty to Assure Defense of Liberty." The story detailed how Aussie citizens were giving up all their basic rights for the war and doing so happily. "Australians have now been asked by their Government to throw their own freedom to the winds until victory has been won."[62]

The *New York Times* said Congress had conferred "on President Roosevelt almost unlimited powers to regulate the nation's emergency effort at home."[63] President Roosevelt's new agency for dealing with censorship said its mission was "partly mandatory, partly voluntary."[64] FDR announced the Censorship Bureau at a press conference, ironically, but he made no bones or apologies about the goals of the new agency. "It is necessary that prohibitions of some types of information contained in long existing statutes be rigidly enforced." He also called on "a patriotic press and radio"; and the new head of the department, Byron Price, a former executive with the Associated Press, made clear his initial target was the U.S. mail—specifically, letters written by private citizens going outside the country.[65]

FDR appeared well, dressed in a gray tweed suit and black tie, but the dark circles under his eyes were noticeable to reporters. There was some light banter with a radio reporter over the rumor that Roosevelt had called the Japanese "dirty yellow bastards." Roosevelt cautioned the reporter to be careful with his consonants, and everybody laughed. When asked, he said he felt "fit as a fiddle."[66] Only the president's doctor knew that FDR was a very sick man. A longtime sufferer of polio, he was plagued with dangerously high blood pressure that went largely unaddressed. The toll of stress and illness was starting to show in his gray pallor and bouts of fatigue. To the rest of the world, though, he seemed as cheerful and vigorous as ever with his trademark cigarette holder stuck in his mouth at the usual jaunty angle. It was one of the greatest deceptions, in a war full of them.

"When he traveled by car, he was lifted in and out of the back seat away from public view. News photographers understood that they were not to photograph the president sitting in his wheelchair or being carried, and when anyone violated that rule the Secret Service confiscated the film," said David Brinkley.[67]

In the face of the new government crackdown on communications, the Justice Department announced that local officials had been going too far in arresting people under the Sedition Act and warned that in the future they must consult with Washington before moving ahead with any apprehensions.[68]

At the same time, the final Selective Service bill was passed by Congress. While all men ages eighteen to sixty-four would be registered, only men ages twenty-one to forty-five would be drafted. But eighteen-year-olds could enlist with their parents' permission. The War Department estimated this new bill would produce an army of 8,000,000 men.[69]

The administration was also moving ahead with a war council among the Allies, to better coordinate land, sea, and air offensive operations and counteroffenses against the Axis powers. FDR hinted that what might be needed was an "Allied General Staff" to blend together the military leadership of all the countries opposing the Axis powers. That evening he ate late and then worked into the night reviewing documents, talking on the phone, and issuing dispatches.[70]

Bills were flying out of Congress. Money for the military, money for more military and defense-related housing, money for civil defense, "increasing the authorized tonnage of the Navy," another granting the navy access to every shipyard in America, publicly owned—or not.[71] A bill was offered to empower the government to take over the machinery in private plants, "an action now forbidden by the Property Seizure Act."[72] The government was now spending money at a rate of roughly $20 billion a year, with approximately 72 percent devoted to the military. With all the spending for the New Deal, Lend-Lease, and the war, the national debt soared to over $55 billion.[73]

New regulations also flew out of Washington dealing with the weight of bicycles, the manufacture of new radios, and even one proposal to essentially nationalize all industry in America. The Treasury Department was looking at a plan "for centralized government control over the flow of capital and the financial conduct of industry."[74] Regardless, a new aviation company saw a bright horizon, and private stock purchases were offered in the Cessna Aircraft Co.

The results of the public spending and the national will were already tangible. The B-17 "Flying Fortress"[75] bomber had been developed only several years earlier, but North American Aviation and the Glenn Martin Aircraft

Co., with plants in Tulsa and Kansas City, announced that two entirely new bombers would begin rolling off the assembly line in early January—only one month after the attack on Pearl Harbor.

These two planes, the B-24 "Liberator" and the B-25 "Mitchell," were being fabricated entirely from automobile parts and machinery supplied by the Ford Motor Company, Chrysler, Goodyear, and the Fischer Auto Body Co.[76] The thirty-one-day turnabout from peacetime manufacturing to an Arsenal of Democracy was no less than astonishing.

American Exceptionalism was a wondrous thing.

CHAPTER 18

THE EIGHTEENTH
OF DECEMBER

"Hawaii Army, Navy Chiefs Ousted; Nimitz Replaces Kimmel"

Los Angeles Times

"Japs in Borneo Peril Singapore"

Washington Post

"Rationing of Tires to Start on Jan. 4"

New York Times

"Jap Victim's Father Tries to Join Navy"

Los Angeles Times

Flag sales were up, but morale was down as the lonely and modest burials taking place daily near Pearl Harbor became known.

The demand for American flags was nothing like it had been on the eve of America's entrance into the First World War when sales skyrocketed 100 percent. In the days after Pearl Harbor, flag sales were up, by industry estimates, some 15 to 25 percent, which was impressive, yet also a bit less than expected.[1] Because of the demand for cotton, muslin, wool, and silk for the military, flags were being made out of rayon, but even these synthetic flags were scarce. The bottom line: there was a pent-up demand, just not much supply. Dealers who had stocked up before December 7 sold out in a matter of hours.

In Hawaii, the young men who had died for that flag were buried. Each afternoon, on the island of Oahu, a group of marines trooped out to a grave site and fired a salute to yet another fallen American soldier or sailor. "A tight lipped group of six-foot marines in olive-drab uniforms raise their rifles and fire three volleys over the fresh earth as nightfall approaches fast. A bugle sounds taps."[2]

These forlorn memorials had begun on December 8 and had been going on for days. "They have been laid to rest on green hills overlooking the sea— there to remain until a peaceful time when the bodies might be returned to their native soil."[3] There were no family members, no politicians, no crowds. Only the brief discharge of guns, the trumpet, and the murmured prayers by men of the cloth punctuated the silence.

Nuuanu Cemetery was initially used for the first of the Pearl Harbor dead. The cemetery overlooked the sea. Then, when all the spaces had been taken, graves were dug on Red Hill, which overlooked Pearl Harbor. "Day after day, just before sunset, with simple dignity befitting the gallantry with which they died for their country, America's finest have been buried at Honolulu."[4]

Each burial observance was accompanied by Navy Chaplain Captain William Maguire and a black-robed priest. The priest blessed the ground with "holy water," and Maguire recited a committal prayer. On the decks of many of the navy vessels, Sunday church services were routine, some beginning at 8 a.m. None took place on December 7. Now prayers were offered every day. "Don't say we buried with sorrow," Captain Maguire said. "Say we buried with conviction. Our men died manfully and we will wipe out the treachery come what may. The spirit of these men lives on. I can feel it."[5]

Each grave was adorned with a floral bouquet, Hawaiian-style, all picked from nearby homes. "Each grave is marked and each body carefully identified for shipment back to the mainland after the war is fought and won—back to home towns." Maguire said he was proud of the sacrifices of these sacred dead. He said, "And while all this heroism was going on, those Japs were still machine-gunning. . . ."[6]

He told of men with arms ripped off, begging to get back into the fight. Men burned, nearly naked, screaming, "I want to get back to my ship. I want to get back to my gun." Other wounded men said, "For God's sake, I am alright."[7] They weren't.

Americans, Maguire said, "would glow if they could see how our boys died. If every American had seen how quietly, yes, quietly men suffered, how gallantly they died, how courageously they thought about the next man, they would glow. They would swear our front line will never give."[8]

In the towns and villages of America, because there were not bodies to bury, many internment ceremonies went forward anyway, as at Georgetown University, with "flag draped catafalque symbolizing the bier of Ensign George Anderson Wolfe who died at Pearl Harbor."[9] Also among the fallen was Billie McCary, seventeen, of Shades Mountain, Alabama. He was on the *Arizona* as a member of the band, for which he played the tuba and the coronet. Just weeks earlier, the band from the *Arizona* had competed with sixteen others in Hawaii, and Billie and his band came away with the gold cup.[10]

The first "white" resident of Birmingham—as noted by the *Birmingham News*—to die at Pearl Harbor was James Mark Lewis, twenty-one, seaman second class. Again the inevitable telegram: "The Navy Department regrets to inform you . . ." Concluding, it said, "The Department extends to you its sincerest sympathy in your great loss. To prevent possible aid to our enemies, please do not divulge the name of his ship. . . . Rear Admiral C.W. Nimitz, chief of Bureau of Navigation." James's dream was to be a navy chaplain, combining his love of boats as a child and his devotion to the Birmingham Tabernacle Gospel. His mother, age sixty, told the paper that, if she could, she would put on a uniform and go fight. The boy's father, "aged . . . sitting in the sun on his back steps his face cupped in his hands said only, 'they stabbed him in the back . . . he didn't have a chance.'" Seaman Lewis's remains had not yet been recovered.[11]

Julius Ellsberry was the first "Negro" resident of Birmingham to be killed at Pearl Harbor, again as noted by the Birmingham paper. "First to be notified here that a son had given his life for his country was a Negro family in Inglenook." Ellsberry, twenty, was a "mess attendant aboard a warship."[12] The paper featured an editorial headlined, "Julius Ellsberry. All Birmingham, white and colored, honors his name." The family got the identical telegram that the McCary and Lewis families had received.[13] The U.S. military may have been segregated, but death was color-blind.

In dying for their country, the boys, Julius, Billie, and James, were not separate but were equal. The price of war kept going up. It was a price equally shared by all social and economic classes. Everyone had a stake in the war; America was experiencing a social cohesion that had not been witnessed before.

In a marvelous public relations stunt, Roosevelt wrote a letter to another president: he wrote it to whomever would be president in 1956, recommending the eighteen-month-old son of downed pilot/hero Captain Colin P. Kelly Jr. for appointment to West Point, fifteen years hence. "In the conviction that the service and example of Captain Colin P. Kelly Jr. will be long remembered, I ask for this consideration in behalf of Colin P. Kelly III."[14]

Nominations to U.S. military service academies such as West Point (for the army) were competitive. While some applicants would be eligible for a presidential nomination by virtue of a parent's service, all U.S. citizens were eligible to compete for a nomination from their congressional representative and senators. A nomination from FDR himself certainly constituted an amazing "trump card." Indeed, the president of the United States in 1956 offered "Corky" a.k.a. Colin P. Kelly III an appointment to the United States Military Academy at West Point, but in true hero fashion, the young Kelly refused, wanting to compete with everybody else for a place; and he did so, graduating from "The Point" in 1963. The president of the United States in 1956 was Dwight David Eisenhower, who in 1941 was an obscure, chain-smoking aide in the office of Army Chief of Staff George C. Marshall and who only months before had been promoted to the rank of general. Before that, he was a clerk for General Douglas MacArthur. Roosevelt loved being president, MacArthur wanted to be president, and Eisenhower hadn't even given it a thought.

The shake-up in the Pacific command finally came, oddly, before FDR's Board of Inquiry had even met to investigate what had actually happened at Pearl Harbor and whether or not anyone really was to blame. Indeed, the board was given the task of finding facts in search of a theory. "They will seek to fix the responsibility for the fact that the armed services were 'not on the alert' on Dec 7."[15]

Admiral Chester W. Nimitz, fifty-six, was named to replace Admiral Husband E. Kimmel, fifty-nine, who was unceremoniously removed as commander in chief of the United States Fleet and as commander of the Pacific Fleet. The position as chief of the navy was a fairly meaningless title, but the position of head of the Pacific fleet was where the rubber met the road. Nimitz would become commander of the Pacific fleet but not "Commander-in-Chief" of the navy itself. Also removed and replaced were General Walter C. Short, sixty-one, commander of the army garrison in Hawaii, and Major General Frederick L. Martin, fifty-nine, commander of the Army Air Corps there.

Stepping in for Short was Lieutenant General D.C. Emmons, fifty-two, and replacing Martin was Brigadier General C.L. Tucker. "The shifts were the direct result of the surprise Japanese attack on Pearl Harbor, December 7, in which the Hawaiian defense forces were caught off guard."[16]

Douglas MacArthur, who could have also been removed because he'd had some warning of an imminent attack, unlike Kimmel and Short, escaped unscathed because he was still fighting a battle in the Philippines, because he got better "press" back home than did the others, and because he was a personal favorite of Roosevelt, despite their political differences. They were kindred spirits in that they were royalty in America. MacArthur was the scion of a famous military family. His father had won the Congressional Medal of Honor for action in the Civil War, and Roosevelt, of course, was the scion of a famous political family. They had worked together before, and there was a friendship, though based on society and not ideology.

In 1932, the Bonus Marchers of the Great War had descended on Washington in the depths of the Great Depression to ask the government to pay early a bonus promised to the doughboys who had answered their country's call. The bonuses had been issued in 1924 but would not come due until 1945; however, many of these heroes who went over there were out of work, starving, and wanted the government to pay ahead of time, even if it meant forgoing the interest. President Herbert Hoover refused and directed MacArthur to rid Washington of the marchers. MacArthur used harsh actions to clean the city of the thousands of Bonus Marchers and their families. In 1936, when Roosevelt had still not solved the Depression, the

Democratically-controlled Congress, over the president's objections, paid the Bonus Marchers.[17]

Kimmel and Short were not American royalty, were frankly scapegoats—sacrificial lambs who had done everything by the book, had not been given all the facts by Washington, and now were being punished for it.[18] They had been as astonished by the attack as anyone else in the world, but had they been given the decoded Japanese communications between Tokyo and their embassy in Washington that the War Department and the White House were intercepting, Kimmel and Short may have had a chance to change or at least alter the course of history. Even the night before the seventh, when shown the next-to-last segment of the fourteen-part Japanese communiqué that presented the Japanese ultimatum, FDR read it and said, "This means war."[19]

That was never communicated to any of the field commanders in the military, especially in the Pacific, who had more than a passing interest in the intent of Prime Minister Tojo and his government.

Adding to this, the War Department and the navy had been tracking a large convoy of Japanese ships, including six aircraft carriers just days earlier, but when the armada turned eastward, U.S. military strategists lost track of it. This too was never communicated to Kimmel or Short. All they ever got were oblique and confusing messages from Washington, reinterpreting the secret coded information going back and forth between Washington and Tokyo. The administration had believed that war was imminent between Japan and the United States, but they wanted Tokyo to commit the "first overt act of war" so a moral case for participation in the war could be made to the American people and the world community.[20]

The Roosevelt administration had successfully squashed any congressional investigation and had gained control of the matter by naming its own board of inquiry. Even so, it was obvious the blame was either going to Roosevelt, Cordell Hull, Henry Stimson, George C. Marshall, Harold Stark, Frank Knox, and the rest of the military and political leadership in Washington, or it was going to two competent, if politically naïve, men who were 6,000 miles away, without access to the press to tell their side of the story or defend themselves. The outcome of this was easy to see. The lead in the *Baltimore Sun* reported, "Without waiting for any more information on the contributing causes of the Pearl Harbor disaster," the men were humiliatingly dumped.[21]

Washington had seen the old "hang 'em out to dry" gambit a thousand times before. Someone had to take the blame, and the master politicians in Washington made sure it was going to be Kimmel and Short, and not themselves. The history of the country was marked with not only heroes but also scapegoats. "Sources" in Washington let it out that Short and Kimmel had not been "on the alert."[22] An unflattering photo of Kimmel was made available to the newspapers. This was all orchestrated: the War Department and the secretary of the navy made the announcement simultaneously. Secretary of War Stimson bluntly said his thinking was in line with Secretary of the Navy Knox regarding the "unpreparedness of the situation of December 7th ... and to expedite the reorganization of the air defenses in the (Hawaiian) islands."[23]

Their demotion was the headline of every newspaper in America, and nearly all used the word "ousted."[24] It was humiliating, especially since Kimmel's new assignment was to stay in Hawaii on "temporary duty." The final humiliation was that he would have to stay to watch Nimitz replace him.

Nimitz, as head of navy personnel, only days before was signing the telegrams notifying the next of kin of the death of their sons. But he'd also seen plenty of sea action in war and peace. Now he would get a chance to lead the friends and brothers and teammates of those fallen at Pearl Harbor into battle. He met that day for an hour in private conference with President Roosevelt.[25]

Chester Nimitz, with a two-rank jump in rank to a full admiral, was being pushed to the center stage of history. Kimmel and Short, having been demoted, left the military in early 1942 and faded into the mist of cruel and unjust history.

The bad news from Malaya continued. The Japanese were driving hard down the peninsula toward Singapore; and British troops were not only on defense, but London was beginning to withdraw some of its troops, which was tantamount to an admission that all was lost there. Events were not faring any better in Hong Kong, where the Japanese demanded the British surrender, but the British refused. The Chinese were attempting a counteroffensive to aid the British, who had received an impossible order from London to "hold on."[26] The Japanese also seized the strategically important Penang Island.[27] And things worsened in the Philippines as well; the Japanese continued moving toward Manila, and it was reported they were using buses to transport the invasion forces.

American forces in Manila did, however, destroy twenty-six Japanese planes. America's first ace of the war, First Lieutenant Boyd D. "Buzz" Wagner, had shot down five enemy planes in the air and was credited with the destruction of many of those twenty-six planes on the ground.[28]

Japanese troops made landfall on the island of North Borneo and Sarawak, both under British protection, both rich in oil, rubber, sugar, coffee, iron, coal, spices, and other treasures of the Earth.[29] Sarawak had an unusual history, to say the least. One hundred years earlier, Sir James Brooke, an English officer, had helped the Sultan of Brunei fight off an insurrection. In gratitude, the Sultan gave Brooke the territory of Sarawak, and his descendants still ruled the area as of the beginning of the Second World War.

Later, the "White Rajah"—Anthony Robert Brooke, son of Sir James— penned an agreement with England to provide protection for his country. When war broke out, the island had been celebrating the centennial of "White Man's Rule."[30] Japanese forces were also invading Dutch-owned islands in the region.

Just north of Sarawak, an earthquake of huge dimensions shook Formosa, China, and Japan; and hundreds were killed. Yet another earthquake hit Turkey, with similar deadly results. Both were a reminder that while war was waged, the forces of nature went on unimpeded.

The eighteenth of December was not a day of gigantic news, unless one counted the ouster of Kimmel and Short, which was huge, as it was the biggest shakeup in the military leadership since the Civil War; but many, it seemed, had expected that Kimmel and Short would be relieved of their commands sooner or later. It had been rumored in the papers and in political and military circles for days, and everybody took it in stride. Some members of Congress had demanded that Kimmel and Short be imprisoned. They had become marked men who, after December 7, were simply marking time, waiting for their sentencing without first being charged or even receiving a fair trial.

The American people had become used to temporary and sudden changes over the past several weeks. The 1940s were looking different than the 1930s, when little seemed to change. Now there appeared to be a point where Americans settled into a routine that involved change on a daily, if not hourly, basis. No announcement, no event, no pronouncement, no decision, no news was outside the realm of possibility, except one saying they would lose the war. No one in America believed that. A new reality had settled across America, and upheaval seemed the new normal.

In the realm of the new reality, the U.S government seized a half million pounds of tin, privately owned, that was being stored in a warehouse in New York City. It was needed for the war effort. No one blinked or protested.

Then the Office of Production Management announced it was "freezing" all tin supplies in the United States.[31] Tin would now be controlled by the director of priorities of the Metals Reserve Corporation, a subsidiary of the Reconstruction Finance Corporation, which eventually developed eight separate subsidiary corporations for the war effort. Washington also announced that, from now on, it would coordinate all air-raid drills and blackout drills. Americans for the first time were being urged to save scrap metal.

Announcements were made. The federal government announced it was hiring shipbuilders and metalworkers for operations in Pearl Harbor. The government also announced that fishing in New England would be limited to clear days only; the government announced it was, well, nationalizing the oil industry in California, citing national security.[32] And "the laundry machine manufacturing industry is going to be called on to fill war orders aggregating millions of dollars."[33]

"Eating habits may be changed a little because of the Jap war," said the *Wall Street Journal*. "All canned pineapple come from Hawaii. Supplies may be cut down due to shipping difficulties. Tuna and sardines for canning and other fish caught off the west coast will be harder to get due to naval regulations and risks to fishermen. Japanese canned crab meat is out."[34]

Airmail to the Pacific was halted for a time, but that came as little surprise. Also, "Northern California was battered by the winter's worst storm the first of this week but until today it was a military secret." The navy and

Weather Bureau brass had withheld the news until it was old enough to not do the Japanese any good.[35]

With the government's edict to limit rubber to almost exclusive military use, Price Administrator Leon Henderson caused a near riot when he said that production of such non-essential items as golf balls and tennis balls might be eliminated. Duffers and strokers swarmed into department stores and sporting goods stores, such as Abercrombie and Fitch, and cleaned them out in a matter of minutes.[36]

The NFL's annual Pro Bowl game, involving the winner of the NFL title and a team of all-stars from the other nine teams, was moved from Los Angeles, where it had always been, to New York.[37] Again, security.

The first refugee ship since the outbreak of formal hostilities between the Axis and the United States arrived in Jersey City. One hundred ninety-one passengers breathed the air of freedom.[38] Reports from the Russian Front and North Africa were good for the Allies. The Russians finally appeared to be pushing the Germans back, while the British were also making headway in Libya. However, some analysts thought the Germans were simply reassessing and would mount a strike against Russia, farther south.

A navy bomber carrying six men crashed in Norfolk, killing all aboard,[39] and a plane carrying a general on a seemingly routine flight from New York to California disappeared,[40] but these noncombat-related crashes were now commonplace. There wasn't a day that went by without a report on a crash of a military plane. Meanwhile, civilian pilots now had to carry photo identification, something previously unheard of. Yet another rumored attack on the West Coast was reported, but this time it was a submarine and not a mystery plane.[41]

In FDR's confidential papers that day, there was no mention of Kimmel or Short, or Nimitz for that matter. Some of the documents dealt with the deficient number of airplanes at the disposal of the navy: "The Navy has on hand an even 100 Douglas torpedo bombers known as TBD. This number is barely sufficient to meet minimum operating requirements."[42] A second memo noted that the navy only had 768 "aircraft torpedoes." Complicating things, "unfortunately, there is no such thing as a universal torpedo." It was noted hopefully that "a new Government torpedo plant is being erected in Chicago by the American Can Company, but this factory will not be in production until the end of 1942."[43]

Cubans uncovered a Gestapo plot to set up a signaling system in a mountain range overlooking the Atlantic. Two arrested operatives of Nazi Germany were found with charts and plans detailing the plot.[44] Nazi agents were also foiled in an attempt to blow up railway tracks in Bolivia that were used to ship tin and lead to the United States. Mexican officials discovered Japanese operatives attempting to install a radio transmitter. With all the attempts by the Axis powers to commit sabotage in Central and South America, a conference representing all the Americas was announced for January 15 in Rio. Part of the approved agenda was to "curb the activities of 'undesirable aliens' in the Western Hemisphere."[45]

Sales of the "series E" bond—known as the "people's bond"—continued to skyrocket, up 146 percent over the previous week.[46]

All the government mandates to Detroit were bound to have an effect on employment in the car industry. Not only were up to 1 million assembly line workers affected, but also 44,000 new-car dealers, showroom managers, car salesmen, secretaries, swab boys, mechanics, tire salesmen, advertising and marketing executives . . . the list of those affected went on and on. At the end of 1941, when it became known that no new cars would be made for the foreseeable future, new-car dealers did a land office business but it was only temporary. "Backbone of the dealer's business is the sale of new cars and trucks and such accessories as tires and tubes, radios, heaters, etc. Production of nearly all such goods, for the market in which he sells, is being severely restricted where not eliminated entirely."[47]

Some workers in Detroit would be rehired as the factories were retooling for the war, but many others would not. "Vastly increased output of military trucks and tanks, warplanes and aircraft fuselages and engines, marine motors, guns and shells and hundreds of other industry-made munitions will create jobs practically immediately for tens of thousands of laid off automotive workers. By late next year—possibly sooner in some cases—the serious unemployment problem now facing automotive centers should be wholly or largely solved," said the *Wall Street Journal*.[48]

The disposition of the thousands of "enemy aliens" who had been picked up by G-men in the hours and days after the attack at Pearl Harbor had still not been settled. The wheels of justice were turning especially slowly in this regard, and one of the first hearings for the thirty-six Japanese, German, and Italian nationals being held at, among other locations, the East Boston Immigration Detention Center would not take place until Monday, December 22.[49] In New York, some were being held at—ironically—Ellis Island.[50]

The port of embarkation had been closed for fifteen years, but now it was being used for something altogether different.[51] "Although no specific charge had been disclosed, presidential warrants for their arrest were based on a blanket allegation that their liberty was 'dangerous to the public peace and safety of the United States.'"[52]

Even if not being held in detention, an "enemy alien" could not "have in his possession firearms or other implements of war; short-wave receiving or transmitting or signal devices, codes or ciphers, cameras, and documents in which there may be invisible writing. Photographs, sketches, pictures, drawings, or maps or any military or naval equipment are also banned." An order came down actually telling the "enemy aliens" to surrender these items.[53]

The U.S. attorney for Massachusetts, Edmund J. Brandon, said, "While enemy aliens are not 'criminals' in the ordinary sense of the word, neither are they entitled to the rights set forth in the Bill of Rights. The latter applies only to citizens and aliens of countries other than enemy countries."[54] Brandon elaborated that the disposition of the alien enemies in captivity was entirely the prerogative of the president and that any American citizens who turned in a suspected alien enemy who was working to undermine the United States would receive the full protection of the Department of Justice.[55]

In Canada, all Japanese were being registered, regardless of status.[56] The national government in Vancouver alone had confiscated 1,035 Japanese fishing boats.[57]

Acting on a tip, the Chicago office of the FBI arrested the head of the consulate there, Kiagachiro Ohmori. The consulate office there was shut down and sealed. They also arrested an Austrian inventor, Dr. Fritz Hansgrig, who was working at a magnesium plant in California. The FBI did not elaborate on why Dr. Hansgrig was arrested.[58]

Still unresolved was the status of the diplomats of the Japanese and German legations in Washington. The Japanese, it was known, were drinking heavily, as witnessed by the chauffeur for the widow Mrs. William Howard Taft, who accidently got himself stuck for a time in the Japanese embassy on Massachusetts Avenue in Washington. According to David Brinkley in *Washington Goes to War*, the Japanese envoys were imbibing heavily the night of December 6, which accounted in part for the slowness in transcribing the last of the fourteen-part message for delivery to Cordell Hull on the day of December 7. The "embassy staff had been drinking Scotch whiskey all night and the translators were still drunk the next morning."[59]

American diplomats in Berlin had already been moved out of the city to a "comfortable hotel" until an exchange could be worked out, and the United States responded in kind, taking the German diplomats to an equally "comfortable hotel."[60] Switzerland was now representing the interests of the United States "in all belligerent countries."[61]

While men rushed to enlist, the need to bolster the ranks was great enough to discuss the possibility of drafting married men.[62] "The Government will become hard-boiled about drafting husbands whose wives are self-supporting, the Senate was told today, as military leaders made known their view that this country must have an Army much larger than 4,000,000 men."[63] Allowance would be made, but General Lewis B. Hershey, head of the Selective Service, said that a four-million-man army in that era was not practical. He explained to the Senate that the army "may have to go to the bottom of its manpower." He compared it to the Civil War, during which more than 2 million soldiers were twenty-one or younger, more than 1 million were eighteen or under, more than 800,000 were seventeen and below, and two dozen or so were just ten years of age. Germany, said Hershey, had a standing army of 8,000,000.[64]

The University of Kentucky announced that it would grant college credit to any of its underclassmen who either enlisted or were drafted for military service.[65] Not waiting to be drafted into the army, Japanese American brothers Benjamin and Fred Kuroki, of Grand Island, Nebraska, enlisted in the U.S. Navy. The story of two Japanese brothers enlisting ran on all the wire services.[66]

The women who wanted to serve finally got their wish when it was announced the military needed 50,000 nurses immediately. The army had 6,811 nurses on active duty, and the navy had only 828 trained nurses. Initially, the new nurses would serve as part of the Red Cross, but the idea was floated again of drafting women directly into the military.[67] Thousands of women had already stepped forward to volunteer their skills.

Eastman Kodak Company had developed "color prints direct from color negatives, the latest Eastman contribution to the progress of color photography for the masses." It was called "Kodacolor" and came in rolls that, once exposed, were sent for developing to the Kodak plant in Rochester, New York, and then sent back to the customer. It was a revolutionary development.[68]

But not every invention caught on immediately. With only several days left until Christmas, toy manufacturers were working overtime to fill orders for what was shaping up to be one of the biggest gift-buying seasons in years. "Plastic toys have not attracted the buying public, so far," said a spokesman for the Milton Bradley Company. He said, "It takes a new idea a little while to make itself felt in the market and also because plastics . . . are expensive."[69]

CHAPTER 19

THE NINETEENTH
OF DECEMBER

"Enemy Aliens Will Be Kept in Camps in the Southwest"

Christian Science Monitor

"British-Canadian Garrison Is Still Holding Hong Kong"

Lethbridge Herald

"Japanese Bomb Panay Island in Philippines"

Washington Post

President Roosevelt's new proposal for an Allied Grand Council that would bring together all the countries of the Allied powers ran into headwinds: he wanted it based in Washington, but Winston Churchill wanted it nearer the front, in London. America had been in the war a little over a week, American troops hadn't even set foot on the European continent, and already there was intramural squabbling among the Allies. FDR would only say the discussions on the Grand Council were "in progress" and that they had been conferring for a week, but he would not elaborate beyond that at his press conference.[1] Nevertheless, the first meeting took place in . . . London.

A draft of a "Memorandum of Agreement" for a Supreme War Council was prepared for Winston Churchill, FDR, Stalin, and the "Generalissimo of the Armies of the National Government of the Republic of China . . ."[2] Chiang Kai-Shek, who had already had a fabled career.

The document was very specific on theaters of operation, unity efforts, a "common agreement" not to make peace with any enemy until all the Allied powers made peace with that enemy, and so forth.[3] Curiously, the Allies could never get it straight on what to call the operation.

The day before, President Roosevelt held a ninety-minute meeting with his American "war council," including new member Admiral Chester Nimitz. Nimitz was anxious to get to his new command but told reporters, "I am very sensible to the fact that I am being entrusted with a very great responsibility which I intend to discharge to the utmost of my ability."[4] Nimitz's wife, Catherine, could not join her husband right away, as she was at their vacation home in Wellfleet, on Cape Cod.

Roosevelt spent another long day, mostly at his desk, in meetings and "hacking away at the mound of memos and reports in the big wire basket on his desk."[5]

The government finally made a decision on the thousands of enemy aliens it was holding in various locations around the country. The plan was announced to build internment camps in the remote deserts of the American Southwest, but the War Department refused to reveal their exact locations. It did leak out, though, that a handful of enemy aliens were also being shipped to Montana.[6]

"Thousands of enemy aliens in the United States, ordered interned, after hearings held by the Justice and War Departments, will be sent to permanent concentration camps to be constructed in the Southwestern States, it was announced today."[7] Initially, three camps were planned for construction, and the aliens, already held at various army and civilian locations around the country, to be held for the duration of the war.

Just days after December 7, Attorney General Francis Biddle said the bulk of the arrests of aliens was over, but a mere two weeks after he made that statement, the arrests continued unabated. "Under special wartime powers the Federal Government is continuing the summary arrest and detention of any Japanese, Germans and Italians above the age of 14 who may have been deemed 'dangerous to the public peace or safety of the United States,' by the Attorney General or the Secretary of War." Nearly 500 "axis aliens" had been picked up in the Los Angeles area alone. FBI officials pointed out that "there are hundreds of dangerous aliens who came to this country as agents of sabotage and destruction, awaiting the day when, behind the lines, they could strike a blow for Japan, Germany or Italy."[8]

The internees were dressed in old army uniforms and given three square meals a day, but little else.[9] So as to avoid confusion and "embarrassment," Chinese Americans nationwide began wearing lapel pins and buttons bearing American and Chinese flags, distributed by the Chinese consul general's office in New York.

The diplomats representing the Axis powers had it better. Germany's 145 attachés and nationals were being held in a posh resort hotel in White Sulphur Springs, West Virginia, and the Japanese envoys were holed up at a posh resort hotel in Hot Springs, Virginia. Rumors had it that both groups of diplomats were drinking heavily.[10]

Laura Ingalls, a popular, petite, and pretty aviatrix of the 1930s, was, it turned out, a Nazi stooge. Winner of many speed races and records, the thirty-eight-year-old was arrested and incarcerated in Washington on charges of being on the payroll of the Nazis without reporting either the money or her work. The FBI had her dead to rights as taking money over the years from agents of the Third Reich. She'd been a familiar sight to Washingtonians, having flown her silver low wing plane over the capital and "bombarded the city with peace pamphlets."[11]

What looked like altruism at the time may have been just another ploy by the Germans to keep Americans out of the European conflict. At the time, she was the head of the "Woman's National Campaign to Keep [the] United States out of War." Ingalls had spoken often at America First gatherings.[12]

The fight for the Philippines was rapidly deteriorating for the Americans, even as General MacArthur and Admiral Thomas Hart put up a brave front, claiming battle victories. But it was noticed that navy documents were being burned in an incinerator, a sure sign that things were not going well for the American side.[13] Some Filipino troops were battling the onslaught with only sharpened bamboo poles and knives.[14] Heavy bombing was reported over Manila in what was described as "hit and run tactics"[15] and the Japanese claimed that U.S. forces were "in retreat." Three waves of Japanese planes hit the island of Panay especially hard, including a religious school located there. Civilians were killed, and a great deal of property was damaged on the sugar-producing island.[16]

The situation in Hong Kong was even worse, as Tokyo had gained a strong forward-command position, cutting off communication between the British forces there and the outside world. No one knew if the British garrison was still holding on and, if so, how long it could hold. "The Japanese made landings at several places thus making the dispersal of the British forces necessary to cope with the various assaulting parties." However, "the Anglo-Canadian garrison on the island is 'comparatively small with a considerable area to defend.'" The Japanese propaganda agencies "claimed that British resistance in Hong Kong was collapsing and that the capture of the crown colony, which they described as already half-conquered, was only a matter of hours."[17]

The word "claim" was liberally used in the public relations war between the Allies and the Axis. Winning or the perception of winning was important for the military, the politicians, and the citizenry. Morale was everything to all involved, and both sides were guilty of putting things in the best light or minimizing the damage done by the enemy. There was no question that the Allies were far more honest with their citizens than the Axis, perhaps because part of the glue that holds democracies together is the truth, while part of the glue that holds despotic governments together is lies. Lying comes easily for those whose aspiration is to control other people.

Wake Island was holding on by its fingernails, subjected to round-the-clock bombing from warships and airplanes. Japanese ships, troops, and bombers were carrying out widespread offensive campaigns against American and British military outposts, while opening up new fronts in Dutch New Guinea and advancing toward the Burma Road. Supply lines were becoming an issue for the Allies. "Imperial Tokyo headquarters . . . asserted that Japanese troops operating from Aparri, 250 miles north of Manila, had seized a U.S. Army base and were driving southward. The Tokyo high command claimed furthermore that the Philippines air defenses had been virtually knocked out as a result of Japanese bombing attacks on flying fields. Britain's struggle to halt the Japanese drive toward Singapore took a darkening turn as British and Indian troops were acknowledged to have withdrawn below the southern border . . . apparently yielding the 115-mile-long Malayan Peninsula state to the Japanese."[18] The *New York Times* reported that the Japanese troops fought with a "fanatical disregard . . . of a constantly high death toll."[19]

Frantically, a private naval message marked "Secret" ended up on Roosevelt's desk, pleading "there is no time to lose. We must at all costs hold Singapore . . . the operations which are being hailed in the press are largely illusory. Due to the events of the past week, there is a dangerous undercurrent in certain powerful official circles which deprecates American and English prestige and our ability to win this war. That it is already too late is even being said by some."[20]

A source in London confirmed that British troops were evacuating the island of Penang, an "important . . . base . . . one of Singapore's major outer defense posts." American newspapers made unconfirmed reports that American troops had been dispatched to Singapore to help the Brits hold on to the vitally important outpost, but this never came to be. Americans had their own hands full.[21] Wake Island was bombed yet again; there was nothing to the little atoll, and it was a miracle anything was left of it. Some reports in the United States said there had been a lull in the fighting in the Far East, but you could not tell that to a flyer or an infantryman or the marines on Wake. Apparently an American submarine had sunk a Japanese troop transport in the region, while an American fighter pilot, Lieutenant Samuel H. Merett, his plane shot up, flew it and himself into the side of a Japanese transport.[22]

The British navy was faring better in the Mediterranean than in the Far East. They were literally blowing Italian warships out of the water on what seemed to be a daily basis. On the eighteenth alone, the Italians had lost 1 destroyer, 2 cruisers and 5,000 men.[23] The carnage was such that the Germans restarted their airplane attacks on British ships operating there.

The seasonal rains had begun, complicating the situation for the American troops in the Far East. The Japanese were accustomed to jungle fighting, mud, and guerilla warfare. The Americans were not. A news report said the Japanese had attempted a landing at New Guinea, which, if true, meant they were opening yet another front in the Western Pacific. The Japanese were cunning and knew exactly what they were doing. Strike fast before the Allies could effectively respond and then attack everywhere, as they had the advantage of position. Then bleed the Allies dry of men and materiel before London and Washington could effectively reply and rearm. After seizing the territory, fortify it and make it impossible for the Allies to regain possession. Their plan was working beautifully.

Concern was so high over the Japanese game plan of permanent offense that some started to speculate that the Panama Canal was also vulnerable. Knocking out the canal would add thousands of miles to any journey of an American naval vessel from the East Coast to the West Coast. Plus navigating the Straits of Magellan at the bottom of South America meant traversing some of the worst waters on the face of the earth. Locations along the Straits were named "Fatal Bay, Fury Island, Last Wreck Point, [and] Isolation Harbor."[24] Security around the Canal increased many-fold.

Roosevelt temporarily promoted MacArthur to a full general, "a rank customarily reserved for the chief of staff of the army." There was also some talk around Washington about MacArthur, having just received his fourth star, being awarded the rank of supreme commander of the allied forces in the Far East."[25] The promotion was warmly endorsed by many editorial pages, including those of the *Washington Post*.[26]

War was hell in the air, on the ground, and at sea. A British bomber had ditched in the North Atlantic, and the crew floated for days with little water or food. To make bad matters worse, they were harassed by sharks: "One of the sailors had a large chunk taken from his chest and died five minutes later. All of them had a bad case of sun poisoning and were blistered. Their bodies were swollen."[27]

The armies of the world had taught soldiers how to fight; their faiths told them how to die; and doctors helped them with their wounds; but no one taught or prepared them how to survive. Survival was as important to war as any other aspect, and yet it had been completely overlooked by the planners and tacticians and strategists. Survival equipment was nonexistent, but new drugs were coming on line that would save the lives of many wounded men. Among them were anti-bacterial "sulfa" drugs that were the precursors to penicillin. The production and sales of sulfa drugs grew rapidly after their discovery in 1935. By 1941, more than 15 million people were treated with sulfa drugs every year.[28] They proved a godsend on the battlefield.

On the domestic side, just as government officials were telling the American people that there was no cause for alarm and there would be plenty of food for the citizenry during the crisis, stories began to appear suggesting otherwise, that change might come in just a few months. "It's true those old meatless days, motorless Sundays, one lump sugar and weaker coffee are not in prospect now. Tea, pepper, tapioca and possibly soap will be scarce." It was also noted that meats, canned goods, and cigarettes would be available, but more expensive. Christmas turkeys were going up in cost.[29] Reports said that Italian Americans, French Americans, and other "hyphenated Americans" had no worries as there were plenty of Christmas "eels" available for their dinner tables.[30]

New tires and new cars were out, as were new radios, new vacuum cleaners, new kitchen appliances, and most other household goods. Gas rationing on the East Coast was forecast for the spring, and Washington was still deliberating across-the-board controls over prices. It was already controlling the price of grains. Civilians were also asked to stay off the long-distance phone lines or at least keep their calls brief. War was one thing and sacrifices were expected, but it tried men's souls when the flow of wines and liqueurs from the occupied countries of Europe "dried up."[31]

Not all the citizens who volunteered or made sacrifices or went without for the war effort had the best of intentions. In Los Angeles, "marauding gangs of self-appointed air-raid wardens who molest citizens on the pretense that they are 'aiding defense'" were a problem in the city of not-all-angels.[32] On the other hand, in San Diego, a "Minuteman" group of "crack marksmen" was formed with the help of local law enforcement. The job of the volunteer riflemen was to "crush any attempts at local sabotage."[33] Many were affiliated with local gun clubs and the National Rifle Association.

More and more death notices from the Pacific, including the Philippines, were appearing in the broadsheets. And more stories appeared of grief-stricken parents, fathers enlisting or trying to enlist, and mothers joining the volunteer cause. In order to help boost morale for the American citizenry, the War Department produced the first motivational poster for the American effort. It was, at best, mediocre. The placard depicted five "ape-like figures in German uniform singing the Horst Wessel song."[34] Better, though, was the reemergence of syndicated columnist Ernie Pyle after a four-month sabbatical. His wife had been ailing, and he had taken time off to care for her. Now one of America's famous scribes came roaring back, and millions of readers were delighted.

A recruiting office in New York held a poster competition. The first prize was a full, one-year scholarship to the Art Student League of New York City. The winning poster was excellent, creative, "portraying the undercarriage of an Army pursuit plane striking a tarmac" with the banner headline reading, "Be a U.S. Army Aviation Cadet." The private sector was always more creative than the public sector, and excellent submissions came from "children, housewives, doctors, lawyers, green grocers, students, and salesmen."[35]

The concept of a "just war" had been a difficult notion for religious leaders and for people who had been taught and who believed that all violence was against the laws of God and man: peace was always the way. However, these were new and horrific enemies of all that was decent, and they were equipped with instruments of mass destruction.

Pacifism was one thing, but letting evil win the earth was quite another, especially when good had the means to fight back. The military announced it needed thousands more chaplains in order to minister to the spiritual needs of the American fighting man. Robert Paterson, undersecretary of war, said that a soldier needed two things: "a firm faith in his country's cause and spiritual strength. The comforts the chaplains give the soldiers are beyond any reckoning."[36]

The Catholic Bishops of America, following in the footsteps of Pope Pius XII, endorsed the American efforts as a "war for peace" and promised to work with the U.S. government without becoming political in an earthly fashion. The Catholics said it was their mission "to try to help, as becomes churchmen, our Government in being the instrument of Almighty God for the setting up of a new era in which human rights, human dignity, human freedoms, and a sane human solidarity will offer to all peoples prosperity and a chance for the pursuit of happiness."[37]

In reflection, several writers were somberly remembering the millions in aid the United States had given to the Japanese people during the devastating earthquake of 1923. "In the United States, more than fifteen million yen was raised for relief work. The United States Army contributed several million dollars worth of supplies, the United States Navy two million dollars worth. Of course, the flyers who bombed Hawaii did not pause to think of the ancient and profoundly honorable duty of gratitude."[38]

Criticism continued over the dishonorable lobbying activities and the egregious fees received by former Roosevelt associates, Tommy Corcoran and Charles West. The report from Senator Harry Truman's investigating committee "demolishes the theory that New Deal reformers are any different really than their brethren of the old Deal."[39]

Another lobbyist, with an elixir that would have made ancient alchemists green with envy, turned a $42,000 investment into $34,000,000 in war contracts. Queried by tough-as-nails Truman about how this was possible, Frank Cohen, the beneficiary of his own largesse, replied, "We were just good natured damned fools, that's all."[40] Unfortunately, noted some editorialists, there were almost no regulations dealing with the access-selling industry, which was flourishing in Washington.

America went forward anyway. The new movie for children, *Dumbo*, was a big hit, as was the performance of Corporal Jimmy Stewart, who in a national radio broadcast several days earlier had commemorated the Bill of Rights. Stewart had enlisted a year earlier, was assigned to Moffett Field around San Francisco, and had been out of the Hollywood spotlight for months. Stewart had been drafted in 1940 but was rejected because he weighed too little. After working out with a Hollywood trainer, he put on enough weight to be accepted into the Army Air Corps. Flying and music, not acting, were always Stewart's first loves, even as he received the best actor award for his performance in the marvelous 1941 screwball comedy about social manners, *The*

Philadelphia Story. An actor with a quintessentially American screen persona, Stewart was able to take time off from his duties to participate with other actors and actresses in commemorating the Bill of Rights. He spent hours writing his own script, demonstrating a deep knowledge and appreciation of American history.

Upon hearing it, Spencer Tracy said, "One of the most deeply-moving patriotic deliveries I ever heard. If that's Army training maybe a lot of us who think we can act ought to join up," to Hollywood columnist, Harold Heffernan.[41] By the time of his retirement, Stewart had reached rank of brigadier general and was awarded a DFC, a high French commendation, and other medals. Stewart was a decades-long film star, a family man, religious, successful, an American hero, and finally the iconic everyday man. A wonderful life, indeed.

The *Wall Street Journal* calculated the odds of a young American male being drafted. If you were twenty-one to twenty-eight years of age, classified 1-A, and had not yet been called, guess what? Your number was up, and you would be drafted. It was a 100-percent certitude. If you had dependents, the odds were 1 in 7 of being called. If your work was classified as "essential," the odds were 1 in 4 that you would still be drafted. Except if you were a "farm boy." The army inducted 1,000 of these young men and then released them to go back to their work on the farm because their fathers needed them. Up in the air were boys who were still aged nineteen to twenty-one years of age. Roosevelt had wanted them drafted, but many in Congress only wanted them registered at this time.[42]

Then Secretary of War Henry Stimson abruptly announced that army enlistments would soon cease.[43] Since the seventh, the patriotic outpouring of young men wanting to sign up—such as "farm boys"—was depriving many war industries of skilled workers. The army would depend on the Selective Service to weed out the 1-As from the 4-Fs. The Selective Service had over a dozen different designations, including Conscientious Objectors (1-A-O) to 4-A, for the sole surviving son of a family. Such a designation would be employed more than once in this new war.

New laws were also passed to make it difficult for creditors and banks to get at the men in uniform and for those not in the military. When not thinking about the war or volunteerism or things of immediate concern, the men in uniform were thinking about the economy and their own situation. The country was going through one massive dislocation as it was switching almost instantly from a peacetime to a wartime economy. Before the seventh, the stock market had been unreliable, up and down. Housing starts were down massively in November, and many small businesses were barely holding on. No doubt war was good for economies, as Lend-Lease had breathed life into the torpid American economy, but it came with a price. As men and women were hired for war work, men and women were fired because of war work. The secretary of war put out an all-points bulletin hiring an "unlimited number" of "men and women stenographers." They were needed immediately, though it was open to question how many men were in the workforce who knew how to type, write shorthand, and take dictation.[44] And 300,000 auto workers had already been laid off in Detroit.[45] Until the economy could actually grow and consume on a large scale, creating a demand for goods and services, the economic situation would be tenuous.

The nineteenth was the Friday before Christmas, and because many G.I.s could not make it home, the towns and villages and families of America took the young men in uniform to their bosom. Parties were organized, dances, meals, music, gifts. In Fayetteville, North Carolina, the main drag of the town was closed to traffic, and a massive street party was held for "the boys." Sixty-two thousand soldiers descended for a barbecue feast.[46] It was the same at Camp Blanding in Florida, where the locals laid out a massive spread for the soldiers; the same story was repeated all over the country. Churches in Baltimore were also feting thousands of soldiers. And the old hero of the First World War, Alvin York, was on a morale tour of American military installations.[47]

Roosevelt and the First Lady wanted the White House Christmas—despite the presence of antiaircraft guns throughout the area—to go forward as normally as possible. The massive spruce tree had been placed inside the fence on the South Lawn, as opposed to its usual location on the Ellipse, for security reasons. Nonetheless, the plan was to open up the White House lawn on Christmas Eve to 30,000 well-wishers and carolers and to enjoy a

performance by the Marine Band. FDR was scheduled to speak just after
4 p.m., and then he and Mrs. Roosevelt would attend services at Foundry
Methodist Church.[48] A White House staff party was also in the works for
Christmas Eve.

Christmas was tough at the home of J. E. Ingraham of Eastaboga, Alabama,
as he mourned the loss of his son, George. George Ingraham had been killed
the morning of the seventh—just after mailing his father a Christmas card.[49]

Despite the war, or perhaps because of it, meetings in Washington on the
future of the new medium, television, were going forward. Few in America had
a television, but some government officials and executives with the National
Broadcasting Company saw its potential, primarily as a learning device and
tool to alert many people on war developments. "The current discussions by
N.B.C. are based on three main points: Increased use of television as a training device through programs dealing with air-raid precautions, fire control,
first aid, etc; large screen television to be used in public auditoriums for civilian defense programs; and entertainment."[50]

The government considered moving nonessential agencies out of Washington
to accommodate all the new military personnel and war industry civilians
flooding into the city. Officials were also making plans to evict—forcibly, if
necessary—private companies from their places of business as well. To meet
the needs of the navy alone, huge temporary buildings made out of aluminum were constructed on the Mall, row after row of them. They looked like
giant mobile homes and were horrendously ugly. The temporary buildings
were still on the Mall twenty-eight years later when President Richard Nixon
ordered them dismantled, as they should have been at the end of the war.

FDR "asked" the governors of the forty-eight states to consolidate all their
public employment services "under the federal government" so as to "facilitate the rapid recruiting of defense workers." Yet a new agency, the State and
Territorial Employment Services, was set up immediately. FDR said that a

meeting in Washington to discuss the matter was "waste motion."[51] In essence, Roosevelt was federalizing the states' labor forces.

His new Bureau of Censorship began to flex its muscles, but the more it did so, the more some civil libertarians questioned the wisdom of such an agency. On the one hand, FDR abhorred censorship and said so. On the other, he saw the usefulness in chilling leakers and potential leakers, while putting a fright into anyone who might step over the line and communicate too much information from the government, on the radio or via a private letter. Congress was going one step further, though. A bill that would "permit President Roosevelt to take control of telephone and telegraph facilities" was approved by the Interstate Commerce Committee. Potentially, it meant FDR could also control the "transmitting equipment of press services."[52] The Associated Press and United Press were the lifeblood of hundreds of newspapers around the country, and without the wires, their newspapers would be reduced to covering only farm reports and social doings.

Congress was still considering a plan to make Daylight Savings Time the law of the nation in order to ameliorate many problems associated with blackouts and air raids, while at the same time lengthening the workday.[53] Also under active consideration were federal laws enforcing and taking control of the blackouts in all the states.[54]

The head of the federal office of Civil Defense, New York mayor Fiorello La Guardia, was under fire. "Responsible sources reported that high official White House circles were displeased over the Mayor's handling of the civil defense problem." Specifically, "under criticism were the false air raid alarms in New York last week, the air raid drill staged for newsreels in Times Square . . . and the complete failure . . . of the well-advertised test of a giant siren that proved virtually inaudible."[55] These were just three of the hundreds of expensive mistakes going on in the country.

Even at its most efficient, war is nothing if not expensive. The cost of war kept spiraling upward. It was calculated that in December 1941, it cost the country an appalling $729 per second, but by 1942, it would be up to an astounding $1,400 per second.[56]

Some in academia had been slow to join the war effort. Two weeks after the declaration of war, the presidents of Wesleyan College, Colby College, and other schools pleaded with their undergraduate males to stay with their studies and get their degrees (and continue paying their tuitions), while others, including Harvard, finally got into the swing of things.

The president of Harvard said third-year law students could receive "war degrees" on a case-by-case basis with an abbreviated last year. Smith College organized an Ambulance Corps, Brown University added "14 military courses," Yale was offering degrees in three years, and Simmons College in Massachusetts was holding evening courses in national defense.[57]

By the afternoon of Friday, December 19, the Japanese were claiming to have taken Hong Kong, in spite of the claims of the British military. If the Japanese claim were true, it would be devastating. Just hours earlier, Secretary of the Navy Frank Knox spoke to the 1942 graduating class of Annapolis, whose graduation had been accelerated by six months because of the war. He told the 547 graduates that the army and the navy had repulsed a third attack by the Japanese at Pearl Harbor, but this was false as there had been no third attack. He also asserted that with thirty minutes notice, the Japanese air invasion would have been blown out of the sky. "There is no question at all, in light of what transpired, that half an hour's warning of the approach of the Japanese planes would have made all the difference."[58] Who knew?

However, Knox also told the young men in white dress uniforms what was becoming obvious to all now: the Japanese had by far the largest naval force in the Western Pacific.

"By far."[59]

CHAPTER 20

THE TWENTIETH
OF DECEMBER

"U.S. Reveals Foe Operating Subs off East Coast"

Birmingham News

"Hong Kong Defenders Staging Last Ditch Fight"

Yuma Daily World

"12 U.S. Agencies, 10,000 Leaving D.C."

Washington Post

"Heavy Philippine Battle Rages; Japs Land Anew"

Sun

As news days go in a new war, Saturday the twentieth was a relatively measured one even as planes were downed, ships were sunk, soldiers were killed, and civilians were marched off to their own extermination. A determined march was working inexorably against America and the Allies.

The war news—such as it was—was getting worse for the Allies. The newspapers began using phrases like "bad news from the East" and "heavy raid reported close to London." A headline in the *Boston Evening Globe* screamed,

"Hong Kong Doomed."[1] The Saturday evening edition of Baltimore's *Sun* newspaper reported as if Hong Kong had already fallen, but in fact, the British garrison was fighting on, holding on, hanging on.

Winston Churchill once said that "the power of an air force is terrific when there is nothing to oppose it."[2] To illustrate Churchill's point: for years a man had flown Christmas gifts to lonely lighthouse keepers and their families up and down the New England coast, but the navy grounded the "Flying Santa," fearing he might be mistaken for an enemy plane and shot down.[3] So much for Christmas spirit.

Still, Americans could take heart and draw on their own history for inspiration and resolve. After all, the twentieth was also the 164th anniversary of another beleaguered time in American history: when George Washington and his ragged and demoralized men straggled into Valley Forge, Pennsylvania, to make camp. Among his troops was Private Henry Cone of Lyme, Connecticut.

Congress was moving toward a break, even after a pledge by Speaker Sam Rayburn that the House would not go out of session because of the war. The plan now was to go into recess until January 5.

Since the attack at Pearl Harbor, the national legislature had moved with lightning speed over long days to declare war on three nations, appropriate billions of dollars for defense, grant the president unprecedented war powers, create a restructured Selective Service bill, which was finally headed to President Roosevelt for his signature, and hold hearings on all sorts of war-related matters, including corruption.

The head of the Selective Service, General Louis B. Hershey, sent Roosevelt a memo outlining his concerns that men in war-related industries should stay put and not be allowed to join the armed forces. "In many instances they are men of skills who should stay in war production or vital civilian activities." He advocated that recruiting stop and that the military depend instead on a draft.[4] Memos Roosevelt reviewed that day dealt with the disposition of loyal Japanese on the West Coast[5] (authored again by John Franklin Carter), memos on the Dutch East Indies,[6] memos on Russia,[7] and

Stalin's desire for "the Baltic States . . . but also . . . expansion to the west, presumably by advancing the Lithuanian borders into East Prussia" and obtaining "naval and air bases in Finland . . ."[8]

No wonder Roosevelt was tired and cranky.

He also received a detailed memo from the office of the legal advisor at the State Department explaining how, while the Constitution was clear on declaring war, it was silent on declaring peace. "The Constitution itself contains no specific grant of power to any branch of the Government to make peace." It had been discussed at the Constitutional Convention in August of 1787 "to give Congress the power to declare both war and peace. The motion was unanimously rejected." This power had been in the Articles of Confederation. Any conclusion of hostilities required a treaty, and that required the approval of the U.S. Senate. However, the fabled document gave the president broad powers. According to constitutional experts, "It is the right of the president, and not of Congress, to determine whether the terms [of peace] are advantageous, and if he refuses to make peace, the war must go on." Even Woodrow Wilson said only the Senate could ratify peace.[9]

A House special investigating committee also released a report that said "thousands of Nazis, Fascists, Japs are active there" in South America. In Argentina alone, it was charged that over 2,000 Gestapo agents were operating, and there "was reason to believe that a large contingent of Storm Troopers has been organized and that secret drilling is now in progress." Also, the committee report claimed that there were 90,000 Nazis in the Buenos Aires area alone.[10] The German embassy in that city was little more than a printing press for propaganda.

The German embassy had taken the speeches of Charles Lindbergh, put them in a brochure, and distributed them widely throughout Argentina.[11] Lindbergh, erstwhile American hero, would suffer a permanent blow to his reputation and prestige because of his previous pro-German, isolationist stance. The congressional report on these matters was comprehensive and had been assembled in a short period of time. Senator Harry Truman's steadfast work rooting out corruption was also impressive.

Whether one agreed or disagreed with all the actions of Congress, those actions were nonetheless impressive in speed and scope.

It was time for the editors of the United Press to poll themselves and rank the top ten stories of 1941. The attack at Pearl Harbor was the lead-pipe cinch for first place. Of the succeeding nine, all were war-related, from Lend-Lease to the Atlantic Charter to the pitched sea battle between the *Bismarck* and the *Hood* in the Atlantic. Not even Joe Louis's epic title defenses or Joe DiMaggio's fifty-six game hitting streak or Ted Williams's phenomenal season hitting over .400 made the top ten stories.[12]

In Washington, a former silent screen star, Corrine Griffith, and her husband, "wealthy Washington (D.C.) laundry operator George Marshall," were granted full custody in the adoption of two young girls. Buried at the bottom of the small newspaper item, it was also noted that Marshall was the owner of the "Washington professional football Redskins."[13]

The national debt was announced at $57 billion dollars.[14]

Initially, the War Department had put out a call for skilled welders and steel-workers needed to help build ships at Pearl Harbor, but it was revealed several days later that, in fact, the workers were needed to "help repair the damage" at the war-torn island. "Those needed include mechanics, laborers and helpers. Among the journeyman trades the pay will vary from $1.02 an hour to $1.30 an hour, depending on the type of work. One hundred laborers at 62 cents an hour and 100 helpers at 74 cents an hour are needed. Single men are preferred . . . all applicants will be subjected to . . . [a] Federal Bureau of Investigation fingerprint test."[15]

The war industry continued to ramp up speedily as the president set higher and higher production quotas. Exhibiting his usual knack for the inspirational phrase, FDR called America's massive manufacturing might the Arsenal of Democracy. At first, business leaders as well as Congress (which had to come up with the astronomical funding) balked at some of his ambitious demands. Soon, though, the war economy was firing on all cylinders and producing weaponry and materiel at levels previously deemed utterly impossible. Germany and its Axis partners were about to get a taste of America's will. At a plant in Johnsville, Pennsylvania, new dive bombers were near to being turned out only weeks after the factory opened. Without revealing any details, the designers of the new plane promised it would fly circles around the German Stuka. The new American plane's initial name was "Buccaneer."[16]

To build planes, trains, automobiles, tanks, ships, guns, etc., raw materials were needed—and lots of them. So the government's requisitioning of privately owned material accelerated. "OPM Priorities Director Donald M. Nelson yesterday announced the seizure by the Navy of more than one million dollars worth of critical scarce materials being held in warehouses and railroad terminals for shipment to foreign countries. The requisitioning, first under new powers granted to the Office of Production Management by Executive Order, included more than 13 million pounds of steel, 3½ million pounds of copper, 34,000 pounds of tin and 70,000 feet of teakwood. The steel had been located by OPM research and statistics bureau's survey of lost, hidden and frozen inventories . . . . The owners of the property taken . . . will be compensated for the value of the materials."[17] The navy also helped itself to "four of [the] Gulf's finest yachts" in Mobile, Alabama.[18]

With astonishing speed, the U.S. government had not only identified privately held metals, woods, and other materials but had also taken them for the war effort. Government was all-pervasive by the twentieth. Not since the special powers that President Lincoln had appropriated for himself during the Civil War had the centralized authority of the U.S. government moved with such alacrity and such trampling of private property, if not of the Constitution, for that matter. During the existential crisis of the Civil War, Lincoln used his war powers to suspend the writ of habeas corpus, proclaim a blockade, and spend funds without congressional authorization. Most of his actions were subsequently upheld by Congress and the courts. Now, America faced another existential crisis, and FDR had precedent for dispensing with a few inconvenient democratic niceties.

The *Wall Street Journal* fretted about the new war powers granted FDR by Congress. "President Roosevelt now holds greater powers over life and property than any President before him. Legislation to give him still more power already is being planned. Two additional legislative grants of power are to be asked soon, government officials disclose. Also, it is anticipated that the President will soon ask Congress to eliminate the Tabor amendment to the Property Requisitioning Bill." If eliminated, it would allow outright seizure of factory equipment by the government for the war effort.[19] Unlike some editors in the Civil War who had been ordered imprisoned by Lincoln because their opposition had displeased him, Roosevelt made no such move against newspapers that opposed him, including the *Journal.*

The Office of Production Management was being reorganized. This, for the few defenders of an unfettered free market, was cause for concern. The OPM regulated just about everything already, from rubber to salad oil. Now it was poised to directly manage all of industry and the entire workforce, including "the curtailment of production for civilian use." It was also preparing to take over the "pulp and paper; printing and publishing; lumber and building materials; plumbing and heating; electrical appliances; automobiles; transportation and farm equipment; industrial and office machinery." The list just continued on and on.[20]

Because of the rapid expansion of the federal war bureaucracy, some government functions were actually suggested to be outsourced to other locations around the country to make room for the war effort in Washington. All in all, twelve federal agencies including the Patent Office, the Rural Electrification Administration, the Fish and Wildlife Service, and others were proposed to be moved to New York City, St. Louis, and Chicago, among others. For the 10,000 federal workers potentially being displaced, the government promised to pay their moving costs and help them find adequate housing, or, if they could not move, the government promised to help them find comparable jobs.[21] The forced private-sector layoffs came with no such guarantees.

America's medical schools on the East Coast announced that becoming a board certified physician would now take only three years, as opposed to the usual four-year plan because of the desperate need for doctors in military hospitals. A "Victory Book" campaign was organized nationally to get people to send works of fiction and nonfiction to servicemen for their reading pleasure. The Girl Scouts organized a "Senior Scout" program to train their elder girls "in emergency feeding, messenger service, care of children, preparation of emergency shelters and packing of emergency rations and equipment."[22] A contingent of members of the Canadian Air Cadets came through New York on a publicity tour, with the idea of starting a similar program for American boys. The ages of the air cadets were fourteen to eighteen, and they were described as the "kindergarten of the Royal Air Force."[23]

Perhaps because of the Christmas season, the city of Washington was displaying a public spiritedness not normally associated with the Capitol of Cynicism. Dupont Circle and Glover Park organized air-raid watching groups, as did Takoma Park in Maryland. A "D.C. Committee of 70" was set up to collect scrap paper, rubber, metal, and old rags.[24]

Blind Americans were also doing their part for the war effort. At "fifty-four workshops for the blind in twenty-seven states," they were churning out for the military "brooms, mops, deck swabs, mattresses, cocoa mats, pillow-cases, whisk brooms, mailing bags, mop handles and similar articles."[25]

Because skilled labor was needed, some of the new vocational and academic teaching programs for the blind came about as a direct result of the war effort. Over 2,000 patriotic sightless citizens working in these various plants wanted to kick the stuffing out of the Axis thugs too.

Even Fido was being recruited for the war effort. The commander of the Los Angeles harbor, Colonel W. W. Hicks, put out an all-points bulletin for "canine recruits." He "said the dogs could be of all sizes or breeds, but must be in good health and sufficiently intelligent to pass the canine equivalent of the Stanford universal achievement test." What the lucky dogs would be engaged in was termed a "military secret." It was recalled that "in the last war, they were used at the front to carry messages."[26]

It may have been the holiday season that brought people together, but marriages still ended and some badly. In order to secure a divorce, a public notice ran in the New York Times: "My wife, Phyllis Zenerino, having left my bed and board . . . [I] will not be responsible for her debts. Frank Zenerino, 608 9th Avenue, New York."[27]

The spirit of Christmas and esprit de corps and sacrifice were almost everywhere else, though. In the Philippines, the 6,000 criminals of the penitentiary offered to donate blood for the Allied cause and to fight the Japanese if released. "The prisoners reaffirmed their faith in the United States and the Philippines."[28] A group of thirteen criminals, most of them serving life sentences at San Quentin, went one better and offered themselves to FDR as a "suicide squad." They wrote a letter to Roosevelt, which the warden allowed to go to the White House and in which they proposed "to serve as human torpedoes to help crush the Japanese. It is far better to sacrifice one life than to lose thousands," the missive said.[29] Sacrifice for a higher calling, even among crooks, was deep in the American creed.

Across America, religious and seasonal Christmas songs burst forth in department stores, on city sidewalks, in government buildings, in public schools, on radios, and all across the country. Everybody wished everybody else "Merry Christmas!" and no one was offended. Bibles were everywhere, as were crèches—scenes of the manger where Christ was born. Big write-ups in all the papers detailed planned church festivities, and there were extensive stories in the Washington papers of the planned activities of the Roosevelt clan on Christmas Eve. Christmas lighting had been kept to a minimum, but the sacrifices of war made the American people all the more resolute and, indeed, righteous in wanting to celebrate the birthday of Jesus Christ. The fact that America was fighting for its life made the Christmas of 1941 deeply meaningful because it represented, to most people, the very thing that made fighting worthwhile. Understandably, beneath the Christmas joy was a seriousness of purpose among the people.

So much so that many factories were humming and operating on December 25. "To supply steel for war, many plants in the industry, will operate on Christmas Day for the first time in 24 years, or since the first World War." Some of the plants that would be open included Carnegie-Illinois Steel Corporation, Republic Steel, and, appropriately, Bethlehem Steel. All workers would receive time-and-a-half, and the president of Carnegie, J. L. Perry, remarked, "It is no longer a question of how much steel can be provided to industry but how quickly. Delay in the production of steel means delay in the production of material vital to national welfare."[30]

Christmas was being celebrated in Hawaii, albeit it in a truncated manner.

Blackouts were still in effect, but during the day, navy enlistees in their white uniforms were spotted carrying packages on the streets of Honolulu. "Nobody seems downhearted. Nevertheless, the territorial office of civilian defense has established a public morale section to promote loyalty to the United States and interracial harmony . . . This section is headed by an American, with one Chinese assistant and another of Japanese-American ancestry."[31]

But what was on everybody's mind in Hawaii was when the bars and nightclubs and liquor stores would open back up.[32]

Even with the massive disruption in the national economy, consumer spending was projected to increase greatly in 1942 "despite higher taxes and rising prices."[33] After years of grim deprivation during the Depression, there was a huge pent-up demand for consumer goods and a better life. Anticipating the upswing in the economy, the Spiegel Company of Chicago, a department store and mail-order house, announced it was for the first time offering a credit plan for mail orders, with no interest charges, only a small "carrying charge."[34] Adding to the holiday spirit was the release of a new Shirley Temple movie, *Kathleen*, after a two-year hiatus for the hugely popular young movie actress.[35]

Reality was always deeply woven into the fabric, however. There were ongoing discussions about canceling the annual New Year's Eve festivities in Times Square in New York City. Boston's archbishop, William Cardinal O'Connell, canceled the traditional midnight Mass for Christmas Eve because of the fear of what could happen to a large group of unsuspecting churchgoers. "The action was taken in a move to co-operate with defense authorities by eliminating the possibility of congestion of hundreds of persons after dark in the event of an emergency."[36] A letter had gone out to every Catholic church in America to be read at Mass on Sunday, the twenty-first, asking all parishioners to get involved in war work.

The Jews of Europe were also grounded in reality, a monstrously horrible one: "the Paris municipal government ordered new measures against Jews in the German-occupied capital and surrounding Seine department." Jews were required to notify Gestapo officials of any change in their addresses. "For the last week, the Gestapo has been rounding up Jews and sending them to concentration camps. Travelers arriving at Vichy said several thousand had been arrested."[37]

Navy sources also revealed that German U-boats had been sighted off the Eastern Seaboard, sometimes within eyesight of land. The main Philippine island of Luzon was under increased assault by Japanese forces, which had made yet another successful beachhead on the island.[38] American and Filipino soldiers and flyers were doing their best under impossible circumstances.

Just a few weeks earlier, most Americans could probably not find Luzon on a map. Now they were learning about faraway places they had never before heard of, with odd and even funny names, but which were quickly becoming very important to them and their country. Just that day, they learned that American forces on Mindanao near the town of Davao were engaged in "some of the most serious battling of the war," where the Japanese had opened yet a new front in the fight for the Philippines. Meanwhile, the British had taken Derna and El Mekili in North Africa.[39]

From the Russian front, "Tarussa, sixty-five miles northeast of Kaluga, and the town of Kanino, southeast of Kaluga, also were reported captured. Kaluga is an important rail junction on the line running south to Bryansk and Kiev."[40] They also learned that American fighter planes had downed four Japanese bomber planes over Chungking.[41] However, twenty-four Japanese planes bombed, again, this time hitting the U.S. base at Cavite near Manila Bay.

The situation in Hong Kong worsened for the British. Giant fires were seen in the area, and there were reports of hand-to-hand fighting in the streets. Wake Island was enduring its thirteenth day of attack. They'd been undergoing an underreported story of "long hammering by bombs and shells, of endless hours without rest or sleep, of the dogged spirit which has turned aside attack after attack in more than 300 hours of almost constant attack."[42] The island was no more than 2,600 acres, and "the highest point above sea level is 15 feet."[43] The tough marines and navy seamen on the island repelled another two attempts by the Japanese to take the little atoll.

The leaders of the Marine Corps were getting ready to roll out their new recruiting poster for billboards across the country. It featured a "rough and ready marine, against a background of the sea and ships, holding his hand out to greet prospective enlistees." The caption read, "Want Action? Join the United States Marine Corps."[44] The battle for Wake Island certainly served as an inspiration for the poster and for the American people. The Japanese had, at the outset of the war, claimed they had captured Wake Island, but the marines and the navy would continue the battle until finally surrendering on December 23.

Enlisting was one thing. That only began the process. Young enlistees only had a few days to settle their civilian affairs; break the news to alternatively angry, scared, and proud parents; tell their friends and employers, maybe a girlfriend or at least the girl next door; pass the physical and then report to a recruiting office to swear their loyalty to the Constitution of the United States and to follow the orders of the president of the United States and their superior officers. A recruiting doctor observed that Northern boys had "good feet and bad teeth," while Southern boys had just the opposite. His theory was boys in the South liked to go barefoot, while boys in the North ate "too much candy and soft foods."[45] Ironically, both bad teeth and flat fleet could earn a young man a 4-F designation, though other restrictions against serving, including hernias, hay fever, or a "nasal deformity," had been lowered.[46]

Often, towns would hold parades for the young men with good teeth and good feet, cheering and watching them march off even as they were still in "civvies," with bands, and crowds, and fanfare, before they boarded a bus or a train and headed for six weeks of hell in boot camp. It was all rough going, learning how to kill other men, eat lousy food, and live in drafty barracks with no air conditioning and poor heating, and drill instructors yelling at them all the time. One "boot" at Fort Dix swore the breakfast sausages were stuffed with sawdust. At no time did any "boot" have any privacy. They marched together, ate together, showered together, and slept together. They went into the military as little more than boys but came out as men, forever changed. The marines had the roughest boot camps of all, complete with hazing and harassing. Of the first twenty-eight days in camp, nine were spent learning how to shoot and handle a rifle.[47]

There had never been a military man in the history of the nation who said service in uniform did not change his life forever. Friendships also sprang up, some that lasted a lifetime—however short that might now be.

The day had been relatively quiet on the Malayan Peninsula, but most thought the Japanese were regrouping for a massive assault on Singapore. American and British troops were earning their combat pay. American military leaders told reporters that, despite all the problems, they believed MacArthur would hold on to the Philippines with his 130,000 troops, despite the fact that supplies were running perilously low. MacArthur also had maintained the warm support of Philippine president Manuel Quezon.[48] It would be difficult. The Philippines, all told, had over 300 separate islands and atolls that, combined, made up more shoreline than that of the entire continental United States.[49]

It was not known if the island redoubt of Corregidor had yet been attacked, but the telltale smoke associated with antiaircraft gunfire was seen over the island. Also, the Philippines were overrun with Japanese sympathizers. At one location, American servicemen discovered a mirror in a tree, obviously put there as a signal to Japanese bomber pilots.[50]

One of the cushiest U.S. Army assignments of the war may have been to the new garrison on the island of Bermuda. The closest the island came to war was having the British name one of their bomber planes after it, or maybe a visit from the occasional German submarine. True, it was out of harm's way, away from the action, but if eating cold K-rations in a wintry foxhole in Europe was not your cup of tea or if sweating out the war in the engine room of a warship in the Pacific was not up your alley, then pulling easy duty on a balmy island while still getting a ribbon on your chest was a good way to go. And to top it off, there were regular Pam Am Clipper fights between the island and Miami.

Meeting the press the day before, FDR was in a lousy mood, "his face graven and serious, his manner brusque and preoccupied. Mr. Roosevelt started talking without preamble, without a trace of a smile. As somber as his heavy black suit and the lines bracketing his mouth, the President paced off his conference quickly." After a long day, he slipped out for a "pre-dinner swim and an evening of work." The president's health was markedly deteriorating, but this fact was kept hidden from an anxious nation that needed confidence in its leaders. The White House staff also was burning the midnight oil.[51]

A mini-crisis developed over the weekend when Secretary of State Cordell Hull had to angrily knock down a rumor that the State Department had "asked the Navy to suspend patrolling activities west of Hawaii during his pre-war negotiations with Japanese diplomats here." He blamed Fifth Columnists for "spreading the foulest reports that the most mendacious mind can conceive."[52] The accusation was that Hull wanted to create a peaceful atmosphere by having the navy stand down, as it would send a signal to the Japanese that the United States did not suspect them of possible dirty pool. It would have been the ultimate white flag.

The issue of a congressional investigation into the events at Pearl Harbor was slipping once again out of its box, having already been scotched twice by the White House. Senator Robert Taft, Republican of Ohio, spoke out and said that just because Roosevelt had created his own blue ribbon committee, it should not preclude a Capitol Hill inquiry from going forward.[53]

Another mini-crisis coming out of FDR's Business-Labor meeting was that unions were balking now at abiding by a no-strike pledge if they could not protect their "closed shops." As more and more men and women were coming into the war industries, it was not clear that they had to be compelled to join unions as they had for years. The goal had been to get unions to agree to no strikes for the duration of the war, but when this became a sticky wicket, Congress threatened more legislation expanding the no-strike laws.

The next day, Sunday the twenty-first, was the championship game for the NFL. The game, to be played in Chicago, would feature the "Monsters of the Midway," the Bears, against the New York Giants. The Bears, the defending champions, were heavily favored, and were coached by the legendary George Halas, aka "Papa Bear." But with everything going Chicago's way in advance of the game, ticket sales were way off, and game officials were not expecting anything close to a sellout.

Fans could be forgiven for having other things on their minds.

CHAPTER 21

THE TWENTY-FIRST
OF DECEMBER

"Report Sub Attacks Off U.S."

Chicago Sunday Tribune

"Son Is Not Dead, Navy Apologies, Gloom Vanishes"

Boston Sunday Globe

"Arab Cheers Greet British at Derna"

Washington Post

If Saturday the twentieth had been a day of big little news, Sunday the twenty-first was a day of little big news. Under giant black headlines: "The Navy said . . . it had received unconfirmed reports that two oil tankers had been attacked by submarines . . . and that one had sent out an S.O.S." The two ships were the 6,912-ton ship *Emidio* and the 6,771-ton *Agriworld*.[1]

The *Agriworld* had been only a hundred miles from San Francisco, en route to Los Angeles.[2] The crew of the *Agriworld* put on their life belts, fearful of being sunk. Despite being fired upon repeatedly by the submarine's deck gun, rolling seas threw off the aim of the gun crew, and she survived. The attack on the *Emidio*, less lucky, was off Blunts Reef, near the tiny California town of Eureka, only fifteen miles off shore. The ship had "sustained a torpedo attack." The navy later sighted the crippled ship and radioed that it was riding "low in the water." Both ships escaped, despite the *Emidio* being hit repeatedly by shells from the unidentified submarine. The crews for both ships clearly identified submarines, however no markings.[3]

Navy and army planes searched for the attacking warships, but to no avail. Several days earlier, an unidentified submarine had been sighted off Puget Sound and military planes had engaged the vessel, firing on it, but this was only revealed later.[4] Some officials suspected the Japanese had a hidden sub base in Latin America. One man claimed he'd seen Japanese fishing boats hauling cement there for years.[5]

These attacks on the oil tankers, plus the new sightings of German U-boats off the East Coast, brought the war much closer than it had been before. After two weeks of unremitting war news and emergency announcements, the American people could be forgiven if they'd become a bit disconsolate. Telltale signs emerged of flagging morale. Still, "news of the submarine actions of San Francisco did not disturb the outward calm of Los Angeles. Church bells echoed all the morning and the roads were clogged with the usual Sunday traffic."[6]

It was also confirmed that an American commercial vessel, the *Cynthia Olson*, with a cargo of lumber some 700 miles from the West Coast, had been fired upon and hit by a Japanese submarine on the day of December 7.[7] The *Cynthia Olson* had been sunk with all hands lost.

More bad news came from the Far East when it was learned that communications with the city of Davao on the island of Mindanao had been cut off. The Japanese had made landfall the day before and now General MacArthur could not get any information out of that battle zone.[8] "No word has been received from there since yesterday afternoon." It was reported the Japanese had come ashore "in fairly substantial forces . . . [T]he Davao campaign may develop into the most important land battle yet in the Philippines archipelago."[9] The goal of the Japanese was to quickly build airfields on conquered territories and establish air supremacy as soon as possible.

The situation was also deteriorating in Manila. Douglas MacArthur warned that looters would face the death penalty. Before the blackout came, reports got out that the Moro tribe, a tough bunch of bolo-swinging native warriors, joined the fight against the Japanese on Mindanao.[10]

MacArthur then discovered, to his dismay, that twenty Japanese ships including destroyers and submarines were engaged in the battle for the Philippines, more than he'd previously known about.[11] The odds were stacking up against the optimistic general.

Underestimating the Japanese was proving costly. The Japanese were thorough and had well-developed plans. Several months before the attack on Hawaii and other military installations—including Guam—it turned out that a Japanese ship suffered a deliberate wreck at Guam just so the officers and crew could get a close good look at the island's defenses—defenses they later overcame.[12]

Hong Kong was teetering. "The Japanese say they have the city of Victoria and that lorries flying the scarlet ball of the rising sun are roaring through the streets, packed with disarmed British soldiers; the remnants of the British garrison are encircled on the peak of the island, Mount Victoria."[13] The Japanese had already captured or destroyed large quantities of oil, rice, vehicles, and medicines, and much of the colony was aflame. The slim hope was for relief by Free Chinese forces. No relief for the gutsy British troops hiding and fighting a last-gasp guerilla battle was contemplated by London.

While the loss of Hong Kong to the Japanese would be devastating, the loss of the strategically located Singapore would be cataclysmic. Singapore had deep sea anchorages, docks for repairing large ships, "workshops for machinery and guns, one of the most powerful transmitting stations in the world, and huge underground oil and armament depots." But Britain's "crown jewel" was even more than that. "The vital significance of Singapore is not simply because it lies athwart trade routes supplying both the United Kingdom and the United States; it is the one spot in that part of the world able to accommodate large fleets in an emergency."[14] From Singapore, attacks could be launched against Sumatra, Borneo, and Australia. For the U.S. fleet to have a port in the Far East from which to wage war, it had to be Singapore. The facilities at Guam were unfinished and had been lost to the Japanese; the facilities at the Philippines were inadequate. If the navy lost Singapore, it would push the United States back thousands of miles.

For all of these reasons and many others, the Allies were fighting hard to hold on to Singapore. "British units fighting along the 400-mile Malaya penin-sula leading to Singapore include English infantrymen, Scottish Highlanders, Australians, Sikhs, Moslem riflemen, Gurkhas and Malayans."[15]

Not all the news was bad. Wake Island was still holding on. "Three days after the Japanese had claimed the island, two days after the President had warned the nation to expect its loss, the isolated band of heroes sent out one of the most astounding communiqués of the war. They still held Wake. They had repulsed four landing attacks. They had succeeded in sinking a Japanese cruiser and a destroyer. Whether they held the island indefinitely depended upon rein-forcements and supplies but already they had taught Nippon that what looked like a pushover on paper can be hell on earth when it is defended by the United States Marines. It was in the tradition . . . of the Argonne, Chateau Thierry, and Belleau Wood, where Marine marksmanship and Marine bayonets liter-ally exterminated the pride of the German Army," boasted the *Boston Sunday Globe*.[16] Now, of course, there was a new German army to defeat.

The *Saturday Evening Post* ran a long story that detailed how the Third Reich was planning for a five-year war against the Allied powers. Like the citi-zens of England, Japan, and America, their government was not only asking for sacrifices from the citizenry, they were demanding it. Propaganda Minister Joseph Goebbels went on state radio to call on the German people to donate blankets to their soldiers on the Russian front.[17] The Nazis meanwhile were embarking on a massive shipbuilding program. Their shipyards were operat-ing twenty-four hours a day.

War was not only all hell, it was also vile. As the German troops fell back from their thrusts into Russia, they desperately needed transportation of any kind. As a rouse, they announced in Russian towns that free salt was available. Peasants came from everywhere via horse and sleigh when the word spread of the free salt. Except there was no free salt. The Germans took the horses, and sleighs, and shot any Russians who protested the theft.

For Hitler and Nazi Germany, there were no longer civilians, women or children. Any human being, in any circumstance, was fair game. The German people themselves would eventually learn the terrible consequences of total war on their own soil, but that would come later, when the tables had turned against them. In 1941, at the apex of their power, the Nazi conquerors cut a murderous swath through every invaded country, with no compunction and with complete impunity. They were particularly savage toward the Russians, whom they considered *untermenschen*, subhuman.[18]

The War Department, concerned about the nation's morale, began churning out stories of heroes and of American successes. The tale of Captain Colin P. Kelly Jr., who had sacrificed his life to sink a Japanese war ship, had been in the paper for days. It was later learned Captain Kelly had ordered six of the crew in his plane to parachute to safety, leaving him and two others to finish the mission in their shot-up and battered plane. After his demise, he was posthumously awarded the Distinguished Service Cross by Douglas MacArthur.[19]

Yet another daring pilot was thrilling Americans with his exploits, Colonel Claire Chennault, of the now-famous "Flying Tigers." Chennault had volunteered to fight with the Chinese against the Japanese like so many other young American adventurers; however, to do so, he had to "resign" from the Army Air Corps. That was before December 7 changed everything. Chennault was a ruggedly handsome Texan and natural leader who shot down numerous Japanese planes, flew the "Hump" over Burma, was a virulent anti-communist, and graced the covers of *Look* and *Time* magazines.[20]

Roosevelt was pushing hard to organize a Supreme War Council, and the name of Wendell Willkie was floated to either chair or at least serve on the committee. "The Council members would be given broad policy-making powers and authority over all segments of the Nation's wartime life—from civilian activities to actual naval and military operations. They would be responsible only to Mr. Roosevelt." The council was described by one White House insider as "embryonic." On the surface, the White House seemed in command and organized, but if the surface was scratched, human beings would be found who were just as disorganized and panicky as anyone else in the country. FDR was also still trying to get a planning operation going that would involve the British, American, Russian, Chinese, Dutch, "and other governments allied in the world-wide war against the Axis."[21]

Joe Stalin was being a pain in the ass, as per usual. The British foreign minister, Anthony Eden, had been in Moscow for days, holding the Soviet dictator's hand, trying to get him to play nice with everybody else. In a confidential telegram to Secretary of State Cordell Hull, a British official wrote it became "apparent at the most recent meetings between Eden and Stalin that it would be impossible to reconcile the British and Soviet drafts of the proposed pacts on the joint war effort and European post-war problems, in view of the Soviet attitude with respect to the recognition of the 1941 frontiers." Stalin was also delusional as he told Eden "he had expressed the belief that Germany will be defeated within one year and Japan possibly within six months."[22]

All told, FDR had five big items on his "to do" list, including "reorganization of the machinery of the United States and British governments to integrate and expedite the war tasks of the two nations."[23] He met that Sunday with the British ambassador, Lord Halifax, to begin the work on an agenda for a planned meeting that week of the Allies. Though the Russians still hadn't declared war on Japan, they wanted in on the talks.[24]

Curiously, even as of two weeks after the beginning of the war, it was still not commonly being referred to as "World War II" or the "Second World War." Nor was the "Great War" being commonly referred to as "World War I." These appellations appeared here and there in one form or another but would take time to take root in the common lexicon.

Willkie had been on the radio just the evening before, giving the American people what for, telling them they were not sacrificing enough and that they had to get used to a future of "Spartan simplicity and hard work."[25] If his 1940 GOP presidential opponent was willing to play bad cop, FDR was more than happy to play good cop.

In his 1940 effort, hundreds of "Associated Willkie Clubs of America" had sprung up. By 1941, they had become the "Independent Clubs of America." By December 1941, they had become nothing, disbanding to concentrate on the war effort.[26] The chairman of the Republican National Committee, Joe Martin, sent a letter to all GOP state chairmen informing them of his decision to cancel the party's annual meeting in Washington in January. However, Martin did suggest that countrywide "Lincoln Day dinners" be held on the anniversary of the sixteenth president's birthday as "patriotic demonstrations."

He continued, "Let us publicly proclaim our support of the Administration in an irresistible effort to win the war."[27]

FDR already had a "War Cabinet" working on solving the problems facing the American military and he'd met with them on Saturday, in the Cabinet Room of the White House. It was an amalgamation of White House staff, such as Harry Hopkins and cabinet officials like Attorney General Francis Biddle and Labor Secretary Frances Perkins.[28] A bit of good news greeted the War Cabinet in Washington and Winston Churchill's war planners in London when the British army scored another breakthrough in Libya against the German tank corps. As the Brits rolled into Derna, Libya, they were greeted by "cheering and smiling Arab tribesmen."[29]

Just days before, the government was assuring the American people that food was plentiful and would be so for the foreseeable future, and nothing like the last war. Then Paul McNutt, Federal Security Administrator, told the National Defense Gardening Conference that Americans needed to conserve food and that the "meatless Mondays" of the last war were not inconceivable.[30] Fearing a run on sugar would drive up prices, the government stepped in and froze the cost.[31]

Whereas several days earlier American flags sales were only up modestly, toward the end of the month, they had increased sharply—at least for the thirty flag manufacturers in the greater Chicago area. "Orders by the thousands are pouring into the some 30 companies which manufacturer the 'Star-Spangled Banner' and other patriotic insignia. It's the war, of course."[32] Washington was encouraging all Americans to display the stars and stripes.

The American Institute of Public Opinion, headed by the up-and-coming pollster George Gallup, took a survey of the American people and asked if they would be willing to work an extra eight hours a week in order to help the war effort. An astonishing 88 percent said yes and only 12 percent said no. "Despite long working hours in many war plants, the overwhelming majority of defense workers interviewed indicated their willingness to work an extra eight hours a week in order to speed production."[33]

Washington was moving ahead with what it hoped would be a streamlining of labor, bringing the state and local governments effectively under the control of the national government. The plan was to have a workforce that responded "rapidly" to the needs of the war effort. "President Roosevelt, acting to utilize the man power and woman power of the country for armament production to the fullest extent, ordered creation of a national industrial recruiting agency, which would merge the State and territorial affiliates of the United Sates Employment Services." The plan included "more effective use of those already employed through transfer of needed workers from less essential jobs to war production."[34]

Private property was being confiscated left and right, especially in Washington. One example was a picture-frame shop across from the White House. It had been there for years, filling the orders of presidents as far back as Teddy Roosevelt. It was taken for the war effort and the old building razed. "The land, it seems, is needed for construction of a Government building. Spared were the historic Decatur and Blair houses."[35]

While the government was seizing private property for the war effort, it was also taking control of some twenty foreign-owned plants in the Philadelphia area. The Axis-owned factories were taken over by Treasury officials, after the FBI identified their ownership. "Treasury agents, following a pre-arranged plan, moved in quietly to prevent sabotage and insure maximum production of defense products."[36]

Like their German counterparts, American shipbuilders were also working overtime and ten navy ships slid into the water in one day. "Destroyers, submarine chasers, cargo ships and tankers were represented in the launchings, many of them going into the water far ahead of schedule." Ships were launched in Charleston, South Carolina, New York, and Chester, Pennsylvania.[37] In Charleston, two ships "splashed" within ten minutes of each other. Of course, it had already been determined that these shipyards would be fully operational on Christmas Day.[38]

Three Republican senators came forward to say they would not be "gagged" by the war, despite FDR's power and popularity. This ran contrary to a proclamation the Republican National Committee had issued some days earlier.

The chairman of the RNC and the chairman of the Democratic National Committee issued a joint communiqué and sent a telegram to FDR pledging to set aside partisanship for the duration of the emergency. The pledge lasted nearly two weeks—pretty impressive, considering politicians made the promise.

The three who decided to battle the headwinds of near-unconditional national support for Roosevelt were Wayland "Curly" Brooks of Illinois, Styles Bridges of New Hampshire, and "Mr. Republican" himself, the redoubtable Robert Taft of Ohio and the leader of conservatives in America, such as they were in 1941.

The three represented three differing viewpoints of the GOP, which may have explained their apparent permanent minority status since 1932. Brooks was an out-and-out isolationist, bitterly opposing FDR, Bridges was an out-and-out internationalist, supporting FDR, and Taft was somewhere in the middle. Taft told the Associated Press that he did not believe that all of FDR's "recommendations . . . must be accepted blindly." Elaborating, he said, "Certainly in all fiscal matters we must exercise our own judgment." The three said they planned on critiquing civilian decisions but not those by the military, and they promised not to try to "run the war in Congress."[39]

Others joined the flow with enthusiasm. The publisher of the *Chicago Tribune*, Colonel Robert R. McCormick, a fierce opponent of Roosevelt's for years and a champion of the America First movement, significantly announced from his own radio station, WGN, that America would someday rule the waves and that America would someday have "command of the sea" and "command of the air."[40] Heads must have shaken in the White House when they heard of the internationalist address by McCormick.

McCormick wasn't anything if he wasn't a patriot, though. Two weeks after the attack, American newspapers were still filled with angry editorials and tough cartoons attacking the Germans, the Italians, but most especially, the Japanese. McCormick's *Tribune* was no exception. One of his reporters had an unusually salient point. At the 1932 Olympics, the Japanese swimmers had done surprisingly well, especially in the shorter competition. It was later learned that the swimmers had been pumped full of fresh oxygen. The *Tribune's* point was that if the Japanese cheated then, and had cheated two weeks earlier at Pearl Harbor, they could be counted on to continue cheating.[41]

As it was the weekend before Christmas, Americans were engaged in last-minute shopping. There were only three shopping days left. For women, jewelry, slippers, quilted robes, lounge pajamas, house coats, and gowns were suggested, while smoking jackets, pajamas, White Owl cigars, a Palmolive shaving kit, and shirts were offered for men. Portable radios were also suggested by retailers as good gifts—for war news of course—as were albums of Nelson Eddy and Rise Stevens, Kate Smith, and the "Dorsey Brothers Favorites."[42]

For girls, baby buggies, rag dolls, and tricycles were dancing in their heads. While for boys, BB guns and bicycles were what kept them mostly nice and not naughty.

It was an especially busy season as shopping, cooking, wrapping, church services, caroling, decorating, and school plays intermingled with meetings and lectures on incendiary bombs and the ethics of leaving children in school during air raids as opposed to parents taking them home. The *Post* took note of "Gay Caroling Ushers in Christmas Week."[43]

As always, Americans were flocking to their favorite movie theaters to see their favorite actors and actresses. One new film had no actors, though. It was a documentary entitled *Target for Tonight*, and the newspaper ads for it shouted, "How Would You Like To Bomb Germany Tonight?" The film was a feature-length depiction of an RAF squadron from takeoff to dropping bombs over Germany, dodging harrowing antiaircraft fire and attempting to return safely to England.[44] Still, the Motion Picture Board that represented women's and civic clubs selected *Citizen Kane* as the best picture of the year, followed by *How Green Was My Valley*. Also appearing on the list were *Dumbo* and *Meet John Doe*.[45]

War bonds were also popular Christmas gifts, especially Series E. They sold in denominations of $25, $50, $100, $500, and $1,000, but this was their value at maturity after ten years. Their purchase price, respectively, was $18.75, $37.50, $75, $375, and $750. They paid a respectable 2.9 percent interest annually and could be cashed in for their full face amount after ten years. Of course, the full faith and credit of the U.S. government backed up the principle and the interest of every bond. For the small patriotic investor including tykes, war stamps were available at 10 cents, 25 cents, 50 cents, $1, and $5. Bonds were also available in Series F, but these were large amounts, beyond the reach of nearly all Americans, going as high as $10,000.[46]

Americans—at least those of a marriageable age—also had something on their minds, namely matrimony. The Cook County clerk said a new record was set for marriage licenses, 350 in one day, on December 19. "The spurt was attributed to the presence in Chicago of many soldiers, sailors and marines on Christmas leave." Conversely, the county also reported that the number of divorces had plunged since December 7.[47] The Post Office reported voluminous mail[48] and crime was reportedly down across the nation.

An early Christmas present came for the family of navy man Oscar Thompson, 21, of Geneva, Illinois, whose family had received a telegram ten days earlier that their son was missing and presumed dead. Then his father, Fred, received a telegram saying that Oscar "was among the survivors, and there were apologies about the previous report being untrue."[49]

For the first time since December 7, navy recruiting offices would close from 4 p.m. on Christmas Eve to 8 a.m. on the twenty-sixth. The navy also announced that all recruits, both active duty and on reserve, could go home for Christmas if they could make it. It was generous, as they would have off the twenty-second until the twenty-seventh.[50]

Before December 7, many servicemen and officers wore their civilian clothing as much as possible, as a military career was not held in high regard by many Americans. Now, everybody held them in high regard, especially those in the services themselves, who wore their uniforms with unbridled pride.

Most civilians had a tough time telling a staff sergeant from a seaman or a colonel from a corporal. To help Americans distinguish ranks and services, many of the papers helpfully displayed the stripes and stars of shoulder boards for generals and admirals as well as the insignias of lesser ranks.

Army servicemen wore khakis and a black tie, tucked neatly into their shirt between the second and third button, with the "overseas" cap that looked like a large #10 envelope when laid on a table. The army was updating its officers' uniforms, dropping the great looking Sam Browne belt that for years featured a leather strap over the coat that crossed the chest from the right shoulder to the left hip.

Some thought the navy had the best uniforms, both officers and swabs.

The officers wore dress whites in summer, dress blues in winter, and for day-time dress, khaki suits. For the summer, they also had the option of white shorts, short sleeve shirts, stretch white socks, and white bucks. Some of their formal uniforms were eye-catching. The seamen also had dress white and blue uniforms for going ashore and got to wear dungaree pants and denim shirts when shipboard. The round "gob's" cap was classic, as were the buttoned-not-zippered pants with bellbottoms and the flap on the back of their pull-over tunics. The flap was popularized by the British navy to keep uniforms from being soiled by greasy pigtails (not an issue for American sailors in 1941).

For many, the marines had the others beat hands down, both for the offi-cers and the lowly privates. The mix of light blue, dark blue, red trim, and white officer cap for their formal dress uniform was smashing. That the most important general in the marines wore the same dress uniform as the men in the ranks told of a singleness of purpose which screamed "always faithful."

Two admirals who had new braid added to their uniforms were Admiral Ernest J. King, whom Roosevelt promoted to commander in chief of the United States Naval Fleet, replacing Admiral Husband Kimmel; and Rear Admiral Royal E. Ingersoll, who was appointed commander of the Atlantic Fleet. The replacement of Kimmel was pro forma, as he'd already been relieved of com-mand of the Pacific Fleet.[51] King was unique among the elder gentlemen of the navy in that he knew how to fly an airplane and had served aboard subma-rines, as well as ships during the Spanish-American War. He was one of the most well-rounded and experienced men in the navy.[52] Because King outranked Chief of Naval Operations Admiral Harold Stark, he only had to report to Secretary of the Navy Frank Knox and the president of the United States. King was tall, no nonsense, described as "a pleasant gentleman ashore but a tough hombre at sea."[53] King's nickname at Annapolis had been "Old Eagle Eye."[54]

At train stations and bus depots, volunteers for the Red Cross and the Salvation Army, often pretty girls, were there to hand out free coffee and doughnuts as well as pencils and writing papers.

Restaurants and coffee shops in those terminals were jammed with trav-elers. At some of those restaurants and at others across the country, owners were in the process of changing their menus and "rechristening Italian spa-ghetti" as "Liberty Noodles."[55]

CHAPTER 22

THE TWENTY-SECOND OF DECEMBER

"Major Battle Is Raging in Philippines"

Birmingham News

"GOP Chiefs Agree Party Must Keep Eye on New Deal Actions"

Birmingham News

"Holiday Mail Breaks Record"

Los Angeles Times

"Three More Attacks On U.S. Ships by Jap Submarines Revealed"

Evening Star

U.S. attorney general Francis Biddle began creating seventy "Alien Enemy Hearing Boards" situated around the country to determine the fate of the thousands of Japanese, Germans, and Italians being held by the government at various detention centers. "The quasi-judicial panels, which start functioning as soon as they are appointed, will hear the cases of all enemy aliens brought before them individually and will make recommendations to the attorney general, who will render the final decisions."[1]

Like the local draft boards, the Enemy Hearing Boards would be comprised of civic leaders, businessmen, local politicians, and clerics. Each board, after reviewing each case, could recommend to Biddle the "unconditional release" of the incarcerated individual, his parole, or that he be "interned for the duration of the war." Further, "the alien enemy may be accompanied by a relative, friend or adviser, but will not be permitted to be represented by anyone in the capacity of an attorney."[2]

Among the 35,000 reported Japanese nationals living on the various Hawaiian islands, 272 were being held as accused Fifth Columnists. (The number of Japanese in both America and the Hawaiian islands swung wildly around.) All known subversives were imprisoned, but the search continued for others.[3]

The treatment of Germans, Italians, and especially Japanese living in the United States was on the minds of many. The *Washington Post* generally supported the internment policy but also urged caution. "How necessary is the roundup, how strict must be the security, needs no emphasis after the revelation of what the Fifth Column did in Hawaii. We must give the benefit of doubt to our own security." However, the paper also noted the need to not jump to conclusions over "inoffensive, loyal aliens. The best way to create disaffection among an otherwise loyal alien population would be to treat them as enemies in our midst."[4] The *New York Times* also addressed the matter in an editorial entitled, "The Slanting Eye."[5]

Americans were worried, though. Over the weekend, civilian guards and Santa Barbara police at the Miguelito Canyon Reservoir had gotten into a gun fight with unknown saboteurs, suspected of wanting to destroy the water supply for the city and nearby Camp Cooke. It was the second attempt, and though they were chased off, "a dozen leaders in colonies of Japanese vegetable workers in the vicinity were rounded up . . . and sent off to Midwest concentration camps."[6] There was also the occasional violence against Japanese. In Los Angeles, unidentified assailants had shot a Japanese man in the back.[7]

Roosevelt received yet another in an interminable and unceasing line of memos on "Dealing with the West Coast Japanese Problem," authored again by his secret operative, John Franklin Carter. The document complained about overblown comments by Navy secretary Frank Knox about "Fifth Columnists. This term is loose and has been widely abused." Yet it also went into great detail about saboteurs, but mostly doubting the danger they posed.

The document counseled caution for FDR. "The loyal Japanese citizens should be encouraged by a statement from high government authority . . . Their offers of assistance should be accepted . . ." Other documents that day making their way to the president covered North Africa, food supplies, the Supreme War Council, and more British memoranda.[8]

Roosevelt also met that day with his cousin, Theodore Roosevelt Jr. That afternoon, he and Eleanor had cocktails in the Red Room, and several hours later hosted a dinner with seventeen guests including Churchill, Lord Beaverbrook, Hull, Hopkins, and others. Roosevelt turned in just before 1:00 a.m.[9]

Henry Luce, publisher of *Life* magazine and *Time*—both hugely influential publications—had been all for going to war in the guise of Charles Foster Kane, beating the war drums for months. Luce's magazines had also been cruelly dismissive of any point of view other than total internationalism.

Luce had his own ideas on how to treat "aliens." Now that America was at war with Japan, both of his publications ran side-by-side photos of Chinese and Japanese, complete with diagrams and charts, explaining how Americans could tell the difference between the two races. Discussing the reason for the full-page depictions, *Life* magazine explained, "U.S. citizens have been demonstrating a distressing ignorance on the delicate question of how to tell a Chinese from a Jap."[10] For the Japanese subject, Luce picked a photo of General Tojo—not the most popular man in America as of late December 1941. For the Chinese subject, he chose a low-level "Chinese public servant." Whereas the Chinese subject had "lighter facial bones" and a "higher bridge," the Japanese had a "flatter nose" and "earthy yellow complexion" and a "broader, shorter face," the publication patiently explained.[11]

The Chinese had received better press in America than had the Japanese for a number of years, thanks in part to Pearl Buck's hugely popular novel, *The Good Earth*, about American missionaries in China, which won a Pulitzer in 1932; Frank Capra's movie *Lost Horizon*; and Charlie Chan, the popular B-movie detective.

Biddle's efforts were proving more successful than others in the administration, who were running into bureaucratic resistance over moving the Patent Office out of Washington. Patent lawyers deluged the White House with letters and protests and the staff of 1,400 complained over the moving of 20,000,000 files. They estimated those files weighed 4,717 tons and the cabinets they were stored in weighed another 3,325 tons. Through all the previous wars, the Patent Office had stayed put, even during the War of 1812, when their records were stored in the only government building not burned by the British.[12]

The Roosevelt White House held the hand of the Patent Office employees and reassured them that they would only have to move to New York for the duration of the war. The government had agreed to pay for the cost of moving the employees and their household items, but not the cost of moving their families. The bureaucrats spent the better part of December thumbing "through law books . . . trying to find a law under which transportation costs of an employee's dependents could be paid. They found none."[13]

The Federal City had other problems. It had conducted its first air-raid alarm, which on the surface seemed successful. Lights flashed, radio bulletins went out, and phone calls were hurriedly made. Buses, trains, and cabs stopped. The police stopped traffic. "But the defense establishment in the Wardman Park Hotel heard no whistle. . . ." Off in the far distance, people in the city heard a whistle or a siren but only if they strained to listen. "The Willard Hotel wardens" from five blocks away "heard faintly a whistle in the distance."[14] Compared to those of other locales, D.C.'s drill, with the exception of the mute sirens, was a smashing success, though one local paper called the whole thing a "fiasco."[15]

Byron Price had already been sworn in as head of the Censorship Bureau. His oath of office included the part where he promised to defend the Constitution against all enemies, foreign and domestic. Very few pointed out the incongruity of his job and his oath. A columnist, Blair Bolles of the *Evening Standard,* was one of the few. "One day last week President Roosevelt made a speech about the glories of the Bill of Rights. Two days later he appointed a national censor, whose business it is to infringe on the Bill of Rights' guarantee of freedom of the press. Nobody protested. War is paradoxical, and we accept the idea that even in a war fought to protect the system of which the Bill of Rights is a part, free publication of information must be restricted."[16]

The paradox went unaddressed as Price's mission was to stop all information that could aid the Axis powers—very often a subjective determination. Who was to determine what really aided the enemy and what the American people had a right to know? This was no debate over how many Founding Fathers could dance on the head of a pin: it went to the core of the very existence of the American Republic. Was it necessary to sublimate the Constitution in order to save it?

The matter had been fought between Jefferson and Hamilton; over the Sedition Acts of the early 1800s; over the actions of Abraham Lincoln during the Civil War when he imprisoned, without due process, newspaper editors who wrote articles that displeased him; or over the powers granted Woodrow Wilson during the Great War and what some thought was his low regard for the Constitution, seeing it as an impediment to executive progress.

Without even flinching, the National Association of Broadcasters had gone right along with the new state of censorship in America and in many ways, took the policy one step further, on its own and without government coercion. The NAB issued their own new guidelines against "sensationalism, carelessness and second-guessing in news broadcasts—as well as 'ad lib' broadcasts on the street or in the studio. . . . Other 'do nots' included the second guessing of military officers, over-estimating American military power or under-estimating enemy strength, broadcasting unformed reports, and the use of sponsors of news as a springboard for advertising 'commercials.'"[17]

Radio had already been banned from broadcasting weather reports, and now the NAB said broadcasts designed to "increase tension" were "do nots." The guide also stated, "An open microphone accessible to the general public constitutes a very real hazard in times of war. Any question regarding the war or war production might make trouble."[18]

Anxious over a surprise attack by the enemy during Christmas week, civil defense units asked their thousands of volunteer spotters all over America—

but especially on the East Coast—to organize platoon systems and be on the watch for enemy planes, twenty-four hours a day for the duration of Christmas week. In Neshaminy, Pennsylvania, O. P. Titus, a seventy-seven-year-old widow, walked her post every day from 11 a.m. to 1 p.m., surely convinced her town was of vital importance to the enemy.[19]

On the West Coast, all private planes within 150 miles of the coastline were abruptly ordered grounded until further notice.[20]

Americans who had already signed up for civil defense were more than happy to do so and did so, but if the photos that were guiding them on Japanese planes were anything like those running in *Life* magazine, they were woefully out of date, by five to ten years at least. *Life* published photos as a guide for Americans, but they were of biplanes and open-cockpit planes, neither of which was in use by the Japanese for combat for years.[21]

Eyes toward the sky were helpful, but it paid to be watchful of the waves as well. The Pacific Ocean, including along the California coastline, now resembled a shooting gallery. After the shock that two oil tankers had been attacked so close to the California coast, the U.S. Navy announced that enemy submarines had several days earlier attacked other American vessels close to the Golden State. Both the steamships *Samoa* and *Lahaina* were attacked and the latter sunk en route to San Francisco.[22]

The tanker *L. P. St. Clair* reported that torpedoes had been fired on her and the Coast Guard said another tanker, *H.M. Storey*, owned by the Standard Oil Company, had been fired upon off the coast of Santa Barbara.[23] A coast guardsman saw the whole thing from the shore, including the *Storey's* on-deck gun firing and missing the sub as it slipped beneath the surface.[24] Navy patrol boats dropped depth charges after responding to the attack. Other captains fought back as well. The skipper of the *Agriworld*—previously fired upon—actually attempted to ram the unidentified sub assailing his tanker.[25]

New details emerged about the attack on the *Emidio*, including the atrocious actions of the unknown sub on defenseless seamen. After being torpedoed, the crew abandoned ship and hunkered down in three lifeboats alongside. The enemy submarine then turned its deck gun on the unarmed and helpless civilian seamen, blasting repeatedly. The first reports indicated no casualties, but follow-up reports said all twenty-two seamen were believed dead. The ship had issued an S.O.S. and American planes responded within ten minutes, dropping depth charges, but it was unknown if the sub had been hit.[26]

The Atlantic was also a shooting gallery, but this time it was favoring the United States. Secretary of the Navy Frank Knox announced that fourteen German U-boats had either been hit or sunk, though it was not said when the actual fighting took place. FDR had, in fact, issued his "shoot on sight" order several months before.

Knox had a meeting the day before with the president, and upon its completion, immediately issued his statement to refute "any thought in the public mind that 'the Navy has done nothing about' the daring approach of Axis sea 'rattlesnakes' to United States shores . . . [giving] assurance that 'appropriate counter measures' have been taken."[27] Americans indeed had been wondering, since December 7, about the U.S. Navy.

Citizens had heard about the exploits of the army and the marines and the daring deeds of Army Air Corps pilots and the American volunteers with the RAF and the Chinese, but little about the navy. Indeed, this announcement by the navy was the first official acknowledgment of any sea action whatsoever against "sub-surface fight craft."[28] The storyline was that FDR wanted to keep the Germans guessing, since they were still sinking American commercial ships with impunity, but now it seemed clear the greater worry was the morale of the American people. Of course, no details involving ships or complements were released. Knox hinted also that the "silent service" was engaged in the battle for the Philippines and the navy was taking steps to deal with the enemy subs running amuck on the West Coast. But they would have their hands full.

"Activity of Jap undersea boats near the Pacific coast, coupled with a stepped up assault on the Philippine Islands, led to the belief the enemy in the West has thrown out a submarine screen to prevent reinforcement of hard-pressed United States forces in the Pacific."[29]

The Japanese claimed they had sunk nine Allied submarines and had taken prisoner an untold number of Dutch, American, and British officers.[30]

The War Department estimated that Tokyo had as many as forty submarines that could reach the West Coast of America from their home waters. At least half the Japanese submariner fleet, Congress was told, was capable of distances in the neighborhood of 14,000 to 18,000 miles, without refueling. The distance from Seattle to Yokohama Bay was just over four thousand miles. This gave the Japanese navy a considerable cushion to do the maximum damage along the American West Coast. And if they refueled along the way in the Marshall or Caroline Islands, they could patrol the West Coast even longer.[31]

Some were also capable of laying up to sixty floating mines. The Japanese sub fleet was brand new, with not one submersible older than three years. On the surface, they made twenty knots, giving them plenty of speed to catch up to tankers and cargo ships.[32]

The situation in the Philippines was desperate. Douglas MacArthur was now facing an all-out invasion of the main island of Luzon. The Japanese were all in, committing somewhere between 80,000–100,000 troops to the invasion. At least eighty troop transports were landing on the island, only 150 miles from Manila. Whereas MacArthur had once been confident of fighting off the invading Japanese, a spokesman could only say the American and Filipino soldiers were "behaving well."[33] The *Washington Post* put the best light on the situation, saying, "General Douglas MacArthur's headquarters has anticipated an attempted landing in force there and preparations have long been completed to meet just such an eventuality."[34]

The Japanese bombed the hometown of Philippine president Manuel Quezon, which was bad enough. His town of Baler was obscure, inland, was considered an "open city," and the only reason to bomb it would be to undermine Filipino morale. But Japanese troops also encountered a busload of young girls and boys who were students at the University of Manila trying to get to their home province of Batangas. The bus driver and the boys rushed forward to defend the girls and were machine-gunned down. The Japanese soldiers then "mistreated" the girls. "The whole community . . . relatives of the students, is reported to be infuriated while word of the outrage is spreading throughout the province."[35]

A *Time* correspondent on the scene filed this report. "Manila this evening was very tense . . . smoldering fires started in the noontime raid . . . Civilians are assuming wartime posts of censorships, patrols, evacuating, bandage-making . . . Talking to already stubble-bearded, grimy Yank soldiers at undisclosed posts: 'I'd like another crack at those low-flying bastards. Write my mother I'm a hero. I'll stay here. I'll stick it out' . . . Night sounds: howling dogs, shouts from sentries, douse that cigarette, turn off those lights, shrill police whistles . . . the babble of Filipino and American voices. . . ."[36]

In Hong Kong, the British "Tommies" were holding on by the skin of their teeth. The Japanese were carrying out a furious campaign to destroy what was left of the British garrison, and the Allies' only hope was relief from the Chinese. The battle "raged across Happy Valley," ran one report with no obvious sense of irony. Artillery, aided by naval guns, shelled British shore batteries and fortifications. Japanese accounts said one after another British strong point was being reduced on the rock-bound island and that complete control was only a matter of time."[37] The Japanese had also bottled in 100 ships and as many as half had been sunk, including destroyers, gunboats, tankers and transports. King George VI sent a message to his men telling them "thoughts of all at home [are] with you." A radio message crackled back, "organized resistance continues . . . heavy fighting." The Union Jack was still flying over parts of Hong Kong but "the defenders" were "doomed" to a "certain death or war-long captivity."[38]

The story was somewhat better in Singapore, where the British were mounting a counteroffensive after first retreating forty-five miles to regroup. "British forces, drawn up on a new line across the Malay peninsula about 300 miles north of Singapore, were reported today to have smashed heavily at Japanese forces gathering. . . ."[39] The Allies needed to hold on to Singapore and were throwing everything into the fight.

For their part, the U.S. Marines were still holding on to Wake Island, still repelling the Japanese. U.S. relief ships had been repelled by the Japanese, but the marines kept fighting. "The valiant chapter in the history of warfare being written by a handful of United States marines on Wake Island in the Pacific yesterday gained another few lines. Isolated and alone, beyond the possibility of immediate help, dependent on what food and ammunition they have with them, this little force yesterday still held out after two weeks of constant attack."[40]

The day before, Wake had been hit two more times by bombing planes. And still it held on. So too did Midway, apparently.

A small Associated Press story moved on the wires, though many papers chose not to run it. But the *Birmingham News* did print it under the head-line, "Nazis Execute 5 Jews in Occupied France." The story, as picked up from Vichy Radio, said the executions were punishment for "renewed attacks" on the German military.[41]

There was an air of desperation blowing in Berlin. For the first time in years, there would be no Christmas furloughs for the German army. Every man was ordered to stay at his post. They were also dealing with a huge out-break of typhus among their troops in Russia, as well as their faltering mili-tary campaigns in Libya and Russia.

Illustrating how tenuous their positions had become on the Eastern Front and in North Africa, Berlin began pulling troops out of Norway and reassign-ing them to the two battle zones. Norway had been occupied by Germany, though the Norwegians were a courageous people with an active underground working to trip up the Germans. Crown Prince Olav was a thorn in the side of the Germans but they dared not execute him. He was hugely popular, in part because of his frank way of speaking. He wanted to join the Allies and declare war on Japan but lamented, "We can't get a parliament together to do it."[42]

Hitler fired his top military commander and took over direction of the German army personally, after telling the German people he did so because of an "inner call."[43] In light of his stunning early successes, Hitler fancied himself a military genius. However, even though his bold gambles had paid off in the beginning of the war, he was a mediocre military strategist whose stubbornness paved the way for many colossal blunders, as would soon become apparent. But he was riding high in 1941, and no German officer dared oppose him—yet.

The Monor family of Ft. Myers, Florida, got an unexpected Christmas gift. Previously notified by the War Department that their son, Kenneth, had been killed at Pearl Harbor, they received another notice—this one saying that the telegram was in error and their boy was alive after all.[44]

The news was not the same in other homes. In Humboldt, Tennessee, Mr. and Mrs. V. A. Kennington learned of their double loss at Pearl Harbor, sons Cecil, 21, and Milton, 20. When informed by the navy, Mr. Kennington said, "I have four more sons. I will give them all and I, too, would fight to put down such sneaking and deadly enemies as the Japs, Hitler and Mussolini." The family had already lost their eldest son fighting "in the first World War."[45]

The Barber family in New London, Wisconsin, received the terrible news in triplicate. The three eldest sons, Malcolm, 22, LeRoy, 21 and Randolph, 19, had all been aboard the *Oklahoma*, serving as firemen. Just hours before attending services at the Most Precious Blood Catholic Church, Mr. and Mrs. Peter Barber received the horrible report. All three of their boys died in the attack. The family priest, Fr. Raymond Fox, announced the news to the stunned congregation. "I am glad they died like men and could give their lives for their country," said Peter, their dad. The parents told of how their sons had asked the navy to serve together and how in Hawaii they had met the actor and singer Gene Autry, who then hosted the three in his home in California when the Barber boys had received a furlough. Mr. and Mrs. Barber still had two sons left at home, aged 16 and 9, and the father said, "When their brothers are old enough, I am sure they will avenge their deaths."[46]

Their church planned a requiem high mass for the lost sons of New London.

Revenge was also on the mind of Fletcher Lindsay, 20, of Alabama. His big brother James, 23, had been killed on the *Arizona*. The young man walked into a navy recruiting office in Mobile and signed up only twelve hours after finding out his brother was dead. Fletcher's mother signed his papers without hesitation. Bereaved and angry brothers all over America were swearing revenge.[47]

Lou Boudreau received an early Christmas gift when he was appointed manager of the Cleveland Indians. This made the shortstop the youngest manager in the history of major league baseball.

The day also marked the sixty-second birthday of Josef Stalin. Two years earlier, when they were uneasy allies, Hitler had sent "Uncle Joe" a birthday greeting. "Accept my most sincere congratulations on your sixtieth birthday, my best wishes for your personal wellbeing and a happy future for the Soviet people."[48] That was before Hitler invaded his country, an act which tended to put a damper on friendships of convenience and strategic alliances. The strange fact was, the incessantly suspicious Stalin had actually trusted the German dictator. Stalin was genuinely shocked when Hitler violated their nonaggression pact and sent his Panzers rolling toward Moscow. The rest of the world was less surprised.

Not everybody in America was interested in home and hearth for the holidays. Many liked to travel, and though cruises to South America were still available, the seas seemed uncertain to many and travel and touring closer to home was becoming more attractive by the minute. The government of Alabama took out big ads in the *New York Times* "inviting Winter tourists to visit Alabama on the trips South. The ad advised travelers to take time to see Alabama's giant power dams, huge defense industries, army camps, surging cities, stately ante-bellum homes, cotton fields, fine herds of cattle, historic scenes of the Civil War and glorious azaleas of Mobile."[49]

Congress was looking at a national sales tax as a means of raising even more revenue for the war. It was proposed as an alternative to the "so-called withholding tax which the Treasury suggested for consideration a few weeks ago and which employers would be required to deduct from workers' pay checks."[50]

A national sales tax was seen as a "less painful" way to collect new revenue. A Republican member of the House, Bertrand Gearhart of California, touted the sales tax and believed it "would lose much of its 'bugaboo' when contrast with such proposals as the 15 percent withholding tax being proposed by Secretary of the Treasury Morgenthau." Others fretted that the sales tax would adversely affect those "least able to pay," while others argued for increasing the excess profits tax on corporations.[51]

More and more evidence of the effects of the war appeared in the daily lives of the American people. At first they were told there would be plenty of food, then that story changed, and then it changed again. Now the government advised exactly what foods they should stock in their pantries. Government nutritionists recommended the following: sixteen cans of evaporated milk, cans of beans, cans of corn, cans of "meat or fish," cans of peas, cans of tomatoes, cans of sauerkraut, cans of luncheon meat, cans of salmon, cans of sardines, cans of tomato juice, cans of grapefruit juice, soda crackers, whole wheat crackers, sixteen bars of chocolate, chocolate syrup, sugar, jam, coffee, peanut butter, tea, and "one pound of prunes."[52]

Women were advised that while there was not a foreseeable shortage of gloves, they should engage in "wise buying."[53] Doctors were advising Americans of the healthfulness of whole milk. "For the adult, whole milk alone and without fortification can serve for complete nutrition for a long time," said Professor E. B. Hart of the University of Wisconsin. Of course, he advocated that if people tried to live by milk alone—for, say, six months—they might try "fortifying their diet with copper, iron and manganese."[54]

Just as the government warned people not to hoard sugar, Americans did precisely that, cleaning out stores in many parts of the nation. There appeared to be no shortage of booze, however. All sorts and manner were recommended to help with the holiday cheer. "What every woman wants to know about a man. . . . That he is adept in mixing holiday cheer . . . and equally considerate in choosing the whiskey he gives and serves his friends. Old Schenley."[55]

To get to the supermarket or department store or liquor store and stock up on groceries and milk and gloves and whiskey, the Goodyear Tire and Rubber Co. came out with the "War Tire." It was made from regenerated rubber. The idea behind it was to keep "the civilian wheel of America from coming to a stop."[56] The contrivance was flimsy and unreliable.

Goodyear was in danger of losing its rubber plantations in Sumatra, just across from Malaya, where the fierce fight for Singapore was raging on. The president of the Goodyear Company, P. W. Litchfield, told the American consumer his company could keep rolling out War Tires indefinitely as long as automobile operators did not drive "over 35 miles per hour."[57]

CHAPTER 23

THE TWENTY-THIRD
OF DECEMBER

"Churchill In Unity Talks At White House"

New York Times

"U.S. Ship Fired On Only Six Miles Off Pacific Coast"

Birmingham News

"Japs Land on Luzon"

Evening Star

"Japs Land on Wake Island"

Lethbridge Herald

In the low, backwater country around Orlando, Florida, a "cracker" hurried into a navy recruiting office, demanding an immediate haircut and shave for his excessively long locks and beard. The chief machinist mate who was in charge of recruiting inquired why he wanted it so badly and why now. "Well, I'll tell you. I been out huntin' and fishin' down on the St. Johns—kinda away from things. An' by doggo, I just found out them danged Japs is a-fighin' us."[1]

The people pushing into the ranks of the U.S. military came from all walks and ways: oldsters, youngsters, blue collar, white collar, Sun Belt, Farm

Belt, Bible Belt, Mid-West, Mid-Atlantic, West Coast, East Coast, Gulf Coast, Confederates, Yankees, city slickers, country boys, black men, white men, Hispanic men, Asian men, fathers, sons, grandfathers, and even a few elected officials. The army said over 28,000 men had enlisted in the first two weeks after December 7.[2] Of course, some women wanted to go and fight too.

"Although the Army has called most of the lieutenants, captains and majors in the . . . Field Artillery Reserves to active duty, for the present at least it does not need its commanding officer, Col. Harry S. Truman, junior Senator from Missouri, and his confidential aide, Lieut. Harry Vaughan, it was learned yesterday." As it turned out, Truman and Vaughan had been berating the War Department for days to put them into active duty. "They volunteered to serve as soon as this war was declared, but were told that they have a more useful function to fulfill as Senator and Senator's aide."[3] Truman was then fifty-seven years old, only two years younger than FDR.

With all the men pouring into the lists, they were draining the work pool. The male labor shortage was such that the owner of a large cab company in San Diego complained that with all the men either going into war industries or enlisting, he might be forced to hire women to drive his taxis. He "petitioned the City Council for 'chauffeurette' licenses."[4] A New York legislator was advocating the full use of the thousands of prisoners in the state penitentiaries to be mobilized to make up the country's labor shortage.[5]

The day after the NFL championship—the most poorly attended in league history—the annual college draft began. Because of their records, the Pittsburgh Steelers and the Washington Redskins went first. The Redskins drafted Bill DeCorrevont of Northwestern and the Steelers took Bill Dudley of Virginia. Dudley went on to a Hall of Fame career as a star running back in the forties and fifties. DeCorrevont—in four seasons for the Redskins, Chicago Cardinals, Chicago Bears, and Detroit Lions—rushed 75 times for 233 yards and a 3.1 yard-per-carry average, fumbling on eight occasions, which meant he gave up the ball over 10 percent of the time. At quarterback, he threw for 155 yards, tossing ten interceptions and only three touchdown passes, completing just 42 percent of his passes. DeCorrevont went into the rug-cleaning business in Chicago after his less-than-illustrious pro-football career. At the end of his career and with little left to give the game, Dudley finished his remaining days with the Redskins.[6]

FDR was more astute in his draft choices than the Redskins. He nominated, for U.S. attorney for Northern Ohio, Don Miller, who in a previous incarnation had been one of the famous "Four Horsemen" of the great Notre Dame teams coached by Knute Rockne.[7] At 5:00 p.m. that day, FDR again had cocktails in the Red Room with Eleanor and some guests.[8]

In the battle of wills, the U.S. Patent Office stared down the FDR White House, so rather than moving to New York, a frantic search was on to find suitable office space elsewhere in Washington or even in suburban Virginia, or at last resort, as far south as Richmond.

The government agency, like all the others, came to the battle well-armed and well-flacked. Of the 153 government bureaucracies in Washington, all told, they had nearly 35,000 "press agents" ready to do battle to trumpet their good works, protect their fiefdoms and live and die by their code: the first rule of the bureaucracy is to protect the bureaucracy. "They agree on one point— the value of the work they describe and the indispensability of the agency engaged in it," sniffed the *Birmingham News*.[9]

Roosevelt's Labor-Business conference was still deadlocked over the issue of the closed shop and a war-long no-strike pledge. The union and corporate bureaucracies had been at loggerheads for days with no resolution in sight.

Gossip columnist and Roosevelt acolyte Walter Winchell was still pushing the rumor that Charles Lindbergh and his wife, Anne Morrow Lindbergh, were headed for a divorce. Why? Because she'd been spotted dining with her mother, sans husband Lindbergh. In his characteristically snide manner, Winchell referred to the aviator as "the Lone Dodo."[10] In Winchell's mind, anyone who ran afoul of him wasn't merely an opponent—they were an enemy who had to be destroyed. Winchell was a supporter of FDR and his policies; after the war, the hugely influential opinion-maker would sing a different and considerably darker tune, embracing the McCarthyism of the day to smear many of his former Democratic friends as communists, homosexuals, and spies. Winchell always trimmed his sails to the prevailing winds. In 1941, he tacked toward the winds of war.

The heroine of the South, Margaret Mitchell, authoress of *Gone with the Wind*, journeyed above the Mason-Dixon line to attend the launching of the USS *Atlanta*, a new cruiser. Garbed in a Red Cross uniform, photographed at the Brookwood station, she looked happy for the entire world to see, though she was painfully shy.[11]

Incredibly, yet another American tanker was fired upon—and sunk—off the California coast. The 400-foot-long *Montebello* went to the bottom, though four life boats did make it to shore, but not before they too were fired upon by the submarine. The seamen cursed and yelled at the sub, wishing for their own weapons. "Sherriff Murray C. Hathaway said longboats and fishing craft trying to rescued [sic] survivors from the *Montebello* were [also] shelled and fired on by machine guns from the attacking craft."[12]

Another American ship, the *Larry Doheny*, was fired upon as well, though not sunk. "It was the eighth submarine attack on American freighters and tankers in nearby Pacific waters since opening of the war with Japan."[13] Overnight, people along the coast around Morro Bay and Estero Bay heard loud gunfire and explosions.[14]

Americans were getting jumpy, and rightly so. An American freighter was making for San Diego under full steam, bellowing a thick trail of black smoke out of her stack. Thinking a naval battle was underway, nervous residents along the West Coast called the police and other officials.[15]

The dribble of announcements of the dead or missing from Pearl Harbor and other battle scenes became a torrent. In San Diego, four young men, all city natives, were revealed to have been killed.[16] In Alabama, a seaman in his forties who had been called back to active duty in August of 1940 was missing in action.[17] In Los Angeles, the first of many of the sons of the city, Lieutenant Commander Charles Michael, who'd been lost on the *Utah*, was announced as among the dead.[18] Then two sons of an employee of the *Los Angeles Times*, Wesley Heidt, 24, and Edward J. (Bud) Heidt, 25, both firemen–first class on the *Arizona*, were both reported missing.[19]

As part of a campaign to buck up American morale, the War Department made available some of the survivors of the attack on Pearl Harbor to give their firsthand accounts of what happened. "Graphic first-hand narratives of what happened at Pearl Harbor December 7 [were] told with dramatic coolness today by three naval officers who had leading parts in the titanic defense of giant warships against a sky full of Japanese planes that pounced on them suddenly 'from out of nowhere.'" They told of the attacks, heroism, and tragedy. "During the early morning attack a marine said to an officer, 'Pull this piece of metal out of my back.' It was a bomb splinter so hot the officer had to use a rag to remove it. The wounded marine returned to his machine gun and remained on duty until late that afternoon."[20] There were hundreds of such tales of can-do Americanism. This was the first of such revelations about the attack, though Washington officials were still guarded about the extent of the damage.[21]

Another story from CBS radio told of Lt. Walter Cross, an Army Air Corps pilot whose aircraft had been hit by enemy planes. Cross bailed and hit the silk, as Japanese planes buzzed around him, taking turns shooting at him as he floated helplessly to earth. Miraculously, they failed to hit him, "and his only injury was a pair of blistered feet in an eight-day hike back to Manila through mountainous terrain inhabited only [by] savage tribesmen."[22]

Another pilot found himself in a similar situation. As he floated to the ground, natives waited. They were going to tear him to shreds. Their village had already been bombed by the Japanese, and to them all airplanes and pilots were alike. That's when the American flyer doffed his airman's cap. "This intruder definitely was not a Japanese—he had a shock of flaming red hair."[23]

By now America thought it was immune to surprise. Who should show up for breakfast the morning of the twenty-third, but British prime minister Winston Churchill!

Only a handful knew of his and FDR's plans to meet in Washington and nary a word of it leaked out. Some reporters intimated that they knew in advance but that such reporting was now verboten and writing about it before the prime minister completed his sojourn could get them into a lot of hot water. He'd actually arrived late Monday and went directly to the White House, getting there around 5:40 p.m.[24]

A brief statement was issued: "The British prime minister has arrived in the United States to discuss with the president all questions relevant to the concerted war effort. Mr. Churchill is accompanied by Lord Beaverbrook and a technical staff."[25] They had many things to discuss, large and small, from the size of the Allied army to how to handle Ireland and how to convince the Irish to allow Allied sub bases there. They would later be joined by Canadian prime minister Mackenzie King. The Nazis believed Churchill had left London and suspected he was headed for conferences in the Middle East, but did not rule out Moscow or Washington.[26]

White House press secretary Steve Early knew, of course, but could not tell the press or confirm or deny that the historic meeting was forthcoming. Only until an announcement was made in Great Britain could he go ahead and tell the press corps. "Early's desk will never look the same. In the scramble for mimeographed statements a lamp was knocked over, a porcelain donkey was broken, gadgets and knickknacks were jumbled." The *Boston Globe* noted, "Three days before the birth anniversary of the Prince of Peace two great leaders were deep in discussion of war."[27]

It was the second time in six months that Roosevelt and Churchill had met, but this time Churchill was already in the White House, deep in conversation over drinks and dinner with Roosevelt before the Americans knew "Winnie" was in the country. Their first meeting was aboard the HMS *Prince of Wales* in August of 1941, when they devised the Atlantic Charter. Churchill's mother, Jennie Jerome, had been born in America and in later years visited the United States four times: the first in 1890, the second at the invitation of Mark Twain in 1900, and again in 1929 and 1931 on lecture tours.

FDR set an "all hands" conference for the next day at 6:00 p.m. On Tuesday, top brass and civilian leadership were to meet with the Prime Minister and the eighty political and military experts who had accompanied him on his boat trip across the Atlantic. Churchill's presence in the United States was a tonic to the country's morale and to FDR's morale.

Roosevelt so looked forward to seeing Churchill, he went by car to an unidentified nearby airport to meet his friend as he flew into Washington. Churchill arrived in a navy-blue "pea jacket" and "dark yachting cap." The uniform was that of the Trinity House Lighthouse Service, "a semi-governmental organization concerned with life-saving and the operation of lighthouses."[28] In his hand, he carried a cane, equipped with a flashlight for blackouts. Roosevelt was in a gray double-breasted business suit whose pant legs, while cuffed, appeared too long. The snap brim of his fedora was turned up, befitting the style of the obliging nobles of the era. "The car slipped in through the gates of the southgrounds, then rolled up at the entrance looking out across the still-green lawn and to the towering Washington monument in the distance."[29]

Churchill's trip—which had been his idea—had been risky to say the least. He'd boarded a blacked-out train in London, then made a crossing over the war-torn Atlantic to Massachusetts, and then took a flight into Washington. It took a number of days to complete and rumors floated around London and Washington as to his whereabouts. "The White House would neither confirm nor deny the reports, but issued warnings of the possible grave consequences of speculation or mention of the subject in any way."[30] Despite the arduous journey, Churchill looked in good health.

Upon his arrival at the White House, the two men posed briefly for photographs and Churchill hid his cigar for a moment. FDR was using his leg braces, a cane in his right hand, and his left hand was gripped on the arm of White House naval attaché Captain John R. Beardall.[31] "The sheer drama of the meeting on American soil ... should have salutary psychological reactions...."[32] Just over their heads were parts of the White House that had been painted over to cover the scorch marks made by the fire the British had set to the White House in the War of 1812, nearly burning it to the ground. Then, the two countries were bitter enemies. Now they were allies "forged" by a fire set in a different century.[33]

While waiting for Churchill to arrive, FDR had met that day with his fifth cousin, Teddy Roosevelt Jr., who was a brigadier general.[34] Most of the day, he was in the Oval Office, in one-on-one and small meetings with foreign dignitaries accompanied by Vice President Henry Wallace.

FDR also went through paperwork, including sending a memo to John Franklin Carter, responding to an obliquely circuitous memo in which "Jack" (which FDR called him) discussed at length their concerns about security in New York. Carter, between the lines, was suggesting the creation of an independent security force comprised of individuals "now debarred by reason of age, formal education . . . ." He had already identified some willing to help and said they did not lack for "funds or facilities. The individuals . . . seem to be able, intelligent and know what they are doing." He suggested to Roosevelt that in recruiting a certain kind of help in the New York area, what was needed was "a relaxation of red tape, especially at the moment when rapid expansion of functions and activities is essential."[35]

After darkness had covered Washington, FDR went to the south portico entrance, got into a car, and went to meet Mr. Churchill.[36] That evening, FDR and the British prime minister stayed up talking until 1 a.m.[37]

The next morning, the two world leaders, exhausted, slept in. "Both rose long after the White House staff was bustling with its duties of the day."[38]

The rest of that Tuesday brought more unwanted news. Japanese forces had finally made a landing on Wake Island after a dozen or more strikes against the marines and navy seamen. But there was no word from the G.I.s that they'd surrendered or that they were still fighting. "The invaders landed Tuesday morning, the navy said. Information was not immediately forthcoming whether the 'leatherneck' defenders were still resisting."[39]

The Japanese had also made yet another landing on Luzon, where the American forces were attempting to throw them back into the sea, and though the battered British garrison was holding on in Hong Kong, two top Canadian officers were killed there. Worse, the Japanese claimed they had taken over a thousand prisoners in Hong Kong. Many news reports on the situation in Hong Kong took note of the hour of the day, so as to keep a running story in perspective. It was reported that on Monday alone, "about 100 bombs fell on the island." The tenacious Brits, Indians, and Canadians had destroyed a bridge and two enemy ships.[40] If they were going down, they were going down fighting.

The Japanese had landed and taken Borneo, but found only burnt offerings left behind by the British. "Three men of the Royal Engineers said they began putting the torch to wells, pipe lines, pumping stations and refineries a few days after war broke out."[41]

The fighting on Luzon was described as "intense." Douglas MacArthur was issuing hopeful statements, still saying he had things "well in hand," but his tanks and artillery were more useful in fighting off the enemy surge.[42] Commanding the troops in the field under MacArthur was a capable man, Major General Jonathan M. Wainwright.[43] U.S. forces had reportedly sunk "47 Nipponese Troop Transports," which was welcome news. But Japanese planes had also bombed a civilian center on Luzon where many Filipino government officials were being housed. The Japanese had also landed a strong contingent at the Lingayen coast, some 150 miles north of Luzon, an apparent "pincer" move.[44]

In spite of his brave public statements, MacArthur was sending fraught telegrams to the War Department, pleading for reinforcements. "PURSUIT AND DIVE BOMBER REINFORCEMENT BY MEANS OF AIR-CRAFT CARRIER STOP PRESENT ENEMY ENCIRCLEMENT PERMITS INTERRUPTION OF FERRY ROUTE TO SOUTH DUE TO DAY BOMBARDMENT MINDANAO FIELDS STOP EARLY REINFORCEMENT BY CARRIER WOULD SOLVE PROBLEM STOP CAN I EXPECT ANYTHING ALONG THAT LINE . . . IN THIS GENERAL CONNECTION CAN YOU GIVE ME ANY INKLING OF STRATEGIC PLANS PACIFIC FLEET . . . MACARTHUR."[45]

Time magazine wryly observed, "The U. S. had been reacting to 'other people's' war. It was now in its own war."[46] Between Hawaii, Guam, Wake Island, the Philippines, the waters of the West Coast and Midway, America knew all too well. Guam hadn't been heard from since the tenth. The last message from the navy said, "Last attack centered at Agana. Civilians machine-gunned in streets. Two native wards of hospital and hospital compound machine-gunned. Building in which Japanese nationals are confined bombed."[47]

Curiously, even with all the action in the Pacific occupying the American forces and with so little action against Germany so far, the Gallup polling organization surveyed the American people and found that, by a whopping margin of 64 percent to 15 percent, they considered Germany to be the greater threat to America than Japan.[48] The poll results presaged what would become a continual source of tension and debate among American and British military leaders: which theater of war deserved the most attention, Europe or the Pacific? From the beginning of the global conflict until V-E day, the effort in Europe would take precedence. Despite the desperate lobbying of generals such as MacArthur, who wanted ever-more resources to combat the Japanese, the Nazis were always perceived by FDR and Churchill as the greater menace. Hitler would have to be dealt with, first and foremost. As early as December 1941, American opinion in this regard was influenced by the news of yet another sinking by the Germans, this time of the British carrier *Formidable*. The loss of the 23,000-ton ship had a devastating effect on the war effort and on public opinion.[49]

In Hong Kong, some of the fiercest fighting was taking place on the "broad playing fields of the Happy Valley recreation areas east of Victoria."[50] News reports of Hong Kong noted the upbeat tones of the British forces, even as the reports also called the soldiers there "beleaguered."[51] Some 20,000 British soldiers were fighting on, standing their ground while also defending "3,000 white women and children who remained [and] are now living in caves. . . ."[52] The Japanese had been blasting away at Hong Kong by plane and warship for days and now their troops were closing in on the desperately outnumbered Brits.

Some observers said the fall of Hong Kong would not be as devastating as the loss of Singapore. But in point of fact, Hong Kong was an excellent natural harbor, strategically important. "Japan gains a fine naval anchorage behind the fortified rocky island, a good airfield only 600 miles from Manila, and some shipbuilding facilities and three dry docks. . . . Hong Kong was the Gibraltar of the East and well named that."[53] From Hong Kong, the Japanese could intensify the fight south. Australia knew that if the Philippines fell and Malaya fell, it would only be a matter of time before the Japanese landed on their northern shores.

Churchill was becoming a beloved figure in America—described by the *Atlanta Constitution* as a "rotund little fighting premier"[54]—perhaps more popular in the land of his mother's birth than in the land of his father's birth. Indeed, some of his political adversaries held his mother's country of birth against him.[55] "Britain's ruling class still considers him brilliant, erratic, unsafe."[56]

His arrival in America was reported on widely and enthusiastically. He was an extrovert and a character, again like his mother, with a knack for tossing off the perfect bon mot. Once at a dinner party, he told his seat mate, "We are all worms. But I do believe that I am a glow-worm."[57]

He'd been up and down in British politics, and had changed parties several times; it was sometimes difficult to keep track of the state of his career. But beginning in the early 1930s, he saw the German military buildup and began to loudly protest it, despite the claims of the status quo in Parliament that he was wrong and that Hitler would abide by the Treaty of Versailles. Even as Hitler moved into other European countries, the British pooh-poohed it. They simply had no more stomach for war. After the Germans invaded Poland—with whom England had a mutual defense agreement—in September of 1939, the die was cast.

Churchill was a Renaissance man. A soldier, a statesman, a writer, and many other guises, he'd seen battles, both military and otherwise, including many political battles he'd started himself. After losing a seat in Parliament in 1923, he packed his troubles and his brushes and went to Egypt to paint scenery. He'd won medals in 1895, 1897, and in 1916 for helping the Spanish in Cuba; for his bravery in India; and for action in the Sudan, in the Boer Wars, and service on the Western Front. "Soldier, newspaper man, adventurer, lecturer, artist, bricklayer, politician and statesman, Churchill has served in more wars, held more offices and practiced more arts than any man of his time in the British Empire. In the middle of the last war, Churchill was a colonel in charge of a regiment. In a foxhole being shelled, he was urged to move on by a superior officer saying, 'I tell you, this is a very dangerous place.' Churchill replied, 'Yes sir, but after all this is a very dangerous world.'"[58]

The day before, Sunday, December 21, Roosevelt asked Americans to pray and declared that January 1, 1942, would be a national day of prayer. "We are confident in our devotion to country, in our love of freedom, in our inheritance of strength. But our strength, as the strength of all men everywhere, is of greater avail as God upholds us." He declared January 1 "a day of . . . asking forgiveness for our shortcomings of the past, of consecration to the tasks of the present, of asking God's help in days to come."[59] The proclamation was widely reported in the press without cynicism or rancor or question.

Unlike Woodrow Wilson, who canceled all his press conferences during the Great War, FDR was holding them on an almost daily basis now. From the night of the eighth, when he'd broadcast a national radio message to the country from the basement of the White House, already partially blacked out—where he'd invited reporters and photographers in—right up through the coming of Christmas and beyond, Roosevelt courted the press, seeing them as an important ally, unlike Wilson, whom the press turned on. "Mr. Roosevelt met the press, lectured them on what they might and might not print. He looked calm, rested, cheery and buoyant."[60]

Archbishop Francis J. Spellman was the military vicar of the United States. He gave a radio broadcast over the CBS radio network and in front of a live audience of three hundred military and civic leaders in New York at the National Catholic Community Service clubhouse. In this, his first speech as the military vicar, he asked the American people not to go on strike, but the speech went much, much further. It was a testament to the high moral plane upon which he believed America operated and the direness of the world situation. "What will it profit us, however, to emerge victorious over attacks from abroad if at the same time we do not preserve the ideals of democracy at home and their indispensable supports of religion and morality."[61]

Spellman had worked on the address for hours, poring over news clippings. At one point he quoted publisher Henry Luce. "The high resolve is yet to come . . . [I]t would be better to leave America in a heap of smoking stones than surrender it to the mechanized medievalism which is the Mikado, or to the Antichrist which is Hitler."[62] The speech was a magnificent testament to the "American Century" of the country's charity and selflessness, of its moral bearings, but also a warning to not lose its moral compass. Luce had coined the term, "American Century."[63]

Even with the surprise visit of Churchill and his huge entourage and all the comings and goings in the White House due to the war, it still promised to be a quiet Christmas for the Roosevelts. All four sons were now on active duty. "For the first time since the Roosevelts moved into the White House, there won't be a child or a grandchild home for Christmas."[64] Mrs. Roosevelt was busy, though. Because of her duties as assistant civilian defense director, she had meetings to attend and speeches to give. She also attended a "slum clearance project" where Christmas carols were sung. There, "a tiny Negro woman edged up to her . . . very elderly but very pert." She was introduced to Mrs. Roosevelt as "Betty Queen Anne." When her age of ninety-seven was mentioned to the First Lady, the elderly woman replied, "Lordy, I'm more dan dat." Betty claimed she had been a slave near Fredericksburg, Virginia.[65]

When Eleanor Roosevelt arrived back at the White House, a dinner had to be prepared for Churchill and his aides. She also hung a stocking in the Oval Office containing a bone for Fala, the family pooch.[66]

Before the meeting of the "War Council," Churchill and FDR sat together behind the president's untidy desk cluttered with keepsakes in the Oval Office and faced the journalists in an historic press conference, which lasted about half an hour.[67] The setting was described as "electric."[68]

Churchill pulled on his customary cigar, and the president smoked several Camel cigarettes, attached as always to his ivory cigarette holder clamped between his teeth. Roosevelt was in a gray suit and was still wearing the mourning band on his left arm for his mother. Churchill was in "formal striped trousers and a dark blue coat. He was wearing [a] polka-dot blue and white bow tie."[69] The New York Times said he stared "unperturbedly into space" as he waited for things to begin.[70] As always, Harry Hopkins was standing off to the side.

The reporters in the back could not see the two men, so Roosevelt asked Churchill to stand for a moment "while those in the crowded back rows could get a glimpse of him." Churchill, 67, immediately jumped to his feet but still could not be seen, so he clambered onto his chair "grinning broadly and waving his cigar."[71] The reporters applauded and cheered.

During the course of the press conference, the leaders said "the key to the whole conflict is the resolute manner in which the American and British democracies are going to throw themselves into this war." The Evening Star reported, "Pulling on his cigar from his mouth, [Churchill] smiled wryly then as he remarked that someday the Allied nations might wake up and find themselves short of Huns."[72] Asked about how long the war might take, the prime minister remarked that it would take twice as long if it were managed "badly." FDR and the reporters laughed. "The reporters hurled a barrage of questions—and soon found the prime minister adept in swift replies."[73] The prime minister was eloquent, and "displayed his marked gift for turning phrases—a gift which has made his speeches and writings literary achievements."[74]

Churchill also announced he would broadcast a Christmas Eve message to the American people the next day and said there was much to thank God for. Earlier, they'd met with State Department officials.[75] Roosevelt announced yet another new bureaucracy, this one the new Office of Defense Transportation.[76]

Following the press conference, reporters filed out and political and military aides filed in for a two-hour meeting. No real details were made public at the time, but the two men wanted to address "all questions related to the concerted war effort."[77]

What Roosevelt and Churchill had in mind was a "Victory Program" to create an Allied force of such magnitude it would simply roll over Axis opposition. They were talking in terms of producing 1,500 four-engine bombers a month, a Supreme Commander in the Far East (MacArthur was the popular and logical choice) as well as a Supreme Commander in Europe and a standing army of 20,000,000 men among all the Allied powers. They also divided the world into four war zones: "Europe[;] the Middle East and North Africa[;] The North Atlantic[;] and The Pacific and Far East."[78]

Speculation was rife that Hitler would mount a renewed offensive against Russia, or would invade England, or would invade Spain. There were also rumors of discord within his military command. The fact was that little was really known of what the next plans were for the Third Reich. Churchill had told war planners "that he looked for a new German offensive in some theatre to counter-balance the humiliating reverses in Russia. He mentioned a thrust towards the Mediterranean and an invasion of Britain . . . but said frankly that he did not know where it would come."[79]

Attending the "War Council" meeting were all the top administration officials, including the Secretary of War Henry Stimson, Secretary of State Cordell Hull, Chief of Naval Operations Harold Stark, Secretary of the Navy Frank Knox, the new commander in chief of the fleet, Admiral Ernest King, and as always, FDR's friend and confidant, Hopkins. Attending for the British were Sir Dudley Pound, admiral of the fleet; Sir Charles Portal, Air Chief Marshal; and Sir John Dill, Field Marshal.[80] The goal was straightforward: the eradication of Hitlerism from the world, as Roosevelt said. They saw Japan as an extension of Germany. "The matter of immediate urgency is, of course, the Battle of the Pacific...."[81] This was untrue.

A plan was coming together to accomplish total victory, though: "Worldwide strategy and worldwide supply leading to worldwide victory."[82]

FDR and Churchill had mutually decided that nothing less than unconditional surrender of the Axis scourge would be acceptable.

CHAPTER 24

THE TWENTY-FOURTH OF DECEMBER

"Californians See Sub Attack U.S. Ship"

Evening Star

"Wake Marines, Fighting to End, Sink Two Ships"

Washington Post

"Fall of Philippine Isles Inevitable Japanese Boast"

Birmingham News

Winston Churchill, FDR's guest in the White House, was surprised to find he was served not one but two eggs with his breakfast. All of Great Britain had been on a ration of one egg per day and to set an example, Churchill followed suit. "Mrs. Franklin D. Roosevelt confided today that the White House's distinguished guest had interrupted war conferences with President Roosevelt to eulogize his breakfasts—breakfasts of fruit juice, eggs, bacon, toast and coffee that are just routine in many American homes this side of the Atlantic." In addition to his solitary egg, the prime minister normally had only toast and tea. This was a gustatory moment, and he enthused about it "with boyish glee."[1]

The reviews were coming in for their performance the day before from the press and they were all favorable. "Two great statesmen-showmen, sharing the star parts in a world drama that will be read and studied for centuries to come, played a sparkling and unique scene at the White House yesterday. There was Roosevelt, debonair and facile as usual, and Churchill, jaunty and ruddy. Their audience was composed of 200 hand-picked Washington correspondents, described by Mr. Roosevelt as the 'wolves' of the American press, and including a score of foreign journalists."[2] It was a surreal scene, reporters milling about, letting their cigarette ashes fall to the floor.

Still, both men made it abundantly clear that the Allies were on the defensive and would be for a long time before they could engage in offensive operations and begin rolling back the Axis. "Mr. Churchill promised the utmost in defensive operations until such time as favorable conditions permit the beginning of a general offensive."[3]

His appearance was of some fascination to the media and the American public, as was often the case when someone met a person whom they had only known through photos and newsreels. "He has a pinkish complexion, blue eyes and a wisp of reddish-gray hair remaining on his nearly bald head. These features, plus a roundish countenance, give him a look that has been described as cherubic. There are times when he assumes an expression that has led his countrymen to hail him as the personification of Britain's bulldog courage. His mouth tightens into a straight line, his jaw hardens and his blue eyes flash." A reporter used the American slang "lick," which Churchill was not familiar with, but otherwise it had been a smashing performance.[4]

Christmas Eve promised to be a busy day for the president and the First Lady and their extraordinary guest, as well as all of official (and some of unofficial) Washington. It was also, as all knew, the busiest day of the year for a flying wonder of the world whose permanent home was someplace north of the Arctic Circle.

The good-natured Santa Claus planned to make a visit to Sing Sing, the notorious maximum-security prison in Ossining, New York, to give its hardened inmates talcum powder, safety razors, candy, clean white shirts, shaving cream, and tobacco." The 29 men in the death house awaiting execution would receive the same gifts—except for the razors."[5]

The navy suspended its annual custom of inviting poor children on board their ships because of the war but would still host parties for the children of its various posts.[6]

Mrs. Roosevelt's itinerary was crammed. In the morning there was the Central Union Mission, where twelve hundred children would be "entertained." At 12:30 p.m. she would speak to the Volunteers of America party, where some five hundred baskets would be distributed to the needy of Washington. Then there was the Salvation Army at 1:30; she was to hand out the first of the toys for poor children. Following that, she would participate in the lighting of the tree on the South Lawn at 4:30 p.m., after which Christmas carols would be sung. There was also the White House Christmas party to attend to, as well as her own family with a new grandbaby boy, courtesy of their son, Franklin Delano Roosevelt Jr.[7]

Roosevelt spent the day in meetings with Churchill. Much of the discussion centered on how to best allocate the resources of the other members of the Allied powers in combating the Axis. "The American and British experts in strategy working here together on the master-plan for the war against the Axis are fitting Russia and the other allies closely into their world-wide battle scheme...."[8]

They also went over a detailed memo analyzing the political state of the world, including relations between the Third Reich and the Arab World. "The Führer has always supported the Arab cause and deplored the vicissitudes suffered by the Arabs at the hands of the British and the Jews." The memo noted the "Mufti" had been given a place of honor on the occasion of the delivery of Hitler's speech of December 11."[9] From an intercepted Arab news report: "The Tripartite powers are fighting against the Anglo-Saxon plutocrats, the Jews and the Bolsheviks and are therefore fighting for the Arab cause."[10] This was temporary expediency on the part of the Nazis, of course. Little did the Arabs fathom Hitler's true contempt for what he regarded as their unclean, inferior race. In his mind, a German "solution" would come to the swarthy tribes of the Middle East, in good time.

FDR also reviewed piles of paperwork, including a memo from John Franklin "Jack" Carter, Roosevelt's personal aide, whose job it was to snoop around government bureaus and Washington and report exclusively back to the president. Carter generated a mound of confidential memos, all for Roosevelt's eyes alone. On the twenty-fourth, Carter asked FDR to give him a letter, which he could present to government bureaucrats to explain his "authority . . . to avoid embarrassment."[11] He also gave FDR a memo on security problems in the "Long Beach Naval Defensive Sea Area."[12]

Earlier that day, the White House announced that Churchill and Roosevelt would attend church together the next day at the Foundry Methodist Church for the 11:00 a.m. service. Security would be tight. Unless someone were a regular congregant or a member of the prime minister's entourage or the White House staff, or they held a special ticket, there was little chance of getting in. Special tickets were printed and had to be shown to get into the building. "Even cabinet members who have not obtained tickets will be barred by secret service men who will direct admission."[13]

Mrs. Roosevelt had sympathized earlier that day with Churchill, lamenting that he was "so far away from home on Christmas." He replied, "Holidays and work days are just the same. Until this war is over, there is nothing else but work that can be in our minds."[14]

As far as the rest of the city, "The glad tidings of Christmas will be sung in the half-darkened streets of Washington this week, but the upsurge of the season's spirit already is expressed in excited announcements of events to be both gay and religious."[15] Charity seemed to be everywhere with no one high-hatting, at least for one day. Except, of course, for Hollywood.

Warner Brothers studios gave itself a gift as only the moguls of Tinsel Town knew how. Assuming it was a prime target for high-level enemy bombers, the studio built itself a bomb shelter to outdo all other bomb shelters. It was actually four cavernous underground havens, large enough to house thirty-five hundred employees. "The completed shelters are concrete basements, reinforced with sandbags, and equipped with hospital units, beds, water in gas-proof containers, kitchens and gas protection."[16] They also had access to ambulances, and "field telephones have been installed all over the lot."[17]

Whether champagne and bartenders were available in the plush shelters is uncertain. But one thing was certain: the immigrant Jews who invented the motion picture business and founded Hollywood saw World War II as their biggest chance yet to gain long-coveted legitimacy in American society. The war was an opportunity to banish their sense of being outsiders and to prove that they were loyal Americans. For their part, the Warners wired President Roosevelt that "personally we would like to do all in our power within the motion picture industry and by use of the talking screen to show the American people the worthiness of the cause for which the free peoples of Europe are making such tremendous sacrifices."[18] Patriotic pictures also were good box office.

In the nation's capital—as in the rest of the country—movie attendance, gift giving and other forms of consumer activity were up over the previous year. The department stores—especially in Washington—were jammed with last-minute shoppers. Nationwide, public school and parochial school kids were already out for Christmas break.

Even the "Ambassador Extraordinary and Plenipotentiary of His Majesty the Son of Heaven," Admiral Kichisaburo Nomura, put his pants on one leg at a time. This was also true with his underwear, which is why an attaché still at the Japanese Embassy in Washington went shopping for "drawers" for Nomura. The attaché was surrounded by a "brace of FBI agents." The day before, a Christmas tree had been spotted being delivered to the Embassy.[19] FDR had received a letter that very day from Generalissimo Chiang Kai-shek, expressing his gratitude to Roosevelt and explaining his idea for a "Supreme War Council" to effectively fight the Axis and, especially, the Japanese.[20]

The Germans were less celebratory of the Christmas season. In the town of Folkestone, England, in the Kentish Coastal District, as children sang Christmas carols in some of the towns that dotted the White Cliffs of Dover, huge explosions punctuated the tranquil evening. The Germans, with their big guns in France, were lobbing shells at the civilian targets, all the way to the South of England, some twenty-two miles across the English Channel. "The children's voices trembled, but they sang on while the explosions echoed along the cliffs of Dover."[21]

The RAF, possessed of more Christmas spirit than the Germans, suspended their bombings for Christmas Eve and Christmas Day.[22]

British radio intercepted a German message in which they announced completion of "intensive fortification works along the Atlantic coast of Europe" after eighteen months of labor. Miles and miles of reinforced batteries and "bombproof shelters for submarines [were] built and camouflage shelters erected for land troops." Ideally, they could be used for "a complete base and support for offensive operations against Britain." Also, the Germans noted the emplacements would not only give them an offensive capability but also "security against invasion of Europe."[23]

Two more commercial ships were attacked along the West Coast, one American and one Canadian. The *Absaroka* and the *Rosebank*—both freighters—had been torpedoed within an hour of each other. The *Absaroka* was apparently sinking, and all hands had abandoned ship. The attack was in the morning, and spectators on the shore could clearly see the attacking submarine on the surface. "Onlookers on shore watched as a crew of approximately 35 took to lifeboats."[24] The *Rosebank* had been thought to have been sunk but it was later learned it had limped back to a harbor.

The *President Harrison* had been in "Far East waters" when the war broke out and while many civilian liners made it through safely, the Japanese did capture this ship.[25] Packet boat service between Los Angeles and Catalina Island was suspended because of the repeated attacks.[26]

Another commercial ship, the *Lahaina*, had been torpedoed repeatedly by a Japanese sub on December 11, hitting the huge freighter as many as twelve times before it sank. Thirty of the crew made it into a lifeboat designed for seventeen men and then drifted for over twenty days—armed with only a makeshift sail and a single compass. They finally washed up on the shore at Maui, where they were first mistaken for invaders. A couple of the men had died at sea from exposure, though their tiny boat was well-supplied with vegetables and fruits.[27] For these men to wash up on a speck of an island in the middle of the enormous Pacific had to be considered a Christmas miracle.

Navy officials had not heard from Wake Island for more than a day and conceded it had probably been lost to the Japanese. The navy would only say that "an enemy force effected a landing on Wake Island the morning of the 23rd."[28] The fourteen-day battle by the U.S. Marines was the stuff of legends. Commanded by Major James P. S. Devereux, the garrison had no more than 385 men on three little islands not much bigger than the campus of a small university. Together, the three totaled some 2,600 acres. Devereux only had twelve fighter planes at his disposal and a "small quantity of weapons."[29] He had some anti-aircraft guns also, but that was about it.

One of the last reports from Wake was they had managed to sink two more Japanese ships before apparently succumbing to the invaders. The enemy had already claimed they had conquered the territory and conceded that they'd lost two ships.[30] The Japanese may have been aided by the cover of a dark and stormy Monday evening.

All knew the garrison could not hold on indefinitely, but still the loss was yet another blow. A small amount of solace could be taken in the moral victory that the marines had held on so long and that they had taken so many Japanese men and so much materiel down with them, but the United States already had plenty of moral victories. It was time for some real victories.

The navy issued a one-sentence statement: "Radio communication with Wake Island has been severed."[31] The Japanese had also restarted their shelling of Palmyra Island and Johnston Island.

The British were in no better shape in Hong Kong but were fighting just as valiantly as the American marines. The attempts by the Chinese to relieve the British troops had not come. As far as London knew, the Chinese contingent was too small and too far away to be of much good to the struggling and dug-in Brits, Indians, and Canadians in the "crown colony." They were given "little chance of holding out unless aid could be gotten through to them."[32] "The hopelessly outnumbered defenders . . . were losing heavily, and the situation was acknowledged to be critical."[33]

On the Malayan Peninsula, the British seemed to have regrouped and had, it appeared, slowed the Japanese drive toward Singapore.

The Dutch in the Western Pacific knew something about real victories. So far, they had sunk one Japanese ship per day on average with their fighter and bomber planes. The Dutch government announced that "the Japanese, in retaliation, had bombed and machine-gunned outlying Netherland islands, inflicting civilian casualties."[34]

In the Philippines, the situation was worsening quickly. Overnight, the Japanese had landed more men "in heavy numbers." They were also bringing tanks ashore now. General MacArthur's forces were now outnumbered, and in at least four areas on Luzon murderous fighting was going on. "Enemy airplanes have been particularly active in supporting landing and shore operations."[35] Air raids had become a commonplace occurrence and the Japanese bombing campaigns had created numerous fires near Ft. McKinley. "The enemy is exerting 'great pressure,' an army spokesman said of the Lingayen battle."[36]

The islands were impossible to defend, especially with the relatively small army MacArthur had at his disposal. He'd estimated that he needed at least 500,000 men to adequately defend the country, and he had far less than that, even with the Filipino troops at his disposal. "With the Philippine defenders said to be outnumbered and hard pressed north and south of the capital, the War Department announced the appearance of enemy troop ships off Batangas on the southern tip of Luzon Island, about 65 miles southwest of Manila."[37] The Japanese propagandists claimed they had complete dominion over all aspects of the battle for the Philippines.

The department also announced the first seventy-five recipients of the Distinguished Flying Cross, some awarded posthumously, including Captain Colin P. Kelly, whose saga of his heroic actions against a Japanese ship, and who died in the line of duty had, like the marines on Wake, become the stuff of folklore. Possibly one pilot who deserved the DFC was Lt. Hewitt Wheless, whose B-17 bomber was attacked by no less than eighteen Japanese Zeros, hitting the plane fifteen hundred times yet not bringing it down. "When we got back, the plane looked like a sieve," the calm lieutenant said. "But the holes just gave us more fresh air inside. These babies (the Flying Fortress) sure live up to their reputations."[38]

The award, which had been authorized by Congress in 1926, was for anybody in the Air Corps who had "distinguished himself by heroism or extraordinary achievement in an aerial flight." The seventy-five recipients were not just those who piloted the planes, but those who attended to them as well.[39] Master sergeants, staff sergeants, corporals, and privates were among the awardees.

The sports writers of the Associated Press voted the Cleveland Indians the biggest disappointment of 1941. The year before, they'd missed the American League pennant by the skin of their teeth, by just one game, and the Yankees took it. In 1941, the Indians finished twenty-six games out of first place. The best fight of the year was voted the Joe Louis and Billy Conn fight. The worst fight of the year was voted the Joe Louis and Lou Nova fight.[40]

Box office star Mickey Rooney, 21, and the unknown aspiring secretary, Ava Gardner, 17, announced their commitment to life-long fidelity and matrimony.[41] The film industry was working with the government to ensure the government did not censor the film industry. "President Roosevelt has appointed Lowell Mellett, Director of the Office of Government Reports, as coordinator of Government films during the war emergency with the statement that he wants no censorship of motion pictures."[42]

The Southern Bell Telephone and Telegraph Company took out large newspaper ads pleading with readers not to make any long-distance phone calls on Christmas Day and New Year's Day and possibly jam the lines, when the government needed them.[43]

For the first time since December 7, the War Department had allowed journalists and photographers to inspect the damage done at Hickam Field. "Tattered skeletons of huge hangars at the army's Hickam Field stood Wednesday as gaunt evidence of the surprise Japanese attack on this placid pleasure spot, and in them lay . . . the twisted and charred wreckage of the many once-mighty guardians of Hawaiian skies . . . The baseball field was covered with bomb craters."[44] Most of the casualties at the field had occurred while men were still in their barracks, many still in bed. Some, as at Wheeler Field, never got off the ground. "American pilot casualties at Wheeler were . . .

two killed by strafers as they were taking off, and one as he was boarding his plane to attack."[45] They never had a chance.

The lion and the lamb settled down together and gave FDR and the country an unexpected Christmas gift. The business and labor conference, which just the day before had seemed at an impossible impasse, came to an historic agreement. Labor would agree to no strikes for the duration of the war if business agreed to no lockouts. Jaws dropped all over the country when the two old antagonists, labor and business, further agreed to settle all disputes by "peaceful means," including the matter of closed shops.[46] America was united in purpose; patriotism trumped even economic self-interest.

Congress had mostly fled the city for their home districts and home states, but a few members still remained, including some on the House Ways and Means Committee, who were trying to determine how to raise the massive funds needed to support the war effort. Some members "predicted the bill might bite huge chunks out of individual and corporation incomes. . . ."[47] An "unlimited tax" was under advisement. Setting an income cap for all Americans, after which the government would take everything, was bandied about. Other radical plans were also discussed including collecting tax in the actual tax year. But some members thought "it was premature to discuss suggestions that the 1942 tax bill be collected immediately on 1942 incomes. Federal taxes normally are collected in the year after which income is received."[48]

Marshal Pétain broadcast a gloomy Christmas message to the people of France, telling his conquered countrymen that peace was a long way off and that many families in France had already been separated by the Nazis, due to imprisonment.[49] Rumors were thick in political and diplomatic circles that the Germans were getting ready to push Pétain out of his feeble and emasculated position as head of the French Vichy government. The plan was to replace him with a new figurehead who was out-and-out pro-Nazi.[50]

Meanwhile, Pope Pius XII issued his annual Christmas Eve message from Vatican City in which he issued a Five-Point Plan for a post-war world. In a broadcast on Vatican Radio, Pope Pius XII called for the elimination of aggression, "oppression of minorities," against future wars and armaments and "persecution directed against religious sects or churches because faith 'is one of the rights of mankind.'"[51] His remarks were carried live in the United States on the Mutual Radio Network.[52]

That afternoon, as the sun dipped over the horizon, Churchill and FDR both addressed a crowd of twenty thousand on the South Lawn of the White House (attendance estimates varied widely) and the nation by radio, as the president flipped the switch to light the big Christmas tree. It was the first time the White House Christmas tree had ever actually been placed on the White House grounds. Previously, it had been on the Ellipse, Lafayette Park, or Sherman Square. The Marine Band played and the crowd sang Christmas songs just before the lights of the cedar tree were turned on. The songs included "Joy to the World" and "Silent Night." The band had played "God Save the King" and "The Star Spangled Banner," which, of course, commemorated the American success over Churchill's forebearers at the battle of Ft. McHenry in the War of 1812. The invocation was given by Father Joseph Corrigan of Catholic University.[53]

It was noted that some in the crowd had waited as much as a whole hour before being admitted through the Southwest and Southeast gates, which opened just after 4:00 p.m. and where army tents had been erected to check individuals. Because no packages or cameras were allowed on the grounds, they were lined up along the fencing to wait until their owners returned to claim them. Some women—called by the *Washington Post* the "indomitable species"—asked soldiers on duty to hold their packages but the men in uniforms refused, albeit politely.[54] After a time, the gates were closed and no one inside would be allowed out until the proceeding had been completed.

The weather had been unseasonably warm with daytime temperatures in the low sixties. "The sunset gun at Fort Myer boomed just before the two men walked onto the portico. A crescent moon hung overhead. To the southward loomed the Washington Monument, a red light burning in its lofty window."[55]

FDR and Churchill appeared on the south portico and both stood to give their remarks. "Over the traditional ceremony hung the pall of war, but there were signs of merriment and good cheer." At 5:00 p.m., their remarks were carried live across the nation on all radio networks. In his plummy aristocratic baritone, the Englishman opened by saying, "I have the honor to add a pendant to the necklace of that Christmas goodwill and kindness with which my illustrious friend the President has encircled the homes and families of the United States. . . ." He spoke eloquently of his home, of his mother's "ties of blood" to America, and "the commanding sentiment of comradeship in the common cause of great peoples who speak the same language, who kneel at the same altars, and to a very large extent pursue the same ideals. This is a strange Christmas eve. Almost the whole world is locked in a deadly struggle." He also spoke of the "terrible weapons which science can devise."[56] There was a marvelous rhythm to his remarks, and his cadence was mesmerizing. Churchill was a dynamic leader, but he also was a gifted writer and speaker.

Continuing, he said, "I cannot feel myself a stranger here in the center of the summit of these United States. I feel a sense of unity and fraternal association, which through all your kindness, convinces me that I have a right to sit at your fireside and share your Christmas joys."[57]

Churchill said to the gathering that the young across the globe "shall not be robbed of their inheritance or denied their right to live in a free and decent world." Concluding with a climactic poetic grace, in a way that only Churchill could, he intoned, "Here then, for one night only, each home throughout the English-speaking world should be a brightly lit island of happiness and peace . . . And so, in God's mercy, a Happy Christmas to you all."[58]

Roosevelt had spoken first and then introduced the British prime minister as one of the "great leaders" in the world. A newspaper noted that it may have been the only time FDR had "played second fiddle" to a superior public speaker. It was noted that the crowds were silent as Churchill spoke and "restless" when FDR addressed them.[59]

In his "Yule Message," Roosevelt's remarks were sprinkled heavily with reference to the war and sacrifice but also of hope and the Christian philosophy of love and charity. "The year 1941 has brought upon our Nation a war of aggression by powers dominated by arrogant rulers whose selfish purpose is to destroy free institutions . . . Our strongest weapon in this war is that

conviction of the dignity and brotherhood of man which Christmas signi-
fies—more than any other day or any other symbol."[60]

In his gracious and eloquent comments, he never mentioned Germany
or Japan by name, but made clear that the forces of the Allies represented the
forces of light and the Axis powers represented the forces of darkness. "The
new year of 1942 calls for the courage and the resolution of old and young to
help win a world struggle in order that we may preserve all we hold dear."[61]

Their remarks were broadcast live on radio, coast to coast. The Reverend
Oscar Blackwelder of the Washington Federation of Churches gave the benediction. The whole program, from the lighting of the tree, which had been
placed near the fence bordering the South Lawn, through the playing of the
bands and the speeches and remarks lasted but thirty-five minutes, just as
stars in the sky began to twinkle. Yet those in attendance knew they had seen
something special.

Roosevelt had also sent a Christmas message to the Armed Forces of
America, and if there was anyone who needed prayers at the time, it was the
boys and girls in blue and khaki:

> To the Army and Navy: In the crisis which confronts the Nation, our
> people have full faith in the steadfastness and the high devotion to duty
> demonstrated by the men of all ranks of our Army and Navy. You are set-
> ting an inspiring example for all the people, as you have done so often in the
> past. In sending my personal Christmas greeting to you I feel that I should
> add a special measure of gratitude to the admiration and affection which I
> have always felt and have expressed in other years. I am confident that dur-
> ing the year which lies before us you will triumph on all fronts against the
> forces of evil which are arrayed against us.
>
> Franklin D. Roosevelt, Commander in Chief.[62]

That evening, Churchill joined the Roosevelts for Christmas Eve dinner, where instead of the British favorite of goose, he dined on turkey and
cranberries.[63]

CHAPTER 25

THE TWENTY-FIFTH
OF DECEMBER

"Government and U.S. Forces May Leave Manila;
200,000 Japanese Estimated Landed on Luzon"

Washington Post

"Japs Claim Capture of Hong Kong"

Birmingham News

"Submarines Attack More U.S. Vessels"

Evening Star

"War Cast Shadow Over Christmas Joy Throughout Land"

New York Times

T he enemy was closing in on Douglas MacArthur from what seemed to be all sides. Enemy troops were coming ashore at Lamon Bay, near Manila, and at a half dozen other hard-to-pronounce but easy-to-understand locations. Ferocious ground fighting was everywhere and large armadas of transports filled with fresh Japanese troops ready to come ashore were reported south of Manila. No one in the American military had anticipated or prepared for this avalanche of enemy soldiers. They certainly hadn't been sighted.

Japanese planes had swarmed over Luzon most of the day and were deliberately bombing the business and civilian areas of the island. Discussions were held to consider declaring Manila an "open city" so as to halt the bombing. Brussels, Paris, Belgrade, and other cities had been declared in such a manner so as to save the lives of civilians while preserving the culture and architecture of those cities. The Quezon government fled the city.[1]

MacArthur was now facing possibly 200,000 Japanese fighting men who had landed on the island since the beginning of hostilities, and they were advancing quickly on American and Filipino strongholds. "Japanese hordes swarmed toward Manila from all directions today and this city was thrown into a supreme battle for its freedom on Christmas Day. . . ." A message the night before "told of heavy Japanese reinforcements lying off Luzon; at least 100 enemy transports accompanied by strong naval and air escort. . . ."[2]

The War Department issued a brutally frank statement. "Though American and Philippine troops are greatly outnumbered, they are offering stiff resistance to the Japanese forces in a series of delaying actions."[3] Delaying actions only meant to delay the inevitable. The number of War Department communiqués was going up, but American morale was going down.

Given the situation on the ground, the United States announced that it might have to withdraw its forces from the Philippines. That made it one of the lousiest Christmases for Franklin Roosevelt and the American citizenry in recent memory, certainly since 1777 and Valley Forge, in which the embers of a newborn nation were nearly snuffed out, or the Christmases of 1812 and 1813 or 1861 through 1863, again when those embers almost died.

There was an additional sense of loss and distress because of Wake Island. Post-mortems were filed in many papers, speculating on what happened to the surviving marines. "What became of the little garrison is not known."[4] The Japanese were not known for their charity toward prisoners of war. Profiles of the fearless commander, Major James Devereux, along with his wife and ten children began appearing in the press. Devereux was a career Marine and hailed from a family of military men.

Military leaders had wanted a base on Wake because it had a protected cove which they were dredging of coral heads and, once constructed and outfitted with oil tankers, runways, buildings, docks and the like, would be an excellent forward base of operations against the Japanese in the Pacific. It was a link in a chain from the West Coast to Hawaii to Midway to Wake to Guam to Manila. Now the chain was broken.

Just a few days earlier, no one in America knew Wake Island from Treasure Island. It was a dot in the middle of the vast Pacific and only became more widely known after Pan Am had erected a seaplane operation there a few years earlier. Human footprints were rarely found on the island. It was a strategic defeat in a young war in which America had yet to win anything. In relation to its small size, the island's loss was an outsized psychological blow to the morale of Americans, who knew the flag of the Rising Sun now flew over former U.S. territory. The defenders of Wake had held out two days longer than the defenders of the Alamo, a fact which the marines noted with solemn if disconsolate pride.

The tattered British garrison at Hong Kong finally succumbed to the Japanese as well, making this Christmas lousy for Winston Churchill and the British too. The Japanese government made the announcement of the British capitulation, and London did not deny the claim. Tokyo's propagandists twisted the knife when they announced on state radio that the island was a "Christmas gift" from the military to the Japanese people.[5] Of course, the Japanese were not Christian, but rather Shinto and Buddhist.

"The last-ditch defense of Hong Kong has broken under relentless assault by land, sea and air and the crown colony which for a century has been a British bastion off the southeast China coast has fallen to the Japanese. So ends a great fight against overwhelming odds," the British Colonial Office said.[6] By the early evening of the twenty-fifth, Japanese officials were meeting with the British governor of Hong Kong, Sir Mark Young, to discuss the terms of surrender and the disposition of civilians and combatants.[7]

A confidential memo from British ambassador Lord Halifax to Franklin Roosevelt spelled out the problems in Hong Kong. "During previous 24 hours enemy kept up incessant attacks and local raids accompanied by intensive bombardment by artillery mortars and dive bombers. Troops very tired." Halifax told FDR that water had been cut off, "food supplies greatly reduced by enemy action." The memo went on to review the world in the eyes of the British, and with the exception of Libya, it wasn't very pretty.[8]

Churchill was quickly becoming a popular boarder in the White House. He often got up early, as he was still on London time—five hours ahead—but he worked diligently and quietly, armed with an endless supply of Cuban cigars. Around 4:00 p.m., he would take a break and retire for a nap that would last an hour or two and then go back to work, often by transatlantic telephone or cable, until 1:00 a.m. "He has endeared himself to the White House staff with his sense of humor, his entertaining quips, and an amazing vitality and capacity for work."[9]

He was also without shame. As Jon Meacham noted in *Franklin and Winston*, "Churchill, fresh from his bath, was in his guest room at the White House, pacing about naked—'completely starkers,' recalled Patrick Kinna, a Churchill assistant who was taking dictation from the dripping prime minister. There was a tap at the door, and Churchill said, 'Come in.' Roosevelt then appeared and, seeing the nude Churchill, apologized and began to retreat. Stopping him, Churchill said, 'You see Mr. President, I have nothing to hide from you.' Roosevelt loved it.

"'Chuckling like a school boy, he told me about it later,' said presidential secretary Grace Tully. 'You know Grace . . . I just happened to think of it now. He's pink and white all over.'"[10]

Churchill went to church in the same car as Eleanor and Franklin Roosevelt. The prime minister was in a "dark blue topcoat" and carried a cane for the 11:00 a.m. service. Security was extremely tight and government agents and police were everywhere; only a few of the onlookers caught a glimpse of the two men. Many regular congregants had to stand outside of their own place of worship, the Foundry Methodist Church, unable to get in. FDR walked in holding a cane in one hand and the arm of his ever-present naval aide, Captain John Beardall, on the other. While in church, they were spotted singing out the carols, Churchill wearing his reading glasses and FDR with his trademark pince-nez eyewear.[11]

After the service, Churchill and Roosevelt spent much of the day in war planning. The White House let it leak out that Roosevelt was "too busy" to open his Christmas gifts but even the most ardent Rooseveltians had to roll their eyes at this too-obvious public relations ploy. "Although a day behind schedule, aides said he expected to find a spot during today's heavy engagement calendar to call Fala, his Scotty, and open their presents."[12]

The White House looked surreal that evening. Most windows had been shrouded in blackout fabric as seen from the south. No other lights appeared except those on the Christmas tree on the South Lawn and some ground lights that illuminated the South Portico.

Given the news of the day, Christmas dinner was somber, though the meal itself was sumptuous enough. The menu included oysters on the half shell, soup with sherry, roast turkey with chestnut dressing, giblet gravy, venison sausage, olives and fresh vegetables, sweet potato casserole, grapefruit salad, cheese crescents, plum pudding, cake and ice cream, and even bonbons.[13]

Churchill and the Roosevelts were joined by Harry Hopkins and his daughter, Diane, for the dinner, along with 60 guests, according to his schedule. It was followed by "movies and carols." That night, FDR and Churchill met alone in the prime minister's room for over an hour, past 1:00 a.m.[14] Hopkins's wife, Barbara, had died of cancer in 1937, and he and his daughter now lived in a suite in the private residence of the White House. Hopkins had three older sons, all of whom served in the military, including Stephen, a Marine, who was killed in the Pacific.

Following dinner the plan was to call friends and family members separated by the war. The Roosevelts were keen to speak with their far-flung sons. Via a transatlantic phone call, the prime minister's wife, Clementine, and their daughters "sent their greetings" to their father and husband.[15] Roosevelt also sent "Mrs. Churchill" a cablegram wishing her a Merry Christmas. "It is a joy to have Winston. He seems very well and I want you to know how grateful I am to you for letting him come. Franklin D. Roosevelt."[16] Clementine Churchill responded two days later, thanking the Roosevelts for their kindnesses, mentioning "how good you both have been" to her husband.[17] Roosevelt received a note from Lord Halifax conveying the Christmas wishes of "His Royal Highness the Duke of Kent: 'My very best wishes for Christmas and the New Year—George.'"[18]

Even with a world at war, Christmas was celebrated around the globe in some fashion or another, even as in many war zones and battlefields no truces had been called. The Philippines were, it was noted, "the only Christian Nation in [the] Orient."[19] A little girl there asked her mother if the Japanese would allow Santa Claus through. No packages for servicemen had made it through the Japanese blockade. Of course, no lights were allowed on to celebrate the day of enlightenment.[20]

"Lack of food and materials, the separation of families, the blackouts, and other restrictions reduced festivities in many lands."[21] Even so, pilgrims streamed into Bethlehem as bells pealed "amid the crags of the Judean Hills" to attend services at the Church of the Nativity, praying for peace on an earth that, as of December 25, had virtually no peace."Hundreds of pilgrims, among them uniformed Czechs, Polish, Greek, Yugloslav, Free French and British soldiers, stood outside the adjacent church of the Covenant of St. Catherine where the Latin patriarch, Msgr. Louis Barlassina, intoned the pontifical high mass accompanied by a Franciscan choir."[22] Bethlehem was celebrating a Christmas for those who prayed for peace more than anyone else, the soldiers.

The atheistic Soviets saw the propaganda value in Christmas. They distributed cards with the caption "Tannenbaum, Tannenbaum" complete with a "dead German soldier under a lighted, snow-laden Christmas tree." The newspaper of the Russian army, the *Red Star*, "published its own Christmas card. It portrayed Santa Claus giving Hitler a calendar opened at the date December 22. It said 'Congratulations Herr Führer! Today is just six months since the start of your six-week march on Moscow.'"[23]

In England, Brits went back to London to attend religious services in many bombed-out places of worship. They were warned that the Germans may attack at any time but returned nonetheless to their "shell-bruised churches." Worldwide, British subjects were celebrating Christmas Day as best they could. "In Africa the British troops who were pursuing the Axis legions westward in Libya had no time for Christmas celebrations, except for a hasty gulp of plundered Italian and German wines which they found on the way. Hundreds of cases of beer and other luxuries, however, were flown from Egypt to British units in the rear."[24]

Charity and kindness were rampant. Women made blankets for the elderly in nursing homes, gift packages were delivered to orphanages, and the vacant house of Oliver Wendell Holmes Jr., a justice of the Supreme Court, was opened as a home for girls who had come to Washington, desperate for work. "If a girl arrives in town without any place at all to go—as is often the case these days—she can find lodging" at the large house. Holmes had died in 1935, leaving his entire estate to the federal government. The house had been empty since his death but found a new purpose in giving safety and refuge to hundreds of homeless girls. At one point, the house on I Street NW had almost been a victim of the wrecking ball to make room for a parking lot.[25]

The *Evening Star*, NBC, and Warner Brothers studios gave out hundreds of gifts and meals for poor children, but as a matter of fact, all the newspapers across the country engaged in many forms of charity and not just at Christmas. Many, such as the "Jimmy Fund" in Boston, were boosted throughout the year.[26] CBS, the army, and the navy arranged for some children in America to talk with their fathers who were stationed in England.[27] In Baltimore, "65 Negro children patients" had a Christmas party with ice cream, cake, presents, and a visit from Santa Claus.[28]

At Long Beach, the navy put on a Christmas party for some 2,500 navy children, including some who had lost fathers at Pearl Harbor. It was "heart-rending," according to the *Los Angeles Times*.[29] The climax of the party was the appearance of the omnipresent Santa Claus. Indeed, St. Nick had made so many appearances so quickly and efficiently around the country, one might be forgiven for suspecting that there was more than one jolly fat man.

Treasury secretary Henry Morgenthau and his wife threw a party for the 125 soldiers who were permanently billeted at the Treasury Department since the beginning of the war. "The soldiers were given packs of gum, cigarettes, handkerchiefs, razors, candy and toiletries," recounted one report. But there were more festivities to come. "This afternoon, Treasury girl employees will dance with the soldiers in the corridors to the music of an orchestra provided by the Red Cross."[30]

In preparation for Christmas Day, the War Department ordered 1,500,000 pounds of turkey for the men who had not been granted a leave for Christmas. The Quartermaster Corps was preparing a lavish spread for the twelve thousand cafeterias and mess halls around the country.[31] Crowding their serving of turkey, the men had sage dressing, mashed potatoes and

Hubbard squash, buttered peas, soups, fruits, nuts, mince pie, ice cream, mints, and candy.[32]

It could be a sad and lonely time for those young men with loved ones and sweethearts far away and the military wanted to do what it could to help keep morale and spirits up. The halls were seasonably decked with holly, poinsettias, crepe paper, ribbons, and decorated Christmas trees. After dinner the boys were treated to "'an informal entertainment session' . . . with army songs and Christmas carols." To meet the spiritual needs of the men, army chapels featured special Christmas services.[33] All told, "[a] long list of dances, church services, carol 'sings,' open house programs and musicals are available to service men on Christmas leave. . . ."[34]

Christmas in Honolulu took on a serious and sober air of its own. Several days after the seventh, things had loosened a bit but now officials tightened things up even more. On guard to the point of paranoia about another surprise attack, officials imposed the strictest possible blackout measures and martial law was enforced, including a prohibition of all hard liquor. "Service men were not allowed to leave their posts and stations. Honolulu remained on the alert, not to be caught off guard again." Purchases of gas were restricted to 10 gallons per month and stores had to close by 3:30 so workers could be home by 4:00 p.m. Sightseeing was banned. A year before, Christmas in Hawaii had been a rollicking movable feast of fun, but this year, "many men were spending Christmas digging bomb shelters."[35]

The contents of the few Japanese planes shot down on December 7 were released for the first time to the American people. There was the usual propaganda material, as expected, including bad drawings of FDR. Yet also, "the planes were stocked with well-aged whisky, concentrated foodstuffs, cider, soda pop, candy, chocolate paste impregnated with whisky, hardtack, tooth powder and chopsticks."[36]

More importantly, the first casualities from Pearl Harbor who could be moved appeared by ship in San Francisco Bay on Christmas Day. "Ambulances moved away through the barricades while mothers stood in a steady rain, watching with hopeful eyes as the passengers emerged."[37] The name of the ship was not released for security reasons, but from Hawaii to California, it had to pursue a "zigzag" course to avoid possible torpedoes from enemy submarines. The Army Nursing Service put out an all-points-bulletin asking for volunteer women to step forward and help with the wounded.[38] All of the men had stories of bravery and death. They were, the *New York Times* noted, "Filled with cold anger at the Japanese. . . ."[39]

Because of the new restrictions on tin and the limitations on paper, Americans were asked to save their wrapping paper and take them to recycling centers. The Rogers Peet Company of New York, a men's clothier, suggested as Christmas gifts officers' uniforms for the army, navy, and Marine Corps.[40] Sealtest Ice Cream hosted a Christmas special radio show that featured the great actor Lionel Barrymore, reading *A Christmas Carol* to millions of listeners.[41]

The *Los Angeles Times* held their annual Christmas party for their more than 750 paperboys, complete with entertainment by Bob Hope.[42] The new movie, *The Maltese Falcon*, starring Humphrey Bogart and Mary Astor, had opened to favorable reviews, and the top box office draw for 1941 was Mickey Rooney, followed by Clark Gable, Judy Garland, and Spencer Tracy.[43] Another new movie debuted, *You're in the Army Now*, starring Phil Silvers, Jimmy Durante, and an up-and-coming comedic actress, Jane Wyman.[44] In 1941, every studio started churning out service comedies. In this offering from Warner Bros., Silvers and Durante played hapless vacuum-cleaner salesmen mistakenly inducted into the army; zany antics predictably and humorously ensued.

A memo was posted in the navy's headquarters in New York, warning the men to be careful of women spies. "Women are being employed by the enemy to secure information from navy men, on the theory they are less liable to be suspected than male spies. Beware of inquisitive women as well as prying men. See everything, hear everything, say nothing."[45]

The war dominated everything. Even as children had gone to bed the night before, thinking and hoping for gifts under the tree, "titanic world events cast their shadow over the spirit of the holiday throughout the land."[46]

For the first time, members of Congress were required to carry photo identification for security reasons to enter the U.S. Capitol, because, while the

Capitol Police recognized the members, the new soldiers guarding Capitol Hill did not.[47] The business of government went on despite the holiday. The Office of Price Administration announced price controls on shoes and many other leather products. The Office of Production Management put out a call for old flashlights, urging Americans to find their old ones before purchasing new ones. "Stubbed toes during blackouts can be averted," a Washington official averred.[48]

Yet another commercial freighter, the *Dorothy Phillips*, was torpedoed close to the California coastline. This time, however, American planes responded quickly and it appeared they nailed the enemy submarine. The army said a debris field had been spotted floating in the water.[49] The whole country was on a high state of alert, thinking the enemy would enjoy nothing more than to hit America again hard on December 25. "Extra precautions were taken throughout the country in all vital industries and installations lest there be a concerted enemy attempt to sabotage important facilities. On the Pacific Coast, the navy declared a 'double alert' against surprise attacks."[50] The army warned the governors of the Western states to be on the alert for "Fifth Columnist" activities.

The prime minister of Ireland, Eamon De Valera, gave a national radio broadcast in which he announced his decision to stay neutral and keep the Irish out of the war. "It is our duty to Ireland to try to keep out of war. And with God's help, we hope to succeed." He offered the Americans his "sympathies," but nothing more. He offered the British nothing.[51]

King George VI made a brilliant and moving Christmas radio broadcast speaking of the sacrifices of the British people and exhorting them to great efforts. "I am glad to think millions of people in all parts of the world are listening to me now . . . if skies before us are still dark and threatening there are stars to guide us on our way. Never did heroism shine more brightly than it does now, nor fortitude, nor sacrifice, nor sympathy, nor neighborly kindness. And with them, the brightest of all stars is our faith in God. These stars will we follow with his help until light shall shine and darkness shall collapse."[52]

Seventy-seven years earlier, Henry Wadsworth Longfellow penned,

> I heard the bells on Christmas Day
> Their old, familiar carols play,
> And wild and sweet
> The words repeat
> Of peace on earth, good-will to men![53]

That poem, *Christmas Bells*, was written as America was hurtling through a war with itself, over what kind of country—or countries—it would be. Three quarters of a century later, many of the old internal debates in America still existed, but a larger debate had taken over: Would the world allow itself to be enslaved by the Axis forces, or live free? The factionalism inside America had mostly been set aside. At least for the time being, the story was not a Farewell to Arms but a Call to Arms.

Eloquence was at its best on this day, and many of the newspapers had superb and moving commentaries on the meaning of Christmas in the context of a world at war.

> The greatest miracle of all time is celebrated today by all Christendom. Two thousand years ago a child was born in a humble crib in the little town of Bethlehem, and the event brought a unity to mankind and an impulse....
>
> It is sometimes said we are entering upon a new Dark Ages. All the outwards signs, to be sure, point to it. The Dark Ages were ushered in by the scourges which assailed mankind in the early centuries of the Christian era. The scourge was the irruption of the Germanic barbarians, who overran the Roman Empire, under the aegis of which Christian civilization grew up. It was Christian England, and England alone of all the Roman provinces, that escaped being overwhelmed and kept the flame alight . . . No Christian order can be recaptured, no Christian civilization can be saved, till the Christian world rediscovers its integrity.... It is easy under the pressure of danger to develop a common front for fighting a common enemy. It is less easy to develop an common front for living together . . . Our main hope that a Christian shape will be given to tomorrow's life is that the star is shining—the same star that shone on the shepherds as they watched their

flocks on the Bethlehem hillside and in the morning led the wise men of their East to the inn in the town. Thither our wise men must also repair.[54]

Yet another concluded, "The American people recognize in Christmas the symbol of the purpose for which they toil and fight. With firm reliance upon a Merciful God, they anticipate the happier Christmases yet to dawn."[55]

The love manifest in the celebration of Christmas threw all of these great global issues into sharp relief. However, regardless of their particular religion—whether it was Christian, Jewish, Muslim, Hindu, or any of the myriad forms of worship—civilized people the world over knew that the Axis represented unadulterated evil.

"I don't see much future for the Americans. It is a decayed country. My feelings against Americanism are feelings of hatred and deep repugnance . . . . Everything about the behavior of American society reveals that it's half Judanized and the other half Negrified."[56] So proclaimed the Prince of Evil, Adolf Hitler.

Rarely had all of the races and creeds of humanity faced such a stark choice between civilization and barbarism, between decent society and a thousand years of darkness.

CHAPTER 26

THE TWENTY-SIXTH
OF DECEMBER

"Manila Declared 'Open City'"

Chicago Daily Tribune

"War Tide to Turn by 1943, Churchill Says"

Evening Star

"Enemy Submarine Sunk Off California"

Hartford Courant

Winston Churchill's historic address to a joint session of Congress was decided upon only at the last minute and took place in the Senate chamber rather than the House chamber, where nearly all such Capitol Hill addresses occurred, for the simple reason the lower had more seating space than the upper. But Congress was out of session and most members had gone home and, as such, had not received sufficient notice to get back in time for the momentous remarks. Even House Speaker Sam Rayburn was out of town. "Despite the fact that many Senators and Representatives had gone home for Christmas, both houses had unexpectedly large delegations present."[1]

The smaller Senate room also had better acoustics. After the representatives, first dibs for seats went to the diplomatic corps and government bureaucrats. "Chairs for House members, the Supreme Court Justices and the President's cabinet will be placed among the 96 desks of the Senators."[2] The Soviet ambassador, Maxim Litvinoff, was seated next to Lord Halifax, the British ambassador. The envoys for other countries including Belgium, Luxembourg, South Africa, Denmark, Poland, Greece, and others were present while astonishingly the representatives for Canada and Australia—both part of the greater British Commonwealth—were "not in evidence."[3] And nearly as surprising, both Secretary of State Hull and Secretary of War Stimson were also absent.

But the public was barred "from the history-making ceremonies because of the limited accommodations. Only people with access cards could get in, and the only people who could get access cards were congressional members, government officials, and those in the diplomatic corps."[4] These restrictions did not stop hundreds of Americans from queuing in a long snaking line in a vain attempt to get into the U.S. Capitol.

All indications were that the prime minister was just as eager. The legislature opened for business at noon, and Churchill rose to speak at exactly 12:30 p.m. to an overflowing crowd. The attendees had their cameras taken away, but, for the first time in the history of the Senate, a live broadcast was allowed and, again for the first time, movie cameras were also allowed in. Procedurally, the body was actually in recess though "unanimous consent was granted by the Senate to have the proceedings printed in the Congressional Record. . . ."[5] It was an unusual method for accommodating an invited speaker who was not a member of the Senate. The Marquis de Lafayette had addressed the Senate in such a fashion during his farewell tour in 1824, and yet another rare speaker to that body had been, ironically, the King of Hawaii, Kalahaua, in December of 1874.[6]

The prime minister stood in the well of the Senate, surrounded by a forest of microphones in front of him—from CBS, NBC, MBS, and others—and a handful of politicians seated behind him including Vice President Henry Wallace and Majority Leader Alben Barkley of Kentucky, while sound cameras could be heard whirling in the balcony. In front of Churchill were many though not all of the members of Congress, nearly all men. But, curiously enough, "women predominated" in the galleries which surrounded the room on three sides.[7] Sentries were everywhere. Churchill was sporting a dark bow tie and three-piece Oxford gray suit, his left hand often gripping his lapel, his right index finger slashing the air for effect. Other times, his hands were on his hips, thumbs forward, or were gripping both lapels. He was a master showman and like many showmen, more at ease in front of big crowds than in small settings.

He was introduced by the president of the Senate, Vice President Henry Wallace, simply as "the Prime Minister of Great Britain!"[8] Churchill then took a bronze green case out of his pocket and removed a pair of spectacles, which he settled on his nose and ears.

The air was electric and it was simply one more thrilling moment in a town that should have become used to thrilling moments long ago. He began with a joke. "I can't help but reflect if my father had been American and my mother British, instead of the other way around, I might have gotten here on my own."[9] The appreciative Americans roared with laughter.

Churchill made a fleeting reference to his own long and "not . . . uneventful" life. He also shared the kind and gracious remarks any Englishman was known for, including a self-deprecating wit. Had he made it to Congress on his own, he joshed, "I would not have needed any invitation, but if I had it is hardly likely that it would have been unanimous."[10] A human quote machine in the best British traditions of Shakespeare, Wilde, Dickens, and Disraeli, Churchill was such a profoundly literate and memorable man that a term already was being coined in the American press to describe his style: *Churchillian.* He said America had "drawn the sword for freedom and cast away the shadow."[11] And, "Now we are the masters of our fate."[12]

Gesturing for emphasis, Churchill didn't pull any punches, in the character of the British government under his rule. Since he had ascended to the prime ministership, Churchill had quite deliberately rejected the "gloss it over" happy talk, and ignored the threat tenures of Stanley Baldwin and Neville Chamberlain. Part of his falling-out with Baldwin was over Churchill warning the British people of the military buildup by Nazi Germany and Adolf Hitler. Baldwin and the status quo he led in London wanted to appease Hitler or simply ignore him. Churchill felt this was irresponsible, but most did not agree with him until September 1, 1939, when Germany invaded Poland. Churchill was proven right, but because the Poles had a mutual defense treaty with the British, it meant a new war for England.

Churchill had little regard for his fellow Tory, Baldwin. "Stanley occasionally stumbles over the truth, but he always hastily picks himself up and hurries on as if nothing had happened."[13]

This conservative member of Parliament from Epping and relatively new prime minister hit the British subjects right between the eyes with the truth.

Now he did the same with Congress and the American people.

Early in his political career, he started out as a conservative, left to become a liberal, and then later in life, returned to the conservative fold. As Churchill put it: "Anyone can rat, but it takes a certain amount of ingenuity to re-rat."[14] He was a conservative like Baldwin and Chamberlain, but a far different kind, embracing in many ways the American conservatism of the Founders, which was essentially an anti-status quo movement of ideas. Churchill never feared or looked down on the citizenry, again like the American Founding Fathers. "I am a child of the House of Commons. I was brought up . . . to believe in democracy; trust the people."[15] He embraced his predecessor, the great Benjamin Disraeli, when Disraeli lamented that the world in his time was "for the few and for the very few."[16]

While never mentioning Lincoln, Churchill scored impressively by taking a populist position against "privilege and monopoly," saying, "I have always steered confidently toward the Gettysburg ideal of government of the people, by the people, for the people." He gave the inwardly looking Americans a quick thumb-nail sketch of his life and career in Parliament where members were "servants of the state, and would be ashamed to be its masters."[17]

In his half-hour speech, he said that while 1942 would start off badly for the Allies, the year—or maybe not until 1943—would finish much better as the full industrial and political might of America would become felt in the war. "He predicted that in a year or 16 months the flow of munitions in the United States and Britain will produce results in war power 'beyond anything that has been seen or foreseen in the dictatorial states.'" Expanding, he said it was reasonable to "hope that [the] end of 1942 will find us quite definitely in a better position than now and the year 1943 will find us able to take the initiative on an ample scale."[18] It took a lot of courage to tell the citizens of the Allied powers they might not taste victory for another year or more. And yet he also saw hope.

"But here in Washington, in these memorable days, I have found an

Olympian fortitude which, far from being based upon complacency, is only the mark of an inflexible purpose and the proof of a sure, well-grounded confidence in the final outcome." He was interrupted repeatedly with applause and huzzahs. He spoke of the common bonds and common mission of Great Britain and the United States. "Now that we are together, now that we are linked in a righteous comradeship of arms, now that our two nations, each in perfect unity, have joined all the life energies in a common resolve, you will see milestones upon which a steady light will glow and brighten."[19]

He concluded by telling the American legislators of his faith and mission. "I will say that he must indeed have a blind soul who cannot see that some great purpose and design is being worked out here below, for which we have the honor to be the faithful servant. It is not given to us to peer into the mysteries of the future; yet, in the days to come, the British and American peoples will, for their own safety and for the good of all, walk together in majesty, in justice and in peace."[20]

When he finally sat down, he was showered with several minutes of applause. The Senate chamber hadn't heard such eloquence and oratory since the "Great Triumvirate" of Daniel Webster, Henry Clay, and John C. Calhoun. As he left, Churchill raised his right hand and with his index and middle fingers, formed the "V" for victory sign. The audience went wild again and he left to the sound of thunderous approbation.

With characteristic irony, he once said that history would be kind to him because he intended to write it. With this extraordinary speech to Congress, he wrote a big chapter in that history of his life and times. On Capitol Hill, they called it "Churchill Day." One of those attending, Senator Ernest McFarland of Arizona, mentioned to Churchill that his wife missed the event because she was ill and in the hospital. With that, Churchill telephoned the woman to say he "hoped she would have a speedy recovery."[21]

Roosevelt listened on radio, along with millions of Americans and Brits. Afterwards, the precise articulation of Churchill was uniformly praised by the often tongue-tied and inarticulate politicians of Washington.

After a lunch with the congressional leadership, the British prime minister left the Capitol, but spotting a group of fans and supporters, "he strolled across the Capitol Plaza until he was within a few feet of the cheering crowd of spectators gathered there. Bowing and smiling and waving his black hat at the crowd which was dotted with sight-seeing American soldiers, he bade them farewell with the 'V' sign."[22]

That day, Churchill also met with FDR to discuss the economics of war. They had already covered the military aspects and the diplomatic. Now they had to figure out how to pay for it and how much it would cost to win the world by winning a war. They met with economists and budget experts from their respective governments, both civilian and military. Estimates of the cost to the Allies for 1942 alone totaled $40 billion.[23] The cost alone for three indoor shooting ranges at Ft. Dix, New Jersey, was over $100,000.[24]

In the Senate, a national lottery was proposed as a means of raising needed revenue.[25] The plan behind the lottery was also to put the government in direct competition with illegal gaming in the country. Its goal would be to "kill the numbers racket, slot machines, pinball nickel grabbers and bookie establishments." Prizes would range from $100 to $1,000 dollars.[26]

Churchill and Roosevelt were guided in their discussions by a detailed memo on the "Victory Program" authored in abstruse bureaucratese by Henry Stimson. The cost of ginning up a worldwide machine to wage war and destroy the enemy would be put to paper in black and white. Everything from "Planes, Spare Engines and Parts" to "Small Arms and Automatic Weapons and AC Cannon" were covered in a budget of $33,347,460,905 for 1942 but this was just for the Army and the Air Corps. Stimson was still reviewing the navy's and the Maritime Commission's budget needs.[27] President Roosevelt also reviewed a memo authored by Army Chief of Staff George Marshall that made recommendations on the Africa campaign and putting troops in Casablanca.[28]

Before Pearl Harbor, the president tended to be cautious in his projections of public spending, reluctant to antagonize a frugal-minded Congress. On December 7, all of that changed—irrevocably. The very same Congress that had almost voted against the draft was now, after Pearl Harbor, endorsing new and colossal funding requests from FDR that previously were unthinkable. Roosevelt was setting ostensibly far-fetched production goals, and in response, a newly quiescent Congress simply opened the spending floodgates. The mobilization for war was releasing sweeping political and economic forces that would forever transform American society. Washington would never again be a relatively small, southern town.

Even though Congress was out of session in recognition of the holidays, congressional committees kept meeting to go over the financing of the war and slash projected or hoped-for billions from domestic programs to help pay for the military. To win the war, the New Deal would have to be shelved. Progressive senator Robert La Follette of Wisconsin pitched a fit, denouncing the suggested elimination or cutbacks of the Farm Security Administration, the National Youth Administration, and the Civilian Conservation Corps, saying this would "knock some of the major props of Federal support out from under our social structure in the lower income levels."[29]

More motivational posters were coming out now, definitely better than the first ones of the war. The Red Cross released one of a downright sexy brunette nurse, shapely with full lips, in white nurse's garb and blue cape, with Uncle Sam standing behind her, his left hand gently on her shoulder.[30] Others told civilians "DON'T 1) Talk Loosely to Strangers 2) Spread Rumors." This poster, it was reported, "was designed for taverns . . . to warn drinkers against inadvertently passing on valuable military information or causing trouble by spreading rumors. Loose talk is dangerous in wartime!"[31] Another encouraged buying (what else?) war bonds.

It would take more than posters and bonds to see the United States through the days ahead. Churchill was right in preparing the American and the British people for more bad news because it was coming hour by hour and day after day. After all, the Allies were up against "wicked men," but in the end, they "would be called to terrible account."[32] Some of that bad news included word from Wake Island that the Japanese captured almost four hundred marines and another thousand civilians, mostly construction workers on the island.[33]

News from Europe was grave as well. The Russian counteroffensive against the German invasion appeared to have slowed and the Germans were digging in, resisting harder. Even the Soviet propaganda tabloid *Izvestia* reported that "the Germans had heavily fortified this place and exerted every effort to stop our offensive. Stubborn street engagements ensued. . . ."[34] The *New York Tribune* reported that "German resistance is increasing all along the front."[35] And the German war industry was turned up even higher, as more and more of their women went to work in the factories. The Germans also had another brutal advantage: slave labor from the occupied territories.

The Germans claimed they had sunk twenty-seven British ships in the month of December alone. The Japanese claimed they'd destroyed forty British planes in the air and another eight on the ground in a new assault on Rangoon, Burma.[36] The Japanese were occupying Thailand and had, since the first hours of the war, with nary a squeak from the Allies, who were too busy holding on by their fingernails to other territories in the Western Pacific.

New reports were coming from Hong Kong that suggested civilian riots had broken out there in the last days as the Japanese had cut off the water supply. The outpost had been bombed forty-five times in eight days by planes, not including the constant shelling from the sea.[37]

There was good news from Midway. For the first time in days, Allies received communications from its embattled forces there, and amazingly it appeared as if the marines had successfully held the island. "We are still here," flashed one message.[38] "The Navy said today its force of Marines on Midway Island is still holding out. The Midway garrison was in communication with headquarters here yesterday but the Navy would not discuss the messages nor how the Marines were faring on the mid-Pacific isle."[39]

The really bad news was rolling in from Manila. The Japanese forces were advancing on the city from two directions, laying waste to everything in their path, military and civilian. They "intensified a two-way assault on Manila, with an artillery fight northwest of the capital and a tank battle to the southeast, where Japanese pressure has been increased an Army communiqué declared late today. Casualties were reported heavy in the tank battle."[40] The Japanese trickle of tanks put ashore had rapidly become a caravan. Tokyo made public claims that they had destroyed the entire American fleet operating in the waters around the islands of the Philippines.

The threat to the civilian population of 600,000 had forced the decision on Douglas MacArthur to declare Manila an "open city," meaning it would be neutral and that all warring parties would agree to not conduct any battles there. He did so, he declared, "to spare the metropolitan area from the possible ravages of attack. . . ."[41] Japanese planes flew over the city, but stopped dropping bombs and American antiaircraft guns stopped firing on those planes when over the city. Under the rules of engagement, all belligerents were supposed to steer clear of such designated areas. Douglas MacArthur had already departed his headquarters in Manila to take personal command of the army in the field.

The Roosevelt administration was faced with the very real possibility of losing the Philippines to the Japanese. "Washington reports conceded that eventual loss of the Philippines archipelago was distinctly possible as Japanese hordes poured onto Luzon, and Manila was threatened from several sides simultaneously."[42]

All through history, military battles were planned by old men, but executed by young men. This war was no different. The American army and navy were comprised of downy-faced boys, not much removed from being tucked into feather beds by their mothers; but if possible, the Japanese troops were even younger, some as young as fifteen years of age, sweating it out and struggling and fighting in the jungles of the Philippines, whose people were also putting what were essentially little more than boys into the life-and-death struggle of the fight.

In the background of the national debate of late December 1941 were the beginnings of a small pushback against the "First War Powers Act of 1941," as it had become known, and all the power granted President Roosevelt over most forms of private or privately owned communications in America as of December 18, 1941.

The Espionage Act of 1917 had never been repealed. The more radically restrictive Sedition Act of 1918 had been repealed by 1921. Essentially, one had the freedom of expression in America, but only up to a point. Among the verboten verbiage were "false statements to interfere with the success of the United States," which was so open to interpretation as to cause a chilling effect on the ability of anybody and everybody to express their own opinions. Only the overt act of treason was a constitutional offense. That standard was a bit more fixed; an individual had to act to topple the government by "levying war" against the United States or "give aid and comfort to the enemy," as specified in Article Three, Section Three.[43]

Perhaps Churchill and his government's bluntness, as opposed to the often less-than-forthcoming U.S. government, led a small but hardy band of civil libertarians to wonder how many public facts of the war the government should be left in control of. After all, it was December 26, and Americans still had not been told all the facts of Pearl Harbor or the other battles raging in the Pacific. The Roosevelt government often confused the facts of the war with the secrets of the war.

The U.S. Supreme Court expressed its own opinions on censorship when it ruled seven to zero that corporations and businesses had the right to speak out against labor unions and labor problems without it being considered a violation of the Wagner Act. Organized labor considered the 1935 Wagner Act to be the Holy Grail of the labor movement, as it severely restricted what businesses could do in the face of labor organizing and activities. By overturning this key portion of the Wagner Act, the high court gave the American people a moment to pause and reflect on the power of government to censor and just how much power it should really have.

Previously, Woodrow Wilson had made it clear that he felt the Constitution and the Bill of Rights was an impediment to progressive society, and he proved it shortly after the beginning of the First World War by asking Congress for broad powers to censor. His bill called for life imprisonment for anybody who distributed in wartime any information deemed to interfere with U.S. war policies. The goal was to shut down political opposition to Wilson. The bill passed the Senate but died in the House. Yet another bill offered by Wilson after America's entry into that war would have made it a crime for anyone to publish anything the chief executive deemed to be of use to the enemy. American newspapers rose up in opposition, led by the Hearst newspaper chain, and the bill was heavily amended.[44]

It was the simple nature of some men to want to control the knowledge and freedom of other men, and the debate had been at the core of the American experiment since before the days of the Founding Fathers.

Government bureaucrats were not only capable of dumb mistakes and over-reaching, they were also often guilty of dumb overreacting. Deep in the heartland of Pennsylvania, the eternal flame at Gettysburg, signifying a great victory for the United States, was doused by the National Park Service, fear-ful that the light would be an attractant for enemy bombing of the ancient battlefield and cemetery.[45]

Other inanities were mercifully reversed. The "Flying Santa" of New England, a pilot who flew gifts each year to lonely lighthouse keepers and their families, had been initially grounded by military officials. At the last minute they relented, realizing they had gone too far, and the Flying Santa was airborne again, spreading goodwill and cheer up and down the coast.

The bountiful nature of Washington was such that nearly five thousand more meals were prepared for Christmas Day than there were soldiers to eat them. The best laid plans of the District Defense Committee were to arrange for dinners to be prepared in five thousand homes where families had vol-unteered to take in soldiers for the day. The meals all arrived and everything had been carried out except for one thing: they were missing soldiers. At the last minute, Washington had been declared a war emergency zone and all leaves were canceled. Servicemen and officers had to stay on base or on their ships for Christmas Day. No one had bothered to tell the organizers, who had expended thousands of hours in an attempt to provide a home-cooked meal for serviceman away from home. Finally, a call was placed to a local post and the officer who answered haughtily replied, "You people in Washington don't seem to realize that a war emergency does exist."[46]

Actually, the civilian population was all too familiar with the issues of life and death, of sacrifice and charity, and of peace and war. In just a two-day period, over 400 people, including many children, had died in America because of accidents. "Death stalked the highways . . . but also struck 97 times in other forms—fire, guns, lightening, planes."[47] A group of ten in St. Louis had attended midnight Mass, boarded a bus, got into an accident, and the ensuing fire killed them on Christmas Day.[48]

In New York, a former school teacher, Isabelle Hallin, 32, was found dead by her own hand on Christmas Day, the unlit gas pilots in her stove open. Four years earlier, she'd been falsely accused of serving alcohol to members of the Saugus, Massachusetts, drama club by the town harpy, who a wire story said was a "prominent Saugus clubwoman."[49] The *Boston Daily Globe* said her accuser was the wife of a local minister.[50] Hallin, who was described as a "pretty blonde," lost her job, sued for libel, won the case, and left town to take a job as a copywriter in New York, but the false accusations crushed her spirit and she finally took her life. She left no suicide note.[51] Massachusetts had a long and cherished history of smearing and ruining people in the name of righteous mean-spirited busybodies.

Of all the sad stories of December of 1941, the death of Howard Lusk was one of the saddest. He'd been an orphan in Michigan, not knowing anything about any member of his family. He ran away from orphanages continuously until, at age sixteen, he was discovered on the mean streets of Baltimore in the darkest and deepest days of the Great Depression. He was penniless, disheveled, and hungry and was taken in by the Travelers' Aid Society. Eventually, an unknown sister was discovered, who had also been abandoned as a child, like Howard. He'd travelled on the rails for years, north and south, east and west, in a vain attempt to find his parents.

Eventually, Howard found a home in the army, and then as a private in Pearl Harbor on December 7, 1941, found death at the age of 25.[52]

CHAPTER 27

THE TWENTY-SEVENTH
OF DECEMBER

"Japs Blast Undefended Manila"

Birmingham News

"Papers in U.S. Hit New Peak in Circulation"

Atlanta Constitution

"Ban Tires for Family Cars"

Chicago Daily Tribune

O n Christmas Day in Rhode Island, Henry "Daddy" Johnson celebrated his 107th birthday. Henry was a former slave who had met
Abraham Lincoln after the Emancipation Proclamation and was
in remarkably good health, perhaps because he chose to never marry so he
could "stay out of trouble." Until the prior year, he'd lived unaided in a rough
cabin in the woods of the tiny state.[1] Andrew Jackson was president when
Johnson was born.

In Missouri, General John M. Claypool, 95, of the former Confederate
army of the Confederate States of America and, by 1941, the national commander of the United Confederate Veterans, was photographed signing
up for civil defense work in St. Louis.[2] James K. Polk was president when
Claypool was born.

Meanwhile in Georgia, William Jones, 105, led more than three dozen former slaves in prayer "that this country may be victorious, as the Atlanta Ex-Slave Association held its annual Christmas party."[3] Martin Van Buren was president when Jones, a former slave himself, was born.

In 1941, the grandsons of slaves and grandsons of Confederate generals took up arms together, united to fight a common enemy which had embraced a perverted aim of elevating a "Master Race" over the rest of humanity. Ironically, the U.S. Armed Forces were, at the time, racially segregated, mirroring the color barrier throughout the rest of American society. This great paradox would be tackled with full force, but not until after the war.

Just then the Democratic political machine in Chicago was having its own problems with race, as the chief justice of the Windy City's Municipal Court, Edward Scheffler, refused to recognize the appointment of a black attorney, Patrick B. Prescott Jr., as an associate justice on the same bench. The appointment of Prescott was made by the Illinois Republican governor, Dwight Green.[4]

There was a bond growing between Churchill and Roosevelt. Philosophically, they disagreed on much—one the liberal, the other conservative—but they liked each other personally and respected each other's political skills. They also shared the same basic worldview, particularly against the backdrop of Nazism. Certainly their love of the sea was an important bond as well. During the First World War, Roosevelt had been assistant secretary of the navy, the same time that Churchill had been First Lord of the Admiralty in Britain.

They both had suffered political reversals and rejections and had come through those trials as hardened and tougher men. They'd first met in 1918, when they were far younger, somewhat callow, and neither carried a cane. Both were the children of rank and privilege, though Americans would sometimes complain they had no royalty. The Roosevelts, the Vanderbilts, the Rockefellers, the Whitneys, the Cabots, and the Lodges defied that hollow protest. Classless society, indeed. A mordant ditty made the rounds, among high society and hoi polloi alike: "New England, land of the bean and the cod, where the Lodges talk only to the Cabots, and the Cabots talk only to God."

The next time they met wasn't until, fittingly, on a ship called the *Augusta* in August 1941 to produce the Atlantic Charter. The document was not a mutual defense treaty, but instead a framework for how democracies should conduct themselves in relation to other democracies. Churchill had sailed to Newfoundland to confer with Roosevelt on the *Prince of Wales*, the very same battleship sunk later by the Japanese.

While both men were known for their humor, Churchill's was more intellectual; he could be devastating but was also self-deprecating. At his lunch with the congressional leadership the day before, Senator Josiah Bailey of North Carolina told him that ever since the Boer War, "I have always believed that you would be Prime Minister of Great Britain," to which Churchill replied, "Senator you are wrong. My future is behind me."[5]

The after-action reports continued to roll in for his landmark speech to Congress and they were 100 percent favorable. Everybody knew when the *Atlanta Constitution* editorialized, "It was a great speech. It was moving, inspiring and full of power" and then singled out his reference to Gettysburg for accolades that the world had indeed changed in those twenty days since December 7, that America was a changed country. Factionalism—at least for the moment—had been set aside.[6]

The only countries where, predictably, it had been badly reviewed were Germany and Italy. The German "view is that the catastrophic situation in Anglo-American conduct of war has led to this meeting." The Italian press said it was one more "step by England along [the] path of political submission to United States."[7] In one other regard were Roosevelt and Churchill similar: they were supreme egotists, obsessed with praises but also brickbats.

Some saw it in a broader context that Congress, even with the bombing of Pearl Harbor and with America losing the war for the Pacific, still needed to hear from Churchill to gain a greater perspective on what was at stake in the war for the world. Churchill had to remind his American audience that his people also "had the same feeling in our darkest days."[8]

Said syndicated columnist David Lawrence, "He brought with him a tonic of reassurance and confidence that makes long range planning for victory seem comprehensible in spite of the setbacks and defeats of the immediate future. Nothing compares with it. . . ."[9]

That Saturday, FDR had eight separate meetings, all dealing with the war, and Churchill attended six of them. Some of the meetings dealt with better communications and coordination among not just Great Britain, Russia, and America but also Australia, Norway, and Belgium, the latter [two] having "refugee governments." They also met with Soviet ambassador Maxim Litvinov who, like all the Russians it seemed, had to be handled with kid gloves.[10]

The war planners were also still trying to decipher the Third Reich's next move. Some thought it might be renewed effort in North Africa, where the British had finally gained the upper hand, or an invasion of Turkey or an invasion of Spain. Hitler's surprise moves of the past seven years had kept his enemies guessing and had not changed.

Meanwhile, another man of the sea, Admiral Chester Nimitz, reported to Pearl Harbor to assume his new command as head of the Pacific fleet.

The Japanese agreement with General MacArthur to treat Manila as an "open city," and thus not to be touched by either's military, lasted exactly one day. By the twenty-seventh, the Japanese renewed their heavy bombing campaign, apparently waiting only for MacArthur to move his antiaircraft guns out of the city so they could attack with impunity. In all the destruction falling from the sky, not one shot was fired from the ground in retaliation to the silvery and glistening twin-engine bombers.[11]

Attacking an unarmed city filled with innocent civilians offended sensibilities, no less so than if a country attacked another and then declared war after the attack. War, according to the Geneva Conventions, was supposed to be conducted civilly and that meant not making unnecessary war on noncombatants. "Rivaling if not surpassing the stab-in-the-back assault on Pearl Harbor, the raiders visited terror upon the helpless metropolis . . ."[12] They sank one and badly damaged another ocean-going liner at anchor in the Manila harbor while also damaging two American war ships. While bulletins and news reports on the battle for the Philippines were readily available, very few photos of the carnage and destruction were appearing in any of the nation's broadsheets. Many of the stories were angry and graphic, though, including the strafing of civilians in the Intramuros district of the old city.

Even the normally unruffled and fact-based Associated Press wire-service hotly reported, "Japan treacherously violated the laws of human decency anew Saturday when Japanese bombers savagely attacked Manila, killing many and setting fires, 24 hours after the Philippine capital had been declared an open, undefended city." Much of the bombing campaign had focused on the area around a large hotel "where several hundred Americans and Britons were sheltered."[13] Dozens of planes over many hours pounded the city and the first estimates were of fifty killed and many wounded, but the count of the dead multiplied as the day went on.

A 350-year-old church, Santo Domingo, was hit by Japanese bombing planes and caught fire. Much of the old walled portions of the city built hundreds of years earlier by the Spanish were leveled. A radio report said the church had been "smashed by one direct hit."[14] Japanese ground troops were even closer to the city now, just over sixty miles away. American and Filipino forces were falling back, again and again. The bombing campaign by the Japanese had pretty much wiped out what was left of MacArthur's air corps and air fields. Oil fires were everywhere, the Manila port was a bombed-out wreck and the U.S. naval base at Cavite had been spewing black smoke for over two days. Explosions of gas and ammo dumps were frequently heard.

Cordell Hull, Roosevelt's secretary of state, was asked his opinion of the Japanese regard for the international law and the civility of war. The normally understated elderly man let loose, comparing the behavior of the Japanese to that of Nazi Germany, saying they were "practicing the barbaric methods of cruelty and inhumanity that Hitler had been using in Europe." He noted the cruelty also of the Japanese when they invaded China in 1937. Senator Burton K. Wheeler, Democrat of Montana and noted isolationist before December 7, said of the Japanese, "We face only a half-civilized race and in the future they have to be treated as such."[15] Then he could not resist a shot at FDR and Lend-Lease saying how much he regretted not having the bombs to "bomb the hell out of" Japanese cities because "we have given them away!"[16]

Bert Silen, an NBC broadcaster in Luzon, said over the air, "The cry is for help—help from America. And if this does not come soon, all of us have resigned ourselves to the inevitable."[17] The Japanese were reportedly dropping bombs all over the island, and while Tokyo said nothing about violating the rules dealing with open cities, Berlin radio ridiculously said the Japanese did not recognize it as such because MacArthur had not consulted with the civilian population before announcing his decision. The Berlin broadcast was picked up by NBC short-wave radio.

Late in the evening of the twenty-sixth, the War Department issued a communiqué on the crisis in the Philippines. "Philippine theatre. Fighting in the Lingayen Gulf area north of Manila, is of desultory character. Combat operations in the southeast, in the general vicinity of Lamon Bay, are very heavy. The enemy is being continually reinforced from fleets of troopships in Lingayen Gulf and off Atimonan. Enemy air activity continued heavy over all fronts. There is nothing to report from other areas."[18] Lamon Bay was on the east coast of the Philippines, Lingayen was on the west coast of the Philippines, and Manila was right in between.

The Japanese navy minister, Shigetaro Shimada, went before the Diet and claimed that the Japanese had nearly destroyed the British and the American navies and air forces operating in the Western Pacific. "He asserted British and American naval losses included seven battleships sunk, three heavily damaged and one less seriously damaged; two cruisers sunk and six damaged; a destroyer sunk and four damaged; nine submarines, nine gunboats, seven torpedo boats and sixteen merchant [ships] sunk and fifty captured." He also said they had destroyed 338 American planes in the Philippines and together, including British planes lost, had destroyed 803."[19] Again, the Allies did not dispute the enormous and impressive claims and again, all this was widely printed in the Western newspapers, and there was little the U.S. government could do to censor the stories or gloss them over. The word "retreat" appeared in a number of those stories.[20]

Bulletins appeared about how friends and associates of General MacArthur feared for his life. In the "world war" he was known to take risks—some which were thought to be reckless—and his capture by the Japanese would be a huge propaganda victory for Tokyo and equally disheartening for Americans. "MacArthur's headquarters staff in Manila went to an air-raid shelter each time Japanese planes approached, but the general remained in his office, smoking and studying war maps."[21] Of great concern too was the safety of his wife, Jean, and their son, Arthur. Of the fight for the Philippines, the American high commissioner, Francis B. Sayre, summed it up in one short sentence: "We will fight to the last man."[22]

The Japanese were not only destroying, they were also restoring. In Borneo, retreating British engineers had laid waste to some 150 oil wells, in the hopes of denying or delaying the precious liquid for the enemy. The ploy failed as the Japanese, within days, brought seventy of them back on line, producing by their estimate some 700 tons of oil a day.[23] The Japanese alacrity in restoring the oil wells underscored the degree to which their conquest of East Asia was in large part predicated on their strategic need to capture rich oil resources, once controlled by the British. The Japanese knew full well that without sufficient oil to power their war machine, their aspirations for a greater Empire would be futile.

In capturing the area of Sarawak from the British, the Japanese gained tons of precious tin, rubber, guns, "armor[ed] cars," and other spoils of war.[24] Additionally, a report from the British colonial office said the Japanese were now "operating" in the Gilbert Islands, which were approximately halfway between the Hawaiian Islands and Australia. "The announcement expressed fears that some European residents of the little chain of 16 coral atoll islands might have been taken prisoners."[25]

Americans were following the news of their country and the news of the world as newspaper circulation reached an all-time high, according to *Editor and Publisher*.[26] Morning papers were up, afternoon papers were up, and Sunday papers were up. Most papers cost 2 to 3 cents.

For weeks, women had been warned that the days of silk stockings—at least during the war effort—were probably over and now it appeared they were, as many department stores had pushed their purchase hard for the Christmas buying season. The National Association of Hosiery expected inventories to run out, as there had been a run on them since December 7. Silk would be needed for more important roles including parachutes and the powder bags for the large guns on warships if the Allies were going to get a leg up over the Axis powers.

Washington finally got its policy together on civilian purchases of new tires during the war and the course of action was essentially, "Hit the road, Jack." Plain, everyday citizens had no hope (at least legally) of getting new tires, but neither did cabbies nor those who lived in rural areas. Tires in 1941 were not steel-belted or vulcanized or pneumatic or nylon-belted, and did not last for thousands of miles. They were essentially a thin rubber balloon inside a hard circle of rubber that wrapped around a steel rim, and the contraption did not last long. A board with nails, glass in the road—these were daggers at the throat of these poorly made tires. Even if they did not meet their demise due to puncture, they wore out very quickly as did the tread. Getting stuck in snow, ice, and mud was an everyday occurrence and the solution for many people was to place chains around their tires, which destroyed the soft tar of city streets. An outright ban on tires was essentially a ban on driving. This was not an inconsequential decision by the government. The cessation of the sale of new tires had a broad and potentially devastating ramification for the economy. As many people drove their cars to work each day or took cabs, it would definitely have an effect on employment. Goodyear pitched their flimsy contrivances by saying, "You can safely run your tire until the non-skid tread design practically disappears. Then you can have them safely regrooved. Later, if your tire carcasses are sound, you can safely have them retreaded and drive them nearly as far again."[27]

"The nation's 32,000,000-odd motor car owners today face an almost complete tire famine," said one story.[28] Local rationing boards were set up with three members from each community, like the Draft Boards and the Enemy Alien Boards. The members would be appointed by each state's governor and would be empowered to issue certificates for purchase "to those few operators that come under the classifications outlined by Washington and all law enforcement agencies have been asked to aid in enforcing the rationing rules."[29]

The rubber shortage was such that people were advised against going for Sunday drives, to walk more, and to only drive for essential reasons, and when one did, combine all their errands together. Comedian Bob Hope was depicted in newspaper ads astride a Schwinn bicycle.[30]

New tire sales were limited to police and fire departments, doctors, nurses, veterinarians, trucks that delivered oil, farm tractors and other equip-ment needed for the production of food, and delivery trucks for scrap metals and trucks for "garbage removal."[31] For delivery vehicles like milk trucks, it was no-go. The Office of Production Management later amended their rules to allow for the manufacture of fire hoses.[32] American farmers were urged to plant a Russian imported dandelion, as some scientists saw the weed as being able to produce a modicum of rubber to replace at least some of the shortage, according to the National Chemurgic Council.[33] One side effect of the new rule: "Stores were quickly cleaned out of golf balls."[34]

City fathers in Detroit of all places made plans to bring out of retirement over a hundred streetcars to fill the need for public transportation created by the tire shortage.[35] The shortage was so severe in Great Britain, the Minister of Supply issued an outright ban on anything made out of the now-rare substance including "corsets . . . golf tees and garden hoses."[36]

With all the seriousness of purpose in America, it was sometimes difficult to remember that the country also still had a seedy underside, fueled by easy money, notoriety, and booze. Young millionaire heiress Gloria Vanderbilt was so often in the news it was reasonable to assume she employed an army of publicists. But she was also a "Jonah," bringing trouble and bad luck to everybody around her, it seemed. At her engagement party, two men who claimed to be princes got into a fistfight and this made the newspapers, even as war was raging all around and even as young American boys were fighting and dying.[37]

Just as American families were getting over the weeklong food festival of Christmas week, they were staring down the barrel of yet another festival of food and fun during New Year's week. Still, with the new regulations on tires, Americans would have plenty of opportunity to walk off the extra poundage they gained over the holiday season. Ralph's, a chain supermarket in the Los Angeles area, was touting all sorts of meats, fruits, vegetables, and staples for customers to restock their shelves. Interestingly, of all the staples listed, including salt and pepper, Maxwell House coffee (1 pound was just 31 cents), and potatoes (10 pounds for 27 cents), sugar was nowhere to be found in their print ads. They also now carried the new disclaimer at the bottom, "We Reserve the Right to Limit Quantities."[38]

They would also have plenty of jobs in manual labor to sweat over, building the arsenal of democracy. Government planners in myriad agencies, including the National Youth Administration, were conceiving new job training programs for men and women, as there was a "skilled labor gap." The effort involved "federal, state and local agencies" who were "cooperating in an all-out program to provide skilled workers to fill the wide gaps in industrial plant rosters growing out of the acceleration of production to meet war needs." The plans included moving workers around the country to meet the needs of various industries. Also, women would be "encouraged" to join the work force. "As a first big step, the big-scale employment of women looms, hence they are now being trained for jobs now reserved for male workers. Women soon will dominate in many machine shops, drafting rooms, engineering departments, light assembly divisions, light riveting and spot welding."[39]

The American government continued its crackdown on "enemy aliens" in the country. In Alabama, fruit orchards owned by Japanese nationals were seized by the Department of the Interior, while the Justice Department issued a terse statement that all "Japanese, German and Italian nationals in seven Pacific coast states" had until 11 a.m. on Monday, the twenty-ninth, to surrender to authorities any radio-transmitting equipment, especially short-wave radios, as well as any cameras they owned. Those states the edict applied to were Washington, California, Utah, Montana, Oregon, Idaho, and Nevada.[40] A second group of twenty-three enemy aliens was trucked from San Francisco to "a Missoula internment camp. . . . About 100 local aliens previously have been sent to Montana. Several carloads of Southern California aliens were scheduled to be placed aboard the same train at Sacramento."[41]

Security measures were becoming even tighter in America—if that were possible—three weeks after the outbreak of war. Additional cordons were thrown up around defense plants, identification cards for workers were being issued and were tightly controlled, and law enforcement officials often pulled over drivers for no apparent reason. Washington tightened even further the border with Mexico, not allowing anyone to carry any form of correspondence across the boundaries. All letters would be confiscated.[42]

While nobody used the phrase "police state," a blanket of state-sponsored security—along with the acquiescence of most Americans—was settling over the country. The Santa Anita thoroughbred racing meeting was canceled for the first time ever. Public officials were debating banning any gathering of more than 10,000 people. To enter the Los Angeles harbor—as with others around the country—specially issued photo identification was needed, but this identification also contained "fingerprint, status of citizenship and physical description of the holder."[43]

The harbor had already been designated a "navy sea defense district" by presidential order. "Photographing in the area is prohibited and no one can divulge movements of shipping or naval activities under penalty of violation of the Espionage Act or other Federal or state laws...."[44]

The costs for civil defense had gone up exponentially. As a result, money available for other municipal programs was severely restricted. The lead editorial in the Los Angeles Times read, "Where to Cut to Save Money for War." Editorials in the New York Times, the New York Herald-Tribune, the Indianapolis News, and others applauded the new restrictions and offered advice to citizens on how to stay out of trouble.[45]

If anybody did complain about all the censorship, shortages, rationing, checkpoints, blackout drills, ubiquitous guards, and any number of other infringements and inconveniences, the Pavlovian response was, "Don't you know there's a war on?" as if the questioning party was somehow unpatriotic.

The matter of the Japanese, German, and Italian legations was still to be resolved, though the United States pledged to abide by the international conventions. The German staff and ambassador had been removed from Washington and were comfortably ensconced at the Greenbrier Hotel in West Virginia, mostly eating and drinking too much. They were awaiting their deportation, which was delayed because of the niceties of diplomats, the intermediary Swiss, and foot-dragging bureaucrats.[46] The Germans, though, weren't in any hurry to leave.

Further, the Roosevelt administration pledged that in the matter of Japanese prisoners of war, here it too would abide by the 1929 articles of Geneva endorsed and ratified at the time by forty-seven countries. Ominously, Japan never ratified the conventions. "The United States has informed the Japanese government that all Japanese prisoners captured by American armed forces will be treated in accordance with the prisoner-of-war convention. . . ." The Americans expected the Japanese to reciprocate and "grant all American prisoners of war reciprocal fair and humane treatment."[47] It was asking a lot.

The Japanese already had a sizable number of American POWs, including the marines taken at Wake Island, in China, and at Guam, plus the sailors taken off a gunboat captured in Shanghai. The Americans only had a handful including several pilots shot down in Pearl Harbor and the crew of one of the "midget" submarines captured in that battle. According to the 1929 document as created by the International Red Cross, prisoner exchanges had to be arranged and POW camps opened for international inspection.

Representatives of the World Alliance of the Young Men's Christian Association, including Dr. Darius Davis, had gone on an inspection tour of the Russian, German, French, and English POW camps and found that each was generally abiding by the Geneva Convention, although the Germans fed their Soviet prisoners less than prisoners "of other nationalities." Each day, the Russians were given "a cooked turnip 'with a little codfish thrown in.'"[48] Many governments sent "supplementary" food to their captive men. Davis was asked if prisoners could survive without supplementary food and he remarked that the Serbs and the Poles got nothing from home, "and they are still able to live."[49] No inspections had yet been made of Japanese POW camps and, of course, there was no mention of the German concentration camps where the extermination of millions of human beings was just getting underway.

As abruptly as the torpedo attacks along the California coast had begun, they now largely ceased. No doubt the increased surveillance by civilians and the law enforcement along the shore, as well as vastly increased overhead flights by the military and the additional precautions taken by ship captains, combined to have a positive effect. However, it could also have been that the subs—presumably Japanese—had run low on fuel and supplies and were thus forced to withdraw to safer waters to re-provision. Still, fishing on the West Coast was severely restricted because boat insurance had jumped up and with it, the cost of sardines.[50]

The American people had digested the situation with more than some aplomb. There was panic but never chaos among the populace, and given what submarines were capable of doing to defenseless ships and shore emplacements, they would have been justified in panicking more. Shipping along the coast was vitally important to the local economy at the time. There were few roads up and down the West Coast.

Airplanes were not big enough to haul sufficient quantities of food and other goods, so it was up to ships and trains to carry the load. The very thought of commercial ships being sunk at random could have caused pandemonium, sending food prices spiraling upwards with runs on grocery stores, and yet, those Americans along the West Coast had now taken the whole matter in stride, perhaps inured a bit to the new vicissitudes of war.

For them, war and sacrifice already had become a way of life. Little could Americans realize, in those heady first days of rekindled patriotism, just how long and costly this global conflict would prove to be.

CHAPTER 28

THE TWENTY-EIGHTH
OF DECEMBER

"Japanese Bombs Fire Open City of Manila;
Roosevelt and Churchill Fix War Strategy"

New York Times

"Japs Demand Filipinos 'Cease All Resistance'"

Atlanta Constitution

"Night Shifts for Women in Plane Plants Seen"

Los Angeles Times

T he twenty-eighth marked the third week after Pearl Harbor. It was also the last Sunday of the year, and the churches of America were packed with congregants and parishioners listening to ministers and priests asking them to pray for their president, for Winston Churchill, for their elected leaders, but most importantly for the people on the front lines fighting for America.[1] The archbishop of Chicago, Samuel Stritch, asked his parishioners to pray for Roosevelt and against the "Godless . . . fury."[2] The day before, in a synagogue in New York, Rabbi Elias Solomon spoke to his flock about FDR and Churchill, "Like Joseph of old, they seem to have been chosen to preserve life and liberty for all men and nations."[3]

It would be nice to imagine that the national emergency and the holiday season might cool the partisanship and mean-spiritedness in America, but not so. In addition to getting on Roosevelt's nerves over his mismanagement of the Office of Civil Defense, Fiorello La Guardia, as mayor, ordered the head of the Office of Commissioner of Markets in New York City, William Morgan Jr., to fire Mrs. Preston Davie, whom newspaper accounts said was a "blue-blooded leader in Republican women circles."[4]

La Guardia was a Republican in only the most casual and tissue-thin interpretation. In 1941, the Republican Party was home to many moderates and liberals, especially in the Northeast. La Guardia was a New Dealer through and through and had campaigned for Roosevelt in 1936 and 1940. La Guardia won Gracie Mansion by running against corruption and then ran the city like a little dictator rather than a "Little Flower." He also ran for mayor on the ticket of the American Labor Party, an ultra-liberal organization. Mrs. Roosevelt had been installed by her husband as the assistant director of the Office of Civil Defense to keep an eye on La Guardia for FDR, and because she herself had been mildly critical of his stewardship of the OCD.[5]

When Morgan refused to fire Mrs. Davie, La Guardia got tough and one of his lackeys referred publicly to Mrs. Davie as Morgan's "girlfriend."[6] Morgan threw up his hands and resigned.

Candor was the Western watchword in the waning days of December. Australian prime minister John Curtin gave a speech before his parliament in Canberra in which he warned of more and more reversals for the Allied powers. The leaders of the Allies had little choice but to tell people this as the news each day seemed to become gloomier and gloomier. The best they could do against Japan, Curtin said, was to "slow the enemy down."[7]

Curtin also understood what he and the Allies were up against. "We face an enemy nurtured in the tradition that to die for the nation is the highest virtue."[8] Not everyone was convinced that the Allies felt that defeating the Japanese carried the same weight as defeating Nazi Germany, including many, not surprisingly, in the Pacific. Indeed, in the war conferences in Washington, on at least one occasion, Allied representatives suggested that the war in the

Pacific could wait. "Diplomatic circles reported . . . that one of the premises basic to the conference was that Hitler's Germany was the chief and, at present, perhaps the most vulnerable enemy and that Japan, if she could be checked at Singapore and its approaches including the Philippines, could be taken care of later."[9] The premise was dangerous and foolish because even a cursory look at the broadsheets of the days made clear that the battles for Singapore and the Philippines were not going at all well for the Allies. There might not be much, later.

Another harsh critic of the "Europe First" policy, Sir Keith Murdoch, publisher of the *Melbourne Herald*, took Churchill to task, denouncing him for being "Atlantic-minded" and said in no uncertain terms that if Singapore fell, then the Churchill government would fall. "Some of those in office are ready to say we can finish the Japanese after beating the Germans," he stormed.[10] Australia was not a member of FDR's "War Council," but many thought she should be, including Murdoch. The *New York Times* editorially called for "Anglo-American Unity."[11] Sir Keith eventually sired a son named Rupert, who inherited his father's publishing empire, greatly expanded it, and went on to display the same pugnacious streak.

To Murdoch's point, it was announced that the Japanese had seized two of the Gilbert Islands, Makin and Abalang. The islands were a part of the British Commonwealth and only 2,000 miles from Hawaii.[12]

FDR had his own problems with publishers, one in particular. Basil Brewer, the publisher of the *New Bedford Standard-Times*, went hard after the Roosevelt administration over the Philippines, the lack of adequate defenses there, and Douglas MacArthur's decision to declare Manila an open city. "The stupidity of removing defenses from Manila and declaring it an open city with the expectation that Japan would respect its civil population finds its expected answer in the death and destruction wrought there today." Brewer ripped FDR even further, saying his decisions contained a "profound lack of realism."[13]

With the Japanese rapidly moving down the Asian coastline, gobbling up one country, colony, and outpost after another, the Australians' impatience was understandable. They were nervous about the Japanese and had recent history on their side to point to. At some juncture, having taken everything else, the Japanese could be counted on to invade Australia and while the Aussies had a standing army of about 300,000 men, their equipment and training was considered poor. They had a small navy and virtually no air force.[14] With no significant prior threats, Australia had never seen the need to invest in their military and was now looking to the United States and Great Britain.

But the British had their point of view as well and they considered it valid. From where Churchill sat, Hitler was more of a threat to the bulk of the British people than Japan. The British Empire may have had 500 million people—factoring in India and other parts of the Commonwealth—but not all of them voted and not all of them had been bombed day and night by the German Luftwaffe. The British in private sometimes shook their heads about the American reaction to the bombing of Pearl Harbor. During their blitz, it wasn't unusual for London to be hit hundreds of times in a single day by thousands of bombs.

Plus, the war with Germany was over two years old. The war with Japan was only three weeks old. First things first.

Out of those war conferences arranged in Washington by President Roosevelt came a consensus for the conduct of the war against the Axis. Speaking for the nearly three dozen countries arrayed against the Axis— all now members of the Allied powers—"President Roosevelt and Prime Minister Churchill [assumed] dramatic leadership of the ... war against Axis aggression, spread before the accredited representatives of 33 nations yesterday the advanced blueprints for marshaling every economic and fighting resource of this globe-encircling front."[15] No details were of course revealed, but the mere fact that so many countries could agree on anything was in and of itself a miracle. Even America's allies, the Russians and the Chinese, were in agreement. Other countries sending representatives included Mexico, Costa Rica, Honduras, Cuba, and Paraguay and in fact, nearly all the countries of Central and South America were on hand. Roosevelt said they had made "excellent progress."[16]

White House press secretary Stephen Early handed out a statement from FDR which read, in part:

As a result of all these meetings, I know tonight that the position of the United States and of all the nations aligned with us has been strengthened immeasurably. We have advanced far along the road toward achievement of the ultimate objective—the crushing defeat of those forces that have attacked and made war upon us. The present overall objective is the marshaling of all resources, military and economic, of the world-wide from opposing the Axis.[17]

A surprisingly happy addition to the Allied efforts was the Netherlands as a result of their victories in the Far East against Japanese ships and planes. Truth be told, their military successes in the early days of the Pacific war were greater than those of either America or Great Britain. Just the day before, the Dutch had sunk two Japanese warships. The minister for the Netherlands, Dr. Alexander Loudon, was granted a private audience with Roosevelt and Churchill.[18] The Free French were not present at the meeting and it may have been because both Washington and London were miffed at Charles De Gaulle for taking two tiny islands off the coast of Newfoundland without first checking with them. The French then banned any ship from any country to make port in either St. Pierre or Miquelon.[19]

Some of the representatives simply had to step out of their embassies and hail a cab to take them to the White House for these meetings; but others had more harrowing journeys, including the representatives of eight refugee governments who had been "driven from their homelands or have bowed to the exigencies of war to transfer their principal activities to new centers."[20] Some of them were included in the final meeting of the day: Poland, Denmark, Luxembourg, Greece, Czechoslovakia, and others. One more meeting was postponed until the next day because Churchill and Roosevelt had been going non-stop and needed a break after the long Saturday. Churchill would be leaving the next day.

On Sunday, Churchill departed via train for Ottawa, where he was to give a speech before the Canadian Parliament. He climbed aboard a private car at Union Station in Washington at 2:15 p.m. and headed north through Baltimore and Philadelphia before stopping in New York at 6:10 p.m. It took three hours to get to Springfield, Massachusetts, where he arrived at 9:40 p.m. In and out of White River Junction, Vermont, after 1:00 a.m., he did not arrive in Ottawa until 9:00 a.m. the next morning.[21]

Cigarettes and the tobacco industry were hugely important to the civilian population and military government, and it was big news when a new brand came out or, heaven forbid, manufacturers raised the price on a pack of cigarettes. The Office of Price Administration raised a stink when American Tobacco wanted to raise its prices by 57 cents on every 1,000 cigarettes. The increase to the consumer would be about one penny for a pack of 20 cigarettes and the OPM pressured nine other tobacco companies not to follow suit.[22] The cost of a pack of cigarettes was, depending on where you lived, around 20 cents, and over sixty percent of all smokers smoked filterless Lucky Strikes, filterless Camels, or filterless Chesterfields.

Big advertisements filled the magazines of America featuring soldiers and sailors and marines in uniform with cigarettes dangling from their mouths with the screaming headline, "WE WANT CAMELS!"[23] Other ads featured kindly looking doctors with silver-haired temples, dressed in white lab coats, assuring smokers of the healthful benefits of certain cigarette brands. To preempt growing anxieties about the bad physical effects of smoking, tobacco companies increasingly featured bogus "medical evidence" that their brands were actually good for you. They also actively curried favor with physicians and physician groups, leveraging the enormous respect and authority that the medical profession enjoyed in society.

Now, with America at war, cigarette advertisements were starting to feature heroic doctors in battle, supplying fighting men with the medical attention—and cigarettes—that they so desperately needed. As one advertisement had it: "[The medical man] well knows the comfort and cheer there is in a few moments' relaxation with a good cigarette . . . like Camel . . . the favorite cigarette with men in all the services."[24]

Meanwhile, another government entity, the Office of Production Management, issued new orders of its own to makers of farm equipment. The companies were told to "curtail" the manufacturing of new equipment while stepping up the "output of repair parts." "The purpose is to conserve scarce metals while assuring that farmers will be able to keep presently-owned machinery in good working condition." The order, it was said, affected everything "from windmills to wheelbarrows." At the time, some fifty thousand Americans were employed in the farm manufacturing industry, in which there were approximately a thousand companies churning out milk cans, tractors, combines, harrows, hoes, shovels, pickaxes, spades, and spade shovels; the tools for the men and women who had wrought miracles out of the American wilderness and with those tools, their hands, and their fortitude had fed millions of Americans with high-quality and low-cost food.[25]

In the cities, where the sophisticates sometimes looked down their noses at their country cousins, they were getting ready for New Year's Eve. To most farmers, it was simply another day, but to the city slickers, it was an excuse to get dolled up, men in black tie, women in furs and flowing fur coats. A dinner jacket at Raleigh's Haberdasher in Washington was going for $55, enough to feed a family of four for a month. For the police and fire departments of New York, New Year's Eve would be spent patrolling the Great White Way, looking for saboteurs on the ground and bombers in the air. Big crowds were expected as with each New Year's Eve and officials thought the throngs would be a tempting target to the enemy. The city had been under pressure to cancel the reverie on December 31, but they went ahead and made sure seven hundred of New York's finest were out and about to ensure no harm befell the partiers.

For the women, before going out, print ads reminded them—sometimes in the bluntest terms—to take care of their hygiene. "Go to bed, Mary," said one ad for Mum deodorant. "That phone won't ring tonight. No one ever calls Mary anymore. No one ever calls on any girl who is careless about underarm odour [sic]. You need Mum to prevent odour to come." Other ads advised women that if they had any chance at all for a man, they'd better use Lux Soap, or Palmolive Soap, or Cashmere Bouquet Soap. "That exquisite, lingering scent is the success secret of your romantic rival. . . ."[26] Ivory Snow laundry detergent was recommended for women's increasingly rare silk stockings because "perspiration is acid."[27]

Print ads in Los Angeles newspapers urged people to make their reservations now for the Hollywood Palladium where Tommy Dorsey "and his trombone and orchestra" would perform for the revelers on the Palladium's opening night.[28] On the bill for that evening was a wafer-thin twenty-four-year-old kid from Hoboken, New Jersey, named Frank Sinatra.

For those who wanted to party on New Year's Eve in Hawaii, "intoxicating liquor" was still not available by order of the military governor. The only way to obtain beer, liquor, or wine was with a prescription written by a physician. If the "sick" individual was in the military, then his liquor prescription could only be filled by a military pharmacist. If the "sick" individual was a civilian, well, this one gave new meaning to bureaucracy. "Prescriptions written by civilian physicians, dentists and veterinarians must be submitted in duplicate form to the pharmacist who is required to note on the duplicate the action he takes. Then the pharmacist must forward daily the copy with his notation to the controller of civilian medical supplies. . . ."[29] The runaround to getting a drink was enough to drive a man to drink.

J. B. Poindexter, the military governor, was cracking down in other ways. Beginning on December 31, all residents of Hawaii over the age of six years old would have to be registered and fingerprinted. Only military personnel were exempted. The entire "Hawaiian Defense Act" took up a full page in mouse type in the December 28 *Honolulu Advertiser*. Anything and everything in the islands from gasoline consumption to residences to curfews had rules and regulations. The paper also was running classified ads selling bomb shelters. "Can be installed immediately."[30]

Irony was a part of war. It was reported that "several" of the Japanese pilots who had been shot down on December 7 were wearing class rings issued by the University of Hawaii and McKinley High School.[31]

Local radio stations in Honolulu came on no earlier than 6:30 a.m. and their broadcasting day ended at just after 10 p.m. No longer would an enemy use the overnight broadcasting of a radio station as a homing beacon as the Japanese had done early in the morning of December 7. The first show on KGMB was, appropriately, "Dawn Patrol."[32]

The number of Japanese, Germans, and Italians deported from the West Coast and shipped to Montana was increasing. Prisoners who had been held in the Terminal Island Federal jail in the Los Angeles area were cleaned out "and moved to an internment camp." Further, "This was disclosed yesterday with reports that more than 100 Japanese and German nationals had been transported to the internment camp together with a group from San Francisco."[33] Also, all the Japanese-owned shops in the Terminal Island "settlement" were closed.[34]

Across the country, rumors went around that employers were dismissing workers of Italian, German, and Japanese descent, even though they were either American citizens or legal aliens and loyal to their adopted country. Attorney General Francis Biddle cautioned Americans against racism and xenophobia. "Among those who died fighting off the treacherous attacks upon Manila and Pearl Harbor were men named Wagner and Petersen and Monzo and Bossini and Mueller and Rasmussen. To bar aliens from employment is both short-sighted and wasteful."[35] The government then made a high-profile arrest of a "Bund Leader" in Los Angeles, Herman Max Schwinn, "one-time alleged West Coast chieftain of the German-American Bund and many other Nazis and Italians have been arrested for investigation by G-men in a surprise and sensational roundup of aliens in Southern California."[36] Biddle would be an unsung hero of the era, successfully arguing to FDR that the mass internment of Japanese, favored by the military and others, was wrong.

FBI director J. Edgar Hoover took credit for busting a German spy ring operating in the United States long before the war started. Thirty-three were arrested, and by mid-December fourteen had been convicted in federal court and the remaining nineteen had pleaded guilty. The spies used invisible writing and a "complicated code based on pages from the novel *All This and Heaven, Too.*"[37] Hoover was a master at promoting himself and for taking credit for the hard work of subordinates; this was no exception.

Possibly to make amends to Roosevelt, La Guardia's Office of Civil Defense announced its new operating hours, which was all the time. Employees would, for the duration of the war, work twelve-hour shifts. *Time* magazine described La Guardia's operations there as "confused and unprepared" and he as "hen-shaped."[38]

Adjustments in work schedules were also being considered in airplane plants on the West Coast. Though operating on a twenty-four-hour basis, the regulations prevented women from working the "graveyard" shifts unless they were paid overtime, even as the men who worked those hours were paid at the normal rate. It was recommended that this rule be amended or changed because of the national emergency "and because the airplane plants already pay far above the legal minimum wage for women."[39]

The Office of Production Management also "requested" of defense plants, nationwide, that they put in a regular work schedule on New Year's Day. "Since the men at the front, are not taking time off to celebrate New Year's Day, we feel that this should not be considered a holiday for defense plants."[40]

Sub attacks on American vessels had declined dramatically, in part because of increased surveillance by the military and decreased provisions for the subs. Navy officials also credited the decline to quiet citizens. Two phrases popped up: "A slip of the lip may sink a ship" and "That friendly chap may tell a Jap." The Office of War Information and the navy launched a public relations campaign to ask Americans not to talk about "disclosure of . . . ship movements." One official said, "Much of this information is undoubtedly obtained by enemy agents and fifth columnists from conversations which they initiate or overhear in public places." He then put an edge on it with the threat: the "federal Espionage Act . . . carries a maximum penalty of 20 years imprisonment for communicating, either directly or indirectly, information relating to national defense."[41] Mum's the word.

In its lead editorial the *Los Angeles Times* took up the military's lament against so-called Monday morning quarterbacks, "arm-chair generals, table-cloth admirals and all-round amateur runners-of-the-war." The long editorial berated readers for all real or imagined complaints against the conduct of the war and defended the War Department. "Our military and naval leaders are among the ablest of their professions in the world."[42] Most of the complaining came from editorialists and columnists. To wit, an editorial the same day criticized the U.S. military for being taken in by the Japanese, for being foolish enough to believe they would abide by the rules of engagement pertaining to open cities—in this case, Manila—after the Japanese surprise attack. "We should have known that a government capable of such a monstrous crime as was perpetrated at Honolulu would not hesitate at the mere bombing of an open city in defiance of the international code of war."[43] This hard-hitting editorial ran second to the lead in the *Los Angeles Times*. Few have successfully made a charge of consistency stick to the American press.

The siege of Manila and the Philippines now dominated much of the news and with it, the utter and complete denunciation of the Japanese for their bombing of innocent civilians. Inexorably, Japanese troops were driving toward Manila, and Senator Burton K. Wheeler of Montana declared the enemy "an inhuman and half-civilized race."[44]

The death toll overnight had risen and part of Manila seemed to have more bomb craters than standing buildings. One bomb reportedly hit a church, killing eighty people and wounding twenty more. Several nuns were killed.[45] The famed Santo Domingo Church, built by the Dominicans in 1590, had been destroyed in the bombings, according to reports.[46] Despite the fires and the carnage and the danger, many of the residents of the heavily Catholic city attended Mass on the 28th.

The citizenry begged MacArthur to return with the American army in tow to defend the city. But the notion was taking hold that America was going along with Churchill's plan to put the main emphasis of the Allies in Europe. "Despite the Manila news and a steady Japanese advance northward and southward through Luzon, it was reported in Washington that Britain and the United States had agreed, in the interests of a wider strategy, to concentrate on Germany."[47] The Japanese broadcast a message over Tokyo radio which was tantamount to an ultimatum to the Filipino people: lay down your arms and we will stop bombing Manila. A CBS listening post picked up the broadcast. The Japanese demand "was greeted with scorn and derision."[48] A town only 55 miles from Manila, Lucena, now flew the Japanese flag of the rising sun and up to 15,000 ground troops were estimated just in this one area.[49] Despite the threat, the Filipino people refused, in part because they believed, as did MacArthur, that American aid was forthcoming. There was no aid coming.

Fortunately, the monument to Ferdinand Magellan, who brought Christianity and western civilization after he discovered the islands in 1521, was untouched amid the destruction.[50] A small victory. Meanwhile, the streets were strewn with bodies, body parts, blood, and "tattered school books and examination papers from the bombed Intramuros Catholic elementary school...."[51]

The Japanese attack of the day before was enraging to all. They bombed at almost a leisurely pace, wave after wave after wave of planes, doing so in almost three hours, knowing there was no danger from antiaircraft guns.

They also bombed Kuala Lumpur on Saturday and destroyed an ancient mosque, described as one of Malaya's "oldest and finest."[52] The bombing had taken place when many Muslims were there praying.

Washington politicians were lamenting how America had been "twice burnt" and many thundered for direct retaliation against Japan's cities. Senator Alben Barkley was practically offering to carry the bombs to Tokyo on his back. He accused the Japanese of "sadistic cruelty."[53] Problem was, those cities were too far off for American land bombers to make the round trip from any airfields controlled by the Allies. And America had no available planes in the area at the time and no secret airfields.

CHAPTER 29

THE TWENTY-NINTH
OF DECEMBER

"Our Fleet 'Is Not Idle,' the Navy Declares"

New York Times

"Russia, England Agree on Method of War Conduct"

Birmingham News

"Positive Aid Pledged by Roosevelt and Navy in Philippine Fighting"

Sun

The Japanese bombed Manila again around noon, on the twenty-ninth. The city had done everything possible to make it clear it was open for peace, short of taking out ads in the Tokyo newspapers. Any remaining ships in Manila Harbor were towed out—so not to be confused by the Japanese with naval warships—and blown up and sunk.[1]

"The second day of savage, unopposed air-raids left Manila an inferno of burning churches and office buildings. Many persons lay dead among the debris."[2] The second attack of the day also involved repeated strafing of Ft. Murphy, which General MacArthur had already evacuated. The most famous Catholic statue in Manila, "Our Lady of the Rosary," was fortunately saved from the bombing campaign "by priests and church servants who braved the flames and entered the church shortly after bombs had wrecked the bell tower and roof" of the Santo Domingo cathedral.[3] But tragically, a priceless library at the church went up in smoke, destroying 200,000 folios and books. In that library was a complete record of every Filipino dialect spoken over the past 300 years in the islands. "Ironically, the library also contained original manuscripts from Dominican missions in China and Indo-China. They were brought to Manila a few months ago to save them from the ravages of war on the Asiatic mainland."[4]

The Japanese state media, Domei, announced that the government intended to have the Philippines conquered and catalogued by New Year's Day, which was a big holiday in Japan.[5]

President Roosevelt, under pressure to do something, pledged aid to the beleaguered country and to one of his favorite generals, MacArthur. Late the day before, he went on short-wave radio and proclaimed his "solemn pledge that their freedom will be redeemed and their independence established and protected. The entire resources of the United States, in men and materiel, stand behind that pledge, the President's message assured."[6] Almost immediately, the navy issued a statement claiming, "The Fleet is not idle. The United States Navy is following an intensive and well-planned campaign against the Japanese forces which will result in positive assistance to the defense of the Philippine Islands."[7] It was bluster, or disinformation. Other than submarines, there was no attempt or planned attempt involving American surface ships to come to the defense of the Philippines.[8]

Even if Washington had the ability to send anything, a Japanese blockade of the Philippines was forming up to keep anything from getting in. Some wondered about the whereabouts of the American Pacific fleet, such as it was, and a knowledgeable source said, "Be patient." Strategic reasons necessitated silence, but the nation was reassured that the navy would strike when the time was right.[9]

The navy as much as admitted that there had been no military contact between U.S. ships and the Japanese since the beginning of the war. "Naval strategists believe that major contact between the Japanese and United States navies will not occur for some time, maybe months—perhaps a year or more."[10] Of course, without naval "contact," there would be no re-provisioning of the Philippines. The Japanese had complete air superiority over Luzon, so that option was out for the American forces. The Japanese saturation bombing of Clark Field and Nichols Field had obliterated hundreds of planes on the ground, and those that escaped were eventually shot down or were grounded for a lack of replacement parts.

Navy secretary Frank Knox claimed the fleet was at sea and that "the main body of the fleet with its battleships, cruisers, aircraft carriers and submarines was '. . . seeking contact with the enemy.'"[11] The contradictory information coming from naval sources—other than announcing their submarines' successes—was the first real information of any kind since the week after Pearl Harbor. The navy may have been engaged in a disinformation campaign so as to not reveal to the Japanese the true location of the fleet. "The Japanese government is circulating rumors for the obvious purpose of persuading the United States to disclose the location and intentions of the American Pacific fleet. It is obvious that these rumors are intended for and directed at the Philippine Islands."[12]

Among all the services, the navy was in the worst shape when it came to men and materiel. The Air Corps had lost hundreds of planes at Hickam, but airplanes were easier to replace than destroyed or damaged warships, which tended to take longer to refloat.

Despite the rush at recruitment offices, large ads continued to run looking for "College Men . . . to be Naval Officers." No sugar-coating, the ads practically begged that "the Navy needs 7000 Seniors now in college or college graduates as prospective officers. In addition, the Navy needs 5000 men now in their Junior year in college as prospective officers." Upon completion of training, "you will be commissioned as an Ensign, U.S.N.R., at $125 a month and allowances." However, the navy also needed "15,000 men now in their Senior, Junior or Sophomore years . . . as prospective Naval aviators. As full-fledged Naval Aviators their pay will be $205 per month plus allowances."[13]

But as far as the final word on the disposition of the Pacific Fleet, columnist Paul Mallon, who wrote the "News Behind the News" syndicated column, said, "The truth probably is that our naval command has decided not to risk heavy ships in waters where the enemy has air superiority, especially after what happened to the *Prince of Wales* and the *Repulse*. It is also probable a third of the fleet was in the Atlantic when the blow fell. A redistribution of naval forces is obviously necessary. The British should have enough of their own capital ships to take care of the Atlantic. . . ."[14] Mallon was an unusually trenchant columnist.

Japanese parachutists were spotted floating down over Manila, a prelude to invasion and occupation. "Filipino police, sole-remaining defenders of Manila, rushed through the bomb-ravaged and burning city early this morning hunting Japanese parachutists who were said to have been seen swooping down during the night, apparently attempting to prepare the way for invading armies."[15] The Japanese War Office broadcast a statement in which they refused to recognize Manila as an open city. "The Japanese will not consider their action at all limited by such 'arbitrary and unilateral announcements' and will proceed to carry out their war objectives," they said.[16]

American antiaircraft guns—what few there were outside the city— scored a couple of hits and brought down three Japanese planes, but the bombings and the invasion continued. The Japanese advised the remaining civilians in the city to evacuate, via air-dropped pamphlets. They were told to go to two refugee centers, Antipolo and Montalban. It wasn't that the Filipino and American troops weren't up to the challenge. They were; they fought bravely and tirelessly and by all accounts their equipment was better, but they were now facing overwhelming numbers of Japanese troops. "Outnumbered American and Philippine troops dug in among the coconut groves fringing the Tiaong River . . . for a stand against 10,000 to 15,000 Japanese invaders pushing up the Tabayas Isthmus. Their stand was costing the Japanese ten men for every fallen defender."[17]

MacArthur had been training these troops for several years, and it had paid off in a superior fighting soldier, but as a substitution for victory, he would have gladly accepted more tanks, planes, and men, had they been forthcoming from Washington. One American anti-tank gun was, on average, taking out three Japanese tanks along with field guns.[18] "This question of reinforcement is difficult because the Philippines lie 7,000 miles from the United States and are amid Japanese island positions that hold a constant threat to reinforcement by air or sea." The best Washington could realistically offer MacArthur was "Hopeful."[19]

The Japanese storm continued to rage across the entire Pacific. They had finally gained a toe-hold in the mineral-rich Dutch East Indies. The move was a strategic one, aimed at possessing bases near Singapore to stop re-supply and aid from getting to the battered British garrison there.[20] Inhabitants of the East Indies were warned not to run out of their homes when the Japanese dropped leaflets, as it was a ploy.

In Penang, on the Malaya Peninsula, leaflets had been dropped and then Japanese planes strafed the individuals who came out to read the paper which said the Japanese wanted peace.[21]

The Japanese were also dropping paratroopers onto the Malaya Peninsula and claimed they now controlled one third of the isthmus. Singapore announced it had received assurance from both London and Washington that help was on the way, and the Australian Expeditionary Force was mounting a resilient and valiant effort against the Japanese invaders.[22] British leaders were already vowing to take back Hong Kong, but that was so much blue sky over the Pacific as they didn't have the manpower to stop the Japanese advance, much less actually defeat them in open battle. That very day, the Japanese held a triumphal troop review in Hong Kong while announcing they had captured six thousand British troops and fifteen thousand Indian troops.[23]

The final chapter of the American presence in China was written when the Japanese seized the consul there and with it, some sixty noncombatants, who were taken into custody, including Kenneth Yearns, the U.S. consul.[24] It was an open question whether it would also be the final chapter in the American presence in the Western Pacific if the Philippines fell. At this point, Japanese troops had closed to within forty miles of Manila.

A mound of paper crossed President Roosevelt's desk that day but none of it apparently dealing with the Philippines. FDR's inbox was especially heavy on the twenty-ninth. There were memos from Secretary of State Cordell Hull on Borneo,[25] copies of British diplomatic memoranda, including a memo defining "Security," and another on the organizational problems in localities where various agencies were crowding and stepping on each other's toes.[26]

As was often the case, there was a confidential memorandum from John Franklin Carter, a writer (and covert White House operative) who worked out of the National Press Club building in Washington. His memos went directly to FDR, and no one else, as if he was a free agent on the outside, beyond any chain of command, working exclusively and directly for the president. His memos littered Roosevelt's desk.

A new one, dated the twenty-seventh, dealt with "Intelligence Problems in the New York Area."[27] "After discussions with F.B.I., O.N.I. [Office of Naval Intelligence] . . . I am convinced . . . Civil Service should be asked to waive or modify some of its rules on recruiting civilian personal for intelligence services." In so many words, Carter was advocating the creation of a network of private individuals, including Mafiosi and wise guys, to act as covert operatives on behalf of the U.S. government. "There is a need for greater pooling of intelligence reports and services on the New York Area at least."[28] Roosevelt wrote back and advised Carter to take the matter up with William H. McReynolds and Vincent Astor.[29] McReynolds was a White House aide who carried a portfolio with a wide latitude and extensive contacts in the agencies, and Astor was a New York socialite who, because of his connections to horse racing, presumably had contacts in Gotham's underworld.

He also received a copy of a classified British memo on how Great Britain was dealing with their alien problem. "The initial policy was to impose on enemy aliens restrictions graduated according to their estimated potential danger. . . . the Executive advised a policy of general internment . . ."[30] Roosevelt also sent a note on White House stationery to "H.H." saying, "Will you read this over and I will talk with you about it later? F.D.R."[31] The H.H. was Harry Hopkins, and widespread internment of Japanese loomed on the horizon.

The survivors of yet another previous Japanese attack on a civilian American ship in the Pacific washed ashore at Hawaii. But there were only thirteen men out of a complement of thirty-four aboard the *Prusa*, a 7,000-ton freighter.[32]

Life magazine published the most comprehensive set of photos of the carnage of Pearl Harbor, but the bulk dealt with the damage done to civilian targets and not the military in the Harbor or at Hickam Field. "First pictures of Jap onslaught show death & destruction at American base."[33] Still, few military targets were shown and no images of torpedoed ships were printed. Only the photo of a blasted-out hangar and a B-17 that had been forced to belly land were published along with those of some destroyed P-40s that never got off the ground. One surprisingly gruesome photo was of seven dead civilians in the morgue: "[S]even corpses—three men, three women and one child—lie sheeted in an emergency morgue." The publication claimed, "Now for the first time they [readers] may look on the bodies of their own dead."[34]

To end on a happier note, this being the Christmas season, *Life* ran a montage of boys in uniforms saying goodbye to loved ones. At an undisclosed location, up to four troop trains stopped daily.

"As each arrives, volunteer agents of the local Red Cross, the Knights of Columbus or the U.S.O. quickly appears with baskets of books, magazines and jig-saw puzzles which they give away, cartons of cigarets [*sic*] which they sell at any cost." Because of the short stay, the young men were not allowed to get off. "As trains vanish into the night the soldiers shout goodbye to the girls on the platform 'See you again,' they cry 'We'll bring you a necklace of Jap ears.'"[35]

Henry Luce's *Life* magazine seemed to have a direct pipeline into the War Department. In this pre-television era, government publicists saw the splashy, picture-intensive magazine as an important tool in telling the story of the American military and to boost civilian and military morale. Features ran the gamut, from the "Anatomy of Bombs"[36] and the personal story of "Buzz" Wagoner and how he bagged two Japanese Zeros in the Philippines,[37] to the story of the marines and "parachutists,"[38] to "How Nazi Planes May Bomb New York."[39] The thick, visually compelling weekly was filled with the stories and tales of the American fighting man, including full-sized photos of handsome young G.I.s in uniform.

One feature profiled Ensign George T. Weems, a handsome, six-foot-tall specimen of American manhood with everything going for him. Humorously, *Life* also mentioned his one weak spot. The young navy man whose career goal was to become an admiral suffered from "seasickness."[40]

That same week, Luce's *Time* magazine sported a flattering profile of MacArthur in the Pacific, with a quote from the general saying, "When George Dewey sailed into Manila Bay on May 1, 1898, it was Manifest Destiny working itself out. By God, it was Destiny that brought me here. It was Destiny." MacArthur smoked a cigarette as he watched Japanese bombs drop from the sky.[41] The lengthy and gushy two-page profile reviewed his career, that of his father's, his devotion to the Philippines, and his physical courage, as proved in Europe beginning in 1917.

Interestingly, the magazine opened by opining, "For the first time in nearly 10 years of publication, *Time* finds itself unable to tell its readers freely and frankly of all the things it [knows]."[42] While this may have been true, the Luce publishing empire found itself in a position to tell Americans a lot more than what they were getting from other publications and broadsheets, even down to Admiral Chester Nimitz's nickname, "Cottonhead."[43] Indeed, the periodical had dozens of stories about the war and the men conducting the war in great detail, practically swimming in facts.

The magazine that week also had the complete insider dope on how poorly Fiorello La Guardia was running the Office of Civil Defense. The story and the extensive details could have only come from sources close to a White House, very down on the mayor's stewardship. "Indications were that Mr. Roosevelt . . . was getting ready to pluck the Little Flower from OCD."[44]

As FDR and Churchill were wrapping up their historic meeting outlining a plan for defeating the Axis powers, it was revealed that Anthony Eden, foreign secretary in the Churchill government, had made a secret trip to Moscow to meet with Marshall Josef Stalin and his generals to work out the plans to defeat the Axis as it pertained to Russia. It was a "momentous" development, "paralleling the Roosevelt-Churchill meetings in Washington," said the Associated Press.[45] Discussions between the British and the Russians were also held on a post-war world and a "communiqué [outlined] the Anglo-Soviet exchange of views regarding [a] post-war organization of peace provide much useful material which will facilitate further elaboration of concrete proposals on the subject."[46] The Eden-Stalin meetings were termed "friendly."[47]

Several names had been devised to identify what the Roosevelt adminis-tration called the "War Council" but the press also called it the "Supreme War Council," the "Allied Command," and the "World G.H.Q." Roosevelt was also exploring a sort of "National War Council" whose composition and purpose was "to consist of a few top military men and civilians; with broad execu-tive powers to order coordination of the domestic war effort on the military, industrial, civilian and labor fronts . . . Meanwhile through the government men snapped orders and made decisions that changed or would change the lives of millions . . ." According to sources, as many as six thousand new gov-ernment employees were headed to Washington each and every month to join the war effort.[48]

These reports didn't explicitly dwell on what was obvious at the time: the Allies were on the defensive. The Axis powers had been chopping up the world piecemeal, taking one territory at a time—and at quick clip. Japan fol-lowed this tack in the Pacific, and the Third Reich had perfected this strategy in Europe, taking nation after nation. Though the invasion of Russia was of questionable efficacy, in December 1941, the German army still had a huge if embattled presence inside the country. For all the recent ballyhoo about Soviet pushback, they were fighting on their own soil. However, the Germans were withdrawing from Yugoslavia, where a ragtag guerrilla army of Serbs had beat the stuffing out of Reich soldiers. Three times the Germans had launched offensive operations to root out the tough Serb nationals and neu-tralize the country, and three times they were forced to withdraw.

The idea of a united front—an "Allied High Command"—did not originate with FDR or with Winston Churchill but interestingly, with Generalissimo Chiang Kai-shek, leader of the Free Chinese forces in Asia. Immediately, Churchill ordered "General Sir Archibald Wavell to further British cooperation with China" and directed Eden to Moscow to hold the paranoid hand of Joe Stalin and brief him on the plan.[49] Roosevelt sent a clas-sified letter to Chiang suggesting an immediate meeting of the representatives of all the nations warring against the Axis powers.

"It is our thought that, in order to make such command effective, a joint planning staff should at once be organized consisting of representatives of the British, American and Chinese governments. If you consider it practicable, and Russia agrees, a Russian representative might be included. This staff should function under your supreme command. Your views in this matter will be greatly appreciated by me. ROOSEVELT."[50]

The Allies knew they needed to defend their six strongest naval positions: England, Gibraltar, Singapore, Pearl Harbor, Suez, and the Panama Canal. Despite Roosevelt's public pronouncements to the contrary, the Philippines were not on the list. Each of these was an important chokepoint, and from each of these assaults could be launched against the Axis. And each of these was in the crosshairs of the Axis powers as they knew exactly what the Allies knew. "These fortresses are the key points in the Allies mobility, vitally necessary if the Allies are to continue helping each other fight on farflung battlefields. By breaking any two of those key points, the Axis could virtually cut hemisphere from hemisphere." Gibraltar was a concern because the British "suspected Spain and were not sure of Portugal." Germany had invaded North Africa in the hopes of controlling the Mediterranean and still had a strong force there, and the Japanese were making progress in their drive down the Malayan peninsula toward their goal of capturing Singapore. The "Allied High Command" was beginning "the battle of the world" very much on the defensive.[51]

Stitching together another part of the Allied High Command, Winston Churchill arrived in Ottawa on schedule, to the wild cheers of the Canadians. As he stepped off the train, with a cigar stuck in his mouth, he doffed his hat with one hand and gave the "V" sign with his other hand. He'd arrived in Roosevelt's own special Pullman car, "with the crew of porters and Secret Service men who normally look after the president's safety and comfort."[52]

The Ottawa station was jammed with admirers, and the Royal Canadian Mounted Police and Boy Scouts tried to maintain control. Even in the deep of the Canadian winter, clerks and secretaries in the nearby office building flung open their windows to get a glimpse of one of the most famous men in the world.[53]

The wire story noted that Churchill had left Washington in "wartime secrecy" and then proceeded to relay every detail of the trip, including his departure time from Washington and the stops in New York and Springfield where the local police cleared the platforms of all people. He'd made the trip with Canadian prime minister MacKenzie King and spent much of the trip, which carried them through a Massachusetts snow storm, in deep conversation with his parliamentary counterpart. He also worked late into the night on the speech he would deliver on Tuesday to the Canadian Parliament.

On the trip, he slipped into his favorite "Teddy Bear" coveralls. During the London Blitz, on cold evenings, it became uncomfortable and inconvenient to try to switch from pajamas to suits, so Churchill took to wearing the zippered garment. "The gray . . . coveralls gave the Prime Minister the appearance of a jovial Kewpie puffing on a cigar as he lounged and worked. He has both lights and heavies, and the red flannel weather of Vermont and Quebec called for the heavies."[54]

With Churchill gone, Washington got back to the business of running a wartime economy. Since rubber usage had been so severely restricted, gasoline consumption was now under study as well. Gas was plentiful, oil stocks were high, and ever since Great Britain had returned some tankers she'd borrowed the year before, the East Coast restrictions had been lifted. Also, it was noted that "petroleum supply in the United States, which possess great resources of oil, is principally a matter of transportation." Still, the "petroleum coordinator," who reported to Secretary of the Interior Harold Ickes, was ordered by Ickes to make a feasibility study of a gas rationing plan. The initial figure bandied about was a 35 percent reduction in gas usage for 1942.[55]

The citizens of Manila were astonished to wake up and hear over station KGEI that Japanese planes were bombing San Francisco and it was already in flames. It was a hoax; officials suspected that the Japanese had used a more powerful transmitter to interrupt the regular broadcast by an "English speaking announcer" reading "Flash" bulletins several times. "The interference obviously came from a powerful Japanese station deliberately intruding on the KGEI wave[length]."[56] A government official said, "This was the first evidence of an apparent new propaganda technique by the Japanese—an effort to create panic by means of the direct lie."[57]

Government officials began a public awareness campaign aimed at curbing venereal diseases especially, they said, around industrial plants and among the military. "The American Social Hygiene Association, at the urgent request of the army [and] navy . . . is playing an indispensible role in the nation's all-out effort to protect soldier, sailor and marine from syphilis and gonorrhea." An editorial in the *Birmingham News* said, "The problem, however, remains to be solved, and in wartime, naturally, it becomes more acute. This is true not only with respect to our armed forces, but also with regard to industrial workers, particularly those in the war industries."[58]

At the same time, ill-mannered women were the target of a new, "anti-profanity campaign." Arthur S. Colborne was on a one-man mission to wipe out swearing in America. Not just the garden-variety, four-lettered words either, but also "hell" and "gee-wizz" and "doggone" and "dad burn it," because as far as he was concerned, these were "leader-on words" (gateway drugs, as some might later think of them). He said women in bars were the worst offenders. They, in turn, thought he was full of ... well, it's better left unsaid. Curiously, Colborne was also the founder of the "Safe and Sane Fourth of July Movement."[59]

A young, ill-mannered German woman in New Jersey, Helga Schlueter, was arrested and convicted on the charge of "defiling" the American flag. During a firefighters' parade in Lakewood in 1940, in full view she tore up a flag and threw it on the ground. She was in the custody of the FBI, although she had already been sentenced to two years in a reformatory for women. The New Jersey state Supreme Court had already upheld her conviction by an Ocean County court.[60]

Another woman of ill fame, "heiress Gloria Vanderbilt," as she was commonly known, finally got married in Santa Barbara after day upon day of stories about her, her money, her much older fiancé, her family, her controversial young life—all printed ad nauseum in the country's newspapers.[61] There were plenty of photos in the papers of the pretty young heiress. The righteous were also quite prurient at times.

The Reverend Samuel Shoemaker of the Calvary Episcopal Church thought he knew what was ailing America. It lacked, he said, a "national philosophy. The strength of the enemy countries lies in their unity, and their unity comes from the way they as nations look upon life. I believe that Christianity is the forgotten ideology of America."[62] The Reverend Dr. Norman Vincent Peale said what was needed in America was a "Spiritual Army."[63]

A woman of no fame, just good spiritual character, was volunteering in New Jersey to spot for enemy planes. Lavina Mount Minton was no stranger to war, having once nursed injured Civil War soldiers. Lavina was 97 years old and going strong. "I've lived through three horrible wars and I'll see the finish of this one."[64]

At an army base in Illinois, a young, lonely private, Joseph Dee Everingham, sent a letter to the *Chicago Tribune*, announcing: "I am certainly the loneliest private this side of the Mississippi." Within days, his barracks were deluged with cards, letters, cakes, and "lots of lonely girls sent along their pictures. Even a Lonely Hearts club sent a list of wealthy widows." He received cookies, lobsters, candy, sweaters, socks. "He got enough Sunday dinner invitations to last him through the emergency."[65]

As was now an everyday occurrence, another young man thought dead in the Pacific turned up alive. Carl Frank Stewart, 19, had been mistakenly thought to have been killed and the navy notified his mother, who for three weeks through her grief could not bring herself to believe it was true. She took to her bed, dreaming of her boy. She refused to accept the proceeds from an insurance policy on young Carl's life. Then she got another missive from the navy, advising her that Carl was not dead but had been wounded "seriously, but will recover."[66] Perhaps it was mother's intuition.

Without any fanfare, a gentleman by the name of George Herman Ruth Jr. walked into the Manhattan bond office and quietly ordered $100,000 worth of war bonds. Told that the restrictions only allowed for the purchase of $50,000 per year, the man, who went by the nickname of "Babe," bought $50,000 and left an order for another $50,000 to be picked up on January 2, 1942.[67] War bonds and defense stamps had become so interwoven in society, appliance stores offered them for free with the purchase of washers, dryers, and ranges.[68]

The archbishop of New York, Francis Joseph Spellman, donated $1,000 to the Red Cross for the war fund and "disclosed that he had contributed one pint of ecclesiastical blood for the blood bank."[69]

And the archbishop of Canterbury, following Franklin Roosevelt's suit, called for the British to be in church on New Year's Eve and New Year's Day. "Throughout this country members of the various religious faiths will join with their co-religionists in the United States in observing a day of prayer."

The Anglican archbishop fired a rhetorical shot across the bow of his church's old adversary saying, "We recommend that in all Catholic churches there be prayers."[70] Lambs did not always play well together.

A former associate of Mr. Ruth, Lou Gehrig, had died several years earlier but Hollywood thought so much of him, his life, and his courage in facing death, it decided to make a movie about him and announced Gary Cooper would portray the "Iron Man." Hollywood also announced the beginning of filming of a new Tarzan movie starring Johnny Weissmuller, who was, for a generation, the best and the only "Ape Man."

Japanese, German, and Italian "Axis Aliens" began showing up at police stations all over the West to surrender thousands of cameras and massive amounts of radio equipment, per the directive of the federal government. For each item, a receipt was given "if Federal authorities release it at some future date."[71]

More war songs were pouring forth, but not the type found in church. The popular band leader Sammy Kaye penned, "Remember Pearl Harbor." The lyrics revealed Kaye's Catholicism: "We'll always remember Pearl Harbor, Brightest jewel of the blue southern sea, Our lips will be saying 'Pearl Harbor', On each bead of our rosary."[72] As many as 260 patriotic songs were submitted to Tin Pan Alley, slang for the group of music publishers clustered in New York City who dominated songwriting in America at the time. The very first song about the war they rushed out was "We Did It Before and We Can Do It Again," by Dinah Shore and Eddie Cantor. Other song titles by various artists included, "You're a Sap, Mr. Jap," and this particularly blunt tune, "We're Going to Find a Fellow Who is Yellow and Beat Him Red, White and Blue."[73]

In accordance with the new restrictions in Hawaii, all 215 buses of the Honolulu Rapid Transit Company had their roofs painted black.[74] All movie theaters in Hawaii stopped showing films at 4 p.m., including the Roosevelt, Waikiki, Kaimuki, Kapahulu, Kewalo, Kalihi, and Wahiawa theaters.[75]

New information and tales kept coming out about the attack.

A young wife, Margaret Bickell, 20, was in Oahu on December 7 with her husband, First Lieutenant George Bickell, 25, eating breakfast when they heard the first attack. Lt. Bickell reported immediately to his base and got up and flew against the Japanese until being shot down and crashing in the ocean, right in front of his wife. She then saw her husband swim to shore, get another plane, take off, and resume the fight.[76]

Mrs. Bickell also told of "sullen Japanese servants" in Oahu who, after December 7, had turned on lights during blackouts and smoked cigarettes out of doors when the general order was to not light anything for fear the enemy would spot it.[77]

CHAPTER 30

THE THIRTIETH
OF DECEMBER

"Britain Bombed Heaviest in Weeks"

Sun

"F.D.R. 'Pushed Europe into War Against Me,' Nazi Leader Complains"

International News Service

"Red Men Bury Hatchet to Aid War on Axis"

Associated Press

A s a means of helping Germany with their war effort, a committee of Frenchmen appointed by Vichy French president Marshal Pétain seriously considered demolishing the Eiffel Tower and salvaging the 1,000 tons of steel in the edifice worth at the time some $1,000,000. "Paris' 984-foot Eiffel Tower, known to millions since it was built 52 years ago, may be scrapped by a national metal collection committee working under Marshal Pétain. . . ."[1]

The committee's stated purpose was to identify buildings that lacked any real artistic or historical value. Surprising as it might seem, the tower didn't make the cut. One member of the French Academy, writer Henry Bordeaux, deemed Alexander Eiffel's 1889 creation for the World's Fair "an insult to aesthetic taste."[2] However, although controversial when it was first erected, the pioneering steel tower soon became an object of affection and veneration for Parisians—and a symbol of France itself.

After June 1940, the French Tricolor no longer flew from the Eiffel Tower but rather the flag with the menacing black spider of the Third Reich. German troops had marched into what had been known as the City of Light with near impunity, save the tears of a few old Frenchmen pining for the days of lost Napoleonic glory.

The news of the tower's intended destruction arrived to the world by a circuitous path. "Tokyo radio tonight carried a *Domei* agency dispatch from Lisbon quoting a dispatch from New York based on a British broadcast heard by American shortwave listeners." It had originated on Berlin radio coming from an official announcement from Vichy.[3]

Small wonder Winston Churchill had little respect for the men of the Seine. In his speech to the Canadian Parliament he acidly said,

> The British Empire and the United States . . . are going to fight out this new war against Japan together. We have suffered together and we shall conquer together. But the men of Bordeaux, the men of Vichy they would do nothing like this. They lay prostrate at the foot of the conqueror. They fawned upon him.
>
> What have they got out of it?
>
> This fragment of France which was left to them is just as powerless, just as hungry as, and even more miserable, because more divided, than the occupied regions themselves. Hitler plays from day to day . . . with these tormented men.[4]

There was still a huge debate raging in Washington over sources of new revenues for the national emergency. In the month of December alone, the war effort had cost nearly $2.2 billion dollars.[5]

War bonds, stamps, and the current tax structure wouldn't suffice, according to many of the bureaucrats responsible for having opinions on such matters. Funding for the war was already consuming some 23 percent of the national income, but it would shortly rocket up from there.[6] Henry Morgenthau, secretary of the Treasury, hired a new tax aide, Randolph Paul, who had some interesting notions on tax policy. "Prime obstacle to an effective tax structure . . . is the fact that taxpayers (at least in peacetime) have an insufficient 'sense of debt to society and little intelligent interest in the continuation of the conditions which enable satisfactory living."[7] Paul did not stop there. He made fun of companies for wanting to keep "surplus accumulations." Expanding, he continued that "the primary function of consumption taxes should be to control production, not raise revenue." Paul had helped Congress write the "Excess Profits Tax" which the government slapped on businesses in 1940 with the rate of earnings—weighted—of "not more than 10%."[8]

War was not only hell, it was expensive. As Roosevelt and his advisors tallied things, to effectively prosecute the war would take roughly half the national economy by midyear 1943; that was about fifty billion dollars. Yet another name was coined for the effort. It would be called, imaginatively, "The War Program." Even as the president told the press about such enormous sums, he pooh-poohed the money owed the United States by Britain under Lend-Lease. "Bookkeeping and questions of repayment . . . are almost a thing of the past," he breezily asserted.[9]

He also announced that the government was seriously considering going on "Daylight Savings" for 1942. "Mr. Roosevelt recalled that estimates were made that as much as 500,000 kilowatt hours of electric energy would be saved each day by a country-wide program extended from the spring to the fall. That, he added, is an awful lot of power."[10]

Funding had already gone forth, though, for a massive building program of Liberty Ships, which would become famous as the backbone of the Maritime navy. The very first Liberty ship, the *Patrick Henry*, had been completed in September of 1941 but was commissioned in December. The initial plan of the Maritime Commission was to build 312 of these workhorse boats, which were used for all manner of transporting goods and troops. The *Patrick Henry* was quickly followed by the *John Randolph* and the *American Mariner*, and shortly, hundreds more would be splashed with little fanfare, but much admiration.[11]

Bond sales had exploded in the month of December as Americans bought more than $400 million worth of the paper notes signifying their loan to the U.S. government; but Treasury officials said, when all is said and done, the total haul could go as high as $500 million. Many banks and bond offices had actually run out, because of the run on bonds. November saw less than half that number, around $220 million. "War probably was the big stimulus," the Associated Press dryly noted.[12]

Congressman W. Disney, Democrat of Oklahoma, was not fantasizing when he proposed a massive $11 billion tax increase to pay for the national emergency.[13] Morgenthau said in no uncertain terms that to conduct the war successfully meant a "considerable rearrangement of people's finances."[14]

Part of the cost of the new war would go for the proposed new women's volunteer army. A supplement to the regular army, "Women volunteers in khaki uniforms would be enrolled as privates and officers of the U.S. Army under a plan approved . . . by the War Department and now awaiting congressional action."[15] The plan for voluntary women to back up the men was the brainchild of Congresswoman Edith Nourse Rodgers, a Republican from Massachusetts. The inspiration had come from the auxiliary organizations of women in Great Britain who worked in uniform in the front office to support the men in uniform at the front. Secretary of War Henry Stimson was all for it.

The women, it was proposed, would be stationed right along with the men at military bases around the globe and the pay would be similar to that of the men. These women, it was envisioned, would practice close-order drilling and the officers and noncommissioned officers would be picked by merit. "They would live in barracks and be subject to military discipline. Outside of several drill hours weekly they would do clerical and secretarial jobs and work as teleprinter operators, cooks, bakers, dieticians, pharmacists, telephone operators and hospital and laboratory technicians."[16] Stimson also envisioned they could take over the entire air warning system in the country, replacing the voluntary hodgepodge set up by the Office of Civil Defense.

Cigarettes would not go up in cost after all, at least for the foreseeable future. The millions of smokers in America, from the president down to the neighborhood paperboy, heaved a smoky sigh of relief when the government stepped in to prevent the hike. The American Tobacco Company had refused the request to hold the line on a price increase by the Office of Price Administration, so the OPM changed the request to an edict that no tobacco companies could raise the price of a pack of cigarettes. Americans were free to smoke abundantly and cheaply.[17]

Washington also ordered that manufacturers of soap and paint were barred from hoarding eighteen hundred different kinds of fats and oils. Everything from cottonseed to "lemon, camphor, clove, wintergreen and citronella" was covered by the directive from the OPM.[18] The OPM was also displeased with the allocation of all raw materials to the war effort and one official called for the control of all such supplies from the "bottom up."[19]

The nation's capital was laying in the final plans for the mandated tire-rationing program to begin January 5, 1942. "The ordinary civilian motorist probably has bought his last new tire for a long time to come." The administration of much of the program would be laid off on the state governments to administer. One governor, when told his state would handle the bureaucracy responded, "Where's the money coming from?"[20] Companies such as the Firestone Tire and Rubber Co. took out full-page ads in publications explaining essentially why they could no longer sell new tires. They also produced a booklet entitled, "How to Get More Mileage from Your Tires."[21]

Some saw the silver lining in the rubber rationing. According to a Gallup survey, a majority of Americans did nothing for exercise, and the walking that came with the new realities was a benefit because "health authorities [urged] Americans to take more exercise." The survey noted that among those Americans who did walk, "the medium average distance walked in any one day is only about one and one half miles."[22] These paternalistic assertions must have come as a surprise to the many Americans who hoed fields, worked with their hands, operated heavy equipment, lifted dirty laundry, shoveled snow off their sidewalks, raked yards, threw newspapers while they pedaled bicycles, carried groceries out of the store and into the kitchen, lifted barges, and toted bales.

Meanwhile, officials of the National Stockyards reported a "marked increase" in purchases of horses and mules.[23]

As New Year's Eve was fast approaching, women were buying out the remaining stocks of silk stockings for those under-exercised legs. The previous August, the government had mandated that no more silk stockings be manufactured but retailers could sell out their inventories, though "promotion of Nylon and new constructions of other fibers are expected to expand to cushion exhausting of the all-silk product."[24]

Rumors were going around military circles that Adolf Hitler would be ousted in a military coup in 1942 and replaced by a military junta. Rumors were also circulating that German generals had secretly flown to Ireland for God knows what. A Luftwaffe plane had made a forced landing in Ireland recently, but there was no one above the rank of a sergeant in the plane. German planes were, however, over London in large waves for the first time in a long time, as it was the first anniversary of the giant firebombing of the old city by the Luftwaffe. This bombing lacked the punch of earlier Nazi over-flights, and the stiff-upper-lipped Brits brushed off the attack as they would a buzzing mosquito. "[D]amage nowhere was serious and the number of casualties were small," ran one report.[25]

Rumors were rampant in the Dutch East Indies "that Allied reinforcements were on their way to the Pacific and that a general offensive against Japan could be expected soon."[26] There were no reinforcements coming.

Great Britain retaliated to the renewed bombing of London, by bombing Nazi-held installations along the coast of France all the way to Norway, a thousand-mile front. The British hit munitions plants, synthetic rubber plants, sunk eight ships, blew up oil stores, ammunition dumps, and hit other assorted targets.[27] The British attack had more sting with their Mosquito bombers than did the Germans with their Junkers.

Adolf Hitler sat down for an interview with the famed war correspondent Pierre J. Huss, British correspondent for the International News Service. When asked who was the cause of the war, the Führer said, "Ja, Herr Roosevelt—and his Jews." He also dismissed the rumor that he "chews rugs" when irate. The setting could have been that of a pleasant grandfather—roaring fire, rain pelting at the window, a dog—with a "swastika collar strolled lazily up to Hitler and nuzzled his hand. He stroked the head. . . ." His paranoia of FDR was evident, though. "He wants to run the world and rob us all of a place in the sun. He says he wants to save England but he means he wants to be ruler and heir of the British Empire. I first saw this some years ago when Roosevelt began his undeclared war on me through speeches, boycotts and political intriguing in all chancelleries of Europe. Every time I reached forth my hand he slapped it down. When I began to show him that meddling in European affairs was not so easy and might be dangerous, he lost all control of himself and began his campaign of vilification." He also made reference to the "sabotage of Munich" and how this too was Roosevelt's fault. He made an anti-Semitic allusion to "Roosevelt and his golden calf."[28]

Huss knew otherwise, of course. Being there with this monster, he said, "[gives] you the uncomfortable feeling that none but the führer should be heard or seen, lest perhaps a blitz of unrestrained temper and authority hit the man nearest this volcano." Huss referred to Hitler's aides as "flunkies with booted black pants . . . ."[29]

This portion of the historic interview concluded with the Führer ranting that Roosevelt had broken political tradition in America by seeking a third term but even so, he could outwait FDR because, "I am young and healthy. Roosevelt is not."[30]

The circle was closing on Manila and Singapore. Overnight, Japanese planes had raided Singapore four times, bombing it heavily. Since Christmas Eve, bombs had fallen on Manila, but then they went silent. However, no one thought for a minute that the Japanese had changed their minds and withdrawn their forces. They just had a new target to go after: Corregidor.

The Japanese began bombing Corregidor Island, only thirty miles from Manila. For three hours, they blasted at the island with a "very large force of enemy aircraft."[31] The tactic was designed to weaken the fortification strength of the Allied military there as a possible prelude to the Japanese navy steaming into Manila Harbor. "Corregidor is of natural rock formation and is about 6½ miles long. It is five miles from the northern mainland shore, about midway at the bay's mouth." The island was surrounded by several smaller islands, also fortified. Corregidor was honeycombed with caves where supplies had been stored "for any siege and where its defenders could shelter from air-raids and artillery barrages from the mainland."[32] Since it bristled with big guns, no navy commander in his right mind would attempt to enter Manila Bay without first neutralizing Corregidor.

But Douglas MacArthur did have a new ally in the war for the Philippines. The Balugas, a pygmy tribe whose men stood no taller than five feet, announced their opposition to the empire of Japan, led by "King Alfanso."[33] They lived in the mountains on the island of Luzon and as tribute to the Allies, turned over to the Americans three Japanese soldiers who had parachuted into their domain.

The Japanese propagandists had tried to divide the Filipinos from the Americans, but there was a bond and a history between the two that ran deep. MacArthur, who had a long and warm history with the Philippines—his own father, Arthur MacArthur, had served there as civilian governor—had raged and denounced the Japanese for the bombings of Manila, which he himself had declared an open city. But there was little other than that which he could do against the surging tide of the Japanese invasion.

MacArthur noted what seemed to be a deliberate attempt by the Japanese to obliterate the religious culture of Manila. "The great Cathedral of the Immaculate Conception was a special target of Japanese bombs. It was sought out and attacked on three successive days. The College of San Juan Lateran, with its irreplaceable library of original manuscripts, was likewise attacked. Repeated attacks on successive days were made on Santa Rosa Convent and Santa Catalina Convent. The San Juan Dedios Hospital was also the object of vicious attacks."[34]

Things were faring better for the Americans who had volunteered to fly and fight with the Chinese air force. The American Volunteer Squadron had, on December 26th alone, shot down 26 Japanese planes in dog fights over Rangoon. The Americans, led by the legendary Col. Claire Chennault, meanwhile had lost only two planes.[35]

As soon as Winston Churchill returned to Washington from Ottawa, Franklin Roosevelt planned on convening another "War Council" meeting. "Military and naval . . . experts have been laboring on a master strategy plan for the past week."[36] Churchill, while in Ottawa, gave a sterling speech to the Canadian Parliament. It was there that he assured Australia, another parliamentary government and member of the Commonwealth, and their nervous if also steely prime minister, John Curtin, that the Allies would not leave their friends down under to the mercy of the merciless Japanese. But his speech was also vague and news reports only said that "Churchill and President Roosevelt have decided on definite measures of defense for both British and American interests in the Pacific."[37]

Churchill had hailed the Canadian contribution to the war and mocked the Axis powers, interrupted often by the applauding audience in the House of Commons. He said the war "must be an assault on the citadel and homeland of the guilty powers, both in Europe and Asia." The British prime minister said the goal was straightforward: "the total extirpation of Hitler tyranny, Japanese frenzy and the Mussolini flop." Churchill loved tormenting Benito Mussolini. The Italian dictator was a preening and vain egomaniac, obsessed with his own machismo. These qualities made Il Duce an easy target of ridicule; even his ally Hitler considered him to be an embarrassment. "[Churchill's] speech was filled with jibes and taunts at the Axis partners which moved the crowded chamber to cheers and laughter, but most of it was a calm, confident review of the road already travelled and the road still left to travel."[38]

His praise of Roosevelt was generous and heartfelt. "I have been all this week with the President of the United States, that great man whom destiny has marked for this climax of human fortune."[39] The crowds inside and outside Parliament Hill went wild. Loudspeakers broadcast his speech to the thousands standing in the cold and snow. "Hitler and his Nazi gang have sown the wind—let them reap the whirlwind."[40]

For Winston Churchill and the people of Great Britain, it had been a long and lonely quest as they had been the only major power opposing Nazism. At one point, observers felt there was a real chance England could fall to the Third Reich. No sane person wished for war, but the only way to end this new conflict was for more countries to declare war, and by the end of December 1941, 90 percent of the countries of the world were at war with someone. Though his headcount clashed with that of the U.S. State Department, Churchill told the Canadians "more than 30 States and nations" were arrayed against the Axis; the striped pants set of Foggy Bottom, ever cautious, low-balled it to 29.[41]

He concluded his peroration, as only the old master could: "The power of the enemy is upon us," he said. "Let us then, sir, address ourselves to our task, not in any way underrating its tremendous difficulties and perils; but in good heart and sober confidence, resolved that whatever the cost, whatever the sufferings, we shall stand by one another, true and faithful comrades, and do our duty, God helping us to the end."[42]

As with all his wartime speeches, Churchill's remarks were a pleasure to read and a joy to hear. The words and phrases cascaded over his listeners, convincing them of Churchill's righteousness and why they needed to join in his cause. There is no doubt that he saved England from Hitlerism and by extension, saved the world from a new Dark Age. At few times in history had a man been so clearly and perfectly thrust forward to fulfill his destiny.

Other volunteers were springing forth. Under one of the most awful headlines of the month, the Associated Press moved a story: "Red Men Bury Hatchet to Aid War on Axis." It detailed how California's Indian tribes, having been at odds with Washington since 1850, "patched up their differences and will support the United States in its war against the Axis. The Mission Indian Foundation, with 3,000 . . . members, telegraphed President Roosevelt . . . 'a message of loyalty and readiness to serve our great nation.'"[43]

A reclusive college professor ensconced in Princeton, a sleepy college town in New Jersey, gave a rare interview just before he was to address the American Physical Society. The organization was dedicated to the pleasure of knowledge, not the flesh. "Dr. Albert Einstein, renowned German Jewish refugee scientist and once a militant pacifist, said tonight the democracies eventually would win over the totalitarian powers but that 'we must strike hard and leave the breaking to the other sides.'" The interview with the sixty-two-year-old mathematician "with the great shock of unruly white hair" was conducted in his modest, green-shuttered home, as he smoked a pipe and pondered the often inane questions of his journalistic inquisitors. When asked about conditions in Nazi Germany—3,000 miles away—he replied, "I have no methods of observation" there.[44] His books had been banned for years in the Third Reich. The brilliant Einstein, whose groundbreaking Theory of Relativity had forever changed humankind's basic notions of the physical universe, had been hounded by the Nazis for practicing what they mocked as "Jew science." Like many of his talented colleagues, Einstein had seen the writing on the wall in Hitler's Germany and fled to the United States before the outbreak of war. Luckily for the civilized world, the Nazis had chased from their midst the very geniuses who could have given Hitler the atomic bomb.

Other scientists were also pondering the practical application of science to killing the enemy. Naturally, they met in Cleveland.[45] "Astronomy is turning practical for wartime to increase the range and accuracy of guns and to advance aerial photography, the American Astronomical Society heard tonight. Scores of astronomers now are applying their knowledge of mathematics and telescopes to ballistics . . . The problem of an astronomical body moving peacefully through the ether is much the same mathematically as that involving a bullet moving through the air."[46]

Yet another obscure scientist said the theory of the expanding universe was all wet. After six years of staring each night through the largest telescope in the world at Mt. Wilson in California, Dr. Edwin P. Hubble stated his belief that the universe was static, not dynamic, filled with approximately one hundred million Milky Way galaxies.[47]

And in a startling announcement, scientists said that there was absolutely no doubt about it, water existed on Mars! They weren't sure though if oxygen existed on the "Red Planet."[48]

The territorial civilian governor of Hawaii, Joseph Poindexter, had already announced the mandatory fingerprinting of all island residents, but other new strictures were announced in the *Honolulu Advertiser* and other papers. Long forms were printed in the broadsheets for everybody to fill out including the number of radios owned, and questions about their make, were they long wave, short wave, did the individual have either a receiver or transmitter? Number of beds in place of residences, and were the beds doubles, singles, or three quarter? The government also wanted to know the number of bathrooms in one's domicile. Would the renter or owner be willing to take in evacuees? With all the questions about fingerprints, nationality, "Racial Extraction," etc., the curiosity of the government seemed limitless.[49]

Poindexter was also granted executive authority over all bakery goods under the "M-Day Act." It said, "Bakery products may be offered for sale as long as they are fit for human consumption. . . ."[50] Something no doubt rarely considered before his administration.

The paper also had a long list of civilian residents of Hawaii whom friends and loved ones on the "mainland" had not been able to get a hold of since December 7. Worried individuals had been contacting the Red Cross asking for their assistance and got the cooperation of the newspaper to do so. "It will be appreciated if anyone whose name appears below will call the local American Red Cross office . . . and notify their present status, in order that a reply might be cabled to the National Headquarters in Washington as soon as possible."[51]

Residents of the islands, who had served in the military of any country other than the United States, had to turn themselves in to the local police station immediately. Regulations were also issued for fishing boats, including all boats to be painted white, fish only in designated areas and in designated hours, and only American citizens were allowed to own fishing licenses.[52]

An elaborate air-raid system was being constructed on the various islands of Oahau, Kauai, Maui, and Hawaii in the hope that all the residents could know at the same time if another attack was forthcoming. "The new system will be ready for operation in the very near future and installation is now contingent only upon the arrival of equipment."[53]

Fantastic stories of the overt operations of "Fifth Columnists" operating in Hawaii were emerging, including a United Press story, published in the *New York Times*, in which the navy secretary said huge arrows were cut in the "sugar fields pointing to hangars, munitions" and that some Japanese routinely strolled around the Schofield barracks. He detailed the "general espionage and sabotage network," including shopkeepers, a "host of spies, chiefly proprietors of small stores, restaurants, cafes . . . Japanese naval intelligence, which ran a much more extensive organization . . . its agents included fishermen and seamen." After saying such, came the clarification that this was not "an indictment of all Japanese in Honolulu. On the whole, they were industrious, dependable and well behaved. But enough of them were fifth columnists to make the attack successful."[54]

The order by the attorney general to "enemy aliens" to turn over camera equipment and radio broadcasting equipment was, by all accounts, enthusiastically obeyed. Francis Biddle's directive was originally aimed at seven states in the West but then was extended to the rest of the country. In the Los Angeles area alone, some four thousand now-contraband items had been surrendered to the local police, including "several hundred [firearms], mostly rifles and shotguns. . . ." The Los Angeles Board of Equalization also revoked the liquor licenses of all German, Italian, and Japanese aliens, affecting several hundred businesses.[55]

Roosevelt's secret operative, John Franklin Carter, got the go-ahead to start hiring civilian operatives in the New York area who were not part of civil service. Per FDR's directive, Carter had taken the matter up with others and they advised him under "Executive Order No. 8564" that the Office of Naval Intelligence and Army Intelligence could recruit their own civilian operatives. Euphemistically, Carter made reference to the "pooling of certain Intelligence functions in the New York Area." He also indicated that some of the more stuffy individuals in government intelligence, including Bill Donovan, thought his idea was nuts. "I am doubtful that any of the services will be co-operative," he said.[56] And again, while Carter never put it in writing, it seemed clear his intention was to recruit underworld figures to help the U.S. government defeat a bigger set of criminals.

Gloria Vanderbilt was back in the news. In Beverly Hills, she and her sister were held up and had $4,000 worth of jewelry stolen by a gunman "at their palatial Beverly Hills home."[57] She also received an "extra" allowance from her estate now that she was married. The robber—who had posed as a chauffeur—had second thoughts as one of the pins he'd stolen was a diamond encrusted "V" for victory brooch, valued at $1,000. The robber returned to the scene of the crime and, knocking on the door, pushed a package into the hands of a maid. Inside was the "V" pin along with a note from the Captivating Crook. "Mon Dieu et mon droit"—"My God and My Right."[58] Hollywood often had some of the most charming crooks in America.

Americans along the West Coast had been skittish for days now, after so many submarine attacks, and at Ft. MacArthur, servicemen thought they spotted more. "The guns were trained on the two shadowy objects in the water but before the command to fire was given, another observer flashed the signal: 'Whales.'"[59]

The war in the Pacific had gone badly for America and it was getting worse. The Japanese propaganda machine was in full force, the Domei news agency falsely reported at least sixteen American submarines sunk and far more damage from December 23 to the 27th. Yet the War Department, at this time, did not openly refute these claims or the braggadocio of the Domei.[60] Again, MacArthur was forced to withdraw his lines of defense as more Japanese troops came ashore. "In the last few days the enemy has been heavily reinforced by several infantry divisions, tank regiments and horse cavalry. Japanese units are composed of veteran soldiers with modern equipment."[61] He also had to concern himself with up to four thousand American civilians scattered throughout the Philippines.

On the Malaya Peninsula in both the east and the west, Japanese troops had broken through the defensive lines and were marching along some excellent roads, right into the city of Singapore. Despite the fact that the Dutch seemed the only Allied nation who knew how to fight the Japanese, even their own East Indies were threatened. Again, proximity and easier supply lines were contributing to their problems. If the Japanese gained this strategically important stretch of islands, they could launch strikes all over the areas including at Singapore and Australia. "The Japanese now threaten the Netherlands Indies from bases in North Borneo, from Mindanao in the Philippines and from Penang, which is only 200 miles across the Strait of Malacca from the well-developed and wealthy region of Northeast Sumatra."[62]

The Atlantic was no better. Not only was the U.S. Navy not scoring there, a German submarine sunk the freighter *Sagadahoc* as she steamed for South Africa.[63] Nor was the Russian front looking good; Germans were effectively parrying the Soviet counter-attacks. But the Axis had troubles of its own: Hitler had asked Benito Mussolini "for ten more Italian divisions for Russia, but Il Duce refused on the grounds that Italian soldiers were not inured to the Russian climate."[64]

Charles Lindbergh was trying to re-enlist in the Army Air Corps, but was getting the runaround from a government that mostly despised him. At his press conference, FDR was asked about the application of the "Lone Eagle" to be reinstated in the Air Corps Reserves so he could go on active duty, but he brushed aside the question, saying he had "no information" on the matter.[65]

General "Hap" Arnold, chief of the Air Corps, was anxious to have Lindbergh rejoin. "Lindbergh's act indicates a definite change from his former isolationist stand."[66] Others around the White House were less enthused about the reinstatement of their old antagonist.[67]

American morale could reach no lower than when it was learned that the Statue of Liberty, in following police blackout orders, would not be brilliantly illuminated. "Instead of being a blaze of glory, the Statue of Liberty will throw just enough light to indicate her presence in the bay." Before the beginning of the war, plans had been made to "install three new 3,000-watt-mercury-vapor lamps, to replace the thirteen 1,000-watt incandescent bulbs," but now that had been junked. The lamp beside the Golden Door was darkened.[68]

The entire Statue of Liberty—great symbol of American Exceptionalism, all 151 feet one inch of her, and in the middle of New York Harbor—was to be lighted with just two measly 100 watt bulbs.[69]

Nonetheless, Lady Liberty's gaze remained steady, in confident anticipation of brighter days ahead.

CHAPTER 31

THE THIRTY-FIRST
OF DECEMBER

"Manila Radio Falls Silent as Japan Attackers Near"

Honolulu Advertiser

"50 Billion a Year is Set by President as Our War Outlay"

New York Times

"Churchill Thinks Japs Are In For Surprises Before War Ends"

Birmingham News

A s the year ends, the Grand Alliance looming upon the horizon is perhaps the most astonishing in history."[1] So wrote the great Anne O'Hare McCormick, Pulitzer Prize-winning columnist for the *New York Times*. Indeed, recent events had been astonishing. The world had changed radically—it was aflame with war, but prayers for peace were prevalent too. The United States had also changed greatly and was aflame with a unity never seen before. A "National Will" was afoot in the land.

Even in England, on New Year's Day, there was a "religious festival at Albert Hall [for] the national day of prayer. The Archbishop of Canterbury and Cardinal Arthur Hinsley will give short addresses."[2] If the Church of England and the Church of Rome could get along in their own Grand Alliance, then anything was possible.

They knew, however, what it was they were fighting for. "The object of the meeting is to emphasize the fact to those here and elsewhere that the Allies are fighting for the restoration and preservation of Christendom."[3] Nearly the entire British government, clergy, and royal family were on hand, save Winston Churchill.

On the desks of many professionals in 1941 was a calendar, one page for each day of the year, usually placed in a cheap plastic holder with two rings in which to insert the pages. When all three hundred and sixty-five pages had been turned, a new year was placed in the desk calendar and the process began once again. This last day of 1941 was turned on desks across the country and with it a page of history.

It was New Year's Eve in America and Benny Goodman was entertaining in the Terrace Room of the Hotel New Yorker. The hotel hit handsomely dressed patrons with a $10 cover charge to listen to the "King of Swing" and his magical clarinet. Yet as McCormick noted, "We are at the end of our careless, easy years. . . ."[4]

Six thousand miles away, another man who often wore a formal white jacket, Admiral Chester Nimitz, was due to assume command of the crippled Pacific fleet the next day, January 1. The decision by President Roosevelt to replace Admiral Husband Kimmel with Nimitz would prove to be monumental, but this ceremony, in white day uniforms, would be a formality, with Nimitz actually replacing Vice-Admiral William Pye, who had temporarily replaced Kimmel.

Also scheduled in New York for the big night was Broadway star Kitty Carlisle, singing with Dick Gasparre and his orchestra in the Persian Room at The Plaza, which had a $15 cover charge. Meanwhile, at Billy Rose's Diamond Horseshoe in the Hotel Paramount, the minimum was only a dollar. Around the world, from Los Angeles to New York to Sydney, New Year's Eve celebrants were warned about excessive rejoicing. "Don't congregate. Keep moving outside. Celebrate—mildly, please—indoors."[5] Fiorello La Guardia asked New Yorkers not to blow horns. The Little Flower was still under severe disapproval. "I have suffered too much during the last six months absorbing the criticism, the abuse, the smears and jeers of people including some of the press, who wouldn't cooperate when we were seeking to train people for just this emergency," he whimpered.[6] The barrel-chested, staccato-speaking Italian was a character right out of the newspaper movie, *His Girl Friday*.

The city of Boston imposed a midnight tariff on food, and the *Globe* noted that "despite taxes and the Axis, capacity crowds will welcome the New Year here."[7] CBS, NBC, and Mutual Radio planned to broadcast an evening of big band and orchestra music. They would intersperse local "pickups" around the country with radio men interviewing citizens on the street, asking them about New Year's, their resolutions, and how they were enjoying the evening.

In London, because of heavy Christmas consumption, it was unknown if there would be enough wine and whiskey for the New Year's festivities.[8] Of course, liquor had already been banned in Hawaii and the police were cracking down heavily on bootleggers. The big radio station, KGMB, was due to end its broadcasting day at 10:30 p.m., after the news and fifteen minutes of popular swing music. Because of the island-wide curfew, there would be no nightclubbing around Honolulu or any other part of the territory on December 31. Fireworks were banned in Oahu. The provost judge, Lt. Colonel Neal D. Franklin, had already handed out fines for blackout violations.[9]

Hawaiians could take comfort, though, knowing that they had an over-supply of bananas which they could consume "for health and as a means of saving money."[10] The next day, the Daughters of Hawaii planned on placing leis and flowers on the graves of the men killed on December 7.[11] "At noon, there will be a Hawaiian chant, and a group of Hawaiians will sing 'Aloha Oe.'"[12]

Besides the Hotel New Yorker, in Baltimore, the Caribbean Tea Room, Twenty-One, Nates & Leons, and Marty's all planned bashes for New Year's.[13] Tommy Dorsey and his trombone were set to ring in the New Year at the Palladium in Los Angeles with special guests Frank Sinatra and the drummer Buddy Rich. Sinatra and Rich, two of the most talented (and headstrong) men in the jazz world, despised each other. Dorsey's band only had room for one breakout star, and they each vied for that honor. The personal enmity between Sinatra and Rich would one day erupt into fisticuffs. In the meantime, for the New Year's soiree they headlined, a $5.00 cover charge got the patron a private table, dinner, and party favors.[14] Still, "the World War which engulfed the United States in 1941 cast a dark shadow over . . . efforts to celebrate the arrival of the New Year with a rollicking fling."[15]

One hundred and ninety-nine years had passed since George Frederick Handel's *Messiah* had first been heard in Dublin and now, many churches throughout the West were planning on bringing in the New Year with a choral rendition of the oratorio. Many Americans had opted on this night to celebrate the ringing in of the New Year on their knees, but sober.

Factories were working at full steam, 24/7, including on New Year's Eve, while government doctors were spewing forth about American diets and American marriages. For Rosie the Riveter and her husband, Walt the Welder, a diet that included the daily consumption of "eggs, leafy vegetables, fresh fruit, milk, cheese, meat and bread" was recommended as the way to go.[16] Bananas were not specifically mentioned. The American marriage was thought because of the war to be in better health than at any time recently.

But the workers at the Ford Motor Company, where employees worked ten-hour shifts to make machines for the Willow Run airplane factory, had a problem. First, the men wanted some time off during those ten hours to "rest and wash up."[17] To make matters worse, management opposed the men smoking cigarettes, pipes, and cigars while they operated heavy equipment. The paternalistic Henry Ford, known for his abstemious nature, expected the same of his workers. Fighter planes and bombers were already "rolling off the production lines of U.S. manufacturers at the rate of 2,000 a month." Tanks were being built at the rate of almost 3,000 per month.[18]

The reality of war was all around. It was announced that Mt. Palomar, the site of the famed giant telescope in San Diego, was closed for the duration of the war.[19] On campuses, opinion was divided over whether sports programs should be cut back or participation made mandatory, as means of preparing the young men for combat. Government officials estimated there was a ready supply of some 25 million American males qualified for combat duty.

Thursday the first was officially a holiday, but many of the 200,000 federal workers had been "asked" by the various agencies to "contribute their holiday in the interests of an 'all out'—war effort and work New Year's Day."[20]

A new campaign by the government, "Salvage for Victory!" also reminded Americans that even on this night the war was never very far from their doorstep. "Save waste paper, rags, old skates, bicycle tires, rubber boots, children's toys . . ."[21] One government official puffed out his chest and proclaimed, "in a shooting war our planes, tanks, ships and guns have enormous appetites for metal. Mr. and Mrs. America have already made sacrifices. They must be prepared to make still more sacrifices."[22] The Office of Production Management came up with another slogan, "Get in the Scrap!" extolling Americans to save and salvage, as a way to join the war effort.[23]

As investors predicted, railroad stocks climbed sharply. With the new restrictions on rubber, people would turn back the pages of time and traverse the country as before, on the B&O and the Lehigh Valley, the Reading and the Erie Lackawanna. Among the various railroad companies, a hundred thousand new boxcars were ordered to accommodate the war effort and the shift by the civilian population from cars and trucks, to trains. While not taking Americans "back to horse and buggy days," the ban did push the railroads again "to the forefront as movers of passengers and freight."[24] The president of the Association of American Railroads, J. J. Pelley, wrote the presidents of colleges and universities asking that their football teams not travel by train "and keep student travel to a minimum so that we can devote our passenger facilities to troop movements."[25] Stocks in tire companies had plummeted, though, and theft became widespread.

Some worried that American women's style would falter in the face of the war, but right there on the fashion pages was a shapely model posing in what was sure to be popular haute couture for 1942. "Today's defense worker (or shall we call them war workers?) are going about their jobs efficiently in sturdy denim fashions adapted from men's work clothes. This mechanic's suit is styled for comfort."[26]

Ted Williams was voted baseball's "Man of the Year" by the *Sporting News*, making up for the fact that he'd lost out to Joe DiMaggio for MVP.[27] He was the first ballplayer to bat over .400 since 1930. The Chicago Bears, winners of the NFL championship, were on their way to New York for the annual All-Star game pitting the defending champs against a team made up of the best players from the rest of the league.

Baseball in January of 1942 was declared essential by the president personally, but even so, so many ballplayers left to join the fight that the quality of the game fell precipitously. It stumbled through using has-beens, never-weres, old men, young men, and in St. Louis, the joke-of-the-league Browns, used a one-armed ballplayer, Pete Gray, in the outfield because he could not serve in the military. The Browns won the American League pennant in 1944.

Citizen Kane was chosen as picture of the year by the New York Film Critics, and the annual list of the ten best-dressed women in the world was released.[28] Topping it for 1941 was the Duchess of Windsor, the twice-divorced and many-loved Wallis Simpson, for whom a man gave up a throne, a crown, and an Empire (and in so doing, changed the course of history for Great Britain and the world). Sentimentalized in the press as the "Love Story of the Century," the reality behind Simpson and Edward was actually quite tawdry. Unknown to the public at the time, Simpson remained promiscuous, even while married to Edward. For his part, the weak-willed Edward showed Nazi sympathies and proved such a security risk that an angry Churchill demanded that the erstwhile king be isolated from any secrets of state. The public saw the Duke of Windsor as a romantic figure, when, in fact, he would prove a royal embarrassment for many years to come.

After one last transmission from General MacArthur's command, all official communication stopped from Manila as of 3:35 a.m. the morning of December 31. "The enemy is driving in great force from both north and south. His dive-bombers practically control the roads from the air. The Japanese are using great quantities of tanks and armored units. Our lines are being pushed back," was the last message heard.[29]

A Tokyo broadcast was monitored calling on the American forces to cease all resistance in the Philippines "to assure the safety and protection of lives and property in Manila."[30] The Dutch press reported that Allied relief was just over the horizon. "Allied reinforcements were reported by Dutch newspapers tonight to be en route to the Pacific war theatre. . . ."[31] No such luck. It was also reported that Winston Churchill had cabled Australian prime mister John Curtin with assurances that resources would be made available to defend his country. But there was, again, no mention of the Philippines. The Philippines eventually fell and MacArthur was forced for a time onto the tiny island of Corregidor and then ordered off that island fortress by FDR and sent to Australia. Meanwhile, thousands of American, British, Australian, and Filipino troops fell into the hands of the murderous Japanese and faced a long death march in Bataan.

Things continued to go badly for the Americans in the Western and Central Pacific in 1942 with ships such as the *Langley*, the *Edsall*, and the *Peary* and many others sunk by the Japanese, until Chester Nimitz, with three aircraft carriers and a hell of a lot of luck, sank four of the Japanese fire line carriers at the Battle of Midway in June of 1942. All four of the carriers had been used in the attack on Pearl Harbor and everybody marinated themselves in the joy of revenge. Still, some members of Congress called for Nimitz's impeachment because he did not—they felt—more aggressively pursue the badly damaged and limping Japanese armada.

His predecessor knew something about being unfairly hounded. Admiral Husband Edward Kimmel, broken and bitter, took an early retirement in 1942 and spent most of the rest of his life trying to pick up the pieces of his shattered reputation, even as his son Manning was killed aboard a navy sub in 1944.

Twenty years after his command was destroyed before his very eyes, he wrote a book called simply *Admiral Kimmel's Story*, attempting to exonerate himself, but the book was filled with bitter recriminations against Roosevelt. The foreword to the book could only muster this defense of Kimmel: "It must be remembered that Admiral Kimmel was never formally charged with dereliction of duty . . . ."[32] Admiral Husband Kimmel, in his book, went so far as to call Roosevelt a "criminal."[33]

General Walter Short also retired from the military in early 1942. He moved to Dallas and seemed less obsessed with restoring his name than Kimmel. Short died in 1949 of heart disease.[34]

Kimmel and Short were exonerated on several occasions in later years, through studies, papers, and reports; but as a result, rather than being scape-goats, they morphed into victims and no real fighting man wanted to be regarded as either.

An act of Congress in 1947 allowed every man in uniform to receive the lifetime benefits of his highest rank in the war, except for two: Kimmel and Short.

Singapore had been hit again in late December of 1941 four times by Japanese bombers and looting broke out as the social structure began to break down. The pattern that was playing out in the Philippines and had played out in Hong Kong and Guam and Wake Island was now playing out in the Malaya city. Blitzkrieg bombings occured night and day to neutralize the enemy planes and ground batteries while unnerving the civilian populations and were followed by a massive, quick-striking invasion, all supported by a naval bombardment. Martial law was declared in Singapore to help stabilize the state of affairs. Spain, while officially neutral, was unofficially acting as a leader in the cheering section for Japan when the state radio in Madrid said the Japanese, in bombing Manila, had only hit military targets. Madrid said it had Tokyo's word on that.[35]

Douglas MacArthur and other American officials had assured and reas-sured the people of the Philippines that a relief effort was on the way; in fact Washington had ordered most of the American navy to withdraw to Australia to save what ships it had left, operating in the Western Pacific. Only a number of U.S. subs remained. "The little Asiatic Fleet, based in the Philippines, was never intended as anything other than a harassing and delaying fleet . . . it was never expected to prevent Japanese landings."[36] This, plus the fact that the only reliable port was in Singapore, also crippled the navy's operations in the South China Sea, and the U.S. subs that were operating got poor reviews. In fact, the navy would not take any significant action until February of 1942 when the *Yorktown* and the *Enterprise* attacked the Japanese in the Marshall and Gilbert Islands.[37]

In one of his final communiqués before evacuating his command post, MacArthur promised to mete out revenge for the bombing of Manila.

Eventually, he moved his family and forces to the Bataan section of Luzon and then, onto the island of Corregidor for one last stand before he could return.[38]

Word was spreading that MacArthur's position was tenuous, faltering. "Private advices received in New York indicate that the fall of Manila is imminent." MacArthur had attempted to evacuate three hundred wounded by ship.[39] "Yankee and Filipino soldiers fought desperately to block the assault, but the sheer weight of Jap numbers and equipment forced our men slowly back towards the capital."[40]

The Japanese were crowing about their successes in the Pacific, claiming to have destroyed over 540 American, British, and Dutch aircraft, and to have sunk or badly damaged 33 large warships and four smaller vessels. They also claimed to have killed over 3,000 Allied troops while capturing 7,000 POWs.[41]

One sailor they did not kill, but whose own government thought they had, was Clifford Kickbush, 19, who "saw a grave marked as his own and talked to a friend who thought he had helped bury him in the Hawaiian Islands informed his parents he was very much alive." He contacted his very relieved parents and assured his startled shipmate that he had not seen a ghost. "What the devil! I helped bury you yesterday."[42] The story only became public three weeks after the attack.

Most Americans had assumed that the Burma Road was a vital link to China and the Free Chinese Forces, along which munitions, medicine, and materiel passed from the Allies; in truth, the road was a highway of pirates, privateers, con men, crooks, and murderers. "It has been, and still remains both a national scandal and a national disgrace. Because the Burma Road has for years been dominated by racketeers and war profiteers . . . 10,000 Chinese soldiers have gone without rifles, hand grenades or munitions."[43] Thousands of tons of materiel destined for the Free Chinese never made it, left alongside the long road, stolen, destroyed, or which ended up on the black market, ever since its opening in 1938.

Mohandas Gandhi, the "Little Leader," stepped down as the head of the All-India Nationalist Congress because of his commitment to nonviolence. India, where opposition to British colonial rule was brewing, conditionally supported England. Some there wanted to leverage support for England in exchange for independence, but Gandhi would have none of it. "I could not identify myself with opposition to war efforts on the ground of ill-will against Britain." In essence, he would not support violence in exchange for peace. "If such were my view and I believed in the use of violence for gaining independence . . . I would consider myself guilty of unpatriotic conduct."[44] The decision by the Indian government was a practical one, though. The Japanese were threatening to bomb Calcutta. The Japanese were also suspected by the navy of having opened up submarine operations in the waters off Alaska.

Closer to home, the U.S. Congress wrapped up a rather eventful first session. In the 77th Congress, all they did was declare war on three countries, pass a huge new defense budget, give the president extraordinary authority under the War Powers Act, including the ability to censor just about anybody and any entity, pass a huge tax increase, pass the Lend-Lease Act, undo most of the Neutrality Acts of the 1930s, reinstitute Selective Service, and conduct numerous investigations, including corruption and fraud in defense lobbying.

Legislation they did not get around to passing included anti-lynching laws, stopped by a ferocious filibuster in the Senate. Proponents of the law thought that 1941 would be their year to finally get federal laws against lynching moved through Congress, but it was not to be so. The *Birmingham News*, while opposing a federal law against lynching, said, hopefully, that in all of 1941, there had only been four in the country, according to the Tuskegee Institute. This was down from thirty-nine lynchings in the years 1936 to 1941, and over three hundred from 1922 to 1936. "Almost any year now the nation may be able to go through an entire 12-month period without a lynching. This would be about the best answer to those who persist in agitating for a federal anti-lynching law."[45]

They also did not get the planned investigation into war propaganda in the movies, but by December it was a moot point. With the government's complicity, Hollywood had helped manufacture a consensus in favor of war.

Then "the Senate passed resolutions for sine die adjournment Jan. 2 and convening of the new Congress Jan. 5," at which time they would consider legislation to allow FDR the executive authority to direct the country to abide by daylight saving. The House did likewise. One of the first bills they would take up in 1942 was the "establishment of a separate air force."[46] The 77th Congress began 1941 riddled with factionalism and petty bickering, Democrats versus Republicans and Democrats versus Democrats. There simply weren't enough Republicans to fight amongst themselves. They also began the year arguing over a $17 billion federal budget. Twelve months later, they were in near unanimous agreement that the country needed a $61.5 billion budget, all of it save $8 billion slated for national defense.[47] Capitol Hill in January of 1941 was dominated by isolationists. In December of 1941, it was dominated by internationalists.

The city of Washington finally staged a successful blackout drill, after numerous failed attempts to do so. All it took was twelve thousand air raid wardens bellowing throughout the city for residents to get off the streets and turn off their lights. "By intent, it was only a partial blackout. Street lights were extinguished only in the downtown section and even there lights continued to glow . . . for the order in such cases were simply to use as little light as possible."[48]

Via his odious propaganda minister, Joseph Goebbels, Adolf Hitler addressed the German people on New Year's Eve. So, too, did Marshal Pétain address the French people on that day. Hitler claimed to have been behind the Japanese attack on Pearl Harbor, but a confidential memo to FDR from Rome refuted that. There, Hermann Goering had a conversation with an undercover British operative in which the German signaled his interest and approval of the Japanese operations in the Pacific. Although out of favor with Hitler for the recent failures of his Luftwaffe, Goering probably would have known if there had been any coordination between Berlin and Tokyo on December 7. Goering said, "I should consider it a great pleasure if Japan would be so kind as to instruct me in their method of conducting these operations. I feel that I have made a great mistake in not giving more study to the matter of launching aerial torpedoes."[49]

In the continuation of his exclusive interview with Pierre Huss of the International News Service, it was clear Hitler was still paranoid, ill-informed, insecure, and delusional. "He may have heard that astrologers are saying in the eighth year of his favorable sign in the heaven is the last. It is a worrisome thing." One thing was for sure. Adolf Hitler was absolutely obsessed with Franklin Roosevelt.[50]

The rumor was still going around that Hitler would be overthrown by his generals in 1942 and they would immediately sue for peace. A memo from the Office of Naval Intelligence laid it out, saying the German military was divided between "two factions, the first—Extremist, the second—Conservative. The Extremists are strong adherents of Hitler . . . Marshal Goering is now inclined toward the Conservative group, which is the real reason for his present alienation from Hitler. He and other members of the Conservative faction are under close surveillance of the Gestapo." The memo continued, "The Conservatives aim at final liquidation of the Nazi party at the earliest opportunity . . . ."[51]

In an earlier broadcast, he'd referred to President Roosevelt as "Frau Roosevelt."[52] British astrologers also forecast a bad 1942 for Adolf Hitler.

Still ringing in the ears of the Allies were the immortal words of Churchill: "There will be no halting or half measures. There will be no compromise or parley. These gangs of bandits have sought to darken the light of the world . . . and thence march forward into their inheritance. They shall themselves be cast into the pit of death and shame, and only when the earth has been cleansed and purged of their crime and of their villiany will we turn from the task which they have forced upon us . . . The enemies have asked for total war. Let us make sure they get it."[53]

Mr. Churchill was due back in Washington on January 1st and few men fired up the American people as did the British prime minister.

The first time Churchill and Roosevelt met in London in 1918, they did not like each other, though they did share a fondness for "tobacco, strong drink, history, the sea, battleships, hymns, pageantry, patriotic poetry, high office and hearing themselves talk." But they grew to respect each other, and on Churchill's part, there was a genuine fondness. He once said that FDR was like opening a new bottle of champagne, and FDR once said to Churchill, "I am glad we live in the same decade."[54]

At the stroke of midnight on January 1, 1942, America had been at war 27 days since the attack on Pearl Harbor. On December 8, President Roosevelt had made it official and then he did so again on December 11. America was thrust into a new world war; one in which she had vowed never to be involved; one that polling established the vast majority of the American people opposed; and one that had been forced upon a reluctant nation and indolent capital. "A languid Southern town with a pace so slow that much of it simply closed down for the summer grew almost overnight into a crowded, harried, almost frantic metropolis struggling desperately to assume the mantle of global power, moving haltingly and haphazardly and only partially successfully to change itself into the capital of the free world."[55]

Once forced into battle, the American people quickly rallied to the cause of patriotic grace, passion, desire, commitment, fear, revenge, love, hate, anger—all the emotions one would expect when one's country is unfairly and maliciously and sneakily attacked. Especially if that country was America in 1941, with its particularly strong streak of patriotism and sense of fair play.

The events of December 7, 1941, changed America forever. They sent the country careening off on a wildly different path of history than the one it had traveled in the days before that fateful morning. In the two hours of the attack, the navy lost more men than in World War I and the Spanish-American War combined. However, the nearly 3,000 dead did not come close to representing or reflecting the dimensions of the radical changes to America.

On December 6, 1941, America was an old body at rest. By the afternoon of December 7, it was a young body in motion. Action had been initiated and now America was obliged to engage in reaction. Yet it was more than just mere physics.

On December 6, 1941, America was in many ways a tired and run down country and many thought she had seen her best days. The cloud of the Great Depression hung over the country despite the best (and, some said, harebrained) efforts of the New Dealers. The "Brain Trust" advisers around FDR, who had come into power in 1933 full of promise and full of themselves, had, by 1941, drifted away, frustrated with their failures. FDR was essentially alone with only his last New Deal companion, Harry Hopkins, still at his side, still believing that government could prime the pump.

In joining the Allied effort against the Huns, as they had in 1917, America took the lead but also learned from the mistakes at the Treaty of Versailles; the French insisted on humiliating the German people, giving rise to Adolf Hitler, giving rise to a new world war. No one in America really knew why the world went to war in August of 1914, except Barbara Tuchman. The assassination of the Archduke Ferdinand by Gavrilo Princip is cited as the flashpoint, which triggered a series of mutual defense treaties, but European countries had battled each other for hundreds of years and it was often difficult to tell the good guys from the bad.

The war had revived a dying, wandering, and meandering America, without national purpose. And it changed the country forever. Never at any point in American history had the country been as united as it had been following December 7. Not on July 4, 1776, not on September 17, 1787, not for the War of 1812, certainly not in April 1861, not for the Spanish-American War, and not for the War to End All Wars. Indeed, in 1917 Congress debated for days before voting to support Woodrow Wilson, and even then, dozens of members voted against the War Resolution. After 1919, Americans asked themselves, "What did we get out of the first world war but death, debt, and George M. Cohan?"[56] It was a good question.

Never again would America be an isolationist country as it had been after 1919, refusing to join the League of Nations. After this war, America took the lead in creating the United Nations. Rather than turning its back on the empire of Japan and Nazi Germany, America chose instead to rebuild those war-torn countries and, going even further, implement the Marshall Plan as a means of rebuilding other countries in Europe, to protect them and America from Soviet advances, even as an Iron Curtain fell across Europe. It changed the USSR, too, leading to a Cold War, in turn leading to America's victory over the Soviets.

It forever changed the culture of America, kicking off a new realization of human rights for women and blacks.

It forever changed the economy as a heretofore unknown "Middle Class" sprung into being. It changed education, as the G.I. Bill, one of the greatest and kindest pieces of legislation ever passed by a grateful country, gave access to the academy to millions of G.I.s. It changed labor in America and the view toward government. The gentility of the past melted away. A brutality was evident at the end of the war that was not there at the beginning. For months after Pearl Harbor, American publications did not print photos of dead American soldiers. The subject was confined to private memos that ended up on Roosevelt's desk, as on December 11, when "Cincpac" Fleet surgeon Elphege A.M. Gendreua wrote, "The dead were fingerprinted, where possible, identification marks and teeth charted, bodies marked with attached wooden tag, and wrapped in canvas."[57]

It changed the airplane from a marginally important player in economics and warfare to a central role in the world. Roosevelt's first Secretary of War, George H. Dern, dismissed the airplane in war as "the fantasy of a dreamer."[58] Airplanes fought during World War II as the Army Air Corps, making a decisive difference on the battlefield. In the end, the war would hinge on who controlled the skies. The U.S. Air Force became its own armed service in 1947, marking the undisputed primacy of air power in warfare. After the war, the country was awash in commercial airlines and had plenty of experienced pilots to fly for them. It changed science, as rockets, once thought of as kids' stuff, became a reality in war and then in peace, leading to satellites, men in space, and walking on the moon.

This war, beginning in 1939, was easier to comprehend and it was easier to tell the good guys from the bad guys. It was *The Good War*, as Studs Terkel so memorably dubbed it.[59]

Newspapers across the country contained full-page ecumenical ads entreating Americans to go to the church of their choice for "A Universal Day of Prayer" as called for by President Roosevelt just a few days earlier.[60] New Year's Day was celebrated in the Catholic Church as the Feast of Circumcision, but all churches throughout America would be open from early on the morning of January 1, 1942, until well into the evening for prayer, communion, and supplication.

This prayer—recited in America and across the globe—had been marked "Triple Priority" for the American Embassy because it was to be read in London as well:

The year 1941 had brought upon our nation, as the past two years have brought upon other nations, a war of aggression by powers dominated by arrogant rulers whose selfish purpose is to destroy free institutions. They would thereby take from the freedom-loving peoples of the earth the hard-won liberties gained over many centuries.

The new year of 1942 calls for the courage and the resolution of old and young to help win a world struggle in order that we may preserve all we hold dear.

We are confident in our devotion to country, in our love of freedom, in our inheritance of courage. But our strength, as the strength of all men everywhere, is of greater avail as God upholds us.

In making this first day of the year 1942 a day of prayer, we ask forgiveness for our shortcomings of the past, consecration to the tasks of the present, and God's help in days to come.

We need His guidance that this people may be humble in spirit but strong in the conviction of the right; steadfast to endure sacrifices and brave to achieve a victory of liberty and peace.[61]

—Franklin Delano Roosevelt

America had the will to succeed; this much was certain. But to do so would require the necessary "blood, toil, tears and sweat."

EPILOGUE

"A failure of imagination . . ."

After the devastating fire of 1967 in which *Apollo One* astronauts Gus Grissom, Ed White, and Roger Chafee were burned alive on the ground in a seemingly routine drill, another astronaut, Frank Borman, was ordered to head up the NASA investigation.

He was hauled before a hostile congressional committee and toward the end was asked, "How could this have happened? How are three men killed in a ground test of the *Apollo* capsule?" Borman, a taciturn man, thought for a moment and replied to New Mexico senator Clinton Anderson, "Senator, it was a failure of imagination. . . ." Elaborating, Borman said, "No one ever imagined . . . [we] just didn't think that such a thing could happen."

So it was with the attack by the Japanese on December 7, 1941. Sure, memos had been written and hypotheticals discussed, but when it got down to cases, no one—until it was too late—really ever thought the Japanese could sail thousands of miles undetected and attack Pearl Harbor.

No one in America imagined that the Japanese would have the cunning and tenacity to attempt such a feat, and yet they succeeded because of a failure of imagination on the part of those in power in Washington, both civilian and in the military. It had been speculated, war-gamed, theorized, but nobody really thought it could happen.

There is not one shred of evidence that President Roosevelt somehow manipulated events to get America into the war. At the most, the War

Department believed, as of November 28, "Japanese future action unpredict-able, but hostile action possible at any moment."[1] FDR had also been given several severe warnings about the Japanese in confidential memos, some of which specifically mentioned Hawaii, yet even still, the idea was so farfetched so as to be dismissed by nearly all. Everybody believed the next Japanese move would be an invasion of Thailand.

Carl Jung, the great Swiss philosopher, fashioned the notion of "synchronic-ity," which he called "a causal connection of two or more psycho-physic phe-nomena. . . ." Events, he said, were not only grouped by cause but by meaning as well. What might seem coincidental was, in fact, often part of a larger inter-connectivity of unfolding events, according to Jung.[2]

Few things in American and world history illustrate synchronicity better than the attack on Pearl Harbor. Events conspired to help the Japanese, and hurt America and the world in the short run, but ironically hurt Japan and helped America and the world in the long run.

"December 7, 1941 . . . will live as one of the most brilliant military per-formances of all time. Superbly planned and superbly executed. . . ." And that was the analysis of the American military. The question why was answered by Admiral Isoroku Yamamoto with his directive of November 5, 1941. The Japanese desired to "drive Britain and America from Greater East Asia," a long-cherished goal.[3] Consider that Franklin Roosevelt runs for an unprec-edented third term and wins, breaking the "no third term" rule, which had governed all previous second-term presidents. This liberates him and begins a seemingly unrelated chain reaction of events that winds its way through history, from December 7, 1941, right up until today. He initiates both Lend-Lease and the Atlantic Charter, both revolutionary developments, neither of which might have gone forward, either the year before, or if Wendell Willkie were elected president in 1940. Willkie made staying out of Europe the cen-terpiece of his campaign.

In the fall of 1941, Congress decided by one vote to preserve a standing army, by maintaining a draft. At the time, there were few enlistees and those who wanted to join up were by and large poor physical specimens.

A beautiful American spy living in Europe, Amy Thorpe Pack, had been recruited by the British Security Coordination to make use of her red hair, flashing green eyes, and feminine wiles to steal German decoding technology called "Enigma." This technology was called "the greatest secret and most spectacular intelligence achievement of the war."[4]

The Americans thought themselves safe because of the discovery, assuming that they would know as soon as the Japanese diplomats knew of any military actions by the war-like Axis power. War warnings were sent to Kimmel and Short, but with no amplifying details, and while the Philippines and other locations were mentioned, Hawaii was not.[5] The headline of the *Hilo Tribune Herald* on November 30, 1941, shouted, "JAPAN MAY STRIKE OVER WEEKEND."[6] The premature warning cooled enthusiasm a tad for the stolen technology. Meanwhile, analysts were unduly and increasingly confident about their own ability to interpret the subtle and "enigmatic" oriental mind.

Just months earlier, FDR angered some navy admirals, including James Richardson, who happened to be the head of the Pacific Fleet at the time, by ordering the fleet to move from San Diego to Honolulu. This set off a chain of events with the Japanese, who saw the move as provocative and a challenge. Roosevelt, angered at Richardson, removed him and replaced him with Admiral Husband E. Kimmel, whose stewardship of the fleet in Hawaii became an important part of this storyline.

Plans went forward in Tokyo to destroy the fleet and secure the Western and Central Pacific, the main target being the American carriers. The whole idea of the bombing came from the astonishingly successful aerial strike by the British on the Italian navy at Taranto.

To Jung's point, all wars of the time seemed to begin on a Sunday. The Archduke Franz Ferdinand was shot on a Sunday, and his assassination kicked off World War I. Germany invaded Belgium and France on a Sunday, some weeks later. Great Britain and France both declared war on Germany on a Sunday in September of 1939 after the German invasion of Poland. Greece was invaded by Italy on a Sunday in World War II and Germany invaded Russia on a Sunday in June of 1941. How surprising was it that Japan attacked America on a Sunday?

The attack was not as successful as the Japanese had hoped. The

American carriers were not present at Pearl Harbor, and the Japanese failed to destroy the fuel dumps and the dry docks, which allowed the Americans to rebuild quickly.

The attack triggered the German declaration of war on America and thereby pushed the reluctant country into the European conflict, signaling the eventual demise of the Nazis and the rise of the Soviet state. Had America not entered, it is possible that an armistice might have been signed by Great Britain and Nazi Germany with London allowing Chancellor Hitler to keep his new territories. Had the Japanese not attacked Pearl Harbor, the Americans would have most likely never entered the Pacific War or the European conflict.

If Germany started her invasion of Russia in April or maybe even as late as May, the invasion of Russia would have become another spectacular success for Hitler and, with a new Eastern Border, he could have devoted more men and materiel to North Africa, defeating the British there and thus devoted more men and materiel to an invasion of Great Britain. To the end, Hitler had blamed "international Jewry" for the war and managed to exterminate over six million Jews, giving rise just a few years later to the creation of the modern nation-state of Israel.

The world was changed in great earth-shattering ways and small painful ways too. The attack was a pebble dropped in a pool and the concentric circles moved outward, forever.

Ellsworth Westbook Shirley had to quit his thriving life insurance business because it included delivering checks to the parents of boys who had died in the war, just as his oldest son, "Barney," had. When the parents to whom he brought the checks began crying, he did too, and finally could not take it anymore. He sold the business and went into another line of work. His wife Georgia's hair went white in a matter of weeks after hearing about the death of her eldest son. Ellsworth's mother, Cora Shirley, was never the same again, nor were Barney's aunts, Lola and Maude, nor were Barney's two brothers, Eddie and Ronnie.

The departed was our uncle Ellsworth Abbott "Barney" Shirley, who was killed by Japanese troops in French Indo-China in January of 1945. He'd dropped out of high school in 1943 and enlisted in the navy at the age of eighteen with his parents' permission. He became a radio operator on a TBF-1 Avenger plane on board the *Essex*.

On his twentieth birthday on January 10, 1945, Airman Second Class Shirley volunteered for a mission to bomb Japanese docks in Indochina. He needed the air hours to be promoted to Airman 1C. He must have had an omen that day, though; before taking off, he gave away all his priceless possessions in his footlocker while telling his bunkmates he didn't think he was coming back. The plane took off the morning of January 10, 1945.

After acquiring the target and dropping their bomb, the pilot, Donald Henry of Drummond, Idaho, radioed the squadron leader that he still had one bomb left and circled back to make a second pass at the docks.

Instead, the plane was shot down by Japanese antiaircraft fire and crashed in a park in Saigon. Japanese troops discovered the badly wounded Airman Shirley in the wreckage of the plane and killed him. Henry survived the crash and was secreted away by the French Underground, but was later discovered by the Japanese and killed too.

He was called Barney because when he was born, a grandfather exclaimed, "Why, he's got great big eyes, just like Barney Google!" Google was a character in the popular comic strip, "Barney Google and Snuffy Smith."

Like millions of others, the lives of the Shirley family were forever altered by the events of December 7, 1941.

The world was also changed for American blacks because of December 7. In that battle, a new hero emerged. Doris "Dorie" Miller, mess attendant, was picking up laundry on board the *West Virginia* when the attack began. He was initially ordered to help move wounded soldiers and then told to man a 50-caliber antiaircraft gun. Miller stayed at his post, firing repeatedly at Japanese planes, as torpedoes hit his ship, bullets whizzed by, and men died around him. Miller never flinched and only left his duty station when ordered after the situation had become hopeless.

For his bravery Miller was awarded the Navy Cross in early 1942 by another Texan, Admiral Chester Nimitz. In presenting the award to Cook Third Class Miller, Nimitz said, "This marks the first time in this conflict that such high tribute had been made in the Pacific Fleet to a member of his race and I'm sure that the future will see others similarly honored for brave acts."[7] Two years later, Miller was killed with 646 other seamen aboard the escort carrier *Liscome Bay*. Miller received the Purple Heart, the American Defense Service Medal, the Asiatic-Pacific Campaign Medal, a Fleet Clasp, and the Victory Medal. In 1973, the ship USS *Miller*, a frigate, was commissioned.

Dorie Miller's body was never recovered.

Douglas MacArthur, who could have been another scapegoat except for his war-zone command, his savvy skills, his rapport with the American people, and his close relationship with Roosevelt, went to Australia, became the Supreme Commander of the Southwest Pacific forces, and with little resources and men, mounted one of the most brilliant counteroffensives in military history. As his troops were closing in on invading Japan, atomic bombs detonated over Hiroshima and Nagasaki, killing tens of thousands of civilians as per the order of the new president, Harry Truman. Roosevelt died before seeing the successful victory in the world war which he, more than any other man on the face of the earth, was responsible for winning.

MacArthur's brilliant occupation of the defeated country should have earned him the Nobel Peace prize. Several years later, duty called the old general once again and he went to Korea, where he once again mounted a dazzling counteroffensive. After America was lied to by the new Red Chinese government and watched them invade Korea, the general tried to take control of the mess. In so doing he ran afoul of President Truman and was fired from his post.

MacArthur came home to a hero's welcome, revered and beloved by the American people. Truman, who sought another term in 1952, was badly embarrassed in the New Hampshire primary, saw his approval rating fall to the mid-20s, and finally withdrew from the race. His departure opened the door for yet another general, Dwight D. Eisenhower, to serve two underappreciated presidential terms, while the country enjoyed peace and prosperity and saw unprecedented growth and development in civil rights, technology, education, transportation, and medicine. Truman went home to Independence, Missouri, and though he lived to be eighty-eight, he never saw the resurrection of his reputation and presidency. By the mid-1970s, historians had finally come to appreciate the accomplishments and wisdom that characterized the seven years the failed haberdasher was in the White House. Truman would never have been president if Roosevelt had not run again in 1940.

America emerged from the Second World War as the only unchallenged superpower, but that status didn't last long. Another Evil Empire rose up to replace the Third Reich and enslaved the very same Eastern European countries the Germans had ground under their boots. This new empire proved even more vicious and immoral than the Third Reich, if that were possible.

In one of the great historical ironies, Japan and Germany emerged as American allies against Moscow, rebuilt as prosperous democracies by the United States. An organization to settle international disputes—once rejected by the United States—was created with American leadership. English emerged as the international language of all pilots, as the only planes flying after World War II were American and British.

The Cold War took hold. Moscow and Washington, the unchallenged superpowers, eyed each other carefully, and their competition led to an unprecedented arms race only outpaced by a science race with an American eventually walking on the moon, a direct result of America's entry into World War II.

In 1961, another man ascended to the presidency. Had he not been a hero in the Pacific and skillfully used that heroism in his congressional and presidential campaigns, John Kennedy would have likely been dismissed as a rich, philandering playboy, and history would have been drastically altered yet again. It was he who committed the United States to landing a man on the moon before the end of 1970. He was soon assassinated by a loyal follower of Soviet communism. Before his assassination, he committed U.S. troops in a ground war on the Asian continent and years later, after the loss of more than 57,000 Americans, the United States lost her first war and with it, for a time, her sense of national purpose, and of national destiny.

The country stumbled through the 1970s, an embarrassing shell of its former greatness, until another man was elected and summonned forth the greatness of the country one again, scaring the hell out of the elites but beloved by the uncommon men and women of his country. He called Soviet Communism what it was: an Evil Empire. He rejected the containment and détente policies of the past 35 years and embarked on a campaign to destroy the Soviet Union and win the Cold War.

That new Evil Empire eventually collapsed as America and the West defeated it both economically and militarily, setting millions free who had once been imprisoned by the Soviet state and whose parents and grandparents had been threatened and imprisoned and murdered by Hitler and Stalin.

The city of Washington changed radically because of the war and became, because of the attack, the headquarters for the Free World. A city that once had been little more than a bumpkin byway became an awkward player on the world stage, even as it accumulated along the way all the trappings of power including corruption, greed, and one of the highest rates of venereal disease in the country, perhaps confirming that power is the ultimate aphrodisiac.

Because of Pearl Harbor, the culture of America changed radically. Women only partially retreated from the factory floor back to the kitchen floor. More and more women, men, and blacks who never thought about college began attending, especially the returning G.I.s under one of the greatest pieces of legislation ever conceived: the G.I. Bill.

America never again retreated from the world stage, as it did in the early 1800s, as it did after the Spanish-American War, and as it did in 1919 after the end of the First World War. After World War II, the philosophy changed from "America First" to "America First In."

Another president, Ronald Reagan, a former New Dealer, whose movie career unraveled because of Pearl Harbor, unraveled the agreements of Yalta made by FDR and Churchill in which whole chunks of Eastern Europe and the Baltics were handed over to the evil and monstrous thug Josef Stalin.

A wall went up. A wall came down. What had been free and independent was free and independent again after 1991, as the periods of servitude first under Hitler and then under Stalin were finally ended.

The world changed over many times, but the attack on Pearl Harbor was the lynchpin that set off a global synchronicity, whose effects are still being felt today.

NOTES

PREFACE
1. Franklin Delano Roosevelt Presidential Library and Museum, "Japanese Intelligence and Propaganda in the United States During 1941," December 4, 1941, Hyde Park, NY, 2.
2. Franklin Delano Roosevelt Presidential Library and Museum, "Japanese Intelligence and Propaganda in the United States During 1941," December 4, 1941, Hyde Park, NY, 4.
3. Franklin Delano Roosevelt Presidential Library and Museum, "Japanese Intelligence and Propaganda in the United States During 1941," December 4, 1941, Hyde Park, NY, 12–13.
4. Bill Henry, "By the Way," *Los Angeles Times*, December 9, 1941, A1.
5. Jack Shafer, "Who Said It First? Journalism Is the 'First Rough Draft of History,'" *Slate Magazine*: Posted August 30, 2010, http://www.slate.com/id/2265540/.
6. *Boston Globe*, "388 to 1," December 9, 1941, 18.

CHAPTER 1: THE FIRST OF DECEMBER
1. *New York Times*, "Daily Newspapers Sell 42,385,807 a Day," February 18, 1942, 17.
2. *Dunkirk* (NY) *Evening Observer*, "Pétain Ready to Give Rest of His Nation to Nazis," December 1, 1941, 1.
3. *Time*, "Army: Battle of the Carolinas," December 1, 1941, 32.
4. Associated Press, "U.S. Army Will Use Live Ammunition in 1942 Maneuvers," *Washington Evening Star*, December 1, 1941, A7.
5. *Time*, "Navy: World's Mightiest," December 1, 1941, 34.
6. *Time*, "Huck's New Boat," December 1, 1941, 76.
7. *Life*, "Japanese Bow and Grin for the Camera But Get Nowhere in Washington," December 1, 1941, 36.
8. F. Tillman Durdin, "Singapore Doubts Japanese Threats," *New York Times*, December 4, 1941, 5.
9. Associated Press, *Baltimore Sun*, December 1, 1941, 1.
10. Associated Press, "FR, Hull Confer; No Final Answer Filed from Tokyo," *Bismarck* (ND) *Tribune*, December 1, 1941, 1.
11. *Emporia* (KS) *Daily Gazette*, December 1, 1941, 5.
12. *Emporia* (KS) *Daily Gazette*, December 1, 1941, 5.
13. Edward E. Bomar, Associated Press, "String of Military Bases," *Ironwood* (MI) *Daily Globe*, December 1, 1941, 1.
14. United Press, "British Navy Reinforced in Pacific," *Coshocton* (OH) *Tribune*, December 1, 1941, 1.
15. International News Service, "Tojo Statement Ends Vacation for Executive," *Charleston* (SC) *Gazette*, December 1, 1941, 1.

16. Dewitt Mackenzie, "Nazi Setbacks Stop the Japs," *Emporia* (KS) *Daily Gazette*, December 1, 1941, 1.
17. Constantine Brown, "This Changing World," *Washington Evening Star*, December 1, 1941, A11.
18. Constantine Brown, "This Changing World," *Washington Evening Star*, December 1, 1941, A11.
19. *Time*, "National Affairs: Advice to Japan," December 1, 1941, 14.
20. Associated Press, "R.A.F. Drops 150 Tons of Bombs on Hamburg," *Bakersfield Californian*, December 1, 1941, 3.
21. Associated Press, "Flashes," *Bakersfield Californian*, December 1, 1941, 1.
22. *Coshocton* (OH) *Tribune*, "Home From Russia," December 1, 1941, 4.
23. United Press, "Goebbels Says U.S. Can't Save England," *Dunkirk* (NY) *Evening Observer*, December 1, 1941, 1.
24. Associated Press, "Brett's Plane Fired Upon by Axis Warship," *Greeley* (CO) *Daily Tribune*, December 1, 1941, 2.
25. Associated Press, "F. D. R. Envisioned Nazi Effort at World Dominance in 1939," *Birmingham* (AL) *News*, December 1, 1941, 1.
26. *Life*, "The Pursuits Fly from Any Level Meadow," December 1, 1941, 92.
27. *Life*, "Even the Bombers Operate Out of Dispersion Fields," December 1, 1941, 96.
28. *Bakersfield Californian*, "Air School," December 1, 1941, 6.
29. Hanson W. Baldwin, "Sees Big Losses for Army in War," *New York Times*, December 1, 1941, 10.
30. William A. Baker, "1,400 Conscientious Objectors Toil in 20 Camps at Own Expense, Without Pay," *Tucson* (AZ) *Daily Citizen*, December 1, 1941, 12.
31. Associated Press, "1800 'Over Age' Men of 29th Division Soon to Be Released," *Cumberland* (MD) *Evening Times*, December 1, 1941, 1.
32. Paul Mallon, "News Behind the News," *Bakersfield Californian*, December 1, 1941, 15.
33. Associated Press, "Call of the Sea Brings 'Pop' Back to Navy," *Birmingham* (AL) *News*, December 1, 1941, 3.
34. U.S. Census Bureau, *Historical Statistics of the United States: Colonial Times to 1970* (Washington, D.C., 1960), 70.
35. *New York Times*, "Powerful New Gun Developed By U.S.," December 4, 1941, 13.
36. *Bakersfield Californian*, "A Future Problem," December 1, 1941, 15.
37. Alexander D. Noyes, "Stock Market Averages Go to Lowest Since 1938—Strike Troubles and Japanese Deadlock," *New York Times*, December 1, 1941, 27.
38. *New York Times*, "Stock Market Averages," December 1, 1941, 28.
39. Associated Press, "Pay Roll Tax Can Finance Pensions, Downey Claims," *Bakersfield Californian*, December 1, 1941, 6.
40. *Time*, "Public Opinion: Fear, But Not of Entanglement," December 1, 1941, 18.
41. David Brinkley, *Washington Goes to War* (New York: Alfred A. Knopf, 1988), 17.
42. *Life*, "Army Fires Businessman," December 1, 1941, 30.
43. Thomas Wolfe, *The Complete Short Stories of Thomas Wolfe*, ed. Francis E. Skipp (New York: Simon and Schuster, 1989), 192.
44. *Life*, "Parker," December 1, 1941, 1.
45. *Time*, "Delivering the Goods for Uncle Sam," December 1, 1941, 1.
46. *Time*, "Soap Suds That Turn Into Rubber," December 1, 1941, 1.
47. *Life*, "Plymouth: The Low-Priced Car Most Like High-Priced Cars," December 1, 1941, 1.
48. *Life*, "Columbia," December 1, 1941, 16.
49. *Life*, "Schwinn-Built Bicycles," December 1, 1941, 88.
50. *Coshocton* (OH) *Tribune*, "Defense Expected to Limit New Car Buyers' Choice," December 1, 1941, 1.
51. *Albuquerque Journal*, December 1, 1941, 8.
52. *Life*, December 1, 1941, 7.
53. *Life*, December 1, 1941, 8.
54. *Life*, "Stromberg—Carlson," December 1, 1941, 86.

55. *Time*, "Radio: From Washington," December 1, 1941, 50.
56. Richard Kluger, *Ashes to Ashes: America's Hundred-Year Cigarette War, the Public Health, and the Unabashed Triumph of Philip Morris* (New York: Random House, 1997), 192.
57. *Washington Evening Star*, "Camel—the Cigarette of Costlier Tobaccos," December 1, 1941, B10.
58. *Boston Daily Globe*, "Something New Has Been Added," December 1, 1941, 11.
59. *Life*, "Call for Philip Morris," December 1, 1941, 113.
60. *Life*, "Grandpa Goes Modern," December 1, 1941, 54.
61. United Press, "Oregon State and Duke to Play in Famed Rose Bowl," *Brainerd* (MN) *Daily Dispatch*, December 1, 1941, 8.
62. *Brainerd* (MN) *Daily Dispatch*, "Meet Joe DiMaggio III," December 1, 1941, 8.
63. *Fitchburg* (MA) *Sentinel*, "Leaving Fenway?" December 1, 1941, 8.
64. *Beatrice* (NE) *Daily Sun*, "Mountaineer and Child Bride," December 1, 1941, 2.
65. *Portsmouth* (NH) *Herald*, "Parents Protest New York Crime Wave," December 1, 1941, 5.
66. United Press, "Gov. Talmadge Refuses to Pardon Six Floggers," *Fitchburg* (MA) *Sentinel*, December 1, 1941, 3.
67. *Life*, "The Governor of Georgia Remembers That He Was Once a Flogger Himself," December 8, 1941, 40.
68. *Coshocton* (OH) *Tribune*, "Communist Hires Willkie as Counsel," December 1, 1941, 1.
69. *Life*, "Latin-American Black Is New," December 8, 1941, 99.
70. *Kingsport* (TN) *Times*, "Social Calendar," December 1, 1941, 3.
71. *Greeley* (CO) *Daily Tribune*, "Modest Maidens," December 1, 1941, 6.
72. *New York Times*, "The Robin Moor, Reportedly Torpedoed, May Be First U.S. Victim of a Nazi Attack," June 10, 1941, 1.
73. Charles Herd, "Reuben James Hit," *New York Times*, November 1, 1941, 1.
74. Associated Press, "Tale of Heroism Aboard the Kearny After Torpedo Hit Told by Ensign," *New York Times*, November 4, 1941, 4.
75. United Press, "Kearny Fought U-Boat Pack," *New York Times*, December 4, 1941, 3.
76. Associated Press, "Seven Americans Lost," *New York Times*, December 4, 1941, 3; Associated Press, "Navy to Man Guns on Ships If Armed," *New York Times*, October 12, 1941, 5.
77. Associated Press, "Tells Boston Audience Aid Bolsters RAF," *Hartford Courant*, October 31, 1940, 1.
78. Associated Press, "Far Eastern Crisis Grows More Acute," *Hartford Courant*, December 1, 1941, 1.
79. Associated Press, "Far Eastern Crisis Grows More Acute," *Hartford Courant*, December 1, 1941, 1.
80. Associated Press, "FR, Hull Confer; No Final Answer Filed from Tokyo," *Bismarck* (ND) *Tribune*, December 1, 1941, 1.
81. Associated Press, "F.D.R Speeds Back to Capital," *Bakersfield Californian*, December 1, 1941, 1.
82. *Time*, "National Affairs: Advice to Japan," December 1, 1941, 13.
83. International News Service, "Tojo Statement Ends Vacation for Executive," *Charleston* (SC) *Gazette*, December 1, 1941, 1; Associated Press, "FR, Hull Confer; No Final Answer Filed from Tokyo," *Bismarck* (ND) *Tribune*, December 1, 1941, 1.
84. Associated Press, "Americans Advised to Leave Shanghai," *Atlanta Constitution*, December 1, 1941, 1; International News Service, "Yanks Put on Alert," *Charleston* (SC) *Gazette*, December 1, 1941, 1.
85. International News Service, "British Reinforce East," *Charleston* (SC) *Gazette*, December 1, 1941, 1.
86. International News Service, "British Reinforce East," *Charleston* (SC) *Gazette*, December 1, 1941, 1
87. Richard C. Wilson, United Press, "Far East Waits War Outburst," *Bakersfield Californian*, December 1, 1941, 1.
88. Associated Press, "F.D.R Speeds Back to Capital," *Bakersfield Californian*, December 1, 1941, 1; Associated Press, "Japan to 'Redouble Efforts' with U.S.," *Bakersfield Californian*, December 1, 1941, 1.

89. James B. Reston, "4 Powers Ready, Washington Says," *New York Times*, December 1, 1941, 1; United Press, "President and War Chiefs Confer on Oriental Crisis," *Los Angeles Times*, November 26, 1941, 1; Associated Press, "Americans Again Urged to Quit Japan," *Washington Post*, November 26, 1941, 1; John O'Donnell, "F.D. Arrives Today; To See War Cabinet," *Washington Times Herald*, December 1, 1941, 1.

90. Paul W. Ward, "Japan Crisis Ends Vacation of Roosevelt," *Baltimore Sun*, December 1, 1941, 1.

91. *Middlesboro* (KY) *Daily News*, "President Roosevelt Carves Again," December 1, 1941, 1.

92. *Time*, "The Presidency: Battle Stations," December 1, 1941, 15.

93. Frank L. Kluckhohn, "President Is Grim," *New York Times*, December 1, 1941, 1; Associated Press, "F.D.R. Cancels Georgia Vacation," *Atlanta Constitution*, December 1, 1941, 1.

94. *Life*, "Japanese Bow and Grin for the Camera But Get Nowhere in Washington," December 1, 1941, 36.

95. Associated Press, "FR, Hull Confer; No Final Answer Filed from Tokyo," *Bismarck* (ND) *Tribune*, December 1, 1941, 1; James B. Reston, "4 Powers Ready, Washington Says," *New York Times*, December 1, 1941, 1.

96. *Time*, "The Presidency: Battle Stations," December 1, 1941, 15; Associated Press, "F.D.R. Cancels Georgia Vacation," *Atlanta Constitution*, December 1, 1941, 1.

97. Frank L. Kluckhohn, "President Is Grim," *New York Times*, December 1, 1941, 1.

98. Frank L. Kluckhohn, "President Is Grim," *New York Times*, December 1, 1941, 1.

99. *Washington Evening Star*, "Fala 'Announces' President's Return to White House," December 1, 1941, A2.

100. Julius C. Edelstein, "Parley Requested By Jap Emissaries; May Reject Terms," *Washington Times Herald*, December 1, 1941, 1.

101. Otto D. Tolischus, "U.S. Principles Rejected By Japanese as 'Fantastic,'" *New York Times*, December 1, 1941, 1.

102. John Franklin Carter, "Memorandum on Mexican Border Situation (Eastern Portion)," December 1, 1941, Franklin Delano Roosevelt Presidential Library and Museum, Hyde Park, NY.

103. *New York Times*, "Japan's Imports Cut 75% by War," December 2, 1941, 6.

104. Chicago Tribune Press Service, "War's Pinch to Be Widely Felt; Japan to Suffer More Than U. S.," *Chicago Daily Tribune*, December 9, 1941, 31.

105. Associated Press, "FR, Hull Confer; No Final Answer Filed from Tokyo," *Bismarck* (ND) *Tribune*, December 1, 1941, 1.

106. Franklin Delano Roosevelt Presidential Library and Museum, "FDR: Day by Day—The Pare Lorentz Chronology," December 1, 1941.

107. Associated Press, "Both Sides Admit Situation Is Grave," *Portsmouth* (NH) *Herald*, December 1, 1941, 1.

108. *Salt Lake Tribune*, "Summary of Day's News From Europe, Far East," December 1, 1941, 2.

109. Associated Press, "Nazi Reversals Cause Japs to Ask More Time," *Panama City News-Herald*, December 1, 1941, 1.

110. United Press, "Strategic Areas Are Ordered on War-Time Basis," *Idaho Evening Times*, December 1, 1941, 1.

CHAPTER 2: THE SECOND OF DECEMBER

1. *Birmingham* (AL) *News*, "55 Minutes to Atlanta 4 Flights Daily $6.50," December 1, 1941, 11.

2. *Washington Evening Star*, "Fast Non-Stop Commuter Service to New York," December 2, 1941, A7.

3. *New York Times*, "Subway Smokers Beware," December 1, 1941, 21.

4. Associated Press, "Those Service Men on Leave: 'Give Them a Lift,'" *San Francisco Chronicle*, December 1, 1941, 4.

5. Floyd Healey, "'Secession' Movement Is Backed," *San Francisco Chronicle*, December 1, 1941, 1.

6. *Washington Evening Star*, "Yerela, Calif.—Thursday 'Rebels' Show Determination," December 2, 1941, A4.

7. Associated Press, "11 Per Cent Gain Seen in U.S. Use of Gasoline," *Washington Evening Star*, December 1, 1941, A3.

8. *Washington Evening Star*, "Traffic Report," December 1, 1941, A12.

9. *Time*, "Missouri: Scientifically Drunken Drivers," December 1, 1941, 18.

10. *Washington Evening Star*, "Nation's Auto Dealers Told U.S. Will Stop Inflation in Prices," December 1, 1941, A12.

11. Gordon William Prange, Donald M. Goldstein, and Katherine V. Dillon, *At Dawn We Slept: The Untold Story of Pearl Harbor* (New York: McGraw-Hill, 1981), 154.

12. *Time*, "A Few More Billions," December 1, 1941, 32.

13. Associated Press, "Buffalo Sets Stamp Sale Record," *New York Times*, December 3, 1941, 10.

14. *Time*, "Building: More Dirt," December 1, 1941, 72.

15. Associated Press, "House Groups to Air Role of Lobbying in Defense Contracts," *Washington Evening Star*, December 1, 1941, A1.

16. *Washington Evening Star*, "Two Hearings to Open Tomorrow on Defense Contract Lobbying," December 2, 1941, A3.

17. *New York Times*, "Permanence in Workers' Areas Seen by Miss Gladys Miller, Consultant— Number of New Units Equals Slam Razings," December 1, 1941, 16.

18. Associated Press, "Pro Football Title Game Will Be Played December 21," *Washington Evening Star*, December 1, 1941, A1.

19. Associated Press, "American Football Meets to Plan Expansion," *Washington Evening Star*, December 6, 1941, 1A.

20. *Time*, "The Real Thing," December 1, 1941, 49.

21. *Time*, "Words, Words," December 1, 1941, 49.

22. *Boston Daily Globe*, "Lodge Says U.S. Needs a Standing Army of 750,000," December 2, 1941, 2.

23. *Boston Daily Globe*, "R.H. White's Basement," December 2, 1941, 2.

24. *Boston Daily Globe*, "Jordan Marsh Company," December 2, 1941, 3.

25. *Boston Daily Globe*, "Jordan Marsh Company," December 2, 1941, 7.

26. *Boston Daily Globe*, "Conrad's," December 2, 1941, 11.

27. *Washington Post*, "Woodward and Lothrop," December 2, 1941, 4.

28. Associated Press, "O. P. M. Asks Public to Economize on Yule Wrappings," *Washington Evening Star*, December 1, 1941, A12.

29. Associated Press, "Don't Be Too Practical in Yule Buying, Mrs. Roosevelt Urges," *Atlanta Constitution*, December 2, 1941, 4.

30. *Washington Post*, "Indians Here to Demand Fire Water," December 2, 1941, 15.

31. *Time*, "Words, Words," December 1, 1941, 49.

32. *Time*, "Casualties," December 1, 1941, 49.

33. Tallulah Bankhead, *Tallulah: My Autobiography* (New York: Harper, 1952), 101.

34. Eugene S. Duffield, "How'll They Pay? Mr. L, Income $30,000, Adjusts His Savings Plan to Meet Higher Taxes," *Wall Street Journal*, December 1, 1941, 1.

35. *Time*, "The Presidency: The Old Master," December 1, 1941, 13.

36. *Time*, "National Affairs: Advice to Japan," December 1, 1941, 14.

37. *Time*, "Foreign Relations: Aid to Iceland," December 1, 1941, 14.

38. *Time*, "Foreign Relations: How to Beat Rationing," December 1, 1941, 24.

39. *Time*, "Medicine: War & Sanity," December 1, 1941, 54.

40. *Time*, "Medicine: War & Sanity," December 1, 1941, 54.

41. *Time*, "Welcome Stranger!" December 1, 1941, 31.

42. *Washington Evening Star*, "Sugar-Control Bill Passes House Despite Opposition by Hull," December 2, 1941, A3.

43. *Time*, "Music: Juke-Box Divas," December 1, 1941, 36.

44. *Time*, "Art: Artists' Rations," December 1, 1941, 39.

45. *Time*, "Education: First Two R's," December 1, 1941, 57.

46. *Time*, "Education: History Lesson," December 1, 1941, 57.

47. *Atlanta Constitution*, "Today's Radio, Tuesday's Local Programs," December 2, 1941, 17.

48. *Time*, "Cinema: Baghdad-on-the-Pacific," December 1, 1941, 82.

49. *Los Angeles Times*, "Day for Soviet Aid Proclaimed," December 1, 1941, 12.

50. *Birmingham* (AL) *News*, "'Citizen Kane' Will Be Shown Next at Empire," December 1, 1941, 25.

51. *Time*, "Cinema: Baghdad-on-the-Pacific," December 1, 1941, 82.

52. *Time*, "Books: Great Improbabilities," December 1, 1941, 88.

53. *Time*, "Books: Murder in November," December 1, 1941, 92.

54. *Christian Science Monitor*, "U.S.-Tokyo Talks Resumed; Nazi's Face New Soviet Peril; British Push Ahead in Libya," December 1, 1941, 1.

55. Associated Press, "Nazis Fleeing From Rostov Facing Trap," *Washington Evening Star*, December 2, 1941, 1.

56. United Press, "Din of Moscow Battle Heard on Air in London," *New York Times*, December 1, 1941, 2.

57. Franklin Delano Roosevelt Presidential Library and Museum, "Informal Remarks of the President to State Chairmen of Birthday Ball Committees December 2, 1941—5:00 P.M.," December 2, 1941, Hyde Park, NY.

58. Associated Press, "America First Reveals Plan for Role in 1942 Election," *Baltimore Sun*, December 2, 1941, 9.

59. *Look*, "Colgate Dental Cream," December 2, 1941, 25.

60. *Look*, "Chesterfield," December 2, 1941, 68.

61. *Boston Daily Globe*, "Lux Toilet Soap," December 2, 1941, 19.

62. Raymond Clapper, "What Roosevelt Is Not Telling Us," *Look*, December 2, 1941, 11.

63. *New York Times*, "288 Men, 1 Woman Listed in Dollar-a-Year Class," December 4, 1941, 11.

64. Carlisle Bargeron, "'Wall Street Wolf' Protects the Little Businessman," *Look*, December 2, 1941, 18.

65. *Look*, "Café Society Holds a Board Meeting," December 2, 1941, 22.

66. *Look*, "Meet The People: Meet the Men and Women of Russia, Whom Hitler Will Never Enslave," December 2, 1941, 28.

67. Samuel Spewack, "What's Happening to the Rich in England," *Look*, December 2, 1941, 30.

68. *Look*, "Vice-President Wallace Sets a Hollywood Fashion," December 2, 1941, 36.

69. John C. Henry, "76 and 80 Cent Pay Raises Won By Rail Unions," *Washington Evening Star*, December 2, 1941, A1.

70. Associated Press, "18 Convicted of Plot Against Army Face Terms of 10 Years," *Washington Evening Star*, December 2, 1941, A2.

71. Associated Press, "British Report Sinking Italian Destroyer, Two Supply Ships," *Washington Evening Star*, December 2, 1941, A1.

72. Associated Press, "Nazi's Cut Through British Ring to Rescue Force in East Libya; Capture Rezegh in Fierce Battle," *Washington Evening Star*, December 2, 1941, 1X.

73. Matthew Halton, "Libyan Sand Wastes Strewn With Litter of 'Dead' Axis Tanks," *Boston Daily Globe*, December 2, 1941, 21.

74. British Embassy, Washington, D. C., Memo to The Honorable Franklin D. Roosevelt President of the United States of America, December 2, 1941, Franklin Delano Roosevelt Presidential Library and Museum, Hyde Park, NY.

75. Associated Press, "Churchill Proposes Extending Draft to Men 18 to 50," *Washington Evening Star*, December 2, 1941, 1X.

76. Otto D. Tolischus, "U.S. Principles Rejected By Japanese as 'Fantastic,'" *New York Times*, December 1, 1941, 1.

77. Garnett D. Horner, "U.S. Asks Japan to Explain Troop Moves: Prompt Reply Is Requested By President," *Washington Evening Star*, December 2, 1941, A1.

78. Associated Press, "Japanese Troops Drill With Parachutes," *Boston Evening Globe*, December 2, 1941, 19.

79. United Press, "Japan Seizing Private Shipping for Transport Duty," *Boston Evening Globe*, December 2, 1941, 19.

80. Garnett D. Horner, "U.S. Asks Japan to Explain Troop Moves: Prompt Reply Is Requested By President," *Washington Evening Star*, December 2, 1941, A1.

81. Associated Press, "Roosevelt Is Reported Taking Personal Role In Washington Talks," *Birmingham* (AL) *News*, December 2, 1941, 29.

82. Frank L. Kluckhohn, "Roosevelt Calls In Navy Adviser to Hear Hull Report on Orient," *Washington Post*, December 2, 1941, 1.

83. Frank L. Kluckhohn, "A Test for Tokyo," *New York Times*, December 3, 1941, 1.

84. Garnett D. Horner, "U.S. Asks Japan to Explain Troop Moves: Prompt Reply Is Requested By President," *Washington Evening Star*, December 2, 1941, A1.

85. Franklin Delano Roosevelt Presidential Library and Museum, "FDR: Day by Day—The Pare Lorentz Chronology," December 1, 1941.

86. Frank L. Kluckhohn, "Japan Sees Hull," *New York Times*, December 2, 1941, 1.

87. Associated Press, "Roosevelt, Stark Confer Knox Says Fleet Is Ready Tokyo Continues Talks," *Hartford Courant*, December 2, 1941, 1.

88. Associated Press, "F.D.R. Calls Navy Aide in Asia Crisis," *Los Angeles Times*, December 2, 1941, 1.

89. Constantine Brown, "This Changing World," *Washington Evening Star*, December 2, 1941, A9.

90. Garnett D. Horner, "U.S. Asks Japan to Explain Troop Moves: Prompt Reply Is Requested By President," *Washington Evening Star*, December 2, 1941, A1.

91. Associated Press, "Battleship Leads British Flotilla into Singapore," *Washington Evening Star*, December 2, 1941, 1X.

92. Associated Press, "Battleship Leads British Flotilla into Singapore," *Washington Evening Star*, December 2, 1941, 1X.

93. Associated Press, "Japanese Are Not Told," *New York Times*, December 4, 1941, 4.

94. Associated Press, "All Marines Out of Shanghai; Will Remain in Philippines," *Washington Evening Star*, December 2, 1941, 1X.

95. Garnett D. Horner, "U.S. Asks Japan to Explain Troop Moves: Prompt Reply Is Requested By President," *Washington Evening Star*, December 2, 1941, A1.

96. Royal Arch Gunnison, "Philippines Maintain Ceaseless 'War Alert' Against Japanese," *Washington Evening Star*, December 2, 1941, A3.

97. Associated Press, "Just Like '76, Tokyo Says," *Baltimore Sun*, December 2, 1941, 2.

98. Associated Press, "U.S. Revenue Collections Only Third of Spending," *Washington Evening Star*, December 2, 1941, 1X.

99. *Washington Evening Star*, "Knox Plan to Change Navy Cafeteria Setup Brings Controversy," December 2, 1941, 2X.

100. *Washington Evening Star*, "Knox Plan to Change Navy Cafeteria Setup Brings Controversy," December 2, 1941, 2X.

101. The White House, Washington, "Memorandum for the President" by J.R. Beardal, December 6, 1941, Franklin Delano Roosevelt Presidential Library and Museum, Hyde Park, NY.

102. Franklin Delano Roosevelt Presidential Library and Museum, "Memorandum on Poles in U.S.S.R.," December 6, 1941, Hyde Park, NY.

103. Associated Press, "Navy Is Ready for Anything, Knox Asserts," *Atlanta Constitution*, December 2, 1941, 1.

104. *Atlanta Constitution*, "Patrolling the Sea," December 2, 1941, 1.

105. *Washington Evening Star*, "Exit From the Ark Royal," December 2, 1941, A1.

106. Associated Press, "Cruiser May Have Been Sunk By Pocket Battleship," *Washington Evening Star*, December 2, 1941, A3.

107. Associated Press, "48 Merchant Vessels, 11 Naval Craft Sunk in Month, Nazis Say," *Washington Evening Star*, December 2, 1941, A6.

108. Associated Press, "Baltimore Yards Will Launch Six Ships This Month," *Washington Post*, December 2, 1941, 8.

109. Walter Lippmann, "Today and Tomorrow: The Turning Point at Home," *Los Angeles Times*, December 2, 1941, 4.

110. *Washington Post*, "House Asked to Have Pegler Explain Epithets," December 2, 1941, 6.

111. Matthew Frye Jacobson and Gaspar González, *What Have They Built You To Do? The Manchurian Candidate and Cold War America* (Minneapolis, MN: University of Minnesota Press, 2006), 6.

112. Kenneth Goff, *Red Betrayal of Youth* (Enterprise Print, 1946), 29.

113. *Washington Post*, "Parking Fee Control Here Is Proposed," December 2, 1941, 13.

114. Dewey L. Fleming, "One Hostile Tokyo Act May Mean Conflict at Once, Washington Hears," *Baltimore Sun*, December 2, 1941, 1.

115. Franklin Delano Roosevelt Presidential Library and Museum, "FDR: Day by Day—The Pare Lorentz Chronology," December 1, 1941.

116. David Lawrence, "Formula Yet May Save Pacific Peace," *Washington Evening Star*, December 2, 1941, A9.

CHAPTER 3: THE THIRD OF DECEMBER

1. *Washington Evening Star*, "Bureaucrats Blamed for Blocking Plans for Army of Jews," December 3, 1941, A4.

2. John Barry, "War Diary (823d Day—Dec. 3, 1941)," *Boston Evening Globe*, December 3, 1941, 2.

3. *Boston Evening Globe*, "New Zealanders Await With Bayonets," December 3, 1941, 2.

4. John C. Henry, "Roosevelt Pledges Lease-Lend Defense Supplies to Turkey: Move Is Viewed As U.S. Attempts to Thwart Axis," *Washington Evening Star*, December 3, 1941, A1.

5. *Washington Evening Star*, "Aid-to-Russia Policy Stands, White House Replies to Critics," December 3, 1941, A5.

6. *New York Times*, "India Is Reported Getting U.S. Aid," December 3, 1941, 11.

7. Associated Press, "America First Reveals Plan for Role in 1942 Elections," *Baltimore Sun*, December 2, 1941, 9.

8. *New York Times*, "Murrow Sees End of War in Our Hands," December 3, 1941, 9.

9. British Embassy, Washington, D. C., Memo to The Honorable Franklin D. Roosevelt President of the United States of America, December 3, 1941, Franklin Delano Roosevelt Presidential Library and Museum, Hyde Park, NY.

10. H. Ford Wilkins, "Quezon Avows His Loyalty to Roosevelt," *Washington Post*, December 2, 1941, 24.

11. Associated Press, "New U.S. Arctic Base in Far North Atlantic to Check Nazis Asked," *Birmingham* (AL) *News*, December 3, 1941, 2.

12. Associated Press, "Germans Driven 12 to 24 Miles, Russians Claim," *Washington Evening Star*, December 3, 1941, 1X.

13. Associated Press, "Nazis Threaten Moscow Anew; Rout From Rostov Continues," *Atlanta Constitution*, December 3, 1941, 11.

14. Associated Press, "British Re-form Lines for New Battle in Libya," *Birmingham* (AL) *News*, December 3, 1941, 1.

15. Edward Kennedy, Associated Press, "British in Libya Established on Strong Offensive Line," *Washington Evening Star*, December 3, 1941, 2X.

16. *Washington Evening Star*, "Examples Are Cited," December 3, 1941, A6.

17. United Press, "Hull Pessimistic About Far East," *Boston Evening Globe*, December 3, 1941, 1.

18. *Washington Evening Star*, "Wheeler Criticizes Policy," December 3, 1941, A6.

19. *Christian Science Monitor*, "The Isolationists Put on a Show," September 10, 1941, 24.

20. Associated Press, "Lewis Indorses Sen. Wheeler For Presidency," *Washington Post*, July 3, 1940, 3.

21. Associated Press, "All Thumbs Real or In Films," *Washington Evening Star*, December 3, 1941, A15.

22. Dorothy Thompson, "On the Record: America First Committee's Attitude Called Hindrance to U.S. in Japanese Negotiations," *Washington Evening Star*, December 3, 1941, A11.

23. J.A. O'Leary, "Far-Reaching Measure Passed 252 to 136," *Washington Evening Star*, December 3, 1941, A1.

24. *San Francisco Chronicle*, "State Farmers: Laws to Curb Sabotage of Defense Program Urged," December 3, 1941, 9.

25. George Gallup, "Big Majority Would Forbid All Defense Strikes By Law," *Tucson (AZ) Daily Citizen*, December 3, 1941, 5.

26. Associated Press, "NLRB Benefits Denied Unions With Bundists, Reds in House Move," *Birmingham (AL) News*, December 3, 1941, 1.

27. Editorial, "Where There Is No 'Right to Strike,'" *Los Angeles Times*, December 3, 1941, 4.

28. Associated Press, "20 C.I.O. Aides Cited as Having Police Records," *Washington Post*, December 3, 1941, 1.

29. *New York Times*, "Red Activities Laid to City Students; Coudert Committee Sees Real 'Peril,'" December 3, 1941, 1.

30. Dale Harrison, "Everybody's New York," *Birmingham (AL) News*, December 3, 1941, 9.

31. *New York Times*, "Dentistry to Cut Army Rejections," December 2, 1941, 18.

32. *Hartford Courant*, "5 Negroes Among 197 Given Tests," December 2, 1941, 5.

33. *Portsmouth (NH) Herald*, "30 to Take Selective Service Exam Tomorrow," December 2, 1941, 1.

34. *Atlanta Constitution*, "State Receives Draft Order for 707 More Men," December 3, 1941, 24.

35. *Atlanta Constitution*, "Alleged Draft Evader Pleads for Chance 'To Serve Country,'" December 3, 1941, 24.

36. Associated Press, "Draft-Age Mexicans Need Entry Permits," *Washington Evening Star*, December 3, 1941, A16.

37. *Atlanta Constitution*, "Defense Program Causes Rush for Birth Certificates," December 3, 1941, 5.

38. Frank Bristol, "Globe Exclusive: Nazis Train Mexican Youth for 'Foreign Legion' Service," *Boston Daily Globe*, December 3, 1941, 24.

39. Dale Harrison, "Everybody's New York," *Birmingham (AL) News*, December 3, 1941, 9.

40. Tom Treanor, "The Home Front," *Los Angeles Times*, December 3, 1941, 1A.

41. *San Francisco Chronicle*, "Inland Shipyard: Denver to Share Work," December 3, 1941, 5.

42. Associated Press, "Prison Labor Shares in Wage Bonuses," *Christian Science Monitor*, December 3, 1941, 3.

43. Blair Bolles, "$5,503 Fee for Arms Contracts Totaling $16,572 Revealed," *Washington Evening Star*, December 3, 1941, 1X.

44. *Washington Evening Star*, "560 Are Disqualified for Federal Jobs by Loyalty Tests," December 3, 1941, A1.

45. Associated Press, "Pacifist Duke of Bedford Takes Seat With Lords," *Washington Evening Star*, December 3, 1941, A1.

46. Associated Press, "Lady Astor Charges Churchill Draft of Women Is Too Weak," *Washington Evening Star*, December 3, 1941, 1X.

47. *Atlanta Constitution*, "Poll Reveals Britain Approves Defense Conscription of Women," December 3, 1941, 2.

48. Dan E. Clark II, "Angelenos Vote Against Draft Law for Women," *Los Angeles Times*, December 3, 1941, 9.

49. Dorothy Dix, "Be a Square Shooter and Hold Your Husband," *Boston Daily Globe*, December 3, 1941, 27.

50. *New York Times*, "Japan's Imports Cut 75% by War," December 2, 1941, 6.

51. Associated Press, "Episode Considered Effort to Determine Tokyo's Good Faith," *Atlanta Constitution*, December 3, 1941, 1.

52. Associated Press, "Japan Asked to Explain War Moves," *Los Angeles Times*, December 3, 1941, 1.

53. Associated Press, "F. D. Pushes Tokyo Showdown; Demands Japan State Aims in Indo-China," *Boston Daily Globe*, December 3, 1941, 1.

54. Frank L. Kluckhohn, "A Test for Tokyo," *New York Times*, December 3, 1941, 1.

55. Garnett D. Horner, "Showdown in Pacific Hinges on Tokyo's Reply to U.S.," *Washington Evening Star*, December 3, 1941, 1X.

56. Lloyd Lehbras, Associated Press, "F.D.R.'s Jap Query May Hurry Nippon to Take Her Choice," *Birmingham* (AL) *News*, December 3, 1941, 1.

57. Associated Press, "Washington Awaiting Japan's Answer," *Birmingham* (AL) *News*, December 3, 1941, 8.

58. Frank L. Kluckhohn, "A Test For Tokyo," *New York Times*, December 3, 1941, 1.

59. Frank L. Kluckhohn, "A Test For Tokyo," *New York Times*, December 3, 1941, 1.

60. Dewey L. Fleming, "Roosevelt Asks Tokyo Just What Its Plans Are," *Baltimore Sun*, December 3, 1941, 1.

61. Wilfrid Fleisher, "Japanese Deny Tojo Made 'Purge' Speech," *Washington Post*, December 3, 1941, 2.

62. Claude A. Mahoney, "Situation in Pacific Prompts Naval Speed, Bard Declares," *Washington Evening Star*, December 3, 1941, B24.

63. Associated Press, "Navy Aware of Japanese Naval Power, Bard Says," *Baltimore Sun*, December 3, 1941, 4.

64. Hedley Donovan, "Reply on Troops in Indo-China May Settle Issue of Peace or War," *Washington Post*, December 3, 1941, 1.

65. *Washington Post*, "Tokyo Must Explain Actions," December 3, 1941, 1.

66. Hedley Donovan, "Reply on Troops in Indo-China May Settle Issue of Peace or War," *Washington Post*, December 3, 1941, 1.

67. United Press, "Japan to Exhaust All Peace Avenues; Tokyo Reported Reconsidering Points in Reply to Hull," *Washington Post*, December 3, 1941, 2.

68. Hedley Donovan, "Reply on Troops in Indo-China May Settle Issue of Peace or War," *Washington Post*, December 3, 1941, 1.

69. Lloyd Lehbras, Associated Press, "F.D.R.'s Jap Query May Hurry Nippon To Take Her Choice," *Birmingham* (AL) *News*, December 3, 1941, 1.

70. Clark Lee, "Japanese Reported Massing Huge Forces in South Indo-China," *Washington Evening Star*, December 3, 1941, 1X.

71. Office of Naval Intelligence, "Bulletin," December 3, 1941, Franklin Delano Roosevelt Presidential Library and Museum, Hyde Park, NY.

72. Larry Rue, "London Papers See U. S. Action if Japs Attack," *Chicago Daily Tribune*, December 2, 1941, 5.

73. Royal Arch Gunnison, "Dutch Are Reported Pressing British to Move Into Thailand," *Washington Evening Star*, December 3, 1941, A8.

74. Editorial, "Eating His Own Words," *Chicago Daily Tribune*, December 2, 1941, 14.

75. *Chicago Daily Tribune*, "The Tribune's Platform: Save Our Republic," December 2, 1941, 14.

76. Frank L. Kluckhohn, "Japanese See Hull," *New York Times*, December 2, 1941, 1.

77. Associated Press, "U.S. Navy Can Shoot Straight, Connally Warns Japanese," *Washington Evening Star*, December 3, 1941, 2X.

78. *Baltimore Sun*, "Japan Decides to Continue Her Discussions With Us," December 2, 1941, 12.

79. *Atlanta Constitution*, "War Imminent in Vast Orient," December 3, 1941, 11.

80. *New York Times*, "Saks Fifth Avenue," December 2, 1941, 11.

81. Associated Press, "Soldiers Are Polled on Gift Desires, and Money Leads," *Washington Evening Star*, December 3, 1941, A6.

82. *New York Times*, "Tell Macy's Where He Is," December 3, 1941, 9.

83. *Washington Evening Star*, "George's Radio Co.," December 3, 1941, A16.

84. *Washington Evening Star*, "Radio Program, Wednesday, December 3, 1941," December 3, 1941, B22.

85. *Atlanta Constitution*, "Next Friday Night Will Be 'Shirley Temple Time,'" December 3, 1941, 21.

86. *Washington Evening Star*, "Coal: High Quality—Low Prices," December 3, 1941, B24.

87. *Washington Evening Star*, "Furloughs Forecast Record Travel for Holiday Season," December 3, 1941, A7.

88. *Atlanta Constitution*, "Camel," December 3, 1941, 11.

89. Ralph McGill, "Soldier Stretches 10-Day Pass Into 22 Years, But Comes Back," *Atlanta Constitution*, December 3, 1941, 1.

90. *Baltimore Sun*, "U.S. $5 Auto Tax May Be Repealed," December 2, 1941, 13.

91. Associated Press, "Taxes Have Reached Near-Peak Levels, Senator George Says," *Washington Evening Star*, December 3, 1941, A2.

92. *Washington Post*, "Treasury Spends $3 for Every $1 Revenue," December 3, 1941, 29.

93. Associated Press, "Senators Discuss Special Treatment for Small Firms," *Washington Evening Star*, December 3, 1941, A3.

94. Walter W. Ruch, "Says Reich's Debt Is Near 18 Total," *New York Times*, December 3, 1941, 7.

95. Associated Press, "U.S. Purchases Chile's Secondary Metal Output," *Washington Evening Star*, December 3, 1941, A4.

96. Associated Press, "Use Statues for Bullets, Congressman Proposes," *Atlanta Constitution*, December 3, 1941, 7.

97. *Chicago Daily Tribune*, "U. S. Lets Huge Aluminum Pile Go to Waste," December 2, 1941, 1.

98. Stephen Trumbull, "Puerto Rico Called U. S. Headache," *Hartford Daily Courant*, December 3, 1941, 9.

99. Stephen Trumbull, "Poverty and Disease Make Puerto Rico Problem for Army," *Washington Evening Star*, December 3, 1941, A5.

100. E.M. Castro, "U.S. Navy Is on Patrol Duty as Brazil Bolsters Defenses," *Washington Evening Star*, December 3, 1941, B6.

101. *Los Angeles Times*, "Irish Expect Attacks at Sea," December 3, 1941, 7.

102. *Los Angeles Times*, "Axis Planes Stranded Liner," December 3, 1941, 7.

103. *Washington Evening Star*, "Decrease in Atlantic Sinking 'Good Story' Knox Tells Press," December 3, 1941, A3.

104. *Los Angeles Times*, "America Turning Out Ship a Day," December 3, 1941, 9.

105. United Press, "Warships Launched Daily by the Navy," *New York Times*, December 3, 1941, 1.

106. *Los Angeles Times*, "Shipping News," December 3, 1941, 26.

107. *Los Angeles Times*, "Air Mail Schedule," December 3, 1941, 26.

108. Judson Bailey, Associated Press, "Mel Ott Named Playing Manager of Giants, Succeeding Terry; Bill 'Promoted' Into General Manager Role," *Atlanta Constitution*, December 3, 1941, 16.

109. Associated Press, "Boudreau Picks Aides," *Atlanta Constitution*, December 3, 1941, 16.

110. Ron Kaplan, "From Pike to Hirsch: Jews on First (and Second, and . . .)," *Jewish News*, December 21, 2006, 10.

111. Jack Troy, "All in the Game," *Atlanta Constitution*, December 2, 1941, 17.

112. Associated Press, "Griffith Joins Nats," *Atlanta Constitution*, December 3, 1941, 16.

113. Associated Press, "Morris Brown Can Win Negro Title Saturday," *Atlanta Constitution*, December 3, 1941, 17.

114. *Los Angeles Times*, "Slave's Son, 100, to Wed," December 3, 1941, A1.

115. *Washington Evening Star*, "Airport Coffee Shop Refuses to Serve Colored Quartet," December 3, 1941, A6.

116. Associated Press, "Jury Convicts Ex-Warden in Negro's Death," *Atlanta Constitution*, December 3, 1941, 1.

117. Associated Press, "Georgia Negro Troops Seize Tampa Air Field in Blackout," *Atlanta Constitution*, December 3, 1941, 7.

118. Otto D. Tolischus, "Japan Still Says U.S. Must Give In," *New York Times*, December 3, 1941, 4.

119. Associated Press, "Nazi Peace Move Seen," *New York Times*, December 3, 1941, 4.

CHAPTER 4: THE FOURTH OF DECEMBER

1. Franklin Delano Roosevelt Presidential Library and Museum, "Japanese Intelligence and Propaganda in the United States During 1941," December 4, 1941, Hyde Park, NY.

2. Franklin Delano Roosevelt Presidential Library and Museum, "Japanese Intelligence and Propaganda in the United States During 1941," December 4, 1941, Hyde Park, NY.

3. *Washington Evening Star*, "Randolph Protests Moving U.S. Bureaus to Crowded Cities," December 4, 1941, A-2. United Press, "Jap Evacuates Ship Sails After Mail Is Ordered Taken Off," *Tucson (AZ) Daily Citizen*, December 3, 1941, 2.

4. *Washington Evening Star*, "Leaders to Tell Plans for War Office Roads," December 4, 1941, B1.

5. Associated Press, "Army Plans to Add 38,728 Acres to Site of Hill Reservation," *Washington Evening Star*, December 4, 1941, B13.

6. *Washington Evening Star*, "Fingerprints to Be Required of Many D.C. Licensees," December 4, 1941, 1X.

7. *Washington Evening Star*, "Defense Units Study Means to Protect Girls Hired by U.S.," December 3, 1941, A2.

8. *Washington Evening Star*, "Roomers in 'A' Zones," December 5, 1941, A-1; *Washington* 1941, B1.

9. *Washington Evening Star*, "Defense Units Study Means to Protect Girls Hired by U.S.," December 3, 1941, A2.

10. Wyona Daswood, "To Change the Subject: The Other Side of the Picture," *Christian Science Monitor*, December 6, 1941, 13.

11. *Washington Post*, "D.C. Rent Czar Will Be Chosen By Weekend," December 3, 1941, 3.

12. *Washington Post*, "Bundles for U.S. Bluejackets to Warm Them on Patrol," December 3, 1941, 9.

13. *Washington Post*, "Government Girl, 19 Years Old, Reported Missing," December 3, 1941, 1.

14. *Washington Post*, "Capitol's First Woman Air Raid Warden Enrolled," December 3, 1941, 21.

15. *Birmingham (AL) News*, "No Man's Land: Lulu Tells Betty What's Going On in Washington," December 7, 1941, B1.

16. *Washington Post*, "2,000 Cars of Troops Move Through Capital," December 4, 1941, A3.

17. Associated Press, "Slow Drivers' War Continues," *Los Angeles Times*, December 4, 1941, I16.

18. *Washington Evening Star*, "Densest Fog in Years Hits Traffic in D.C., East and Midwest," December 4, 1941, A8.

19. *Boston Globe*, "The War's to Blame as Banshee Wails Rend Boston's Fog," December 4, 1941.

20. *Washington Evening Star*, "Senator Complains Uniform Is 'Unwelcome' in District," December 4, 1941, 2X.

21. *Washington Evening Star*, "Randolph Says He Won't Drop Suffrage Fight," December 4, 1941, B12.

22. *Washington Evening Star*, "If You Have Cold Stay Home, Say Health Chiefs," December 4, 1941, B18.

23. Associated Press, "Industrialists Urge Ban on Antidefense Strikes," *Los Angeles Times*, December 4, 1941, A1.

24. Franklin R. Kent, "The Great Game of Politics," *Los Angeles Times*, December 4, 1941, B1.

25. Associated Press, "Ford Making Munitions, but He Still Hates War," *Los Angeles Times*, December 4, 1941, 7.

26. *Washington Post*, "Men Trailer Redcaps to Check Upon Their Tips Hearing Told," December 3, 1941, 11.

27. *Washington Post*, "Air Attaché and Mrs. Kenny Honored at Informal Party Given by Canadian Minister," December 4, 1941, B3.

28. *Washington Post*, "Nelson Rockefellers Are Dinner Hosts," December 4, 1941, B3.

29. Hope Ridings Miller, "Capital Whirl," *Washington Post*, December 3, 1941, 19.

30. *Washington Evening Star*, "Army Orders," December 3, 1941, B15.

31. *Washington Evening Star*, "Radio Program; Short-Wave Programs," December 4, 1941, D8.

32. Devon Francis, "Plant Is Dedicated as 'Breeding Nest' for Dive Bombers," *Washington Evening Star*, December 4, 1941, A2

33. *New York Times*, "War Victims to Be Aided," December 3, 1941, 11.

34. *New York Times*, "President of Cuba Asks Extra Powers," December 3, 1941, 11.

35. *New York Times*, "Argentina Seeking to Thaw U.S. Credits," December 3, 1941, 11.

36. K.W.B. Middleton, *Britain and Russia*, (England, U. K.: Hutchinson, 1947), 177.

37. Royal Arch Gunnison, "'War Alert': The Entire Far East Is on a War Footing—The Next Move Is Up to Japan," *San Francisco Chronicle*, December 3, 1941, 3.

38. Daniel T. Brightham, "Russians Smash to Taganrog; Turks Get Lease-Lend Help; Hull Not Hopeful on Japan," *New York Times*, December 4, 1941, 1.

39. H. O. Thompson, Associated Press, "Solon Predicts Pincer Move By French and Japs," *Idaho Evening Times*, December 3, 1941, 1.

40. H. O. Thompson, Associated Press, "Solon Predicts Pincer Move By French and Japs," *Idaho Evening Times*, December 3, 1941, 1.

41. Jay G. Hayden, "Peace Means Revolution for Japan," *Washington Evening Star*, December 4, 1941, A13.

42. Jay G. Hayden, "Peace Means Revolution for Japan," *Washington Evening Star*, December 4, 1941, A13.

43. Associated Press, "Envoys Deliver Note Contents Undisclosed; Sees Chief of Army," *Washington Evening Star*, December 5, 1X.

44. Associated Press, "Japanese Diplomats in Mexico Speed Up Plans to Go Home," *Washington Evening Star*, December 4, 1941, A1.

45. Associated Press, "Tokio Agency Calls Hull Plan Unacceptable," *Washington Evening Star*, December 4, 1941, A1.

46. National Geographic Society, "Where Are They Fighting," *Washington Evening Star*, December 4, 1941, A19.

47. Associated Press, "Tokio Agency Calls Hull Plan Unacceptable," *Washington Evening Star*, December 4, 1941, A1.

48. United Press, "Collapse of Pacific Parleys Expected," *Los Angeles Times*, December 4, 1941, 1.

49. *Washington Evening Star*, "Japan's Intentions," December 4, 1941, A12.

50. *Washington Evening Star*, "Japan's Intentions," December 4, 1941, A12.

51. Associated Press, "Roosevelt Sees Congress Chiefs on Far East," *Washington Evening Star*, December 4, 1941, 1X.

52. INS News Agency, "Hopes of Japanese-American Agreement Fading Hourly: Secretary Hull Is Pessimistic on Main Issues," *Atlanta Constitution*, December 4, 1941, 15.

53. Associated Press, "Germans Are Caustic on U.S. Extending Aid to Turkey," *Washington Evening Star*, December 4, 1941, A3.

54. Associated Press, "Germans Are Caustic On U.S. Extending Aid to Turkey," *Washington Evening Star*, December 4, 1941, A3.

55. Associated Press, "Sees Japan Joining U.S.," *New York Times*, December 4, 1941, 5.

56. Associated Press, "Japan's Privy Council Discusses Crisis at 2-Hour Meeting," *Washington Evening Star*, December 4, 1941, A2.

57. INS News Agency, "Hopes of Japanese-American Agreement Fading Hourly; Secretary Hull Is Pessimistic on Main Issues," December 4, 1941, 15.

58. Associated Press, "Tokyo Reply Awaited in Washington," *Hartford Courant*, December 4, 1941, 1.

59. Royal Arch Gunnison, "Fleet at Singapore to Curb Japanese and Halt Nazi Raids," *Washington Evening Star*, December 4, 1941, A9.

60. Associated Press, "Australian Cruiser Sunk After Destroying Raider," *Daily Boston Globe*, December 3, 1941, 16.

61. Associated Press, "Reuben James Survivor Wants to Get Back to Sea," *Washington Evening Star*, December 4, 1941, A7.

62. Associated Press, "U.S. Would Take Cash for Sinking," *Tucson Daily Citizen*, November 3, 1941, 1.

63. Associated Press, "Article 3," *New York Times*, December 4, 1941, 11.

64. Associated Press, "German Parachutist Arrested in Dublin," *Washington Evening Star*, December 4, 1941, A4.

65. Associated Press, "Nephew of Churchill, Canadian War Pilot, Missing in Action," *Washington Evening Star*, December 4, 1941, A6.

66. *Washington Post*, "Navy Launching a Ship a Day," December 3, 1941, 8.

67. Chicago Tribune Press Service, "U.S. Navy Bares 'Possible' Hit in Battling U-Boat," December 5, 1941, 5.

68. Associated Press, "Sub Apparently Was Damaged, Navy Is Told," *Washington Evening Star*, December 4, 1941, A1.

69. *Los Angeles Times*, "Japan Sends Ships to Indo-China Base," December 5, 1941, 6.

70. United Press, "Japan to Exhaust All Peace Avenues," *Washington Post*, December 3, 1941, 2.

71. *Washington Evening Star*, "Speedup in Delivery of Liberty Ships Sought," December 4, 1941, A5.

72. Associated Press, "Three Axis Divisions Are Locked in Battle With Serb Guerillas," *Washington Evening Star*, December 4, 1941, 1X.

73. United Press, "Siege of Belgrade By Serbs Reported; Ankara," *New York Times*, December 3, 1941, 7.

74. Associated Press, "36 Nazi Prisoners Killed as German Plane Bombs Them," *Daily Boston Globe*, December 4, 1941, 23.

75. Associated Press, "189 More Firms Put on U.S. Blacklist," *Washington Evening Star*, December 4, 1941, 1X.

76. Associated Press, "189 More Firms Put on U.S. Blacklist," *Washington Evening Star*, December 4, 1941, 1X.

77. Associated Press, "189 More Firms Put on U.S. Blacklist," *Washington Evening Star*, December 4, 1941, 1X.

78. Associated Press, "Nazis Set Deadline for Surrender of French Terrorists," *Washington Evening Star*, December 4, 1941, A18.

79. Associated Press, "Nazis Set Deadline for Surrender of French Terrorists," *Washington Evening Star*, December 4, 1941, A18.

80. United Press, "Inquiry Turns to Remington," *Telegraph-Herald*, December 5, 1941, 11.

81. Associated Press, "Workers at Bell Warplane Plants Vote to Strike," *Daily Boston Globe*, December 1, 1941, 8.

82. *Atlanta Constitution*, "Nobody Can Argue With a Paid Check," December, 4, 1941, 5.

83. *Atlanta Constitution*, "Nobody Can Argue With a Paid Check," December, 4, 1941, 5.

84. Chesly Manly, "F.D.R.'s War Plans," *Chicago Daily Tribune*, December 4, 1941, 1.

85. *Washington Evening Star*, "Source of War Plans Story to Be Probed, Early Says," December 4, 1941, A2.

86. *Washington Evening Star*, "Source of War Plans Story to Be Probed, Early Says," December 4, 1941, A2.

87. Associated Press, "Roosevelt Sees Congress Chiefs on Far East," *Washington Evening Star*, December 4, 1941, 1X.

88. *Washington Evening Star*, "Source of War Plans Story to Be Probed, Early Says," December 4, 1941, A2.

89. *Washington Evening Star*, "Source of War Plans Story to Be Probed, Early Says," December 4, 1941, A2.

90. *Washington Evening Star*, "Source of War Plans Story to Be Probed, Early Says," December 4, 1941, A2.

91. Dorothy Thompson, "America-Firsters Japan's Ace in Hole, Thompson Charges," *Atlanta Constitution*, December 4, 1941, 1.

92. *Washington Evening Star*, "Give Sports the Lasting Gift," December 4, 1941, A4.

93. *Washington Evening Star*, "Her Husband Was a Stranger," December 4, 1941, B13.

94. *Washington Evening Star*, "Roger Smith Hotel," December 4, 1941, B14.

95. *Washington Evening Star*, "The Pall Mall Room," December 4, 1941, B14.

96. *Washington Evening Star*, "Cocktails—Dancing—Entertainment," December 4, 1941, B14.

97. Associated Press, "Juke Box Mardi Gras Hits Carolina Towns as 29th Says Adieu," *Washington Evening Star*, December 4, 1941 B16.

98. "For Maximum Defense Economy, The New 1942 Crossley," December 4, 1941, A20.

99. *Washington Post*, "Tops For Breakfast; These Cool Mornings," December 2, 1941, 7.

100. *Daily Boston Globe*, "Baldness Can Be Prevented," December 4, 1941, 5.

101. *Boston Evening Globe*, "Wake Up Clearheaded," December 4, 1941, 6.

102. Associated Press, "Baer to Be Welcomed Back to Native State," *Sarasota Herald-Tribune*, December 4, 1941, 7.

103. *Atlanta Constitution*, "Dickens 'The Life of Our Lord' Will Appear in Constitution," December 4, 1941, 1.

104. Associated Press, "Anti-Nazi Offices Raided," *Washington Evening Star*, December 4, 1941, A6.

105. Associated Press, "Moore Draws $500 Fine for Striking Auld," *Atlanta Constitution*, December 4, 1941, 3.

106. *Los Angeles Times*, "Car Hop Shoots Herself; Draft Feared for Boy Friend," December 4, 1941, 4.

107. *Daily Boston Globe*, "Our Army," December 4, 1941, 12.

108. *Daily Boston Globe*, "OK if Mistaken for Southerners,' Says Y-D Officer," December 4, 1941, 13.

109. *Los Angeles Times*, "U.S. Not 'Bluffing' LaGuardia Says," December 4, 1941, 16.

110. *Daily Boston Globe*, "U.S. Sub Halibut Launched at Yard in Portsmouth," December 4, 1941, 16.

111. Associated Press, "Output of 50,000 Planes for 1942 Now Held Likely," *Boston Evening Globe*, December 4, 1941, 5.

112. Frederick R. Barkley, "New Defense Bill Brings Total Near 68 Billions," *New York Times*, December 4, 1941, 1.

113. Associated Press, "Troops for Air Raid Defense Maneuvers to Arrive Today," *Los Angeles Times*, December 4, 1941, 6.

114. Associated Press, "Troops for Air Raid Defense Maneuvers to Arrive Today," *Los Angeles Times*, December 4, 1941, 6.

115. Celestine Sibley, "1941 World's Champion Typist Shows Atlanta How It's Done," *Atlanta Constitution*, December 4, 1941, 4.

116. *Atlanta Constitution*, "Auto Takes Dip," December 4, 1941, 30.

117. *Los Angeles Times*, "Down the Decades with Los Angeles," December 4, 1941, 22.

118. *Los Angeles Times*, "Down the Decades with Los Angeles," December 4, 1941, 22.

119. *Los Angeles Times*, "Down the Decades with Los Angeles," December 4, 1941, 22.

120. Associated Press, "Too Much Radio Grounds for Divorce," *Los Angeles Times*, December 4, 1941.

121. *New York Times*, "The Siege of Japan," December 4, 1941, 24.

122. *New York Times*, "The Siege of Japan," December 4, 1941, 24.

123. Dewey L. Fleming, "U.S. and England Ready for Blockade of Japan if Tokyo Provokes War," *Baltimore Sun*, December 4, 1941, 1.

124. *Atlanta Constitution*, "Mrs. Roosevelt Speaks on 'Town Meeting' Show," December 4, 1941, 27.

125. Associated Press, "Mrs. Roosevelt Assures Fairness to Aliens," *Washington Evening Star*, December, 4, 1941, A18.

CHAPTER 5: THE FIFTH OF DECEMBER

1. Thomas R. Henry, "Of Stars, Men and Atoms," *Washington Evening Star*, December 4, 1941, A12.

2. Frank Carey, "British and Nazi Astronomers Exchange Views Despite War," *Birmingham* (AL) *News*, December 8, 1941, 4.

3. Associated Press, "Amateur Operator Develops New Radio Which Quiets Static," *Washington Evening Star*, December 4, 1941, B18.

4. Associated Press, "Boom in Plastics Industry May Avert Post-War Slump," *Washington Evening Star*, December 4, 1941, B19.

5. *Washington Evening Star*, "Wild Hedges Found Rich in Vitamins," December 5, 1941, A5.

6. Thomas R. Henry, "Of Stars, Men And Atoms," December 6, 1941, A10.

7. *New York Times*, "Powerful New Gun Developed By U.S.," December 4, 1941, 13.

8. Associated Press, "70-Ton Flying Boat Catches Fire During Tests at Baltimore," *Washington Evening Star*, December 5, 1941, A1.

9. *Washington Evening Star*, "Rain Here Last Night Totaled More Than in All of November," December 5, 1941, 1X.

10. *Atlanta Constitution*, "Sanitary Precautions Seen as Major Factor in Prolonging Life," December 5, 1941, 3A.

11. George Gallup, "Gallup Poll Reveals: U. S. Public Is Food Conscious," *Atlanta Constitution*, December 5, 1941, 7A.

12. Uncle Dudley, "Why Thailand?" *Boston Daily Globe*, December 4, 1941, 18.

13. Pertinax, "Vichy Assent Hinted In Japanese Move into Indo-China," *Washington Evening Star*, December 5, 1941, A6.

14. Walter Lippmann, "U. S. Declared to Be on Verge of All-Out War," *Boston Daily Globe*, December 4, 1941, 18.

15. *Baltimore Sun*, "Realities in the Pacific as Mr. Hull Loses Hope," December 5, 1941, 16.

16. F. Tillman Durdin, "Singapore Doubts Japanese Threats," *New York Times*, December 4, 1941, 5.

17. Associated Press, "Russians Admit Nazi Big Guns Shell Moscow," *Washington Evening Star*, December 5, 1941, A1.

18. Associated Press, "Red Drive Futile Germans Insist," *New York Times*, December 6, 1941, 5.

19. Associated Press, "British Repulse 3 Axis Attacks Near Tobruk," *Washington Evening Star*, December 5, 1941, 1X.

20. Associated Press, "Pepper and McNary Clash Over Defense Support," *Washington Evening Star*, December 5, 1941, A5.

21. *Washington Evening Star*, "Representative Fish Testifies Before Jury Probing Propaganda," December 5, 1941, 1X.

22. *Washington Evening Star*, "Stimson Denounces Publication of Story on U.S. 'War Plans,'" December 5, 1941, 1X.

23. Associated Press, "Nipponese Army Reported in Skirmish With Reds on Border," *Washington Evening Star*, December 5, 1941, 1X.

24. Associated Press, "Night Clubs Bar Uniformed Men, Senator and General Charge," *Washington Evening Star*, December 5, 1941, 2X.

25. *Washington Evening Star*, "On Week-End Leave?" December 5, 1941, A17.

26. *Washington Post*, "Yule Spirit to Greet Service Men," December 6, 1941, 18.

27. *Washington Evening Star*, "On Week-End Leave?" December 5, 1941, A17.

28. *Washington Evening Star*, "On Weekend Leave?" December 5, 1941, A16; *Washington Post*, "Clubs Offering Fun for Service Men," December 6, 1941, 18.

29. Associated Press, "Army Plans to Train 10,000 Bombardiers Within Next Year," *Washington Evening Star*, December 5, 1941, A2.

30. *Washington Post*, "War Department Building Takes Shape," December 4, 1941, 14; *Washington Evening Star*, December 5, 1941, A3.

31. Associated Press, "Export Violation Case Indictment," *Christian Science Monitor*, December 5, 1941, 9.

32. Associated Press, "South American Presidents May Meet on War," *Washington Evening Star*, December 5, 1941, A1.

33. *Washington Evening Star*, "Restricted Covenants in Land Sales Upheld," December 5, 1941, 2X.

34. Associated Press, "Court in New Jersey Reverses Bund Case, Voids Race Hatred Law," *Washington Evening Star*, December 5, 1941, A2.

35. Associated Press, "Bergdoll Is Denied Parole for Christmas Homecoming," *Washington Evening Star*, December 5, 1941, A1.

36. Associated Press, "Americans in France to Broadcast to U.S.," *Washington Evening Star*, December 5, 1941, A1.

37. Associated Press, "German Major Wounded in New Paris Attack," *Washington Evening Star*, December 5, 1941, 1X.

38. Associated Press, "Serb Flanking Movements Against Nazis, Reported," *Washington Evening Star*, December 5, 1941, 1X.

39. Overseas News Agency, "King Michael Reported Nazi Prisoner as Plot Leader," *Boston Daily Globe*, December 5, 1941, 1.
40. Associated Press, "'V' Army Ordered to Become Active," *Washington Evening Star*, December 5, 1941, A1.
41. *Washington Evening Star*, "Far East Reported Preparing for Early U.S. Tokyo Break," December 5, 1941, 1X.
42. *Washington Post*, "President's Day," December 6, 1941, 2.
43. *Washington Post*, "President's Day," December 6, 1941, 2.
44. John C. Henry, "Reply to U.S. Cites Vichy's O.K. on Army," *Washington Evening Star*, December 5, 1941, A1.
45. John C. Henry, "Reply to U.S. Cites Vichy's O.K. on Army," *Washington Evening Star*, December 5, 1941, A1.
46. *Washington Evening Star*, "Far East Reported Preparing for Early U.S. Tokyo Break," December 5, 1941, 1X.
47. Associated Press, "Nipponese Army Reported in Skirmish With Reds on Border," *Washington Evening Star*, December 5, 1941, 1X.
48. Associated Press, "Nipponese Army Reported in Skirmish With Reds on Border," *Washington Evening Star*, December 5, 1941, 1X.
49. Associated Press, "Japan 'Cannot Accept' Terms, Tokyo Is Told," *Atlanta Constitution*, December 5, 1941, 1A.
50. Associated Press, "Tokyo Hedges on War; Britain in New Warning," *Christian Science Monitor*, December 5, 1941, 1.
51. Associated Press, "Japan 'Cannot Accept' Terms, Tokyo Is Told," *Atlanta Constitution*, December 5, 1941, 1A.
52. *Boston Daily Globe*, "Hull Under Fire in Japan for Baring U. S. Terms," December 5, 1941, 1.
53. Associated Press, "Nipponese Army Reported in Skirmish With Reds on Border," *Washington Evening Star*, December 5, 1941, 1X.
54. Associated Press, "Alexander Warns Japan Aggression Won't Pay," *Washington Evening Star*, December 5, 1941, A9.
55. Paul Mallon, "News Behind the News," *Birmingham* (AL) *News*, December 5, 1941, 1.
56. Associated Press, "Faster Draft Rate Expected to Keep Up Strength of Army," *Washington Evening Star*, December 5, 1941, A4.
57. Oliver Wendell Holmes and Richard A. Posner, *The Essential Holmes: Selections From the Letters, Speeches, Judicial Opinions, and Other Writings of Oliver Wendell Holmes, Jr.* (Chicago: University of Chicago Press, 1997), XIV–XV.
58. Jonas Klein, *Beloved Island: Franklin & Eleanor and the Legacy of Campobello* (Forest Dale, VT: Paul S. Eriksson, 2000), 228.
59. *Washington Evening Star*, "Hard to Determine When Subs Are Sunk, President Says," December 5, 1941, A10.
60. Uncle Dudley, "Sea Battle," *Boston Daily Globe*, December 5, 1941, 26.
61. "Bulletin," December 5, 1941, Franklin Delano Roosevelt Presidential Library and Museum, Hyde Park, NY.
62. "Report on Talk With Vincent Astor," December 5, 1941, Franklin Delano Roosevelt Presidential Library and Museum, Hyde Park, NY.
63. *Washington Evening Star*, "Bill Signed to Pay Man $830 for Capitol Injury," December 5, 1941, A14.
64. Frank I. Weller, "Shift From China Cuts Fabulous Pay of U.S. Marines," *Washington Evening Star*, December 5, 1941, C10.
65. *Birmingham* (AL) *News*, "Americans Itching: To Get After Japs," December 5, 1941, 1.
66. Pertinax, "Vichy Assent Hinted in Japanese Move Into Indo-China," *Washington Evening Star*, December 5, 1941, A6.

67. Constantine Brown, "The Changing World: Diplomats Giving 100-to-1 Odds That War Will Break Out Involving Japan," *Washington Evening Star*, December 5, 1941, A13.

68. Constantine Brown, "The Changing World: Diplomats Giving 100-to-1 Odds That War Will Break Out Involving Japan," *Washington Evening Star*, December 5, 1941, A13.

69. Associated Press, "Karl Decker, Famous War Correspondent, Dies in New York," *Washington Evening Star*, December 5, 1941, A14.

70. Associated Press, "Martin and Landon Plead for Return to Two-Party System," *Washington Evening Star*, December 5, 1941, A18.

71. Associated Press, "Mrs. Roosevelt Buys Bedroom Sleepers For 22 Children," *Washington Evening Star*, December 5, 1941, A18.

72. *Washington Evening Star*, "Activities of Interest to Diplomatic and Official Circles Here," December 5, 1941, B3.

73. Associated Press, "W.C.T.U. Puts Liquor Cost Since Repeal at 50 Billions," *Washington Evening Star*, December 5, 1941, B6.

74. *Washington Evening Star*, "Hershey Milk Chocolate," December 5, 1941, C6; *Washington Evening Star*, "Super Specials: Anacin Tablets," December 5, 1941, C6.

75. Associated Press, "13 Recommendations Made by N.A.M. on Post-War Economy," *Washington Evening Star*, December 5, 1941, A20.

76. Sheilah Graham, "Bruno Walter Defends Playing of Music of German Masters," *Washington Evening Star*, December 5, 1941, B18.

77. Sheilah Graham, "Bruno Walter Defends Playing of Music of German Masters," *Washington Evening Star*, December 5, 1941, B18.

78. *Washington Evening Star*, "U.S. Movies Continue to Hold Popularity in Unconquered Europe," December 5, 1941, C4.

79. Harold Heffernan, "Actresses' Worst Enemy Is Nervous Breakdown," *Washington Evening Star*, December 5, 1941, D5.

80. Eleanor Roosevelt, "My Day: The President's Dog Misses Georgia Visit," *Atlanta Constitution*, December 5, 1941, 8A.

81. United Press, "Sport Just Won't Be Downed by Mere Train or Automobile," *Birmingham* (AL) *News*, December 5, 1941, 17.

82. Associated Press, "Cat Rescued After 3 Days in Well," *Boston Daily Globe*, December 5, 1941, 14.

83. *Washington Evening Star*, "Radio Program: Friday, December 5, 1941," December 5, 1941, D10.

84. *Atlanta Constitution*, "Shirley Temple Bows Tonight on Radio Hour," December 5, 1941, 7F.

85. Associated Press, "Ten Georgia Colleges Suspended From Southern Accredited List Because of 'Political Interference': Suspension to Take Effect in September," *Atlanta Constitution*, December 5, 1941, 1A.

86. Sam Clarke, "Georgia Farmers Have Folding Money This Holiday Season," *Atlanta Constitution*, December 5, 1941, 7A; United Press, "New Holiday Sales Record Predicted," *Washington Post*, December 5, 1941, 19; Paul Gesner and John Beckley, "Families Are Urged to Readjust Spending to Offset High Prices," *Birmingham* (AL) *News*, December 5, 1941, 2.

87. *Wall Street Journal*, "Treasury Offering Today $1 Billion 2s, $500 Million 2s; Subscription Rules Tightened to Cut Speculation," December 4, 1941, 8.

88. *Birmingham* (AL) *News*, "Alabama Power Company: Restriction of Power Use Lifted," December 5, 1941, 3.

89. *Atlanta Constitution*, "Georgia Power Company: Blackout Lifted," December 6, 1941, 7.

90. *Birmingham* (AL) *News*, "Parisian's Christmas Sale," December 5, 1941, 25.

91. *Boston Daily Globe*, "Rogers Jewelers: 5 Tube Radio," December 5, 1941, 20.

92. *Saturday Evening Post*, "General Electric," December 6, 1941, 7.

93. Associated Press, "Loot From 1852 Mail Robbery Found in Philadelphia Attic," *Washington Evening Star*, December 5, 1941, A2.

94. *Birmingham* (AL) *News*, "Americans Itching: To Get After Japs," December 5, 1941, 1.

95. Editorial, "On All Fronts, Including the American," *Los Angeles Times*, December 5, 1941, A4.

96. Associated Press, "Tokyo Envoy to Mexico Ordered Home as U.S.-Japan Crisis Grows: Many Others, Fearing War, Plan to Leave," *Baltimore Sun*, December 5, 1941, 1.

CHAPTER 6: THE SIXTH OF DECEMBER

1. Associated Press, "Feller to Enlist in Service, But hopes To Pitch on Weekends," *Atlanta Constitution*, December 6, 1941, 17.
2. Associated Press, "Feller Will Reveal His Plans Next Week," *Washington Post*, December 6, 1941, 20.
3. Walter Winchell, "Walter Winchell on Broadway; Things I Never Knew and Still Dunno," *St. Petersburg* (FL) *Times*, December 8, 1941, 7.
4. *Calgary* (Alberta, Canada) *Herald*, "Japs Can't Equal U.S. Naval Power," December 8, 1941, 5.
5. Naval History and Heritage Command, "Ships Present at Pearl Harbor, 0800 7 December 1941," http://www.history.navy.mil/faqs/faq66-2.htm.
6. Robert Cressman, *The Official Chronology of the U.S. Navy in World War II* (Annapolis, MD: Naval Institute Press, 2000), 57.
7. Robert Cressman, *The Official Chronology of the U.S. Navy in World War II* (Annapolis, MD: Naval Institute Press, 2000), 57.
8. Robert Cressman, *The Official Chronology of the U.S. Navy in World War II* (Annapolis, MD: Naval Institute Press, 2000), 59.
9. John B. Lundstrom, *The First Team: Pacific Naval Air Combat From Pearl Harbor to Midway* (Annapolis, MD: Naval Institute Press, 2005), 27.
10. Marc T. Greene, "U.S. Air Force Grows in Pacific," *Baltimore Sun*, December 7, 1941, 17.
11. *Washington Evening Star*, "Surrounded by Fog, Stimson Gets a Lift Home," December 7, 1941, A4.
12. *Christian Science Monitor; Weekly Magazine Section*, "Battle of Fifth Avenue," December 6, 1941, 12.
13. *Baltimore Sun*, "Hitler & The US; Manifesto By 16 Pastors," December 6, 1941, 11.
14. Associated Press, "Japanese Accuse U.S. of Trying to 'Pass Buck,'" *Hartford* (CT) *Courant*, December 6, 1941, 3.
15. Associated Press, "Japan Justifies Troop Movements into Indo-China," *Hartford* (CT) *Courant*, December 6, 1941, 1.
16. Richard L. Strout, "Tokyo Reply Keeps Door Open," *Christian Science Monitor*, December 6, 1941, 1.
17. *Christian Science Monitor*, "Göttliche Führung," December 6, 1941, 12.
18. Joseph G. Harrison, "Intimate Message: Washington," *Christian Science Monitor*, December 6, 1941, 13.
19. Otto D. Tolisch, "Japan Confident Talks Will Go On," *New York Times*, December 6, 1941, 2.
20. *Los Angeles Times*, "Where Silence Seems Superfluous," December 6, 1941, A4.
21. Lloyd Lehrbas, "Second Tokio Reply Awaited Here; Peace Talks Are Delayed," *Washington Evening Star*, December 6, 1941, 1X.
22. Bertram D. Hulen, "Japanese Answer; Says Troops in Indo-China Do Not Exceed Limit in Pact with Vichy," *New York Times*, December 6, 1941, 1.
23. Associated Press, "Joint U.S.-Japan Commission Is Proposed to End Deadlock," *Atlanta Constitution*, December 6, 1941, 1.
24. *New York Times*, "Japan Institute Here Is Closing," December 6, 1941, 2.
25. Associated Press, "Joint U.S.-Japan Commission Is Proposed to End Deadlock," *Atlanta Constitution*, December 6, 1941, 1.
26. *Christian Science Monitor*, "Draft for Overseas Service Major Issue in Australia," December 6, 1941, 11.
27. Associated Press, "Australia Calls for Execution of 'ABCD' Military Measures," *Constitution*, December 6, 1941, 4.

28. Associated Press, "Britain Takes Up Battle Posts in Far East as Crisis Grows," *Christian Science Monitor*, December 6, 1941, 1.

29. Associated Press, "Singapore Alert Sounded; Manila Evacuation Seen," *Birmingham News*, December 6, 1941, 1.

30. Henry W. Harris, "Crisis Finds Foes of Japan Strong," *Boston Evening Globe*, December 6, 1941, 2.

31. Henry W. Harris, "Crisis Finds Foes of Japan Strong," *Boston Evening Globe*, December 6, 1941, 2.

32. Walter Robb, "Macarthur Prepared if Japan Strikes Blow," *Los Angeles Times*, December 6, 1941, 5.

33. Otto D. Tolischus, "Needn't Fear Air Attacks Japan Told," *Washington Post*, December 6, 1941, 2.

34. Henry W. Harris, "Crisis Finds Foes of Japan Strong," *Boston Evening Globe*, December 6, 1941, 2.

35. *Christian Science Monitor*, "House Votes Eight Billions for Defense," December 6, 1941, 1.

36. Associated Press, "Army Recreation Delay Ridiculed," *Christian Science Monitor*, December 6, 1941, 11.

37. Sheilah Graham, "Navy Air Cadets Talk Girls and Planes, Not War, Reporter Says," *Washington Evening Star*, December 6, 1941, 2X.

38. Associated Press, "State Drops Charges In Naval Plane Killing," *Washington Evening Star*, December 6, 1941, A2.

39. *Washington Evening Star*, "Temporary Buildings' Removal Following Emergency Indicated," December 6, 1941, A4.

40. *Wall Street Journal*, "Vinson Tries to Work Up Steam for Profits Limit Bill, But Congress Is Not Responsive," December 6, 1941, 2.

41. *Wall Street Journal*, "Vinson Tries to Work Up Steam for Profits Limit Bill, But Congress Is Not Responsive," December 6, 1941, 2.

42. *Wall Street Journal*, "Defense Contracts Awarded," December 6, 1941, 6.

43. *Baltimore Sun*, "Dr. Lazaron Tells of Britain at War," December 7, 1941, 8.

44. *Baltimore Sun*, "Germans Plan to Ask U.S. to Repay Blacklist," December 6, 1941, 1.

45. Honor Croome, "The Nazi Economy," *Christian Science Monitor*, December 6, 1941, 10.

46. Earl C. Behrens, "Propoganda Drive Centers in Schools," *Los Angeles Times*, December 6, 1941, 1.

47. *Baltimore Sun*, "Dies Group Probes Pro-Nazi Influence in America First," December 6, 1941, 1.

48. *Baltimore Sun*, "Dies Group Probes Pro-Nazi Influence in America First," December 6, 1941, 1.

49. F.R. Kent Jr., "Widening of Dies Probes Revealed," *Baltimore Sun*, December 7, 1941, 15.

50. *Washington Post*, "Youth Rally Hears Pepper Assail Hitler," December 6, 1941, 19.

51. Gordon William Prange, Donald M. Goldstein, Katherine V. Dillon, *At Dawn We Slept, The Untold Story of Pearl Harbor* (New York: Penguin Books, 1991), 70.

52. *New York Times*, "Nazis Bar Sales By Jews," December 6, 1941, 7.

53. *New York Times*, "Nazis Bar Sales By Jews," December 6, 1941, 7.

54. Jerome Frank, "Red-White-and-Blue Herring," *Saturday Evening Post*, December 6, 1941, 9.

55. Jerome Frank, "Red-White-and-Blue Herring," *Saturday Evening Post*, December 6, 1941, 9.

56. Jerome Frank, "Red-White-and-Blue Herring," *Saturday Evening Post*, December 6, 1941, 9.

57. Jerome Frank, "Red-White-and-Blue Herring," *Saturday Evening Post*, December 6, 1941, 9.

58. Jerome Frank, "Red-White-and-Blue Herring," *Saturday Evening Post*, December 6, 1941, 9.

59. Joe Morton, "American Concentration Camp," *Greeley* (CO) *Daily Tribune*, December 6, 1941, 4.

60. Frederick Kuh, "Britain Declares War on Finland, Hungary, Rumania," *Idaho Evening News*, December 6, 1941, 1.

61. *Hartford* (CT) *Courant*, "That Ickes Oil 'Shortage,'" December 6, 1941, 8.

62. *Hartford* (CT) *Courant*, "That Ickes Oil 'Shortage,'" December 6, 1941, 8.

63. J. I I. Carmical, "10% Cut Is Likely In 'Gas' Efficacy," *New York Times*, December 6, 1941, 1.

64. *Saturday Evening Post*, "Partners in Power for the Nation's Defense," December 6, 1941, 33.

65. *Saturday Evening Post*, "I Keep 500 'Horses' on Their Toes," December 6, 1941, 90.

66. *Saturday Evening Post*, "All-out Aid for a Hungry Man!" December 6, 1941, 31.

67. *Saturday Evening Post*, "When You Have a Smokers Cough—It's Time to Change to Spuds," December 6, 1941, 75.

68. *Washington Post*, "Seasonal Sale! Brand New '41 Models," December 6, 1941, 18.

69. *Washington Post*, "Seasonal Sale! Brand New '41 Models," December 6, 1941, 18.

70. *Christian Science Monitor*, "War Dines Heartily at New World Table But Essential Foods Are Still Plentiful," December 6, 1941, 6.

71. *Christian Science Monitor*, "War Dines Heartily at New World Table But Essential Foods Are Still Plentiful," December 6, 1941, 6.

72. *Washington Evening Star*, "Work of Colored Artist in Library of Congress," December 6, 1941, A4.

73. *Atlanta Constitution*, "Todays Radio; Saturdays Local Program," December 6, 1941, 11.

74. Associated Press, "Honduran President Reveals Nazi Plots in Central America," *Washington Evening Star*, December 6, 1941, A1.

75. Associated Press, "Russian Armies Slash at Foe in Flank Attacks," *Washington Evening Star*, December 6, 1941, A1.

76. Associated Press, "Russian Armies Slash at Foe in Flank Attacks," *Washington Evening Star*, December 6, 1941, A1.

77. Associated Press, "British Submarine Sunk Off Norway, Nazis Claim," *Washington Evening Star*, December 6, 1941, A2.

78. *Christian Science Monitor*, "Prisoners: Pawns of Nazi Conquest," December 6, 1941, 7.

79. *Baltimore Sun*, "Cannibalism Is Reported in Germany's Prison Camp," December 7, 1941, 3.

80. *Baltimore Sun*, "Cannibalism Is Reported in Germany's Prison Camp," December 7, 1941, 3.

81. Angus Thuermer, "Prisoners Make Arms for Nazis," *Hartford* (CT) *Courant*, December 7, 1941, 5.

82. Associated Press, "British Free Admiral's Wife," *Christian Science Monitor*, December 6, 1941, 11.

83. Jesse A. Linthicum, "Sunlight on Sports," *Baltimore Sun*, December 1, 1941, 14.

84. Bill Dismer Jr., "Banta of Eagles Aims to Show Redskins They Passed Up Ace," *Washington Evening Star*, December 6, 1941, A18.

85. Associated Press, "Tommy Breaks Up With Fifth Wife," *Evening* (OH) *Independent*, December 6, 1941, 2.

86. Ida Jean Kain, "Rita Hayworth Does Not Diet; Stays Thin by Dancing, Sports," *Washington Evening Star*, December 6, 1941, 15.

87. *Washington Post*, "Bible for President," December 6, 1941, 8.

88. Edgar Ansel Mowrer, "Japan Believed Certain to Fight," *Los Angeles Times*, December 6, 1941, 5.

89. *Washington Post*, "U.S.-Japan at End of Talk, He Asserts," December 6, 1941, 4.

90. *Christian Science Monitor*, "World Golden Rule Week Calls For Self-Denial and Generosity," December 6, 1941, 14.

91. *Christian Science Monitor*, "Tokyo Regime Called Bluff; China Stiffer," December 6, 1941, 14.

92. *Christian Science Monitor*, "Tokyo Regime Called Bluff; China Stiffer," December 6, 1941, 14.

93. United Press, "Japanese Council Defies Effort of United States to Bar 'New Order,'" December 6, 1941, 1.

CHAPTER 7: THE SEVENTH OF DECEMBER

1. Joint Committee on the Investigation of the Pearl Harbor Attack, *Pearl Harbor Attack: Hearings Before the Joint Committee on the Investigation of the Pearl Harbor Attack*, 79th Cong., 1st sess., 1946, Government Printing Office, Exhibit no. 17, Memorandum for the President, "Subject: Far Eastern Situation," November 27, 1941, 1083.

2. Joint Committee on the Investigation of the Pearl Harbor Attack, *Pearl Harbor Attack: Hearings Before the Joint Committee on the Investigation of the Pearl Harbor Attack*, 79th Cong., 1st sess., 1946, Government Printing Office, Exhibit no. 17, Memorandum for the President, "Subject: Far Eastern Situation," November 27, 1941, 1083.

3. Joint Committee on the Investigation of the Pearl Harbor Attack, *Pearl Harbor Attack: Hearings Before the Joint Committee on the Investigation of the Pearl Harbor Attack*, 79th Cong., 1st sess., 1946, Government Printing Office, Exhibit no. 17, Memorandum for the President, "Subject: Far Eastern Situation," November 27, 1941, 1083.

4. Joint Committee on the Investigation of the Pearl Harbor Attack, *Pearl Harbor Attack: Hearings Before the Joint Committee on the Investigation of the Pearl Harbor Attack*, 79th Cong., 1st sess., 1946, Government Printing Office, Exhibit no. 17, Memorandum for the President, "Subject: Far Eastern Situation," November 27, 1941, 1083.

5. Joint Committee on the Investigation of the Pearl Harbor Attack, *Pearl Harbor Attack: Hearings Before the Joint Committee on the Investigation of the Pearl Harbor Attack*, 79th Cong., 1st sess., 1946, Government Printing Office, Exhibit no. 17, Memorandum for the President, "Subject: Far Eastern Situation," November 27, 1941, 1083.

6. Husband E. Kimmel, *Admiral Kimmel's Story* (Chicago, IL: Henry Regnery Company, 1955), 15.

7. Husband E. Kimmel, *Admiral Kimmel's Story* (Chicago, IL: Henry Regnery Company, 1955), 19.

8. Gerald Griffin, "President Makes Move As Convoys Are Sighted Bound for Gulf of Siam," *Baltimore Sun*, December 7, 1941, 1.

9. Doris Kerns Goodwin, *No Ordinary Time: Franklin and Eleanor Roosevelt: The Home Front in World War II* (New York: Simon and Schuster, 1955), 286.

10. *Honolulu Advertiser*, "Housing Aid Appeal Sent to Governor," December 7, 1941, 1.

11. *Honolulu Advertiser*, "See Santa Today," December 7, 1941, 1.

12. *Honolulu Advertiser*, "'Clean Shave' Drive Started," December 7, 1941, 1.

13. United Press, "Week's War Preview," *Honolulu Advertiser*, December 7, 1941, 7.

14. Associated Press, "Man Dies Without Learning His Identity," *Los Angeles Times*, December 7, 1941, 8.

15. United Press, "Japanese Herald 'Supreme Crisis,'" *New York Times*, December 7, 1941, 3.

16. United Press, "Singapore Forces Recalled to War Stations; Base Ready to Act in Any Emergency," *Honolulu Advertiser*, December 7, 1941, 7.

17. Associated Press, "Australia and Allies Reported in Accord on Pacific Defense," *Washington Evening Star*, December 7, 1941, A2.

18. Blair Bolles, "Roosevelt Sends Note to Hirohito; Japanese Convoys Near Thailand; U.S. Takes Over Finnish Vessels: President's Action Looked on Here As Last Step," *Washington Evening Star*, December 7, 1941, 1.

19. Franklin Delano Roosevelt Presidential Library and Museum, "Roosevelt's Appeal to Hirohito to Avoid War," December 6, 1941, Hyde Park, NY.

20. Franklin Delano Roosevelt Presidential Library and Museum, "Roosevelt's Appeal to Hirohito to Avoid War," December 6, 1941, Hyde Park, NY.

21. Franklin Delano Roosevelt Presidential Library and Museum, "Roosevelt's Appeal to Hirohito to Avoid War," December 6, 1941, Hyde Park, NY.

22. *New York Times*, "New Troop Moves," December 7, 1941, 1.

23. Blair Bolles, "Roosevelt Sends Note to Hirohito; Japanese Convoys Near Thailand; U.S. Takes Over Finnish Vessels: President's Action Looked on Here As Last Step," *Washington Evening Star*, December 7, 1941, 1.

24. Blair Bolles, "Roosevelt Sends Note to Hirohito; Japanese Convoys Near Thailand; U.S. Takes Over Finnish Vessels: President's Action Looked on Here As Last Step," *Washington Evening Star*, December 7, 1941, 1.

25. Associated Press, "F.D.R. Puts Jap Crisis Up to Emperor: Personal Message Sent to Mikado Amid Reports of Fresh Troop Moves," *Birmingham* (AL) *News*, December 7, 1941, 1.

26. Associated Press, "Japanese Head for Thailand," *Los Angeles Times*, December 7, 1941, 14.

27. Fredric L. Borch, Daniel Martinez, *Kimmel, Short, and Pearl Harbor* (Annapolis, MD: Naval Institute Press, 2005), 56.

28. United Press, "London Prepares for Fighting," *New York Times*, December 3, 1941, 4.

29. Associated Press, "Special Commission Urged," *New York Times*, December 7, 1941, 3.

30. Associated Press, "U.S. Stalling, Says Tokyo," *Los Angeles Times*, December 7, 1941, 1.

31. Associated Press, "U.S. Stalling, Says Tokyo," *Los Angeles Times*, December 7, 1941, 1.

32. Associated Press, "Roosevelt Insincere, Stalling in Talks, Japanese Press Says," *Washington Evening Star*, December 7, 1941, A4.

33. Associated Press, "U.S. Helps Guard South Pacific," *Calgary* (Alberta, Canada) *Herald*, December 2, 1941, 3.

34. Associated Press, "Roosevelt Insincere, Stalling in Talks, Japanese Press Says," *Washington Evening Star*, December 7, 1941, A4.

35. Associated Press, "Australia and Allies Reported in Accord on Pacific Defense," *Washington Evening Star*, December 7, 1941, A1.

36. Associated Press, "British Forces Recalled to Singapore Posts," *Washington Evening Star*, December 7, 1941, A3.

37. Associated Press, "Britain Goes to War Against Finland Quietly and Formally," *Washington Evening Star*, December 7, 1941, A1.

38. Associated Press, "Move Synchronous With British War Declaration," *Washington Evening Star*, December 7, 1941, A1.

39. Associated Press, "Finn President Warns Britain and U.S. of Soviet Friendship," *Washington Evening Star*, December 7, 1941, A4.

40. Associated Press, "French Fleet Declared Active in Mediterranean," *Washington Evening Star*, December 7, 1941, A1.

41. Associated Press, "British Credit American Planes for Biggest Victory in Libya," *Washington Evening Star*, December 7, 1941, A1.

42. Associated Press, "Russia May Get Wheat From Pacific Northwest," *Washington Evening Star*, December 7, 1941, A1.

43. Associated Press, "Moscow Facing New Peril From Enemy Hordes," *Washington Evening Star*, December 7, 1941, A1.

44. *New York Times*, "Navy Is Superior to Any," December 7, 1941, 1.

45. *New York Times*, "Dentistry to Cut Army Rejections," December 2, 1941, 18.

46. Department of the Navy, Memorandum for the President, "Subject: Report on Enlisted Personnel, United States Navy," December 2, 1941, Washington, D.C.

47. *Birmingham* (AL) *News*, "Experts With Radios Are Needed By Navy," December 7, 1941, 14.

48. *Washington Evening Star*, "21-Year-Olds Face Call to Army Duty At Least by July 1," December 7, 1941, A5.

49. Associated Press, "Doctor Scores His Profession," *Indiana* (PA) *Evening Gazette*, December 5, 1941, 1.

50. *Washington Evening Star*, "Revlon Nail Enamel," December 7, 1941, A7.

51. Martin Caidin, *Golden Wings* (New York: Random House, 1960), 104.

52. Martin Caidin, *Golden Wings* (New York: Random House, 1960), 104.

53. Drew Pearson and Robert S. Allen, "Merry-Go-Around," *Palm Beach* (FL) *Post-Times*, December 14, 1941, 4.

54. Martin Caidin, *Golden Wings* (New York: Random House, 1960), 104.

55. Associated Press, "Japs Strike at U.S.," *Emporia* (KS) *Gazette*, December 1941, 1.

56. Associated Press, "Eyewitness Report of Air Raid," *Baltimore Sun*, December 8, 1941, 2.

57. Martin Caidin, *Golden Wings* (New York: Random House, 1960), 106.

58. Bill Henry, "By the Way With Bill Henry," *Los Angeles Times*, December 9, 1941, A1.

59. Bernard C. Nalty, *War in the Pacific Pearl Harbor to Tokyo Bay: The Story of the Bitter Struggle in the Pacific Theater of World War II* (Norman, OK: University of Oklahoma Press, 1999), 32.

60. *Time*, "The U.S. at War, Tragedy at Honolulu," December 15, 1941, 22.

61. Thomas Yarbrough, "Writer Learns Hawaiian Raid No 'War Game,'" *Atlanta Constitution*, December 13, 1941, 1.

62. Jim Hopkins and Michelle Kessler, "Unlike Pearl Harbor, This Tragedy Was Live," *USA Today*, September 25, 2001, 8B; Geoffrey C. Ward and Ken Burns, *The War: an Intimate History, 1941–1945* (New York: A.A. Knopf, 2007), 1.

63. Jim Hopkins and Michelle Kessler, "Unlike Pearl Harbor, This Tragedy Was Live," *USA Today*, September 25, 2001, 8B; Geoffrey C. Ward and Ken Burns, *The War: an Intimate History, 1941–1945* (New York: A.A. Knopf, 2007), 1.

64. United Press, "Hawaii Under Martial Law, Islands Quiet; Blackout Enforced, Violators Punished," *New York Times*, December 11, 1941, 6.
65. Gerald Eckert, in discussion with the author.
66. Thomas E. Henry, "Capital Retains Outward Calm Despite Shock of War News," *Washington Evening Star*, December 8, 1941, A8.
67. Shirley Povich, "War's Outbreak Is Deep Secret to 27,102 Redskin Game Fans," *Washington Post*, December 8, 1941, 24.
68. Shirley Povich, "War's Outbreak Is Deep Secret to 27,102 Redskin Game Fans," *Washington Post*, December 8, 1941, 24.
69. Shirley Povich, "War's Outbreak Is Deep Secret to 27,102 Redskin Game Fans," *Washington Post*, December 8, 1941, 24.
70. Associated Press, "Struck Before Declaration, Tokyo Admits," *Washington Post*, December 8, 1941, 8.
71. Paul S. Dull, *A Battle History of the Imperial Japanese Navy, 1941–1945* (Annapolis, MD: Naval Institute, 1978), 16.
72. Paul S. Dull, *A Battle History of the Imperial Japanese Navy, 1941–1945* (Annapolis, MD: Naval Institute, 1978), 16.
73. Associated Press, "Japs Open War on U.S. With Bombing of Hawaii; Fleet Speeds Out to Battle Invader," *Los Angeles Times*, December 8, 1941, 1.
74. Associated Press, "Child Among the Dead," *New York Times*, December 8, 1941, 13.
75. Richard Haller, International New Service, "Honolulu Caught By Surprise Raid," *Charleston (SC) News and Courier*, December 8, 1941, 7.
76. Associated Press, "Eyewitness Report of Air Raid," *Baltimore Sun*, December 8, 1941, 2.
77. Associated Press, "Many Americans Die in Bombing of Hawaii; Fires Set in Honolulu," *Baltimore Sun*, December 8, 1941, 1.
78. Associated Press, "Eyewitness Report of Air Raid," *Baltimore Sun*, December 8, 1941, 2.
79. Associated Press, "Eyewitness Report of Air Raid," *Baltimore Sun*, December 8, 1941, 2.
80. *Newsday* (NY), "How Radio Reported '41 Attack," December 7, 1941, 15.
81. Video Material, *Tora! Tora! Tora!*, Craig Shirley Collection.
82. Associated Press, "2 Big U.S. Battleships Reported in Action Now," *Baltimore Sun*, December 8, 1941, 3.
83. Mark S. Watson, "Dawn Air Raid Finds U.S. Forces on Islands Not Ready for Action," *Baltimore Sun*, December 8, 1941, 4.
84. *Maryville* (MO) *Daily Forum*, "Japs Attack Manila," December 7, 1941, 1.
85. *Maryville* (MO) *Daily Forum*, "Reports Staggers London," December 7, 1941, 1.
86. *Maryville* (MO) *Daily Forum*, "Far East Crisis Explodes!" December 7, 1941, 1.
87. *Maryville* (MO) *Daily Forum*, "News Spreads," December 7, 1941, 1.
88. Associated Press, "Two Japanese Bombers Appear Over Honolulu; Unverified Report Says a Foreign Warship Appears Off Pearl Harbor," *Maryville* (MO) *Daily Forum*, December 7, 1941, 1.
89. *Washington Post*, "War Brings a Tense Day to White House Press Room," December 8, 1941, 4.
90. Margalit Fox, "Frank Tremaine, 92, Reporter Who Broke Pearl Harbor News, Dies," *New York Times*, December 27, 2006, C11.
91. Susan McShane, in discussion with the author, September 12, 2011.
92. Susan McShane, in discussion with the author, September 12, 2011.
93. Gerald Eckert, in discussion with the author.
94. Associated Press, "U.S. at War! Japan Bombs Hawaii, Manila," *Washington Post Extra*, December 7, 1941, 1.
95. *Washington Post*, "War Brings a Tense Day to White House Press Room," December 8, 1941, 4.
96. Edward T. Folliard, "Hawaii Attacked Without Warning With Heavy Loss; Philippines Are Bombed," *Washington Post*, December 8, 1941, 1.
97. Gerald Griffin, "Tempo of War Apparent at White House," *Baltimore Sun*, December 8, 1941, 3.

98. Frank L. Kluckhohn, "Guam Bombed; Army Ship Is Sunk," *New York Times*, December 8, 1941, 1.

99. *Washington Post*, "War Brings a Tense Day to White House Press Room," December 8, 1941, 4.

100. *Washington Post*, "War Brings a Tense Day to White House Press Room," December 8, 1941, 4.

101. *Washington Post*, "War Brings a Tense Day to White House Press Room," December 8, 1941, 4.

102. *Washington Post*, "War Brings a Tense Day to White House Press Room," December 8, 1941, 4.

103. *Washington Post*, "War Brings a Tense Day to White House Press Room," December 8, 1941, 4.

104. *Washington Post*, "War Brings a Tense Day to White House Press Room," December 8, 1941, 4.

105. Richard Haller, "Hawaii Attack Is Described By Eyewitness," *Washington Post*, December 8, 1941, 3.

106. *Washington Post*, "War Brings a Tense Day to White House Press Room," December 8, 1941, 4.

107. Edward T. Folliard, "Hawaii Attacked Without Warning With Heavy Loss; Philippines Are Bombed," *Washington Post*, December 8, 1941, 1.

108. Associated Press, "All Jap Nationals Ordered Arrested," *Maryville* (MO) *Daily Forum*, December 7, 1941, 1.

109. Thomas R. Henry, "Capital Retains Outward Calm Despite Shock of War News," *Washington Evening Star*, December 8, 1941, A6.

110. Scott Hart, "Crowds Gather at White House As News of Attack Spreads," *Washington Post*, December 8, 1941, 3.

111. *Washington Post*, "News of War With Nippon Stuns Civilians, Service Men Alike," December 8, 1941, 7.

112. Richard Turner, Associated Press, "Bursting Jap Bombs Bring War to Hawaii," *Boston Daily Globe*, December 8, 1941, 11.

113. *Washington Evening Star*, "Washington Quickly Turned Into a Wartime Capital," December 8, 1941, B19.

114. Gerald Griffin, "Tempo of War Apparent at White House," *Baltimore Sun*, December 8, 1941, 3.

115. Richard L. Strout, "War Comes to Washington—On a Sunday Afternoon," *Christian Science Monitor*, December 8, 1941, C1.

116. Associated Press, "Bombers Attack Philippine Points," *New York Times*, December 8, 1941, 8.

117. Associated Press, "Army Bombers Roar North," *New York Times*, December 8, 1941, 8.

118. Royal Arch Gunnison, North American Newspaper Alliance, "No Bombing of Manila," *New York Times*, December 8, 1941, 8.

119. Associated Press, "Nichols Field Gas Supply Reported Destroyed," *Washington Post*, December 9, 1941, 3.

120. C. P. Trussell, "Congress Decided," *New York Times*, December 8, 1941, 1.

121. C. P. Trussell, "Congress Decided," *New York Times*, December 8, 1941, 1.

122. Robert Schlesinger, *White House Ghosts* (New York: Simon and Schuster, 2008), 26.

123. Franklin Delano Roosevelt Presidential Library and Museum, "FDR: Day by Day—The Pare Lorentz Chronology," December 7, 1941.

124. *Time*, "The U.S. at War: National Ordeal," December 15, 1941, 18.

125. Peter Grier, "Pearl Harbor Day: How FDR Reacted on December 7, 1941," *Christian Science Monitor*, December 7, 2010.

126. Franklin Delano Roosevelt Presidential Library and Museum, "Diary Entry of Agriculture Secretary Claude R. Wickard," December 7, 1941, Hyde Park, NY.

127. *Time*, "The U.S. at War: National Ordeal," December 15, 1941, 18.

128. *Baltimore Sun*, "Congress Leaders Take Part in Cabinet Session to Discuss U.S. Action," December 8, 1941, 2.

129. Edward T. Folliard, "Hawaii Attacked Without Warning With Heavy Loss; Philippines Are Bombed," *Washington Post*, December 8, 1941, 1.

130. Edward T. Folliard, "Hawaii Attacked Without Warning With Heavy Loss; Philippines Are Bombed," *Washington Post*, December 8, 1941, 1.

131. *Washington Evening Star*, "All-Night Vigil Kept at Navy Department; 1,000 at Decks," December 8, 1941, B8.

132. *Washington Evening Star*, "All-Night Vigil Kept at Navy Department; 1,000 at Decks," December 8, 1941, B8.

133. Franklin Delano Roosevelt Presidential Library and Museum, "Diary Entry of Agriculture Secretary Claude R. Wickard," December 7, 1941, Hyde Park, NY.

134. Associated Press, "Tojo Promises Japan Victory Over America," *Washington Post*, December 8, 1941, 3.

135. Associated Press, "Tokyo Acts First," *New York Times*, December 8, 1941, 1.

136. Associated Press, "Tokyo Acts First," *New York Times*, December 8, 1941, 1.

137. Blair Bolles, "Japanese Diplomats to Be Guaranteed Safe Return Home," *Washington Evening Star*, December 8, 1941, A5.

138. Paul W. Ward, "Japanese Embassy Guarded by Washington Police Squad," *Baltimore Sun*, December 8, 1941, 4.

139. Paul W. Ward, "Japanese Embassy Guarded by Washington Police Squad," *Baltimore Sun*, December 8, 1941, 4.

140. *Washington Post*, "Irish Mother of Six Can't Leave Embassy," December 8, 1941, 3.

141. Paul W. Ward, "Japanese Embassy Guarded by Washington Police Squad," *Baltimore Sun*, December 8, 1941, 4.

142. *New York Times*, "Burning of Papers Watched By 1,000," December 8, 1941, 5.

143. *Washington Post*, "Embassy Row Bustles as War Comes to U.S.," December 8, 1941, 3.

144. *Time*, "The U.S. at War, the Last Stage," December 15, 1941, 26.

145. *Washington Evening Star*, "F.B.I. Rounding Up Japanese Citizens Throughout Nation," December 8, 1941, B1.

146. *Baltimore Sun*, "Boys Hang Effigy," December 8, 1941, 11.

147. Associated Press, "Clipper Reaches Hawaii Safely," *Washington Post*, December 8, 1941, 2.

148. Thomas M. Coffey, *Hap: The Story of The U.S. Air Force and The Man Who Built It, General Henry "Hap" Arnold*, (New York: Viking Press, 1982), 242.

149. Elizabeth Henney, "Beautiful, Friendly Honolulu, Asking Only Peace, Is at War," *Washington Post*, December 8, 1941, 5.

150. Bill Henry, "Japan's Daring Attack on Hawaii Designed to Cripple U.S. Fleet; Suicide Bomb Raid Perfectly Timed," *Los Angeles Times*, December 8, 1941, 1D.

151. Franklin Delano Roosevelt Presidential Library and Museum, "Memorandum for The President," Box 1, December 7, 1941.

152. Franklin Delano Roosevelt Presidential Library and Museum, "Transcript of Telephone Conversation Between FDR and Treasury Secretary Henry Morgenthau, Jr." Box 515, December 7, 1941, Hyde Park, NY.

153. T. J. King, *Joint and Naval Intelligence Support to Military Operations* (Darby, PA: Diane Publishing, 2011), V12.

CHAPTER 8: THE EIGHTH OF DECEMBER

1. Charles Hurd, "Stark's Report Stresses Speed, Day Before Japan Attacks," *Washington Post*, December 8, 1941, 27.

2. Frank L. Kluckhohn, "Guam Bombed; Army Ship Is Sunk," *New York Times*, December 8, 1941, 1.

3. George Fielding Eliot, "Jap Raid Believed Hindering Action," *Los Angeles Times*, December 8, 1941, 1C.

4. Editorial, "We Shall Win," *Baltimore Sun*, December 8, 1941, 16.

5. *Los Angeles Times*, "Public Believed First War Reports Only Gag," December 8, 1941, 2.

6. *Los Angeles Times*, "Air Guards, Attention!" December 8, 1941, 1.

7. Carroll Kilpatrick, "Visitor to White House Criticizes American Defense in Hawaii," *Birmingham* (AL) *News*, December 8, 1941, 8.

8. Gordon William Prange with Donald M. Goldstein and Katherine V. Dillon, *Dec. 7, 1941: The Day the Japanese Attacked Pearl Harbor* (New York: Wings Books, 1991), 376.

9. *Washington Evening Star*, "Gasoline Dump at Nichols Field Believed Fired," December 8, 1941, A1.

10. *Boston Daily Globe*, "Japan Strikes Over Wide Area," December 8, 1941, 4.

11. *Washington Evening Star*, "Gasoline Dump at Nichols Field Believed Fired," December 8, 1941, A1.

12. Bill Henry, "Japan's Daring Attack on Hawaii Designed to Cripple U.S. Fleet," *Los Angeles Times*, December 8, 1941, 1D.

13. *Washington Evening Star*, "Gasoline Dump at Nichols Field Believed Fired," December 8, 1941, A1.

14. United Press, "Japanese Premier's Story," *New York Times*, December 8, 1941, 5.

15. *Washington Evening Star*, "Gasoline Dump at Nichols Field Believed Fired," December 8, 1941, A1.

16. Woody Klein, *All the Presidents' Spokesmen: Spinning the News—White House Press Secretaries from Franklin D. Roosevelt to George W. Bush* (Westport, CT: Praeger Publishers, 2008), 38.

17. William L. O'Neill, *A Democracy at War: America's Fight at Home and Abroad in World War II* (Cambridge, MA: Harvard University Press, 1995), 5.

18. Hazel Rowley, *Franklin and Eleanor: An Extraordinary Marriage* (New York: Farrar, Straus and Giroux, 2010), 246.

19. Philip M. Seib, *Broadcasts from the Blitz: How Edward R. Murrow Helped Lead America Into War* (Dulles, VA: Potomac Books, 2006), 157.

20. James MacGregor Burns and Susan Dunn, *The Three Roosevelts: Patrician Leaders Who Transformed America* (New York: Grove Press, 2001), 442.

21. Dan Van Der Vat, *Pearl Harbor: The Day of Infamy—An Illustrated History* (New York: Basic Books, 2001), 74.

22. Peter Grier, "Pearl Harbor Day: How FDR Reacted on December 7, 1941," *Christian Science Monitor*, December 7, 2010, http://www.csmonitor.com/USA/2010/1207/Pearl-Harbor-day-How-FDR-reacted-on-December-7-1941; Emma Brown, "'Air raid, Pearl Harbor': Who Said It?," *Washington Post*, January 19, 2011, http://voices.washingtonpost.com/postmortem/2011/01/air-raid-pearl-harbor-who-said.html.

23. *New York Times*, "Army, Navy Order Wide Censorship," December 8, 1941, 8.

24. Associated Press, "Espionage Act Violators Face Death Penalty," *Boston Daily Globe*, December 8, 1941, 6.

25. *New York Times*, "Army, Navy Order Wide Censorship," December 8, 1941, 8.

26. John G. Norris, "All Dangerous Japanese Face Arrest by U.S.," *Washington Post*, December 8, 1941, 7.

27. John G. Norris, "All Dangerous Japanese Face Arrest by U.S.," *Washington Post*, December 8, 1941, 7.

28. Drew Person and Robert S. Allen, "Merry–Go–Round," *Birmingham* (AL) *News*, December 14, 1941, 5.

29. *Washington Post*, "Armed Plants Told to Work 24 Hours a Day," December 8, 1941, 23.

30. *Washington Post*, "Heavy Guard Thrown Around Capital's Most Vital Spots," December 8, 1941, 3; *New York Times*, "Patterson Asks All Plants Guard Against Sabotage," December 8, 1941, 4; Associated Press, "Emergency Measures Enforced in Nation," *Boston Daily Globe*, December 8, 1941, 20.

31. C.P. Trussel, "Congress Decided," *New York Times*, December 8, 1941, 1.

32. *New York Times*, "The Day in Washington," December 9, 1941, 4.

33. *New York Times*, "La Guardia Acts to Guard Cities," December 8, 1941, 3.

34. Associated Press, "Britain Declares War on Japs, Allying Herself With U.S.," *Washington Evening Star*, December 8, 1941, A2.

35. Associated Press, "Text of Address by Churchill," *Washington Post*, December 9, 1941, 19.

36. Associated Press, "Costa Rica at War With Japan," *Atlanta Constitution*, December 8, 1941, 1.

37. United Press, "China Goes to War With Axis States," *New York Times*, December 9, 1941, 9.

38. *New York Times,* "Australia Declares War on the Japanese," December 8, 1941, 2; Associated Press, "Netherlands Join in War on Japan," *New York Times,* December 8, 1941, 7.

39. Associated Press, "Nicaragua Takes Stand," *New York Times,* December 8, 1941, 15.

40. *New York Times,* "Canada Declares War Upon Japan," December 8, 1941, 14.

41. Associated Press, "Carpenter Union Declares War on Japanese as War Flares," *Atlanta Constitution,* December 8, 1941, 11.

42. *Atlanta Constitution,* "Island of Hilo Open to Attack, Says Atlantan," December 8, 1941, 11.

43. Associated Press, "North Borneo Attack Reported," *Washington Evening Star,* December 8, 1941, A1.

44. *Washington Evening Star,* "Gasoline Dump at Nichols Field Believed Fired," December 8, 1941, A1; Frank L. Kluckhohn, "Guam Bombed, Army Ship Is Sunk," *New York Times,* December 8, 1941, 1.

45. United Press and International News Service, "Jap 'Chute Troops Seen in Honolulu," *Washington Post,* December 8, 1941, 2.

46. John Franklin Carter, "Memorandum on Japanese Problem (West Coast, Mexican Border)," December 8, 1941, Franklin Delano Roosevelt Presidential Library and Museum, Hyde Park, NY.

47. United Press, "Jap Attack Under Way for 2 Weeks," *Washington Post,* December 8, 1941, 1.

48. Associated Press, "Believe May Have Used Suicide Squads," *Washington Post,* December 8, 1941, 3.

49. *Washington Post,* December 8, 1941, 1.

50. Associated Press, "Japan Strikes All Over Pacific," *Boston Daily Globe,* December 8, 1941, 1.

51. Associated Press, "1,500 Dead in Hawaii," *Boston Evening Globe,* December 8, 1941, 1.

52. Frank L. Kluckhohn, "Guam Bombed; Army Ship Is Sunk," *New York Times,* December 8, 1941, 1.

53. United Press, "Report Nazis to Act," *Boston Daily Globe,* December 8, 1941, 10.

54. *Washington Evening Star,* "Gasoline Dump at Nichols Field Believed Fired," December 8, 1941, A1.

55. Blair Bolles, "Japanese Diplomats to Be Guaranteed Safe Return Home," *Washington Evening Star,* December 8, 1941, A5.

56. Associated Press, "Wave After Wave of Japanese Planes Attack Hawaii," *Washington Evening Star,* December 8, 1941, A5.

57. *Washington Evening Star,* "Gasoline Dump at Nichols Field Believed Fired," December 8, 1941, A1.

58. United Press, "Jap Transport Hit," *Boston Daily Globe,* December 8, 1941, 15; Associated Press, "Aircraft Carrier Used in Attack on Pearl Harbor Reported Sunk," *Boston Daily Globe,* December 8, 1941, 1.

59. United Press, "Tokyo Bombers Strike Hard at Our Main Bases on Oahu," *New York Times,* December 8, 1941, 1.

60. Frank L. Kluckhohn, "Guam Bombed; Army Ship Is Sunk," *New York Times,* December 8, 1941, 1.

61. Associated Press, "Many Americans Die In Bombing of Hawaii; Fires Set in Honolulu," *Baltimore Sun,* December 8, 1941, 1.

62. Associated Press, "Wave After Wave of Japanese Planes Attack Hawaii," *Washington Evening Star,* December 8, 1941, A5.

63. Thomas R. Henry, "Capital Retains Outward Calm Despite Shock of War News," *Washington Evening Star,* December 8, 1941, A6.

64. Associated Press, "Rome Radio Denies Saying Axis Is at War With U. S.," *Washington Evening Star,* December 8, 1941, A2.

65. *Washington Evening Star,* "Gasoline Dump at Nichols Field Believed Fired," December 8, 1941, A1.

66. Blair Bolles, "Japanese Diplomats to Be Guaranteed Safe Return Home," *Washington Evening Star,* December 8, 1941, A5.

67. Blair Bolles, "Japanese Diplomats to Be Guaranteed Safe Return Home," *Washington Evening*

Star, December 8, 1941, A5; United Press, "Japanese Consulate Booed in New Orleans," *Washington Post*, December 8, 1941, 3.

68. Associated Press, "Japanese Beaten Up by New York Trio," *Boston Evening Globe*, December 8, 1941, 2.

69. *New York Times*, "Plains Guard City From Air Attacks," December 9, 1941, 1.

70. Associated Press, "Huge Naval Stronghold Is Bombed," *Boston Daily Globe*, December 8, 1941, 2.

71. Associated Press, "1500 Dead In Hawaii," *Boston Evening Globe*, December 8, 1941, 1.

72. Associated Press, "Manila Planes Roar North," *New York Times*, December 8, 1941, 5.

73. Hedley Donovan, "Aid to Allies Won't Falter, U.S. Pledges," *Washington Post*, December 9, 1941, 1.

74. United Press, "Latest War Bulletins," *Los Angeles Times*, December 8, 1941, 1.

75. Louis P. Lochner, "Nazis Try to Put Blame on Roosevelt," *Washington Post*, December 9, 1941, 14;

76. Associated Press, "Germans, Blaming Roosevelt, Silent on Aid to Japanese," *Los Angeles Times*, December 9, 1941, 4.

77. *New York Times*, "The International Situation," May 28, 1941, 1.

78. Frank L. Kluchkhohn, "Fifth Column Curb," *New York Times*, June 17, 1941, 1.

79. John C. Henry, "Roosevelt Says Date of Attack in Pacific Will Live in Infamy," *Washington Evening Star*, December 1941, 1; *Washington Post*, "Roosevelt Message to Be Broadcast," December 8, 1941, 27.

80. Associated Press, "Oakland Schools Closed as Air Raid Precaution," *Washington Evening Star*, December 8, 1941, A4.

81. *Honolulu Star-Bulletin*, December 7, 1941, 1.

82. Associated Press, "Markets at a Glance," *Washington Evening Star*, December 8, 1941, A1.

83. *New York Times*, "A Pause on the Stock Exchange to Listen to The President," December 9, 1941, 53.

84. *Washington Evening Star*, "Tense Throng Fills Grounds as President Goes to Capitol," December 8, 1941, 1.

85. C.P. Trussel, "Congress Decided," *New York Times*, December 8, 1941, 1.

86. *Washington Post*, "Roosevelt Message to Be Broadcast," December 8, 1941, 27.

87. James B. Reston, "History Is Heard: Studies Here as President Asked for Declaration of War," *New York Times*, December 9, 1941, 5.

88. James B. Reston, "History Is Heard: Studies Here as President Asked for Declaration of War," *New York Times*, December 9, 1941, 5.

89. Frank L. Kluckhohns, "Unity in Congress," *New York Times*, December 9, 1941, 1.

90. Robert C. Albright, "Calm Congress Accepts Challenge with But One Dissenting Vote; Long Ovation Given President; Packed Galleries Applaud Speech," *Washington Post*, December 9, 1941, 1.

91. James B. Reston, "History Is Heard: Studies Here as President Asked for Declaration of War," *New York Times*, December 9, 1941, 5.

92. John C. Henry, "Roosevelt Says Date of Attack in Pacific Will Live in Infamy," *Washington Evening Star*, December 8, 1941, A1.

93. *Time*, "The U.S. At War: National Ordeal," December 15, 1941, 18.

94. *Time*, "The U.S. At War: National Ordeal," December 15, 1941, 18.

95. Associated Press, "Aids Twice in War Steps," *New York Times*, December 9, 1941, 5.

96. *Birmingham* (AL) *News*, "No Man's Land in Washington," December 14, 1941, 1.

97. F. R. Kent Jr., "Notables Pack Capitol for War Declaration," *Baltimore Sun*, December 9, 1941, 2.

98. *Time*, "The U.S. At War: National Ordeal," December 15, 1941, 18.

99. Associated Press, "Administration Foes Issue Calls for Unity in War on Japan," *Washington Evening Star*, December 8, 1941, A8.

100. Louis M. Lyons, "Again a U.S. President Asks for Declaration of War," *Boston Daily Globe*, December 8, 1941, 20; F. R. Kent Jr., "Notables Pack Capitol for War Declaration," *Baltimore Sun*, December 9, 1941, 2.

101. Louis M. Lyons, "Again a U.S. President Asks for Declaration of War," *Boston Daily Globe*, December 8, 1941, 20; Charles Mercer, "Service Chiefs, Envoys Attend Joint Session," *Washington Post*, December 9, 1941, 2.

102. Mona Dugas, "Wives of Cabinet Members and Diplomats Fill Gallery to Hear War Declaration," *Washington Evening Star*, December 8, 1941, B3.

103. James B. Reston, "History Is Heard: Studies Here as President Asked for Declaration of War," *New York Times*, December 9, 1941, 5.

104. Alistair Cooke, *The American Home Front: 1941–1942* (New York: Grove Press, 2007), 12.

105. Alistair Cooke, *The American Home Front: 1941–1942* (New York: Grove Press, 2007), 13.

106. James B. Reston, "History Is Heard: Studies Here as President Asked for Declaration of War," *New York Times*, December 9, 1941, 5.

107. Louis M. Lyons, "Again a U.S. President Asks for Declaration of War," *Boston Daily Globe*, December 8, 1941, 20.

108. Franklin D. Roosevelt, "To The Congress of the United States," The White House, December 8, 1941, Collection Grace Tully Archive, Franklin Delano Roosevelt Presidential Library and Museum, Hyde Park, NY.

109. The United States National Archives and Records Administration, "Teaching With Documents: 'A Date Which Will Live in Infamy,'" http://www.archives.gov/education/lessons/day-of-infamy/.

110. Ron Powers, *Dangerous Water: A Biography of the Boy Who Became Mark Twain* (Cambridge, MA: Da Capo Press, 2001), 174.

111. Lyle C. Wilson, "Senate's Vote Unanimous; House Ballots 388 to 1. Victory Pledged," *Pittsburgh* (PA) *Post-Gazette*, December 8, 1941, 1.

112. Louis M. Lyons, "Again a U.S. President Asks for Declaration of War," *Boston Daily Globe*, December 8, 1941, 20.

113. Gould Lincoln, "Jeannette Rankin Casts Only Vote Against War," *Washington Evening Star*, December 8, 1941, A2.

114. John C. Henry, "Roosevelt Says Date of Attack in Pacific Will Live in Infamy," *Washington Evening Star*, December 1941, 1.

115. Chesly Manly, "Congress Votes War on Japan in Speedy Session," *Chicago Tribune*, December 9, 1941, 7.

116. John C. Henry, "Roosevelt Says Date of Attack in Pacific Will Live in Infamy," *Washington Evening Star*, December 1941, 1.

117. Gould Lincoln, "Jeannette Rankin Casts Only Vote Against War," *Washington Evening Star*, December 8, 1941, A2.

118. Gould Lincoln, "Jeannette Rankin Casts Only Vote Against War," *Washington Evening Star*, December 8, 1941, A2; F. R. Kent Jr., "Notables Pack Capitol for War Declaration," *Baltimore Sun*, December 9, 1941, 2.

119. *Boston Daily Globe*, "388 to 1," December 9, 1941, 18; Louis M. Lyons, "War Declared Swiftly After F.D. Speaks," December 9, 1941, 1.

120. F. R. Kent Jr., "Notables Pack Capitol for War Declaration," *Baltimore Sun*, December 9, 1941, 2.

121. Ruth Cowan, "Republican Women Happy Over Victory," *Washington Post*, November 5, 1942, 4.

122. Associated Press, "55 Who Missed Vote on War Declaration All Approved It," *Washington Evening Star*, December 9, 1941, A2.

123. *New York Times*, "The President Signs the Declaration of War," December 9, 1941, 1; *Washington Post*, "Rep. Rankin Again Votes Against War," December 9, 1941, 2.

124. *New York Times*, "Four-Hour Chronology of Declaration of War," December 9, 1941, 3.

125. James B. Reston, "History Is Heard: Studies Here as President Asked for Declaration of War," *New York Times*, December 9, 1941, 5.

126. *Time*, "The U.S. at War: National Ordeal," December 15, 1941, 18.

127. *Washington Evening Star*, "Recruiting Offices Here Crowded With Men Eager to Enlist," December 8, 1941, B1.

128. *Washington Evening Star*, "Recruiting Offices Here Crowded With Men Eager to Enlist," December 8, 1941, B1.

129. *Washington Evening Star*, "Senator Chandler Volunteers for Army Duty," December 8, 1941, B1.

130. *Atlanta Constitution*, "Women Offered Defense Courses," December 8, 1941, 12.

131. Associated Press, "Ted Williams Is Still Rated in Class 3-A," *Atlanta Constitution*, December 8, 1941, 17.

132. Associated Press, "Hundreds of Women Offer Services for Defense Work," *Baltimore Sun*, December 9, 1941, 4.

133. C. P. Trussell, "Unanimous Senate Acts in 15 Minutes," *New York Times*, December 9, 1941, 6.

134. Franklin Delano Roosevelt Presidential Library and Museum, "FDR: Day by Day—The Pare Lorentz Chronology," December 8, 1941; John C. Henry, "White House Indicates War Crisis Is 'Bigger' Than Clash in Orient," *Washington Evening Star*, December 9, 1941, 1X.

135. Associated Press, "Emergency at San Francisco," *New York Times*, December 8, 1941, 6.

136. *Los Angeles Times*, "Jap Boat Flashes Messages Ashore," December 8, 1941, 6.

137. *Boston Globe*, "U.S. Government at the Panama Canal," December 8, 1941, 2.

138. *Christian Science Monitor*, "Outbreak of War Halts Strikes in New England Area," December 8, 1941, 2.

139. *Christian Science Monitor*, "Harvard's Role in Country at War Topic of Meeting," December 8, 1941, 2.

140. Associated Press, "Arrest of Japs Dangerous to U.S. Ordered," *Atlanta Constitution*, December 8, 1941, 1.

141. *Washington Evening Star*, "F. B. I. Rounding Up Japanese Citizens Throughout Nation," December 8, 1941, B1.

142. Associated Press, "Arrest of Japs Dangerous to U.S. Ordered," *Atlanta Constitution*, December 8, 1941, 1.

143. *Washington Evening Star*, "F. B. I. Rounding Up Japanese Citizens Throughout Nation," December 8, 1941, B1.

144. *Baltimore Sun*, "Judge Denies Citizenship to 34 Aliens," December 9, 1941, 28.

145. *New York Times*, "Japan, U.S. Close 88 Years Peace," December 8, 1941, 2.

146. *Washington Evening Star*, "F. B. I. Rounding Up Japanese Citizens Throughout Nation," December 8, 1941, B1.

147. Associated Press, "Japanese Firms Grabbed by U.S," *Spokesman-Review* (WA), December 9, 1941, 2.

148. Associated Press, "U.S. Takes Over All Japanese Businesses and Funds, Rounds Up Nearly 1000 Nationals," *Washington Post*, December 9, 1941, 8.

149. Associated Press, "Morgenthau's Order Bans Communication With Japan or 'Allies,'" *Washington Evening Star*, December 8, 1941, A9.

150. Associated Press, "Communicating or Trading with Japanese Barred," *Washington Post*, December 8, 1941, 9; Associated Press, "U.S. Takes Over All Japanese Businesses and Funds, Rounds Up Nearly 1000 Nationals," *Washington Post*, December 9, 1941, 8.

151. *New York Times*, "Japan's Holdings Here Impounded," December 8, 1941, 7.

152. Associated Press, "Morgenthau Bans Dealings with Japanese," *Baltimore Sun*, December 8, 1941, 3.

153. *Los Angeles Times*, "Little Tokyo Banks and Concerns Shut," December 9, 1941, 4.

154. *Los Angeles Times*, "Little Tokyo Carries on Business as Usual," December 8, 1941, 2.

155. *Los Angeles Times*, "Troops Rush to Posts Here," December 8, 1941, 4.

156. *Washington Evening Star*, "Washington Quickly Turned Into a Wartime Capital," December 8, 1941, B14.

157. *Boston Daily Globe*, "Navy in New England Switches to War Basis," December 8, 1941, 6; *Boston Evening Globe*, "Antisabotage Moves by F. B. I. and Timilty," December 8, 1941, 5.

158. *Boston Daily Globe*, "America First Undecided About Lindbergh Rally," December 8, 1941, 16.

159. *New York Times*, "Isolation Groups Back Roosevelt," December 9, 1941, 44; *Washington Post*, "'Forced Upon, We Must Fight,' Hoover Says," December 8, 1941, 15; Associated Press, "America First Backs War, Says Gen. Wood en Route to Boston," *Boston Daily Globe*, December 8, 1941, 19; *New York Times*, "'No Choice,' Says Landon" December 8, 1941, 6.

160. United Press, "U. S. Provoked War, Nye Says," *Washington Post*, December 8, 1941, 8; *Time*, "The U.S. at War: Man Without a Cause," December 15, 1941, 19.

161. Associated Press, "War Fails to Halt Anti-War Rally," *Baltimore Sun*, December 9, 1941, 28.

162. *Boston Daily Globe*, "Cancel Permits for Ships Leaving Boston for Abroad," December 8, 1941, 15; *Boston Daily Globe*, "Railroads Won't Sell Japs Tickets," December 8, 1941, 15.

163. *New York Times*, "Entire City Put on War Footing," December 8, 1941, 1.

164. John MacCormac, "Tax Rise Hinted by Morgenthau," *New York Times*, December 9, 1941, 35.

165. *New York Times*, "Navy Acts Here to Guard Coast," December 8, 1941, 7.

166. *New York Times*, "Entire City Put on War Footing," December 8, 1941, 1.

167. Associated Press, "First Casualty List in War With Japan," *Washington Evening Star*, December 8, 1941, A2.

168. Associated Press, "Wave After Wave of Japanese Planes Attack Hawaii," *Washington Evening Star*, December 9, 1941, A5.

169. *New York Times*, "Drastic Control Marks War News," December 9, 1941, 7.

170. Associated Press, "Large U.S. Losses Claimed by Japan," *New York Times*, December 9, 1941, 1; *Washington Evening Star*, "'Dim Out' Is Tasted by Capital But 'Don't Walk' Signs Glow," December 8, 1941, A14; *Washington Evening Star*, "Nearby Communities Organize to Guard Against Sabotage," December 8, 1941, B1.

171. Associated Press, "Lindbergh Asks United Stand in War Effort," *Washington Evening Star*, December 8, 1941, A1; *Boston Daily Globe*, "Lindbergh Silent; All Callers Barred at Vineyard Estate," December 8, 1941, 7.

172. Associated Press, "America First Urges All-Out Hostilities Against Japanese," *Washington Evening Star*, December 8, 1941, B23.

173. *Washington Evening Star*, "The Christmas Campaign," December 8, 1941, A2.

174. *Washington Evening Star*, "National Airport Goes on Virtual Wartime Basis," December 8, 1941, A9.

175. *Washington Evening Star*, "Nearby Communities Organize to Guard Against Sabotage," December 8, 1941, B1.

176. *Washington Evening Star*, "'Dim Out' Is Tasted by Capital But 'Don't Walk' Signs Glow," December 8, 1941, A14.

177. *Washington Evening Star*, "Mrs. Roosevelt Challenges Women in War Crisis," December 8, 1941, A14.

178. *Washington Post*, "With All Uncertainty Gone, We're Ready, First Lady Says," December 8, 1941, 5.

179. Associated Press, "G. M. on War Basis," *Washington Evening Star*, December 8, 1941, A4.

180. Associated Press, "Welders Rescind Order Calling Off Nation-Wide Strike," *Washington Evening Star*, December 8, 1941, A4.

181. Associated Press, "Patterson Requests Munition Productions On 24-Hour Basis," *Washington Evening Star*, December 8, 1941, B23.

182. Associated Press, "45th's Only Japanese Soldier in Guardhouse," *Washington Evening Star*, December 8, 1941, A11.

183. Associated Press, "West Coast Musters Emergency Strength for Possible Attack," *Washington Evening Star*, December 8, 1941, A12.

184. Associated Press, "Canal Zone Guarded, Panama to Intern All Japanese Residents," *Washington Evening Star*, December 8, 1941, A12.

185. Associated Press, "Emergency at San Francisco," *New York Times*, December 8, 1941, 6; Associated Press, "Private Planes Except Airliners Are Grounded," *Washington Evening Star*, December 8, 1941, B1.

186. Associated Press, "West Coast Musters Emergency Strength for Possible Attack," *Washington Evening Star*, December 8, 1941, A12.
187. *Los Angeles Times*, "City Springs to Attention," December 8, 1941, 1.
188. *New York Times*, "West Coast Acts for War Defense," December 8, 1941, 6; *Los Angeles Times*, "Port Black-Out Ordered by Navy," December 8, 1941, 1C.
189. *Los Angeles Times*, "City's Airfield Blacked Out," December 8, 1941, 1E.
190. *Los Angeles Times*, "Terminal Island Isolated as Defense Precaution," December 8 ,1941, 1F.
191. *Washington Evening Star*, "500 Radio Amateurs in Washington Area Silenced by War," December 8, 1941, B18.
192. Garnett D. Horner, "Final Japanese Note, Flouting U. S. Offer, Rouses Hull's Anger," *Washington Evening Star*, December 8, 1941, A3.
193. Associated Press, "Secretary Hull's Statement, U.S. Note of Nov. 26 and Japan's Reply," *New York Times*, December 8, 1941, 10.
194. Garnett D. Horner, "Final Japanese Note, Flouting U. S. Offer, Rouses Hull's Anger," *Washington Evening Star*, December 8, 1941, A3.
195. Cordell Hull, *The Memoirs of Cordell Hull in Two Volumes Volume II* (New York: The McMillan Company, 1948), 1095.
196. *Time*, "The U.S. At War, In Mr. Hull's Office," December 15, 1941, 26.
197. Corbis Images, "Ambassadors Nomura and Kurusu on December 7, 1941," http://www.corbisimages.com/stock-photo/rights-managed/NA008645/ambassadors-nomura-and-kurusu-on-december-7.
198. *Washington Evening Star*, "Japan's War Declaration," December 8, 1941, A11.
199. *New York Times*, "Entire City Put on War Footing," December 8, 1941, 1.
200. Hanson W. Baldwin, "War of the World," *New York Times*, December 8, 1941, 7.
201. Edward T. Folliard, "Hawaii Attacked Without Warning with Heavy Loss; Philippines Are Bombed," *Washington Post*, December 8, 1941, 1.
202. *New York Times*, "Entire City Put on War Footing," December 8, 1941, 1.
203. Associated Press, "3,000 Killed and Hurt in Jap Attack on Hawaii; Two U.S. Warships Sunk," *Birmingham* (AL) *News*, December 8, 1941, 1.
204. Doris Kearns Goodwin, *No Ordinary Time Franklin and Eleanor Roosevelt: The Home Front in World War II* (New York: Simon and Schuster, 1995), 289.
205. Peter Grier, "Pearl Harbor Day: How FDR Reacted on December 7, 1941," *Christian Science Monitor*, December 7, 2010, http://www.csmonitor.com/USA/2010/1207/Pearl-Harbor-day-How-FDR-reacted-on-December-7-1941.
206. *Los Angeles Times*, "Death Sentence of a Mad Dog," December 8, 1941, A; *New York Times*, "Newspapers Call for Meeting Foe," December 8, 1941, 5.
207. Frank L. Kluckhohn, "Guam Bombed; Army Ship Is Sunk," *New York Times*, December 8, 1941, 1.
208. *Atlanta Constitution*, "Comment Here Flare Against Move by Japan," December 8, 1941, 2.
209. Editorial, "Death Sentence of a Mad Dog," *Los Angeles Times*, December 8, 1941, A.

CHAPTER 9: THE NINTH OF DECEMBER
1. Associated Press, "New York Has Two Air Raid Alarms; Planes Reported Near; Hostile Aircraft Said to Be Flying Toward East Coast," *Birmingham* (AL) *News*, December 9, 1941, 1.
2. *New York Times*, "City Nonchalant as Sirens Wail," December 10, 1941, 14.
3. *New York Times*, "City Nonchalant as Sirens Wail," December 10, 1941, 14.
4. *New York Times*, "2 False Air 'Raids' Upset New Yorkers," December 10, 1941, 14.
5. *New York Times*, "City Nonchalant as Sirens Wail," December 10, 1941, 14.
6. *New York Times*, "2 False Air 'Raids' Upset New Yorkers," December 10, 1941, 14.
7. *New York Times*, "What to Do in an Air Raid," December 10, 1941, 14.
8. *New York Times*, "What to Do in an Air Raid," December 10, 1941, 14.
9. *Los Angeles Times*, "Registration of Defense Volunteers Will Continue Throughout Week," December 9, 1941, A14.

10. *Boston Evening Globe*, "War Extra! Air Raid 'Dress Rehearsal,'" December 10, 1941, 1.
11. Associated Press, "New York Has Two Air Raid Alarms; Planes Reported Near; Hostile Aircraft Said to Be Flying Toward East Coast," *Birmingham* (AL) *News*, December 9, 1941, 1.
12. Associated Press, "New York Has Two Air Raid Alarms; Planes Reported Near; Hostile Aircraft Said to Be Flying Toward East Coast," *Birmingham* (AL) *News*, December 9, 1941, 1.
13. *Boston Daily Globe*, "Antiaircraft Guns Put on Coast," December 9, 1941, 14.
14. *Boston Daily Globe*, "Near-Panic Reported in Several Schools; Many Teachers Weep," December 9, 1941, 14.
15. *Boston Daily Globe*, "Boston-Bound Cars Stopped in Cambridge," December 9, 1941, 14.
16. *Boston Daily Globe*, "Raid Signals Go on in Eastern Mass.; Warning on Panic," December 9, 1941, 14.
17. Associated Press, "More Plains Off Frisco, New Raid Alarm Sounded; About 30 Craft Fly Over West Coast Sector, Then Leave, Army Says," *Baltimore Sun*, December 9, 1941, 1.
18. Associated Press, "Big Air Squadron Driven Back from San Francisco; Navy Sends Three Warships to Hunt Intercepted Planes," *Atlanta Constitution*, December 9, 1941, 1.
19. Lawrence E. Davies, "Turn Back To Sea," *New York Times*, December 9, 1941, 1.
20. Associated Press, "Army and Navy Are on Prowl for Pacific Aircraft Carrier," *Birmingham* (AL) *News*, December 9, 1941, 1.
21. Associated Press, "More Plains Off Frisco, New Raid Alarm Sounded; About 30 Craft Fly Over West Coast Sector, Then Leave, Army Says," *Baltimore Sun*, December 9, 1941, 1.
22. Associated Press, "Alaska Prepares Against Possible Attack by Japanese Fleet in Swing Northward," *New York Times*, December 9, 1941, 28.
23. *Birmingham* (AL) *News*, "Japs Believed Trying to Panic U.S. Into Calling Fleet Back Home," December 9, 1941, 2.
24. Associated Press, "Seattle City Scene of Wild Blackout Acts," *Cumberland* (MD) *Evening Times*, December 9, 1941, 1.
25. Associated Press, "All Pacific Northwest Feels Impact of War," *Birmingham* (AL) *News*, December 9, 1941, 15.
26. *Washington Evening Star*, "Alarms a Rehearsal Safety Officials Say; 'Alert' Ordered Here," December 9, 1941, A1.
27. Associated Press, "Reports of Japanese Planes Over Pacific Coast Stirs Alarms," *Washington Evening Star*, December 9, 1941, 1X.
28. John Barry, "War Diary 829th Day—Dec. 9, 1941," *Boston Evening Globe*, December 9, 1941, 12.
29. *Boston Evening Globe*, "War Extra! Air Raid 'Dress Rehearsal,'" December 10, 1941, 1.
30. Associated Press, "2 'Rehearsals' In N. Y.; General Still Dubious," *Boston Evening Globe*, December 1, 1941, 1.
31. Associated Press, "Hitler Reported Told Six Days Ago That War Was Coming in Pacific," *Birmingham* (AL) *News*, December 9, 1941, 1.
32. Associated Press, "Army Still Give Troops Yule Holidays," *Birmingham* (AL) *News*, December 9, 1941, 1.
33. Associated Press, "Tokyo Insists Planes Sunk 2 Battleships, *Boston Daily Globe*," December 9, 1941, 3.
34. Associated Press, "Reports 2 American Battleships Sunk, 4 Others Damaged," *Washington Post*, December 9, 1941, 7.
35. Associated Press, "Air Reinforcements Rushed to Hawaii," *Boston Daily Globe*, December 9, 1941, 3.
36. Edward E. Bomar, "Temporary Loss of Superiority by U. S. Fleet Seen," *Atlanta Constitution*, December 9, 1941, 7.
37. Associated Press, "F. D. R. to Talk on Japanese Attack Tonight," *Atlanta Constitution*, December 9, 1941, 9.
38. John C. Henry, "Plant Expansion Also Planned as War Measure," *Washington Evening Star*, December 9, 1941, A1.

39. Amy Porter, "Hundreds of Women Overrun Defense Centers Offering to Aid," *Atlanta Constitution*, December 9, 1941, 2.

40. *Atlanta Constitution*, "Women Rush to Offer Help in War Work," December 9, 1941, 7.

41. Associated Press, "Jap Troops Land on Island Near Philippine Capital," *Atlanta Constitution*, December 9, 1941, 1.

42. United Press, "10 R.A.F. Planes Lost in Raids Over France," *New York Times*, December 9, 1941, 7.

43. Associated Press, "U.S. May Have to Put Up 150 Billions in War," *Birmingham (AL) News*, December 9, 1941, 1.

44. Associated Press, "Army's First Casualty List Names 37 Killed in Honolulu," *Birmingham (AL) News*, December 9, 1941, 1.

45. Associated Press, "War Casualties," *Hartford Courant*, December 10, 1941, 13.

46. Associated Press, "Army Casualty List Released," *Los Angeles Times*, December 10, 1941, 1C.

47. *Washington Evening Star*, "News Operator Repeats Role in World War I," December 10, 1941, B6.

48. Associated Press, "Official Army Casualty List," *Baltimore Sun*, December 10, 1941, 4.

49. Associated Press, "House Acts Today to Send Army to Fight Anywhere," *Boston Daily Globe*, December 10, 1941, 19.

50. *Boston Evening Globe*, "A Message From the U.S. Treasury," December 9, 1941, 1.

51. Associated Press, "No Picnic, but Will Buy a Defense Bond," *Boston Evening Globe*, December 9, 1941, 12.

52. Associated Press, "Fighting Songs Call Sounded," *Los Angeles Times*, December 9, 1941, 7.

53. *Birmingham (AL) News*, "Alabamians Flock to Answer Nation's Summons to Defense," December 9, 1941, 12.

54. *Boston Daily Globe*, "Boston Recruiting Offices Swamped; '17 Mark Broken," December 9, 1941, 1.

55. *Los Angeles Times*, "Lindbergh Beacon on Top of City Hall Turned Off," December 9, 1941, A1.

56. Associated Press, "Volunteers Swamp Recruiting Offices Throughout Nation," *Washington Evening Star*, December 9, 1941, A4.

57. Associated Press, "Greenberg Gives up Plans for Baseball to Rejoin Army," *Washington Evening Star*, December 10, 1941, A21; Hugh Fullerton Jr., "Athletic Programs Held Sure to Be Curtailed by War," Washington Evening Star, December 9, 1941, A13.

58. John Lardner, "Louis Given New Song for Christmas Present," *Hartford Courant*, December 10, 1941, 17.

59. Associated Press, "American Eagles Ask Crack at Japs; Some May Leave England," *Birmingham (AL) News*, December 9, 1941, 15.

60. *Birmingham (AL) News*, "Merchants Are Urged to Help Government Catch Moonshiners," December 9, 1941, 6.

61. Associated Press, "280,000-Man Civil Air Patrol Is Asked," *Birmingham (AL) News*, December 9, 1941, 6.

62. Carroll Kilpatrick, "Call Issued for Alabama Farmers to Step Up Their Production," *Birmingham (AL) News*, December 9, 1941, 6.

63. Associated Press, "Union Vow Loyal Work," *Los Angeles Times*, December 9, 1941, 15.

64. Associated Press, "Union Vow Loyal Work," *Los Angeles Times*, December 9, 1941, 15.

65. Associated Press, "Prison Meted 18 Socialists," *Los Angeles Times*, December 9, 1941, 15.

66. Dorothy Thompson, "Declare War on All of Axis Partners Now," *Boston Daily Globe*, December 8, 1941, 14.

67. Possible Form of Declaration of War Against Japan, 1941 December 8, Henry Lewis Stimson Papers (Microfilm edition, reel 105), Manuscripts and Archives, Yale University Library, New Haven, Connecticut.

68. Telegram from William Loeb to Henry Stimson, 1941 December 8, Henry Lewis Stimson Papers (Microfilm edition, reel 105), Manuscripts and Archives, Yale University Library, New Haven, Connecticut.

69. Letter from Douglas Palmer to Henry Stimson, 1941 December 10, Henry Lewis Stimson Papers (Microfilm edition, reel 106), Manuscripts and Archives, Yale University Library, New Haven, Connecticut.

70. Henry Lewis Stimson, Council on Foreign Relations, Royal Institute of International Affairs, *The Far Eastern Crisis* (New York: Harper & Brothers, 1936), 1.

71. Jennet Conant, *Tuxedo Park: A Wall Street Tycoon and the Secret Palace of Science That Changed the Course of World War II* (New York: Simon and Schuster, 2003), 24.

72. *New York Times*, "Attack Long Planned, Evidence Indicates," December 8, 1941, 2.

73. Frank L. Kluckhohn, "Japan Wars on U.S. and Britain; Makes Sudden Attack on Hawaii; Heavy Fighting at Sea Reported," *New York Times*, December 8, 1941, 1.

74. Frank L. Kluckhohn, "Japan Wars on U.S. and Britain; Makes Sudden Attack on Hawaii; Heavy Fighting at Sea Reported," *New York Times*, December 8, 1941, 1.

75. Associated Press, "Tokyo Radio Broadcasts a Talk on 'Good Morals,'" *New York Times*, December 8, 1941, 5.

76. *New York Times*, "Text of Roosevelt's Message to Hirohito," December 8, 1941, 12.

77. James B. Reston, "Japan Out to Get Our Cargo Ships," *New York Times*, December 8, 1941, 5.

78. *Washington Post*, "What's Going On and Where," December 9, 1941, 32.

79. *New York Times*, "Wake and Guam Reported Taken," December 9, 1941, 12; *New York Times*, "Japanese Aerial and Ocean Forces Strike in Widening War in the Pacific," December 9, 1941, 4.

80. *New York Times*, "Wake And Guam Reported Taken," December 9, 1941, 12.

81. Hanson W. Baldwin, "Japan's War Pattern: Swift Blows Reveal the Grandiose Aims and Underline Our Defense Problem," *New York Times*, December 9, 1941, 20.

82. Associated Press, "Langley Not Bombed, Navy Advises Bulletins," *Washington Post*, December 10, 1941, 1.

83. Associated Press, "Nichols and Clark Air Fields, Fort McKinley Among Targets," *Washington Post*, December 9, 1941, 3.

84. F. Tillman Durdin, "Malaya Thwarts Push by Japanese," *New York Times*, December 9, 1941, 1.

85. *New York Times*, "Hong Kong Raided Twice in a Day," December 9, 1941, 11.

86. *New York Times*, "Japanese in Singapore Celebrate Before Attack," December 9, 1941, 11.

87. United Press, "Great American Navy Defeat Hinted by War Correspondent," *Los Angeles Times*, December 9, 1941, 1C.

88. Associated Press, "Navy's Pacific Chief Tough Customer," *Baltimore Sun*, December 8, 1941, 6.

89. Associated Press, "Move Is Brewing to Courtmartial Island Defenders," *Birmingham* (AL) *News*, December 9, 1941, 1.

90. Associated Press, "Move Is Brewing to Courtmartial Island Defenders," *Birmingham* (AL) *News*, December 9, 1941, 1.

91. Associated Press, "Move Is Brewing to Courtmartial Island Defenders," *Birmingham* (AL) *News*, December 9, 1941, 1.

92. Associated Press, "War at a Glance," *Birmingham* (AL) *News*, December 9, 1941, 1.

93. C.P. Trussell, "Navy Criticized as Caught Asleep," *New York Times*, December 10, 1941, 1.

94. *New York Times*, "Attack on Sunday Held to Show Study of West," December 8, 1941, 2.

95. *New York Times*, "Japan, U.S. Close 88 Years' Peace," December 8, 1941, 2.

96. Bill Henry, "Japan's Daring Attack on Hawaii Designed to Cripple U.S. Fleet: Suicide Bomb Raid Perfectly Timed," *Los Angeles Times*, December 8, 1941, 1D.

97. *New York Times*, "Hull Often Said 'Japan' in Hitting Croquet Ball," December 8, 1941, 7.

98. Hedley Donovan, "Japan Lied 'Infamously,' Hull Says," *Washington Post*, December 8, 1941, 1.

99. Hedley Donovan, "Japan Lied 'Infamously,' Hull Says," *Washington Post*, December 8, 1941, 1.

100. Associated Press, "Secretary Hull's Statement, U.S. Note of Nov. 26 and Japan's Reply," *New York Times*, December 8, 1941, 10.

101. *New York Times*, "Japan, U.S. Close 88 Years' Peace," December 8, 1941, 2.

102. Nobel Foundation, "The Nobel Peace Prize 1906," http://www.nobelprize.org/nobel_prizes/peace/laureates/1906/roosevelt-bio.html#.

103. Associated Press, "Bulletins," *Baltimore Sun*, December 9, 1941, 1.

104. Associated Press, "Canal Zone Seizes Nationals of Axis," *New York Times*, December 9, 1941, 7.

105. *Birmingham* (AL) *News*, "First Alien Roundup Is Begun in Alabama; Seven Nabbed By FBI," December 9, 1941, 12.

106. *Boston Daily Globe*, "Germans, Italians Taken by Federal Agents Here," December 10, 1941, 10.

107. *New York Times*, "Japanese Arrests in Country At 345," December 9, 1941, 40.

108. Associated Press, "Roundup; U. S. Seizes Enemy Businesses, Nationals," *Boston Daily Globe*, December 9, 1941, 30.

109. Craig Thompson, "Britain Joins U.S. Against Japanese," *New York Times*, December 9, 1941, 14.

110. *Washington Post*, "Bulletins," December 8, 1941, 1.

111. *New York Times*, "West Coast Acts for War Defense," December 8, 1941, 6.

112. *Los Angeles Times*, "Japanese Aliens' Roundup Starts," December 8, 1941, 1.

113. *New York Times*, "West Coast Acts for War Defense," December 8, 1941, 6.

114. Thomas J. Hamilton, "Japanese Seizure Ordered by Biddle," *New York Times*, December 8, 1941, 6.

115. Thomas J. Hamilton, "Japanese Seizure Ordered by Biddle," *New York Times*, December 8, 1941, 6.

116. Thomas J. Hamilton, "Japanese Seizure Ordered by Biddle," *New York Times*, December 8, 1941, 6.

117. Associated Press, "Support Pledges Flood Olson," *Los Angeles Times*, December 9, 1941, 9.

118. Associated Press, "Unimaginable," *Los Angeles Times*, December 8, 1941, 2.

119. *Los Angeles Times*, "Japan Consul 'Quite Sorry,'" December 8, 1941, 2.

120. *Los Angeles Times*, "Planes Guard City from Air Attack," December 9, 1941, 1.

121. *Washington Evening Star*, "Scientists Concede It's Difficult to Tell Japs from Chinese," December 10, 1941, A5.

122. Associated Press, "Chinese Get Buttons to Distinguish from Japs," *Boston Evening Globe*, December 9, 1941, 6.

123. *New York Times*, "United China Relief," December 9, 1941, 29.

124. *New York Times*, "Planes Guard City from Air Attacks," December 9, 1941, 1.

125. Thomas J. Hamilton, "Japanese Seizure Ordered by Biddle," *New York Times*, December 8, 1941, 6.

126. *Los Angeles Times*, "Disaster Plan Use Imminent," December 9, 1941, A1.

127. *Los Angeles Times*, "City Springs to Attention," December 8, 1941, 1.

128. *Los Angeles Times*, "City Springs to Attention," December 8, 1941, 1.

129. *Los Angeles Times*, "City Springs to Attention," December 8, 1941, 1.

130. *New York Times*, "Fire Siren Blast to Warn of Raids," December 9, 1941, 27.

131. *Los Angeles Times*, "Navy's Intelligence Office Hums in Night," December 8, 1941, 6.

132. Associated Press, "Censors Shut Off News to Axis; U. S. Papers Get Restrictions," *Chicago Daily Tribune*, December 9, 1941, 13.

133. *Chicago Daily Tribune*, "Army and Navy Act," December 9, 1941, 13.

134. *Los Angeles Times*, "Auxiliary Volunteers Swamp Police Stations," December 9, 1941, 7.

135. Associated Press, "West Coast Marshals Forces to Meet Crisis," *Los Angeles Times*, December 9, 1941, 4.

136. Associated Press, "West Coast Set to Meet New Danger," *Hartford Courant*, December 9, 1941, 10.

137. Associated Press, "LaGuardia Issues Air Raid Instructions," *Atlanta Constitution*, December 9, 1941, 11.

138. *Los Angeles Times*, "J. J. Haggarty," December 9, 1941, 2.

139. *Birmingham* (AL) *News*, "Nash," December 9, 1941, 2.

140. Malvina Lindsay, "The Gentler Sex," *Washington Post*, December 8, 1941, 17.

141. Dorothy Dix, "Men Are Slaves to Beauty, Yet When Marry They Pass up Looks," *Baltimore Sun*, December 8, 1941, 25.

142. H.I. Phillips, "The Once Over," *Washington Post*, December 8, 1941, 13.
143. William F. Kerby, "All Consumption Curbs Due to Be Stiffened; Scarcity List Will Grow," *Wall Street Journal*, December 8, 1941, 1.
144. William F. Kerby, "All Consumption Curbs Due to Be Stiffened; Scarcity List Will Grow," *Wall Street Journal*, December 8, 1941, 1.
145. William F. Kerby, "All Consumption Curbs Due to Be Stiffened; Scarcity List Will Grow," *Wall Street Journal*, December 8, 1941, 1.
146. Thomas J. Keller, "Civilian Uses of Copper, Lead, Zinc and Other Vital Metals to Disappear; Increased Output Will Be Pushed," *Wall Street Journal*, December 8, 1941, 2.
147. Thomas J. Keller, "Civilian Uses of Copper, Lead, Zinc and Other Vital Metals to Disappear; Increased Output Will Be Pushed," *Wall Street Journal*, December 8, 1941, 2.
148. Associated Press, "Welders End Strike at Ordnance Plant," *New York Times*, December 8, 1941, 18.
149. Henry Rose, "Japan Almost Wholly Dependent on Imports for Oil; Her Supplies Are Sufficient for 1 to 2 Years," *Wall Street Journal*, December 8, 1941, 5.
150. Alfred F. Flynn, "Ship Schedules, Priorities Being Revised Based on Longer Routes and Use of Convoys," *Wall Street Journal*, December 8, 1941, 4.
151. *Wall Street Journal*, "Secret Plans to Protect Defense Plants Put in Immediate Operation," December 8, 1941, 4.
152. Associated Press, "Free French Declare War on Japan," *Los Angeles Times*, December 9, 1941, 8.
153. Editorial, "This, Too, Is War," *Birmingham* (AL) *News*, December 9, 1941, 8.
154. Walter Lippmann, "U. S. Must Fight Axis Combination on All Fronts," *Boston Daily Globe*, December 9, 1941, 18.
155. Uncle Dudley, "Dedication," *Boston Daily Globe*, December 9, 1941, 18.
156. Uncle Dudley, "Dedication," *Boston Daily Globe*, December 9, 1941, 18.
157. *Washington Evening Star*, "Smoke at German Embassy Indicates Burning of Papers," December 9, 1941, A1.
158. Associated Press, "Reichstag May Meet Tomorrow to Hear Stand on New War," *Washington Evening Star*, December 9, 1941, A3.
159. Garnett D. Horner, "Rumors of Nazi War on U.S. Heard By Hull," *Washington Evening Star*, December 9, 1941, 1X.
160. John C. Henry, "White House Indicates War Crisis Is 'Bigger' Than Clash in Orient," *Washington Evening Star*, December 9, 1941, 1X.
161. Associated Press, "Germany May Declare War at Any Moment," *Boston Evening Globe*, December 1, 1941, 1.
162. Associated Press, "Reichstag May Meet Tomorrow to Hear Stand on New War," *Washington Evening Star*, December 9, 1941, A3.

CHAPTER 10: THE TENTH OF DECEMBER

1. Ruth Cowan, "Roosevelt Shows Little Effect of Strain in Directing War," *Washington Evening Star*, December 10, 1941, A3.
2. Ruth Cowan, "Roosevelt Shows Little Effect of Strain in Directing War," *Washington Evening Star*, December 10, 1941, A3.
3. David Brinkley, *Washington Goes to War* (New York: Alfred A. Knopf, 1988), 105.
4. Ruth Cowan, "Roosevelt Shows Little Effect of Strain in Directing War," *Washington Evening Star*, December 10, 1941, A3.
5. David Brinkley, *Washington Goes to War* (New York: Alfred A. Knopf, 1988), 252.
6. *Washington Evening Star*, "President Defines Duties and Curbs on Resident Aliens," December 9, 1941, 2X.
7. *Washington Evening Star*, "President Defines Duties and Curbs on Resident Aliens," December 9, 1941, 2X.
8. *Baltimore Sun*, "Full Navy Department Shakeup Demanded as Result of Hawaii Defeat," December 10, 1941, 2.

9. J. Edgar Hoover, "J. Edgar Hoover to Edwin M. Watson," December 10, 1941, Federal Bureau of Investigation, President's Official File 10-B: Justice Department; FBI Reports, 1941; Box 15, Franklin Delano Roosevelt Presidential Library and Museum, Hyde Park, NY, 1.

10. Henry N. Dorris, "Senate, House Groups Vote Bills to Keep All in Service During War," *New York Times*, December 10, 1941, 1.

11. *Washington Evening Star*, "U.S. Control of All Radio Authorized," December 10, 1941, A-1.

12. Frank L. Kluckhohn, "Army, Navy Get Control of Radio," *New York Times*, December 11, 1941, 3.

13. *Washington Evening Star*, "Gen. Pershing, 81, Offers Services to President," December 10, 1941, A1.

14. Associated Press, "President's Power Greatly Enlarged," *New York Times*, December 9, 1941, 7.

15. Associated Press, "President's Power Greatly Enlarged," *New York Times*, December 9, 1941, 7.

16. Associated Press, "President's Power Greatly Enlarged," *New York Times*, December 9, 1941, 7.

17. John C. Henry, "Roosevelt Summons State and Military Leaders to Parley," *Washington Evening Star*, December 10, 1941, A1.

18. John C. Henry, "Roosevelt Summons State and Military Leaders to Parley," *Washington Evening Star*, December 10, 1941, A1.

19. Associated Press, "Real Teeth in Price-Control Bill Urged," *Boston Daily Globe*, December 10, 1941, 19.

20. *Birmingham (AL) News*, "Strict Censorship Is on But Feverish Activity Is Apparent," December 9, 1941, 14.

21. Associated Press, "Alien Enemies in U.S. Under Rigid Rules," *Boston Daily Globe*, December 10, 1941, 19.

22. Lawrence E. Davies, "Carrier Is Hunted off San Francisco," *New York Times*, December 10, 1941, 20.

23. Associated Press, "Hawaii Calm Since Blitzkrieg, Governor Says; Food Control Planned to Conserve Supplies," *New York Times*, December 9, 1941, 13.

24. Associated Press, "Seek Exchange of American for Japanese," *Boston Evening Globe*, December 9, 1941, 3.

25. United Press, "Japan to Protect Enemy Nationals," *New York Times*, December 9, 1941, 15.

26. Associated Press, "Americans, Britons Rounded Up," *New York Times*, December 9, 1941, 15.

27. Associated Press, "U.S. Warships in Battle off Manila, Berlin Says," *Baltimore Sun*, December 10, 1941, 1.

28. Associated Press, "Superior Knowledge of Languages Seen as Aid to Japan," *Washington Evening Star*, December 10, 1941, A15.

29. C.P. Trussell, "Navy Criticized as Caught Asleep," *New York Times*, December, 10, 1941, 1.

30. C.P. Trussell, "Navy Criticized as Caught Asleep," *New York Times*, December, 10, 1941, 1.

31. Associated Press, "Wheeler Calls for Support of Roosevelt," *Boston Daily Globe*, December 8, 1941, 11.

32. Winston S. Churchill, *The Grand Alliance* (New York: Houghton Mifflin, 1950), 652–655.

33. Walter Robb, "Clique Pushed Japan Into War, Says Writer," *Los Angeles Times*, December 8, 1941, 4.

34. Glenn Babb, "Japanese Run True to Form—Striking at U.S. Without Warning," *Birmingham News*, December 9, 1941, 13.

35. Glenn Babb, "Japanese Run True to Form—Striking at U.S. Without Warning," *Birmingham News*, December 9, 1941, 13.

36. *Boston Daily Globe*, "Madness Infects Japanese, President of Tufts Asserts," December 9, 1941, 7.

37. *Christian Science Monitor*, "U.S. Navy Suffers a 'Scapa Flow'; Allies Quick to Declare War on Japan," December 11, 1941, C1.

38. Carroll Kilpatrick, "Army Does Not Plan Expeditionary Force Against Japs at Once," *Birmingham News*, December 9, 1941, 14.

39. Carroll Kilpatrick, "Army Does Not Plan Expeditionary Force Against Japs at Once," *Birmingham News*, December 9, 1941, 14.

40. Helen Lombard, "Admiral Leahy's Warning on Japan Recalled, Wanted to 'Clean Up' After Panay Was Sunk," *Washington Evening Star*, A5.

41. David Lawrence, "U.S. Learns, Lesson in Attack," *Washington Evening Star*, December 9, 1941, A11.

42. Jay G. Hayden, "U.S. Navy Caught off Guard," *Washington Evening Star*, December 9, 1941, A11.

43. Associated Press, "Preparedness of Defenses Is Questioned: Capital Hears Queries About Functions of Hawaii Off-Shore Patrol," *Baltimore Sun*, December 9, 1941, 1.

44. *Baltimore Sun*, "Full Navy Department Shakedown Demanded as Result of Hawaii Defeat," December 10, 1941, 2.

45. *Baltimore Sun*, "Full Navy Department Shakedown Demanded as Result of Hawaii Defeat," December 10, 1941, 2.

46. *Baltimore Sun*, "Full Navy Department Shakedown Demanded as Result of Hawaii Defeat," December 10, 1941, 2.

47. Jack Bell, "Hitler Promised to Aid Japs, Says Senator Gillette," *Evening Independent*, December 9, 1941, 1.

48. Husband E. Kimmel, *"Admiral Kimmel's Story,"* (Chicago, IL: Henry Regnery Company, 1955), 32.

49. Husband E. Kimmel, *"Admiral Kimmel's Story,"* (Chicago, IL: Henry Regnery Company, 1955), 2.

50. *Washington Post*, "Strategy at Hawaii," December 8, 1941, 12.

51. *New York Times*, "The Rendezvous with Destiny," December 12, 1941, C24.

52. *New York Times*, "Drastic Control Marks War News," December 9, 1941, 7.

53. Associated Press, "Raid Manila; Seize Guam Call Hawaii Loss 'Disaster,'" *Chicago Daily Tribune*, December 9, 1941, 1.

54. Associated Press, "60 Years Later, Pearl Harbor Pilots Recall Attack," *Mount Airy News*, December 6, 2001, 8A.

55. *Washington Post*, "Strategy at Hawaii," December 8, 1941, 12.

56. *Washington Post*, "Strategy at Hawaii," December 8, 1941, 12.

57. Associated Press, "Reports Plane Mother Ship Sunk," December 9, 1941, 13.

58. *New York Times*, "Large U.S. Losses Claimed By Japan," December 9, 1941, 1.

59. Winston Churchill, *"The Grand Alliance."* (New York, NY: Rosetta Books, 1948), 551.

60. *New York Times*, "Japan Says Allies Are Broken at Sea," December 11, 1941, 1.

61. *New York Times*, "Japan Says Allies Are Broken at Sea," December 11, 1941, 1.

62. F. Tillman Durdin, "Japanese Ashore in Force in Malaya," *New York Times*, December 10, 1941, 1.

63. Associated Press, "Britain and Japan Hurl Reinforcements Into Malayan Jungle Battle," *Baltimore Sun*, December 10, 1941, 4.

64. Associated Press, "Heroism in Philippines," *Baltimore Sun*, December 10, 1941, 4.

65. Associated Press, "Tokyo Claims Seizure of 200 Merchantmen," *Baltimore Sun*, December 10, 1941, 4.

66. Associated Press, "Tokyo Claims Seizure of 200 Merchantmen," *Baltimore Sun*, December 10, 1941, 4.

67. Associated Press, "Tokyo Claims Seizure of 200 Merchantmen," *Baltimore Sun*, December 10, 1941, 4.

68. Franklin Delano Roosevelt Presidential Library and Museum, *Halifax to FDR Letter Regarding Military Situation: Military Report from London, December 10, 1941*, December 12, 1941, Hyde Park, NY.

69. Associated Press Wire Photo, "Casualty Error," *Evening Star*, December 10, 1941, A2.

70. *New York Times*, "2 False Air 'Raids' Upset New Yorkers," December 10, 1941, 1.

71. *New York Times*, "Blackout Ordered for Capitol Dome," December 10, 1941, 18.

72. International News Service, "The Presidents Day," *Washington Post*, December 11, 1941, 2.

73. *New York Times*, "The President's Address," December 10, 1941, 1.

74. *New York Times*, "The President's Address," December 10, 1941, 1.

75. *New York Times*, "The President's Address," December 10, 1941, 1.

76. *New York Times*, "The President's Address," December 10, 1941, 1.

77. *New York Times*, "The President's Address," December 10, 1941, 1.

78. *New York Times*, "The President's Address," December 10, 1941, 1.

79. *New York Times*, "The President's Address," December 10, 1941, 1.

80. International News Service, "The Presidents Day," *Washington Post*, December 11, 1941, 2.
81. International News Service, "The Presidents Day," *Washington Post*, December 11, 1941, 2.
82. Associated Press, "New Air Raid Alarm Sounded in New York After 2 False Scares," *Washington Evening Star*, December 10, 1941, A2.
83. Associated Press, "New Air Raid Alarm Sounded in New York After 2 False Scares," *Washington Evening Star*, December 10, 1941, A2.
84. Associated Press, "New Air Raid Alarm Sounded in New York After 2 False Scares," *Washington Evening Star*, December 10, 1941, A2.
85. Thomas R. Henry, "Innocent Inquiry 'Alerts' Northeast Seaboard," *Washington Evening Star*, December 10, 1941, B1.
86. Lawrence R. Davies, "Carrier Is Hunted off San Francisco," *New York Times*, December 10, 1941, 20.
87. Lawrence R. Davies, "Carrier Is Hunted off San Francisco," *New York Times*, December 10, 1941, 20.
88. *New York Times*, "The Day in Washington," December 10, 1941, 7.
89. C. P. Trussell, "Navy Criticized as Caught Asleep," *New York Times*, December 10, 1941, 1.
90. C.P. Trussell, "Navy Criticized as Caught Asleep," *New York Times*, December 10, 1941, 1.
91. Associated Press, "Senate Committees Refuse to Question Defense Strategy," *Washington Evening Star*, December 10, 1941, A5.
92. Paul W. Ward, "Navy and Army Criticized For Hawaii Defeat," *Baltimore Sun*, December 10, 1941, 3.
93. C.P. Trussell, "Navy Criticized as Caught Asleep," *New York Times*, December 10, 1941, 1.
94. *New York Times*, "Arrests of 12,850 Revealed in Vichy," December 10, 1941, 7.
95. *New York Times*, "Arrests of 12,850 Revealed in Vichy," December 10, 1941, 7.
96. *New York Times*, "Arrests of 12,850 Revealed in Vichy," December 10, 1941, 7.
97. Associated Press, "Germany Cuts Off Press Relations with America," *Washington Evening Star*, December 10, 1941, A1.
98. *New York Times*, "Enlistments Rise to New Highs Here," December 10, 1941, 22.
99. Associated Press, "Bulletins: Report U.S. Burning Papers," *Hartford (CT) Courant*, December 10, 1941, 1.

CHAPTER 11: THE ELEVENTH OF DECEMBER

1. Associated Press, "Germany and Italy Declare War on U.S. and Sign New Axis Alliance," *Washington Evening Star*, December 11, 1941, A1.
2. Associated Press, "Dictators Give Views on Conflict," *Kingsport (TN) Times*, December 11, 1941, 1.
3. Associated Press, "Dictators Give Views on Conflict," *Kingsport (TN) Times*, December 11, 1941, 1.
4. Associated Press, "Dictators Give Views On Conflict," *Kingsport (TN) Times*, December 11, 1941, 1.
5. Associated Press, "Mussolini War Statement," *New York Times*, December 12, 1941, 4.
6. Associated Press, "Dictators Give Views on Conflict," *Kingsport (TN) Times*, December 11, 1941, 1.
7. Associated Press, "How Hitler Declared War on U.S.," *Christian Science Monitor*, December 11, 1941, 10.
8. Associated Press, "How Hitler Declared War on U.S.," *Christian Science Monitor*, December 11, 1941, 10.
9. Associated Press, "Germany and Italy Declare War on U.S. and Sign New Axis Alliance," *Washington Evening Star*, December 11, 1941, A1.
10. Michael Barone, *Our Country: The Shaping of America from Roosevelt to Reagan* (New York: Free Press, 1990), 145.
11. Brett Gary, *The Nervous Liberals: Propaganda Anxieties from World War I to the Cold War* (New York: Columbia Univ. Press, 1999), 301.
12. *Washington Evening Star*, "Axis Envoys Notifying U.S. of War Received By Under-Officials," December 11, 1941, A2.

13. Bertram D. Hulen, "Hull Very Frigid to Visiting Envoys," *New York Times*, December 12, 1941, 3.

14. *Washington Evening Star*, "Axis Envoys Notifying U.S. of War Received By Under-Officials," December 11, 1941, A2.

15. Associated Press, "Germany and Italy Declare War on U.S. and Sign New Axis Alliance," *Washington Evening Star*, December 11, 1941, A1.

16. *New York Times*, "Charges in German Note," December 12, 1941, 5.

17. Associated Press, "Sequence of Nazi Aggression Leading to Break With U.S.," *Christian Science Monitor*, December 11, 1941, 6.

18. *New York Times*, "Submarine Warfare," February 20, 1940, 18.

19. *Washington Evening Star*, "Axis Envoys Notifying U.S. of War Received By Under-Officials," December 11, 1941, A2.

20. *Washington Evening Star*, "Italian and German Embassies Are Calm at War Declaration," December 11, 1941, A3.

21. *New York Times*, "Our Declaration of War," December 12, 1941, 1.

22. *New York Times*, "City Calm and Grim as the War Widens," December 12, 1941, 1.

23. Frank L. Kluckhohn, "War Opened On Us," *New York Times*, December 12, 1941, 1.

24. Associated Press, "Miss Rankin Voted 'Present' in Weak Voice; Clerk Had to Call Her Name a Second Time," *New York Times*, December 12, 1941, 6.

25. *Chicago Daily Tribune*, "Montana G. O. P. Head Demands Rep. Rankin Change Vote on War," December 9, 1941, 4.

26. Robert C. Albright, "Declaration Laid On President's Desk Three Hours After Two Houses Meet," *Washington Post*, December 12, 1941, 1.

27. Associated Press, "U.S. Troops Released for War Abroad," *Kingsport* (TN) *Times*, December 11, 1941, 1.

28. Drew Pearson and Robert S. Allen, "Washington Merry-Go-Round," *Kingsport* (TN) *Times*, December 11, 1941, 4.

29. Associated Press, "Grim-Visaged F.D.R. Signs War Papers," *Atlanta Constitution*, December 12, 1941, 6.

30. Associated Press, "Proof Democracy Can Move Swiftly," *Atlanta Constitution*, December 12, 1941, 6.

31. Associated Press, "U. S. Answers Axis Challenge, Declares War," *Atlanta Constitution*, December 12, 1941, 1.

32. Associated Press, "U.S. Troops Released for War Abroad," *Kingsport* (TN) *Times*, December 11, 1941, 1.

33. Associated Press, "Tobey Renews Demands for Navy Inquiry," *Washington Evening Star*, December 11, 1941, A1.

34. Associated Press, "Tobey Renews Demands for Navy Inquiry," *Washington Evening Star*, December 11, 1941, A1.

35. Associated Press, "Senators of Both Parties Demand Investigation of Hawaii Attack," *Kingsport* (TN) *Times*, December 11, 1941, 4.

36. Drew Pearson and Robert S. Allen, "Washington Merry-Go-Round," *Kingsport* (TN) *Times*, December 11, 1941, 4.

37. *New York Times*, "Silent Galleries Watch War Vote," December 12, 1941, 5.

38. *Washington Evening Star*, "Roosevelt Accepts Offer of Parties to Drop Politics," December 1, 1941, A9.

39. Associated Press, "Democrats and Republicans Adjourn Domestic Politics," *Los Angeles Times*, December 11, 1941, 17.

40. Associated Press, "Japs May Have Timed Attack By U.S. Army's Down Patrol," *Washington Evening Star*, December 11, 1941, A8.

41. Gordon W. Prange, *At Dawn We Slept* (New York: McGraw-Hill, 1981), 70–77.

42. *New York Times*, "Stimson Asks Time for Facts on Hawaii," December 12, 1941, 11.
43. George Fielding Eliot, "Bomb Hits of Japanese Hint New Device Used," *Los Angeles Times*, December 11, 1941, 5.
44. *Washington Post*, "Suicide Pilots' Dove Straight Into Ships, U.S. Officers Think," December 11, 1941, 1.
45. *Washington Post*, "Congressmen Halt Hawaiian Investigation," December 11, 1941, 26.
46. Charles Hurd, "U.S. Fliers Score," *New York Times*, December 12, 1941, 1.
47. Associated Press, "Churchill Expects U.S. Losses to Cut Help for Britain," *Washington Evening Star*, December 11, 1941, A2.
48. Winston S. Churchill, *The Grand Alliance* (New York: Houghton Mifflin, 1950), 620.
49. Associated Press, "130 Officers Saved With 2,200 Men from Wales and Repulse," *Washington Evening Star*, December 11, 1941, A3.
50. Winston S. Churchill, *The Grand Alliance* (New York: Houghton Mifflin, 1950), 590.
51. Canadian Press, "British-U.S. Navies Still Superior To Joint Axis Fleets," *Lethbridge Herald* (Alberta, Canada), December 11, 1941, 1.
52. Associated Press, "Brown of CBS, Rescued from Sea," *Atlanta Constitution*, December 11, 1941, 1.
53. O. D. Gallagher, International News Service, "Repulse Survivor Walked Down to Sea as on Sloping Sidewalk," *Atlanta Constitution*, December 11, 1941, 1.
54. *New York Times*, "The Admiralty's Christmas Card of Good Cheer Becomes a Message of Sorrow," December 11, 1941, 7.
55. *Washington Evening Star*, "Officials Consider Air Raid Shelters for Washington," December 11, 1941, A1.
56. Associated Press, "Capitol Hums with War Activity; One Senator Blocks FDR Bill," *Atlanta Constitution*, December 11, 1941, 2.
57. *Washington Post*, "Navy to Clean Up Merchant Marine," December 11, 1941, 7.
58. Associated Press, "Late War Bulletins," *Washington Evening Star*, December 11, 1941, A1.
59. Alfred Friendly, "U.S. Bans Tire Sales; Will Seize All Imports," *Washington Post*, December 11, 1941, 1.
60. Alfred Friendly, "U.S. Bans Tire Sales; Will Seize All Imports," *Washington Post*, December 11, 1941, 1.
61. Associated Press, "Capitol Hums with War Activity; One Senator Blocks FDR Bill," *Atlanta Constitution*, December 11, 1941, 2.
62. Drew Pearson, Robert S. Allen, "Washington Merry-Go-Round," *Kingsport* (TN) *Times*, December 11, 1941, 4.
63. Doris Kearns Goodwin, *No Ordinary Time* (New York: Simon & Schuster, 1994), 291.
64. Doris Kearns Goodwin, *No Ordinary Time* (New York: Simon & Schuster, 1994), 265–266.
65. Frank L. Kluckhohn, "Army, Navy Get Control of Radio," *New York Times*, December 11, 1941, 3.
66. Franklin Delano Roosevelt Presidential Library and Museum, "Memo from Chief of Naval Operations Harold Stark to President Roosevelt" December 12, 1941, Hyde Park, NY.
67. Clark Lee, Associated Press, "Landings in North Are 'In Heavy Force,'" *Washington Post*, December 11, 1941, 6.
68. Constantine Brown, "This Changing World," *Washington Evening Star*, December 11, 1941, A13.
69. *Washington Post*, "Bulletins: Japs Seize U.S. Consuls at Hanoi," December 11, 1941, 4.
70. United Press, "U.S. Bombs Fire Japanese Battleship; Army Smashes Main Philippine Invasion," *Washington Post*, December 11, 1941, 1.
71. United Press, "Philipines Fight; Army Reports Invasion Under Control, With a New Effort Repulsed," *New York Times*, December 11, 1941, 1.
72. William Safire, Leonard Safir, *Words of Wisdom* (New York: Simon & Schuster, 1989), 54.

73. William Manchester, *American Caesar, Douglas MacArthur 1880–1964* (Boston: Little, Brown and Company, 1978), 152.

74. *Life*, "Commander of the Far East," December 8, 1941, 1.

75. *Life*, "Commander of the Far East," December 8, 1941, 8.

76. *Washington Evening Star*, "Navy Calls Member of House for Duty," December 11, 1941, A13.

77. Robert A. Caro, *Means of Ascent: The Years of Lyndon Johnson* (New York: Alfred A. Knopf, 1990), 20.

78. Robert A. Caro, *Means of Ascent: The Years of Lyndon Johnson* (New York: Alfred A. Knopf, 1990), 24–25.

79. *Kingsport* (TN) *Times*, "Go Ahead—Surprise Her! With a Diamond," December 11, 1941, 5.

80. *Kingsport* (TN) *Times*, "Give Her Glamour . . . You Can Do So With . . .," December 11, 1941, 6.

81. *Kingsport* (TN) *Times*, "To Show Your Devotion Nothing Will Thrill Her More Than a Gorgeous . . .," December 11, 1941, 6.

82. *Washington Evening Star*, "Jordan's Corner 13ᵗʰ & G Sts.," December 11, 1941, A3.

83. *Washington Evening Star*, "Haley's Photo Album," December 11, 1941, A3.

84. Ovid A. Martin, Associated Press, "Housewives Assured Food Supplies Ample for Nation," *Kingsport* (TN) *Times*, December 11, 1941, 7.

85. *Los Angeles Times*, "Vegetables Found Free of Poisons," December 11, 1941, Part II, 2.

86. *Washington Evening Star*, "Grand Opening! Bladensburg D.G.S. Mkt.," December 11, 1941, A15.

87. *Washington Post* "'Give Gifts That Pour'; Clark's," December 11, 1941, 7.

88. Gladwyn Hill, Franklin Mullin, Wide World, "Nation's Corn Crop Will Be Basic Factor in Deciding War End," *Birmingham* (AL) *News*, December 11, 1941, 2.

89. Associated Press, "Government Okays New Army Helmets," *Washington Post*, December 11, 1941, 10.

90. Associated Press, "1,000 Heavy Bombers Monthly New Goal of U.S. Industry," *Atlanta Constitution*, 3.

91. Associated Press, "War Brings Peace to Labor Front: Threatens Propeller Output," *Washington Post*, December 11, 1941, 10.

92. *Birmingham* (AL) *News*, "Two Alabamians Die in Fighting Around Hawaii," December 12, 1941, 1.

93. *Boston Globe*, "Lynn, Hingham Youths Killed at Honolulu," December 12, 1941, 1.

94. *Washington Evening Star*, "Army List of 87 Killed," December 11, 1941, A4.

95. *Washington Evening Star*, "More Victims," December 11, 1941, A4.

96. Associated Press, "This Soldier Is Very Much Alive," *Washington Post*, December 11, 1941, 12.

97. Associated Press, "Admiral Kidd Dead in Action in Hawaii," *New York Times*, December 11, 1941, 4.

98. *New York Times*, "Award 62 Medals to Heroes of Navy," March 15, 1942.

99. Associated Press, "Eleven Frenchmen Shot By Germans," *Kingsport* (TN) *Times*, December 11, 1941, 2.

100. Associated Press, "U.S. Writers Restrained in Germany," *Hartfort* (CT) *Courant*, December 11, 1941, 13.

101. Associated Press, "Nazis Seize Americans Equal to Number Arrested in U.S.," *Washington Evening Star*, December 11, 1941, A4.

102. *Washington Evening Star*, "Italian Embassy Staff Stocks Up With Vitamins," December 12, 1941, B21.

103. *New York Times*, "U.S. to Exchange Axis Reporters," December 12, 1941, 7.

104. *Washington Post*, "Navy to Clean Up Merchant Marine," December 11, 1941, 7.

105. Associated Press, "5ᵗʰ Columnist Hunt Started by F.B.I.," *Boston Globe*, December 11, 1941, 18.

106. Associated Press, "Justice Department Starts Check on Potential Quislings," *Los Angeles Times*, December 12, 1941, Part 1, 8.

107. *Washington Post*, "Navy to Clean Up Merchant Marine," December 11, 1941, 7.

108. *Los Angeles Times*, "Axis Aliens Have Citizenship Right," December 14, 1941, 11.

109. *Washington Post*, "Navy to Clean Up Merchant Marine," December 11, 1941, 7.

110. United Press, "U.S. Bombs Fire Japanese Battleship; Army Smashes Main Philippine Invasion," *Washington Post*, December 11, 1941, 1.

111. *New York Times*, "Bulletins: N.Y. Harbor Mined, Navy Warns Shipping," December 11, 1941, 33.

112. Associated Press, "Navy Will Bury Dead Where They Lost Lives," *Atlanta Constitution*, December, 11, 1941, 4.

113. *Washington Evening Star*, "Army Mounts Guns to Protect U.S. Buildings and Workers," December 12, 1941, A3.

114. *Atlanta Constitution* "City Defense Corps Formed; Blackout Planned Next Week," December 11, 1941, 1.

115. *Boston Globe*, "Japanese War Propaganda Here, Says Speaker," December 11, 1941, 5.

116. *Los Angeles Times*, "Everything Normal in Hawaii, Brother Phones Angelino," December 11, 1941, Part 1, 9.

117. *Washington Evening Star*, "D.C. Emergency Don'ts," December 11, 1941, A9.

118. F. R. Kent Jr., "A Blitz Veteran Writes On: Air Raid Behavior," *Baltimore Sun*, December 11, 1941, 30.

119. Howard W. Blakeslee, Wide World, "Here's How to Teach Yourself to See Better in Blackouts," *Birmingham* (AL) *News*, December 11, 1941, 2.

120. *Washington Post*, "Skip War Talk with Children, OCD Urges," December 11, 1941, 25.

121. *Washington Post*, "Capital Eager to Do Its Share: We Can Be of Great Service By Observing These Don'ts," December 11, 1941, 1.

122. *Washington Post*, "Tin Pan Alley Declares War on Japan," December 12, 1941, 11.

123. *Washington Post*, "Japan's Mark Is Taboo," December 11, 1941, 8.

124. David Brinkley, *Washington Goes To War* (New York: Alfred A. Knopf, 1988), 25.

125. *Washington Post*, "Japan's Mark Is Taboo," December 11, 1941, 8.

126. *Washington Post*, "Military Guard's Shot in Air Stops Thief; U.S. Buildings Install Blackout Curtains," December 11, 1941, 25.

127. Mark Eliot, *Walt Disney: Hollywood's Dark Prince* (New York: Carol Publishing, 1993), 163–166.

128. Louella O. Parsons, International News Service, "Cheers for Cartoons," *Washington Post*, December 11, 1941, 17.

129. Hedda Hopper, "So They Take Busmen's Holidays," *Washington Post*, December 11, 1941, 16.

130. John Lardner, "Slapsie Maxie Gets Set For Babe Ruth's Arrival," *Hartford* (CT) *Courant*, December 11, 1941, 19.

131. Associated Press, "Axis powers Pledge No Separate Peace, Japan Announces," *Washington Evening Star*, December 11, 1941, A6.

132. International News Service, "The President's Day," *Washington Post*, December 11, 1941, 2.

133. "Employment Status of the Civilian Noninstitutional Population, 1940s to date," Last Modified: April 11, 2011, http://www.bls.gov/cps/cpsaat1.pdf.

134. *Washington Post*, "Valuable U.S. Documents May Be Hidden in Maryland," December 11, 1941, 7.

135. Doris Kearns Goodwin, *No Ordinary Time* (New York: Simon & Schuster, 1994), 298.

136. Associated Press, "Panama Canal Closed From 6 P.M. to 6 A.M.," *Boston Globe*, December 11, 1941, 9.

137. *Los Angeles Times*, "Planes Search Skies for Japs," December 11, 1941, 1.

138. Associated Press, "Unidentified Planes Circle Los Angeles," *Washington Post*, December 11, 1941, Part 1, 9.

139. *Los Angeles Times*, "Plans Made to Provide Bomb Shelters Here," December 11, 1941, Part 1, 9.

140. *Los Angeles Times*, "San Diegan Killed in Black-out Crash," December 11, 1941, Part 1, 12.
141. *Los Angeles Times*, "Thunderbolts During Storm Cause Bomb Scare," December 11, 1941, Part 2, 1.
142. *New York Times*, "End of Air Raid Alarm Confusion Sought by Army, Navy and City," December 11, 1941, 1.
143. *Boston Globe*, "N.E. Rectifies Mistakes of Its First Air Raid Alarm," December 11, 1941, 1.

CHAPTER 12: THE TWELFTH OF DECEMBER
1. *Washington Evening Star*, "Strong Jap Attacks Dent British Lines on Malayan Border," December 12, 1941, 1.
2. *Washington Evening Star*, "Strong Jap Attacks Dent British Lines on Malayan Border," December 12, 1941, 1.
3. Associated Press, "Vessels Slip Away; Attacks on Luzon at Increased Fury," *Birmingham* (AL) *News*, December 12, 1941, 1.
4. Dewitt Mackenzie, "The War Today:," *Birmingham* (AL) *News*, December 12, 1941, 49.
5. *Boston Daily Globe*, "Must Teach Axis Lesson to Remember 1000 Years," December 12, 1941, 24.
6. Richard Overy, *Why The Allies Won* (New York: Norton, W.W. & Company, Inc., 1995), 249.
7. Richard Overy, *Why The Allies Won* (New York: Norton, W.W. & Company, Inc., 1995), 32.
8. David M. Kennedy, *The Library of Congress World War II Companion* (New York: Simon & Schuster, 2007), 480.
9. Associated Press, "Pilot, Killed Sinking Haruna, Called First U.S. Hero in New War," *Washington Evening Star*, December 12, 1941, A6.
10. Associated Press, "Pilot, Killed Sinking Haruna, Called First U.S. Hero in New War," *Washington Evening Star*, December 12, 1941, A6.
11. *New York Times*, "Liners and Carrier Escape Invaders," December 11, 1941, 1.
12. *Washington Evening Star*, "Lone Code Word Puts Pan American Planes on Wartime Plan," December 12, 1941, A15.
13. *Washington Evening Star*, "Our Trial Begins," December 12, 1941, A12.
14. Hanson W. Baldwin, "Air Power Pacific Key," *New York Times*, December 11, 1941, 6.
15. Ernest Lindley, "A Bad Beginning," *Washington Post*, December 10, 1941, 17.
16. *Los Angeles Times*, "If the Battleship is Doomed—," December 11, 1941, 4.
17. Cecil Brown, "Dramatic Death of Battle Cruiser Repulse," *Washington Evening Star*, December 11, 1941, A7.
18. Cecil Brown, "Dramatic Death of Battle Cruiser Repulse," *Washington Evening Star*, December 11, 1941, A7.
19. *Birmingham* (AL) *News*, "Optimists Warned Japs No Pushover," December 12, 1941, 6.
20. Associated Press, "The Japanese Aren't Any Pushover," *Birmingham* (AL) *News*, December 12, 1941, 39.
21. *New York Times*, "This Is an Air War," December 11, 1941, 26.
22. David Lawrence, "America's Courage Faces Test," *Washington Evening Star*, December 12, 1941, A13.
23. Associated Press, "Closer British Watch Kept on Nazi Fleet," *Washington Evening Star*, December 12, 1941, 1.
24. *Boston Evening Globe*, "All Men and Women May Be Registered for Defense," December 12, 1941, 1.
25. *Boston Evening Globe*, "All Men and Women May Be Registered for Defense," December 12, 1941, 1.
26. Associated Press, "Bill to Draft Men 18 to 65 to Get Swift House Action," *Washington Evening Star*, December 12, 1941, A1.
27. *Washington Evening Star*, "Recruiting Stations Report Little Letup in Enlistments," December, 12, 1941, A14.
28. *Baltimore Sun*, "Son Gives His Navy Father a Surprise," December 12, 1941, 30.

29. *Telegraph-Herald*, "Sees Need for 10,000 Nurses," December 11, 1941, 8.
30. *Washington Evening Star*, "D.C. Man Jailed for Attempting to Dodge Draft," December 12, 1941, B1.
31. David Brinkley, *Washington Goes to War* (New York: Knopf, 1988), 81.
32. *Atlanta Daily World*, "S.C. Soldiers Given Bibles," December 13, 1941, 1.
33. *New York Times*, "From Jobs to Marines, 'Privilege' to Serve," December 11, 1941, 4.
34. *New York Times*, "From Jobs to Marines, 'Privilege' to Serve," December 11, 1941, 4.
35. Associated Press, "Billions in War Taxes to Be Sought at Once by Legislators," *Washington Evening Star*, December 12, 1941, A6.
36. *Washington Evening Star*, "Model Air-Raid Shelter Planned in Alexandria," December 12, 1941, B1.
37. *New York Times*, "Making the Rounds with a New York City Air-Raid Warden," December 14, 1941, 64.
38. Grace Tully, *F. D. R. My Boss* (Chicago, IL: Peoples Book Club, 1949), 259.
39. *Washington Evening Star*, "Boat Owners Help 24-Hour Patrols on Potomac Bridges," December 12, 1941, B1.
40. *Boston Daily Globe*, "Air Raid Rules for Autoists: Stop, Park at Curb, Lights Out," December 12, 1941, 3.
41. *Washington Evening Star*, Woodward & Lothrop ad, December 12, 1941, B20.
42. *Los Angeles Times*, "Roundup of Aliens Called Nearly Over," December 11, 1941, 8.
43. *Los Angeles Times*, "Roundup of Aliens Called Nearly Over," December 11, 1941, 8.
44. *Hartford (CT) Courant*, "Local Chinese Has His Troubles Proving It On New York Trip," December 11, 1941, 22.
45. Associated Press, "Body of Chinese, Slain by Headsman, Found in Seattle," *Washington Evening Star*, December 12, 1941, A2.
46. *Los Angeles Times*, "Filipino Knifes Japanese in Car," December 13, 1941, B1.
47. *New York Times*, "Warns Americans of 'Split Loyalty,'" December 11, 1941, 7.
48. *New York Times*, "Warns Americans of 'Split Loyalty,'" December 11, 1941, 7.
49. *New York Times*, "Warns Americans of 'Split Loyalty,'" December 11, 1941, 7.
50. Associated Press, "Hitler Admirer and Aides Seized by F. B. I. on Coast," *Washington Evening Star*, December 12, 1941, A2.
51. *Washington Evening Star*, "Congress Is Warned of Sabotage Danger; F. B. I. Calls 'Alumni,'" December 12, 1941, A4.
52. *Washington Evening Star*, "Army Mounts Guns to Protect U. S. Buildings and Workers," December 12, 1941, A3.
53. *Washington Evening Star*, "Congress Is Warned of Sabotage Danger; F. B. I. Calls 'Alumni,'" December 12, 1941, A4.
54. Frank L. Kluckhohn, "Army, Navy Get Control of Radio," *New York Times*, December 11, 1941, 8.
55. *Atlanta Constitution*, "General Motors Defense Output Beats Schedule," December 12, 1941, 20.
56. Frank L. Kluckhohn, "Army, Navy Get Control of Radio," *New York Times*, December 11, 1941, 8.
57. *Washington Post*, "Blue Pencil," December 13, 1941, 14.
58. *Atlanta Constitution*, "Criticism," December 12, 1941, 16.
59. Walter Lippmann, "On Rising to the Occasion," *Birmingham (AL) News*, December 12, 1941, 16.
60. *Pittsburgh Post-Gazette*, "Raid Alarms to Silence Radio Quickly," December 13, 1941, 6.
61. *Birmingham (AL) News*, "Another Chance to Do Your Bit," December 12, 1941, 39.
62. *New York Times*, "Jailed in Charity Scheme; Five Men Also Fined in Lottery at Paterson Elks Club," December 13, 1941, 12.
63. Robert Quillen, "No Man's Right to Liberty Transcends Another's Right to Life," *Atlanta Constitution*, December 12, 1941, 16.
64. Will Swift, Ph.D, *The Roosevelts and the Royals* (Hoboken, New Jersey: John Wiley & Sons, Inc., 2004), 133.

65. Associated Press, "Van Nuys Introduces Bill Giving President Extra War Powers," *Washington Evening Star*, December 12, 1941, A6.

66. *Washington Evening Star*, "Tobey Knows Nothing of Hawaiian Battle, Roosevelt Declares," December 12, 1941, A14.

67. *Washington Evening Star*, "Upper House Votes to Give Each Senator $4,500 Assistant," December 12, 1941, A2.

68. *Saturday Evening Post*, "Happy Birthday to You," December 13, 1941, 34.

69. Associated Press, "Five Auto Plants Close Under O. P. M. Order for Curtailment," *Washington Evening Star*, December 12, 1941, A2.

70. Associated Press, "Production of Automobiles May Be Halted Entirely After February 1," *Washington Evening Star*, December 12, 1941, A20.

71. Associated Press, "Ford and G. M. Plan War Operations on Seven-Day Week," *Washington Evening Star*, December 13, 1941, A12.

72. Associated Press, "President Asks Press and Radio Not to List War Casualties," *Washington Evening Star*, December 12, 1941, A2.

73. *Washington Evening Star*, "Army Death List From Hawaii Reaches 155, Still Incomplete," December 12, 1941, A6.

74. *Washington Evening Star*, "Tobey Knows Nothing of Hawaiian Battle, Roosevelt Declares," December 12, 1941, A14.

75. *Washington Evening Star*, "40-Hour Work Week and Overtime Stand, President Declares" December 12, 1941, A14.

76. Associated Press, "Kimmel, Bloch Commend Valor Shown at Hawaii," *Washington Evening Star*, December 12, 1941, B28.

77. Associated Press, "Would-Be Hero Admits Hoax in Blast Scare," *Washington Evening Star*, December 12, 1941, A14.

78. David Brinkley, *Washington Goes to War* (New York: Knopf, 1988), 21.

79. Lamar Q. Ball, "Atlanta's Santa Claus Is in War Up to His Ears, on U. S. Side," *Atlanta Constitution*, December 12, 1941, 1.

80. U. S. Census Bureau, Educational Attainment, "A Half Century of Learning: Historical Census Statistics on Educational Attainment in the United States, 1940 to 2000: Detailed Tables," Last Revised: September 22, 2010, http://www.census.gov/hhes/socdemo/education/data/census/half-century/tables.html.

81. U. S. Census Bureau, Educational Attainment, "A Half Century of Learning: Historical Census Statistics on Educational Attainment in the United States, 1940 to 2000: Detailed Tables," Last Revised: September 22, 2010, http://www.census.gov/hhes/socdemo/education/data/census/half-century/tables.html.

CHAPTER 13: THE THIRTEENTH OF DECEMBER

1. Associated Press, "Californians 'Lose Pants' in Jap Cleaning Shop," *Birmingham* (AL) *News*, December 12, 1941, 1.

2. *Los Angeles Times*, "Census Bureau Tells Reason for Crowded Clothes Closets," December 12, 1941, 13.

3. Associated Press, "Sees Open Season on 'Japs,'" *New York Times*, December 12, 1941, 21.

4. *Washington Evening Star*, "Ship, Japan Mail, Has Name Changed to China Mail," December 13, 1941, A12.

5. *Boston Globe*, "Axis Nationals Being Taken Off American Ships," December 13, 1941, 2.

6. Associated Press Wire Photo, "Alien Detention Camp in Canal Zone," *Washington Evening Star*, December 13, 1941, A12.

7. Associated Press Wire Photo, "Alien Detention Camp in Canal Zone," *Washington Evening Star*, December 13, 1941, A12.

8. Associated Press, "Total of 2,541 Enemy Aliens Are Arrested," *Atlanta Constitution*, December 13, 1941, 5.

9. *New York Times*, "Central America Now Fully in War," December 13, 1941, 7.

10. Associated Press, "Housewife's 'Doorstop' Proves to Be 50-Pound Aerial Bomb," *Atlanta Constitution*, December 13, 1941, 2.

11. *Los Angeles Times*, "Gloria Vanderbilt Will Be Married to Di Cicco," December 12, 1941, 1-Part II.

12. *Atlanta Constitution*, "To Amuse Us Today," December 12, 1941, 19.

13. *Atlanta Constitution*, "War Takes Play in Newsreels Showing at Movie Houses Here," December 12, 1941, 19.

14. Associated Press, "A Tokyo Claim—It's Suspect," *San Francisco Chronicle*, December 13, 1941, 1.

15. Associated Press, "Japanese Claim U.S. Battleship Arizona Is Sunk," *Birmingham* (AL) *News*, December 13, 1941, 1.

16. Constantine Brown, "This Changing World," *Washington Evening Star*, December 13, 1941, A9.

17. Associated Press, "Knox Returns From Hawaii; Hurries Here," *Washington Evening Star*, December 13, 1941, 1.

18. *Washington Post*, "Rain and Sleet Slow Washington Traffic; Many Late to Work," December 13, 1941, 2.

19. John C. Henry, "High Naval Officials Called to White House for Consultation," *Washington Evening Star*, December 13, 1941, A3.

20. Associated Press, "Capital Moves to Tap Vast War Reserves," *Atlanta Constitution*, December 13, 1941, 1.

21. Associated Press, "Bombers and More Bombers Likely to Be Cry in War of Pacific," *Birmingham* (AL) *News*, December 13, 1941, 2.

22. International News Service, "The President's Day," *Washington Post*, December 13, 1941, 2.

23. International News Service, "The President's Day," *Washington Post*, December 13, 1941, 2.

24. *Washington Evening Star*, "Encircled Axis Troops Attacked by British West of Tobruk," December 13, 1941, A2.

25. Associated Press, "Army Cancels Coast Blackout to Avoid Hysteria," *Boston Globe*, December 12, 1941, 31.

26. Associated Press, "Warnings Wear Out Fire Engine Sirens," *Washington Evening Star*, December 13, 1941, A9.

27. *Los Angeles Times*, "Man Glows in Blackout," December 13, 1941, 5.

28. *Los Angeles Times*, "Black-out Hint on Calling Doctor," December 12, 1941, D.

29. *Los Angeles Times*, "Windows Dim at Plane Plants," December 12, 1941, 5.

30. *Los Angeles Times*, "Alien Rules Tightened," December 12, 1941, 2-Part II.

31. Associated Press, "Blackout Extended 100 Miles Eastward from San Francisco," *Washington Evening Star*, December 13, 1941, A12.

32. *Los Angeles Times*, "Blue Car Lights Under Ban; Autos Must Halt in Blackouts," December 13, 1941, 1.

33. *San Francisco Chronicle*, "FDR Slaps a 'Keep Out' Order on S.F. Harbor; Navy's in Charge," December 13, 1941, 2.

34. *San Francisco Chronicle*, "FDR Slaps a 'Keep Out' Order on S.F. Harbor; Navy's in Charge," December 13, 1941, 2.

35. *Baltimore Sun*, "Blackout of Baltimore Within 10 Days Planned; Westminster Has Drill," December 13, 1941, 24.

36. Associated Press, "3d Blackout in San Diego; 'Something' Off the Coast," *Boston Globe*, December 12, 1941, 22.

37. Associated Press, "Brief Alert Is Sounded on New England Coast," *Washington Evening Star*, December 13, 1941, A2.

38. *New York Times*, "Veteran Briton Gives Us Raid Pointers; Says Police and Fire Autos Should Use Bells," December 12, 1941, 20.

39. *New York Times*, "Veteran Briton Gives Us Raid Pointers; Says Police and Fire Autos Should Use Bells," December 12, 1941, 20.

40. *Los Angeles Times*, "Weather Bureau Halts Forecasts," December 13, 1941, 1.
41. Associated Press, "New Orleans Won't Have Mardi Gras," *Los Angeles Times*, December 13, 1941, D.
42. *New York Times*, "Churches Prepare for Raids on City," December 12, 1941, 21.
43. *New York Times*, "Theatres to Test Blackout Tonight; Lights in 45th Street Are to Go Out," December 13, 1941, 12.
44. Paul Mallon, "Huge Increase in Army Now Is Imperative," *Birmingham* (AL) *News*, December 12, 1941, 1.
45. Eugene Burns, "Six Vicious Raids by Japs Leave Oahu's Defenders Fighting Mad," *Washington Evening Star*, December 12, 1941, A8.
46. Associated Press, "Japanese Populace Told New York Was Bombed Twice," *Los Angeles Times*, December 13, 1941, A.
47. *Washington Evening Star*, "Day Parking Banned For Christmas Season," December 13, 1941, A7.
48. *Washington Evening Star*, "War Won't Stop D.C. Christmas Tree Program," December 13, 1941, A16.
49. Christine Sadler, "Guns Mounted, D.C. Wardens on 24-Hr. Shift," *Washington Post*, December 13, 1941, 8.
50. Eleanor Roosevelt, "My Day," *Atlanta Constitution*, December 13, 1941, 14.
51. *New York Times*, "City Calm As The War Widens," December 12, 1941, 1.
52. *Boston Globe*, "Says Jap Attack Brings Unanimity of Action to U.S.," December 12, 1941, 4.
53. *Boston Globe*, "National Peace Group Disbands, Votes Funds for Defense Bonds," December 12, 1941, 31.
54. *Los Angeles Times*, "America First to Be Dissolved," December 12, 1941, 8.
55. *Boston Globe*, "Hemisphere Solidarity," December 12, 1941, 26.
56. *New York Times*, "City Calm as the War Widens," December 12, 1941, 1.
57. *New York Times*, "14 Convicted Here as German Spies," December 13, 1941, 1.
58. *New York Times*, "14 Convicted Here as German Spies," December 13, 1941, 1
59. Associated Press, "'Loyalty' Probe Before Civil Pilots Can Fly Again," *Boston Globe*, December 12, 1941, 5.
60. *New York Times*, "Ban Lifted By CAA on Private Airplanes," December 12, 1941, 12.
61. *Boston Globe*, "Manual Cautions Against Pollution of Water Supply," December 12, 1941, 31.
62. Gene R. Casey, "Crack Army Crews Are Constantly Alert at Guns, Searchlights," *Boston Globe*, December 12, 1941, 31.
63. Gene R. Casey, "Key Cities Armed Camps in Greater Boston Now," *Boston Globe*, December 12, 1941, 14.
64. *Boston Globe*, "State Bans Cameras at Boston's Airport Following Complaint," December 12, 1941, 33.
65. Gene R. Casey, "Key Cities Armed Camps in Greater Boston Now," *Boston Globe*, December 12, 1941, 14.
66. *Boston Globe*, "Good for You, Food for You, Guinness," December 12, 1941, 31.
67. *Boston Globe*, "Norman Thomas Tells His Stand on War at Harvard University," December 12, 1941, 33.
68. *Boston Globe*, "Museum Closes to Public Its Jap Art Treasures," December 12, 1941, 23.
69. *Boston Globe*, "Pilgrim Monument Beacon Blacked Out at Provincetown," December 13, 1941, 2.
70. Associated Press, "Lloyd's Discontinues War Risk Insurance on Property in U.S.," *Boston Globe*, December 12, 1941, 22.
71. Associated Press, "Price-Fixing Fines Levied," *Los Angeles Times*, December 12, 1941, 12.
72. Associated Press, "Price Ceilings Are Placed on Fats and Oils," *Atlanta Constitution*, December 13, 1941, 4.
73. *New York Times*, "Japanese Farmers Exempt," December 12, 1941, 3.
74. *New York Times*, "City Votes $25,000 for Raid Sirens," December 12, 1941, 20.

75. United Press, "Japanese Pounded in Luzon, Warships Chased; Russians Rout Nazi Armies on Moscow Front; House Gets Bill to Register All Men 18 to 64," *New York Times*, December 13, 1941, 1.

76. *Saturday Evening Post*, "Smoker's Hack!" December 13, 1941, 60.

77. *Saturday Evening Post*, "Greetings from Philip Morris," December 13, 1941, 64.

78. *Saturday Evening Post*, "Something New has been added!," December 13, 1941, 67.

79. *Saturday Evening Post*, "Merry Crispness," December 13, 1941, 94.

80. *Saturday Evening Post*, "Thirst Asks Nothing More," December 13, 1941, 126.

81. Associated Press, "Guam Probably Taken By Japs, Navy Says, Conferees O.K. 10 Billion For Defense," *Washington Evening Star*, December 13, 1941, 1.

82. Associated Press, "Enemy Is Wiped Out North of Manila by Stubborn Defenders," *Washington Evening Star*, December 13, 1941, 1.

83. Associated Press, "Army Concludes Mopping Up in Lingayen Sector," *Washington Evening Star*, December 13, 1941, 1.

84. Associated Press, "Japs Claim Sinking of Battleship Arizona at Hawaii Sunday," *Washington Evening Star*, December 13, 1941, A2.

85. Associated Press, "4000 Japs Drown," *Boston Globe*, December 13, 1941, 1.

86. David M. Nichol, "'Human Torpedoes' Story Denied by Jap Naval Attache at Vichy," *Boston Globe*, December 13, 1941, 17.

87. Associated Press, "Tokyo Admits Using 'Human Torpedoes,'" *Washington Post*, December 13, 1941, 6.

88. Associated Press, "Pearl Harbor War Widows to Get More," *Pittsburg Post-Gazette*, December 18, 1941, 2.

89. Associated Press, "'I Know He's Happy,' Mrs. Kelly Says on Death of Hero Husband," *Washington Evening Star*, December 13, 1941, A3.

90. United Press, "First Gold Star of 1942 Awarded," *Los Angeles Times*, December 14, 1941, 9.

CHAPTER 14: THE FOURTEENTH OF DECEMBER

1. Associated Press, "Line-Up of Countries Now at War," *Evening Star*, December 13, 1941, A6.

2. Associated Press, "Line-Up of Countries Now at War," *Evening Star*, December 13, 1941, A6.

3. *Washington Post*, "Eire's Stand Unchanged," December 1, 1941, 11.

4. David Brinkley, *Washington Goes to War* (New York: Alfred A. Knopf, 1988), 93.

5. *Baltimore Sun*, "Transit Visas Restricted By Portugal," December 13, 1941, 4.

6. Associated Press, "German Army in Headlong Retreat From Moscow After Utter Defeat," *Atlanta Constitution*, December 13, 1941, 1.

7. Hanson W. Baldwin, "Philippines Delaying Foe," *New York Times*, December 13, 1941, 4.

8. Associated Press, "Nazis Shoot 4 in Paris," *New York Times*, December 13, 1941, 4.

9. By Telephone, "100 Hostages Shot By Nazis in France," *New York Times*, December 14, 1941, 1.

10. *New York Times*, "Reich to Register Americans Over 50," December 13, 1941, 7.

11. W. H. Shippen, "Wherein He Found 'Sanctity of Space,'" *Washington Evening Star*, December 13, 1941, 17.

12. *Washington Evening Star*, "Bolles Urges Dimming Lights to Guard City," December 13, 1941, A16.

13. Associated Press, "U.S. Flyers Battle Japs in Manila Raid," *Sunday Star*, December 14, 1941, 1.

14. Associated Press, "War Insurance Firm Created By Government," *Atlanta Constitution*, December 14, 1941, 9B.

15. David Brinkley, *Washington Goes to War* (New York: Alfred A. Knopf, 1988), xiv.

16. David Brinkley, *Washington Goes to War* (New York: Alfred A. Knopf, 1988), 20.

17. Private Walter Weisbecker, "War and Washington: Soldiers Made to Feel They Belong," *San Francisco Chronicle*, December 14, 1941, 8.

18. *Sunday Star*, "Where to Go What to Do," December 14, 1941, B6.

19. *Atlanta Constitution*, "Attack on Flag Stirred Troops, Atlantan Says," December 13, 1941, 11.

20. *Lethbridge Herald*, "Censor Puts Ban on Kisses in a Row," December 15, 1941, 2.
21. Associated Press, "Plan No Censorship of Domestic Mail," *Boston Sunday Globe*, December 14, 1941, 10.
22. *Los Angeles Times*, "Less Talk Urged on Navy Actions," December 13, 1941, 5.
23. *San Francisco Chronicle*, "U.S. Worried About Gas Protection, Says Mrs. FDR," December 14, 1941, 7.
24. Thomas R. Henry, "Civilian Gas Mask Bill Action Scheduled in Congress Tomorrow," *Sunday Star*, December 14, 1941, A3.
25. *Los Angeles Times*, "Report of Labor Exodus Denied," December 14, 1941, 24.
26. George Gallup, "Air Raid Sentiments Sounded in Gallup Poll," *New York Times*, December 13, 1941, 4.
27. *Washington Post*, "Do's and Don'ts for Handling Fire Bombs," December 13, 1941, 8.
28. *Atlanta Constitution*, "Skull Practice Held Here on Handling Incendiary Bombs," December 14, 1941, 12A.
29. *Sunday Star*, "The Volunteer Overlax of Army Here," December 14, 1941, A4.
30. *Los Angeles Times*, "Draft Objector Ready to Serve," December 13, 1941, 1D.
31. *Atlanta Constitution*, "Georgian Killed in Hawaii Attack," December 13, 1941, 2A.
32. *Birmingham News*, "Lauderdale Negro Killed In Naval Engagement," December 14, 1941, 1.
33. *Boston Sunday Globe*, "Military Honors for Lynn Private Killed in Hawaii," December 14, 1941, 7.
34. *Boston Sunday Globe*, "Schools Asked to Make Stretchers and First Aid Chests," December 14, 1941, 7.
35. Associated Press, "Blind Man Offers Self and Seeing-Eye Dog as Blackout Guides," *Sunday Star*, December 14, 1941, A3.
36. *Birmingham News*, "Boy Scouts to Help," December 14, 1941, 16.
37. *Birmingham News*, "Class at Millport Will Call Off Tour, Buy Defense Bond."
38. *Atlanta Constitution*, "War Writes New Corus to Song," December 14, 1941, 1A.
39. *Atlanta Constitution*, "Auto Clubs Helping Defense," December 14, 1941, 6B.
40. *Sunday Star*, "Gen. Wood Volunteers Services During War," December 14, 1941, A5.
41. *New York Times*, "America First Unit Quits," December 13, 1941, 10.
42. *Sunday Star*, "Gen. Wood Volunteers Services During War," December 14, 1941, A4.
43. Associated Press, "Provisions of Draft Bill," December 13, 1941, 14.
44. *Los Angeles Times*, "Worker Surplus Now Wiped Out," December 13, 1941, 1 Part I.
45. Associated Press, "Studies No Reason For Not Serving," *Washington Evening Star*, December 14, 1941, C1.
46. Associated Press, "Army Officer Urges Rose Bowl Football Game Be Canceled," *Atlanta Constitution*, December 13, 1941, 1A.
47. Walter McCallum, "Ban on Big-Time Competitive Golf by U.S.G.A. for Duration of War Expected," *Sunday Star*, December 14, 1941, C2.
48. *Sunday Star*, "Riggs, Sarah Cooke Get Top Rankings In U.S. Tennis," December 14, 1941, C2.
49. Associated Press, "Frank Capra Quits Films to Join the Signal Corps," *New York Times*, December 13, 1941, 24; Joseph McBride, *Frank Capra: The Catastrophe of Success* (New York: St. Martins Griffin, 2000), 448–460.
50. *Los Angeles Times*, "Frank Capra Awaiting Summons from Army," December 13, 1941, 2.
51. Hedda Hopper, "What Will Public Say?" *Washington Post*, November 2, 1942, B6.
52. *Los Angeles Times*, "Fox West Coast Theaters," December 15, 1941, A15.
53. Associated Press, "Defense Plant Where Explosion Killed Nine," *New York Times*, December 13, 1941, 10.
54. *Lost Angeles Times*, "Drowned Man's Body Found, Probable Victim of Blackout," December 14, 1941, A2.
55. *Christian Science Monitor*, "Oregon Sinking Described at Federal Probe," December 12, 1941, 5.
56. *New York Times*, "Canada to Ration Gasoline April 1," December 12, 1941, 12.

57. Henry E. Rose, "Public to Get Lower Quality Fuel, Means Higher Motorists' Bills," *Wall Street Journal*, December 13, 1941, 1.

58. *Wall Street Journal*, "Heavy Food Buying in Some Areas Forces Grocers to Impose Informal Curbs," December 13, 1941, 2.

59. Associated Press, "O.P.M. Act Bars Sugar Hoarding or Speculation," *Boston Daily Globe*, December 13, 1941, C3.

60. *San Francisco Chronicle*, "OPM Order: Deliveries of Sugar to Big Users Curbed," December 14, 1941, 9.

61. J.S. Armstrong, "Major Shift Seen In War Financing," *Baltimore Sun*, December 13, 1941, 17.

62. George Gallup, "Price, Wage Control Favored," *Atlanta Constitution*, December 14, 1941, 2.

63. Drew Pearson, "President's Bodyguard Strips Jap Newsmen of Their White House Passes; Living Costs Continue Upward Trend," *Birmingham News*, December 14, 1941, 1.

64. *San Francisco Chronicle*, "New York Wrecks Symbol of Goodwill," December 14, 1941, 13.

65. *Baltimore Sun*, "Baltimore Army Nurse 'Well, Safe' in Hawaii," December 13, 1941, 6.

66. *Baltimore Sun*, "Baltimore Army Nurse 'Well, Safe' in Hawaii," December 13, 1941, 6.

67. *Sunday Star*, "Six U.S. Flyers Cited by Army for 'Spectacular Heroism' in Battle to Save Honolulu," December 14, 1941, A1.

68. Celestine Sibley, "54 Women Learning Meaning of Dot-Dash in Classes Here," *Atlanta Constitution*, December 14, 1941, 4B.

69. *San Francisco Chronicle*, "This World" Cover, Col. 5, No. 38, December 14, 1941.

70. Richard H. Minear, *Dr. Seuss Goes to War* (New York: The New Press, 2001).

71. Franklin Delano Roosevelt Presidential Library and Museum, "Report By The Secretary of the Navy to the President," December 14, 1941, Hyde Park, NY.

72. Glen Babb, "There Is No 'One Man' in Japan But Adml. Yamamoto New Hero," *Birmingham News*, December 14, 1941, 8.

73. United Press, "Rear Admiral Kimmel's Death, Reported by Japan, Doubted," *Los Angeles Times*, December 14, 1941, 1.

74. Clarke Beach, "America's Strategic Islands Are Keys to Victory in Pacific," *Sunday Star*, December 14, 1941, B5.

75. Owen L. Scott, "U.S. Facing Long Hard-Fought War," *Boston Sunday Globe*, December 14, 1941, 7.

76. *Sunday Star*, "Kann's Toyland" Advertisement, December 14, 1941, B6.

77. *New York Times*, "Dance Lessons Cost No More at Arthur Murray's," December 14, 1941, X4.

78. *Boston Sunday Globe*, "Gilchrist's" Advertisement, December 14, 1941, 7.

79. *New York Times*, "Saks-34th" Advertisement, December 14, 1941, 17.

80. *Sunday Star*, "Best Sellers," December 14, 1941, E7.

81. *Sunday Star*, "The President" Advertisement, December 14, 1941, D15.

82. Jay Carmody, "Another Year, Another 10-Best List," *Sunday Star*, December 14, 1941, E1.

83. Carolyn Anspacher, "Neediest Families: You Can Help Keep the Home Fires Burning," *San Francisco Chronicle*, December 14, 1941, 9.

84. Blair Bolles, "Total War Between the Democracies and Berlin-Rome-Tokyo Axis Engulfs War," *Sunday Star*, December 14, 1941, B3.

CHAPTER 15: THE FIFTEENTH OF DECEMBER

1. W. E. Lucas, "Fading of Lisbon 'Liberty Beacon' Halts Exodus to America," *Christian Science Monitor*, December 16, 1941, 7.

2. *Boston Daily Globe*, "Hundreds Lose Out on Last U.S. Liner Sailing From Lisbon," December 14, 1941, 10.

3. W. E. Lucas, "Fading of Lisbon 'Liberty Beacon' Halts Exodus to America," *Christian Science Monitor*, December 16, 1941, 7.

4. W. E. Lucas, "Fading of Lisbon 'Liberty Beacon' Halts Exodus to America," *Christian Science Monitor*, December 16, 1941, 7.

5. *New York Times*, "Many Missionaries Listed in War Zone," December 14, 1941, 4.

6. *Life*, "War," December 15, 1941, 27.

7. Associated Press, "Tojo Tells Japanese Diet U.S.-British Fleets 'Crushed,'" *Christian Science Monitor*, December 16, 1941, 7.

8. Franck L. Kluckhohn, "Serious Setback," *New York Times*, December 10, 1941, 1; Charles Hurd, "Two U.S. Isles Holding Out, But Guam Is Believed Lost," *New York Times*, December 14, 1941, 1.

9. *Time*, "The U.S. at War," December 15, 1941, 17.

10. Frank L. Kluckhohn, "Roosevelt Holds Navy Conference," *New York Times*, December 14, 1941, 22.

11. *Time*, December 15, 1941.

12. Waldo Heinrichs, *Threshold of War: Franklin D. Roosevelt and American Entry Into World War II* (Oxford, UK: Oxford University Press, 1990), 18.

13. *Time*, "Labor: Hip & Thigh," November 10, 1941; *Time*, "Letters," December 15, 1941, 4.

14. *Life*, "War," December 15, 1941, 27.

15. United Press, "President Studies First Report on Japs' Surprise Raid on Pearl Harbor," *Yuma (AZ) Daily Sun*, December 15, 1941, 1.

16. Franklin D. Roosevelt Presidential Library and Museum, "Report by the Secretary of the Navy to the President," December 14, 1941.

17. United Press, "President Gives Background of War With Japan," *Yuma (AZ) Daily Sun*, December 15, 1941, 1.

18. Associated Press, "F.D.R. Declares Jap Attack Case of Horror," *Birmingham (AL) News*, December 15, 1941, 1.

19. Associated Press, "Legion Asks Tobey to Demonstrate His Allegiance to U.S.," *Birmingham (AL) News*, December 15, 1941, 6.

20. United Press, "Knox Reveals Six U.S. Warships Lost in Hawaii Attack," *Yuma (AZ) Daily Sun*, December 15, 1941, 2.

21. United Press, "President Gives Background of War With Japan," *Yuma (AZ) Daily Sun*, December 15, 1941, 1.

22. *Time*, "The U.S. At War," December 15, 1941, 18.

23. *Washington Evening Star*, "Secretary Knox's Account of Surprise Attack on Hawaii," December 15, 1941, A1.

24. United Press, "Knox Reveals Six U.S. Warships Lost in Hawaii Attack," *Yuma (AZ) Daily Sun*, December 15, 1941, 1.

25. United Press, "President Studies First Report On Jap's Surprise Raid on Pearl Harbor," *Yuma (AZ) Daily Sun*, December 15, 1941, 1.

26. Charles Hurd, "Heroic Acts Cited," *New York Times*, December 16, 1941, 1.

27. United Press, "Knox Reveals Six U.S. Warships Lost in Hawaii Attack," *Yuma (AZ) Daily Sun*, December 15, 1941, 1.

28. United Press, "Knox Reveals Six U.S. Warships Lost in Hawaii Attack," *Yuma (AZ) Daily Sun*, December 15, 1941, 1.

29. *Washington Evening Star*, "Secretary Knox's Account of Surprise Attack on Hawaii," December 15, 1941, A1.

30. *Washington Evening Star*, "Secretary Knox's Account of Surprise Attack on Hawaii," December 15, 1941, A1.

31. *Washington Evening Star*, "Secretary Knox's Account of Surprise Attack on Hawaii," December 15, 1941, A1.

32. Turner Jordan, "President Roosevelt on All Stations Over Bill of Rights Program," *Birmingham (AL) News*, December 15, 1941, 7.

33. *Los Angeles Times*, "City Unites Today to Honor Bill of Rights Anniversary," December 15, 1941, A1; United Press, "President to Speak Tonight at 8:00 M.S.T.," *Yuma (AZ) Daily Sun*, December 15, 1941, 1.

34. Associated Press, "Bill of Rights Exercises to Be Observed," *Atlanta Constitution*," December 14, 1941, 3.
35. Associated Press, "Allies Are Expected to Take Solemn Vow of No Separate Peace," *Birmingham* (AL) *News*, December 14, 1941, 1.
36. German Radio received by Associated Press, "Axis powers Hold Parley," *Lethbridge Herald* (Alberta, Canada), December 15, 1941, 1.
37. Associated Press, "On Warpath Again," *Lethbridge Herald* (Alberta, Canada), December 15, 1941, 6.
38. United Press, "White House Under Guard; No Longer Goldfish Bowl," *Los Angeles Times*, December 14, 1941, 8.
39. *Los Angeles Times*, "Closed Forest Area Patroled," December 14, 1941, 27.
40. Associated Press, "Patrols to Halt All Ships Nearing Naval Academy," *Washington Evening Star*, December 15, 1941, B20.
41. *New York Times*, "One Plate for New York Autos in 1942, The Other to Be Kept for Use in 1943," December 14, 1941, 1.
42. *New York Times*, "Nazi Citizens are Barred From Liquor Licenses," December 14, 1941, 13.
43. Associated Press, "Stove Firms' Use of Metals Is Cut," *Milwaukee Journal*, December 15, 7.
44. *New York Times*, "11,000 Small Firms Rally for Work," December 21, 1941, 9.
45. *Time*, "Weld It!," December 15, 1941, 44.
46. *Washington Post*, "Coast Guard Takes Over Swedish Liner," December 14, 1941, 1; *New York Times*, "The International Situation," December 13, 1941, 1.
47. *Birmingham* (AL) *News*, "Sandusky, Ohio, Firm Awarded High Honors for Defense Efficiency," December 14, 1941, 13.
48. *Christian Science Monitor*, "Two Refuse Salute; Dismissed From Jobs," December 15, 1941, 3.
49. *New York Times*, "GE Works on Sunday," December 15, 1941, 13.
50. Associated Press, "Jersey Factory Blast Checked by F.B.I., Navy and Police," *Washington Evening Star*, December 15, 1941, A14.
51. *Baltimore Sun*, "War Boosts Total of Blood Donors," December 14, 1941, 16.
52. *Life*, "Movie of the Week: Ball of Fire," December 15, 1941, 89.
53. Associated Press, "Few Things Escape Slang In U.S. Army," *Baltimore Sun*, December 1941, 7.
54. *Life*, "Movie of the Week: Ball of Fire," December 15, 1941, 89.
55. *Life*, "Do You Tell Yourself You Smoke Too Much?" December 15, 1941, 24 and 128.
56. *Los Angeles Times*, "Body of Japanese Found in Canal," December 14, 1941, 27.
57. *Birmingham* (AL) *News*, "Americans Reminded Most Aliens in U.S. Still Loyal Citizens," December 14, 1941, 19.
58. *Birmingham* (AL) *News*, "Americans Reminded Most Aliens in U.S. Still Loyal Citizens," December 14, 1941, 19.
59. *Los Angeles Times*, "Little Tokyo Lid Clamped," December 14, 1941, 1D.
60. Hyung-chan Kim, edit., *Asian Americans and the Supreme Court: A Documentary History* (Westport, CT: Greenwood Publishing Group, 1992), 44.
61. Associated Press, "Japanese Report All-Out Land and Air Offensive Aimed to Capture Hongkong," *Baltimore Sun*, December 15, 1941, 2; United Press, "Enemy Force In Northern Luzon Halted," *Washington Post*, December 11, 1941, 1.
62. Associated Press, "Japanese Drive Forcing British to Quit Kowoloon," *Christian Science Monitor*, December 15, 1941, 1.
63. Associated Press, "King George Marks 46th Birthday," *Los Angeles Times*, December 15, 1941, 2.
64. Canadian Press, "Jungle Fight Is Confused in Malaya," *Lethbridge Herald* (Alberta, Canada), December 15, 1941, 1.
65. Associated Press, "Philippines Declare Emergency State," *Lethbridge Herald* (Alberta, Canada), December 15, 1941, 3; Canadian Press, "Thailand Is Enemy Occupied Country," *Lethbridge Herald* (Alberta, Canada), December 15, 1941, 3.

66. United Press, "How Tables Turned," *Lethbridge Herald* (Alberta, Canada), December 15, 1; Robert C. Freeman and Jon R. Felt, *German Saints at War* (Springville, UT: Cedar Fort, 2008), 205.

67. Associated Press, "New Gains Reported, British Forces Seek Showdown in Libya," *Washington Evening Star*, December 15, 1941, B15; Associated Press, "Indian Troops Reported Repulsing Nazi Forces," *Washington Evening Star*, December 15, 1941, B15.

68. Associated Press, "Marines Are Holding Firm on Tiny Island Despite Air Attacks," *Atlanta Constitution*, December 15, 1941, 1.

69. Associated Press, "80,000 Serbs Hold Germans," *Lethbridge Herald* (Alberta, Canada), December 15, 1941, 2.

70. Associated Press, "Guerrillas Immobilize 24 Axis Divisions, Greeks Report," *Washington Evening Star*, December 15, 1941, A4.

71. Richard L. Strout, "Key Post Seen in Government Seen Probable for Wilkie," *Christian Science Monitor*, December 15, 1941, 3.

72. Richard L. Strout, "Key Post Seen in Government Seen Probable for Wilkie," *Christian Science Monitor*, December 15, 1941, 3.

73. *Washington Evening Star*, "Arnold Named to Be Lieutenant General; 14 Others Promoted," December 15, 1941, B9.

74. Eleanor Roosevelt, "My Day: Ingenuity Replaces Lack of Material," *Atlanta Constitution*, December 15, 1941, 14.

75. Franklin Delano Roosevelt Presidential Library and Museum, "FDR: Day by Day—The Pare Lorentz Chronology," December 15, 1941.

76. Joseph C. Harsch, "Blackouts Find Honolulu Ready for Any Challenge," *Christian Science Monitor*, December 15, 1941, 1.

77. Associated Press, "First Air Passengers Arrive from Hawaii," *Washington Evening Star*, December 15, 1941, B18; United Press, "Honolulu Back on Air," *New York Times*, December 15, 1941, 4.

78. Associated Press, "Rose Bowl Game to Be Played at Duke," *Washington Evening Star*, December 15, 1941, A1.

79. Associated Press, "Launchings Lose Fanfare to Save Money and Time," *Washington Evening Star*, December 15, 1941, A8.

80. *Washington Evening Star*, "Two Men From District Area Killed in Pacific, Navy Says," December 15, 1941, A2.

81. Associated Press, "City Which Gave One Son in '18 Lost Three in Hawaii," *Washington Evening Star*, December 15, 1941, A7.

82. David Lawrence, "Hawaii Attack Held Jap Blunder," *Washington Evening Star*, December 15, 1941, A11.

CHAPTER 16: THE SIXTEENTH OF DECEMBER

1. *Time*, "Wandering Jews," December 15, 1941, 67.

2. *Time*, "Wandering Jews," December 15, 1941, 67.

3. *Time*, "Wandering Jews," December 15, 1941, 67.

4. *Christian Science Monitor*, "Fading Lisbon 'Liberty Beacon' Halts Exodus to America," December 15, 1941, 7.

5. *Christian Science Monitor*, "Fading Lisbon 'Liberty Beacon' Halts Exodus to America," December 15, 1941, 7.

6. *Washington Evening Star*, "Stores Here Report Brisk Demand for Blackout Cloth," December 15, 1941, B1.

7. *Christian Science Monitor*, "Air Shelter Market Booms in New York," December 16, 1941, 6.

8. *Boston Globe*, "Parents! Read This!" December 15, 1941, 11.

9. *Christian Science Monitor*, "Child Registration Planned by U.S.," December 16, 1941, 6.

10. *Christian Science Monitor*, "Strict Wartime Restrictions Imposed on All Ship Traffic in and Out of Boston; Departures and Arrivals Banned During Night Hours," December 16, 1941, 2.

11. *Christian Science Monitor*, "Weather Data Restricted As 'War Secret,'" December 16, 1941, 2.
12. *Christian Science Monitor*, "Birth Control Hearing Jan. 29," December 15, 1941, 2.
13. *Christian Science Monitor*, "Replanning of South End Urged," December 16, 1941, 5.
14. *Christian Science Monitor*, "Great Throng Gives $35,000 to Aid Russia," December 15, 1941, 5.
15. *Christian Science Monitor*, "Great Throng Gives $35,000 to Aid Russia," December 15, 1941, 5.
16. Ella Winter, *Red Virtue: Human Relations in the New Russia* (New York: Harcourt Brace & Company, 1933).
17. *Boston Globe*, "Firewomen of Bay State Lead Nation," December 15, 1941, 1.
18. *Washington Evening Star*, "Dartmouth Speedup to End School Year by May 10," December 15, 1941, B9.
19. *Birmingham* (AL) *News*, "University Students Urged to Keep Calm During War Crisis," December 15, 1941, 6.
20. *New York Times*, "Yale Pledges Support of War," December 15, 1941, 17.
21. *New York Times*, "War Work Rushed at City Colleges," December 15, 1941, 14.
22. *Atlanta Constitution*, "Wants U.S. to Win If It Can—But Don't Deprive Her of a Man," December 15, 1941, 2.
23. *Washington Evening Star*, "Snow Clearance Parking Ban Goes into Effect," December 15, 1941, B1.
24. *Christian Science Monitor*, "U.S. Jews to Rally to Full Aid of Allies" December 15, 1941, 9.
25. James W. Fawcett, "3,000 Here Join in Prayers for Victory, Peace," *Washington Evening Star*, December 15, 1941, B1.
26. James W. Fawcett, "3,000 Here Join in Prayers for Victory, Peace," *Washington Evening Star*, December 15, 1941, B1.
27. *Los Angeles Times*, "Catholics End Prayer Ritual: Processional Honoring Our Lady of Guadalupe Climaxes Peace Services," December 15, 1941, A1.
28. *Atlanta Constitution*, "Minister Resigns; Opposed to War," December 15, 1941, 8.
29. *New York Times*, "Kerrl, Dictator of Reich Churches," December 15, 1941, 19.
30. *Christian Science Monitor* "Draft Unlikely for Men over 35," December 15, 1941, 8.
31. Associated Press, "After All, It Seems Swimming Might Be Handy for Sailors," *Birmingham* (AL) *News*, December 15, 1941, 13.
32. *New York Times*, "Sunday Recruiting Amazes Officers," December 15, 1941, 17.
33. *Atlanta Constitution*, "Domei Writer Denounces Jap Attack on U.S.," December 15, 1941, 8.
34. *Atlanta Constitution*, "Domei Writer Denounces Jap Attack on U.S.," December 15, 1941, 8.
35. Associated Press, "Boy, 16, Army Veteran, Gets His Discharge," *Atlanta Constitution*, December 15, 1941, 9.
36. United Press, "Roads Drop Leave Plan," *New York Times*, December 17, 1941, 30.
37. *Washington Evening Star*, "Defense Sidelights," December 15, 1941, B21.
38. *New York Times*, "'Date Seekers' Are Barred at Enrollment of Boys and Girls for Service in Air Raids," December 15, 1941, 16.
39. Associated Press, "Work Exemption," *Christian Science Monitor*, December 16, 1941, 5.
40. *Wall Street Journal*, "The Electrical Industry," December 16, 1941, 7.
41. *New York Times*, "All Help Pledged by Organizations," December 15, 1941, 15.
42. *New York Times*, "Chief Boatswain Killed," December 15, 1941, 15.
43. *Christian Science Monitor*, "More Japs," December 6, 1941, 8.
44. Associated Press, "Leahy Is Mentioned as Pacific Coordinator," *Birmingham* (AL) *News*, December 15, 1941, 7.
45. *Los Angeles Times*, "Daylight Plan for City Advocated," December 16, 1941, 1.
46. *Christian Science Monitor*, "Short Wave Listening Posts Vital Sources of War News," December 16, 1941, 8.
47. Dewey L. Fleming, "Half of U.S. Income to Go for War Effort Under Roosevelt Plan," *Baltimore Sun*, December 31, 1941, 1.

48. Dewey L. Fleming, "Half of U.S. Income to Go for War Effort Under Roosevelt Plan," *Baltimore Sun*, December 31, 1941, 1.

49. *New York Times*, "Display Ad 21," December 15, 1941, 17.

50. Wide World, "Figuring Your Income Tax (No. 1)," *Birmingham (AL) News*, December 15, 1941, 13.

51. *New York Times*, "Held Under Sedition Act," December 15, 1941, 8.

52. *Christian Science Monitor*, "Moviegoer Is Fined for Booing President," December 16, 1941, 3.

53. *Christian Science Monitor*, "Children Spurn Flag, Mother Gets a Year," December 16, 1941, 9.

54. Associated Press, "U.S. Prepares to Seize Billion in Enemy Assets," *Washington Post*, December 16, 1941, 15.

55. *Christian Science Monitor*, "Office of Bund Seized by U.S.," December 16, 1941, 9.

56. Franklin Delano Roosevelt Presidential Library and Museum, "Memorandum of Summary of West Coast and Honolulu Reports by Munson Etc.," December 16, 1941, Hyde Park, NY.

57. *Christian Science Monitor*, "'Ad Men' Told of Huge Task of Business," December 16, 1941, 2.

58. *Christian Science Monitor*, "Price Curb Vital to Win War Declares Senate," December 16, 1941, 1.

59. Associated Press, "Farm Bloc Endangers Price Controls," *Wall Street Journal*, December 16, 1941, 3.

60. *Los Angeles Times*, "Live Projectile Falls in Yard," December 15, 1941, 1.

61. *Yuma (AZ) Daily Sun*, "New Powers Voted For President," December 16, 1941, 1.

62. Franklin Delano Roosevelt Presidential Library and Museum, "FDR: Day by Day—The Pare Lorentz Chronology," December 10, 1941.

63. Associated Press, "Blast Hongkong as British Defy Surrender Edict," *Chicago Daily Tribune*, December 15, 1941, 4.

64. Associated Press, "Blast Hongkong as British Defy Surrender Edict," *Chicago Daily Tribune*, December 15, 1941, 4.

65. *Christian Science Monitor*, "Fading Lisbon 'Liberty Beacon' Halts Exodus to America," December 16, 1941, 7.

66. *Christian Science Monitor*, "Tojo tells Japanese Diet U.S. & British Fleets 'Crushed,'" December 16, 1941, 7.

67. *Christian Science Monitor*, "Plan for Joint War Council Speeded by Allied Nations," December 16, 1941, 10.

68. *Christian Science Monitor*, "Tojo tells Japanese Diet U.S. & British Fleets 'Crushed,'" December 16, 1941, 7.

69. *Christian Science Monitor*, "Yamamoto Planned Assault; Seeks to Take Whitehouse," December 16, 1941, 7.

70. *Christian Science Monitor*, "Army Flier Tells How He Downed Four Enemy Planes in Hawaii Attack," December 16, 1941, 8.

71. *Christian Science Monitor*, "Yamamoto Planned Assault; Seeks to Take Whitehouse," December 16, 1941, 7.

72. *Christian Science Monitor*, "Educators Take Up Project of Planning World Peace," December 16, 1941, 3.

CHAPTER 17: THE SEVENTEENTH OF DECEMBER

1. *Christian Science Monitor*, "A Penny a Plane Bad News for Axis," December 16, 1941, 8.

2. *New York Times*, "Start Fund for a New Arizona," December 17, 1941, 3.

3. *Christian Science Monitor*, "Donations of Cash to Beat Japan Range From One Cent Up to $200," December 17, 1941, 3.

4. *Christian Science Monitor*, "Reading Girl to Santa: Every Nation Be Free," December 17, 1941, 4.

5. *Christian Science Monitor*, "Aviation Books Free to All Young Fliers," December 17, 1941, 3.

6. *New York Times*, "Congress Speeds Huge War Effort," December 17, 1941, 7.

7. *Baltimore Sun*, "Big Defense Fees Told By Corcoran," December 17, 1941, 8.

8. Robert De Vore, "Large Arms Manufacturer Is Linked to Defense Lobby," *Washington Post*, December 3, 1941, 1.

9. *Washington Evening Star,* "Corcoran Reveals $65,000 Contract Fee," December 16, 1941, 1.

10. *Christian Science Monitor,* "Corcoran Denies Any Fee Concerning Defense Contracts," December 16, 1941, 10.

11. Merrel W. Whittlesey, "Tee to Green . . ." *Washington Post,* April 19, 1942, 5.

12. Gibson, Truman K., Steve Huntley, *Knocking Down Barriers: My Fight for Black America,* (Chicago: Northwestern University Press, 2005).

13. Francis E. Stan, "Baseball's Old Fox Picks Up a Package," *Washington Evening Star,* December 16, 1941, A17.

14. *Los Angeles Times,* "Shrine Game to New Orleans," December 17, 1941, 21.

15. Bill Boni, "Tom Harmon Chosen Outstanding Male Athlete of Year in Poll," *Atlanta Constitution,* December 10, 1940, 21.

16. Hy Hurwitz, "Fear Baseball Leagues Will Suspend in '42," *Boston Globe,* December 17, 1941, 1.

17. Larry Wolters, "W-G-N Program Features Oath by Six Recruits," *Chicago Tribune,* December 20, 1941, 14; Larry Wolters, "Theme of Radio in 1942: 'Keep 'Em Rolling!'" *Chicago Tribune,* January 4, 1942, S4.

18. *Christian Science Monitor,* "Pearl Harbor Widows' Pension to Be Raised to Wartime Level," December 17, 1941, 9.

19. *Christian Science Monitor,* "Pearl Harbor Widows' Pension to Be Raised to Wartime Level," December 17, 1941, 9.

20. *New York Times,* "German-Born Parents Lose Sons in Hawaii," December 17, 1941, 11.

21. *New York Times,* "Midget Submarine Has 2 Torpedoes", December 17, 1941, 8.

22. Franklin Delano Roosevelt Presidential Library and Museum, "Memorandum for the President From the Secretary of the Navy Regarding Assets in the Pacific," December 20, 1941, Hyde Park, NY.

23. Franklin Delano Roosevelt Presidential Library and Museum, "Memorandum for the President From the Secretary of the Navy Regarding Assets in the Pacific," December 20, 1941, Hyde Park, NY.

24. Associated Press, "New Air Attack by Japanese Aimed at Philippine Sea Base," *Christian Science Monitor,* December 16, 1941, 8.

25. *Christian Science Monitor,* "Americans in Air and Sea Attacks but Foe Gains in Borneo and Hong Kong," December 17, 1941, 1.

26. *Christian Science Monitor,* "Hong Kong and Singapore in Serious Danger?" December 16, 1941, 1.

27. Hanson W. Baldwin, "The Threat to Singapore," *New York Times,* December 17, 1941, 8.

28. Walter Trohan, "Enemy Warships Shell 2 Isles in Hawaiian Area," *Chicago Tribune,* December 17, 1941, 2.

29. Associated Press, "Hong Kong Is Facing Threat," *Rock Hill Herald,* December 16, 1941, 1.

30. Franklin Delano Roosevelt Presidential Library and Museum, "First Priority of Military Strategy," December 19, 1941, Hyde Park, NY.

31. Hanson W. Baldwin, "The Threat to Singapore," *New York Times,* December 17, 1941, 8.

32. *Washington Post,* "Bomb Kills 6 Gestapo Men in Paris," December 17, 1941, 3.

33. Associated Press, "Indian Heroes, British Officer Stem Japanese," *Atlanta Constitution,* December 15, 1941, 4.

34. *Washington Post,* "Singapore and Hongkong Peril Admitted," December 17, 1941, 4.

35. United Press, "Hitler at Berchtesgaden, Nerves Torn, Turks Hear," *New York Times,* December 17, 1941, 13.

36. Associated Press, "Germans Wreck Shrines of Three Famed Russians," *Chicago Tribune,* December 17, 1941, 14.

37. Franklin Delano Roosevelt Presidential Library and Museum, "Memorandum from the British Embassy to President Roosevelt Regarding Operational Events Covering the 4th to 11th December, 1941," December 17, 1941, Hyde Park, NY.

38. Porter Barclay, "Nazis Take Stern Measures to Nazify Conquered Youth; Polish Children Executed," *Lethbridge (CA) Herald,* December 17, 1941, Back Page.

39. Hanson W. Baldwin, "The Threat to Singapore," *New York Times*, December 17, 1941, 8.

40. *New York Times*, "Tokyo Version of U.S. 'Losses,'" December 17, 1941, 11.

41. *New York Times*, "4 Young Ensigns Take Ship to Sea in Pursuit of Japs," December 17, 1941, 10.

42. *New York Times*, "1917 Powers Voted," December 17, 1941, 1.

43. *Washington Evening Star*, "Congress Expected to Delay Inquiry on Pearl Harbor," December 16, 1941, A6.

44. Associated Press, "News by Knox Held Amazing," *Los Angeles Times*, December 16, 1941, 1A.

45. *New York Times*, "Hawaiian, With Three Bullet Wounds, Beats Japanese Airman to Death Against a Wall," December 17, 1941, 7.

46. Clarice B. Taylor, "Hawaiian Woman Slays Jap Pilot," *Washington Post*, December 17, 1941, 1.

47. Joseph G. Harrison, "War Powers Granted President; Army-Navy Shake-Up in Pacific?" *Christian Science Monitor*, December 17, 1941, 1.

48. Joseph G. Harrison, "War Powers Granted President; Army-Navy Shake-Up in Pacific?" *Christian Science Monitor*, December 17, 1941, 1.

49. Associated Press, "Pearl Harbor Raid Probers Appointed," *Atlanta Constitution*, December 17, 1941, 1.

50. Husband E. Kimmel, *Admiral Kimmel's Story* (Chicago, IL: Henry Regnery Company, 1955), 78.

51. Joseph G. Harrison, "War Powers Granted President; Army-Navy Shake-Up in Pacific?," *Christian Science Monitor*, December 17, 1941, 1.

52. International News Service, "The President's Day," *Washington Post*, December 17, 1941, 2.

53. *New York Times*, "1917 Powers Voted," December 17, 1941, 1.

54. *New York Times*, "1917 Powers Voted," December 17, 1941, 1.

55. Arthur Krocks, "Hull Warning Unheeded?" *New York Times*, December 17, 1941, 4.

56. *Boston Globe*, "F.D. Labor-Industry Address," December 18, 1941, 9.

57. *New York Times*, "Aid in War Voted By Longshoremen," December 17, 1941, 22.

58. *Boston Globe*, "Rationing Starts on Jan. 4 for Automobile Tires," December 18, 1941, 33.

59. *Christian Science Monitor*, "Don't Neglect Your Pets During Air Raids," December 17, 1941, 3.

60. *New York Times*, "Siren Tests Today; Blast of 15 Minutes Real Raid Warning," December 17, 1941, 1.

61. *Los Angeles Times*, "Daylight Time Plan for City Advocated," December 16, 1941, 1.

62. *Christian Science Monitor*, "Australians Give Up Liberty to Assure Defense of Liberty," December 17, 1941, 9.

63. *New York Times*, "1917 Powers Voted," December 17, 1941, 1.

64. *Nevada State Journal*, "Censor Plan on Out-Going Data Slated," December 17, 1941, 1.

65. *Los Angeles Times*, "Prompt War Censorship Planned by President," December 17, 1941, 11.

66. International News Service, "The President's Day," *Washington Post*, December 17, 1941, 2.

67. David Brinkley, *Washington Goes to War* (New York: Alfred A. Knopf, 1988), 105.

68. Associated Press, "No More Arrests Coming for Alleged Sedition," *Christian Science Monitor*, December 17, 1941, 9.

69. *New York Times*, "1917 Powers Voted," December 17, 1941, 1.

70. Everett R. Holles, "Roosevelt Finds Military Strategy Doing Very Well," *Washington Post*, December 17, 1941, 1.

71. International News Service, "The President's Day," *Washington Post*, December 17, 1941, 2.

72. *New York Times*, "1917 Powers Voted," December 17, 1941, 1.

73. *Atlanta Constitution*, "All Divisions Participate in Bonds' Rally," December 17, 1941, 13.

74. *Wall Street Journal*, "Plans Being Drafted for Wartime Control of Capital if Need Arise," December 17, 1941, 3.

75. "History: B-17 Flying Fortress," *Boeing.com*, 1995–2011. http://boeing.com/history/boeing/b17.html.

76.   Associated Press, "First 'Fabricated' Bomber Ready Soon After Jan. 1," *New York Times*, December 17, 1941, 16.

CHAPTER 18: THE EIGHTEENTH OF DECEMBER

1.   *Wall Street Journal*, "U.S. Flag Prices Up; Material Scarcities Slow Down Production," December 17, 1941, 1.

2.   Associated Press, "Hawaii Buries U.S. Dead Until Peace," *Washington Post*, December 18, 1941, 11.

3.   *Chicago Daily Tribune*, "Army, Navy Dead Buried in Hawaii Until War's End," December 17, 1941, 1.

4.   *Chicago Daily Tribune*, "Army, Navy Dead Buried in Hawaii Until War's End," December 17, 1941, 1.

5.   Associated Press, "Hawaii Buries U.S. Dead Until Peace," *Washington Post*, December 18, 1941, 11.

6.   Eugene Burns, "In the Quiet Hills of Honolulu America's Finest Laid to Rest," *Birmingham* (AL) *News*, December 17, 1941, 1.

7.   Eugene Burns, "In the Quiet Hills of Honolulu America's Finest Laid to Rest," *Birmingham* (AL) *News*, December 17, 1941, 1.

8.   Eugene Burns, "In the Quiet Hills of Honolulu America's Finest Laid to Rest," *Birmingham* (AL) *News*, December 17, 1941, 1.

9.   *Washington Evening Star*, "Mass at Georgetown Honors First Alumnus to Die in War," December 18, B1.

10.   *Birmingham* (AL) *News*, "Birmingham Youth on U.S.S. Arizona," December 17, 1941, 21.

11.   *Birmingham* (AL) *News*, "Tarrant Couple Told of Son's Death in Conflict With Japs," December 17, 1941, 22.

12.   *Birmingham* (AL) *News*, "Birmingham Negro is Killed in Action," December 17, 1941, 29.

13.   *Birmingham* (AL) *News*, "Julius Ellsberry," December 18, 1941, 14.

14.   *Christian Science Monitor*, "To the Future: A Tribute to U.S. War Hero," December 18, 1941, 1.

15.   United Press, "Hawaii Raid Inquiry Opens," *Los Angeles Times*, December 18, 1941, 1A.

16.   John G. Norris, "Nimitz Replaces Kimmel; Emmons Made Successor to Gen. Short," *Washington Post*, December 18, 1941, 1.

17.   William Manchester, *American Caesar: Douglas MacArthur 1880–1964* (New York: Little, Brown and Company, 1978), 149–152.

18.   Husband E. Kimmel, *Admiral Kimmel's Story* (Chicago: Henry Regnery Company, 1955), v.

19.   David Brinkley, *Washington Goes to War*, (New York: Alfred A. Knopf, 1988), 86.

20.   Richard M. Ketchum, *The Borrowed Years* (New York: Random House, 1989), 730.

21.   Mark S. Watson, "Three Highest Officers Relieved of Commands; Successors Appointed," *Baltimore Sun*, December 18, 1941, 1.

22.   United Press, "Two Generals Also Removed," *Los Angeles Times*, December 18, 1941, 1.

23.   Associated Press, "Army, Navy Oust Commanders in Charge During Hawaii Attack," *Atlanta Constitution*, December 18, 1941, 1.

24.   Walter Trohan, "Oust Pearl Harbor Chiefs," *Chicago Daily Tribune*, December 18, 1941, 1.

25.   Franklin Delano Roosevelt Presidential Library and Museum, "FDR: Day by Day—The Pare Lorentz Chronology," December 18, 1941.

26.   Associated Press, "Allies Occupy Portuguese Base as Japan Gains," *Christian Science Monitor*, December 18, 1941, 1.

27.   Associated Press, "Allies Occupy Portuguese Base as Japan Gains," *Christian Science Monitor*, December 18, 1941, 1.

28.   Frank Hewlett, "Motorized Force Lured to Trap; Foe's Casualties Heavy," *Washington Post*, December 18, 1941, 1.

29.   *Christian Science Monitor*, "Sarawak and North Borneo: Rich Lands in Vast Jungle," December 18, 1941, 6.

30. *Christian Science Monitor*, "Sarawak and North Borneo: Rich Lands in Vast Jungle," December 18, 1941, 6.

31. *Wall Street Journal*, "OPM 'Freezes' All U.S. Tin Supplies in Sweeping Control Over Imports and Deliveries; Year's Stock on Hand," December 18, 1941, 3.

32. *Wall Street Journal*, "U.S. Assumes Control of California's Oil Industry to Safeguard War Supplies," December 18, 1941, 2.

33. *Wall Street Journal*, "Laundry Machinery Firms Will Receive Large War Orders," December 18, 1941, 6.

34. *Wall Street Journal*, "Business Bulletin," December 18, 1941, 1.

35. *Washington Post*, "Storm Battered North California," December 18, 1941, 6.

36. *New York Times*, "Golf Ball Rush Causes Rationing," December 19, 1941, 27.

37. Bob Smyser, "Scene of Pro Bowl Game Shifted to New York," *Los Angeles Time*, December 19, 1941, 19.

38. *New York Times*, "Ship Is Here With Exiles," December 17, 1941, 24.

39. Associated Press, "6 Die as Navy Plane Crashes in No. Carolina," *Washington Post*, December 18, 1941, 7.

40. *Washington Post*, "Hunt Pressed for Plane Lost with General," December 19, 1941, 1.

41. Associated Press, "Submarine Attacked on Pacific Coast, General Discloses," *Los Angeles Times*, December 18, 1941, 1.

42. Franklin Delano Roosevelt Presidential Library and Museum, "Memorandum for the President from J.R. Beardall on Naval Aircraft Bombs," December 18, 1941, Hyde Park, NY.

43. Franklin Delano Roosevelt Presidential Library and Museum, "Memorandum for the President from J.R. Beardall on Naval Aircraft Bombs," December 18, 1941, Hyde Park, NY.

44. Associated Press, "Cubans Discover German Plot to Signal Planes," *Washington Post*, December 18, 1941, 2.

45. Hedley Donovan, "Conference at Rio Set for January 15," *Washington Post*, December 18, 1941, 5.

46. *Washington Evening Star*, "Defense Bond Sales Soar 146% in Week," December 18, 1941, D6.

47. Harlan V. Hadley, "Auto Series," *Wall Street Journal*, December 18, 1941, 5.

48. Harlan V. Hadley, "Auto Series," *Wall Street Journal*, December 18, 1941, 5.

49. *Christian Science Monitor*, "Status of Enemy Aliens Is Given by U.S. Attorney," December 18, 1941, 2.

50. *New York Times*, "Trade Promoter for Reich Seized," December 20, 1941, 7.

51. David Brinkley, *Washington Goes to War*, (New York: Alfred A. Knopf, 1988), 27.

52. *Christian Science Monitor*, "Status of Enemy Aliens Is Given by U.S. Attorney," December 18, 1941, 2.

53. *Christian Science Monitor*, "Status of Enemy Aliens Is Given by U.S. Attorney," December 18, 1941, 2.

54. *Christian Science Monitor*, "Status of Enemy Aliens Is Given by U.S. Attorney," December 18, 1941, 2.

55. *Christian Science Monitor*, "Status of Enemy Aliens Is Given by U.S. Attorney," December 18, 1941, 2.

56. *Lethbridge Herald* (Alberta, Canada), "Compulsory Registration of All Japanese Is Now Provided For," December 18, 1941, 13.

57. Associated Press, "1,035 Jap Boots Tied Up in British Columbia," *Washington Evening Star*, December 18, 1941, A20.

58. Associated Press, "FBI Seizes Jap Aide In Chicago," *Baltimore Sun*, December 18, 1941, 2.

59. David Brinkley, *Washington Goes to War*, (New York: Alfred A. Knopf, 1988), 87.

60. Associated Press, "Nazi Diplomats Held in Hotel," *Christian Science Monitor*, December 18, 1941, 9.

61. Associated Press, "Swiss Now Represent U.S. in All Belligerent Countries," *Christian Science Monitor* December 18, 1941, 9.

62. Associated Press, "Husbands of Working Wives Face Induction Into Army," *Christian Science Monitor*, December 18, 1941, 3.

63. Associated Press, "Husbands of Working Wives Face Induction Into Army," *Christian Science Monitor*, December 18, 1941, 3.

64. Associated Press, "Husbands of Working Wives Face Induction Into Army," *Christian Science Monitor*, December 18, 1941, 3.

65. Associated Press, "University to Credit Students in Services," *Christian Science Monitor*, December 18, 1941, 3.

66. United Press, "Japanese-Americans Enlist in U.S. Army," *Christian Science Monitor*, December 18, 1941, 3.

67. *Washington Post*, "Nurses May Be Drafted to Meet Greatest War-Time Demand in Nation's History," December 18, 1941, 9.

68. *Christian Science Monitor*, "Snapshots in Color for All," December 18, 1941, 8.

69. *Christian Science Monitor*, "Toy Makers Race to Fill Yule Orders," December 18, 1941, 5.

CHAPTER 19: THE NINETEENTH OF DECEMBER

1. Associated Press, "Allies are Holding Conferences," *Lethbridge Herald* (Alberta, Canada), December 19, 1941, 1.

2. Franklin Delano Roosevelt Presidential Library and Museum, "Memorandum of Agreement: Supreme War Council," December, 19, 1941, Hyde Park, NY, 1–4.

3. Franklin Delano Roosevelt Presidential Library and Museum, "Memorandum of Agreement: Supreme War Council," 1-4, December, 19, 1941, Hyde Park, NY, 1.

4. *Washington Post*, "Nimitz, War Chiefs Map New Strategy," December 19, 1941, 2.

5. International News Service, "The President's Day," *Washington Post*, December 19, 1941, 2.

6. *Los Angeles Times*, "Camps in West to House Aliens," December 19, 1941, 9.

7. *Christian Science Monitor*, "Enemy Aliens Will Be Kept in Camps in the Southwest," December 19, 1941, 8.

8. *Christian Science Monitor*, "Enemy Aliens Will Be Kept in Camps in the Southwest," December 19, 1941, 8.

9. *Los Angeles Times*, "Roundup of Axis Aliens Jails 442," December 19, 1941, 8.

10. *Christian Science Monitor*, "Enemy Aliens Will Be Kept in Camps in the Southwest," December 19, 1941, 8.

11. *Washington Post*, "Laura Ingalls Jailed in D.C. as Nazi Agent," December 19, 1941, 1.

12. *Washington Post*, "Laura Ingalls Jailed in D.C. as Nazi Agent," December 19, 1941, 1.

13. Royal Arch Gunnison, "Japanese to Find Navy Using Offensive Defense in Far East," *Washington Evening Star*, December 18, 1941, A21.

14. *Lethbridge Herald* (Alberta, Canada), "War Shots from Far East: Manila," December 19, 1941, 5.

15. Associated Press, "Hit-and-Run Planes Raid Vital Area," *Baltimore Sun*, December 19, 1941, 1.

16. Associated Press, "U.S. Subs Sink Transport, Torpedo Jap Destroyer," *Boston Globe*, December 19, 1941, 1.

17. Canadian Press, "News Contact With Island Now Cut Off," *Lethbridge Herald* (Alberta, Canada), December 19, 1941, 1.

18. Associated Press, "Japs Meanwhile Strike Fierce New Blows in Pacific," *Birmingham* (AL) *News*, December 18, 1941, 1.

19. *New York Times*, "Japanese Advance in Malayan Drive," December 19, 1941, 6.

20. Franklin Delano Roosevelt Presidential Library and Museum, "Memorandum from Dillon to FDR," Box 2, a1bb01, December 19, 1941, Hyde Park, NY.

21. *Christian Science Monitor*, "British Garrison Evacuates Penang; Cavite and Wake Attacked Again; U.S. Troops reported at Singapore," December 19, 1941, 1.

22. *New York Times*, "American Flier Crashed His Plane Into Enemy Ship Off Philippines," December 19, 1941, 6.

23. *Christian Science Monitor,* "Two Cruisers, Destroyer Lost By Italians," December 19, 1941, 7.

24. Jack B. Beardwood, Associated Press, "If Canal Is Bombed—Pacific War Focuses New Attention on Historic Straits of Magellan," *Washington Post,* December 19, 1941, 9.

25. United Press, "Macarthur Is Nominated for General's Rank," *Yuma* (AZ) *Daily Sun,* December 19, 1941, 1.

26. *Washington Post,* "MacArthur's Promotion," December 21, 1941, 6.

27. Associated Press, "Dogfish Harassed Dunedin Survivors," *Washington Post,* December 19, 1941, 12.

28. Edward Shorter, *Bedside Manners* (New York: Simon and Schuster, 1985), 181.

29. Paul Mallon, "Civilian Life Change Seen in 60 Days," *Hartford Courant,* December 18, 1941, 3.

30. *Boston Globe,* "Eels for Hyphenated Americans Arrive to Christmas Marts," December 19, 1941, 12.

31. *Lethbridge Herald* (Alberta, Canada), "War Dries Up Imported Liquers," December 19, 1941, 2.

32. *Los Angeles Times,* "Fake Wardens Hit for Tactics in Blackout," December 18, 1941, 6.

33. *Los Angeles Times,* "Crack Riflemen Form Corps of Minute Men," December 18, 1941, Part II-5.

34. *Washington Post,* "First Official U.S. War Poster," December 19, 1941, 10.

35. *New York Times,* "Poster Depicting Army Pursuit Ship Wins 'Keep 'Em Flying' Contest to Aid Recruiting," December 19, 1941, 5.

36. *Washington Post,* "Need Stressed for Chaplains," December 19, 1941, 16.

37. *Washington Post,* "Catholics Back 'War for Peace,'" December 19, 1941, 16.

38. *Washington Evening Star,* "Pictures," December 18, 1941, A10.

39. David Lawrence, "Money Dims Halo About New Dealers," *Washington Evening Star,* December 18, 1941, D8.

40. Robert De Vore, "Firm With $42,500 Capital Shared $34,000,000 War Jobs," *Washington Post,* December 19, 1941, 1.

41. Harold Heffernan, "A Moving Performance: Stars Applaud Jimmy Stewart's Bill of Rights Radio Stint," *Washington Evening* Star, December 18, 1941, D4.

42. *Wall Street Journal,* "Washington Wire," December 19, 1941, 1.

43. Charles Hurd, "Army Will Close Volunteer Rolls," *New York Times,* December 19, 1941, 5.

44. *Baltimore Sun,* "Men and Women Stenographers Sought for War Office Jobs," December 19, 1941, 7.

45. *Baltimore Sun,* "Senate Passes 19-to-45 Draft With Only Two Dissenting," December 19, 1941, 12.

46. *Christian Science Monitor,* "North Carolina Town Entertains the Army," December 19, 1941, 3.

47. Harold Martin, "Doesn't Take Book Learning to Shoot a Rifle, Says York," *Atlanta Constitution,* December 19, 1941, 8.

48. Ruth Cowan, Associated Press, "Roosevelts to Have Christmas as Usual Despite A.A. Guns," *Birmingham* (AL) *News,* December 19, 1941, 49.

49. *Birmingham* (AL) *News,* "More Alabamians Killed in Jap War," December 19, 1941, 51.

50. *Wall Street Journal,* "Future of Television Discussed in Capital," December 19, 1941, 6.

51. *Christian Science Monitor,* "State Governments Mobilize Strength Behind War Effort," December 19, 1941, 1.

52. *New York Times,* "Wire Control Approved," December 19, 1941, 6.

53. Associated Press, "Senators Urge Daylight Savings," *New York Times,* December 19, 1941, 4.

54. *New York Times,* "Laws To Enforce Blackouts Urged," December 19, 1941, 18.

55. *New York Times,* "Mayor Off to Washington; Defense Job Under Fire," December 19, 1941, 22.

56. United Press, "War Costing U.S. $729 Per Second; Next Year, $1400," *Yuma* (AZ) *Daily Sun,* December 19, 1941, 1.

57. Louis M. Lyons, "New England Colleges Move to War Footing," *Boston Evening Globe,* December 19, 1941, 5.

58. Associated Press, "30 Minutes Warning and Japs Would Have Lost at Honolulu," *Birmingham* (AL) *News,* December 19, 1941, 1.

59. United Press, "Know Warns Japs Have Largest Naval Force in Western Pacific," *Yuma* (AL) *Daily Sun*, December 19, 1941, 1.

CHAPTER 20: THE TWENTIETH OF DECEMBER

1. *Boston Evening Globe*, "Hong Kong Doomed," December 20, 1941, 1.
2. Winston Churchill, *The Gathering Storm* (New York: Rosetta Books, 2002), 562.
3. *Boston Daily Globe*, "Flying Santa Claus Grounded by War," December 20, 1941, 6.
4. Franklin Delano Roosevelt Library and Museum, "Memorandum For The President from the Director of the Selective Service Regarding Men in Defense-Related Jobs, Recruiting and the Draft," December 20, 1941, Hyde Park, NY.
5. Franklin Delano Roosevelt Library and Museum, "Summary of Report on Program For Loyal West Coast Japanese from John Franklin Carter," December 19, 1941, Hyde Park, NY.
6. Franklin Delano Roosevelt Library and Museum, "Secretary of the Navy Knox to President Roosevelt Regarding Trans-Pacific Netherlands Shipping," December 20, 1941, Hyde Park, NY.
7. Franklin Delano Roosevelt Library and Museum, "Memorandum Regarding Sharing Information From Moscow Between London and Washington," December 20, 1941, Hyde Park, NY.
8. Franklin Delano Roosevelt Library and Museum, "Memorandum Regarding the Soviet Post-War Desire to Expand into the Baltic States and Further West," December 20, 1941, Hyde Park, NY.
9. Franklin Delano Roosevelt Library and Museum, "Memorandum from the Office of the Legal Advisor of the State Department Regarding Legalities Surrounding Declarations of War and Peace," December 20, 1941, Hyde Park, NY.
10. *Baltimore Sun*, "Bares Axis Spying in Latin America," December 20, 1941, 9.
11. Associated Press, "Thousands of Enemy Agents Are Active in Southern Continent," *Atlanta Constitution*, December 20, 1941, 1, 87
12. *Boston Evening Globe*, "United Press Editors Place Soviet War High," December 20, 1941, 1.
13. Associated Press, "Marshall, Wife Get Full Custody of Girls," *Washington Post*, December 20, 1941, 15.
14. Associated Press, "National Debt Tops 57 Billion," *Los Angeles Times*, December 20, 1941, 2.
15. *Washington Evening Star*, "Workers Are Wanted to Help Fix Damage at Pearl Harbor," December 19, 1941, B1.
16. *New York Times*, "Plant to Produce New Dive Bombers," December 19, 1941, 17.
17. *Washington Post*, "Navy Seizes Scarce Materials Worth a Million," December 20, 1941, 15.
18. *Washington Evening Star*, "Navy Takes Over Four of Gulf's Finest Yachts," December 20, 1941, 16.
19. *Wall Street Journal*, "Roosevelt's Powers Already Greater Than Any Previous President's With More On the Way," December 20, 1941, 1.
20. *Wall Street Journal*, "Streamlining of OPM Activities to Speed Arms Work Taking Form," December 20, 1941, 4.
21. *Washington Post*, "Many More to Go; Government Will Aid Those Moving," December 20, 1941, 1.
22. *Washington Post*, "Senior Scouts Start Civilian Defense Move," December 20, 1941, 15.
23. *New York Times*, "Air Training Plan for U.S. Boys Seen," December 20, 1941, 5.
24. *Washington Post*, "D.C. Committee of 70 Set Up to Direct Salvage of Scrap," December 20, 1941, 17.
25. *New York Times*, "Blind Now Aiding Defense Program," December 19, 1941, 21.
26. Associated Press, "Coast Harbor Defender Calls For Dog Recruits," *Baltimore Sun*, December 20, 1941, 8.
27. *New York Times*, "Public Notices and Commercial Notices," December 19, 1941, 2.
28. *New York Times*, "Japanese Bomb Philippine Port," December 19, 1941, 4.

29. *Yuma Daily Sun*, "San Quentin Men Volunteer for Suicide Squad," December 20, 1941, 1.
30. *Wall Street Journal*, "Factories to Hum on Christmas Day Where Operations Aid War Effort," December 20, 1941, 2.
31. Associated Press, "Christmas in Honolulu," *Baltimore Sun*, December 20, 1941, 4.
32. Associated Press, "Christmas in Honolulu," *Baltimore Sun*, December 20, 1941, 4.
33. *Wall Street Journal*, "Industrial Output Up, Reserve Board Says; BAE Forecasts Rise in '42 Buying Power," December 20, 1941, 2.
34. *Wall Street Journal*, "Spiegel Adopts New Sales Policy; Adds Credit Service Charge," December 20, 1941, 3.
35. *Wall Street Journal*, "Shirley Temple Again," December 20, 1941, 7.
36. *Lethbridge Herald*, "War Shots From Here and There," December 20, 1941, 12.
37. *Lethbridge Herald*, "War Shots From Here and There," December 20, 1941, 12.
38. *Wall Street Journal*, "What's News," December 20, 1941, 1.
39. *Baltimore Sun*, "British Take Derna Airport in Quick Sally," December 20, 1941, 3.
40. *Baltimore Sun*, "German Division Wipe Out, Reds Say; Other Casualties Inflicted," December 20, 1941, 1.
41. *Yuma Daily Sun*, "American Pilots Down Four Jap Bombers, China," December 20, 1941, 1.
42. *Washington Post*, "Embattled Wake Fights Off 2 More Jap Air Attacks," December 20, 1941, 1.
43. *Boston Sunday Globe*, "MacArthur's Army," December 21, 1941, 8.
44. *Baltimore Sun*, "New Marine Poster Will Be Out Next Week," December 20, 1941, 3.
45. *Baltimore Sun*, "Thinks He Knows Causes of Physical Defects," December 20, 1941, 9.
46. Associated Press, "Navy and Marine Corps Relax Recruiting Rules," *Los Angeles Times*, December 20, 1941, 5.
47. *Boston Sunday Globe*, "MacArthur's Army," December 21, 1941, 8.
48. Associated Press, "More U.S. War Aid Sought by Quezon," *Baltimore Sun*, December 20, 1941, 9.
49. *Boston Sunday Globe*, "MacArthur's Army," December 21, 1941, 3.
50. Associated Press, "Jap Fifth Columnists Do It With Mirrors," *Washington Post*, December 20, 1941, 3.
51. International News Service, "The President's Day," *Washington Post*, December 20, 1941, 2.
52. *Washington Post*, "Hull Denies He Asked Navy to Lift Patrol," December 20, 1941, 1.
53. *Washington Post*, "Hull Denies He Asked Navy to Lift Patrol," December 20, 1941, 4.

CHAPTER 21: THE TWENTY-FIRST OF DECEMBER

1. *Hartford Courant*, "Enemy Subs Active off East, West Coasts," December 21, 1941, 1.
2. Joseph J. Cloud, "Enemy Subs Lurking off Bothe U.S. Coasts; Two Vessels Attacked in California Waters; Adm. King Named Chief of All Our Naval Forces," *Washington Post*, December 21, 1941, 1.
3. *Los Angeles Times*, "Jap Subs Raid California Ships," December 21, 1941, 1.
4. Foster Hailey, "West Coast Eyes South for Enemy," *New York Times*, December 22, 1941, 3.
5. Foster Hailey, "West Coast Eyes South for Enemy," *New York Times*, December 22, 1941, 3.
6. Foster Hailey, "West Coast Eyes South for Enemy," *New York Times*, December 22, 1941, 3.
7. Joseph J. Cloud, "Enemy Subs Lurking off Bothe U.S. Coasts; Two Vessels Attacked in California Waters; Adm. King Named Chief of All Our Naval Forces," *Washington Post*, December 21, 1941, 1.
8. Associated Press, "Gen. MacArthur Out of Touch With Davao Defenders," *Boston Daily Globe*, December 21, 1941, 1.
9. Associated Press, "Davao Cut Off by Jap Air and Land Attack," *Chicago Daily Tribune*, December 21, 1941, 6.
10. Associated Press, "Bolo-Swinging Moros Rally to Fight Japs," *Boston Daily Globe*, December 21, 1941, A10.
11. *Chicago Daily Tribune*, "Reveal 20 Jap Ships Engaged in Philippine Raid," December 21, 1941, 8.
12. United Press, "Japanese Wreck Ship at Guam," *Los Angeles Times*, December 21, 1941, 1A.

13. Associated Press, "Fight of British for Hongkong Wins Jap Praise," *Chicago Daily Tribune*, December 21, 1941, 6.
14. *Washington Post*, "Allies Merge to Preserve Singapore," December 21, 1941, 4.
15. *Washington Post*, "Allies Merge to Preserve Singapore," December 21, 1941, 4.
16. Arthur Griffin, "Guns Over Boston," *Boston Daily Globe*, December 21, 1941, B7.
17. Harry W. Hannery, "Germany Faces a Five-Year War," *Saturday Evening Post*, December 20, 1941, 6.
18. Terry Goldsworthy, *Valhalla's Warriors: A History of the Waffen-SS on the Eastern Front 1941–1945* (Indianapolis, IN: Dog Ear Publishing, 2010), 231.
19. International News Service, "Capt. Kelly Gave Life to Save Flaming Bomber's Crew of 6," *Washington Post*, December 21, 1941, 1.
20. Associated Press, "Burma Road: American Flyers Down 4 Jap Planes in First Battle for Chinese," *Boston Daily Globe*, December 21, 1941, A9.
21. Joseph L. Myler, "Supreme Council on War Planned," *Washington Post*, December 21, 1941, 5.
22. Franklin Delano Roosevelt Presidential Library and Museum, "Telegram From Thurston to Hull," December 21, 1941, Hyde Park, NY.
23. James B. Reston, "Allies Link Plans in Talks This Week," *New York Times*, December 22, 1941, 1.
24. James B. Reston, "Allies Link Plans in Talks This Week," *New York Times*, December 22, 1941, 1.
25. *New York Times*, "Spartan Days Face Us, Willkie Warns," December 21, 1941, 13.
26. Associated Press, "Willkie Boosters Suspend for War," *Washington Post*, December 22, 1941, 6.
27. *Washington Post*, "Martin Puts Off GOP Meetings Because of War," December 22, 1941, 18.
28. W. H. Lawrence, "Britain-U.S. Confer," *New York Times*, December 21, 1941, 1.
29. Russell Hill, "Arab Cheers Greet British at Derna," *Washington Post*, December 21, 1941, 10.
30. *Baltimore Sun*, "McNutt Asks Nation to Conserve Its Food," December 20, 1941, 8.
31. Associated Press, "Price of Sugar Is 'Frozen' at Current Level," *Chicago Daily Tribune*, December 21, 1941, 1.
32. Associated Press, "Chicago Flag Trade Booms," *Washington Post*, December 21, 1941, S6.
33. George Gallup, "Defense Labor Ready to Work Longer Hours," *Washington Post*, December 21, 1941, B5.
34. *New York Times*, "Effort of States in War Expanded," December 20, 1941, 9.
35. Gerald G. Gross, "Washington in Wartime," *Washington Post*, December 21, 1941, B3.
36. *Baltimore Sun*, "Plants Under Control of Axis Nationals Seized," December 20, 1941, 8.
37. *Chicago Daily Tribune*, "Ships, More Ships Launched to Aid U.S. War on Seas," December 21, 1941, 3.
38. *Chicago Daily Tribune*, "Makers of War Needs to Work Christmas Day," December 20, 1941, 23.
39. Jack Bell, "Criticism in Order Still, Senators Say," *Washington Post*, December 21, 1941, 13.
40. *Chicago Daily Tribune*, "'U.S. Will Regain Pacific Control'—Col. M'Cormick," December 21, 1941, 4.
41. *Chicago Daily Tribune*, "Japanese Tricks," December 21, 1941, 14.
42. *Boston Daily Globe*, "There's No Better Gift Than an Album of Columbia Records," December 21, 1941, C8.
43. *Washington Post*, "Gay Caroling Ushers in Christmas Week," December 22, 1941, 6.
44. *Leithbridge Herald* (Alberta, Canada), "How Would You Like to Bomb Germany?" December 22, 1941, 2.
45. *Washington Post*, "Board Selects 'Citizen Kane' As Best Movie of the Year," December 22, 1941, 7.
46. *Chicago Daily Tribune*, "Buy Defense Bonds," December 21, 1941, 14.
47. *Chicago Daily Tribune*, "350 Licenses to Wed Issued in Day, A Record," December 21, 1941, 16.
48. *Lethbridge Herald* (Alberta, Canada), "Christmas Mail Sets Record," December 22, 1941, 6.
49. Associated Press, "Son Is Not Dead, Navy Apologizes; Gloom Vanishes," *Boston Daily Globe*, December 21, 1941, A9.

50. United Press, "Navy to Give Yule Leave to All of Its Recruits," *New York Times*, December 21, 1941, 13.

51. *Washington Evening Star*, "Admiral King New Chief of U.S. Fleet," December 20, 1941, 1.

52. Associated Press, "Air Man Given New Navy Post; Outranks Stark," *Boston Daily Globe*, December 21, 1941, C1.

53. Marshall Andrews, "New Head Noted for Strategy; Ingersoll Gets Atlantic Post," *Washington Post*, December 21, 1941, 1.

54. Marshall Andrews, "New Head Noted for Strategy; Ingersoll Gets Atlantic Post," *Washington Post*, December 21, 1941, 1.

55. Gerald G. Gross, "Washington in Wartime," *Washington Post*, December 21, 1941, B3.

CHAPTER 22: THE TWENTY-SECOND OF DECEMBER

1. *Washington Post*, "Biddle Appoints Alien Enemy Board for D.C.," December 21, 1941, 18.

2. *Washington Post*, "Biddle Appoints Alien Enemy Board for D.C.," December 21, 1941, 18.

3. *New York Times*, "Hawaii Holds 273 as 5th Columnists," December 22, 1941, 4.

4. *Washington Post*, "Enemy Aliens," December 22, 1941, 12.

5. *New York Times*, "The Slanting Eye," December 22, 1941, 16.

6. *New York Times*, "Gun Battle Routs Coast Saboteurs," December 22, 1941, 3.

7. *Los Angeles Times*, "Car Believed Used by Gunmen Against Soldiers Located," December 22, 1941, A1.

8. Franklin Delano Roosevelt Presidential Library and Museum, "Full Report on Program For Dealing With West Coast Japanese Problem," December 22, 1941, Hyde Park, NY.

9. Franklin Delano Roosevelt Presidential Library and Museum, "FDR: Day by Day—The Pare Lorentz Chronology," December 22, 1941, Hyde Park, NY.

10. *Life*, "How To Tell Japs From The Chinese," December 22, 1941, 81.

11. *Life*, "How To Tell Japs From The Chinese," December 22, 1941, 81.

12. *Washington Evening Star*, "Patent Office Removal Assailed as Costly And Unwise by Congress Leaders and Lawyers," December 21, 1941, 1.

13. Jerry Kluttz, "Several Agencies to Remain Permanently From Capital," *Washington Post*, December 22, 1941, 1.

14. Scott Hart, "Raid Alarm Test Works Well, Except for Sirens," *Washington Post*, December 22, 1941, 1.

15. *Washington Post*, "Yesterday's Fiasco," December 22, 1941, 12.

16. Blair Bolles, "Press No Longer Wholly Free Under War Censorship Order," *Washington Evening Star*, December 21, 1941, 10.

17. Associated Press, "Broadcasters Adopt Guide for Handling America's War News," *Birmingham* (AL) *News*, December 22, 1941, 8.

18. *New York Times*, "Radio to Outlaw Rumors on War," December 22, 1941, 14.

19. Associated Press, "She's Looking for a Jap," *Washington Post*, December 22, 1941, 8.

20. *Yuma* (AZ) *Daily Sun*, "Local Fliers Are Grounded by CAA," December 22, 1941, 1.

21. *Life*, "Japanese Planes; How to Identify Enemy Craft That Might Attack the U.S.," December 22, 1941.

22. Associated Press, "U.S. Vessels Are Attached," *Lethbridge Herald* (Alberta, Canada), December 22, 1941, 1.

23. United Press, "30 Survivors of Tanker Reach Coast; Freighter Sunk Dec. 11," *Yuma* (AZ) *Daily News*, December 22, 1941, 1.

24. United Press, "30 Survivors of Tanker Reach Coast; Freighter Sunk Dec. 11," *Yuma* (AZ) *Daily News*, December 22, 1941, 1.

25. Associated Press, "U.S. Tanker Captain Tries to Ram Sub," *Washington Post*, December 22, 1941, 2.

26. Associated Press, "Reports Received of Enemy U-Boats off The West Coast," *Nevada Mail*, December 22, 1941, 8.

27. Walter V. Nessly, "14 U-Boats Sunk or Hit in Atlantic Knox Says," *Washington Post*, December 22, 1941, 1.

28. Walter V. Nessly, "14 U-Boats Sunk or Hit in Atlantic Knox Says," *Washington Post*, December 22, 1941, 1.

29. Marshall Andrews, "Survivors of U.S. Ship Are Shelled," *Washington Post*, December 22, 1941, 2.

30. Associated Press, "Tokyo Claims Navy Has Sunk 9 Enemy Subs," *Washington Post*, December 22, 1941, 8.

31. Associated Press, "Japs May Have 40 Subs Able to Reach U.S.," *Washington Post*, December 22, 1941, 2.

32. Associated Press, "Japs May Have 40 Subs Able to Reach U.S.," *Washington Post*, December 22, 1941, 2.

33. Clark Lee, Associated Press, "Japs Try Big Landing Near Manila," *Lethbridge Herald* (Alberta, Canada), December 22, 1941, 1.

34. Associated Press, "U.S. Forces Ready For Attack; Control of Islands at Stake," *Washington Post*, December 22, 1941, 1.

35. H. Ford Wilkins, Copyright by the *New York Times*, "Bombing of Quezon's Home Solidifies Filipinos for U.S.," *Washington Post*, December 22, 1941, 8.

36. *Time*, "The U.S. At War," December 22, 1941, 10.

37. United Press, "King George Sends Defenders Praise and Encouragement," *Washington Post*, December 22, 1941, 8.

38. United Press, "King George Sends Defenders Praise and Encouragement," *Washington Post*, December 22, 1941, 8.

39. Associated Press, "British in Malaya Smash at Japanese from New Positions," *Washington Evening Star*, December 22, 1941, A4.

40. *Washington Post*, "Heroes on Wake Hold Firm Despite Two New Attacks," December 22, 1941, 1.

41. Associated Press, "Nazis Execute 5 Jews in Occupied France," *Boston Daily Globe*, December 22, 1941, 26.

42. Associated Press, "Germany Pulling Troops Out of Occupied Norway, Sending Them to Russia And Libya," *Lethbridge Herald* (Alberta, Canada), December 22, 1941, 5.

43. Daniel T. Brigham, "Brauchitsch Is Out," *New York Times*, December 22, 1941, 1.

44. International News Service, "Sailor Still Lives, Parents Learn After Rites Are Held," *Washington Post*, December 21, 1941, 5.

45. Associated Press, "Parents of Son Killed in World War Lose 2 More at Pearl Harbor," *Baltimore Sun*, December 22, 1941, 3.

46. Associated Press, "Town Mourns Deaths of Three Brothers in Honolulu Attack," *Birmingham* (AL) *News*, December 22, 1941, 13.

47. *Birmingham* (AL) *News*, "Youth Would Avenge Death of His Brother," December 21, 1941, 1.

48. Associated Press, "Birthday Felicitations For Stalin, This Time By Allies, Not Hitler," *Baltimore Sun*, December 22, 1941, 11.

49. *Birmingham* (AL) *News*, "Alabama Press," December 22, 1941, 12.

50. Associated Press, "General Sales Tax Proposal Gains in Favor," *Washington Post*, December 22, 1941, 1.

51. Associated Press, "General Sales Tax Proposal Gains in Favor," *Washington Post*, December 22, 1941, 1.

52. *Washington Post*, "Public Told What Foods It Should Stock," December 22, 1941, 6.

53. Jane Driscoll, "No Glove Shortage Is Foreseen, But Wise Buying Is Advised," *Washington Post*, December 22, 1941, 15.

54. *Washington Post*, "New Research Shows Food Value of Milk," December 22, 1941, 15.

55. *Birmingham* (AL) *News*, "What Every Woman Wants to Know About a Man," December 22, 1941, 3.

56. United Press, "Makes 'War Tires' For 35 M.P.H. Tops," *New York Times*, December 22, 1941, 7.
57. Associated Press, "'War Tire' Ready for Market, But Don't Drive Over 35," *Washington Post*, December 22, 1941, 6.

CHAPTER 23: THE TWENTY-THIRD OF DECEMBER

1. Associated Press, "What? A War? Dixie 'Cracker' Rarin' to Crack a 'Danged Jap,'" *Atlanta Constitution*, December 22, 1941, 5.
2. United Press, "28,363 Join Army In 2 Weeks After War Declaration," *Yuma (AZ) Daily Sun*, December 23, 1941, 1.
3. *Washington Post*, "Sen. Truman's Ready for Army, But Army's Not Ready for Him," December 22, 1941, 8.
4. *Los Angeles Times*, "Women May Drive Taxis," December 22, 1941, 16.
5. Associated Press, "Prison Labor Urged for Use on war Goods," *Atlanta Constitution*, December 22, 1941, 8.
6. Associated Press, "Former Steelers Star Dudley Dies at 88," ESPN NFL, February 4, 2010. http://sports.espn.go.com/nfl/news/ story?id=4887025&campaign=rss&source=NFLHeadlines.
7. Associated Press, "Miller of 'Four Horsemen' Named U.S. Attorney," *Washington Evening Star*, December 23, 1941, A2.
8. Ibid.
9. *New York Herald-Tribune*, "35,000 Press Agents," *Birmingham (AL) News*, December 23, 1941, 6.
10. Walter Winchell, "Walter Winchell: Man About Town," *Birmingham (AL) News*, December 23, 1941, 6.
11. *Atlanta Constitution*, "Margaret Mitchell En Route for Commissioning of Atlanta," December 23, 1941, 6.
12. Associated Press, "Subs Sink U.S. Tanker," *Lethbridge Herald* (Alberta, Canada), December 23, 1941, 2.
13. Associated Press, "Subs Sink U.S. Tanker," *Lethbridge Herald* (Alberta, Canada), December 23, 1941, 2.
14. Associated Press, "Heavy Gunfire Heard Off California Coast," *Birmingham (AL) News*, December 23, 1941, 1.
15. *Los Angeles Times*, "Freighter's Smoke Causes Alarm Along Coast Cities," December 22, 1941, 1.
16. *Los Angeles Times*, "Four Lose Lives Serving Country," December 22, 1941, B16.
17. *Birmingham (AL) News*, "War Victim," December 22, 1941, 14.
18. *Los Angeles Times*, "Eagle Rock Holds Memorial For Lieut. Comdr. Michael," December 22, 1941, 8.
19. *Los Angeles Times*, "Sons of 'Times' Man Missing," December 22, 1941, Part I, 8.
20. Tom Yarbrough, Associated Press, "Japs Not Suicidal at Pearl Harbor, Witnesses Declare," *Washington Post*, December 23, 1941, 5.
21. Tom Yarbrough, Associated Press, "Japs Not Suicidal at Pearl Harbor, Witnesses Declare," *Washington Post*, December 23, 1941, 5.
22. Associated Press, "U.S. Pilot Fired On By Jap Flyers While 'Chuting from Sky," *Baltimore Sun*, December 23, 1941, 3.
23. Associated Press, "U.S. Flyer Is Saved From Savage When They See His Hair," *Baltimore Sun*, December 23, 1941, 4.
24. Frank L. Kluckhohn, "2 Leaders Confer," *New York Times*, December 22, 1941, 1.
25. Associated Press, "Churchill In Washington Big Surprise," *Lethbridge Herald* (Alberta, Canada), December 23, 1941, 1.
26. Associated Press, "Nazis Placed Churchill in Middle East," *Boston Daily Globe*, December 23, 1941, 3.
27. United Press, "Steve Early's Desk Will Never Look the Same Again," *Boston Evening Globe*, December 23, 1941, 26.

28. Associated Press, "Churchill Wears Life Saver's Garb," *New York Times*, December 23, 1941, 5.
29. Associated Press, "Leaders of Democracy at White House to Plan War Against Axis," *New York Times*, December 23, 1941, 16.
30. Dewey L. Fleming, "Prime Minister Makes Sudden, Dramatic Trip; Parleys Start at Once," *Baltimore Sun*, December 23, 1941, 1.
31. Associated Press Photo, *Washington Post*, December 23, 1947, 16.
32. *Washington Evening Star*, "Churchill Says Allies Plan Complete Unity of Action in Pacific," December 23, 1941, A6 continued from A1.
33. Jon Meacham, *Franklin and Winston: An Intimate Portrait of an Epic Friendship* (New York: Random House, 2003), xii.
34. *New York Times*, "The Day in Washington," December 23, 1941, 5.
35. Franklin Delano Roosevelt Presidential Library and Museum, "Memorandum From FDR to Jack Carter on The Summary of Preliminary Intelligence Problems in New York Area," December 23, 1941, Hyde Park, New York.
36. International News Service, "The President's Day," *Washington Post*, December 23, 1941, 2.
37. Associated Press Wirephoto Caption, "Discussing War Strategy," *Boston Evening Globe*, December 23, 1941, 23.
38. International News Service, "The President's Day," *Washington Post*, December 24, 1941, 2.
39. Associated Press, "Japs Meanwhile Effect Landing On Wake Island," *Birmingham* (AL) *News*, December 23, 1941, 1.
40. *Washington Post*, "Hongkong's Valiant Defenders Sink Two Ships; Siege Goes On," December 24, 1941, 2.
41. Associated Press, "Japs Obtained No Oil From Borneo Wells," *Baltimore Sun*, December 23, 1941, 4.
42. *Atlanta Constitution*, "Japs Hurled Into Sea by Luzon Defenders," December 23, 1941, 1.
43. United Press, "Resists Invaders," *New York Times*, December 23, 1941, 2. (Dateline: December 22, 1941).
44. Associated Press, "U.S. Mechanized Forces Rushed Into Luzon Battle," *Birmingham* (AL) *News*, December 23, 1941, 1.
45. Franklin Delano Roosevelt Presidential Library, "Radiogram from Manila to the Adjutant General," December 22, 1941, Hyde Park, NY.
46. *Time*, "The U.S. at War," December 22, 1941, 10.
47. *New York Times*, "Last Guam Message Received on Dec. 10," December 23, 1941, 3.
48. Dr. George Gallup, "The Gallup Poll: Germany Considered Greater Threat to U.S. Thank Japan, Survey of Attitudes Shows," *Washington Post*, December 23, 1947, 2.
49. International News Service, "British Carrier Sunk in Atlantic By Sub, Nazis Say," *Washington Post*, December 23, 1941, 4.
50. Canadian Press, "Casualties of Canadians Said 'Heavy,'" *Lethbridge Herald* (Alberta, Canada), December 23, 1941, 1.
51. United Press, "Gallant Few Still Hold Out at Hongkong," *Washington Post*, December 23, 1941, 1.
52. Associated Press, "British in Hongkong Still Fighting, They Report by Radio to Chungking: Communication Maintained," *New York Times*, December 23, 1941, 4.
53. Frank Oliver, "Prize of War: Hong Kong, Garden of South China," *Washington Post*, December 23, 1941, 19.
54. Associated Press, "Churchill in Washington; Confers With Roosevelt," *Atlanta Constitution*, December 23, 1941, 1.
55. Lloyd Lehrbas, Associated Press, "Introducing Winston Churchill," *Birmingham* (AL) *News*, December 23, 1941, 5.
56. Jon Meacham, *Franklin and Winston* (New York: Random House, 2003), 42.
57. Jon Meacham, *Franklin and Winston* (New York: Random House, 2003), 8.
58. Lloyd Lehrbas, "Introducing Winston Churchill," *Birmingham* (AL) *News*, December 23, 1941, 5.

59. *Washington Post*, "President Asks Country to Pray," December 23, 1941, 4.
60. *Time Magazine*, "The U.S. at War, Full Blast," December 22, 1941, 9.
61. *New York Times*, "No Strikes in War, Spellman Pleads," December 22, 1941, 15.
62. *New York Times*, "No Strikes in War, Spellman Pleads," December 22, 1941, 15.
63. *New York Times*, "Four Freedoms Aim of War Hit by Taft," May 26, 1943, 20.
64. Associated Press, "Fall Schedule Helps Ease Worry For Mrs. Roosevelt," *Sarasota* (FL) *Herald-Tribune*, December 23, 1941, 6.
65. *Washington Post*, "Photo," December 24, 1941, 5.
66. Associated Press, "White House to Have Turkey and Trimmin's," *Los Angeles Times*, December 25, 1941, 10.
67. John C. Henry, "Round Table Talks By War Council to Fix Command," *Washington Evening Star*, December 23, 1941, 1.
68. John C. Henry, "Roosevelt and Churchill Mix Showmanship With Democracy," *Washington Evening Star*, December 24, 1941, A3.
69. John C. Henry, "Roosevelt and Churchill Mix Showmanship With Democracy," *Washington Evening Star*, December 24, 1941, A3.
70. Frank L. Kluckhohn, "Churchill Talks," *New York Times*, December 24, 1941, 4 continued from page 1.
71. John C. Henry, "Roosevelt and Churchill Mix Showmanship With Democracy," *Washington Evening Star*, December 24, 1941, A3.
72. John C. Henry, "Roosevelt and Churchill Mix Showmanship With Democracy," *Washington Evening Star*, December 24, 1941, A3.
73. International News Service, "The President's Day," *Washington Post*, December 24, 1941, 2.
74. John C. Henry, "Roosevelt and Churchill Mix Showmanship With Democracy," *Washington Evening Star*, December 24, 1941, A3.
75. John C. Henry, "Roosevelt and Churchill Mix Showmanship With Democracy," *Washington Evening Star*, December 24, 1941, A3.
76. Associated Press, "Transportation Office Created," *Los Angeles Times*, December 24, 1941, 4.
77. Frank L. Kluckhohn, "2 Leaders Confer," *New York Times*, December 23, 1941, 1.
78. United Press, "F.D. and Churchill Divide War Into 4 Major Actions," *Boston Evening Globe*, December 23, 1941, 3.
79. *Washington Evening Star*, "Churchill, President Studying War Roles For Other Allies," December 24, 1941, 1.
80. Associated Press, "'War Council' to Confer with Churchill: Allied Chieftains Discuss Means of Crushing Axis," *Birmingham* (AL) *News*, December 23, 1941, 1.
81. Associated Press, "'War Council' to Confer with Churchill: Allied Chieftains Discuss Means of Crushing Axis," *Birmingham* (AL) *News*, December 23, 1941, 2 continued from page 1.
82. Associated Press, "'War Council' to Confer with Churchill: Allied Chieftains Discuss Means of Crushing Axis," *Birmingham* (AL) *News*, December 23, 1941, 1.

CHAPTER 24: THE TWENTY-FOURTH OF DECEMBER

1. Associated Press, "Churchill Gets 2-Week Ration of Eggs on His Breakfast Tray," *Washington Evening Star*, December 24, 1941, A2.
2. Associated Press, "Churchill Gets 2-Week Ration of Eggs on His Breakfast Tray," *Washington Evening Star*, December 24, 1941, A2.
3. Associated Press, "Churchill Gets 2-Week Ration of Eggs on His Breakfast Tray," *Washington Evening Star*, December 24, 1941, A2.
4. Edward T. Folliard, "Prime Minister Fences Press U.S. Style," *Washington Post*, December 24, 1941, 4.
5. Associated Press, "Santa Claus To Visit Sing Sing Prison," *Birmingham* (AL) *News*, December 24, 1941, 7.

6. *Washington Post*, "Ceremony at White House on Christmas Eve to Highlight Varied Program of Yule Activity," December 22, 1941, 19.

7. Associated Press, "8-Lb. Baby Boy Born to Mrs. F. D. Roosevelt Jr.," *Boston Daily Globe*, December 22, 1941, 1.

8. *Washington Evening Star*, "Churchill, President Studying War Roles For Other Allies," December 24, 1941, A1.

9. Franklin Delano Roosevelt Presidential Library and Museum, "Telegram from Kirk to Hull," December 24, 1941, Hyde Park, NY, 1-2.

10. Franklin Delano Roosevelt Presidential Library and Museum, "Telegram from Kirk to Hull," December 24, 1941, Hyde Park, NY, 2.

11. Franklin Delano Roosevelt Presidential Library and Museum, "Memorandum for Grace," December 24, 1941, Hyde Park, NY, 1.

12. Franklin Delano Roosevelt Presidential Library and Museum, "Memo From C.V. Munson," Hyde Park, NY.

13. *Washington Evening Star*, "Churchill, Roosevelt Will Attend Church Together Tomorrow," December 24, 1941, B1.

14. Associated Press, "Churchill Gets 2-Week Ration of Eggs on His Breakfast Tray," *Washington Evening Star*, December 24, 1941, A2.

15. *Washington Post*, "Ceremony at White House on Christmas Eve to Highlight Varied Program of Yule Activity," December 22, 1941, 19.

16. Associated Press, "Film Studio Ready if War Should Hit," *Baltimore Sun*, December 23, 1941, 2.

17. *Los Angeles Times*, "Studio Builds Raid Shelters," December 23, 1941, 7.

18. Ronald J. Schmidt, *This is The City: Making Model Citizens in Los Angeles* (Minneapolis, MN: University of Minnesota Press, 2005), 46.

19. International News Service, "Jap Ambassador Buys Drawers," *Washington Post*, December 24, 1941, 1.

20. Franklin Delano Roosevelt Presidential Library and Museum, "Telegram to the President from Generalissimo Chiang Kai-shek, Chungking," December 24, 1941, Hyde Park, NY.

21. Associated Press, "Shells and Carols Mix on Kent Coast," *Washington Post*, December 25, 1941, 6.

22. Associated Press, "RAF Suspends Activity," *New York Times*, December 27, 1941, 8.

23. Associated Press, "Nazis Finish Bases for Use Against Britain," *Washington Evening Star*, December 24, 1941, A1.

24. Associated Press, "35 in Crew Take to Lifeboats in View of Shore," *Washington Evening Star*, December 24, 1941, A1.

25. Associated Press, "Tanker, Turned Back in Pacific, Reaches Port," *Washington Evening Star*, December 24, 1941, A1.

26. *Los Angeles Times*, "Santa Catalina Island Ships Halt Service Temporarily," December 24, 1941, A.

27. Associated Press, "30 Gaunt Survivors of Lahaina Safe After 20 Days in Lifeboat," *Washington Evening Star*, December 24, 1941, A5.

28. United Press, "Wake Island All Now in Jap Hands," *Lethbridge Herald* (Alberta, Canada), December 24, 1941, 9.

29. *Washington Evening Star*, "385 Americans There Led by Maj. Devereux," December 24, 1941, A1.

30. *Washington Evening Star*, "385 Americans There Led by Maj. Devereux," December 24, 1941, A1.

31. *Washington Evening Star*, "Communiques: U.S. Contact With Wake Island," December 24, 1941, A4.

32. Associated Press, "Success Claimed By British in Hong Kong Battle," *Washington Evening Star*, December 24, 1941, A4.

33. Associated Press, "Canadians Hold in Last Stand Fight," *Hartford* (CT) *Courant*, December 24, 1941, 1.

34. Associated Press, "Dutch Report Sea Victories," *Milwaukee* (WI) *Journal*, December 24, 1941, 2.
35. *Washington Evening Star*, "Communiques: U.S. Contact With Wake Island," December 24, 1941, A4.
36. Associated Press, "Strong Units Reported in Coast Area," *Hartford* (CT) *Courant*, December 24, 1941, 1.
37. *Washington Evening Star*, "Japs, Off Batangas, Now Menace Manila from Two New Points," December 24, 1941, A1.
38. Royal Arch Gunnison, "Flying Fortress Defies 18 Foes; Returns With 1,500 Bullet Holes," *New York Times*, December 24, 1941, 3.
39. *Washington Evening Star*, "Spectacular Pacific Flight Wins Flying Cross for 75," December 24, 1941, A2.
40. Whitney Martin, "Louis-Conn Fight Chosen As Year's Best in Roundup," *Washington Post*, December 24, 1941, 21.
41. Sigrid Arne, Associated Press, "Mickey Rooney Loses Heart Under Hollywood's Nose and No One Had Even an Inkling of It," *Washington Post*, December 24, 1941, 23.
42. Associated Press, "Roosevelt to Avoid Film Censorship," *Washington Post*, December 24, 1941, 23.
43. *Birmingham* (AL) *News*, "An Urgent Appeal," December 24, 1941, 7.
44. Tom Yarbrough, Associated Press, "Ruined Hangars Stand As Mute Evidence o Fury of Jap Raid," *Birmingham* (AL) *News*, December 24, 1941, 4.
45. *Washington Post*, "Army Rushes Repair Work on Oahu Isle," December 25, 1941, 2.
46. Alfred Friendly, "Labor-Industry Parley Accepts Stoppage Ban," *Washington Post*, December 24, 1941, 1.
47. Associated Press, "Congress May Seek Every Possible Dollar for Taxes Next Year," *Birmingham* (AL) *News*, December 24, 1941, 7.
48. Associated Press, "'Unlimited' Tax Bill Considered to Meet War Expenditures," *Washington Evening Star*, December 24, 1941, A5.
49. Associated Press, "Pétain Tells France Peace Is Farther Off Than Ever," *Washington Evening Star*, December 24, 1941, A5.
50. Associated Press, "New Efforts to Push Into North Africa," *Hartford* (CT) *Courant*, December 24, 1941, 1.
51. Associated Press, "Pope Lays Down plan For Peace Based on Arms Limitation," *Washington Evening Star*, December 24, 1941, A2.
52. Associated Press, "On the Radio Today," *Baltimore Sun*, December 24, 1941, 1.
53. Gerald G. Gross, "Leaders of Democracies Key Their Speeches to Christmas Spirit at Tree Lighting," *Washington Post*, December 25, 1941, 1.
54. *Washington Post*, "Impatient Comment Stops as Churchill Speaks," December 25, 1941, 5.
55. *Washington Post*, "Impatient Comment Stops as Churchill Speaks," December 25, 1941, 5.
56. John C. Henry, "Churchill Tells U.S. Sacrifice Will Win War," *Washington Evening Star*, December 24, 1941, 1.
57. John C. Henry, "Churchill Tells U.S. Sacrifice Will Win War," *Washington Evening Star*, December 24, 1941, A1.
58. *Washington Post*, "Churchill Text," December 25, 1941, 5.
59. *Washington Post*, "Impatient Comment Stops as Churchill Speaks," December 25, 1941, 5.
60. *Washington Post*, "President's Text," December 25, 1941, 5.
61. *Washington Post*, "President's Text," December 25, 1941, 5.
62. Associated Press, "FDR and Churchill Call for Courage, Predict Victory in Yuletide Messages," *Boston Daily Globe*, December 25, 1941, 1.
63. Associated Press, "Churchill Gets 2-Week Ration of Eggs on His Breakfast Tray," *Washington Evening Star*, December 24, 1941, A2.

CHAPTER 25: THE TWENTY-FIFTH OF DECEMBER

1. *New York Times*, "Government Quits Manila," December 26, 1941, 4.
2. Frank Hewlett, "Foe Gains Two Beachheads 55 Miles from Capital, One Periling Cavite; MacArthur Takes Field Command; Fierce Battles Raging at Two Points," *Washington Post*, December 25, 1941, 1.
3. Frank Hewlett, "Foe Gains Two Beachheads 55 Miles from Capital, One Periling Cavite; MacArthur Takes Field Command; Fierce Battles Raging at Two Points," *Washington Post*, December 25, 1941, 1.
4. John G. Norris, "Marines Held Base 14 Days with 12 Planes, 6 Cannon," *Washington Post*, December 25, 1941, 1.
5. Associated Press, "Colony Governor Meets with Foes, Tokyo Declares," *Washington Evening Star*, December 25, 1941, 1.
6. Associated Press, "Hongkong Surrenders to Japanese," *Los Angeles Times*, December 26, 1941, 1.
7. Associated Press, "Hongkong Colony Falls When Water Mains Blasted," *Daily Boston Globe*, December 26, 1941, 1.
8. Franklin Delano Roosevelt Presidential Library and Museum, "Optel. No. 48," December 25, 1941, Hyde Park, NY.
9. Associated Press, "Guest Churchill Is Sleeping and Eating Well at White House," *Washington Evening Star*, December 25, 1941, A-3.
10. Jon Meacham, *Franklin and Winston: An Intimate Portrait of an Epic Friendship* (New York: Random House, 2003), xvi–xvii.
11. John C. Henry, "Churchill Joins Roosevelt in Victory Prayer," *Washington Evening Star*, December 25, 1941, A1.
12. Associated Press, "President Too Busy to Open Presents," *Los Angeles Times*, December 27, 1941, 2.
13. *Washington Post*, "Traditional Dinner Awaits Churchill," December 25, 1941, 5.
14. Associated Press, "White House to Have Turkey and Trimmins," *Los Angeles Times*, December 25, 1941, 10.
15. Associated Press, "White House to Have Turkey and Trimmins," *Los Angeles Times*, December 25, 1941, 10.
16. Franklin Delano Roosevelt, Joseph P. Lash, *F.D.R.: His Personal Letters* (New York: Duell, Sloan, And Pearce, 1950), 1260.
17. Franklin Delano Roosevelt Presidential Library and Museum, "Message from Clementine Churchill to Roosevelts 12/27/41," December 27, 1941, Hyde Park, NY.
18. Franklin Delano Roosevelt Presidential Library and Museum, "Message from Lord Halifax to Franklin Delano Roosevelt 12/25/41," December 25, 1941, Hyde Park, NY.
19. Associated Press, "Philippines, Only Christian Nation in Orient, Swarms with Invading Hordes on Christmas Day," *Washington Post*, December 25, 1941, 8.
20. United Press, "Pilgrims Steam to Town of Bethlehem for Traditional Christmas Ceremonies," *Washington Post*, December 25, 1941, 11.
21. Associated Press, "War Goes on But Yuletide Touches All," *Hartford Courant*, December 25, 1941, 23.
22. Associated Press, "War Goes on But Yuletide Touches All," *Hartford Courant*, December 25, 1941, 23.
23. Associated Press, "Christmas a Memory in Many World Capitals, but Moscow Enjoys It at Nazis' Expense," *Washington Evening Star*, December 25, 1941, 5.
24. Associated Press, "War Goes on But Yuletide Touches All," *Hartford Courant*, December 25, 1941, 23.
25. Christine Sadler, "Justice Holmes' House Will Be Haven For Girls," *Washington Post*, December 25, 1941, 17.
26. *Washington Evening Star*, "Thousands of Christmas Gifts Distributed Among Needy Here," 25, 1941, 6.

27. *Washington Evening Star*, "Children Talk Over Radio With Army Officers in London," December 25, 1941, B-1.

28. *Baltimore Sun*, "65 Negro Children Patients Are Given Christmas Party," December 25, 1941, 5.

29. *Los Angeles Times*, "Navy Santa Doesn't Forget Children Who Lost Fathers," December 25, 1941, 1.

30. *Washington Evening Star*, "Party Honors 125 Soldiers Quartered at Treasury," December 25, 1941, A-5.

31. Associated Press, "1,500,000 Pounds of Turkey Destined for Army's Tables," *Baltimore Sun*, December 20, 1941, 8.

32. Associated Press, "1,500,000 Pounds of Turkey Destined for Army's Tables," *Baltimore Sun*, December 20, 1941, 8.

33. Associated Press, "1,500,000 Pounds of Turkey Destined for Army's Tables," *Baltimore Sun*, December 20, 1941, 8.

34. *Washington Post*, "Many Parties Arranged for Service Men," December 24, 1941, 17.

35. Associated Press, "Honolulu's Christmas Eve Dry as Army Bans All Hard Liquor," *Washington Evening Star*, December 25, 1941, A1.

36. Associated Press, "Japanese Took Pop, Candy on Hawaii Raid," *Washington Evening Star*, December 25, 1941, A-2.

37. *Baltimore Sun*, "Wounded and Evacuees Reach San Francisco From Hawaii," December 24, 1941, 1.

38. *Baltimore Sun*, "Wounded and Evacuees Reach San Francisco From Hawaii," December 24, 1941, 1.

39. Lawrence E. Davies, "Hawaii Wounded Home, Tell How Defenders Dared Death," *New York Times*, December 26, 1941, 1.

40. *Washington Evening Star*, "For His Christmas!," December 20, 1941, 2.

41. *Atlanta Constitution*, "Dickens Story of Christmas on Vallee Hour," December 25, 1941, 31.

42. *Birmingham* (AL) *News*, "Strongest Stars at the Box Office," December 25, 1941, 15.

43. Vincent Townsend, "'Men of Boys Town' Is Best Box office Picture," *Birmingham* (AL) *News*, December 25, 1941, 15.

44. *New York Times*, "Beware of Women Spies, Navy Men Are Warned," December 25, 1941, 22.

45. *New York Times*, "War Casts Shadow Over Christmas Joy Throughout Land," December 25, 1941, 1.

46. *Washington Post*, "Congressman Now Must Carry Identity Cards," December 25, 1941, 24.

47. *New York Times*, "Congress to Use Identity Cards," December 25, 1941, 10.

48. Associated Press, "U.S. Plane's Direct Hits Filled Air with Debris, Army Says," *Washington Evening Star*, December 25, 1941, A1.

49. John C. Henry, "Churchill Joins Roosevelt in Victory Prayer," *Washington Evening Star*, December 25, 1941, A5.

50. *Baltimore Sun*, "Eire to Stay Neutral, DeValera Declares, Unless Under Attack," December 25, 1941, 2.

51. *Los Angeles Times*, "Dawn of Another Christmas Hailed," December 25, 1941, A1.

52. *Washington Post*, "Christmas," December 25, 1941, 10.

53. Henrt Wadsworth Longfellow, *The Complete Poetical Works of Henry Wadsworth Longfellow* (London: George Routledge & Sons, 1871), 544.

54. *Evening Star*, "Christmas, 1941," December 25, 1941, A8.

55. *Washington Post*, "Christmas," December 25, 1941, 10.

56. John Meacham, *Franklin and Winston* (New York: Random House, 2004), 134.

CHAPTER 26: THE TWENTY-SIX OF DECEMBER

1. *Washington Evening Star*, "Churchill Forecast Allies Will Take War Initiative in 1943," December 26, 1941, A2.

2. *Washington Evening Star*, "Churchill to Make Speech to Congress in Senate Chamber," December 25, 1941, A1.

3. *Baltimore Sun*, "Churchill Captures Capital With Speech," December 27, 1941, 1.
4. *Baltimore Sun*, "Churchill Captures Capital With Speech," December 27, 1941, 1.
5. *Washington Evening Star*, "War Tide to Turn by 1943, Churchill Says," December 26, 1941, A2.
6. *Baltimore Sun*, "Honor to Churchill Single Precedent Found," December 27, 1941, 4.
7. *Washington Evening Star*, "War Tide to Turn by 1943, Churchill Says," December 26, 1941, A2.
8. *Baltimore Sun*, "Churchill With Half an Hour of Oratory Captures Nation's Capital," December 27, 1941, 5.
9. The Churchill Center and Museum at the Churchill War Rooms, London, Speeches, Speeches of Winston Churchill, "Winston Churchill Addresses a Joint Session of Congress on December 26, 1941," http://www.winstonchurchill.org/learn/speeches/speeches-of-winston-churchill/1941-1945-war-leader/288-us-congress-1941.
10. The Churchill Center and Museum at the Churchill War Rooms, London, Speeches, Speeches of Winston Churchill, "Winston Churchill Addresses a Joint Session of Congress on December 26, 1941," http://www.winstonchurchill.org/learn/speeches/speeches-of-winston-churchill/1941-1945-war-leader/288-us-congress-1941.
11. The Churchill Center and Museum at the Churchill War Rooms, London, Speeches, Speeches of Winston Churchill, "Winston Churchill Addresses a Joint Session of Congress on December 26, 1941," http://www.winstonchurchill.org/learn/speeches/speeches-of-winston-churchill/1941-1945-war-leader/288-us-congress-1941.
12. The Churchill Center and Museum at the Churchill War Rooms, London, Speeches, Speeches of Winston Churchill, "Winston Churchill Addresses a Joint Session of Congress on December 26, 1941," http://www.winstonchurchill.org/learn/speeches/speeches-of-winston-churchill/1941-1945-war-leader/288-us-congress-1941.
13. Sydney J. Harris, "Thoughts at Large," *Sarasota Harold-Tribune*, December 28, 1941, 4.
14. Stuart Ball, *Winston Churchill* (New York: NYU Press, 2003), 63.
15. The Churchill Center and Museum at the Churchill War Rooms, London, Learn, Speeches, Quotation, "Famous Quotations and Stories," http://www.winstonchurchill.org/learn/speeches/quotations.
16. Sir Winston Churchill, Martin Gilbert, *The Churchill War Papers: The Ever Widening War, 1941* (New York: W. W. Norton & Company, 2001), 1685.
17. The Churchill Center and Museum at the Churchill War Rooms, London, Speeches, Speeches of Winston Churchill, "Winston Churchill Addresses a Joint Session of Congress on December 26, 1941," http://www.winstonchurchill.org/learn/speeches/speeches-of-winston-churchill/1941-1945-war-leader/288-us-congress-1941.
18. The Churchill Center and Museum at the Churchill War Rooms, London, Speeches, Speeches of Winston Churchill, "Winston Churchill Addresses a Joint Session of Congress on December 26, 1941," http://www.winstonchurchill.org/learn/speeches/speeches-of-winston-churchill/1941-1945-war-leader/288-us-congress-1941.
19. The Churchill Center and Museum at the Churchill War Rooms, London, Speeches, Speeches of Winston Churchill, "Winston Churchill Addresses a Joint Session of Congress on December 26, 1941," http://www.winstonchurchill.org/learn/speeches/speeches-of-winston-churchill/1941-1945-war-leader/288-us-congress-1941.
20. The Churchill Center and Museum at the Churchill War Rooms, London, Speeches, Speeches of Winston Churchill, "Winston Churchill Addresses a Joint Session of Congress on December 26, 1941," http://www.winstonchurchill.org/learn/speeches/speeches-of-winston-churchill/1941-1945-war-leader/288-us-congress-1941.
21. Associated Press, "Churchill Phones Senator's Wife Too Ill to See Him," *Chicago Daily Tribune*, December 27, 1941, 6.
22. *Baltimore Sun*, "Churchill Captures Capital With Speech," December 27, 1941, 1.
23. *New York Times*, "40 Billion Is '42 Arms Goal; Churchill Is Going to Canada," December 27, 1941, 1.
24. *New York Times*, "Fort Dix to Open 2 Target Ranges," December 27, 1941, 9.

25. Associated Press, "National Lottery Urged in New Senate Bill," *Washington Evening Star*, December 27, 1941, A3.

26. Associated Press, "National Lottery Urged in New Senate Bill," *Washington Evening Star*, December 27, 1941, A3.

27. Franklin Delano Roosevelt Presidential Library and Museum, "Memorandum for the President: Subject Victory Program," December 26, 1941, Hyde Park, NY.

28. Franklin Delano Roosevelt Presidential Library and Museum, "Memorandum for the President: Subject: North Africa," December 26, 1941, Hyde Park, NY.

29. Associated Press, "Plans to Curb Spending Hit," *Los Angeles Times*, December 27, 1941, 2.

30. *Hartford Daily Courant*, "New Red Cross By Flagg," December 26, 1941, 13.

31. *Atlanta Constitution*, "A Good Reminder," December 26, 1941, 2.

32. The Churchill Center and Museum at the Churchill War Rooms, London, Speeches, Speeches of Winston Churchill, "Winston Churchill Addresses a Joint Session of Congress on December 26, 1941," http://www.winstonchurchill.org/learn/speeches/speeches-of-winston-churchill/1941-1945-war-leader/288-us-congress-1941.

33. *Washington Evening Star*, "1,000 Civilians on Wake, Navy Announces," December 26, 1941, A3.

34. Associated Press, "Christmas Assaults Retake 100 Villages, Red Army Claims," *Washington Evening Star*, December 26, 1941, A2.

35. Walter B. Kerr, "Nazi Resistance Appears Stiffer," *Baltimore Sun*, December 26, 1941, 1.

36. Associated Press, "Bulletins," *Baltimore Sun*, December 26, 1941, 1.

37. Craig Thompson, "British Garrison Ends 16-Day Siege," *New York Times*, December 26, 1941, 1.

38. *New York Times*, "'We Are Still Here,' Is Midway Greeting," December 26, 1941, 1.

39. *Washington Evening Star*, "Midway Marines Still Holding Out," December 26, 1941, A1.

40. Associated Press, "War Tide to Turn By 1943, Churchill Says Japs Intensify Two-Way Drive on Manila," *Washington Evening Star*, December 26, 1941, A1.

41. John G. Doll, *Battling Bastards of Bataan* (Bennington, VT: Merriam Press, 1988), 24.

42. *Atlanta Constitution*, "Loss of Philippines Considered Possible by Gloomy Capital," December 26, 1941, 1.

43. United States Constitution, Article 3, Section 3.

44. David Nasaw, *The Chief: The Life of William Randolph Hearst* (Boston, MA: Houghton Mifflin Harcourt, 2001), 268.

45. *Boston Daily Globe*, "Gettysburg Eternal Light Extinguished As Raid Precaution," December 26, 1941, 2.

46. *Washington Evening Star*, "4,900 Soldier Dinners Go Uneaten Here on War Zone Order," December 26, 1941, B1.

47. Associated Press, "Accidents Kill 429 in 40 States During Two-Day Period," *Washington Evening Star*, December 26, 1941, B2.

48. Associated Press, "Accidents Kill 429 in 40 States During Two-Day Period," *Washington Evening Star*, December 26, 1941, B2.

49. *Boston Daily Globe*, "Isabbele Hallin, Saugus Beauty, Is N.Y. Suicide," December 26, 1941, 2.

50. *Boston Daily Globe*, "Isabbele Hallin, Saugus Beauty, Is N.Y. Suicide," December 26, 1941, 2.

51. *Boston Daily Globe*, "Isabbele Hallin, Saugus Beauty, Is N.Y. Suicide," December 26, 1941, 2.

52. *Baltimore Sun*, "Traveler's Aid Gets Sad Message," December 26, 1941, 4.

CHAPTER 27: THE TWENTY-SEVENTH OF DECEMBER

1. *Daily Boston Globe*, "Former Slave, 107, Combines Birthday, Yule Celebrations," December 26, 1941, 17.

2. *Atlanta Constitution*, "Fighting Spirit," December 26, 1941, 1.

3. *The Atlanta Constitution*, "Ex-Slaves Offer Victory Prayer At Annual Christmas Party," December 26, 1941, 3.

4. *Chicago Daily Tribune*, "Refuses To Seat Negro Named To Bench By Green," December 27, 1941, 9.

5. Gould Lincoln, "The Political Mill," *Washington Evening Star*, December 27, 1941, 9.

6. Ralph McGill, "One Word More," *Atlanta Constitution*, December 27, 1941, 4.

7. Franklin Delano Roosevelt Presidential Library and Museum, "Memorandum from Ambassador Winant to Secretary Hull Summarizing German and Italian Press Comment on Prime Minister Churchill's Address to the Congress," December 27, 1941, Hyde Park, NY.

8. Associated Press, "Text of Address Delivered by Winston Churchill," *Baltimore Sun*, December 27, 1941, 4.

9. David Lawrence, "Churchill Sets Sights for Victory," *Washington Evening Star*, December 27, 1941, 9.

10. *Washington Evening Star*, "War Strategy Talks Rushed at White House," December 27, 1941, 1.

11. Associated Press, "Death Toll Put at 50 in 3-Hour Air Attack; Property Loss Heavy," *Washington Evening Star*, December 27, 1941, 1.

12. Associated Press, "Helpless People Without a Gun Die Amid Terror," *Birmingham* (AL) *News*, December 27, 1941, 1.

13. Associated Press, "Helpless People Without a Gun Die Amid Terror," *Birmingham* (AL) *News*, December 27, 1941, 1.

14. R.P. Cronin Jr., "Manila Sky Filled with Terror During Unmerciful Jap Attack," *Birmingham* (AL) *News*, December 27, 1941, 3.

15. Associated Press, "Hull Says Japan Follows Hitler's Cruelty Methods," *Birmingham* (AL) *News*, December 27, 1941, 1.

16. Associated Press, "Hull Says Japan Follows Hitler's Cruelty Methods," *Birmingham* (AL) *News*, December 27, 1941, 1.

17. Associated Press, "Helpless People Without a Gun Die Amid Terror," *Birmingham* (AL) *News*, December 27, 1941, 1.

18. Franklin Delano Roosevelt Presidential Library and Museum, "War Department Communique on Lingayen Gulf & Lamon Bay" December 26, 1941, Hyde Park, NY.

19. Associated Press, "Bulletin," *Baltimore Sun*, December 27, 1941, 1.

20. Mark S. Watson, "Retreat in the Philippines," *Baltimore Sun*, December 27, 1941, 1.

21. Vicente A. Pacis, "Fear for Safety of MacArthur on Philippine Front," *Chicago Daily Tribune*, December 27, 1941, 2.

22. Associated Press, "Fighting Is Bitter," *New York Times*, December 27, 1941, 1.

23. Associated Press, "Japanese Expect to Restore 70 Borneo Oil Wells in Month," *Washington Evening Star*, December 27, 1941, 1.

24. Associated Press, "Sarawak and the Brookes," *Washington Evening Star*, December 27, 1941, 8.

25. Associated Press, "Japs in Gilbert Islands; Fear for Europeans," *Chicago Daily Tribune*, December 27, 1941, 2.

26. *Baltimore Sun*, "U.S. Daily Newspapers Reach Circulation High," December 27, 1941, 4.

27. *Chicago Daily Tribune*, "GoodYear," December 28, 1941, 8.

28. Associated Press, "Rules Deny New Tires to Private Cars," *Los Angeles Times*, December 27, 1941, 1.

29. Associated Press, "Tire Rationing Rules Released; They Are Tough," *Birmingham* (AL) *News*, December 27, 1941, 1.

30. *Life*, "Schwinn-Built Bicycles," December 29, 1941, 36.

31. Associated Press "Tire Rationing Rules Released; They Are Tough," *Birmingham* (AL) *News*, December 27, 1941, A1.

32. Associated Press, "O.P.M. Relaxes Rubber Ban to Allow Making of Fire Hose," *Los Angeles Times*, December 27, 1941, A1.

33. Associated Press, "Vast Dandelion Planting Urged for Production of Rubber," *Los Angeles Times*, December 27, 1941, A1.

34. *Life*, "On The Newsfronts of the World," December 29, 1941, 20.

35. Associated Press, "Detroit May Revert to Trolleys in Tire Crisis," *Portsmouth* (VA) *Times*, December 28, 1941, 2.

36. Associated Press, "British Ban Making Rubber Articles," *Los Angeles Times*, December 27, 1941, A1.
37. Associated Press, "Princes Stage One-Round Bout at Gloria Vanderbilt's Party," *Birmingham (AL) News*, December 27, 1941, 1.
38. *Los Angeles Times*, "Ralph's the Year Ahead . . . ," December 27, 1941, 4.
39. *Baltimore Sun*, "Seeking to Fill Up Skilled Labor Gap," December 27, 1941, 4.
40. Associated Press, "Enemy Aliens Must Turn in Radios, Cameras," *Washington Evening Star*, December 27, 1941, 1.
41. Associated Press, "Aliens En Route to Montana Camp," *Los Angeles Times*, December 27, 1941, A2.
42. Associated Press, "Mexico Travelers Halted In Search for Letters," *Los Angeles Times*, December 27, 1941, A2.
43. *Los Angeles Times*, "Identification Cards Needed for Entrance to Water Front," December 27, 1941, B.
44. *Los Angeles Times*, "Identification Cards Needed for Entrance to Water Front," December 27, 1941, B.
45. *Los Angeles Times*, "Where to Cut to Save Money for War," December 27, 1941, 4.
46. Associated Press, "Nazi Envoys to U.S. Housed at Hotel," *Baltimore Sun*, December 27, 1941, 4.
47. Lloyd Lehrbas, "Geneva Pact Governs American Treatment of Jap War Prisoners," *Washington Evening Star*, December 27, 1941, A4.
48. *New York Times*, "U.S. Outlines Stand on War Prisoners," December 27, 1941, 8.
49. *New York Times*, "U.S. Outlines Stand on War Prisoners," December 27, 1941, 8.
50. United Press, "Coastal Subsea Raiding Falls Off," *Los Angles Times*, December 27, 1941, A2.

CHAPTER 28: THE TWENTY-EIGHTH OF DECEMBER
1. *New York Times*, "Support for U.S. Urged in Sermons," December 28, 1941, 11.
2. Rev. John Evans, "Pray Against Godless Foes, Archbishop Says," *Chicago Daily Tribune*, December 28, 1941, 13.
3. *New York Times*, "Support for U.S. Urged in Sermons," December 28, 1941, 11.
4. Associated Press, "Market Commissioner says Dispute Topped List of Incidents," *Washington Evening Star*, December 28, 1941, A2.
5. *Time*, "Civilian Defense," December 29, 1941, 11.
6. *Time*, "Civilian Defense," December 29, 1941, 11.
7. *Bulletin of International News*, Vol. 19, No. 1, (Royal Institute of International News, London, England, 1942) 23.
8. *New York Times*, "Australia Warned of More Reverses," December 27, 1941, 5.
9. *New York Times*, "40 Billion is '42 Arms Goal," December 27, 1941, 1.
10. *New York Times*, "Australia Warned of More Reverses," December 27, 1941, 5.
11. *New York Times*, "For Anglo-American Unity," December 27, 1941, C18.
12. United Press, "Gilbert Islands Believed Seized," *Los Angeles Times*, December 28, 1941, 3.
13. Associated Press, "Publisher Assails Removal of Manila's Defenses," *Sunday (DE) Star*, December 28, 1941, A3.
14. Associated Press, "Australia Reliance in U.S., Premier Declares," *Washington Evening Star*, December 28, 1941, A2.
15. John C. Henry, "Parleys Bolster Allies' Position, Roosevelt Says," *Washington Evening Star*, December 28, 1941, A1.
16. John C. Henry, "Parleys Bolster Allies' Position, Roosevelt Says," *Washington Evening Star*, December 28, 1941, A1.
17. Associated Press, "Has Busy Day of Conferences With Churchill," *Boston Daily Globe*, December 28, 1941, C1.
18. John C. Henry, "Parleys Bolster Allies' Position, Roosevelt Says," *Washington Evening Star*, December 28, 1941, A1.

19. Maj. George Fielding Elliot, "French Still Play Vital Part in War," *Los Angeles Times*, December 28, 1941, 4.

20. John C. Henry, "Parleys Bolster Allies' Position, Roosevelt Says," *Washington Evening Star*, December 28, 1941, A1.

21. John C. Henry, "Parleys Bolster Allies' Position, Roosevelt Says," *Washington Evening Star*, December 28, 1941, A1.

22. *Washington Evening Star*, "Henderson Acts to Block Cigarette Price Increase," December 28, 1941, A3.

23. *Life*, "We Want Camels!," December 29, 1941, 70.

24. Associated Press, "Has Busy Day of Conferences With Churchill," *Boston Daily Globe*, December 28, 1941, C1.

25. Associated Press, "O.P.M. Limits Output of All Types of New Farm Machinery," *Washington Evening Star*, December 28, 1941, A4.

26. *Life*, "Toke Raid Would be Costly and Futile," December 29, 1941, 56.

27. *Life*, "Perspiration Is Acid . . . It Cuts Stocking Life!," December 29, 1941, 68.

28. *Los Angeles Times*, "Tommy Dorsey," December 28, 1941, 4.

29. *Honolulu Advertiser*, "Prescriptions for Liquor Under Control," December 28, 1941, 8.

30. *Honolulu Advertiser*, "Hawaii Defense Act," December 28, 1941, 12.

31. United Press, "Hawaii Boys Flew for Japs," *Los Angeles Times*, December 28, 1941, 2.

32. *Honolulu Advertiser*, "KGMB," December 28, 1941, 12.

33. *Los Angeles Times*, "Aliens Evacuated From Federal Jail," December 28, 1941, 8.

34. *Los Angeles Times*, "Welder Union Votes to Stop Work Today," December 20, 1941, 1.

35. *New York Times*, "Short-wave Sets of Aliens Curbed," December 28, 1941, 4.

36. International News Service, "Nab Alleged Coast Bund Leader," *Honolulu Advertiser*, December 29, 1941, 4.

37. *Life*, "Nazi Spies," December 29, 1941, 24.

38. *Time*, "Civilian Defense," December 29, 1941, 11.

39. *Los Angeles Times*, "End of Curbs in Prospect," December 28, 1941, 3.

40. Associated Press, "Defense Plants Asked to Work on New Year's," *Baltimore Sun*, December 28, 1941, 12.

41. *Los Angeles Times*, "Don't Let Tongue Slip," December 28, 1941, 3.

42. *Los Angeles Times*, "A Word to Amateur War Critics," December 28, 1941, 4.

43. *Los Angeles Times*, "We Shall Not Forget This, Yellow Men," December 28, 1941, 4.

44. *New York Times*, "Washington Asks Revenge Bombings," December 28, 1941, 1.

45. United Press, "Old Area in Ruins," *New York Times*, December 28, 1941, 1.

46. United Press, "Old Area in Ruins," *New York Times*, December 28, 1941, 1.

47. *New York Times*, "The International Situation," December 28, 1941, 1.

48. Associated Press, "Nipponese Broadcast Is Quickly Scorned by Angry Islanders," *Atlanta Constitution*, December 28 1941, 1A.

49. United Press, "Japanese Advance Slowly on Manila," *New York Times*, December 28, 1941, 1.

50. *Honolulu Advertiser*, "Japanese Launch Fresh Manila Attack from Air," December 28, 1941, 1.

51. *Honolulu Advertiser*, "Japanese Launch Fresh Manila Attack from Air," December 28, 1941, 1.

52. F. Tillman Durdin, "New Malaya Push by Japan Starts," *New York Times*, December 28, 1941, 6.

53. *New York Times*, "Barkley Predicts Bombing of Tokyo," December 30, 1941, 3.

CHAPTER 29: THE TWENTY-NINTH OF DECEMBER

1. United Press, Frank Hewlett, "Filipino Police Hunt Chutists in Manila Area," *Honolulu Advertiser*, December 29, 1941, 1.

2. United Press, Frank Hewlett, "Filipino Police Hunt Chutists in Manila Area," *Honolulu Advertiser*, December 29, 1941, 1.

3. Associated Press, "Famed Holy Statue Saved in Manila," *Los Angeles Times*, December 29, 1941, 3.

4. United Press, "Priceless Library in Manila Is Lost," *New York Times*, December 29, 1941, 4.
5. *New York Times*, "Tokyo Is Firm on Manila," December 29, 1941, 2.
6. *Honolulu Advertiser*, "FDR Pledges Full Aid to Filipinos," December 29, 1941, 1.
7. *New York Times*, "Messages on Philippines," December 29, 1941, 1.
8. Associated Press, "Philippines Given Pledge By F.D.R. for 'Redemption,'" *Birmingham* (AL) *News*, December 29, 1941, 1.
9. *Honolulu Advertiser*, "Don't Be Impatient, Navy Urges America," December 29, 1941, 4.
10. *Honolulu Advertiser*, "Don't Be Impatient, Navy Urges America," December 29, 1941, 4.
11. Associated Press, "Philippines Given Pledge By F.D.R. for 'Redemption,'" *Birmingham* (AL) *News*, December 29, 1941, 1.
12. Associated Press, "Philippines Given Pledge By F.D.R. for 'Redemption,'" *Birmingham* (AL) *News*, December 29, 1941, 1.
13. *Life* "College Men Wanted," December 29, 1941, 57.
14. Paul Mallon, "Reverses in Far East May Be Expected," *Birmingham* (AL) *News*, December 29, 1941, 1.
15. United Press, Frank Hewlett, "Filipino Police Hunt Chutists in Manila Area," *Honolulu Advertiser*, December 29, 1941, 1.
16. Associated Press, "War Office Says Attacks Will Continue," *Baltimore Sun*, December, 29, 1941, 4.
17. *New York Times*, "10-to-1 Toll Taken on Southeast," December 29, 1941, 3.
18. *New York Times*, "10-to-1 Toll Taken on Southeast," December 29, 1941, 3.
19. *New York Times*, "Washington Is Hopeful," December 29, 1941, 3.
20. *Honolulu Advertiser*, "British Holding Foe Firmly in North Malaya," December 29, 1941, 2.
21. *Chicago Daily Tribune*, "Jap 'Friendship' Leaflets Lure Many to Death," December 29, 1941, 4.
22. *New York Times*, "Australian Force Ready in Malaya," December 29, 1941, 4.
23. Associated Press, "War Office Says Attacks Will Continue," *Baltimore Sun*, December 29, 1941, 4.
24. *Atlanta Constitution*, "Japs in China Seize U.S. Consul, Others," December 28, 1941, 1.
25. Franklin Delano Roosevelt Library and Museum, "Memorandum from Hull to FDR," December 29, 1941, Hyde Park, NY.
26. Franklin Delano Roosevelt Library and Museum, "Memorandum from FDR to H. Hopkins," December 29, 1941, Hyde Park, NY.
27. Franklin Delano Roosevelt Library and Museum, "Progress Report on Intelligence Problems in the New York Area," December 27, 1941, Hyde Park, NY.
28. Franklin Delano Roosevelt Library and Museum, "Progress Report on Intelligence Problems in the New York Area," December 27, 1941, Hyde Park, NY.
29. Franklin Delano Roosevelt Library and Museum, "Letter from FDR to John Carter," December 29, 1941, Hyde Park, NY.
30. Franklin Delano Roosevelt Library and Museum, "Memorandum Regarding Alien Activity in Great Britain," December 29, 1941, Hyde Park, NY.
31. Franklin Delano Roosevelt Library and Museum, "Memorandum from FDR to H. Hopkins," December 29, 1941, Hyde Park, NY.
32. *Honolulu Advertiser*, "13 Survivors of SS Prusa Arrive Here," December 29, 1941, 1.
33. *Life*, "Attack on Hawaii," December 29, 1941, 11.
34. *Life*, "Attack on Hawaii," December 29, 1941, 18.
35. *Life*, "Troops on the Move," December 29, 1941, 23.
36. *Life*, "Anatomy of Bombs," December 29, 1941, 50.
37. Boyd D. Wagner, "'Buzz' Wagner's Story," *Life*," December 29, 1941, 36.
38. *Life*, "U.S. Marines," December 29, 1941, 43.
39. *Life*, "Anatomy of Bombs," December 29, 1941, 50.
40. Oliver Jensen, "Ensign Weems," *Life*, December 29, 1941, 55.
41. *Time*, "World Battlefronts," December 29, 1941, 16.

42. *Time*, "The U.S. at War," December 29, 1941, 7.
43. *Time*, "The U.S. at War," December 29, 1941, 7.
44. *Time*, "The U.S. at War," December 29, 1941, 11.
45. *Birmingham* (AL) *News*, "Russia, England Agree on Method of War Conduct," December 29, 1941, 1.
46. *Honolulu Advertiser*, "Eden-Stalin Conference Covers Conduct of War," December 29, 1941, 2.
47. *Birmingham* (AL) *News*, "Russia, England Agree on Method of War Conduct," December 29, 1941, 1.
48. *Time*, "The U.S. at War," December 29, 1941, 8.
49. *Time*, "World Battlefronts," December 29, 1941, 9.
50. *Time*, "World Battlefronts," December 29, 1941, 12.
51. *Time*, "World Battlefronts," December 29, 1941, 12.
52. Associated Press, "Churchill Is Cheered Wildly by Canadians on Arrival at Ottawa," *Birmingham* (AL) *News*, December 29, 1941, 2.
53. Associated Press, "Churchill Is Cheered Wildly by Canadians on Arrival at Ottawa," *Birmingham* (AL) *News*, December 29, 1941, 2.
54. *New York Times*, "Churchill in 'Coveralls,'" December 30, 1941, 3.
55. Associated Press, "35 Per Cent Slash in Gas Consumption Studied For Civilians," *Birmingham* (AL) *News*, December 29, 1941, 2.
56. Associated Press, "Californians Warned of Jap Raid Reports," *Birmingham* (AL) *News*, December 29, 1941, 2.
57. Lawrence E. Davies, "Foes Spread 'News' of a Fake Bargain," *New York Times*, December 29, 1941, 7.
58. *Birmingham* (AL) *News*, "Venereal Disease in Wartime," December 29, 1941, 6.
59. Associated Press, "Lady Barflies a Prime Target As Anti-Profanity Week Opens," *Baltimore Sun*, December 29, 1941, 13.
60. *Birmingham* (AL) *News*, "Guilty Flag Defiler," December 29, 1940, 7.
61. *Los Angeles Times*, "Gloria Vanderbilt Wed to Pasquale Di Cicco," December 29, 1941, Part B1.
62. *New York Times*, "National Philosophy Found Lacking Here," December 29, 1941, 12.
63. *New York Times*, "Enlistments Begin In 'Spiritual Army,'" December 29, 1941, 12.
64. Associated Press, "Woman Air Spotter 97; Nursed Soldiers in 1865," *New York Times*, December 29, 1941, 8.
65. *Chicago Daily Tribune*, "A Lonely Yank, a Note, and Wow!," December 29, 1941, 1.
66. Associated Press, "She Refuses to Believe Son Killed and Navy Acknowledges Mistake," *Birmingham* (AL) *News*, December 29, 1941, 7.
67. *Time*, "People: Pluggers & Donors," December 29, 1941, 40.
68. *Honolulu Advertiser*, "Defense Stamps Free!," December 30, 1941, 2.
69. *Time*, "People: Pluggers & Donors," December 29, 1941, 40.
70. *New York Times*, "Britain to Join U.S. in Prayers Thursday," December 28, 1941, 2.
71. *Los Angeles Times*, "Axis Aliens Surrender Radio Sets and Cameras," December 29, 1941, 1.
72. *Time*, "Music: Of Thee I Sing, Baby," December 29, 1941, 46.
73. *Time*, "Music: Of Thee I Sing, Baby," December 29, 1941, 46.
74. *Honolulu Advertiser*, "Buses Black," December 30, 1941, 2.
75. *Honolulu Advertiser*, "At the Theaters," December 30, 1941, 4.
76. *New York Times*, "Flier, Shot Down, Resumed Battle in Another Plane as Wife Watched," December 30, 1941, 5.
77. *New York Times*, "Flier, Shot Down, Resumed Battle in Another Plane as Wife Watched," December 30, 1941, 5.

CHAPTER 30: THE THIRTIETH OF DECEMBER

1. Associated Press, "Eiffel Tower May Be Melted to Scrap Metal," *Birmingham* (AL) *News*, December 30, 1941, 2.

2. Associated Press, "Eiffel Tower May Be Melted to Scrap Metal," *Birmingham* (AL) *News*, December 30, 1941, 2.

3. Associated Press, "How War News Gets Around and Why Editors Go Nuts," *Atlanta Constitution*, December 31, 1941, 1.

4. Churchill Center and Museum, Speeches, Speeches of Winston Churchill, "Preparation-Liberation-Assault," December 30, 1941, Chicago, IL, http://www.winstonchurchill.org/learn/speeches/speeches-of-winston-churchill/106-preparation-liberation-assault.

5. *Hartford* (CT)*Courant*, "U.S. Expenditures . . . December Top World War Record," December 30, 1941, 1.

6. *Honolulu Advertiser*, "Bulletins," December 31, 1941, 1.

7. *Time*, "Mr. Paul's Ideas," December 29, 1941, 54.

8. *Time*, "Mr. Paul's Ideas," December 29, 1941, 54.

9. Dewey L. Fleming, "Half of US Income to Go for War Effort Under Roosevelt Plan," *Baltimore Sun*, December 31, 1941, 1.

10. Gerald Griffin, "President Plans Daylight Saving," *Baltimore Sun*, December 31, 1941, 3.

11. Associated Press, "Defense Bond Sales Reach Highest Mark," *Birmingham* (AL) *News*, December 30, 1941, 3.

12. *Birmingham* (AL) *News*, "Defense Bond Sales Reach Highest Mark," December 30, 1941, 1.

13. *Birmingham* (AL) *News*, "11 Billion Dollar Tax Increase Is Proposed," December 30, 1941, 4.

14. *Baltimore Sun*, "Financial Sacrifice Must Come to Win, Morgenthau Warns," December 30, 1941, 1.

15. *Birmingham* (AL) *News*, "Women Volunteers in Uniforms Given Approval Of U.S. Army," December 30, 1941, 2.

16. *Birmingham* (AL) *News*, "Women Volunteers in Uniforms Given Approval Of U.S. Army," December 30, 1941, 2.

17. *Los Angeles Times*, "Cigarette Price Ceiling Slated," December 30, 1941, 1.

18. *Los Angeles Times*, "Hoarding of Fats and Oils Banned," December 30, 1941, 5.

19. *New York Times*, "Allocation Plan Held Inadequate," December 30, 1941, 12.

20. Ernest Lindley, "Tire Rationing to Serve as Test of Democratic Administration," *Birmingham* (AL) *News*, December 30, 1941, 10.

21. Harvey S. Firestone Jr., "The Rubber Situation," *Baltimore Sun*, December 30, 1941, 4.

22. George Gallup, "The Gallup Poll: Survey Shows Majority of Americans Do Nothing to Keep Physically Fit," *Baltimore Sun*, December 30, 1941, 13.

23. Associated Press, "Tire Curb Sells Horses," *New York Times*, December 30, 1941, 11.

24. Paul Gesner and John Beckley "Round-Clock Defense Work in Sight at Most All Plants," *Birmingham* (AL) *News*, 10.

25. Associated Press, "Nazi Launch Air Assault on Coastal Area," *Baltimore Sun*, December 30, 1941, 1.

26. Associated Press, "Mikado's Troops Move on Capital From Southeast," *Birmingham* (AL) *News*, December 30, 1941, 1.

27. Associated Press, "R.A.F. Blows Climax British Land, Sea and Air Assaults," *Los Angeles Times*, December 30, 1941, 1.

28. Pierre J. Huss, "F.D.R. 'Pushed Europe Into War Against Me,' Nazi Dictator Complains," *Birmingham* (AL) *News*, December 30, 1941, 1.

29. Pierre J. Huss, "F.D.R. 'Pushed Europe Into War Against Me,' Nazi Dictator Complains," *Birmingham* (AL) *News*, December 30, 1941, 1.

30. Pierre J. Huss, "F.D.R. 'Pushed Europe Into War Against Me,' Nazi Dictator Complains," *Birmingham* (AL) *News*, December 30, 1941, 4.

31. United Press, "Planes Blast Luzon's Base for Three Hours," *Los Angeles Times*, December 30, 1941, 1.

32. Rear Admiral Yates Sterling Jr., "Manila Bay Protected by Mighty Corregidor," *Honolulu Advertiser*, December 30, 1941, 1.

33. Associated Press, "Tribe of Philippine Pygmies Joins Allies in War on Japs," *Los Angeles Times*, December 30, 1941, 3.

34. *Birmingham* (AL) *News*, "Gen. MacArthur Urges Reprisals for Manila Raids," December 30, 1941, 1.

35. United Press, "U.S. Volunteer Pilots Bag 26 Enemy Planes," *Honolulu Advertiser*, December 30, 1941, 5.

36. United Press, "FDR to Call War Council," *Honolulu Advertiser*, December 30, 1941, 1.

37. United Press, "Enemy Suffers Heavy Losses in Far East," *Honolulu Advertiser*, December 30, 1941, 1.

38. Associated Press, "Churchill Says War Not To End Until Attack on Nazi Homeland," *Birmingham* (AL) *News*, December 30, 1941, 1.

39. Churchill Center and Museum, Speeches, Speeches of Winston Churchill, "Preparation-Liberation-Assault," December 30, 1941, Chicago, IL, http://www.winstonchurchill.org/learn/speeches/speeches-of-winston-churchill/106-preparation-liberation-assault.

40. Churchill Center and Museum, Speeches, Speeches of Winston Churchill, "Preparation-Liberation-Assault," December 30, 1941, Chicago, IL, http://www.winstonchurchill.org/learn/speeches/speeches-of-winston-churchill/106-preparation-liberation-assault.

41. *New York Times*, "U.S. Lists 29 Nations at War With the Axis; Figure Differs From Churchill's in Speech," December 31, 1941, 6.

42. Churchill Center and Museum, Speeches, Speeches of Winston Churchill, "Preparation-Liberation-Assault," December 30, 1941, Chicago, IL, http://www.winstonchurchill.org/learn/speeches/speeches-of-winston-churchill/106-preparation-liberation-assault.

43. Associated Press, "Red Men Bury Hatchet to Aid War on Axis," *Baltimore Sun*, December 30, 1941, 4.

44. Associated Press, "Hard Blows at Foe Urged By Einstein," *Baltimore Sun*, December 30, 1941, 4.

45. *New York Times*, "Bid Astronomers, Navigate Bombers," December 30, 1941, 1.

46. Associated Press, "Astronomy Called Aid to War Effort," *New York Times*, December 30, 1941, 13.

47. Associated Press, "Astronomer Inclined to Doubt Theory Universe Is Exploding," *Baltimore Sun*, December 31, 1941, 13.

48. International News Service, "Scientists Say Water Exists on Red Planet," *Atlanta Constitution*, December 31, 1941, 6.

49. *Honolulu Advertiser*, "Important Notice to All Residents Of Oahu," December 30, 1941, 2.

50. *Honolulu Advertiser*, "Bakery Goods Sale Regulated By Governor," December 31, 1941, 2.

51. *Honolulu Advertiser*, "Sought By Relatives," December 30, 1941, 3.

52. *Honolulu Advertiser*, "General Orders," December 30, 1941, 6.

53. *Honolulu Advertiser*, "Alarm System Will Warn Four Isles of Raids," December 30, 1941, 6.

54. Wallace Carroll, "Fifth Column Exposed," *Boston Evening Globe*, December 30, 1941, 1.

55. *Los Angeles Times*, "Long Lines of Enemy Aliens Deliver Banned Articles," December 30, 1941, 8.

56. Franklin Delano Roosevelt Presidential Library and Museum, "Second Progress Report on Intelligence Problems in the New York Area," December 31, 1941, Hyde Park, NY.

57. *Los Angeles Times*, "Patriotic Raffles Robs Vanderbilts of Jewelry," December 30, 1941, 1.

58. *Baltimore Sun*, "Newlywed Gloria Gets More Money," December 30, 1941, 1.

59. *Los Angeles Times*, "Whales Fool Fort Gun Crew; Report Submarines Offshore," December 30, 1941, 8.

60. Associated Press, "Bulletins," *Baltimore Sun*, December 30, 1941, 1.

61. *New York Times*, "The Texts of the Day's Communiqués on Fighting in Various Zones," December 30, 1941, 2.

62. F. Tillman Durdin, "Foe Seeks to Ring Singapore; Plan to Take It Intact Seen," *New York Times*, December 30, 1941, 1.

63. *New York Times*, "U.S. Freighter Sunk in Atlantic Dec. 3," December 30, 1941, 13.

64. Franklin Delano Roosevelt Presidential Library and Museum, "Memorandum for the Naval Aide to the President," December 26, 1941, Hyde Park, NY.

65. United Press, "Lindy's Offer to Serve May Be Accepted," *Honolulu Advertiser*, December 31, 1941, 6.

66. Associated Press, "Lindbergh Volunteers Servicesin Air Corps; Reaction Is Indefinite," *Birmingham* (AL) *News*, December 30, 1941, 1.

67. James P. Duffy, *Lindbergh Vs. Roosevelt* (Washington, DC: Regnery, 2010), 209.

68. *Baltimore Sun*, "A Darkened Liberty," December 30, 1941, 3.

69. *Baltimore Sun*, "A Darkened Liberty," December 30, 1941, 3.

CHAPTER 31: THE THIRTY-FIRST OF DECEMBER

1. Anne O'Hare McCormick, "The Outstanding Fact in a Fateful Year," *New York Times*, December 31, 1941, 16.

2. Franklin Delano Roosevelt Presidential Library and Museum, "Memorandum from Ambassador Winant to Secretary Hull Requesting a Presidential Message from President Roosevelt for the National Day of Prayer on New Year's Day 1942," December 30, 1941, Hyde Park, NY.

3. Franklin Delano Roosevelt Presidential Library and Museum, "Memorandum from Ambassador Winant to Secretary Hull Requesting a Presidential Message from President Roosevelt for the National Day of Prayer on New Year's Day 1942," December 30, 1941, Hyde Park, NY.

4. *New York Times*, "The Plaza for New Year's Eve," December 31, 1941, 18.

5. *Los Angeles Times*, "Police Warn New Year's Celebrants," December 30, 1941, 1.

6. *New York Times*, "Mayer Assails Critics," December 31, 1941, 10.

7. *Boston Daily Globe*, "Boisterous Greeting Ready for 1942's Boston Arrival," December 31, 1941, 1.

8. Geoffrey Parsons Jr., "Slim Santa This Year In Britain," *Baltimore Sun*, December 23, 1941, 13.

9. *Honolulu Advertiser*, "License Suspensions Face Speeders Here," December 31, 1941, 2.

10. *Honolulu Advertiser*, "Banana Supply Plentiful Here," December 31, 1941, 3.

11. *Honolulu Advertiser*, "Leis for Dead to Be Received New Year's Day," December 31, 1941, 2.

12. *Honolulu Advertiser*, "Leis for Dead to Be Received New Year's Day," December 31, 1941, 2.

13. *Baltimore Sun*, "It's a Treat to Dine Out," December 31, 1941, 5.

14. *Los Angeles Times*, "New Year's Eve," December 31, 1941, 12.

15. Mary Harris, "Ringside Table," *Washington Post*, December 31, 1941, 16.

16. Jane Holt, "News of Food," *New York Times*, December 30, 1941, 14.

17. *New York Times*, "Rest-Period Demand Costs Hours at Ford," December 31, 1941, 9.

18. *New York Times*, "Rest-Period Demand Costs Hours at Ford," December 31, 1941, 9.

19. *Atlanta Constitution*, "Big California Telescope to Be Barred to Public," December 31, 1941, 10.

20. Ben Gilbert, "War Casts Deep Shadow on New Years Parties Here," *Washington Post*, January 1, 1941, 1.

21. *Birmingham* (AL) *News*, "Don't Throw Anything Away, Save Everything for Defense," December 31, 1941, 3.

22. Martin Lide, "2,800 Tanks a Month Is Goal Soon in View; Gun Totals Are Secret," *Birmingham* (AL) *News*, December 31, 1941, 5.

23. *Los Angeles Times*, "County Ordered to Save Salvage," December 31, 1941, 6.

24. John MacCormac, "Railroads Expect Aid from Tire Ban," *New York Times*, December 31, 1941, 9.

25. *Baltimore Sun*, "Whither Fashion in 1942," December 31, 1941, 10.

26. *Honolulu Advertiser*, "Ted Williams Is Voted Baseball's Man of Year," December 31, 1941, 8.

27. Joan Fontaine Female, "'Citizen Kane' Picked as Top Movie of '41," *Birmingham* (AL) *News*, December 31, 1941, 19.

28. *Honolulu Advertiser*, "No Messages Received Since Late Last Night," December 31, 1941, 1.

29. *Honolulu Advertiser*, "No Messages Received Since Late Last Night," December 31, 1941, 1.

30. Associated Press, "Indies Papers Ask Public to be Patient," *Baltimore Sun*, December 31, 1941, 3.

31. Husband E. Kimmel, *Admiral Kimmel's Story* (Chicago, IL: Henry Regnery Company, 1955), v.

32. Husband E. Kimmel, *Admiral Kimmel's Story* (Chicago, IL: Henry Regnery Company, 1955), 169.

33. *Hartford Courant*, "Short Dies at His Home in Texas," September 5, 1949, 1.

34. Associated Press, "Line South of Manila," December 31, 1941, 1.

35. Hanson W. Baldwin, "What Navy Is Doing," *New York Times*, December 31, 1941, 4.

36. Martin Caidin, *Golden Wings* (New York: Bramhall House, 1960), 108.

37. Associated Press, "Hope Fades in Gotham," *Birmingham* (AL) *News*, December 31, 1941, 2.

38. R. P. Cronin Jr., "Outnumbered Forces of Allies Being Pushed Back by Invader," *Birmingham* (AL) *News*, December 31, 1941, 2.

39. Dewitt MacKenzie, "The War Today: Strengthening of Singapore Now Is Squarely Up to U.S.; Weakness in Air Power Is Cited," December 31, 1941, 2.

40. Associated Press, "Japanese Dive Bombers Control Roads as Tanks Smash Closer to Capital," *Baltimore Sun*, December 31, 1941, 1.

41. Associated Press, "Sailor in Hawaii Sees Grave Marked as His," *Baltimore Sun*, December 31, 1941, 2.

42. Leland Stowe, "Burma Road Scandal," *Boston Evening Globe*, December 30, 1941, 1.

43. *New York Times*, "Gandhi Steps Down in War Policy Rift," December 31, 1941, 6.

44. *Birmingham* (AL) *News*, "Lynchings in 1941," December 31, 1941, 6.

45. *New York Times*, "The Day in Washington," December 31, 1941, 9.

46. Dewy L. Fleming, "Half of U.S. Income to Go for War Effort Under Roosevelt Plan," *Baltimore Sun*, December 31, 1941, 1.

47. Associated Press, "Washington Holds Partial Blackout," *Baltimore Sun*, December 31, 1941, 7.

48. Franklin Delano Roosevelt Presidential Library and Museum, "Memorandum To President Roosevelt From Rome Regarding Covert Conversation with Goering," January 31, 1942, Hyde Park, New York.

49. Pierre J. Huss, "Jap Attack Was Nazis' Secret Weapon Against U.S., Writer Discloses," *Birmingham* (AL) *News*, December 31, 1941, 1.

50. Franklin Delano Roosevelt Presidential Library and Museum, "Memorandum for the Naval Aide to the President, Regarding Factional Strife in Germany; Possible Peace Moves," September 26, 1941, Hyde Park, NY.

51. United Press, "'Frau Roosevelt Named by Hitler," *Boston Evening Globe*, December 31, 1941, 2.

52. Canadian Press, "Prime Minister Churchill's Address to Canadian Parliament," *New York Times*, December 31, 1941, 6.

53. Jon Meacham, *Franklin and Winston* (New York: Random House, 2004), 5.

54. Jon Meacham, *Franklin and Winston* (New York: Random House, 2004), xvii.

55. David Brinkley, *Washington Goes to War* (New York: Alfred A. Knopf, 1988), xiv.

56. David Brinkley, *Washington Goes to War* (New York: Alfred A. Knopf, 1988), 27.

57. Franklin Delano Roosevelt Presidential Library and Museum, "Memorandum to Rear Admiral Ross T. McIntire, (MC) U.S. Navy, The Surgeon General, Bureau of Medicine and Surgery, Navy Department, Washington, D.C., from Elphege A.M. Gendreau, Captain, (MC), U.S. Navy Flight Surgeon, United States Pacific Fleet, U.S.S. Pennsylvania," December 11, 1941, Hyde Park, NY.

58. Martin Caidin, *Golden Wings* (New York: Bramhall House, 1960), 89.

59. Studs Terkel, *The Good War* (New York: Pantheon Books, 1984,) 1.

60. *Baltimore Sun*, "Special Prayers Planned for U.S.," December 31, 1941, 6.

61. Franklin Delano Roosevelt Presidential Library and Museum, "Message From President Roosevelt to the American Embassy London, Triple Priority, National Day of Prayer Message," December 31, 1941, Hyde Park, NY.

EPILOGUE

1. Fred Pulis, *The Impact and Legacy Years, 1941, 1947, 1968* (Victoria, BC: Trafford, 2000), 15.
2. Carl Jung Resources, "What Is Synchronicity?," Last Modified: 2011, http://www.carl-jung .net/synchronicity.html.
3. Martin Caidin, *Golden Wings* (New York: Bramhall House, 1960), 102.
4. David Brinkley, *Washington Goes to War* (New York: Alfred A. Knopf, 1988), 43.
5. Walter Trojan, "Blame 2 for Pearl Harbor!," *Chicago Tribune*, January 25, 1942, 1.
6. *Hilo Tribune Herald*, "Japan May Strike Over The Weekend," November 30, 1941, 1.
7. *New York Times*, "Medals Given to 9 by Admiral Nimitz," May 28, 1942, 8.

BIBLIOGRAPHY

BOOKS

Ball, Stuart. *Winston Churchill.* New York: NYU Press, 2003.

Bankhead, Tallulah. *Tallulah: My Autobiography.* New York: Harper, 1952.

Barone, Michael. *Our Country: The Shaping of America from Roosevelt to Reagan.* New York: Free Press, 1990.

Bartsch, William H. *December 8, 1941 Macarthur's Pearl Harbor.* College Station, TX: Texas A&M University Press, 2003.

Bassett, James. *Harms Way.* New York: The World Publishing Company, 1962.

Beschloss, Michael R. *The Conquerors: Roosevelt, Truman and the Destruction of Hitler's Germany, 1941–1945.* New York: Simon & Schuster, 2002.

Bildner, Phil. *The Unforgettable Season: The Story of Joe DiMaggio, Ted Williams, and the Record-Setting Summer of '41.* New York: Penguin Books, 2011.

Billingsley, Kenneth Lloyd. *Hollywood Party: How Communism Seduced the American Film Industry in the 1930s and 1940s.* Rocklin, CA: Forum, 1998.

Black, Conrad. *Franklin Delano Roosevelt: Champion of Freedom.* New York: Public Affairs, 2003.

Borch, Fredric L., and Daniel Martinez. *Kimmel, Short, and Pearl Harbor.* Annapolis, MD: Naval Institute Press, 2005.

Braeman, Joe. *American Politics in the Twentieth Century.* New York: Thomas Y. Cromwell Company, 1969.

Brinkley, David. *Washington Goes to War: The Extraordinary Story of the Transformation of a City and a Nation.* New York: Random House, 1988.

Brinkley, Douglas. *The World War II Memorial: A Grateful Nation Remembers.* Washington, DC: Smithsonian Books, 2004.

Buchanan, Patrick J. *Churchill, Hitler, and the Unnecessary War: How Britain Lost Its Empire and the West Lost the World.* New York: Three Rivers Press, 2008.

Bulletin of International News, vol. 19, no. 1. Royal Institute of International News, London, UK, 1942.

Burns, James MacGregor, and Susan Dunn. *The Three Roosevelts: Patrician Leaders Who Transformed America.* New York: Grove Press, 2001.

Caidin, Martin. *Golden Wings: A Pictorial History of the United States Navy and Marine Corps in the Air.* New York: Bramhall House, 1960.

Caro, Robert A. *Means of Ascent: The Years of Lyndon Johnson.* New York: Alfred A. Knopf, 1990.

Chaplin, George. *Presstime In Paradise: The Life and Times of The Honolulu Advertiser, 1856–1995.* Honolulu, HI: University of Hawaii Press, 1998.

Churchill, Winston S. *The Grand Alliance.* New York: Houghton Mifflin, 1950.

Churchill, Winston S. *The Second World War: Their Finest Hour.* Boston, MA: Houghton Mifflin, 1949.

Churchill, Winston S., and Martin Gilbert. The *Churchill War Papers: The Ever Widening War, 1941.* New York, W. W. Norton & Company, 2001.

Churchill, Winston. *The Gathering Storm.* New York: Rosetta Books, 2002.

Coffey, Thomas M. *Hap: The Story of the U.S. Air Force and the Man Who Built it, General Henry "Hap" Arnold.* New York: Viking Press, 1982.

Cohen, Adam. *Nothing to Fear FDR's Inner Circle and the Hundred Days that Created Modern America.* New York: Penguin Press, 2009.

Conant, Jennet. *Tuxedo Park: A Wall Street Tycoon And the Secret Palace of Science That Changed the Course of World War II.* New York: Simon and Schuster, 2003.

Connaughton, Richard. *Macarthur and Defeat in the Philippines.* New York: The Overlook Press, 2001.

Cooke, Alistair. *The American Home Front: 1941–1942.* New York: Atlantic Monthly Press, 2006.

Costello, John. *The Pacific War: 1941–1945.* New York: HarperCollins, 1981.

Courtney, Richard D. *Painting the Milkweeds: How One American Family Coped with the Great Depression.* Raleigh, NC: Lulu Press, 2008.

Craig, Gordon A. *Europe Since 1914: Third Edition.* Hillsdale, IL: Dryden Press, 1972.

Cressman, Robert. *The Official Chronology of the U.S. Navy in World War II.* Annapolis, MD, Naval Institute Press, 2000.

Diehl, Lorraine B. *Over Here! New York City During World War II.* New York: Harper Collins, 2010.

Doll, John G. *Battling Bastards of Bataan.* Bennington, VT: Merriam Press, 1988.

Donovan, Hedley. *Roosevelt to Reagan: A Reporter's Encounters with Nine Presidents.* New York: Harper & Row, 1985.

Drea, Edward J. *Japan's Imperial Army: Its Rise and Fall, 1853–1945.* Lawrence, KS: University Press of Kansas, 2009.

Duffy, James P. *Lindbergh Vs. Roosevelt: The Rivalry That Divided America.* Washington, DC: Regnery, 2010.

Dull, Paul S. *A Battle History of The Imperial Japanese Navy (1941–1945).* Annapolis, MD: Naval Institute Press, 1978.

Edey, Maitland A., ed. *Time Capsule 1941.* New York: Time Life Books, 1967.

Edey, Maitland A., ed. *Time Capsule 1942.* New York: Time Life Books, 1968.

Edwards, Anne. *Early Reagan: The Rise to Power.* New York: William Morrow, 1987.

Eliot, Mark. *Walt Disney: Hollywood's Dark Prince.* New York: Carol Publishing, 1993.

Ensign, Clint W. *Inscriptions of a Nation: Collected Quotations from Washington Monuments.* Washington, DC: Elliott & Clark, 1994.

Evans, David C. and Mark R. Peattie. *Kaigun: Strategy, Tactics, and Technology in the Imperial Japanese Navy, 1887–1941.* Annapolis, MD: Naval Institute Press, 1997.

Farago, Landislas. *The Broken Seal: "Operation Magic" and the Secret Road to Pearl Harbor.* New York: Random House, 1967.

Freeman, Robert C. and Jon R. Felt. *German Saints at War.* Springville, UT: Cedar Fort, 2008.

Gallagher, Hugh Gregory. *FDR's Splendid Deception: The Moving Story of Roosevelt's Massive Disability-And the Intense Efforts to Conceal It from the Public.* Arlington, VA: Vandamere Press, 1995.

Gary, Brett. *The Nervous Liberals: Propaganda Anxieties From World War I to the Cold War.* New York: Columbia Univ. Press, 1999.

Gibson, Truman K. with Steve Huntley. *Knocking Down Barriers: My Fight for Black America.* Chicago: Northwestern University Press, 2005.

Gill, Bob. *Jackie Robinson: Pro Football Prelude.* Warminster, PA: Professional Football Researchers Association, 1987.

Goff, Kenneth. *Red Betrayal of Youth.* Enterprise Print, 1946.

Goldstein, Donald M. and Katherine V. Dillon. *The Pearl Harbor Papers: Inside The Japanese Plans.* Dulles, VA: Brasseys, 1993.

Goldsworthy, Terry. *Valhalla's Warriors: A History of the Waffen-SS on the Eastern Front 1941–1945.* Indianapolis, IN: Dog Ear Publishing, 2010.

Goodwin, Doris Kearns. *No Ordinary Time Franklin and Eleanor Roosevelt: The Home Front in World War II.* New York: Simon and Schuster, 1994.

Greenstein, Fred I. *The Presidential Difference: Leadership Style from FDR to George W. Bush.* Princeton, NJ: Princeton University Press, 2004.

Hart, Jeffrey. *From This Moment On.* New York: Crown Publishers, 1987.

Hayes, Carlton J.H. and Margareta Faissler. *Modern Times: The Fresh Revolution to the Present.* New York: The Macmillan Company, 1965.

Heinrichs, Waldo. *Threshold of War: Franklin D. Roosevelt and American Entry Into World War II.* Oxford, UK: Oxford University Press, 1990.

Holmes, Wendell, and Richard A. Posner. *The Essential Holmes: Selections From the Letters, Speeches, Judicial Opinions, and Other Writings of Oliver Wendell Holmes Jr.* Chicago: University of Chicago Press, 1997.

Hull, Cordell. *The Memoirs of Cordell Hull.* vol. 1. New York: Macmillan, 1948.

Hull, Cordell. *The Memoirs of Cordell Hull.* vol. 2. New York: Macmillan, 1948.

Jacobson, Matthew Frye, and Gaspar González. *What Have They Built You To Do? The Manchurian Candidate and Cold War America.* Minneapolis: University of Minnesota Press, 2006.

James, D. Clayton. *The Years of MacArthur Volume 1: 1880–1941.* Boston, MA: Houghton Mifflin, 1970.

Japanese Demobilization Bureaux Records. *Reports of General MacArthur: Japanese Operations in the Southwest Pacific Area.* vol. II, pt. I. Tokyo, Japan: U.S. Department of the Army, 1950.

Kass, Amy A. and Leon R. Kass. *What So Proudly We Hail: The American Soul in Story, Speech, and Song.* Wilmington, DE: ISI Books, 2011.

Kennedy, David M. *The Library of Congress World War II Companion.* New York: Simon & Schuster, 2007.

Kennedy, Kostya. *56: Joe DiMaggio and the Last Magic Number in Sports.* New York: Sports Illustrated Books, 2011.

Ketchum, Richard M., *The Borrowed Years 1938–1941.* New York: Random House, 1989.

Kim, Hyung-chan, ed. *Asian Americans and the Supreme Court: A Documentary History.* Westport, CT: Greenwood Publishing Group, 1992.

Kimmel, Husband E., *Admiral Kimmel's Story*. Chicago: Henry Regnery Company, 1955.

King, T. J. *Joint and Naval Intelligence Support to Military Operations*. Darby, PA: Diane Publishing, 2011.

Klein, Jonas. *Beloved Island: Franklin & Eleanor And the Legacy of Campobello*. Forest Dale, VT: Paul S. Eriksson, 2000.

Klein, Woody. *All the Presidents' Spokesmen: Spinning the News - White House Press Secretaries from Franklin D. Roosevelt to George W. Bush*. Westport, CT: Praeger Publishers, 2008.

Kluger, Richard. *Ashes to Ashes: America's Hundred-Year Cigarette War, The Public Health, And The Unabashed Triumph of Philip Morris*. New York: Random House, 1997.

Klurth, Peter. *American Cassandra: The Life of Dorothy Thompson*. New York: Little Brown & Co., 1991.

Kotani, Ken. *Japanese Intelligentce in World War II*. New York: Osprey Publishing, 2009.

Lapica, R.L. and Charles Freedhand, ed. Facts on File Yearbook, 1941: Persons index of World Events. vol. 1. New York: Facts on File, 1942.

Lash, Joseph P. *Eleanor and Franklin: The Story of Their Relationship Based on Eleanor Roosevelt's Private Papers*. New York: W.W. Norton & Company, 1971.

Leonard, Thomas M. *Day by Day: The Forties*. New York: Facts on File, 1977.

Longfellow, Henry Wadsworth. *The Complete Poetical Works of Henry Wadsworth Longfellow*. London, UK: George Routledge & Sons, 1871.

Lundstrom, John B. *The First Team: Pacific Naval Air Combat From Pearl Harbor to Midway*. Annapolis, MD: Naval Institute Press, 2005.

Lyons, Eugene. *Herbert Hoover: A Biography*. Garden City, NY: Doubleday & Company, 1964.

MacArthur, Douglas. *Reminiscences*. New York: McGraw-Hill, 1964.

Manchester, William. *American Caesar: Douglas MacArthur 1880–1964*. Boston, MA: Little, Brown and Company, 1978.

McBride, Joseph. *Frank Capra: The Catastrophe of Success*. New York: St. Martins Griffin, 2000.

McCullough, David. *Truman*. New York: Simon and Schuster, 1992.

McElvaine, Robert S. *The Great Depression: America 1929–1941*. New York: Three Rivers Press, 1984.

McGuire, Edna, and Thomas B. Portwood. *The Rise of Our Free Nation*. New York: The Macmillan Company, 1947.

Meacham, Jon. *Franklin And Winston: An Intimate Portrait of an Epic Friendship*. New York: Random House, 2003.

Middleton, K.W.B. *Britain and Russia*. London, UK: Hutchinson, 1947.

Mills, Walter, and E.S. Duffield. *The Forestall Diaries*. New York: Viking Press, 1951.

Minear, Richard H. *Dr. Seuss Goes To War: The World War II Editorial Cartoons of Theodore Seuss Geisel*. New York: The New Press, 1999.

Monaghan, Frank. *World War II An Illustrated History*. vol. 1. Chicago: J.G. Ferguson, 1943.

Monaghan, Frank. *World War II An Illustrated History*. vol. 2. Chicago: J.G. Ferguson, 1943.

Morton, Louis. *U.S. Army in World War II The War in The Pacific: The Fall of the Philippines*. Washington, DC: Department of the Army, 1953.

Nalty, Bernard C. *War in the Pacific Pearl Harbor to Tokyo Bay: The Story of the Bitter Struggle in the Pacific Theater of World War II*. Norman, OK: University of Oklahoma Press, 1999.

Nasaw, David. *The Chief: The Life of William Randolph Hearst*. Boston, MA: Houghton Mifflin Harcourt, 2001.

Neustadt, Richard E. *Presidential Power and the Modern Presidents: The Politics of Leadership from Roosevelt to Reagan.* New York: The Free Press, 1991.

Notley, David. *Winston Churchill: Quotations.* Norwich, UK: Jarrold Publishing, 1977.

O'Neill, William L. *A Democracy At War: America's Fight at Home and Abroad in World War II.* Cambridge, MA: Harvard University Press, 1995.

Overy, Richard. *War in the Pacific.* Long Island City, NY: Osprey Publishing, 2010.

Overy, Richard. *Why The Allies Won.* New York: W.W. Norton, & Company, 1995.

Peattie, Mark R. *Sunburst: The Rise of Japanese Naval Air Power 1909–1941.* Annapolis, MD: Naval Institute Press, 2001.

Pietrusza, David. *1948: Harry Truman's Improbable Victory and the Year That Transformed America.* New York: Union Square Press, 2011.

Polenberg, Richard. *The Era of Franklin D. Roosevelt 1933–1945.* Boston, MA: Bedford/St. Martin's, 2000.

Powers, Ron. *Dangerous Water: A Biography of the Boy Who Became Mark Twain.* Cambridge, MA: Da Capo Press, 2001.

Prange, Gordon William, Donald M. Goldstein, and Katherine V. Dillon. *At Dawn We Slept: The Untold Story of Pearl Harbor.* New York: McGraw-Hill, 1981.

Prange, Gordon William, Donald M. Goldstein, and Katherine V. Dillon. *Dec. 7, 1941: The Day the Japanese Attacked Pearl Harbor.* New York: Wings Books, 1991.

Raucher, Herman. *Summer of '42.* New York: G.P. Putnam's Sons, 1971.

Richler, Mordecai, ed. *Writers on World War II: An Anthology.* New York: Alfred A. Knopf, 1991.

Rickenbacker, Edward V. *Rickenbacker.* New York: FawcettWorld Library, 1969.

Roosevelt, Eleanor. *This I Remember.* New York: Dolphin Books, 1961.

Roosevelt, Elliott and James Brough. *A Rendezvous with Destiny: The Roosevelts of the White House.* New York: G.P. Putnam's Sons, 1975.

Roosevelt, Elliott and Joseph P. Lash. *F.D.R. His Personal Letters 1928–1945 I.* New York: Duell, Sloan and Pearce, 1950.

Roosevelt, Elliott and Joseph P. Lash. *F.D.R. His Personal Letters 1928–1945 II.* New York: Duell, Sloan and Pearce, 1950.

Roosevelt, Franklin D. *The War Messages of Franklin D. Roosevelt, December 8, 1941, to April 13, 1945: The President's War Addresses to the People & to the Congress of the United States of America.* Lexington, KY: 2011.

Rowley, Hazel. *Franklin and Eleanor: An Extraordinary Marriage.* New York: Farrar, Straus and Giroux, 2010.

Safire, William and Leonard Safir. *Words of Wisdom.* New York: Simon and Schuster, 1989.

Satterfield, Archie. *The Home Front: An Oral History of The War Years in America: 1941–1945.* Chicago: Playboy Press, 1981.

Schlesinger, Arthur M. Jr. *The Crisis of the Old Order: 1919–1933.* Boston, MA: Houghton Mifflin, 1957.

Schlesinger, Robert. *White House Ghosts: Presidents and their Speechwriters; From FDR to George W. Bush.* New York: Simon and Schuster, 2008.

Schmidt, Ronald J. *This Is the City: Making Model Citizens in Los Angeles.* Minneapolis: University of Minnesota Press, 2005.

Seib, Philip M. *Broadcasts from the Blitz: How Edward R. Murrow Helped Lead America Into War.* Dulles, VA: Potomac Books, 2006.

Shales, Amity. *The Forgotten Man A New History of the Great Depression*. New York: Harper Collins, 2007.

Shirer, William L. *The Rise and Fall of The Third Reich*. New York: Simon and Schuster, 1960.

Shogan, Robert. *Hard Bargain: How FDR Twisted Churchill's Arm, Evaded the Law, and Changed the Role of the American Presidency*. Boulder, CO: Westview Press, 1999.

Shorter, Edward. *Bedside Manners*. New York: Simon and Schuster, 1985.

Shrirer, William L. *20th Century Journey: A Memoir of a Life and the Times: The Start: 1904–1930*. New York: Simon and Schuster, 1976.

Smith, Jean Edward. *FDR*. New York: Random House, 2007.

Smith, Page. *America Enters the World: A People's History of the Progressive Era and World War I*. vol.VII. New York: McGraw-Hill, 1985.

Steinhoff, Johannes, Peter Pechel, and Dennis Showalter. *Voices From The Third Reich: An Oral History*. Washington, DC: Regnery Gateway, 1989.

Stille, Mark. *Imperial Japanese Navy Heavy Cruisers 1941–1945*. Long Island City, NY: Osprey Publishing, 1969.

Stimson, Henry Lewis, and McGeorge Bundy. *On Active Service in Peace and War*. New York: Harper & Brothers, 1948.

Stimson, Henry Lewis, Council on Foreign Relations, and Royal Institute of International Affairs. *The Far Eastern Crisis*. New York: Harper & brothers, 1936.

Swift, Will. *The Roosevelts and the Royals*. Hoboken, NJ: John Wiley & Sons, 2004.

Tansill, Charles Callan. *Back Door to War: Roosevelt Foreign Policy: 1933–1941*. Chicago: Henry Regnery Company, 1952.

Taylor, Robert Lewis. *Winston Churchill: An Informal Study of Greatness*. Garden City, NY: Doubleday, 1952.

Terkel, Studs. *The Good War: An Oral History of World War Two*. New York: Pantheon Books, 1984.

Thomas, Evan. *Sea of Thunder: Four Commanders and the Last Great Naval Campaign 1941–1945*. New York: Simon and Schuster, 2006.

Thompson, Robert Smith. *A Time For War: Franklin D. Roosevelt and the Path to Pearl Harbor*. New York: Prentice-Hall, 1991.

Tremaine, Frank and Kay Tremaine. *The Attack on Pearl Harbor: By Two Who Were There*. Fredericksburg, TX: The Admiral Nimitz Foundation, 1997.

Tuchman, Barbara. *The Guns of August*. New York: Dell Publishing, 1973.

Tully, Grace. *F.D.R. My Boss*. New York: Charles Scribner's Sons, 1949.

Vaccaro, Mike. *1941—The Greatest Year In Sports: Two Baseball Legends, Two Boxing Champs, and the Unstoppable Thoroughbred Who Made History in the Shadow of War*. New York: First Anchor Books, 2007.

Van Der Vat, Dan. *Pearl Harbor: The Day of Infamy—An Illustrated History*. New York: Basic Books, 2001.

Ward, Geoffrey C., and Ken Burns. *The War: an Intimate History, 1941–1945*. New York: A.A. Knopf, 2007.

Winter, Ella. *Red Virtue: Human Relations in the New Russia*. New York: Harcourt Brace & Company, 1933.

PERIODICALS

Albuquerque (NM) Journal

Atlanta Constitution

Atlanta Daily World

Bakersfield (CA) Californian

Baltimore Sun

Beatrice (NE) Daily Sun

Birmingham (AL) News

Bismarck (ND) Tribune

Boston Daily Globe

Boston Evening Globe

Boston Sunday Globe

Brainerd (MN) Daily

Calgary Herald (Alberta, Canada)

Charleston (SC) Gazette

Charleston (SC) News and Courier

Chicago Daily Tribune

Christian Science Monitor

Coshocton (OH) Tribune

Cumberland (MD) Evening Times

Dunkirk (NY) Evening Observer

Emporia (KS) Daily Gazette

Fitchburg (MA) Sentinel

Greeley (CO) Daily Tribune

Hartford (CT) Courant

Hilo (HI) Tribune Herald

Honolulu (HI) Advertiser

Idaho Evening Times

Ironwood (MI) Daily Globe

Kingsport (TN) Times

Lethbridge Herald (Alberta, Canada)

Life

Long Island (NY) Newsday

Look

Los Angeles Times

Maryville (MO) Daily Forum

Middlesboro (KY) Daily News

Milwaukee Journal

Mount Airy (NC) News

Nevada Mail

Nevada State Journal

New York Times

Pittsburgh Post-Gazette

Portsmouth (NH) Herald

Portsmouth (VA) Times

Rock Hill (SC) Herald

San Francisco Chronicle

Sarasota (FL) Herald-Tribune

Saturday Evening Post

Spokane (WA) Spokesman-Review

St. Petersburg (FL) Evening Independent

St. Petersburg (FL) Times

Sunday (DE) Star

Sunday Star

Telegraph-Herald (IA)

Time

Tucson (AZ) Daily Citizen

Wall Street Journal

Washington Evening Star

Washington Post

Washington Times Herald

Yuma (AZ) Daily Sun

NEWS WIRES
Associated Press
Canadian Press
Chicago Tribune Service
International News Service
United Press

ELECTRONIC MEDIA
Tora! Tora! Tora! The Attack on Pearl Harbor. 1970. Craig Shirley Collection.
Midway. 1976. Craig Shirley Collection.
MacArthur. 1977. Craig Shirley Collection.
The March of Time: News Reels. Time. 1931–1967. HBO Archives.
FOX News Reels.

OTHER MATERIALS
Claude Wickard. Secretary of Agriculture Claude Wickard's Diary. Wickard Collection. Franklin D. Roosevelt Presidential Library.
Presidential Records. Franklin Delano Roosevelt Presidential Library and Museum.
Joint Committee on the Investigation of the Pearl Harbor Attack.
Henry Lewis Stimson Papers, Manuscripts and Archives, Yale University Library.
The Churchill Center and Museum at the Churchill War Rooms, London, Speeches,

INTERVIEWS
Gerald Eckert, Interview by Craig Shirley.
McShane, Susan. Interview by Craig Shirley. September 12, 2011.

ABOUT THE AUTHORS

Craig Shirley is the author of two critically praised bestselling books on President Reagan, *Rendezvous with Destiny: Ronald Reagan and the Campaign that Changed America* and *Reagan's Revolution: The Untold Story of the Campaign That Started It All.* His third book *December 1941: 31 Days that Changed America and Saved the World* has appeared multiple times on the New York Times Best Sellers lists in December 2011 and January 2012. It also was named a finalist in the "History" category for *ForeWord Reviews* and the American Library Association's Book of the Year Awards. Craig is the founder of Shirley & Banister Public Affairs, was chosen in 2005 by Springfield College as their Outstanding Alumnus, and has been named the First Reagan Scholar at Eureka College, Ronald Reagan's alma mater, where he taught a course titled "Reagan 101."

His books have been hailed as the definitive works on the Gipper's campaigns of 1976 and 1980. He is a member of the Board of Governors of the Reagan Ranch and has lectured at the Reagan Library, the FDR Library in Hyde Park, and the Dole Institute in Kansas.

Shirley, a widely sought after speaker and commentator, has appeared on many network and cable shows and has written extensively for the *Washington Post*, the *Washington Examiner*, the *Washington Times*, the *Los Angeles Times*, *Town Hall*, the *Weekly Standard*, *Politico*, *Reuters*, and many other publications. He also edited the book *Coaching Youth Lacrosse* for the Lacrosse Foundation. He was the founder of the Ft. Hunt Youth Lacrosse League and coached there for fourteen years.

He is now finishing *Citizen Newt*, a definitive biography of Speaker Newt Gingrich and is beginning work on three more Reagan books. Shirley also has plans for a book about Dr. Howard Snyder, the personal physician to President Dwight Eisenhower, and a book about the George Washington family.

Shirley and his wife, Zorine, reside at "Trickle Down Point" on the Rappahannock River in Lancaster, Virginia, and are parents of four children, Matthew, Andrew, Taylor, and Mitchell. His varied interests include sailing, waterskiing, sport shooting, renovating buildings, and scuba diving. An accomplished carpenter, he has built two houses. He was a decorated contract agent for the Central Intelligence Agency.

Andrew Shirley was the principal research assistant on *December 1941*. He is a graduate of Fort Union Military Academy, is a Navy veteran, and is attending Marymount University in Virginia where he will receive a degree in history. He is now undertaking research on Craig Shirley's new book about President Reagan's final years.

General Paul Xavier Kelley is the 28th Commandant of the Marine Corps, serving from 1950 to 1987. Born in Boston, Massachusetts, General Kelley earned his commission in 1950 following his graduation from Villanova where he received a degree in economics. General Kelley served on active duty in a myriad of billets for thirty-seven years.

As an exchange officer with the British Royal Marines, he became one of the few men, and even fewer foreign men, to earn the Green Beret, which is bestowed upon those who successfully complete the Command Course of the Royal Marines. He then joined the Marine Force reconnaissance community as battalion commander. General Kelley (then Lt. Col.) deployed to Vietnam and continued to distinguish himself by earning the Silver Star, as well as the Legion of Merit and two Bronze Stars with Valor Device. In 1970, the general returned to Vietnam for a second tour, commanding the First Marines and earning his second Legion of Merit with Valor Device.

In 1981 he was promoted to general, and in 1983 he was named commandant of the Marine Corps. Following his retirement in 1987, he served as the chairman of the American Battle Monuments Commission, overseeing the design and construction of the Korean and World War II memorials. General Kelley is the Chairman Emeritus of the Irish-American Partnership and a Reagan Fellow at Eureka College.

ACKNOWLEDGMENTS

During the final course of writing this book, my editor and friend at Thomas Nelson, Joel Miller, was in the middle of doing a wonderful thing. He and his wife, Megan, were in Uganda adopting two young boys. While there for several weeks, he edited *December 1941* on a laptop on a table in the bathroom of his hotel. Their magnificence of kindness and charity and sacrifice puts book writing into perspective. Thank you, Joel.

Thank you also to the marvelous professionals at Nelson: Dave Schroeder, Heather Skelton, Kristen Parrish, Katherine Rowley, Jason Jones, Julie Faires, Brian Hampton, Debbie Eicholtz, Walter Petrie, Rosie Colvin, Ramona Wilkes, and Dean Nelson. In addition to their skills and patience, they also have a very necessary sense of humor.

As in the case of my previous books, this one would not have been possible without the tender ministries, patience, tough editing, long hours, and superior suggestions of my wife and best friend, Zorine. Nor would this have been possible without the encouragement and support of my business partner and our friend, Diana Banister. Thank you, Zorine. Thank you, Diana.

Thanks to Maureen Mackey for her marvelous editing.

Andrew Shirley was superb in his research, editing, fact-checking, and advice. He has dedicated, literally, thousands of hours to this book. This is as much Zorine's and Andrew's book as it is mine. Thank you. Thanks also to Borko and Andreja Komnenovic for their superb work.

Thanks also to our other children, Matthew, Taylor, and Mitchell, for their encouragement and love and help and support. Our children are simply the most important people in Zorine's and my life.

Special thanks to four dear friends: Vic Gold, Fred Barnes, Michael McShane, and Gay Hart Gaines for their support, advice, and wise council. The same goes for Gary Maloney.

And thanks to John Persinos for his advice and input on edits as well as cultural and historical suggestions, and many thanks also to my mother, Barbara Eckert, and my sister, Rebecca Sirhal, for digging up family history for the Dedication, as well as their advice and counsel and love.

In the last two weeks, because of the press of time and the reams of research material, a group of professional researchers came to my assistance to help finish the job, like the Marines coming in over the hill just in the nick of time. Thank you to Kate Maxwell, Kristen Helmstetter, Linda Emery, Inez Feltscher, Jasmina Zahirovic, Scott Whitlock, Megan Higgins, Anna Hyde and Joseph S. Catapano, Queenie Bui, Lauren Elizabeth Merz, Mirah Johnston, Sakari Deichsel, Mark Hensch, and Alex B. Weisman. Each was dedicated and their work invaluable.

Thanks also to the following friends—listed here in no particular order: Newt and Callista Gingrich, Mark Levin, Tony Fabrizio, Ken Cuccinelli, Jennifer Harper, Michael Barone, Bill Kristol, Mark Masters, Robert Schlesinger, Charles Pratt, John McLaughlin, Matthew Dallek, Jim McLaughlin, Grover Norquist, Mark Tapscott, Michael Phelps, Shannon Bream, Tom McDevitt, Ralph Hallow, Rob and Robert Meyne, Paul Begala, Ricky Greenfield, Chuck Todd, Mark Allen, Matt Continetti, Jay Test, Peggy Noonan, Bill Clark, Joanne Herring, Stephen Moore, Roger Stone, Richard Viguerie, Michele Davis, John Fund, Paul and Carole Laxalt, Bill Schulz, Fred Eckert, David Marks, George and Mari Maseng Will, Cleta Mitchell, Tom Loringer, Fred Barbash, David Alpern, Cheryl Rampy, Lee Edwards, Del Quentin Wilber, John Heubusch, Dave Arnold, Mike Murtaugh, Philip Cavalier, John Morris, Joanne Drake, Jewell and Pal Hornung, Rick Perry, Ken Cribb, Jim Burnley, Dick Allen, Ken Khachigian, Stu Spencer, Karen Spencer, Fred Ryan, Carl Cannon, Carolyn Hauer, Pat Nolan, Dennis LeBlanc, Quin Hillyer, Brent and Norma Bozell, Susan McShane, Rick and Sue Johnson, Bruce Baker and Rhonda Lognon, Llewellyn King and Linda Gasparello, Ron Robinson, Frank and Becki Donatelli, Dave Roberts, Peter and Irene Hannaford, Jed Donahue, Dick and Mary Snyder, Lou Cannon, Tom and Lyn Finnigan, Ed Meese, Bill Pascoe, Al Regnery, Tish Leonard, Bob Tyrrell, Jim Pinkerton, Howard Fineman, Kevin and Chris Kabanuk, Dan, Soona, Jinnyn, Dan III, Coury, and Raymond Jacob, Ross, Candy, Elizabeth, and Katherine Bhappu, Manek Bhappu, Dr. Roshan and Perin Bhappu, and Homee Schroff. And to Ellen and Wayne Masters and Nathan, Todd, Eric, and Margaret Shirley. And to Human, Stephanie, Laura, and Ethan Sirhal, Karen Howard, Georgette Mosbacher, and Michelle and John Bae.

Thanks to Tish Leonard, Kevin McVicker, Courtney Nolan, Jameson Cunningham, and Dan Wilson at Shirley & Banister Public Relations. And thanks to Matthew C. Hanson, Archives Specialist at the Franklin D. Roosevelt Presidential Library, and to everybody at the Library of Congress.

In the course of writing and researching this book, I discovered many things about my family I did not know until the papers from the Daughters of the American Revolution were given to me by my mother and sister.

I knew about the many sacrifices of many men in the Shirley, Cone, Abbott, Westbook, Watkins, and McGiveron families in all the wars of America but did not know about Henry Cone of Haddam, Connecticut—on my mother's side—who enlisted in May 1775 in the 1st Company, 1st Regiment. He was "at the siege of Boston in May, and at Bunker Hill in June." Under George Washington's command, our grandfather then "wintered at Valley Forge, 1777–8; was at the battles of Brandywine, Monmouth, and Long Island. In 1781, while still in service, he lost an eye to smallpox. In 1793, he was granted a pension and [died] at Lyme Dec. 15, 1827, aged 83." Henry's son Andrew Diodate Cone—another grandfather—served in the War of 1812.

On my father's side, Private William Watkins was one of the "men who marched from Connecticut Town for the relief of Boston in the Lexington Alarm of April 1775...." Watkins was in the "Third Regiment, under General Putnam, 1775, fifth company."

To all the aforementioned, I am in your debt.

INDEX

mutual war pact signing, 308
need for help, 131
New Year's Eve, 522
Royal Air Force, 6
sea power, vs. Japan, 254
vs. U.S., methods of information sharing, 235
Great Depression, 7, 105, 532
opinion on, 8
Great Dictator, The (movie), 47
Great War
Bonus Marchers of, 351–352
as World War I, 301
Greece, representative at D.C. war conference, 482
Greek guerrillas, 314
Greeley (CO) Daily Tribune, 13
Greenberg, Hank, 191
Greene, Marc T., 110
Greenland, German interest in, 46
Greenwich Observatory, 87
Grew, Joseph C., 100, 150, 162, 194
Griffith, Calvin, 60
Griffith, Clark, 334–335
Griffith, Corrine, 378
Grissom, Gus, 537
grooming, 10–11
Groves, John, 61
Guam, 55, 299, 390
Japanese attack, 146, 153, 156
Japanese claims of control, 195
Japanese control, 304
loss of communications, 284, 421
Pan Am Clipper escape, 252
Gullion, Allen, 152
Gunnison, Royal Arch, 39, 71

H

Haan, Kilsoo K., 193
Halas, George, 387
Halibut (submarine), 84

Halifax, Lord (British ambassador), 16, 37, 46, 137, 151, 393, 454
in Congressional gallery, 231
on Hong Kong, 338
memo to Roosevelt, 443
Haller, Richard, 141
Hallin, Isabelle, suicide, 463–464
Halsey, Bill, 110, 136
Halton, Matthew, 37
"ham" radio operators, 88
Hamilton, Alexander, *Federalist 74*, 212
Hamma, Margaret, 84
Hampton, Horace Woodrow, 49
Hanoi, Japanese in American consulate, 238
Hansgirg, Fritz, FBI arrest of, 358
hari-kari, 303
Harriman, Averill, 251
Hart, E.B., 412
Hart, Thomas C., 20, 251, 363
Hartford Courant, 49
Haruna (Japanese battleship), 238, 252
Harvard, 30, 172, 281, 374
Hatfield Wire and Cable Company, 310
Hathaway, Murray C., 416
Hawaii Calls (radio show), 139
Hawaiian Defense Act, 485
Hawaiian Territory, xii, 213. *See also* Honolulu; Pearl Harbor
army concerns about sabotage, 23
arrests for subversive activities, 271
Christmas in, 448
Dec 7 initial reports, 139
lack of news from, 218
martial law and gradual resumption of activities, 245
memo on Japanese espionage in, 64

new regulations, 515
New Year's Eve, 485
news blackout in, 159
servicemen from *Prusa*, 495
Hawkins, Anthony, Jr., 293
Hayes, Roy E., 158
Hayworth, Rita, 35, 125
Hearst, William Randolph, 15, 31, 304
heating for homes, 56
Heffernan, Harold, 103, 370
Heidt, Edward J., 417
Heidt, Wesley, 417
Helm (destroyer), 110
Henderson, Leon, 356
Henney, Elizabeth, 152
Henry, Bill, xii
Henry, Donald, 541
Hershey, Louis B., 256, 359, 376
Hickam Field, 23, 156, 436
Hicks, W.W., 381
Hill, Edwin J., 325
Hill, F. Leroy, 9
Himmler, Heinrich, 124
Hirohito
declaration of war, 180
efforts to isolate, 214
FDR message to, 131–132, 147, 193–194
Hirokawa, Ernest, 64
Hiroshima, 542
Hiryu (Japanese carrier), 138
Hitler, Adolf, 1, 14, 32, 58, 275, 530–531
Allied view of, 422
American Jews' attitude toward, 119–120
contempt for Arabs, 430
control of German army, 409
genocidal policies, 339
health, 339
interview, 510–511
military strategy of, 409
rumors of military coup, 510, 531
and Russian Front, 123
speculation on plans, 426
speech after declaring war on U.S., 227–228
and Stalin, 411